Anonymous

Records of the Presbyteries of Inverness and Dingwall, 1643-1688

Anonymous

Records of the Presbyteries of Inverness and Dingwall, 1643-1688

ISBN/EAN: 9783337017736

Printed in Europe, USA, Canada, Australia, Japan

Cover: Foto ©Lupo / pixelio.de

More available books at **www.hansebooks.com**

RECORDS OF
THE PRESBYTERIES OF
INVERNESS
AND DINGWALL

1643-1688

Edited, with an Introduction, from the
Original Manuscript, by

WILLIAM MACKAY

EDINBURGH

Printed at the University Press by T. and A. Constable
for the Scottish History Society

1896

INTRODUCTION

The Seventeenth Century Records of the Presbytery of Inverness, so far as known to exist, consist of one volume, containing the proceedings of the Presbytery from 5th April 1670 to 19th September 1688.[1] The minutes of the year 1643 are printed from a copy taken from an older volume, unfortunately now lost; and there is recorded on 2nd July 1672 a copy of the minute of a meeting of the Presbytery held at Boleskine on 26th May 1632, which is the earliest record of the Presbytery now extant. That minute is not flattering to the people of Stratherrick, whose minister complained 'that he could not 'live in Boleskine for the evill neighbourhood of the tenents 'y^{r}of, who would not permitt his goods [*i.e.* his cattle] to 'pasture on his own grasse, and that the Tutor of ffoyer 'attempted not only to denude him of the grass, but also a 'part of the land designed alreadie'; but it is interesting as containing early mention of crofts and crofters, and the earliest account probably now known of the formal designation of a glebe in the Highlands.

The Seventeenth Century Records of the Presbytery of Dingwall now extant consist of three volumes, in which are found the proceedings of that Presbytery between 19th June 1649 and 13th October 1687.[2] It appears, however, from the Minutes of 17th March and 21st April 1653, that there existed in that year an 'old pbrie booke being at the beginning thairoff, 'of the daite 12 Novemb. 1633 zeires, and ending at the daite '18 Octob. 1637.' That old book has, like many another church

---

[1] See footnote, p. 135.   [2] See footnote, p. 366.

register, fallen a prey to the troubles or the carelessness of the olden times.

The editor, with the approval of the Council of the Society, has not always given the full minute in the following pages. Such portions—chiefly of a formal nature—as were in his opinion of no value from a historical or social point of view have been omitted. Again, such paragraphs as are within brackets [ ] only give the *purport* of the minutes to which they refer. Certain lists, however, of persons charged with the offence of supporting Montrose and the Royalist cause, which have been omitted from their proper places, have been given as an Appendix.

The Presbyteries of Inverness and Dingwall were both proposed by the General Assembly in April 1581, and it is probable that they were erected soon afterwards. The Inverness Presbytery is mentioned in 1593:[1] but probably the earliest reference to that of Dingwall is in the records printed in this volume. The bounds of the former embraced in the seventeenth century its present parishes of Inverness and Bona, Kirkhill or Wardlaw, Kiltarlity, Urquhart and Glenmoriston, Dores, Daviot and Dunlichity, Moy and Dalarossie, and Petty; as well as Boleskine and Abertarff, which was disjoined on the erection of the Presbytery of Abertarff in 1724,[2] and Croy, disjoined on the erection of the Presbytery of Nairn in 1773. The bounds of the Presbytery of Dingwall embraced its present parishes of Dingwall, Alness, Contin, Fodderty, Kilmorack, Kiltearn, Urquhart and Logie Wester, and Urray; together with the wide western parishes of Applecross, Gairloch, Kintail (including the present parish of Glenshiel), Lochalsh, Lochbroom, and Lochcarron, which are now within the Presbytery of Lochcarron, erected in 1724. The two Presbyteries thus exercised between them an almost unlimited jurisdiction

---

[1] Scott's *Fasti*, v. 252.

[2] Urquhart and Glenmoriston were within the Presbytery of Abertarff from 1724 till 1884.

over an extensive district stretching from sea to sea across the heart of the Highlands, and inhabited by all sorts and conditions of men, from the peace-loving, money-making shopkeepers of the burghs of Inverness and Dingwall, to the wild, kilted, Gaelic-speaking mountaineers, who to-day followed their cattle in the glens, and to-morrow their chiefs on the field of battle—from the stern Covenanters of Alness and Kiltearn to the careless, easy-minded Roman Catholics of Strathglass, Glenmoriston, and Abertarff. On the history of that district, and the religious and social condition of its inhabitants, these Records throw light of no inconsiderable power and value.

The period covered by them was one of turbulence and unrest, in things temporal as in things spiritual—the last years of Charles the First, the years of Cromwell's rule, and the reigns of Charles the Second and James the Seventh. In 1638, the 'Second Reformation' in Scotland was effected by the Glasgow General Assembly, and Episcopacy for a time gave place to Presbytery. Guthrie, Bishop of Moray, in whose province the Presbytery of Inverness lay, was deposed; and the scholarly Maxwell, within whose diocese of Ross the Presbytery of Dingwall was situated, was deposed and excommunicated. Still, the Covenant of 1638, which was subscribed with enthusiasm in the South, met but with scant welcome in the North, and it was subscribed by few within the bounds of our Presbyteries, except in the parishes of Alness and Kiltearn, which were subject to the influence of Munro of Fowlis. Fowlis and most of his relatives and clansmen were keen Covenanters, and his admiration for 'ye godlie in ye West Cuntrey'[1]—that is, the extreme Remonstrants of the south-west of Scotland—was so great at a later period that he refused to accept any minister for the parish of Kiltearn who was not approved of by them. The inhabitants of our bounds, as a rule, continued faithful to

---

[1] See p. 245.

Episcopacy and the King, and even such of them as had no great objection to the Covenant of 1638, strongly opposed the more revolutionary Solemn League and Covenant of 1643. In every movement of the time in defence of the monarchy, they had their share. They fought under the banner of Montrose in his brilliant first campaign, and thus won for themselves the title of 'Malignants.' They subscribed to the Earl of Seaforth's 'Remonstrance.' They joined the 'Engagement' of 1648, and followed the Duke of Hamilton into England. They followed Lord Reay and Mackenzie of Pluscardine in the rising of 1649 in support of Charles the Second, and before their defeat at Balvenie helped to capture Inverness, and to expel the garrison and demolish the town's walls. And when Montrose landed in Caithness, and entered on his unfortunate campaign of 1650, they openly expressed their sympathy with him, although his defeat before he reached the bounds probably prevented their actually joining him to any considerable extent. These courses led to numerous prosecutions by the Solemn Leaguers, and the Malignant ministers of Dingwall, Contin, Fodderty, Kiltearn, and Urray, were deposed, while the elders of Urray, Lochalsh, Lochcarron and other parishes were declared incapacitated. The few ministers who were thus left in the Presbytery of Dingwall combated Malignancy for a time with vigorous zeal. The guilty were fined, placed on the stool of repentance, and in some cases excommunicated; and, lest they should, before giving due satisfaction, become partakers of the Lord's Supper, ministers and sessions were warned not to administer the Communion to any person without the Presbytery's advice and sanction. But this zeal did not last long. The masterful activity of the English Sectaries, not only in civil affairs, but also in matters spiritual, gradually estranged their Scottish adherents; and when, early in 1651, preparations were being made for that invasion of England which ended so disastrously at Worcester, the Dingwall processes were brought to an end with speed and clemency, to enable the accused to join the expedition. After Worcester, Cromwell's soldiers overran Scotland, planting garrisons, among other places, at Inverness and Brahan within our bounds. 'It were vain,' wrote Mr. James Fraser, a member of the Presbytery of Inverness, who experienced the goodwill and hospitality of the English soldiers, 'to relate what advantages the country had by the Inverness garrison.' The advantages were undoubtedly great—for a time war and spoliation ceased — but nevertheless the presence of the English at Brahan was not liked by the gentlemen who constituted the Presbytery of Dingwall. Probably they had good reason for disliking it. On 16th December 1651, the Presbytery met at Logie Wester privately, 'in regaird of the enemie.' Fifteen days later the brethren were unable to meet at Urray as arranged, 'in respect of ane conventione of the Inglishes at Urray' the same day. At the meeting of 16th March 1654, Mr. Donald Macrae, minister of Urray, 'was excused for his last dayis absence, being impeded and molested be the Englishe garisone.' And in the following December the brethren had not the usual 'exercise,' 'in respect the exerciser was abstracted be quartering on.'

One effect of these unpleasantnesses with the English was to cause the members of the Presbytery of Dingwall to think more kindly of the Malignant brethren who had been deposed. No new ministers had been found to fill the pulpits of these unfortunate men, and for years their stipends were diverted from their proper purposes and applied to such objects as the support of lads at schools and students at college, the building of the bridges of Dingwall and Alness, and the construction of public works within the parish of Contin. A more charitable spirit, however, now took possession of the Presbytery. The vacant stipends were, to some extent at least, employed in relieving the poverty and distress of the deposed and their families, and a few of the deposed themselves were restored to their parishes.

The references in the Dingwall Records to the efforts made to place Charles the Second on his father's throne are not without interest. Charles landed at Speymouth in June 1650, and was enthusiastically received. In July the moderator addressed letters to the other members of the Presbytery, urging 'a present dilligence for collecting ye Levie money' which Royalists were endeavouring to raise among the heritors or landowners; and on the 30th of that month the brethren reported that they had received the letters, 'and accordinglie ' wer useing dilligence, bot hade great difficulties to get y^e ' same.' At the next meeting, ' the Brethren c'sidering the ' necessitie of their using diligence in provyding their propor- ' tiones of the levie money not as zet provyded for ordeins all ' to meete Twesday nixt, and bring the same with them, to be ' delivered to the Modr., and to be sent south with all ' c'venient diligence, and each of them to pay sixtene shillings ' by and attour their proportiones, to be given to a bearer : ' and c'sidering the vacancie of Contin and Fottertie, they ' appoynt a warrant to be given to Mr. Coline Mackenzie for ' seeking and uplifting the proportiones of the said Kirks from ' the Heritors of them respue [respectively].' On 20th August a number of clergymen paid the proportions from their parishes, amounting to one hundred merks each. Charles's adherents, for whom the money was intended, were routed by Cromwell at Dunbar on 3rd September; but steps were immediately taken to raise a new army to follow him into England. Provision was made for the spiritual wants of this army. On 14th January 1651, a letter was read from the Commission of the General Assembly, desiring that clergymen should be sent out of the respective bounds of Presbyteries to minister to the combatants from those bounds. On 11th February it was reported that the heritors of Contin were employed in the West Highlands in connection with the levy. On 20th March a letter was submitted from Mackenzie, Lord Tarbert, requesting that a minister should be nominated for Lord Kintail's regiment, and a letter from the Master of Lovat desiring that Mr. Donald Fraser of Kilmorack should be appointed chaplain of the Fraser regiment. The appointment of Mr. Donald Macrae to the chaplaincy of the Kintail regiment is recorded on 8th April, and on the same day a fast is ordained in connection with which instructions are given to pray 'that God wald be 'pleasit to stirre up the spirits of people for their dewties to 'doe in there places as he calls them, y^t magistrats may be 'faithfull in there place, studying the publick good, and be 'furnished with counsell unto the end y^t officers and souldiers 'may be sanctified and fitted with faithfullnes, abilitie, and 'courage for y^r places'; and, further, 'that God wald make 'his people willing, and stirre them up for the defence of there 'brethren, and blesse and gathere there armies togethere, and 'may sanctifie them to be holie unto and instrumentall for the 'delyverie of his distressed land, and y^t the Lord wald judge 'those who haue unjustlie invaded his kingdome and spoiled and 'trampled and trod downe God's sacred ordinances, and mur-'dered so many of God's dear people.' On 27th May it is recorded that the heritors are absent on the 'present expedi-tion,' and that the land is 'pressed with diverse impositions.' On 19th June and following Sunday, a fast is kept, in connec-tion with which the Lord is earnestly wrestled with, and prayed that He 'wald provyde for the necessare preservation of the 'lives of his people from svord and feared famine, y^t the Lord 'wald mercifullie lead ovt ovr armie, inable everie one y^rin to 'keipe themselves from everie wicked thing, covere there head 'in the day of battell, teach their hands to warre, and there 'fingers to fight, and make them have guid successe y^t the 'enemie may flie and fall before, and y^t the Lord wald grati-'ouslie please by there means to delyvere ovr brethren y^t are 'wnder the foot of the enemie, and preserve the remanent of 'this oppressed kirk and kingdome from the wnjust wiolence of 'the cursed and cruell adversaries.' And on 8th July, Simon Mackenzie of Lochslin, father of the 'Bluidy Mackenzie,' King's

Advocate, is unable to attend the Presbytery meeting, 'in regaird of his imployment in the present expedition.' At the battle of Worcester, fought on 3rd September, the Scots were totally defeated. Many of the Highlanders were seized and condemned to slavery in the West Indies and the American plantations. Others perished in the attempt to reach their homes through an unfriendly country, whose language they neither spoke nor understood. Lochslin, however, returned, and the process against him was resumed, although apparently never brought to an issue.

In 1654 the noted Mr. Thomas Hogg, an earnest evangelist, became minister of Kiltearn, and three years later his almost equally noted friend, Mr. John Mackillican, was admitted to the parish of Fodderty, notwithstanding that he was a native of the lowlands of Moray, and consequently weak in the Gaelic tongue. These two clergymen were extreme Solemn Leaguers, and there was soon bad blood between themselves and certain of the older and more conservative members of the Presbytery. They were especially obnoxious to Mr. John Macrae, minister of Dingwall, a son of the manse of Kintail, who believed in Episcopacy, and who was, 'from his learning and piety, more fit for a chair than the pulpit.' Macrae and his party took to badgering Mackillican. In October 1657 he was somewhat sarcastically ordained 'to indevour to pray in the Irishe [Gaelic] language,' and ordered to own a portion of Strathconon for a part of his parish, which he had previously declined to do. Hogg was at the time moderator of the Presbytery, and Mackillican clerk, and they soon took their revenge. In the minutes of 19th January, 15th February, and 30th March 1658 they record Macrae's needless strife, his great miscarriage deserving sharp censure, his litigiousness, needless contention and untractableness, his stubbornness and wilfulness, his wearying tediousness, his misapplication of Scripture, and his pertinacity and loquaciousness. Matters, indeed, had come to such a pass that some of the brethren were forced to declare 'y^t that part of the ministrie was bitterness to them, 'and wished a destruction of the Presbytery, and to be annext 'to other presbyteries.' The Presbytery was not destroyed, but, probably as the result of the quarrel, there was no meeting between April 1658 and May 1663, when the first meeting under the Episcopacy established by Charles the Second was held. One result of the change in the Establishment was the deposition of Hogg and Mackillican; and Mr. John Macrae, who of course conformed, had the satisfaction of seeing the objectionable minutes deleted, and the expressions 'shamelesse lying' and 'the spirit of lieing and malice' written on their margins. The outed ministers, however, continued to preach to the Covenanters of Easter Ross, and the Records contain notices of attempts made to suppress conventicles in the parish of Kiltearn from time to time down to the year 1686.

With the exception that we meet such titles as bishop, archdeacon, deacon, chancellor, vicar, treasurer, and sub-dean, there is little in the Records to show that any change took place in the Church courts on the establishment of Episcopacy. Presbyteries and sessions still continue, and consist of ministers and elders. Proceedings are conducted in the manner which prevailed when there were no bishops; and delinquents are processed and punished in the old style. Neither was there change in the days and form of public worship, except that under Episcopacy the clergy were 'more mindfull' of the Lord's Prayer and the Doxology, and that they preached on Christmas Day, as well as on the anniversary of the Happy Restoration (29th May), and the King's Birthday (14th October).

For some time after the Restoration comparative peace reigned within the bounds of our Presbyteries in connection with Church affairs. With the exception of Hogg and Mackillican, the clergy of both Presbyteries conformed to Episcopacy; and, except in their cases, and in the case of Mr. Angus Macbean, of Inverness, who was admitted by the bishop, and thereafter

became a Covenanter, there was little suffering within the bounds for conscience' sake. Roman Catholics, indeed, were harassed by the Episcopalians, but their persecution was of a mild type. Not so the persecution of the three Covenanters. Hogg suffered fines and privations, imprisonment on the Bass Rock, and exile on the Continent; but he lived to be restored to his parish after the re-establishment of the present Church of Scotland in 1689. Mackillican also was fined, and imprisoned on the Bass and elsewhere; but he returned to Ross-shire in 1686, and spent the remaining years of his life at Alness in peace. In June 1687, Macbean, who was a son of the laird of Kinchyle in the parish of Dores, began to absent himself from the meetings of his Presbytery, and it was soon ascertained that he 'did disown the Govern-
' ment of the Church of Scotland as it is now established by
' Law, by Archbishops, Bishops, and Presbiters.' He further declared his conviction 'that Presbitrie was the only government that God owned in these nations.' He was at first gently reasoned with, but without result. Instead of returning to the 'Armes of the Church,' which were still open and ready to receive him upon his repentance, he 'publicly demitted his charge of the ministry under the present Government,' went to Ross-shire to preach to the Covenanters of that county, and, returning to Inverness, held a conventicle there, 'and so began
' his schisme in one of the most loyall, orderly, and regular cities
' in the nation.' His brethren, without an exception, joined in urging the Episcopal authorities 'to use all ordinar means for suppressing the schisme begun at Inverness.' In February 1688, he was, after suffering imprisonment, summoned before the Archbishop of St. Andrews, the Bishop of Moray, and other dignitaries, and invited to return to the Episcopal fold. He refused, and was deposed. His sentence was read from the pulpit of the Inverness High Church, 'for vindicating the Church's authority, and Terror of such Back-slyders.' His was the last sentence of deposition under the Episcopal estab-

lishment. The imprisonment and treatment to which he was subjected ruined his health, and he died in 1689, in the thirty-third year of his age. The Covenanters of Ross and the South regarded him with great affection and esteem; but he had few followers within the bounds of his own Presbytery, where, as well as within the greater portion of the bounds of the Dingwall Presbytery, Episcopacy flourished and prevailed for many years after its disestablishment by law.

The repose from war and spoliation which the Highlands enjoyed during the last years of Cromwell's rule came to an end at the Restoration, and reavers began their old work of cattle-lifting. From these evils parsons and people suffered alike. The Highlander's respect for the Church and the ministers of religion is of comparatively recent origin. In Roman Catholic times churches were burnt, and the clergy freely robbed. After the Reformation the state of matters was for generations even worse. The Records throw vivid light on the sufferings of the ministers, from their own heritors and parishioners as well as from outsiders. In 1649, Mr. Donald Macrae's starved condition compelled him to pray the Presbytery to remove him from Urray to another sphere. In 1665, Mr. Murdoch Mackenzie, minister of Lochbroom, was 'constrained to leave his ministry' for want of maintenance. In 1672, the same minister was unable to attend Presbytery 'for fear of caption'—imprisonment for debt. In June 1670 Mr. Thomas Houston, minister of Boleskine, complained that 'his house had been laitly seized upon by
' Lochabber Robbers, himselfe threatened with naked swords
' and drawne durks at his brest, his money and household
' stuff plundered; and seeing that one of their number suffered
' death laitly therefor at Inuerness the rest of them were lieing
' in wait for his life, and threatening his ruine and dammage,
' so that in ye evening he is affrayed to [be] burnt to ashes
' or [i.e. before] morning.' Mr. Houston had reason to be alarmed, for his predecessor had been barbarously murdered.

In March 1671 the minister of Dores complained that 'he had 'no mantenance among them [his gentlemen and elders], nor 'could he gete so much of his own stipend as would carry him 'through the parish to manage his Masters affairs, but was 'keeped as a poor mendicant ever since he came amongst that 'people; that they had no inclination to doe him the least 'duty herein, though he had sought after it in the most 'peacable manner that could be, as if, chameleon-like, he 'could live upon the aire'; and in August following he was unable to attend Presbytery for the reason that his horse had been stolen. Next month, Mr. Duncan MacCulloch, minister of Urquhart and Glenmoriston, complained, with reference to the elders and gentlemen of his parish, 'that 'he had neither countenance nor maintenance among them, 'and that when he is wronged or injured in his person or 'means, they have not that due regard to him as to resent these 'wrongs and injuries.' In 1682 'the straites and indigencies' of Mr. Robert Munro, who had Abertarff and Glenmoriston under his charge, were such that his brethren contributed towards his relief.

Frequently, too, the ministers were without the manse and glebe with which the law was supposed to provide him. In 1649 there was no manse or glebe in Kintail, Lochalsh, Lochcarron, or Lochbroom. In 1671 there was no manse in Dores or Kiltarlity, and none in Daviot or Moy as late as 1678. The churches in which the poor pastors preached were frequently ruinous and unfurnished. In 1649 the church of Kintail was without proper 'thacking' [thatching], because of 'the troubles of the tymes,' and there was no pulpit or desk. In Lochalsh there was 'nothing found in this kirk but the bare walls.' The church of Lochcarron boasted of a stool of repentance, but it had neither pulpit nor desks. In 1665 there was in Lochbroom no 'convenient meeting place for preaching, the kirk of Lochbroom being unthatched'; and in 1681 a general regret is recorded by the brethren of the Presbytery of

Dingwall 'that their churches are werie ruinous.' Until well into the eighteenth century few churches were furnished with pews or seats—the people standing or moving about during service, or, in the case of the aged and infirm, sitting on small stools provided by themselves. Notwithstanding laws and ordinances against 'burials in churches,' the rude but sacred buildings were universally made the last resting-places of the people. In 1684, the minister of Boleskine reported 'that all ' persons of all ranks indifferently buried their dead within his ' church, not only his own parishioners, but some others of the ' neighbouring parishes, so that several coffins were hardly under ' ground, which was like to be very dangerous and noisome to ' the hearers of the word within the said church.' Boleskine was not worse than other parishes. The dogs that followed the people to church fought over the human bones that protruded through the earthen floor; and for the malignant fevers that so often ravaged the country, the foul air which the worshippers breathed while they worshipped was not less responsible than the insanitary condition of their dwelling-houses.

Not only were ministers often deprived of their just rights, but insults and threats were frequently their reward for trying to do their duty. In 1671 the minister of Daviot had occasion to give John Mackintosh, a brother of the laird of Aberarder, the first public admonition from the pulpit in connection with a charge of breach of the Seventh Commandment. John did not like the minister's plain speaking, and at the close of the service he came up to him at the church door and thus addressed him in presence of the whole congregation: 'You ' base raskall, how durst yee bee so peart as to abuse mee this ' day? Yee wes too bold to doe it; yee might hav used your ' own equalls so and not me.' Upon the minister calling the gentlemen of the parish as witnesses Mackintosh retorted: ' You base raskall, think you will I eat my words? Were not ' for little to mee I wold bruiss y^{or} bones.' In 1674 the minister of Boleskine summoned a young breaker of the same commandment before his Session. Instead of obeying, the accused sent his father, Donald dow Mack Conachie nan Each—Black Donald son of Duncan of the Horses—in Glenlia, who 'menaciouslie threatened the minister with many opprobrious 'and barbarous malicious speeches.' In 1652 Mr. John Macrae, the learned minister of Dingwall, is publicly called a knave and a liar; and about the same time Thomas McNaoise confesses his malicious imprecations against the ministry generally, and is condemned to stand in sackcloth in all the churches within the Presbytery of Dingwall. In 1673 Mr. Donald Ross, who is always in trouble, is struck by his church-officer, who is consequently dismissed by the Presbytery and ordained to do penance in the church of Contin.

The ministers were greatly obstructed in their work by the troubles of the times. On 2nd August 1649, Duncan McAlister vic conill dowy—Duncan son of Alexander son of Black Donald—an Urray relapser in adultery, failed to appear before his Presbytery because 'his guids [cattle] were stollen from him, 'and he was upon the pursuit of them.' On the 15th, no elders or people attended a presbyterial visitation of Kintail, 'except 'some few that were not considerable,' for the reason that 'they were on the persuit of guids that were stollen and tacken 'away from the severall corners of the countrie.' Reference has already been made to the charge of obstruction brought against Cromwell's soldiers. In July 1674, Hugh Mac Allister vic ean roy, in Dores, a captain of 'The Watch '—a band of volunteers raised for the purpose of protecting cattle and property—who had been summoned before the Presbytery of Inverness, was unable to appear 'to vindicat himself in thir troublesome 'tymes, wherein thieves and robbers have turned insollent and 'resolute in wickedness'; and in July 1676, the heritors and elders of Daviot and Dunlichity declared their inability to attend a proposed visitation of their parish, 'seeing they are 'necessitat to abyd in the Glens to shelter and keep their 'bestiall and goods from the Lochaber and Glencoa robbers.' Several ministers were absent from the meeting of the Presbytery of Inverness, held on 8th July 1685, because they 'could not wait 'upon the dyet considering the great stirrs that were in the 'countrie in respect of the preparatione to his Majesty's host' —an allusion to the proposed Royalist expedition into Argyllshire in connection with Monmouth's Rebellion; and on 5th September 1688, there only met the Moderator and the minister of Kirkhill, all the rest being absent, 'some by reason of the 'great stirrs that were in the countrey anent the late rebellion 'and bloodshed in Lochaber'—a reference to the fight of Mulroy. These troubles were but the forerunners of the War of the Revolution. In that struggle the great majority of the inhabitants of our bounds sided with King James, and many of them fought under the banner of Dundee. Ecclesiastically, the result was the legal re-establishment of Presbyterianism; but the bulk of the people and the majority of the clergy continued to adhere to Episcopacy, and for many years after the Revolution there was virtually no Presbytery either of Inverness or of Dingwall, and every man within the bounds did what was right in his own eyes.

Notwithstanding their many discouragements, the ministers, whether under Presbytery or under Episcopacy, on the whole faithfully laboured for the good of the people. Members of the better classes—sons of lairds or of the larger tacksmen or farmers—they were, with few exceptions, men of intelligence and education, who far surpassed their perhaps more earnest brethren of the Lowlands in charitableness and toleration. To these Lowland brethren their ways were sometimes strange, especially when they went about, not in the orthodox clerical garb, but in all the glory of the Highland dress. To appear in the Church courts in kilt and bonnet, and wearing their hair long like the ordinary Celt of the time, was in the highest degree barbarous, and attempts were early made to put down the unseemly custom. At a meeting of the Synod of Moray, held at Elgin in April 1624, the 'visitors' or examiners of the Presbytery Book of Inverness reported that the brethren of that Presbytery 'haunts to the Presbytrie with uncomly habits, ' such as bonats and plaides; whairfor the Assemblie ordaines ' them not to haunt the Presbytrie any mair with uncomly ' habitts.' Again, in 1640, the same Synod ordained 'that ' all ministers be grave and decent in their apparell, in their ' carriage and behaviour; that none weare long hair, but that ' bothe in lyfe and habite they may be knowne by their men ' to be the ministers of Jesus Chryst.' But it was difficult to reconcile Highland parsons to Lowland fashions. As late as 1671, the Presbytery found it necessary to ordain Mr. Roderick Mackenzie, minister of Moy, 'to goe in a ministeriall habite whan he went to set about any pairt of his work.' According to tradition, the Highland dress was not entirely discarded by the ministers until after Culloden; and *breacan nan cleireach* (the clergy's tartan) is still reproduced in books on tartans.

The old minister's chief duty was of course to preach. This he did as a rule twice every Sunday—first in Gaelic and thereafter in English. In the burghs of Inverness and Dingwall, where the Saxon tongue was known from very early times, the Gospel has no doubt been preached in that tongue from the period of the Reformation. It is difficult to say when it was first preached in English in the country parishes, where Gaelic was universally spoken. Our Records, however, show that English was preached in several churches within our bounds during the period covered by them. In 1651, Mr. Donald Fraser, minister of Kilmorack, had such a command of that language that his removal 'to ane Inglish congregation' was apprehended, 'if not tymlie prevented.' Mr. Donald Ross, minister of Contin, preached in English at the same period; and so, a few years later, did his neighbour Mr. Mackillican—who, indeed, could hardly preach in Gaelic—in the parish of Fodderty. Mr. Thomas Hogg preached in Kiltearn in both English and

INTRODUCTION   xxi

Irish [Gaelic] in 1654, and his Episcopalian successor, Mr. John Gordon, preached in both languages thirty years later. In 1671, the people of Dores 'were refreshed very much by 'their minister Sabbathly both in the English and Irish 'language'; and on 23rd July 1672, a sermon was preached at Wardlaw (Kirkhill) in 'Irish,' and another in 'Scots.' In these parishes, as in all the parishes within our bounds, divine service is still conducted in both tongues, Gaelic being still the popular tongue—so long does it take a new language to supplant an old, even when the new is the language of culture and of commerce.

The Sacramental fast-day and 'preaching week,' which are now so prominent a feature in the religious life of the North, were unknown within our bounds in the seventeenth century, although they had already established themselves in the South, where they have now all but disappeared. The Sacrament of the Lord's Supper, indeed, was seldom administered. Mr. Robert Munro, minister of Kiltearn, admitted in May 1650 that there had been no Communion in his parish since his entry. In the same year it was reported that in Lochbroom the Sacrament had not been administered during the previous seven years. In 1665 Fodderty had been without it for twelve years; and Glen Urquhart was in the same condition during the whole incumbency of Mr. Duncan MacCulloch—1647 to 1671. Other parishes were as bad. In 1679 the Synod of Moray ordered the members of the Inverness Presbytery to administer it; but on 1st October of that year it was found that the 'bretheren have not given it, and ther reason was 'that the frequent charges that ther people gott to be in 'armes against the Macdonalds obstructed ther friedom to 'that great work.' The Synod's order was again and again renewed; but while it is found in 1681 'that the ministers of 'Inverness, Daviot, and Wardlaw have celebrated the same 'about and after Easter, the not giveing it at all, or but verie 'seldome, is very much to be regrated.' In April 1684 several of the brethren of the Presbytery of Inverness reported that they had given the Sacrament that year; but 'the rest told 'that they were impeded by the greatnes of the stormie 'weather and other inevitable impediments.' In short, any and every excuse was seized to put off the sacred rite. And, as was to be expected, some of the churches were without the necessary furnishings and utensils for it. Daviot, for example, had in 1682 no 'necessaries' of any kind; Petty and Croy each rejoiced in a bare Communion table—'other necessaries were borrowed'; while the learned Mr. James Fraser of Kirkhill 'had a very good large table, two good towels, a basin also; but he borrowed silver cups yearly'—no doubt from the ministers of Inverness, who probably possessed the only silver cups of which the bounds could boast.

Although Sacramental fast-days were unknown, there was no lack of other fast and thanksgiving days, and days of humiliation. Sometimes these were kept on the Sabbath. On the last Sunday of August 1649 a fast was observed by order of the General Assembly for the continuance and increase of sin and profanity, especially the sin of witchcraft; the interruption of the Lord's work in England and Ireland, and sore oppression of His people, by the prevailing party of Sectaries in the one and Malignants in the other; and the King's failure to grant what was necessary for the security of religion, and his making peace with the Irish rebels. Prayer was to be offered on these special points; and the Almighty was also to be entreated to 'regaird the necessitie of the poore 'by giveing a fair and seasonable harvest, and bestow upon 'his people a plentifull measure of the fruits of the earth, for 'preventing the famine threatened and feared, and enabling 'the Kingdome to beare necessarie burdens without repyneing.' After the King's execution and the Scots' quarrel with Cromwell, fasts were observed having special reference to the tyranny of the Usurper's 'proud party of Sectaries,' and to the efforts made to place Charles the Second on the throne.

The reasons for the great fast of June 1651, observed when the country was about to send its best blood into England to fight there for 'Kirk and Kingdom,' are of the most solemn nature, and the prayers ordained must have been joined in by thousands of men and women with unusual fervour, if, in some cases, also with sorrow and anxiety, and painful forebodings as to the fate of loved ones who were to join in the distant and dangerous invasion. Less solemn were the fasts that were in after years held by royal command. When the Dutch War of Charles the Second broke out in 1665, a fast was observed 'in behalf of the Royal Navy, and for a blessed success to the intended war against the United Provinces,' and a month later a public thanksgiving for the short-lived triumph over the Dutch. On 13th September there was a public fast and humiliation 'for the rageing of the plague of ' pestilence in England [the Great Plague] and for preventing ' it in Scotland.' Printed proclamations, issued by Charles the Second, ordaining a fast on 18th December 1678 in connection with the discovery of the Popish Plot, were distributed among the brethren of the Presbytery of Inverness on the 11th of that month. On 9th September 1683 a day of thanksgiving was kept for the happy discovery of the Rye House Plot— 'the late horrid plot against his sacred Majesty, his Royal ' Highness [the Duke of York], and the established govern- ' ment.' Similar thanksgivings were observed on 13th August 1685 for the suppression of the Monmouth and Argyll rebellion; in March 1688 'for her Majesty's being with child'; and on 28th June 'for the birth of the Prince of Scotland'—the unfortunate prince concerning whose parentage doubts were unjustly raised, and whom the Whigs consequently dubbed the Pretender. In addition to these and such incidental fasts, the 29th of May—Royal Oak Day—was for many years annually kept within the bounds as a solemn thanksgiving for the Happy Restoration; religious services were in the reign of James held on the King's birthday; and in the Episcopal time the ministers preached at Easter and on Christmas Day.

During the period of these Records, and indeed until the spread of Puritanism after Culloden, the inhabitants of our bounds were not unduly strict in matters of religion; and, especially, they had little of that Sabbatarian spirit which has characterised, and still characterises, their descendants. Towards the Sabbath the clergy themselves sometimes showed a lax spirit. They married their parishioners on that day, and after the ceremony took part in the festivities. They likewise buried on the Sabbath, frequently deserting the pulpit for the funeral and its entertainment. The Synod of Moray ordained in 1640 'that ministers exhort frome burieing on ye Sabbothe, ' and that heirafter no minister leave his awne flock to ' goe to burialls on ye Sabbothe, unless ye necessitie be ap-' prowen be ye Presbiterie'; and, in regard to marriages, the Synod recorded : ' in respect off ye gryt disorders y^t haw fallen ' out in dyverse parts of ye land by drunkennes and tuilzieing ' [fighting] at pennie brydalls, thairfor it is ordained that thair ' be no pennie brydalls maid on ye Sabbath.' But it was difficult to suppress old customs ; and penny weddings, especially, and the irregularities connected with them, continue to be denounced in the Records. Another institutiou that troubled our Presbyteries greatly was the lykewake, at which the mirth was frequently even more boisterous than at the wedding, the chamber of death being frequently filled night after night with jest, song, and story, the music of the fiddle and the pipe, and the shout and clatter of the Highland reel.

In 1649, Mr. Donald Ross, minister of Lochbroom, was found guilty of selling wine in his house and 'keeping com-' panie with some gentlemen drinking wyne upon the sabbath'; and in 1674 Mr. William Smith, minister of Duthel, got so intoxicated at Inverness on a Saturday night that, instead of preaching next morning at Cawdor according to appointment, he did not go near the church, but travelled home on the

Lord's day. The tavern, which usually nestled close to the church, and did a roaring business before and after divine service, was a great evil; and men sometimes in their drunken excitement forgot the sacredness of the sanctuary. In 1672 two lairds, Martin Macgillivray of Aberchalder, and Alexander Mackintosh of Farr, had a 'ploy' on the Lord's day within the church of Dunlichity; in the same year John M'doir was accused of drunkenness and fighting in the church of Kiltearn; and in 1680 Andrew M'Andrew was found guilty of striking a man within the church of Urquhart of Ferintosh. If there was little regard for the Sabbath within the church there was less for it outside, and until things were changed by the spread of Puritanism already referred to, the old Highlander gave up the greater part of the day to pleasure, sports, and his worldly avocations. From the Dingwall Presbytery's minute of 31st July 1649, it appears that dealers in the famous whisky of Ferintosh carried on their trade on Sunday, as did the fishermen of the district their fishing. In the same year an attempt is made to put down Sunday fishing in Kintail; and in 1650 a number of persons in Lochbroom are ordered to be processed for the same offence.

Closely connected with the minister's pulpit ministrations was the catechising of his parishioners, and the pressing upon them of the duty of family worship. In this work, judging from the Records, he failed. For this he cannot be blamed. There was neither Gaelic Bible nor Gaelic Catechism; and, as few of his flock knew English, home services were well-nigh impossible, and were, we may assume, seldom attempted. The calls upon his own time were too many to admit of anything like regularity or thoroughness in his extra-pulpit teaching; and frequently he wholly neglected the duty. His elders were chosen on account of their social position and influence among the people; and while they were helpful in bringing delinquents to justice, they were utterly unable to assist in purely spiritual things. It was long after the period to which these

Records refer, that 'The Men,' who have for the last century and a half been so noted as catechists and expounders and men of prayer, first appeared within the bounds of our Presbyteries.

The frequency of the Presbytery meetings—sometimes two or three within the month—greatly interrupted and interfered with the minister's pastoral work. To these meetings he rode on horseback, in some cases for fifty or even seventy miles, over rough tracks and through unbridged rivers; and when a visitation of the West Coast churches, or the Highland churches as they are called in contra-distinction to the East Coast or Lowland churches, was on hand, the journey was one of weeks. Attendance at the synod, which, in the case of Moray, met at Elgin, and in the case of Ross, at Tain, was also a serious business, involving—taking the return journey into account—a ride ranging from twenty-five to two hundred miles. No wonder we find more excuses for absence than were offered to the giver of the marriage supper. It is my marriage day, said the minister of Urquhart and Glenmoriston to his bishop and synod, in 1626, and therefore I cannot come. My child is at the point of death, said Mr. John Macrae of Dingwall to his Presbytery in 1649; I pray you have me excused. I am tormented with the worm, wrote Mr. Donald Macrae of Urray in 1650; pray, therefore, pardon my absence. I have taken physic, was the message sent by Mr. Farquhar Maclennan to his Presbytery in 1656, and must stay at home. I am tender, and not able to travel, pleaded the minister of Croy in 1677. On the last day of 1650, Mr. Colin Mackenzie was excused, as he was 'attending Reidcastle, who was at the point of death.' On the same date Mr. John Munro of Alness wrote 'that he came getward to keipe the Presbytrie, 'bot that his horse fell under him, and that he was not able to 'ryde.' It fared worse with the minister of Dores in 1671, for his horse had been stolen. In 1675 Mr. Houston of Boleskine was preparing his flock for a long neglected Communion. Mr.

INTRODUCTION xxvii

Fraser of Kiltarlity is in 1676 'South about some law affaires'; in 1680 he is in Inchgald, or the Hebrides; in 1685 he is in the South again. His namesake of Daviot went even further afield, for in 1682 we find him in England. In 1650 the minister of Ferintosh was attending the Committee of War at Inverness; and his neighbour of Urray was in March 1654 impeded and molested by the English garrison at Brahan, and on 12th December following, abstracted by quartering on by the English. The Moderator was unable to attend a meeting held at Kilchumen (Fort Augustus), on 25th September 1677, 'beeing ordered by the Magistrats to preach that day the elec-'tione sermone for chooseing the Magistrats of Inuerness.' Spates in the river Nairn, which was at the time without a bridge, prevented the attendance of Mr. Mackenzie of Moy on more than one occasion; and there are other instances of members being storm-stayed or 'impeded by the waters.' Funerals, also, interfered. In 1650 an appointed meeting was not held at Dingwall on account of the funeral of Mackenzie of Coul. In 1665 the ministers of Alness and Contin were absent at the burial of Balnagown's brother; and in November 1686 a meeting of the Presbytery of Inverness was put off, 'because the Bretheren did atend the Funeralls of the Right 'Reverend Father in God, Colin, late Lord Bishop of Murray, 'whom God called out of this Life, November 11, 1686, to the 'enjoyment of eternall hapines, whose Funerals were honour-'ably and solemnly celibrat with great greef at Elgin, 'Novemb. 22.'

When a reasonable excuse was offered, it was readily accepted; but absence or unpunctuality without cause was resented and punished. On 28th July 1657 it is recorded in the Dingwall register that 'the Moderator not coming precise-'lie at tenn o'clocke, tho shortlie efter, the rest of the brethren 'for the most part would not stay anie longer then the per-'emptorie houre appointed'—a somewhat severe piece of boycotting, seeing that the Moderator was in all probability without clock or watch. The Presbytery of Inverness suspended brethren who 'willfully thryce or oftener absents themselves ' from the Presbytrie without any excuse'; and the Court of Dingwall had a rule 'that everie brother cuming late should give in a sexpens to be given to the poore.' But it was difficult to enforce such regulations, and on 13th October 1663 there was a lively discussion at Dingwall over the refusal of certain dilatory brethren to pay their sixpences; and the momentous matter was referred to the bishop.

The meeting of Presbytery was opened with prayer, after which a member 'exercised' and another 'added' on a text from Scripture. The exercise and addition were thereafter discussed by the brethren, and usually approved; but sometimes approval was withheld, and on 29th December 1657 the brethren were so much dissatisfied with Mr Donald Ross' 'method, matter, and weaknes' that they 'desyred he should 'be reprehended with a premonire.' At certain meetings 'expectants' or aspirants to the ministry were put through their 'Trials'; and sometimes such common heads were discussed as *De transubstantione, De peccato originali, De extentione mortis Christi, De infallibilitate Ecclesiae, De justificatione, De satisfactione Christi, De gratia universali, De perseverantia sanctorum, De primatu Petri, De potestate clavium, De libero arbitrio, De peccato veniali et mortali, De propagatione peccati originalis, De paedobaptismo, De voluntate Dei, De notis ecclesiae, De justitia originali, De certitudine salutis, De Dei scientia, De praedestinatione, De creatione hominis, De anima, De universali redemptione.*

It was the duty of the members of Presbytery to inquire into each others' diligence and faithfulness in the ministry; and in connection with this we find such charges recorded against ministers as preferring their private business to their public duties; neglect of the Communion, and of catechising and family prayer; celebration of mock and irregular marriages, and the disorderly giving of baptism; drunkenness and swearing; malignancy; worshipping with excommunicated persons; and breaches of the Seventh Commandment. As a rule, however, the minister's life and labour are approved; and sometimes the minutes record some special feature which has met with the brethren's appreciation. In 1649, when political excitement ran high, it is noted with satisfaction that the minister of Kiltearn 'attends his charge and meddles not with civil affairs,' and that his brother of Kilmorack 'is no tryster in civill business.' Would that some of our modern ministers held themselves under equal restraint. In 1677 the Presbytery of Inverness, sitting in Glen Urquhart, blessed the Lord for the good applause the minister of that Glen had of his elders, and for the sweet harmony that prevailed; and in the same year the people of Kirkhill declared that their pastor observed all his ministerial duties, 'and was so panefull that they were ' affrayed that he should thereby shorten his own dayes, in all ' likliehood.' It is pleasant to record that the worthy pastor—Mr. James Fraser, author of the unpublished local history known as the Wardlaw MS., and of one or two other manuscripts, which are now in the Advocates' Library—lived and laboured till the year 1709. The 'Bill of Mortality' kept by him from 1663 to the time of his death—a register of deaths in his parish and neighbourhood, but in which general events connected with the district are also recorded—was discovered in the parish a few years ago and placed in the General Register House, where it now is—the most interesting record of its kind in Scotland.

Next to the brethren's duty of finding out and reporting upon each other's shortcomings and failings was that of detecting and suppressing crime and immorality, Popery and idolatry, witchcraft and superstition, and other evil habits and customs among the people; of searching after truth and justice in quarrels between spouses, and in cases of irregular marriages, disputed paternity, and slander; of providing for the honest poor, and bringing vagrants and sturdy beggars to punishment; and of seeing that no strangers settled in their parishes without certificates of good character and freedom from Church censure. They, in short, exercised in a strangely mixed manner the functions of the modern civil magistrates and police authorities; and when they found themselves with a weak jurisdiction, or experienced difficulty in executing their judgments, they invoked the aid of justices and lairds, with the result that offenders seldom escaped. Thus, the Presbytery of Dingwall, after inquiring into a case of child murder in 1685, 'finding that cryms of that nature were above their ' cognizance and decision, determined to represent the case to ' the civil Judge, quhich was accordingly done, the clerk with ' the desire of the Presbyterie haveing wrote a letter to Sir ' Rorie M'Kenzie of Findon, Shereff Deput of Ross, to that ' effect.' In connection with the discovery of gross superstitions in the remote district of Applecross in 1650, the justices were enjoined by the Presbytery 'to doe there duties in suppressing of the foresaid wickedness': the goodman of Culcowie (Kilcoy) was requested in 1656 to ' interpone his authoritie ' in compelling certain sacrificers on his West Highland estates to appear before the Synod; in 1663 the heritors of Urray were called upon to deal with a disobedient delinquent ' as powerfullie as they could'; and in 1668 Lady Seaforth was urged to cause her chamberlain to make stubborn offenders yield obedience. In 1670 the Presbytery of Inverness appoints the minister of Dores ' to give a list of all the obstinat de- ' linquents within his Parish to Alex^r Chissolme, as Baily of ' Stratharrick and Comissar depute of Inverness, to see if that ' rude people and obstinate generation may be brought to a ' more Christian subjection and orderly conformity'; and in 1682 the minister and elders of Croy were recommended 'quhen ' delinquents were obstinat and refractory in paying penalties, ' to have immediat recourse to the Authority of the Com- ' missary.' The Church officers had sometimes cause to welcome such outside aid. In 1665 the officer of Urquhart of Ferintosh was deforced; and in 1672 the officer of Dunlichity confessed that he was 'affrayed' to summon the delinquents of that parish to the Presbytery. No wonder. The lairds of Aberchalder and Farr, and a brother of the laird of Aberarder, were of their number.

Among the ordinary crimes and offences into which we find the Presbyteries inquiring are murder, wife murder, child murder, assault, adultery (in connection with which the penalty of death is alluded to), incest, perjury, drunkenness, failure to support child, and wife desertion. Sometimes it was the woman who deserted the man. We also meet such offences as taking God's name in vain; scandalous usurpation of the ministerial function by John MacFinlay vic Conil Donich, who disorderly baptized infants in the parish of Contin; blasphemy by a would-be theologian from Ferintosh, who declared 'that Christ Jesus was a sinner all the tyme he lived on earth'; and desecration by Kiltearn drovers, who made a cattle fold of the ancient church of Kilchrist, which had been without roof or door since the Glengarry men destroyed itself and its congregation by fire in the famous raid of 1603.

Breaches of the Seventh Commandment were common within our bounds, as they were in every parish in Scotland; and the Records are full of unsavoury processes. When the wretched offenders tried to escape from punishment and exposure they were followed with marvellous persistency and success. Margaret Fraser, an Inverness schoolmaster's frail daughter who refused to disclose the father of her child, and whom the bishop consequently ordered to be excommunicated, fled the country in 1674, and was traced to London, where for two years or more she was the recipient of unwelcome messages from the Presbytery, conveyed to her on one occasion at least by the Inverness merchants, who journeyed to the great city annually in May to purchase commodities for their Highland customers. In 1676 Donald Miller, a sinner who had escaped from Inverness, is found to be in remote Assynt in Sutherlandshire, and 'the Moderator is desyred to wryt to the minister of Assint to send him back to satisfie the kirk discipline.' Alexander Besack and Janet nein vic Gillmichael (Janet daughter of the son of the servant of St. Michael), fugitives from Inverness, are traced to Orkney, and the ministers there are put on their track with such effect that they are glad to recross the stormy Pentland. Next year they are 'reported ' to be att Tung in Strathnaver,' and the ministers of Inverness ' are ordained to wrytt to the minister of the foresaid place to ' remitt them back againe, quhich they promised to doe *quam* ' *primum*.'

In connection with lapses of this sort the paternity was, of course, frequently denied by the male transgressor. If the minister and session failed to bring him to a confession by ordinary dealing, the Presbytery took him in hand and applied a very drastic test of truthfulness. In 1665 William Macleod was ordained to clear himself by oath before the congregation of Fodderty. The minister of Kiltarlity was in 1677 ordered to take Donald Roy, a sheriff officer who was so obstinate in his denial that there was no 'hope of confession except the ' extraordinarie divyne hand of God work on him,' ' diverse ' Lord's dayes before the pulpit in presence of the whole congre- ' gatione, and to offer him the oath, and pray for him that God ' may open his obdured heart to confess the truth, and if he ' continu obstinat, to tak his oath at last upon the head of the ' child, as is the practise of this Kirk and Kingdome.' In 1684 Donald Bain, who denied the paternity of Agnes Mackenzie's child, ' is ordained to purge himselfe by his oath befor ye con- ' gregation of Inverness with his hand on ye child's head, and in ' presence of ye forsaid Agnes, and that ye Ministers are apointed ' to be at pains w^t him, to sie if it be possible to bring him to ' any aknowledgement.' James Fraser was in 1681 put to a greater trial still—he was to take the oath publickly before the congregation of Kiltarlity, with one hand on the child's head and the other upon the Bible. Few guilty persons even in those wild times, were strong enough in their wickedness to be able to go through so solemn an ordeal, and the fortitude of most men gave way before the oath was administered. Their desire to escape punishment and liability is easily accounted for; but we can only conjecture the reason why Charles Mackenzie, son of the laird of Pluscardine, took his illegitimate child into his own charge, and refused to disclose the mother. She was probably of gentle blood, and he, as became the son of the chivalrous leader of the Royalist rising of 1649, did what he could to save her from public shame, and to atone for the wrong he had done her. In Mr. Rorie Mackenzie, minister of Moy, he found a loyal clansman to baptize the infant. For this Mr. Rorie got into trouble with his presbytery and synod, the latter ordaining him to 'mak search for a mother to the child hee baptised to Charles Mackenzie.' The child was nursed by an honest woman in Moy till it was a year old, when Charles 'and his company' appeared and removed it to Strathglass. It is there lost sight of; and, so far as the Records show, the mystery of its maternity was never solved.

Delinquents were punished by being mulcted in pecuniary penalties; placed in the jougs, which usually adorned the church wall near the principal entrance; made to stand before the pulpit in sackcloth, Sabbath after Sabbath, for weeks if not for years, or to sit on the stool of repentance in the most conspicuous part of the church; and, in the worst cases, placed beyond Christian help and hope, here and hereafter, by the dread sentence of excommunication. They sometimes, as we have seen, fled to other bounds. In 1677 William Macpherson elected to serve in Holland as a soldier rather than stand the censure of the Presbytery of Inverness; and in 1686 Ewen Mac Hucheon, in the parish of Kilmorack, leapt out of the frying-pan into the fire, by 'professing himself a Papist to shun the censure of the Church.' Absolution sometimes tardily came. In 1675, William Macpherson, Inverness, who had

sinned with women married and unmarried, 'haveing appeared
' severall yeares *in sacco,* evidencing his publict remorse for his
' saids gross sinns, supplicated the Presbytrie to be absolved,
' and hee appeareing before them with teares and other signes
' off his repentance, is referred to the ministers of Inverness to
' be absolved, and to report ther diligence.' In special cases
justice was wisely tempered with mercy. In 1679 a Glenmoriston delinquent, Dugald Macconachie vic Conill, pleaded
for a modification of the process against him, and the Presbytery 'judged expedient, because of the distance of the place
' and rudeness of the people, to yeild to his humble demand,
' and the minister [was] exhorted in his owne pastorall prudence
' to use all lenity and meikness to gain such.' And, again, in
1687, John Grant, a son of the laird of that Glen, 'a papist
' excommunicat 20 years ago for ane incestuous mariage, he
' being irregularly maried be a popish priest to his uncle's wife,
' and now she being dead, and the said John haveing forsaken
' the errores of the popish Church, and returned and imbraced
' the Orthodox Religion,' applied to be relaxed from the dread
sentence, and to be received into Mother Church, and, after
inquiry, was encouragingly referred by the Presbytery to the
bishop and synod—the said John ' being a gentleman of good
' accompt in his own countrey, and liveing near by Glengarie,
' the inhabitants of quhich countrey are for the most part all
' papists, and are useing many endeavours to make the said
' John relaps into his former apostacie.'

Popery, indeed, was a source of considerable trouble to our
Presbyteries. Into the Chisholm's country of Strathglass,
lying partly in the parish of Kiltarlity and Presbytery of
Inverness, and partly in the parish of Kilmorack and Presbytery of Dingwall, the doctrines of the Reformation had
scarcely penetrated ; and there were also many Roman Catholics
in the Braes of Glenmoriston, and the district of Abertarff.
One effect of the religious rebound and uncertainty that
followed the Restoration was to make people look with a

kindlier eye on the ancient Church, which appeared to have no variableness or shadow of turning; and a stream of apostasy began to flow within the bounds of our Presbyteries which the Episcopal ministers of the time found it impossible to stem. Sir John Byres, of Coates, near Edinburgh, and his wife, Lilias Grant, daughter of the ultra-Protestant Laird of Grant, apostatised, and, burning with the proselyte's zeal, entertained Romish priests and laymen within the castle of Inverness, of which he was governor. They were excommunicated, but that only added to their zeal. They celebrated Easter, 1674, by holding ' a greatt conventione of papists' in the castle, notwithstanding the Presbytery's appeal to the Sheriff-Depute to prevent the gathering by enforcing 'the last and late strick act of counsell' against the Roman Catholics. They sheltered and encouraged priests, the most prominent of whom were Robert Munro, who acted as their chaplain, and served also in Strathglass; Father Hugh O'Rien, who also laboured in that Strath, ' under the notion of a physician'; Priest O'Neil, who resided for a time in the castle in 1681, and Priest Francis Macdonald, who took Glengarry as his corner of the vineyard. Munro's success in seducing souls was such that the Earl of Moray, principal Sheriff of Inverness-shire, undertook, in 1676, to ' cause secure his persone, that he may not mislead the people any longer.' Next year, the Synod of Moray ordained ' that bretheren take narrow inspectione anent
' trafficking priests their preaching or saying mass in families
' or conventicles, and upon certaine informatione to transmit
' their names to the Bishope '; and in 1682, it ordered the ministers 'to give up to the Bishop the names of seminary
' priests, and such as mary and baptise with them, the obstinat
' to be processt ; and, to the end that letters of intercom-
' muning may be obtained against the excommunicat, the
' brethren at their next meeting not to faile to send to the
  Bishop 14 shillings Scots from every brother for the expense
' of the said letters of intercommuning.' But no serious

attempt was made to put these resolutions in force, and the priests continued to go up and down through the parishes 'avowedly, confidently, and affrontedly,' teaching, marrying, and baptizing. It was complained that they even married persons under process, and baptized their ill-gotten issue. Among those who (in addition to Sir John Byres and his wife, and John Grant, of Glenmoriston, already referred to) came under their glamour and renounced Protestantism, were several members of the family of The Chisholm; Colin Chisholm of Buntait, and his wife; David Baillie, of Dochfour; James Baillie, there, and his wife; Allan Macdonald, of Kyltrie, and his wife, and all his children, servants, and tenants; Donald Macdonald, of Culachie, and Ranald Macdonald, of Pitmean, and their wives, servants, and tenants; Alexander Fraser, of Kinneras; the Rev. Colin Dalgleish, and many others of less note. Dalgleish was brought to see the error of his ways, and made a public recantation of Popery within the High Church of Inverness. After the Revolution many of the other perverts and their families returned to Protestantism. Strathglass, however, which the Dingwall parsons declared, in 1678, to be 'pestered with poperie,' continued, and still continues, to be the pride and the pleasure of devout members of the ancient Church.

Certain idolatrous and superstitious customs which prevailed in pagan and early Christian times lingered on for generations after the Reformation. The image called St. Finane, which the Protestant people of Dunlichity worshipped as late as the year 1643, deserved a better fate than burning at the market cross of Inverness, after sermon. Probably the ministers who did the burning did not know that they were destroying the last representation, rude and imaginary though it might be, of one of the most earnest evangelists of the early Celtic Church. There is reason to believe that other saints had similar effigies. When Mackenzie of Kintail and Macdonald of Glengarry were before the Privy Council in connection with that feud the leading feature of which was the Raid of Kilchrist, Mackenzie proved Glengarry to have been a worshipper of the Coan, 'which image was afterwards brought to Edinburgh, and burnt at the cross.'[1] In that case, also, was destroyed, in ignorance, the effigy of a venerated apostle, that prince of Leinster who in the early centuries of our era renounced the world and devoted his life to the Christianising of the Celt, and who was the patron saint of the Macdonald district of Knoydart, where the ruins of his chapel are still to be seen. But the most extraordinary story of idolatry which we know in connection with the Highlands is that told so graphically in the Dingwall minutes of 5th and 9th September 1656. Fortunately, the heathenish practices which had gathered around the memory of St. Mourie greatly impressed the brethren of the Presbytery, and the clerk records details with the relish of an antiquary, if also with indications of horror at the darkness of the superstition. But in this instance, again, the brethren had no idea that they were dealing with customs which, having their origin in remote pagan times, had, after the introduction of Christianity into the Highlands, engrafted themselves on the memory of an eminent Celtic cleric. 'Whether this Mourie,' wrote the late Rev. Dr. Kennedy of Dingwall, 'was a heathen deity, a 'Popish saint, or one of Columba's missionaries, it may be 'impossible to determine.'[2] Much light has been thrown on such matters within the last forty years, and what baffled the Doctor is now easy of determination. Mourie, or Maelrubha, as his name was originally written, was that distinguished saint who crossed from Ireland to Scotland in 671, founded the church of Apurcrosan, now Applecross, and evangelised the district which, roughly, now forms the county of Ross and Cromarty. After his death, Applecross, which is still known in Gaelic as *A' Chomaraich*—the Sanctuary—became sacred ground and the most noted place of refuge in the

---

[1] Gregory's *Highlands and Isles*, p. 303.   [2] *Days of the Fathers in Ross-shire*, v. 6

Highlands; and around the name of the saint himself customs clustered which strongly savour of paganism, and which no doubt had, before his time, some connection with the heathen religion of the country. These survived for centuries. The Presbytery found, in 1656, that the Protestant inhabitants of Applecross, Lochcarron, Lochalsh, Kintail, Contin, Fodderty, Gairloch, and Lochbroom, were in the habit of sacrificing bulls to the saint on his annual festival day (25th August); of giving the sacrificed meat and other offerings to those poor, mentally deranged persons who were known as St. Mourie's afflicted ones—*derilans*[1]—and who owned his special protection; of making pilgrimages to his monuments of idolatry in various places, including Isle Maree, to which, as well as to Loch Maree, he gave his name; of visiting and 'circulating' ruinous chapels associated with his memory—marching round them sun-wise, no doubt; of learning of the future, 'in reference especiallie to lyf and death in taking of jurneys,' by trying to put their heads into 'a holl of a round stone,' which, if they 'could doe, to witt, be able to put in thaire heade, they ' expect thair returneing to that place; and faileing, they ' conceaved it ominous'; and of adoring 'wells and uther ' superstitious monuments and stones, tedious to rehearse.' So far as divination by the hole in the stone was concerned, the man of small head had evidently an advantage over the great-heads of the period. The Presbytery took such steps as were within their power to suppress the 'abhominations'; but it was difficult to destroy what had flourished for ages. As late as 1678, Hector Mackenzie, in Mellan of Gairloch, and his sons and grandson, sacrificed a bull on St. Mourie's Isle, ' for the recovering of the health of Cirstane Mackenzie, spouse ' of the said Hector Mackenzie, who was formerlie sick and ' valetudinarie'; and the mentally afflicted are to this day taken to the island to be cured.

The custom of adoring and supplicating at holy wells had

---

[1] See footnote, p. 282.

also come to be associated with the memory of the ancient Celtic saints. In pagan times mysterious demons dwelt in certain fountains, which were in a sense worshipped by the people. The saints drove out the evil spirits, and the wells were consequently dedicated to themselves. The old custom was, however, continued, with the difference that the adoration was now offered not to the demon, but to the saint. The manner in which wells were changed by the Christian missionaries from pestilent disease-giving agencies to sources of health and blessing is well illustrated by the story of St. Columba and the fountain, narrated by Adamnan.[1] The pilgrimages to such wells are repeatedly referred to in the Records. In 1626, and again in 1642, the Synod endeavoured to repress them.[2] A Commission of the General Assembly sitting at Auldearn in 1649, ordered Mr. John Macrae 'to be more painfull to ' reforme the evil menners of Dingwall, to be [*i.e.* compel] ye ' residents to refraine from goeing to wells on the Lordes day ;' the well-worshippers of Urquhart of Ferintosh were ordered to be taken in hand by the session in the same year; and in 1678 the Synod of Moray ordained the brethren of the Presbytery of Inverness 'to intimat that persons goeing to superstitious wells are to be censured.' The custom, however, continued into the present century, and has not yet altogether ceased. Among the wells to which pilgrimages are still made is that of Culloden, which is annually visited on the first Sunday of May by hundreds of people from Inverness and neighbourhood. One almost regrets to hear the interesting time-honoured custom still preached against by our clergy as it was two and three hundred years ago.

In the same far-off pagan period originated the practice of pouring milk upon fairy knowes for the purpose of appeasing the fairies,[3] who in Christian times became the representatives of the former spirits of the earth; and of kindling Midsummer

---

[1] *Life of St. Columba*, Book ii. c. x. [2] P. 88, footnote.
[3] P. 282.

fires.[1] The Dingwall Presbytery ordained in June 1655 ' that 'the severall brethren intimate to thair congregationes that 'they desist of the superstitious abuses used on St. Johnes day '[24th June], by burneing torches through thair cornes and 'fyres in thair townes, and thaireafter fixing thair staicks in 'thair Kaileyeards.' The custom, however, continued, and the Synod of Ross passed an act against it in 1671. It has long since died out in the Highlands, but it was at one time known all over Europe, and it still exists in Ireland, Norway, Greece, and, probably, other countries. The minute of July 1655 shows that the oft-repeated statement that kail was not known in the Highlands until recent times is incorrect. In that year, evidently, kailyards were common, and were, along with the corn-fields, made the object of the blessing that came through the ancient sacrifice of the Midsummer Fire.

At a time when witches were burnt in England and the Lowlands in hundreds, one would naturally expect to find similar transactions in the Highlands. But although the capital of Sutherlandshire has the unenviable honour of having burnt the last witch put to death in Scotland, the wretched creature suffered as the result of the tardy introduction into the county of that religious zeal which had already mercilessly enforced in the South the Jewish precept, 'Thou shalt not suffer a witch 'to live.' Generally speaking there was, as has already been indicated, little of the nature of religious fanaticism to be found within our bounds during the period of the Records, and the consequence was that when witches and charmers were brought before the Presbytery they were mercifully spared the cruelties and death which would have been their lot had their lines fallen besouth the Grampians, or in the lowlands of Moray. A notorious Fodderty witch, who rejoiced in the name of Agnes Mor nin vick ean glaish—Big Agnes daughter of the son of John the Pale—publicly 'scolded, lyed, menaced, cursed, and used imprecations' against Mr.

---

[1] P. 323.

Donald Fraser in 1672, and was brought before his Presbytery; but all that the brethren did was to ordain her 'to be publicklie rebuked by her minister after sermon.' The court was equally merciful to Finlay Macconochie vic George and his wife, residents of the still witch-ridden Black Isle, for 'con-
'sulting with a witch for getting the profite of their drink
'[milk], formerlie taken away from them as they alleadge, and
'making use of a charme to that effect, and professing that it
'took effect to their mynd';[1] and to those who used charms for the recovery of Donald Glasse from sickness,[2] for interrupting marital relations between Alexander Mac ean vic Gillireich and his wife,[3] for bringing luck and good fortune in connection with a flitting,[4] and even for raising the devil through the turning of the sieve and the shear.[5] It is curious to note that this last expedient, which was resorted to for purposes of divination, was known during the same period in Ross-shire, England, Ireland, and the south of Scotland. Hudibras, expressing his disbelief in the power of telling the future by the aspect of the stars, declares:

> 'Nor can their aspects though you pore
> Your eyes out on 'em, tell you more
> Than th' oracle of sieve and shears,
> That turns as certain as the spheres.'

And in 1682 a servant lass in Irvine, who had learned the art in Ireland, practised it with marvellous success.[6]

To ensure prosperity in their new house a Dingwall couple in 1673 'cross-cut all the couples' of the old, and 'did take a great quantitie of the earth' of it with them; to all which the owner of the old dwelling naturally objected. Other sorceries to which reference is made are the burying of a lamb under the threshold as a preventive against the death of the rest of the bestial,[7] and the keeping of a 'pocke of hearbs' in the milk 'as a preventative against the tacking away the substance

---

[1] P. 181.   [2] P. 240.   [3] P. 344.   [4] P. 329.   [5] P. 156.
[6] *Domestic Annals of Scotland*, February 1682.   [7] P. 196.

of it.'[1] Against 'witchcraft and devillish practices of that sort' the brethren of Dingwall were in 1649 ordained by the Commission of the General Assembly 'to preach powerfully;' but Northern parsons were not over-zealous, and the probability is that the instruction was pretty generally ignored.

In addition to the duties of promoting the true religion and repressing the false, and of putting down crime and vice and superstition, the ministers were expected to inquire into and, to a certain extent at least, to judge in cases of slander, breach of promise, nullification of marriage, and applications for permission to marry again.

The petition of Patrick Gordon and his wife against Mr. Alexander Clerk, one of the ministers of Inverness, for slander from the pulpit, is amusing reading;[2] and reference may also be made to the cases of Mackenzie of Dochmoluak, whose complaint was that he had been accused of undue familiarity with the goodwife of his neighbour of Dochcarty;[3] John Dingwall, who was falsely said not to have been baptized;[4] Bailie Henry Bain, of Dingwall, who had been maliciously called a murderer;[5] Donald Chisholm, whom Agnes nin Donald Vicay had impudently claimed to be the father of her child;[6] and William Macmiller, against whom Robert Catanach, an honest man who thought he knew his own father, sought redress for having avowed and asserted strongly 'that he wes father to the said Robert.'[7] When the charge was proved or confessed the usual penalty was fine, or censure in presence of the congregation. In more recent times slanderers were sometimes made to stand at the gate of the churchyard while the congregation passed out, and to repeat, in Gaelic, the words, 'This is the lying tongue.'

There are two cases of breach of promise of marriage mentioned. In the first the charge was made by the woman and the man got off.[8] In the second, the man was the aggrieved

---

[1] P. 196. [2] P. 85. [3] P. 314. [4] P. 321. [5] P. 325. [6] P. 362.
[7] P. 341. [8] Pp. 303, 305.

person, and there appears to have been ground for his complaint, for the woman, after he had been contracted with her and the banns had been proclaimed in the church of Alness, 'broke her promise to him and violated Church orders. The 'Presbyterie, taking this to ther consideratione, thought good 'to referr the said supplicant to the Sessione of Alnes, to doe 'in it as they find most convenient, the business being better 'knowen to them then to the Presbyterie.'[1]

Applications for divorce or freedom from the marriage tie are numerous. The most common ground is unfaithfulness in either spouse, or physical defect in the man. The case of Elspit Nickphaile is on 14th September 1670 referred to the Synod in very curious terms; and in the following January she is, on the recommendation of the Synod, 'remitted to the Comissar of Inverness for a nullity'—a course which was generally followed. In the case of Donald Kemp, whose application for divorce from Janet Urquhart was considered by the Bishop of Ross, and his assessors and the Presbytery of Dingwall in August 1666, the Bishop taking into consideration that Kemp 'had deported himself soberly without 'ony known publick scandal, and finding the said suppli- 'catione to be of verity,' undertook 'either to speak the 'Commissars of Rosse, or els to write to the Commissars of 'Edinburgh, for a divorce from the said Jonet Urquhart.'

In 1655 and 1656 the Dingwall brethren carefully considered at several meetings the complaint of Duncan Mac Murchie vic Cuile, whose wife, Agnes Kemp, had refused to cohabit with him from the day of their marriage; 'professing 'hir unwillingnes from the beginning to marie the said 'Duncan, bot moved and threatned be the superior of the 'land.' Witnesses were examined in support of her allegations, but the decision of the Presbytery is not recorded. In another case of connubial infelicity the couple are 'bitterly

---

[1] P. 313.

rebuked' for 'their intoward cariage toward one another,' and 'ordained to behave better in tyme to come.'

Notwithstanding such unhappy experiences it is clear that marriage was not always a failure in the olden times. Sometimes we find women who had already tried the experiment applying to the Presbytery for leave to repeat it.

In June 1665 Mr. John Mackenzie, minister of Killearnan, and archdeacon of Ross, 'advysed with the Presbyterie [of 'Dingwall] in reference to a woman in his Parish whose 'husband being caried to Barbados after the battell of Woster, 'and married ther for certainty, whether the said woman 'might have the benefitt of marriage with another man.' The brethren were unable to decide the difficult question, and referred him to the bishop. In November of the same year Mr. John Gordon was also referred to the bishop for advice on the similar case of Janet Nienan (Ann's daughter) in Kiltearn, whose husband had been transported to Barbados after Worcester, and married there, as 'certified by severalls that have come from Barbados.' And in July 1678 the Minister of Contin was authorised to give Agnes nin Donald Oig vic Finlay (Agnes daughter of young Donald son of Finlay) the benefit of marriage with Muroch MacAllan, she having proved 'that Alister Mac William vic Ean vic Conel '[Alexander son of William son of John son of Donald], 'her former husband, who went to France, was dead by 'drowning.' Evidence to that effect was given by John 'Mac Ean vic ryrie (John son of John son of Roderick) 'who deponed upon oath that he saw the said Alexander 'Mac William vic Ean dead;' and one of the brethren 'declared that the same was told him by others that came 'from France.' The old intercourse with France had evidently not yet been greatly interrupted; but one wonders how men whose only language was Gaelic, and some of whom had not even a surname, but only long Gaelic patronymics, managed to make their way among the French.

There were in the seventeenth century no church collections for home or foreign missions, or for the conversion of the Jews; but collections were, nevertheless, by no means unknown. Some of those mentioned in the Records may be referred to. The Presbytery of Dingwall ordered one in 1652 for 'the destressed people off Glasgowe.' It came 'bot slowe speide;' but at last, on 18th February 1653, the brethren paid the contributions of their congregations to commissioners duly authorised to receive the same, 'and receaved discharges conforme.' A collection was made in the Inverness parishes in 1679 for 'the Glasgow people.' In March 1665, the Moderator of the same Presbytery 'presented a supplicatione ' in behalf of the distrest men of Portpatrick, some whereof ' were captive with the Turks, and others of them totally ' ruined in fortune.' The Turks were no doubt the pirates of Algiers, who frequently seized British seamen and sold them as slaves, and who sometimes ventured even into British waters. In 1665, a collection was made for the relief of ' William Mackay, Merchand in Dumbarton, a sufferer under ' the late usurpatione and rebellione;' and, in 1667, one for Captain William Murray, 'a distressed gentleman'; while in 1684 the congregations within the bounds of the Presbytery of Inverness were appealed to for charity for 'Gilbert Andersone in Keith, newly cutt of the gravell.' In 1679 a collection was made for 'the Montrose merchants'—for what reason is not explained. We also find congregational contributions solicited for such purposes as the repair of the Kirk Street of Dingwall, and the bulwarks of Peterhead, Stonehaven, and Dundee; the improvement of the harbour of Portsoy; the erection of the bridge of Inverness; and the repairing of the ' bruse' or brew-house of Alness. The brethren, considering ' the usefulness of the work,' promptly promised to contribute towards the bruse—an early instance, certain modern politicians might be tempted to say, of the connection between Beer and Bible.

Collections were occasionally made to enable hopeful students to attend the University; and, in addition to this, each Presbytery maintained an 'Irish bursar'—that is, a Gaelic-speaking student—at college, towards whose expenses congregations were expected to regularly contribute. This custom was the result of an Act passed by the General Assembly of 1643, ordaining ' that young students that have the Irish language
' be trained up at colleges in letters, especially in the studies
' of divinity,' and recommending Presbyteries and Universities
' to prefer any hopeful student that have that language to
' bursaries, that they, by their studies, in process of time
' attaining to knowledge, and being enabled for the ministry
' may be sent forth for preaching the Gospel in these High-
' land parts, as occasion shall require.' The bursar, as well as the poor 'Irish' boy, who was sometimes maintained by the Presbytery at school, are continually making their appearance in the Records. Notwithstanding numerous exhortations to the contrary, their money sometimes came slowly and irregularly; and it is painful to read that in February 1664 ' the brethren for the most part declynes to pay the burse to
' Mr. John Mackenzie this year, *pretending* they payed him
' at once for both this yeir and the last.'

The grand parochial educational system, which was the child of the Church of Knox, and which has done so much for Scotland generally, was sadly slow in extending its benefits to the Highlands. Perhaps its success would have been greater and more immediate if the Privy Council, in ordaining that a school be planted in each parish, had not so bluntly given as one of the great objects to be attained, the abolition of the Gaelic language, which, it was declared, 'is one of the chieff
' and principall causes of the continuance of barbaritie and
' incivilitie among the inhabitants of the Isles and Heylandis.' That order was passed in 1616, and was confirmed by Parlia-

INTRODUCTION xlvii

ment in 1631, and again in 1646; but in some Highland parishes it was not given effect to until long after the troubles of the Forty-five. Our Records show, however, that the clergy of our bounds did make an effort to plant schools within their parishes, and that in some instances they were not entirely unsuccessful.

Early in 1649 a Commission of the General Assembly, sitting at Auldearn, ordered 'dilligence to be used for the plantation of Schoolles'; and, later in the same year, a Commission sitting at Chanonry appointed 'that Schooles be erected in ' each parish, and diligence thereanent be reported to the ' next provincial [Synod] of Ross, betwixt this and the next ' visitation at Chanonrie.' There was in that year no school within the bounds of the Presbytery of Dingwall, and probably none within those of Inverness, except in the town itself. In July the minister and elders of Kiltearn promised to join Alness in erecting and maintaining a joint school for these parishes; and next year the latter parish found a schoolmaster in Mr. Donald Monro. In July 1649 the minister of Kilmorack ' presses a school,' and gets his reward in the following February, when Hew Ros is appointed schoolmaster, he having satisfied the Presbytery ' of his good education and conversation' and 'his ' abilitie for instructing of children and fitting them for gramar ' Schooles.' But the honour of establishing the first school within the bounds of the Presbytery of Dingwall belongs to the minister and elders of Urquhart of Ferintosh, who in July 1649 'were goeing about to seik for a man to be scholmaister and clerk to ye session,' with the result that in October William Reid accepted the charge. A Committee of landowners and other persons of influence was appointed in September to assist the clergy in 'tacking course for erection and ' plantation of schooles within the Presbyterie, conforme to ' the tenor of the Act of Parliament'; but it was difficult to get them to act, or even to meet, and on 19th February 1650 they reported that they could do nothing 'till they did sie 'whether the Parliament would allow their books of revaluation of the Shyres of Ross and Inverness, in which ane modification and allocation was made for schooles in everie paroch of the Shyre, which they conceive will be competent if allowed.' To get Parliament to grant exceptional privileges to the Highlands was probably not as easy then as it is now; and we hear no more of the Committee.

Strange to say, the capital of Ross, and the parish in which it is situated, were without a school for years after some of their poorer neighbours had established theirs. In January 1650 the learned Mr. John Macrae 'regrates that he cannot prevaile in the mater of planting of a schoole in Dingwall.' The Committee was appealed to, and Macrae was ordained to summon the magistrates and heritors to appear before the Presbytery. Certain of the heritors accordingly appeared on 5th February, and declared the inability of Dingwall to maintain a schoolmaster, unless the neighbouring parish of Fodderty joined. The Committee was again called upon for assistance; but their work closed with the reference to Parliament on 19th February. Next year Mr. John Macrae was ordained 'to have ane schoole;' but years passed before he succeeded, and we find no further mention of the matter until July 1663, when his namesake, Mr. John Macrae, was schoolmaster of Dingwall and clerk to the Presbytery. In 1667 Mr. Charles Alexander was the schoolmaster, Macrae having risen to the ministry. Alexander soon followed in his footsteps. But, notwithstanding these changes, the school flourished until it acquired the status of a grammar school. In February 1674 Mr. George Dunbar was 'appointed to be readie to have ane oratione, and to give ane exigesis of these words of Boethius, in his booke *de Consolatione Philosophiæ*—

"Tu triplicis mediam natura cuncta moventem
Connectens animam, per consona membra resolvis,"

'and that as a specimen of his abilities to teach the grammare 'school of Dingwall, unto quhich he was latelie presented.' At the March meeting Dunbar 'hade ane oratione in Latine, 'with ane exigesis on the poesie formerlie mentioned, in both 'quhich,' it is pleasant to read, 'he did acquit himselfe to the 'full satisfactione of his hearers.'

So far as the West Coast parishes are concerned, there was not a school within them during the period covered by the Records, and no effort was made by the Presbytery to mend the state of matters.

In 1653 the Cromwellian Governor of Inverness took an interest in educational affairs, and 'directed ane letter to the 'Presbyterie [of Dingwall] for tryall quhat mortifications has 'formalie [formerly?] bene allotted for mantenance of schooles 'in all paroches;' and it was remitted to two of the brethren of Dingwall 'to goe to Inverness to answer the Governor's 'letter, and to be informed in the maner of our procedors in 'erecting of Schooles.' The brethren accordingly waited upon the Governor, and reported to the Presbytery 'that schooles 'ar ordained to be kept, conforme to the Act of Parliament, 'in the severall congregationes;' and the members are ordered 'to intimate the said ordenance in their several congrega- 'tiones, to understand, if they consented thairto, or for the 'better accomodatione a conjunctione of paroches be made 'for acting the work.' The Englishman's interference was no doubt well meant, but it does not appear to have been followed by any practical result.

Although the early records of the Presbytery of Inverness do not now exist to show what steps were taken to enforce the provisions of the Acts of Parliament of 1631 and 1646, and to give effect to the ordinances of the General Assembly and the Governor of Inverness, it is certain that, educationally, the bounds of Inverness were on the whole in advance of those of Dingwall.

Soon after the Reformation a grammar school was established in Inverness, which was reported in 1672 to be 'thriveing.'

Next year it became vacant, and on 5th November Mr. Alexander Ross, son of David Ross of Earlsmill, 'was admitted 'schoolmaster at Invernes, of the towne of Invernes, and 'for his tryalls hade the third ode of Horace, and had his 'oratione *de vanitate hum. scientiae*, and all other tryalls usuall 'in the like case, and was fullie approven in every step of his 'tryalls by the Presbyterie and the magistrates and burgesses 'of Invernes, and was unanimouslie accepted of the magis- 'trates and town of Invernes to be their schoolmaster of 'the Grammar School.' Knowledge of Latin was the great test of the schoolmaster's fitness for his work, and so much was the language studied even by the poorer class of pupils, that wonderful stories are still told of the proficiency to which boys attained in it in the past.

There was a school in Kiltarlity in 1671, the master of which, Mr. George Hutchion, gave satisfaction 'in every thing.' He was perhaps excelled by his successor, Mr. John Munro, to whom the minister and elders, in 1677, 'gave a large 'applaus of his painefullness and diligent attendance on school 'and sessione'—he being, as was usual for the teachers of the time, session clerk, and probably also precentor—'and also 'that he was of a Christian, civill, blameless conversa- 'tione.'

In 1682, Kirkhill had a schoolmaster, Mr. Thomas Fraser, who 'besides his attendance of the schoole, was precentor and 'clerk, and read the scriptures publicly every Lord's Day in 'the Irish, betwixt the second and third bell.' For these services he was paid a 'fixed sallary' of a chalder of victual, together with £20 Scots [equal to £1, 13s. 4d. Sterling] out of the session box, 'and also the baptism and marriage money.' At the same time there was 'a flourishing schoole' in Petty, whose master was 'a great help to the minister.' The fame of the Petty school, in the seventeenth and eighteenth centuries, has come down to our own time. The youth of other parishes flocked to this flourishing institution, and in thoroughness of training it is said to have surpassed even the grammar school of Inverness.

But while these parishes did more or less creditably, the remaining parishes within the Inverness bounds were woefully remiss. Daviot, it is true, had 'a school' in 1672, but the schoolmaster had been 'forced to leave for want of mantenance.' Before 1682, the school itself disappeared, the minister declaring in that year 'that they could not nor had any, ' becaus there was no incurragement for one, nor no mediat ' centricale place quhere they could fix a schoole to the satis- ' faction of all concerned.'

In 1672, there was no school in Moy, 'partlie because the ' townes within the pariochin were far distant one from the ' other.' Boleskine was without one ' in regard the townes in ' the parishe were remote the one from the other, and that ' they hade no convenience of boarding children'; and Dores, Croy, and Urquhart, and Glenmoriston were in the same desolate condition. Most of the Inverness parishes, indeed, as well as the West Coast parishes, were without parochial schools for twenty or thirty years after Culloden.

It must not, however, be supposed that the youth of the period were left wholly in darkness. In 1675, the ministers and elders of Dores, while admitting that they had no public school, declared ' that severall gentlemen had schooles in their own houses for educating and traineing up of their children.' In other parishes the same system prevailed—the lairds, wadsetters, and larger tenants combining to employ some struggling student to teach their children during the college recess. Sometimes the children of the more affluent were sent to be taught at Inverness, Fortrose, or Petty. The result was that during the darkest years of the seventeenth century a few were to be found in each parish who could read and write, and express themselves in fair English, and that even the humblest classes took to committing their transactions to writing.

Early in the eighteenth century was founded the Society in

Scotland for Propagating Christian Knowledge, which opened schools in the more desolate districts, and for more than a century and a half continued to do incalculable good in the cause of education, within the bounds of our Presbyteries, as throughout the Highlands generally.

In reading these Records one cannot but be impressed with the magnitude of the change that has come over church life since the times of which they speak. Many things meet us which are apt to surprise and even pain us; but with reference to these it is right to remember that the conduct of the men of the past ought not to be judged by our modern standard of right and wrong. What may appear to us heinous, may have seemed venial in the eyes of the good people of the seventeenth century; and, so far as the clergy of the Records are concerned, it is clear that the great majority of them were Christian gentlemen, who strove to be a pattern to their people, and who did what they could to keep alive the light of the Gospel during days that were, spiritually, somewhat dark.

The editor has, in conclusion, to express his indebtedness to the members of the Presbyteries, for the use of the Records; to Mr. Law, for willing aid and unfailing courtesy; and to his assistant, Mr. Mill, for the excellent Index, which is wholly his work.

WILLIAM MACKAY.

CRAIGMONIE, INVERNESS,
   Midsummer 1896.

FACSIMILE FROM THE DINGWALL PRESBYTERY RECORDS.

RECORDS OF THE PRESBYTERY OF INVERNESS.

At Invernes, 23 November 1643.

Convened, all the Brethren.

That day report was made to the Presbitrie that there was in the Paroch of Dunlichitie ane Idolatrous Image called St. Finane, keepit in a private house obscurely; the Brethren, Mr. Lachlan Grant, Mr. Patrick Dunbar, and Alexander Thomson, to try, iff possible, to bring the said Image the next Presbitrie day.

At Inverness, 7 December 1643.

Convened, the whole Brethren.

Alexander Thomson presentit the Idolatrous Image to the Presbitrie, and it was delyverit to the Ministers of Inverness, with ordinance that it should be burnt at their Market Corse the next Tuysday, after sermone.

At Inverness, 21 December 1643.

Convened, all the Brethren except Mr. Lachlan Grant.

The Ministers of Inverness declairit that, according to the ordinance of the Presbitrie the last day, they caused burne the Idolatrous Image at the Market Corse, after sermone, upon Tuysday immediatelie following the last Presbitrie day.[1]

At Elgine, Aprile 5, 1670.

The Bretheren of the Presbytrie did meet for setleing and appointing ye first presbyteriall meeting, and did conclude that

---

[1] The volume in which the Minutes of 23rd November and 7th and 21st December 1643 are recorded is now lost—the first volume in the Presbytery's possession commencing 5th April 1670. The above three Minutes are printed from an old copy in the editor's possession.

Wednesday the 4 of May 1670 shuld be the first Presbyteriall meeting after the Synod, and Mr. Roderick Mackenzie appointed to haue the exercise, and Mr. James Sutherland the addition. Text, colloss. 1. 24.

At Innerness, May 4, 1670.

Being Wednesday y\ :sup:`e` first meeting after y\ :sup:`e` Synode, convened y\ :sup:`e` Moderator and remanent breyren of y\ :sup:`e` P'bytrie except Mr. Duncane M\ :sup:`c`\ Culloch, Mr. Thomas Huistone, and Mr. Hugh Fraser, Minister at Croy, and no letter of excuse from any of them. The Lord's name was called upon.

Y\ :sup:`t` day, according to y\ :sup:`e` former ordinance, Mr. Roderick M\ :sup:`c`\ Kenzie exercised, and Mr. James Sutherland added, Colloss. 1. 24. Being both removed, one by one, were approven. Mr. James Sutherland is appointed to exercise, and Mr. James Fraser to adde, y\ :sup:`e` nixt day, text, Coloss. 1. 25.

Y\ :sup:`e` saide day y\ :sup:`e` Moderator exhibited y\ :sup:`e` Synodicall referrs, which were presented and discussed as followeth:

1°. Y\ :sup:`e` Ministers of Inerness are appointed to processe William Troupe, Messenger, for adherence to his wife and giving maintainance to his childe.

2°. Katherine Gordone, Spouse to Lauchlane M\ :sup:`c`\ intoshe, *alias* Maltman, to satisfye as ane Adulteress upon y\ :sup:`e` account of her own dela\ :sup:`on` thereof.

3°. Mr. Alex\ :sup:`r` Fraser, Moderator, and Mr. Alex\ :sup:`r` Clark are appointed to attend the subsynod to hold at Forres, May 24 ensuing.

4°. Y\ :sup:`e` breyren of the P'bytrye were appointed to take up a List of y\ :sup:`e` names of Papists profest or suspected to be within there respective Congregationes, and to remitte the same with the Moderator to the Bishope to y\ :sup:`e` fors\ :sup:`d` Subsynode.

5°. [The Brethren are appointed to supply Aldearn, vacant.]

6°. All y\ :sup:`e` Bretheren deficient are appointed to pay Mr. John Dunbar, Bursar of Divinity, in y\ :sup:`e` Presbytrye of Forress.

7°. The Breyñe are to intimate that if any person supplicat the Bishope for clandestine marriage, The meanest shall pay twenty marks, and those of quality according to y\ :sup:`r` ranks. But because that this act was looked upon as someq\ :sup:`t` obscure, it was recomended to the fors\ :sup:`d` delegates to the Subsynod to inquire qho shuld injoy the benefit of the fors^d Act, that is, Qhither the fors^d twenty marks, less or more according to the quality of y^e persons, were to redounde to the Bishope for granting the licence, or to be made furthcoming to the Church where y^e persons receive the benefit of Marriage, and so to be put into the Church treasurye of the respective parochines, and they are appointed to report ane answer to the Bretheren the nixt Presbytry day.

[Several cases of discipline, including Christian Chambers in the Parish of Dores, who is contumax and ordained to be processed.]

And withall the s^d Mr. James Smith, Minister at Dorres, is appointed to give a list of all the obstinat delinquents within his Parish to Alex^r Chissolme, as Baily of Stratharrick and Comissar depute of Inerness, to see if that rude people and obstinate generation may be brought to a more Christian subjection and orderly conformity.

That day ye Moderator presented a letter from the Bishop of Murray in favours of Mr. James Hay, Student in divinity, and residenter in the toune of Inverness, for admitting of the s^d Mr. James to his tryalls in rela^{o}n to expectancy. The qhich the Breyren takeing to y^r considera^{o}n, haue appointed Mr. James Sutherland and Mr. Hugh Fraser, Minister at Kiltarlity, to confer with the s^d Mr. James Hay, and to get some account from him of his reading, and to know he had improved his time since his manumission and graduation in the Colledge: and to report ther answer ye nixt Presbytrye day, qhich is appointed to hold at Inverness, May 28, 1670.

The Meeting closed with Prayer.

Innerness, May 28, 1670.

Y^t day ye Moderator asked ye Breyren if they had brought with y^m a Catalogue of ye Papists profest or suspected to be such w^{t}in their respective parishes, to qhich it was by the Breyren then present that they had (blessed be God) few or none such known within ther congregations, or if any such shuld be found w^{t}in either of ther resptive bounds they shuld not failie *quam primum* to give ane impartiall liste of them. Only Mr. Thomas Huistone is plagued w^t Papists.

[Mr. James Smith, Dores, on being asked whether he had given the list of delinquents to the Bailie of Stratherrick, 'answered y^t he was taking pains upon y^m at home to bring them to obedience, and if that course shuld failie he shuld follow the Presbytrie's direction as the nixt remede.']

Y^t day Mr. James Sutherland, and Mr. Hugh Fraser, Minist^r at Kiltarlity, reported that they had conferred with Mr. James Hay, and had found y^t ye s^d Mr. James had read Calvins Institu^{ons} and Wendeline his Theological Systeme, w^t Pares, and Ursius Catecheticks, and Willets Synopsis Papismi, and Sharpes Course, etc., and culd give a reasonable accompt of what he had read, and that his conversation had been truely Christian and sober dureing all ye time of his abode at Inverness, and that they were so satisfyed w^t him in everything that they judged him qualified for to be admitted to more publick tryalls in relation to expectancy. Al the Breyren present, takeing ye fors^d report to their consideration, and being satisfied theirw^t, haue appointed the s^d Mr. James to haue a private Homily the nixt Presbytry day in the session house of Inverness, on John 6. 44.

At Inerness, June 8, 1670.

[Mr. James Hay had his homily on John 6. 44, and, being removed, was approven. He was ordained to have the addition, and Mr. James Fraser to exercise, next day on Col. 1. 27.]

Y^t day Mr. James Smith, Minister at Dorres, reported that he had given Christian Chamber there 3 publict admonitions from Pulpit on 3 seuerall Lords days: he is appointed to proceed and to make ye first prayer for her ye nixt Lords day, and so to go on till ye nixt Presbytry day, and to report his diligence to y^t dyet.

Y^t day Mr. Thomas Huistone regrated to ye Breyren that notwithstanding that his Parishioners had solemly ingaged and publickly promised in audience of ye s^d Breyren at the last visita^{on}, holden at Boleskine ye 7th of December 1669, to give him all ye incourragements y^t might contribute to ye advancing of the glory of God and ye work of the Ministry in y^t place, and particularly ingaged (upon their credit and reputation) to give him both countenance and mantinance, yet that he had not security for his life or goods; his house being laitly seized upon by Lochabber Robbers, himselfe threatned w^t naked swords and drawne durks at his brest, his money and household stuff plundered, and seing that one of their number suffered death laitly therefor at Inerness, ye rest of them were lieing in waite for his life, and threatening his ruine and dammage, so that in ye evening he is affrayed to [be] burnt to ashes or morning. Nor yet has he that mantinance of them that the laudable lawes of the Land allow him to maintaine himself and his family, and to breed his children at schooles, seeing that some of them are resting him eight yeers, some seven, some six years stipend,[1] and upon qhilk and many moe considerations he does (finding no redress of these unsuperable evils) make his recourse to his Reverend Breyren of ye Presbytery y^t in a fellow sympathy and condolency, qhich shuld be betwixt ye members of a gracious body, they wold be pleased to grant him the benefit of that remedy which the laudable Lawes of ye Church of Christ haue afforded his servants in such unsupportable straits, by giveing a transportation from ye Ministry in that place to anye place qhere the Lord in Mercy may be pleased to call him.

Ye Breyren, considering these sad reasons and condoling his condition, yet told him that they culd not give him ane Act of Transportation w^{t}out ye Bishop and Synod's order, and therefor the Breyren requested him to haue patiently until the nixt Synod, casting himself upon the Lord for his shelter and refuge against al these dangers and sad discouragements; and so referred him to the Synode.

At Innerness, June 29, 1670.

[Mr. Jas. Fraser exercised, and Mr. James Hay added on Col. 1. 27. Both being removed, were approven. Mr. James Hay ordained to haue the exercise, and Mr. Hugh Fraser, at Croy, to haue the addition next day on Col. 1. 28. Mr. Smith, Dores, reports that he has given Christian Chamber the first prayer, and is appointed to give her the 2^d prayer next Lord's day.]

---

[1] During the period covered by these records the stipends were paid partly by the proprietors and partly by the tenants.

Moreover, the Minister at Dores reported that he was taking great pains on those obstinat delinquents y{t} were w{t}in his parish, but culd not prevaile to bring them to obedience; he is appointed therefore to give a liste of them to the Commissar, qho would compel y{m} to obedience.

At Inerness, July 20, 1670.

[All present, except Mr. Duncan M{c}Culloch, 'qho never keeps meeting w{t} his Breyren, and Mr. Thomas Huistone, qho sent no excuse.' Mr. James Hay exercised, and Mr. Fraser, Croy, added on Col. 1. 28. Both approven. Mr. Hay 'appointed to haue his exegesis the next day, *de Transubstantione*, and to sustain disputes.]

That day Mr. Smith reported y{t} he had given in a liste of all the obstinat delinquents w{t}in his Parish to Alex{r} Chissolme (Bayly of y{t} countrey, and Commissar Depute of Inverness), qho promised to take a course w{t} that obstinat and stiffnaked generation, qreby they might be brought to a more Christian subjection and orderly conformity.

August 10, 1670.

[Mr. James Hay necessarily absent, and his exegesis continued to next day. 'His Theses were distributed.' No account from the Commissar Depute as to the Dores delinquents.]

August 24, 1670.

Y{t} day Mr. James Hay delivered his Comon head *de Transubstantione*, and sustained his disputes, and, being removed, was approven. He is appoynted to haue his Popular Sermon the next day on Heb. 12. 24.

Septr. 14, 1670.

[Mr. James Hay delivers his popular sermon, approven, and is appointed 'to sustaine his questionary tryalls and of the Languages the nixt day.']

That Day, one Elspit Nickphaile, in y{e} Parochin off Wardlawe, compeired and gave in a Bill shewing Qhereas she had been married these 9 yeers ago to one John M{c}in Taylor in Moniake, since qhich time the s{d} John Taylor neiy{r} adhered to her nor performed any duty belonging to a husband in any case qhatsoever, especially in ye wedlock bond, he being *frigidej et impotentis naturej*, as was well known, as ye s^d John Taylor confessed befor ye Presbytry, and y^rfor the s^d Elspet Nickphaile supplicated the Presbytry to declare her marriage null and void, that she might be free to injoy any other qhom ye Lord in his providence should provide for her: ye qhich being takin to considera°n by ye Breyren they do referr ye case to ye Synod for advise how to proceed in this and ye like cases, qhereby women that are tyed to Impotent Men for the present may be keeped from all *vagae libidines* to qhich they may be easily tempted so long as they are tyed to men that are *impotens, frigidi, et ad omnes opus conjugale prorsus inepti*.

Sept. 28, 1670.

Y^t day Mr. James Hay sustained his questionary tryalls, and was examined by the Breyren both anent his knowledge in Chronologie, Reconciliation of Scriptures, Ecclesiasticall Histories, and Greek and Hebrew Languages; and, being removed, was approven. He is referred by ye Breyren to ye Bishop for opening of his mouth.

Y^t day ye Bretheren being removed one by one, and diligent search being made of every Brother's diligence in his respective charge, there was nothing found worthy of reprehension. Qhereupon ye Moderator, in name of the Presbytry, Blissed God in there behalfe, and exhorted them to continue diligent in the work of there Ministry, without spot or blemish, and withall pressed each one of them In ye Lord's strength to keep ye meeting of ye Synode.

Y^e nixt Presbyteriall meeting as to the dyet and place thereof is to be appointed at Elgine. Y^e meeting closed with Prayer.

Inerness, Novemb. 16, 1670.

Y^t day y^r was a letter exhibited at the Presbytry directed from ye Bishop of Murray requiring a collection from ye respective Parishes within ye Presbytry for repairing of ye Bulwark of Dundye, and thereupon ye severall breyren were injoined to provide ye same and to report y^r diligence y^rin to the nixt day.

January 4, 1671.

[Among the 'Referrs' from the Synod read this day, is 'Elspet Niphail, in ye Parish of Wardlaw, is remitted to ye Comissar of Innerness for a nullity upon ye account of her husbands impotency and nonadherence.']

At Invernes, Januar 25, 1671.

The said day ye severall Brethren declared y^r willingness to contribute to ye repairing of ye Bulwark at Dundie, but withall declared that y^r people wer most unwilling and dissatisffyed with the same. Ye ordinance is renewed *ut prius*.

At Innernes, March 8, 1671.

That day Mr. James Smith, Minist^r at Doores, regrated to the Prēsbrie that he had ney^r countenance nor mantenance amongst his hard-hearted Parishoners, that they ney^r frequented ye ordinances within y^r own Congregation, nor any wise concurred with him for curbing and suppressing of sin and vice abounding amongst many of his people by keeping hand to discipline; whereupon ye Breyren resolve and conclude (for rectifica^{o}n of these enormities among that crabbed people) ye next Presbyteriall meeting to be holden at Doores this day 20 dayes, where Mr. Hugh Fraser, Minist^r at Kiltarlity, is appoynted to preach.

At Doores, March 29, 1671.

Conveened ye Moderatour and remanent Breeyren of y^o Prēsbrie, except Mr. Hugh Fraser, of Croy, who sent no excuse.

The name of God was called upon. That day Mr. Hugh Fraser, Minister at Kiltarlity, according to the former ordinance, preached, text, Hos. 4. 4. The qch done, the Moderatour desyred y^o Minister to give in a list of his Elders, qch he did and wer present, to wit, William McIntosh of Borlome, Paul McBean of Kynkyle, Angus McBean of Drummin, John Fraser of Erogy, younger, Hector Fraser of Dundelchak, Lachlan McBeane in Darres.

The Moderatour asked ye forsaid elders if ye visita^{o}n were tymously intimated, and they declared that it was two severall

Lord's dayes from Pulpit, and that besides the officer charged the people at y^r dwelling houses personally to keep y^t meeting. The Moderatour desyred ye Minister, Mr. James Smith, to remove, and y^rafter he posed all the gentlemen and elders present, one by one, how they wer satisfyed with y^r Minister his life and conversa°n, how with his doctrine and discipline, if he catechised his people and visited ye sick within ye parish, with every oy^r query usually proponed at such visita°ns. The said gentlemen and elders answered, one by one, y^t they wer wel satisfyed with him, first as to his doctrine, and that they wer refreshed very much by him Sabbathly both in ye english and irish language, and that his life and conversa°n was ministeriall; only that he was not so frequent in catechising as they could wish. The Minister was called in, and ye elders report of him was declared to him, and he desyred to walk answerable to their large declara°n of him, and further was asked by the Moderatour ye reason why he was not so frequent in examina°n and catechising his people as he ought. To which he answered that of a long tyme bygone he had not any settled residence within the Parish nor mantinance to uphold him in the prosecu°n of ye work of his Ministry: however ye Moderatour desyred y^t he should not be wanting any longer on this part of his ministeriall function.

The Gentlemen and Elders wer removed, and ye Minister being asked anent y^m, and of what encouragement they gave him in his ministry, answered that:

1. He had no mantenance among y^m, nor culd he gete so much of his own stipend as would carry him through ye parish to manage his Masters affairs, but was keeped as a poor mendicant ever since he came amongst that people; that they had no inclina°n to doe him the least duty herein, though he had sought after it in the most peacable manner y^t could be, as if, chameleon-like, he could live upon ye aire.

2. He regrated y^t some of his Parishoners dishaunted ordinances within y^r own parish, and went sometymes to hear oy^rs, and sometymes stayed at home without hearing of any, in contempt of him and his ministry.

3. That all discipline was shaken loose among y^m in regard y^t his elders, who should be eyes and hands to him, straitning

him in y̌ᵉ carrying on of discipline, wer patrons and protectours of obstinat and refractory delinquents, whereby he could not doe yᵉ work of yᵉ Lord with joy, but with great greef, among yᵐ; and yʳupon gave in to yᵉ clerk of yᵉ Presbry a roll of such obstinat and hardened delinquents as wer protected by yʳ Masters,[1] and could not be brought to obedience or orderly walking. Whereupon, yᵉ gentlemen and elders being called in, The Moderatour held forth these greevances unto yᵐ, and first of all told yᵐ, yᵗ it wer a sad thing if yeir Minister should be made to succumb (as very like he was, for lack of yᵗ mantinance qch was alloted by yᵉ law of yᵉ land to that charge of Doores) under his sad burden, and told yᵐ yᵗ it was a signe of a gasping devotion among yᵐ, when they wer so close-handed to yʳ Minister, whose very cold water should not goe unrewarded; and furyʳ yᵗ yᵉ Pharisees should rise up in Judgment against yᵐ, who payed tenth of all they enjoyed.

Whereupon, yᵉ elders and gentlemen yⁿ present promised to doe him duty herein, and yᵗ yʳ should not be reason in any tyme coming for the like complent.

2. The Moderatour haveing asked yᵐ why any of yᵐ dishaunted yᵉ publicke ordinances within yʳ own Congregaᵒn to the great greif and discouragement of yʳ Minister, answered yᵗ they yᵐselves (while yʳ affaires permitted yᵐ to be in the countrey) did constantly keep, and would so doe in tyme comeing: but yᵗ yʳ wer oyʳˢ within yᵉ paroch on whom they had no influence to draw yᵐ to such c'formity; qʳupon yᵉ Moderatour in yʳ present audience ordained yᵉ Minister to draw up a list of these dishaunters of ordinances, to haue the same in readiness (in case of yʳ nonconformity) to be presented to the next ensueing synod, that some more effectuall course might be taken with these slighters of publick ordinances.

3. The Moderatour haveing holden forth to yᵐ the desolaᵒn yᵗ was like to ensue in regard of yʳ slacknesse and unconcernednesse in carrying on of discipline, by reason of yʳ protecting and patronising of obstinat delinquents, they promised, all and every one of yᵐ yⁿ present, to cause such delinquents as wer

---

[1] Masters—applied not only to employers, but also to the proprietors on whose lands the delinquents resided.

within yr respective bounds to give obedience to all sessionall appoyntments, but withall declared yt ye most of these delinquents wer in ye wester parish, where they could not reach unto them, they being oyr independent gentlemen's followers and servants, and yrfore desyred ye Prēsbry to fall upon some way for bringing yr Masters to ye like condescendance. Whereupon the Prēsby, taking this to yr serious considera°n, haue appoynted Mr. Thomas Huiston and Mr. James Smith to meet in ye Wester Parish, and to put ye severall heretours and gentlemen there to ye like condescendance, and to cause every gentleman and heritour to be answerable for yr servants and followers, yt they may be brought to give satisfac°n to ye discipline of ye session of Doores; and they to report yr diligence herein to ye next day.

That day ye Moderatour haveing enquired ye Minister anent his Session book, Answered yt upon the forsaid accounts he had not the samen in readiness at this tyme, but withall promised to have the same in readiness *quam primum*.

The Officer being removed, and ye Minister and Elders being enquired anent him, they all gave him ane honest testimony of him in discharging his office; being called in was exhorted to be diligent and painfull, and so was approven.

This being the last meeting day before ye Synod, the whole Breeyren wer removed one by one and particular inquiry being made anent yr doctrine, lyfe, and conv'sa°n, all of ym had a good report among ye breyren, and were approven, and each of ym exhorted to be carefull in ye Lords worke; only Mr. Rodericke McKenzie was ordained to goe in a ministeriall habite whan he went to set about any pairt of his [work].[1]

At Inverness, August 16, 1671.

No doctrine in regard yt Mr. James Smith, who should hav exercised according to ye former ordinance, was absent, who was excused by his letter, in regard yt ane horse being stollen

---

[1] The question of ministerial dress early troubled the Presbytery and Synod. On 13th April 1624, the Synod placed it on record that: 'The Visitors of ye Book of Inverness . . . affirmes that yo bretheren haunts to ye prēbrie with uncomly habits, such as bonats and plaides; whairfor the Assemblie ordaines them . . . not to haunt ye prēbrie any mair wt uncomly habitts.'

from yᵉ sᵈ Mr. James, and having gotten intelligence of him, he wes yis day to prov yᵉ horse to be his, oyʳwise to lose him.

The sᵈ day Mr. Thomas Huston, Minister at Boleskine, reported yᵉ sad and lamentable stat of yᵉ Parish of Vrqʳᵗ in regard of Mr. Duncan McCulloch, Minister yʳ, his slackness in discipline and neglect of dutie in many things, and absence from his church, qʳby sin and iniquitie is abounding and increasing in yᵉ sᵈ parish. The Breyren, taking yis to yʳ serious consideraᵒne, haue appoynted a visitaᵒne off yᵉ Kirk of Vrqᵗ yᶜ 5 of Sept. nixt, and yᵗ yᵉ sᵈ Mr. Duncan shall be advised yʳoff, and preach at the sᵈ meeting.

As also the Brethren appoynted a visitation off yᵉ Kirk off Kirtarlatie to be wpon yᵉ morrow yᵉ 6 off September, and appoynted Mr. Alexʳ. fraser, Minister at Daviot, to preach at yᵉ sᵈ visitatione.

At Vrchart, yᵉ 5 of Septr., 1671.

Convened yᵉ Moderatour and remanent breyren off yᵉ Presbytrie off Inv'nes. Mr. Duncan McCullach preached, text, I Thes. 5. 17.

After prayer, the meeting being tymously intimat, yᵉ roll off elders and deacones wes given in to read, and most of yᵐ all were present. The Session book of Vrqʳᵗ being formerly delivered to Mr. Hugh Fraser, Minister at Kiltarlitie, to revise yᵉ same, was exhibited, being inquired at yᵉ formalitie yʳoff, Answered yᵗ it was not a register buṭ a minut rayʳ, and yⁿ yᵗ it was deficient, wanting three yeirs unfilled up. The sᵈ Mr. Duncan, being rebooked for yis great oversight, was yʳfore ordeaned by yᵉ Moderator to exhibit a register, and to see qᵗ was wanting yʳin, and yᵗ against yᵉ nixt presbyteriall meeting.

Mr. Duncan being removed, and yᵉ severall gentlemen being asked anent his doctrin, life, and coversaᵒne, were all weill satisfied with him as to yis, but withall they regrated yᵗ he vsed no famely visitaᵒn, nor prayed in yʳ fameles qⁿ he lodged in any of his parishoners houses; and yᵗ he did not catechise nor administer ye sacrament ever since his entrie to yᵉ ministrie yʳ; and yᵗ he is a reproach to yᵉ ministrie and yᶜ Parish in going with so beggerly a habit; and, though much off his stipend be areasted in yᵉ parishoners hands, yᵗ yet he hath no cair to pay his debt, or releiv ye gentlemen from hazard at legal executiones in y^r contrar.

The gentlemen and elders being desyred to remov, and Mr. Duncan called in, was sharply rebooked for all yes omissiones, and was injoyned to mend yes things in tymes coming, and y^t *sub periculo gravioris censurej.*

The s^d Mr. Duncan, being asked anent his elders and gentlemen, q^t satisfaction he had off y^m. He regrated y^t he had ney^r countenance nor maintenance among y^m; and y^t q^n he is wrongd or injured in his person or meanes, they haue not y^t due regard to him as to resent yes wronges and Injuries done to him; q^rfor he would demitt.

The gentlemen and elders being called in, and ye fors^d case being holden out to y^m by ye Moderator, They did promise, all off y^m, to giv y^r Minister all ye contenance and assistance y^t lyes in y^r power.

The Officer being removed, ye Minister and elders being asked anent him, Compleaned on his slacknes; hee was yrfor injoyned to be more diligent, under pane of deposition.

That day ye Session was apoynted to repaire ye Church windowes, and to imploy y^r penalties to y^t use.

The meeting closed w^t prayer.

At Kiltarlatie, 6 Sept. 1671.

The Minister being removed, ye Moderator asked the elders anent y^r Ministers doctrin, liff, and conversation and discipline. They all answered one by one, They were weill pleased with him in all yes [these]. The Moderator asked if he did reside w^tin ye Parish; they answered, not: being asked if y^r Minister did catechise ye people, answered, not; and being inquired if he did visit ye faimlies, answered, not. The Moderator asked why were yes things omited, answered becaus y^r Minister had no sufficient Manse or biging to dwell in.

The elders and gentlemen being desyred to remove, and ye Minister called in, ye Moderator asked him why did he omit yes necessarie duties of Catechising ye people and visita°ne of faimlies and visiting ye sick. Answered y^t he had no Manse and yrfor culd not reseid w^tin ye Parish, q^ch wes ye caus of his omitting ye fors^d dueties: as also y^r wes no diligence vsed for setting up his Manse; q'upon y° Moderator and breyren posed y° Minister to use all legale diligence against y° Heritors for erecting a manse as y° Law provydes, and w'all seeing y° stent for erecting a manse wes condescended upon and subscribed by each particular Heritor, He might y° more easily goe to work and put y^m to it. The Gentlemen and elders being called in, y° Moderator asked y^m anent y° Manse why it was not built. They answered they wold use all diligence to collect money and wictuall to build it. And seeing now winter was drawing on and not fit for work, they should hav all things in reddiness against y° nixt Spring, and y^t they should search for a fitte sufficient man for overseeing y° work, and give him a salarie for his expense so long as y° work were doing. The Moderator earnestly exhorted both heritores and Minister to use all expeditione hearin, y^t y° Minister, having a manse, might be incurraged to goe about his calling.

[The Session Book to be given to Mr. James Fraser, Kirkhill, for examination].

The Moderator enquired y° Minister and Elders anent y^r pnt Schoolmaster, Mr. George Hutchion, Answered they were well satisfyed with him in every thing.

The Moderator having asked concerning y^r officer, Answered y^t they knew nothing of him but y^t he was diligent in his office. Y° Moderator exhorted him to continue diligent in his office.

At Inverness, Sept. 27, 1671.

The s^d day y° Minister of Deviot being inquired anent y° refer of John M^cintosh q^t diligence he hed used, Answered y^t he has given him two publick admonitions. As also y° Minister of Deviot reported that y° day he gev y° s^d John M^cintosh y° first admonitione from pulpit imediatly after divyn worshipe; ye s^d John M^cintosh in presence off y° whole congregation cam and s^d to him at y° Church dore, 'You base raskall, how durst yee bee so peart as to abuse mee yis day? yee wes too bold to doe it, yee might hav used your own equalls so and not me.' Wherupon y° Minister turned about and taks all y° gentlemen off y° Parish witnesses; and q'upon y° s^d John M^cintosh s^d againe, 'You base raskall, think you will I eat my words? were not for little to mee I wold bruiss y^or bones.' The Breyren, taking yis lamentable case to y^r consideraᵒn, and while they were deliberating y^{r}anent, In ye interim ye officer comes and shews y^t ye s^d John M^{c}intosh wes without at ye dore desyreing a word off ye breyren; having gotten access, ye Moderator asked q^t hee wold say, or if hee had anything to say to y^m. The s^d John askt iff they had any thinge to say to him. The Moderator s^d, That besides his former contumacie to ye presbyterie, now off leal y^r was a gross emergent scandall acted by him upon his Minister; q^{r}for ye fors^d opprobrious words being read in his audience he confessed hee spok y^m and y^t hee s^d so much; and yrupon craved God and mans mercie.

The Moderator charged him *apud acta* to compeir befor ye Synod tuisday com eight dayes ye 10 off Octob. *sub periculo*; q^{ch} business is referred to ye Synod.

At Inverness, 15 *Novr.* 1671.

The Bretheren of Prie having (after mature deliberatione) laid the sad conditione of the Parish of Vrqrt to their consideratione through the omissiones of their pñt Minister, Mr. Duncan McCuloch, through his manifold and heavie discouragements in his Parochin through want of mantenance and countenance, and by stealling and robbing of the little he hath, have thought good to appoynt a meeting with Mr. Duncan McCulloch to know if he will hold to his former dimissione verballie past at Vrq^{rt} at the last visitatione of that church the 5 Sepr 1671; and y^t at the Lochend of Lochness the first Wednesday of December; and Mr. Alex^r Clerk, Mr. James Sutherland, Mr. James Fraser, and Mr. Hugh Fraser, Minister at Kiltarlatie, are appoynted to meet, and Mr. Hugh Fraser, Minister at Kiltarlatie, appoynted to writ to Mr. Duncan to keep the meeting the day and place appoynted.

13 *Decr.* 1671.

That day John M^{c}intoshe, broy^r to Aberarder, fors^d, compeired of his own accord, who supplicated the Prīē that the Bretheren should move Mr. Alex^r Fraser, his Parish Minister, to desist from processing him, and that he would yield obedience to Church discipline; the Mod^r desyred the s^d John remove to a litle space, and haveing laid the s^d supplicatione to their serious consideratione thought fitt to move the s^d Mr. Alex^r to accept of the said John to his repentance; being incalled was ordained to goe home and satisfie in sacco till y^r be signes of repentance found in him.

According to the former order the Bretheren appoynted, to wit, Mr. Alex^r Clerk, Mr. James Sutherland, Mr. James Fraser, and Mr. Hugh Fraser, Minister at Kiltarlatie, did meet at the Lochend the day appoynted before, where Mr. Duncan McCulloch, Minist^r at Vrq^{rt}, compeired, who regrated to the brethren then pñt, as he did at the visita°ne at Vrq^{rt} befor, that he hade nether countenance nor yet mantenance nor any kynd of encouragement in his Parochin to goe about the work of his Master in his parochin, and that he could not any longer subsist their, therfor would demitt, and was content that a brother should be sent to declare his church vacant, qlk dimissione he did give to the bretheren in writ sub^t with his own hand, whilk was read in the audience of the Prebrie, whilk is registrat as after followes, and the authentick copie sent to the Bishope and patrone of the said Church of Vrq^{rt}.[1]

The next meeting is appoynted to hold at Croy the third tuesday of Jarij next for visiting the s^d Kirk. Mr. Alex^r Clerk, Minister at Invernes, is appoynted to preach y^r that day. Mr. Hugh Fraser, Minister at Croy, is appoynted to

---

[1] The space left in the record for MacCulloch's demission was never filled up. The demission, however, appears in the records of the Synod of Moray as follows:—'I, Mr. Duncan Macculloch, Minister of the United Churches of Urquhart and Glenmorestoune, for onerous reasons and causes knowen to my selfe and to my reverend Brethren of the Presbytrie of Invernes, doe demitt, renunce, and resigne my cure and ministrie at the forsaid Kirkes into the hands of the right reverend father in God, Murdo, Lord Bishop of Murray, and give hereby full way and heartie consent that hencefurth my cure may be declared vacand, ay and quhill it please God to provid that people with a man that may have more incouragment to serve among them than I have had dureing my service in that place: In consideratione quheroff I ever from the dait hereoff renunce, discharge, and resigne my cure, stipend, manses, and gleibes thereoff in all tym coming: In full testimonie quheroff I have both written and subscrived thir presents with my hand at Davach-in-Craig [Lochend] the first of December 1671 yeirs, befor Mr. Alex^r Clarke, minister at Invernes, and Mr. Hew Fraser, minister at Kiltarlitie.   MR. D. MACCULLOCH.'

'MR. A. CLARK, *Witnes.*'
'HUGH FRASER, *Witnesse.*'

send his session book to Daviot, and the Ministers of Moy and Daviot appoynted to revise the same and be in readines to give y^r Judgment to the Prīe at the s^d visitatione. The meeting closed with prayer.

At Croy, 16 January 1672.

Convened the Lord Bishope of Murray and the remanent bretheren of the Pbrie, except Mr. Alex^r Clerk. Prayer hade.

That day Mr. James Sutherland produced a lr̄e from Mr. Alex^r Clerk showing that he was verie sick and that he could not keep that meeting. He is therfor excused.

The Lord Bishope, w^t consent of the bretheren, thought fitt that this dyet should not hold for ane visitatione in regard the Broy^r that should haue hade the doctrine was absent by reason of his sickness.

The Lord Bishope, with consent fors^d, sent two ministers out to the church yard where the most considerable of the Parochin were attending, showing y^m the reason why they wanted doctrine, and that y^{r}for they could not goe about a visitatione of ye church for that dyet.

The brethren of the Pbr̄ie are appoynted to provide y^r proportiones of money for the commissioners expenses, who are to be sent away the next week.

The breyren are appoynted to supplie Mr. James Sutherland (ane of the Commissioners) his charge till his returne, begining at the younger broy^r, and so going one till his returne.

The next meeting to hold at Inv^{ss} the 7 Febij next, and the exercise to hold *ut prius*. The meeting closed with prayer.

At Inverness, 28 Febrij 1672.

Jo^n M^{c}intosh, broy^r germane to Lachlane off Aberarder, hath not entered to his repentance in regard he is constantlie from home searching for money to pay the Earle of Morray the fyne that was imposed judiciallie on him for his former opprobrious speeches to his Minister one the Lords day; therfor his censure continued for a little tyme.

At Moy, 26 Martij 1672.

The Mod^r desyred the Minister give in a list of ye Elders names, which he did, and were pn̄t, to wit, W^m M^{c}intoshe of

B

Corribroch, Angus M^cintoshe in Moy, Lachlan M^cqueen, Jo^n M^cqueen, Donald McWilliam, W^m. McCulbert, Even Roy. The Mod^r asked the Elders if this visita^o^n was tymouslie intimated, they answered that it was, qlk the meeting in itselfe proported. After the Mod^r hade declared the end of the Pbr̃ies coming to that place, he desyred the Minister, Mr. Roderick, to remove, and y^refter he posed all the gentlemen and Elders pñt, one by one, how they were satisfied with their Ministers life and conversa^one, how with his doctrine and discipline, if he catechised his people, if he did visit the sick, if he did visit the families within the Parochines.

The gentlemen and elders answered that in all these queries, and all that were asked of them anent y^r Minister, that they were well satisfied with him, and that he was painefull and diligint in his ministrie among them, and blessed God for him, and desyred the Pbr̃ie encourage him.

The Minister being incalled, the elders report of him held forth unto him, he was exhorted to walk answerable to his sessioners report of him.

The gentlemen and Elders were removed, and the Minister being asked anent them, and qhat encouragement they gave him in his ministerie among y^m, he answered that he was verie well satisfied with them, and that he hade abundance of concurrence and encouragement of them.

The gentlemen and elders were called in, and the ministers good comendatione of them declared to them, the Mod^r, in name of the pbr̃ie, blessed God for them, rejoiceing in their comelie order and Christian harmony together.

The Moderator asked the Elders if y^r were a school in the Pariochin, they answered that there was not a school in the Pariochin partlie because the townes within the pariochin were far distant one from the other, yet they would meet among themselves to see if they could agree upon the most commodious place for erecting of ane school, and that when they hade closed the sowing of y^r seed betwixt and the first of May next.

[There is a Session book.]

The Mod^r asked the Minister if he hade ane decreet of plat and lr̃s (letters) of horning, he answered that he hade neither of them, but that the pariochiners payed him his stipend as they were in use and wont; the matter referred to the Synode for advise.

The Mod^r ordained the Mins^{tr} and Elders to erect a place for publick repentance, and a sackcloath for the delinquents.

Sicklicke the Mod^r desyred the Min^r and elders repaire the church windows.

At Daviot, 27 Martij 1672.

Convened the Mod^r and remanent Bretheren of the Pbrie. The name of God was called upon.

Mr. Alex. Clerk, Minister at Invernes, preached, text 2 Cor. 5. 20.

The Minister was verie sicke in a fever, who rose then from his bed, who gave in a List of his Elders names who were pñt, to witt, Angus M^{c}intoshe of Daviot, Donald McBean off Falyie, W^m McGillivrey of Larges, Alex^r M^{c}intoshe of Ocht^r Urchall, Alex^r Rose in Culechuinacke, Hector M^{c}intoshe in Craggie, Wm Rose in Belvrait, etc.; these are the elders of the s^d Parochin.

The names of the Elders of the Parochin of Dunleitchitie, Lachlan McIntoshe off Aberarder, Robert Shaw off Torrdaroch, Donald M^{c}gillivrey, tutor of Dunmaglass, Duncan McPhaile of Invererrnie, Even McPhersone off Fleichitie, Lachlan M^{c}intoshe in Drumboy, etc.

The Mod^r asked the gentlemen and Elders if this visitatione was tymeouslie intimated, they answered that it was, whilk the meeting in itself did proport.

The Mod^r did hold forth to the meeting the end of the Pries meeting with them that day, to witt, to know the carriage, life, and conversa°ne of minister and elders, and how the interest of Jesus Christ did thrive in their parochin, and of their own harmony, one with the other. Then desyred the Minister, Mr. Alex^r. Fraser, remove, qlk done, the Mod^r asked ye gentlemen and elders pñt nominatim, how they were satisfied with their Ministers life and conversa°ne, doctrine, and discipline, with all questiones usual at such tymes. They answered that they were well satisfied with y^r Minister in all these things, and in what else was proponed to them by the Mod^r.

The Minister being incalled, the Elders report of him was

declared unto him, and God was blessed for him. He was desyred to walk answerable to their deportment of him.

The gentlemen and elders were removed, and the minister being asked anent them, he answered that he was verie well satisfied with them in all the queries proposed to him by the Mod^r anent them.

The gentlemen and elders were incalled, and the Mod^r declared to them the Ministers good report of them, they were exhorted to continue in well doing, answerable to their Ministers report of them.

[They have a Session Book.]

The Moderator asked the Minister and elders if they had a school, they answered that they hade, but that the Schoolmaster was forced to leave them for want of mantenance, but that they should notice the deficients and move y^m to doe dutie, and that then they would call their Schoolmaster againe.

The Mod^r exhorted the Minister and Elders to repaire the church windowes. Sicklike to erect a place of repentance and a sackcloath.

The officers were approven for their diligence in y^r charge.

Inverness, 1 *May* 1672.

That day some of the Bretheren of the Pbrie regrated that Mr. Alex^r Fraser, Minister at Daviot, did not preach in his parioche churches of Daviot and Dunlechtie since the visitatione of the said Churches, whilk was at Daviot 27 Martij 1672. As also that they had occasione of conference with the s^d Mr. Alex^r, and after long debate *hinc inde*, the s^d Mr. Alex^r s^d that he intended to quit his charge, and that people of whom he formerlie hade the charge off needed not expect anything more of him except a valedictorie sermon, nor yet would he embrace any other charge whatsomever, and that through the dislike and prejudice he caried to the pñt government of the Church by Episcopacie, which he did by severall asseverationes and solemne attestationes. The Bretheren laying the premisses to their consideratione they desyred Mr. Alex^r Clerk, Mod^r, writ to the Bishope aqenting him hereof, withall to crave his advice how the Pbrie shall behaue themselves in the particullare.

[Among the 'Refers' from the Synod read this day, are:

'That Mr. Hugh Fraser, Minister at Kiltarlatie, receed (reside) at his charge, and use dilligence against the heretours for building the Manse of that church—whilks refer the Mod^r did press and urge to be obeyed, and Mr. Hugh promised to use all possible dilligence.'—And 'The Mod^r ordained to instruct the Synods mynd to the pariochners of Kiltarlatie concerning y^r Ministers receiding y^r.']

Mr. James Smith, Minister at Dorres, ordained to goe to Vrq^{r}t before the next pbiall meeting, and preach y^r, and declare that church vacand; withall to exhort the gentlemen and elders y^r to use all possible dilligence to furnish a minister for themselves.

At Invernes, 22 May 1672.

[All present except Mr. Hugh Fraser, Croy, and 'Mr. Alex^r ffraser, Minister at Daviot, who is not to be expected to attend any presbyteriall meeting hereafter in regard of his separa^{o}n.']

That day noe doctrine in regard Mr. Thomas Houstone reported that he was not prepared, and that because he hade been since the last dyet of the Pbrie, imployed in attending the goodwife of Erchet, his mother in law, in her sicknes, who is now departed this life. The s^d Mr. Thomas being removed, and after considera^{o}n of what he hade declared, was not judged relevant; therefor was sharplie rebuked.

The next meeting to hold at Invernes, 12 Junij next, for visiting of the affairs of these churches. Mr. Hugh Fraser, Minister of Kiltarlatie, appointed to preach y^r, and Mr. James Smith and the s^d Mr. Hugh appointed to sight the session book, and give y^r judgment y^{r}of to the next meeting.

That day the Mod^r produced a letter from the Bishope wherein he did regrate the case of Mr. Alex^r Fraser, late Minister at Daviot, as also (if y^r were no hopes of reclaiming him) to cause the Pbrie officer to goe and fix a literall Sumonds on the s^d Mr. Alex^r, charging him to compeir before y^m the next meeting, to answer for his wilffull deserting of his charge.

The Bretheren who had frequent occasione to conferr w^t the said Mr. Alex^r, reported that their was noe hopes of reclaiming him, wherfore the Mod^r with consent of the bretheren, called the Pbrie Officer,   Ross, authorising him to goe to the duelling house of Mr. Alex^r foresaid, personallie apprehending, affixing a literall Sumonds on him, sumonding him to compeir befor the Pbrie the next meeting, to answer for his wilful deserting of his charge.

Mr. James Smith obeyed the ordinance of the Pbrie anent goeing to Urq^{r}t.

[The Min^r of Kiltarlatie is dealing with the Heritors for his accommodation among them.]

At Invernes, 12 *Junij* 1672.

Conveened the Mod^r and remanent Bretheren of the Pbrie, except Mr. Hugh ffraser, minister of Croy, absent without excuse. The name of God called upon.

Mr. Hugh Fraser, Minister of Kiltarlatie, preached, text 2 Cor. 6. 1. The roll of the Elders wer called, and were pñt, to wit, Alex^r Cuthbert, Provost, Robert Rose, late Provest, Alex^r Dunbar, late Provest, Jo^n Hepburne, Baylie, Thomas Schevies off Moortowne, Philip Fraser, Baylie, Alex^r Rose, Baylie, Wm Robertsone, Baylie, etc.

The Mod^r asked the elders if this visitatione was tymeouslie intimated; they answered that it was as the meeting of the Parochiners did proport.

After the Mod^r hade declared the end of ye Presbyterie's comeing y^r that day, he desyred the Ministers of that congregatione remove, and then he posed all the gentlemen and Elders, ane by ane, how they were satisfied with y^r ministers in y^r lives and conversatione, doctrine and discipline, if they did visit the sicke, if they visited the families in towne and land, if they catechised the people, if they did celebrate the sacrament of the Lords supper, w^t all wy^r quæries usuall to be proposed at such tymes.

The gentlemen and Elders replyed and answered to all these quaeries as they were proposed, That they were verie well satisfied with y^r Ministers in all these, and that they were verie painfull and laborious in all y^r ministrie, so that they could not object against y^m. They blessed God for y^m, and desyred the Presb. encourage them.

The Ministers were incalled, and the Elders report of them

held forth to them, They were exhorted to walk answerable to y^r Paroichiners laudable commendatione of them.

The Gentlemen and Elders were removed, and the ministers being asked anent them, what encouragement they hade of y^m in there ministrie, and wy^r questiones usuall, they answered that they were well satisfied w^t y^r gentlemen and Elders, except that they did too much encourage Papists and such as was excommunicat of them, and that by their frequent fellowshipe with them, and kindly salutationes given to them.

The gentlemen and Elders were incalled, and y^r ministers commendatione of them reported, God was blessed for them, and they exhorted to continue in welldoeing. But wer rebuked for y^r frequenting the company of Papists excommunicat, and wy^{r}wayes they were desyred to behave themselves more circumspectlie in the matter hereafter, as they would wish no to offend God and to incur a heavier censure of men. Wilk they promised to doe.

The visitors of the Book reported that they hade read the same, and all therein being formall, was approven.

The Clerk to the Session was well reported be the Ministers and Elders, wherefor was, after removeall, incalled and approven.

The Ministers and Elders were enquired anent their Gramar School, and deportment of the Schoolmaster, they ansuered that they were well satisfied with the thriveing theirof, and reported that they were well pleased with y^r Schoolmaster. He was recommended and exhorted to pietie and continue dilligent in his charge.

That day   Ross, Presb. officer, gave in a formall literall executione showing that he hade apprehended personallie Mr. Alex^r Fraser, late Minister at Daviot, by a literall Summonds to compeir befor the Pbrie that day for his willfull deserting of his charge, and that befor famous witnesses. The said Mr. Alex^r being cited at the Kirk door after the ordinarie manner, not compeiring, the officer was ordained to summond him to the next dyet *pro secundo*.

At Boleskine, 2 Julij 1672.

[All present except Mr. James Fraser, Min^r of Wardlaw, and

Mr. Hugh Fraser, Min^r of Croy. Mr. James Smith preached, text Heb. 10. 32.]

The roll of the Elders were called, and were p̅n̅t, to wit, Alex^r Fraser of Faraline, Donald Fraser of Drummond, James Fraser of Dulcrage, James Fraser of Mickle Garth, Donald Fraser of Little Garth, etc.

[The visitation was timeously intimated, 'as the conventione of the people did proport.']

After the Mod^r hade declared the end of the Pb̅ries comeing to that place, he desyred the Minister remove, then he enquired all the gentlemen and elders p̅n̅t nominatim how they were satisfied with their ministers lif and conversatione, doctrine and discipline, if he did visit the sick, if he did visit families, if he did catechise and celebrate the sacrament of the Lords supper, and wy^r questiones usuall in the like case.

The gentlemen and Elders answered that they were well pleased with their minister in all that was proposed to them and blessed God for him, and that he deserved to be encouraged. The Minister was incalled, and the Elders report of him held forth to him. He was exhorted to walk answerable to y^r commendatione of him. The elders were removed, and the minister asked anent them, what encouragement he hade amongst them in his ministrie; he ansuered that he was well pleased w^t them, except in the matter of his mantenance.

The Elders were called in and the Ministers report of them held forth to them, they were exhorted to continue in doeing good and to pay y^r Minister his stipend better in tyme comeing, whilk they promised to doe.

The visitor of the Book was asked y^{r}anent, who reported that he hade dilligentlie revised the same, and all y^{r}in being formall, was approven.

That day Mr. Thomas Houstone, the Minister, regrated that he could not haue the benefitt of his designatione of Manse and Gleib in his grassing and pastorage, as also the s^d Min^r produced the designatione, whilk was read in audience of the meeting. Whereupyn the Mod^r desyred the Minister possess himself of Manse and Gleib and all things belonging thereto. Wherupon he tooke instrument in Hugh Fraser, Notar Publicke at Invernes, his hand, as also desyred the clerk of the

Prie registrate the designatione in the Pbr̄ie book, with the instrument y^rupon, whilk is insert as followeth.

'*Visitatione of the Kirk of Boleskine, holdin the* 26 *May*, 1632, *at Boleskine, the s^d day and yeir*.

'That day conveened Mr. William Cloggie, Mod^r, Mr. Joⁿ Houstown, Mr. William Fraser, Mr. Patrick Dunbar, Mr. Alex^r Grant, Mr. James Wause, Mr, Lachlan Grant, Mr. Alex^r Fraser, and Alex^r Thomsone.

' Mr. Wm Fraser hade the doctrine.

' The Elders, Thomas ffraser of ffaraline, Taus [1] ffraser of Little-Garth, Hugh ffraser off Dulcrag, James ffraser, Tutor of ffoyer, Alex^r ffraser of Kinmunovie, and Hugh ffraser in Drummond.

' The ordinarie questiones proponed, the Minister removed, the Elders were demanded concerning their Minister his doctrine, life, and conversatione, ansuered that they were satisfied with him as to doctrine, considering his abilities, and knew him to be of ane honest life and conversatione, yet requested the Presbytric to take dealling betwixt him and the familie off foyer who are in a continuall combustione cuncerning the Gleib.

' The Minister being called in, and after approbatione, he was enquired anent his satisfactione of the gentlemen and elders, who ansuered that he was well pleased with them, except that he could not live in Boleskine for the evill neighbourhood of the tenents y^rof, who would not permitt his goods to pasture on his own grasse, and that the Tutor of ffoyer attempted not only to denude him of the grass, but also a part of the land designed alreadie.

' The Presbytrie, mynding themselves of the great paines they were att betwixt the familie of ffoyer and the Minister before, were not well pleased that the same was renewed againe, wherfor, after long and wearisome debats, and great paines takin betwixt them, they went and measured and marched the gleib and grassing thereof as followeth, That is, the Burn at the West called Ault Sulua to be march till it went in the Loch ; and the Burn at the easterside, whilk goes by Gorten na Keirach, and betwixt Lugg-croft to Gillie more and William Moires croft, to be the march till it entered in the Lochness, and that little grass be north the gleib betwixt the forsaid burnes to belong to the Gleib as propertie.

' Together also with sufficient grass and pasturage w^t the tenents, wherever the pasture (except their leyrigges) to sex kine, five

---

[1] Taus, *i.e.* Tavish.

horse, fourtie sheep, and fourtie goats, and this to stand as a constant allocatione and mortificatione to the said Minister and his successors, ministers serving the cure. To which Margaret McKenzie, relick of ffoyer, and James ffraser, Tutor off ffoyer, with the rest of the gentlemen of that famillie and the whole eldership consented to *uno voce*. Whereupon the Minister took instrument in the hands of James Duff, Notar burges of Inverness, and appoynts thir pn̅ts to be registrate in the Pbr̅ie book *ad futuram rei memoriam*.'

> Apud Bolleskine, secundo die mensis Julij, anno Dom. Millesimo sexcentesimo septuagesimo 2º: Regnique præclarissimi principis nostri C. S. D. G. Magnae Brittaniae ffranciae et Hiberniae regis fiddej defensoris anno vigesimo quarto.

In presence of me, Notar Publick underscribing, and Witness underwritin, compeired personallie Mr. Thomas Houstown Minister att Boleskine, within the Paroch Kirk therof, where were conveened for the tyme Mr. Alex^r Clerk, Mod^r to the Pbr̅ie of Inv'nes, Mr. Ja. Sutherland, one of the Ministers of Inv'nes, Mr. Roderick McKenzie, Minister at Moy, Mr. James Smith, Minister at Dorres, and Mr. Hugh ffraser, Minister att Kiltarlatie, all reverend Bretheren of the forsaid Pbr̅ie, Together with the Elders of the fors^d parishe off Boleskine, for visiting of the Church therof, who haveing in his hand ane duble or extract of ane act and Judiciall ordinance Be Mr. Wm Cloggie, then Mod^r of the Pbr̅ie above exprest, with the speciall advise of Mr. Joⁿ Houstown, Mi^r at Kirkhill, Mr. W^m ffraser, Minist^r att Kiltarlatie, Mr. Patrick Dunbar, Minister att Dorres, Mr. Alex^r Grant, Mr. James Wause, Mr. Lachlan Grant, and Mr. Alex^r ffraser, then also breyren of the said Presbytrie, bearing date the 26 day of May 1632 yeires, Makeing mentione that, wheras after long debate and great paines taken betwixt Andrew Dow Fraser, Minister serveing the cure at the said Kirk of Boleskine, immediat predecessor to the said Mr. Thomas Houstowne, and the familie of ffoyer, anent the Gleib belonging to the said Kirk and to him as Minister thereof, together with the grassing and pastorage y^rof. The said Mr. Wm Cloggie, Mod^r above named, and the reverend breyren above specifiet, haveing then taken the controversies and debate *hinc inde* to y^r serious and judicious consideratione and avisandum, they and all of them marched and meithed the fors^d Gleib with one consent and *una voce* as followes, viz. The Burne att the west called Ault Sulva to be the only march till the entrie y^{r}of in Lochness, and the Burne at the east syde that goes by Gorten na Keirach and betuixt Lagg croft to Geillie Moar and Wm Moares croft to be the March whill it entered in the forsaid Lochness, and that litle grassing beneath the gleib betuixt the forsaid Burnes to belong to the said gleib as propertie: Together with sufficient grassing and pasturage with the tennents wherever they pasture except y^r leyrigges, and that for sex cows, five horses, fourtie sheep, and fourtie goats, and further the fors^d divisione and ordinance to stand and continue as a constant alloca^{o}ne and mortifica^{o}ne to the s^d Minister and his successores serveing the cure at the s^d Kirk. Wherunto Margaret M^{c}kenzie, relick of ffoyer, and the Tutor y^{r}of, with the whole gentlemen of that familie who were their pñt, and the Elders above exprest then convened, unanimouslie consented. Whereupon the s^d Minister took Instrument in the hands of James Duff, Notar Publick, as s^d Act and Instrument both of the fors^d date containeing many wy^r articles at greater length proport. Likeas the s^d Mr. Thomas Houstowne, as successor above spēit to the s^d Andrew ffraser, himblie required and desyred the forsaid Mod^r and remanent bretheren above named to homologat to the above writin designa^{o}ne made be the said Presbytrie mett y^{r}anent the tyme and place forsaid, and to corroborat the same after the forme and tennor therof, and to decerne the samen and haile benefitt and casualtie effeiring y^{r}to simpliciter in his favours as successour fors^{ds}. Which designatione and act being judiciallie read be the s^d Mr. James Smith, Presbbytrie clerk, and y^{r}efter seen, considered, and approven be them, The said Alex^r Clerk, Mod^r, with consent of the fors^d Bretheren, and they all with one consent, decerned in favours of the said Master Thomas Houstown according to the mortificatione above exprest, and ordained him to posses himself *sine mora* with the lands, pertinents, and grassings belonging to the said Kirk, according to the former designatione in all poynts, and that but necessitie of any uther declarator to be hade y^{r}anent, as he should be ansuerable to the Bishope and Synode of Murray:

and moreover the s^d Mod^r with consent forsaid ordained thir pnts to be orderlie registrate in y^r Presbytrie book *ad rei memoriam* as ane act made y^ranent beares; wherupon the said Mr. Thomas Houstown required Instrument in the hands of me Notar publick underscriving, thir things now done in the s^d Kirk of Boleskine tuixt tuelf and one ocloak of the day, yeir and moneth above writen, in pns of Donald ffraser of Drumond, Donald ffraser of Little Garth, Jo^n ffraser off Migovie, Hugh ffraser of Leadclune, James and Thomas ffraser in Dunchea, Alex^r Rose, Kirk Officer in Inv'nes, and severall other witnesses heirto speciallie called and required.

> Et ego vero Hugo ffraser nōrius publicus in testimonium veritatis praemissorum rogatus et requisitus hoc praesens publicum Instrumentum signo et subscribo meis, etc.
>
> Hu. ffraser,
Nōrius Publicus.

The Mod^r asked the Ministear and Elders if they hade a school, they answered that they could not haue a school in regard the townes in the parishe were remote the one from the wy^r, and that they hade no convenience of boarding children. They were asked anent y^r officer. They reported that they were well satisfied with him. He was incalled and approven.

That day   Ross, Pbrie Officer, gave in a formall literall executione showing that he hade past a literall summonds one Mr. Alex^r ffraser, late Minister at Daviot, summonding him to compeir befor the Pbrie that day for his wilfull deserting of his charge. The said Mr. Alex^r was cited after the ordinarie maner in the like case, not compeiring, the Officer was ordained to Sumond him to the next dyet *pro tertio*.

At Wardlaw, 23 July 1672.

Mr. James Sutherland preached 2 Cor. 4. 5, for the Irish, and 1 Thes. 5. 19 for the Scots sermons.

The catalogue of the Elders was read, and were pnt, to wit, Alex^r Fraser of Moniack, Alex^r Wright in Inglistowne, Donald McBean y^r, Donald McShoirle, Thomas McWarron in Bunchrwe, Donald McThomas vic Andrew in Inchvarie, etc.

[Visitation duly intimated.]

After the Mod^r hade declared the end of pb̃ries comeing to that place, he dsyred the Minster remove, then he asked the gentlemen and elders, one by one, how they were satisfied with y^r minister in life and conversatione, doctrine and discipline, if he did visit the sick, if he did visit families, if he catechised the people, if he did distribute the sacraments, and wy^r questiones usuall in the like case. The Gentlemen and Elders answered that they were well pleased with their minister in all the quaeries proposed and what could be proposed; they blessed God for him, and said that he deserved to be encouraged.

The Minister was called in, and the Elders report of him held forth to him, he was exhorted to walk answerable to y^r good report of him.

[The Minister declared himself well pleased with the Gentlemen and Elders, who were 'verie willing to contribute w^t him in anything that could doe good among them.' The Session Book found in order.]

The Mod^r asked the Minister and Elders anent the Ministers Manse. They answered that they were now in readiness to goe about the erecting of the Manse, in testimony wherof the meassons were imployed in the work, as was manifest to the presbytrie.

They were asked anent y^r Schoolemaster, Mr. Charles Ritchie; they answered that they were well satisfied with him; he was incalled, and exhorted to pietie, and dilligence in his charge.

They were asked anent y^r officer, they did approve of him; y^{r}for he was commended.

That day Rose, Pb̃rie Officer, gave in a formall literall executione bearing that he hade past a literall Summonds one Mr. Alex^r ffraser, late Minister at Daviot, charging him to compeir that day befor the pb̃rie to answer for his willfull deserting of his charge. The s^d Mr. Alex^r being cited and not compeiring. The Bretheren laying the sad conditione of the s^d Mr. Alex^r Fraser to y^r serious consideratione, they thought fitt before they would refer him to the Synode to take some paines on him, that is, that some of the Bretheren, to wit, Mr. Alex^r Fraser, parsone of Pettie, Mr. James Sutherland, Minister at Invernes, Mr. James Fraser, Minister at Wardlaw, Mr. Hugh

Fraser, Minister at Kiltarlatie, should meet at Muckovie, where the s^d Mr. Alex^r receids for the tyme, and Mr. James Smith was appoynted to acquent some of the most judicious and understanding of his friends in Stratherig to meet the s^d bretheren at the s^d place, the same day 14 dayes, to see if they can solve the s^d Mr. Alex^r of his doubts, and reclame him from his pñt errour, and to give y^r report to the next meeting.

At Invernes, 14 *August* 1672.

Conforme to the former ordinance of the Pbrie the breyren appoynted did meet at Muckovic, Wednesday last, being the day appoynted for conference with Mr. Alex^r ffraser, late Minister at Daviot, but the s^d Mr. Alex^r hade left his own house that he might not meet the bretheren, yet notwithstanding his promises to the contrare to some of the brethren befor that day, therfor y^r goeing was to noe purpose; therfor the Mod^r in name of the Pbrie desyred the Clerk to extract the s^d Mr. Alex^r his proces that the same may be hade to the Synode.

The Presbyterie, considering the sad conditione of the parish off Urq^rt, and the manifold abuses committed y^r, and their loose and unrullie walking through the want of gospell ordinances amongest them: as also the little care they have for providing a minister for themselves, have appoynted Mr. James Smith, Minister at Dorres, to goe to Vrq^rt and preach to the people the last Lords day of August instant, and keep session y^r, and exhort the people to use all possible dilligence for searching out for one able qualified min^r sittled for y^t place, and to that effect that they would send some of their number and meet with the Laird off Grant, the most considerable heritor of the Parish, and Mr. James Stuart, Minister of Inveraine,[1] Patrone of the Parishe of Urq^rt, for their help and assistance in the work: and till they be provided the Gentlemen to keep y^r people under them in good order.

At Invernes, 11. *Sept^r* 1672.

That day the Clerk of the Presb. produced the proces of Mr. Alex^r ffraser, late Minister at Daviot, and was read in

---

[1] Inveravon.

Judgment and found formall, the same was delivered to Mr. Hugh ffraser, minister att Kiltarlitie, to be keeped up till the meeting of the Bishope and Synode, that then it may be delivered up.

Mr. James Smith obeyed the ordinance of the Pbr̄ie in goeing to Urq^{rt} in all steps, and Mr. James Hay supplied from his own charge.

That day the Bretheren being weighted with the frequent absence of Mr. Hugh ffraser, Minister at Croy, that he was only present at three meetings since the last Synode, he was seriouslie enquired anent his absence, answered that he was necessitat to go to the South, which did occasione his absence so often. After he was heard the Mod^r, with consent, desyred him remove till he should enquire the breyren anent him, and after he was called in the Mod^r told him that he should not goe to the South, not haveing aquent his breyren of the Pbr̄ie; he was sharplie rebuked, and was desyred to walk more orderlie and brotherlie hereafter *sub periculo gravioris censurae*.

At Inv'nes, 25 Sep^t 1672.

That day Alex^r Ross, Presbyterie Officer, was appoynted to fix a literall Summonds on Mr. Alex^r Fraser, late Minister at Daviot, charging him to compeir befor the Synode the 8 day of Octob. at Elgine, for his wilfull deserting of his charge.

That day the Mod^r asked Mr. Hugh ffraser, Minister att Kiltarlatie, if he hade used any legall dilligence against the Parochiners of Kiltarlatie anent building the manse; answered that he could not use any dilligence against them in regard he knew not any that did represent the Lord Lovat, the most considerable heritor in the Parochin.

At Invernes, Octob 20, 1672.

Be vertue of a former order from the Bishope, Mr. Jo^n Cuthbert hade a homilie text, 1 Tim. 6. 15, and was approven. [Mr. Cuthbert to add next day.]

[Among the refers from the Synod are: 'Mr. Hugh ffraser, Minister at Kiltarlatie, was appoynted to preach at Daviot and cause Summond Jo^n McIntosh, brother of Aberchalder,[1] to the

---

[1] *Sic*; but should be Aberarder.

Pbrie for his reproaching the Minister on the Lords day.' 'That noe persons be receaved from the Hylands without testimonialls.' 'To intimate the excommuncation of Isobell Davidson, Parish of Keith.' 'That noe young man enter upon tryalls without recomendatione simplic from the Mod^r.']

The Mod^r asked Mr. Hugh ffraser, Min^r at Kiltarlatie, if he hade used legall dilligence against the parochioners of Kiltarlatie for building the Manse, Answered that he did not, neither could he, for the cause aforesaid, yet that he was upon a present course to reseid within his own parish for the good of the people and easing of his own person of the great paines and travell he hade been at formerlie by reseiding at Inverness, and that *quam primum*.

That day their was a letter produced and read q^{lk} came from the Bishope desyreing that Mr. Michael ffraser should add to Mr. Jo^n Cuthbert the next dyet *cum intuitu ad locum* to the Church of Daviot and Dunlechtie united Kirks; as also the Bishope desyred that the Presbyterie should accelerat the tryells of Mr. Michael ffraser to the forsaid Kirks, that is to say, that Mr. Michaell have his Common head Wednesday immediatelie after his additione, and his populare sermon, and the tryell of the languages, with his questionarie tryells, the Presbyterie meeting y^{re}after. Mr. Michaell is appoynted to haue his theses in readiness against the next day, the subject of his commone head being *De peccato originali*.

At Invernes, 27 Novr., 1672.

Mr. Michael Fraser was appoynted to haue his Commone head this day eight dayes, *De peccato originali*. He delivered his theses to be disputed that day.

The breyren reported that they did intimat the excommunic°ne of Isobell Davidsone, in the Parish of Keith, from y^r respective pulpets.

That day compeired Mr. James Grant, Expectant, who produced a presentatione from Mr. James Stuart, Lawfull patrone of the Kirk of Urq^{rt}, to the same Kirk, as also a letter from the Bishope desyreing to put Mr. James Grant to his tryells *cum intuitu ad locum* to the Church of Urq^{rt} how soone Mr. Michael Fraser hath closed his tryells.

The next meeting to hold at Invernes, 4 Decr. next. The meeting closed w^t prayer.

4 Decr. 1672.

That day Mr. Michaell Fraser delivered his *exegeses de peccato originali*, sustained his disputs, and was approven.

He is appoynted to haue his populare sermon, and what else was enjoyned and prescribed befor, to the next meeting.

Mr. Roderick McKenzie is appoynted to preach the next Lords day at Daviot, and carie along with him ane Edict sūbt be the Mod^r and clerk of the Pb̄rie relating Mr. Michael Fraser to be their future Minister.

18 Decr. 1672.

That day Mr. Michael Fraser hade his populare sermon text Ephes. 3. 8, with the tryell of the languages, and his questionarie tryells, and wes approven in these and all tōy^r [t'other] steps of his tryells, Therefor was recommended to the Bishope for ordinatione and collatione and institutione, and the clerk appoynted to draw up his testificat to that effect.

Mr. John Cuthbert is appoynted to haue his commone head *de extentione Mortis Christi*, and sustaine the disputs of his theses, that day.

Mr. James Grant is appoynted to haue his homilie the next day, text Jo^n 3. 16.

Mr. Roberick McKenzie preached at Daviot conforme to the former ordinance, and served Edict y^r, and gaue execution y^{r}upon.

Because the Officer of Dunlechitie was affrayed to summond the delinquents of the Parochin of Dunlechitie to the Pr̄ie, the Mod^r, with consent of the breyren, appoynt Alex^r Ross, Pb̄rie officer, to goe to the fors^d Parochin and summond Jo^n M^{c}intoshe, broy^r to Lachlane M^{c}intoshe of Aberarder, for his former guilt, Martcin McGillivrey of Aberchaliter and Alex^r M^{c}intoshe of Far for y^r former ploy in the Church on the Lords day, and that to the next dyet of the Pr̄ie.

At Invernes, 8 *Janry.* 1673

Mr. James Grant hade his homilie text Jo^n 3. 16. They were approven.

That day Alex^r Ross, Pbrie Officer, gave in a formall literall executione showing that he hade summoned the delinquents of Dunlechtie, to wit, Martein McGillivrey, Alex^r M^cintoshe, and John M^cintoshe, to this day; they being cited, non compeired except Jo^n M^cintoshe fors^d, who after rebuke confessed guilt in that he should haue spoken unreverentlie to his parochin minister; whereupon Mr. James Smith, Minister at Dorres, was appoynted to goe to the Kirk of Dunlechtie, and preach y^r to the people on ane Lords day befor the next dyet, and receave the s^d Jo^n *in sacco*, upon signes of repentance.

The Officer fors^d is appoynted to summond Martein McGillivrey and Alex^r M^cintoshe to the next meeting.

29 Janrij 1673.

Mr. James Grant is appoynted (w^t advise of the Bishope) to have his exercise and additione the next dyet, text Col. 2. 19.

Mr. James Smith preached at Dunlechtie conforme to the former order and Jo^n McIntoshe, broyer germane to Lachlan M^cintoshe of Aberarder, was receaved.

[Martin McGillivrey and Alex^r McIntoshe, not appearing, to be summoned to next meeting.]

26 Febrij 1673.

Mr. James Grant hade his exercise and additione, text Col. 2. 14, and was approven. Mr. James Grant was appoynted to haue his common head to the next dyet *de infallibilitate Ecclesiej*, and deliver his theses to be disputed the day y^refter. That day the Pbrie officer reported that he could not meet w^t Martein McGillivery, nor with Alex^r M^cintoshe, and y^rfor did not summond them to this day. The Pbrie thought fitt to continue them till the place be settled with a minister.

That day the Mod^r did present and exhibit a letter from the Bishope desyreing to suspend Mr. Jo^n Cuthbert from the exercise of preaching the gospell because of some dissatisfactione, and that because the s^d Mr. Jo^n Cuthbert went to preach at Daviot contrare ane express formerlie from the Bishope, the tenor of the pnt letter is insert as follows:

'Mr. Johne,—I perceive by your appologetick letter to me that ye haue advisedly transgressed that express injunctione whereby I did discharge you to preach in the Church of Daviot the last Lords day, being the sexteenth instant, far against my expecta^{o}ne of your moderatione and peaceable temper. But seeing ye haue been pleased to abuse that license granted to you be me, and with ane high hand verie contemptuouslie hes vilified and transgressed my order to you, I doe by these p̄nts suspend my licence of preaching granted to you, and I doe suspend you from preaching the gospell anywhere within this diocess of Morray untill the next Provinciall Synode to be holden at Elgine the second tuisday of Aprill in this instant yeir, and I doe by these straitlie require you to compeir befor the Synode the s^d day, with certifica^{o}ne if ye transgress in the performance of these premisses ye shall incur farder ecclesiasticall censure as accords, and I enjoyne the Mod^r of the exercise at Invernes to intimat this sentence to you presbyteriallie, lest you pretend ignorance of the same. Given at Elgine judiciallie (with advice of my bretheren) the 19 day of Febrij 1673.

'Sic subscribitur   MURDO,
                        'Bp. off Morray.'

In obedience to the fors^d letter the Mod^r called Mr. Jo^n Cuthbert and declared him judiciallie to be suspensed from the exercise of preaching till the next Synode, as also *apud acta* charged the s^d Mr. Jo^n to be at the Synode the second tuisday of Aprile next.[1]

That day compeired the Laird of Calder for himself, and produced three seuerall charters each of them containeing his right of patronage to the Parochin of Dunlechtie, and in respect the saids Kirk of Dunlechtie and Daviot are united in ane parochin alledged this to be his vice of the patronage and right to present a minister to these united Parishes now vacand through the depositione of Mr. Alex^r Fraser late Minist^r y^{re}of, who was p̄nted by the Bishope of Morray, and protested against the admissione, colla^{o}ne, and institutione of Mr. Michaell ffraser to the saidis united Kirks or cure and that anything that hath been done by the Bishope or may be done by the Presbyterie not prejudge his right, and further made offer of Mr. Donald McPhersone, p̄nt Minister at Calder, to the s^{ds} cure, he required

---

[1] It was only on 29th January 1673 that Cuthbert passed his final trials before the Presbytery. He was 'approven in all the steps of his tryells,' and 'recommended to the Bishope for a licence to preach the Gospell.'

ane extract of the saids protestatione, which is ordained to be given whenever the same is required.

That day the Mod^r declared in name of the Pbrie that they would admitt Mr. Michael ffraser to the United Kirks of Daviot and Dunlechtie the 4 March in this pnt yeir 1673. Mr. Alex^r Clerk is appoynted to preach. Mr. James Sutherland, Mr. Roderick M'Kenzie, Mr. James ffraser, and Mr. Hugh ffraser, Minister at Kiltarlatie, appoynted to be pnt that day for to bear witness to his admissione.

At Invernes, 12 Martij 1673.

Mr. James Grant hade his commone head *de infallibilitate Ecclesiae* and sustained his disputs, and was approven.

The Mod^r and Breyren went the 4 March last to the Church of Daviot and admitted the s^d Mr. Michaell ffraser to the Kirks of Daviot and Dunlechtie conforme to the former order, and Mr. Alex^r Clerk, Mod^r, preached that day, text Act 8. 29, 33, 31 verses.

Mr. James Grant is appoynted to have his populare sermon to the next dyet, text Mat. 8. 12, as also the tryell of the languages, with the questionarie tryells. Mr. Hugh Fraser, Minister at Kiltarlatie, appoynted to goe to Urq^{rt} the next Lords day and serve his edict.

At Invernes, 26 Martij 1673.

Mr. James Grant hade his populare sermon, text Mat. 8. 12, as also his questionarie tryells, and the tryell of the languages, and was approven in all the steps of his tryells. Wherfor he is remitted to the Bishope to receave ordina°ne, collatione, and institutione.

Mr. Hugh Fraser, Minister at Kiltarlatie, preached at Urq^{rt} the last Lords day for serving of Mr. James Grant his edict, and gaue executione y^rupon.

That day compeired Joⁿ Grant of Corrimony for himself and commissionat be the rest of the Parochiners of Urq^{rt}, supplicating the Pbrie that they would send them Mr. James Grant, whom they are most willing to receave as their minister, promiseing to him dutie according to y^r power, and that in giveing him countenance and mantenance, as also that they will concur with him in discipline and what else may contribute for helping one Gods service to Gods glorie and to his encouragement.

The Mod^r did renew the refer anent Mr. Hugh ffraser, Minister at Kiltarlatie, who told that he did not use any legall dilligence against the Parochiners of Kiltarlatie for building the manse for the cause aforesaid, yet that he did reseid in his own pariochin in the most commodious place he could find for the good of the pariochin and pariochiners.

At Inverness, 7 May 1673.

Be vertue of ane order form the Bishope of Morray, Mr. Hugh ffraser, Minister at Kiltarlatie, went the last Lords day to Urq^{rt}, and preached to the people, and admitted Mr. James Grant to be future Minister y^r, haveing used all the ceremonyes usuall in the like case: the whole parochiners did accept of the s^d Mr. James upon the terms forsaid.

The said Mr. James receaved colla°ne, institutione, and impositione of hands, and the right hand of fellowshipe, with everything usuall in the like case, at Elgine the nynth of Aprill last, in this p͠nt yeir 1673.

At Invernes, 4 Junij 1673.

That day Mr. Hugh ffraser, Minister at Croy, p͠nted a letter to the Pb͠rie from the Bishope of Morray anent the affaires of the Churches of Daviot and Dunlechtie, insert and registrat verbatim as followeth :

'*For Mr. Alex^r Clerk, Mod^r, and remanent Ministers of the Pb͠rie of Invernes, These—*

'*Elgine, 25 Ap͠rill* 1673.

' REVEREND BREYREN,—If I had seen the Laird of Calder's right sooner to the patronage of Dunlechtie it might possiblie have prevented some of our differs anent the planting of that Kirk. But now haveing seen the Laird of Calder's fors^d right (and out of our desyre to settle things amicablie) I thought fitt to show you that I haue resolved and promised to remove Mr. Michaell Fraser betuixt and the fifteenth day of October next, that the Laird of Calder may present ane other the next vice to the united Kirks of Dunlechtie and Daviot, and this is not to derogate from Mr. Michaell, or to inferr any blame on him who is found to be sufficientlie qualified.

But purelie for preserving the Laird of Calder's right of patronage, and that he may haue ane more comfortable ministry els where. I desire thir p̃nts to be recorded in the Pb̃rie Books of Invernes, and commending you to the grace of the Lord, I rest.

'I desyre also that the parochiners oblidgment in y^r letter presented herewith for attending the publick ordinance dureing Mr. Michaell his service of the cure at the s^d Church be recorded also in the s^d register.

'Your affectionat broy^r in Christ,
Sic subscribitur   MURDO,
Bp. of Morray.'

As also Mr. Hugh Fraser fors^d p̃nted ane other letter, to wit, the Parochiners of Daviot and Dunlechtie y^r obligatione to Mr. Michaell, insert as followeth :

'*For my Lord Bishope of Morray, These—*

'MY LORD,—Being informed that your Lo. and the Laird of Calder are agreed anent the patronage of this Kirk and that your Lo. hes promised to remove Mr. Michaell Fraser befor the next Synode to the effect the Laird of Calder may present the next vice, and that wee should in the mean tyme countenance Mr. Michaell Fraser in the administra°ne of divine ordinances, and concur in discipline in that place, wee thought fitt to show your Lo. that we aquiesced to the termes of agreement, and therefor declare and promise that wee will countenance Mr. Michaell dureing the space fors^d, your Lo. always according to your promise removeing Mr. Michaell Fraser betuixt and the Synode appoynted, and shall at p̃nt say noe more but that we rest

'Your Lo. humble servants,
Sic subscribitur   L. M^{c}INTOSHIE.
DONALD M^{c}BEAN.
—— M^{c}INTOSHIE.[1]
ROBERT SHAW.
WILLIAM M^{c}GILLIVREY.
D. M^{c}PHAILE.'

At Invernes, 9 Julij 1673.

That day compeired Wm Robertsone and Alex^r Fraser, two of the Baylies of Inv'nes, and supplicated the Presbytric that

---

[1] Initial illegible.

they would lay to y^r consideratione the conditione of Invernes through the sickness of Mr. James Sutherland, by sending some of their number to preach to them till the s^d Mr. James his recoverie.

The Pbrie, considering the case of Inv'nes, for the cause asserted, they have concluded that they shall preach in the church of Inv'nes every one per vices, and to begin at the youngest minister, and so goe an to the eldest, and Mr. James Grant to begin and preach in Inv'nes the ensueing Lords day.

At Invernes, 20 *July* 1673.

Mr. Hendrie Baylie exercised, and Mr. John Cuthbert added, text Col. 2. 19. They were approven.

Bessie Dean in Invernes was referred from the Session of Invernes to the Pbrie for tryell because she had brought forth a child alledged noe to be her husbands, in regard that her husband hade gone from Inv'nes to France the 7 day of May 1672, and her child was brought forth the 16 day of March 1673, y^r being one moneth and nyne dayes in differ.

The s^d Bessie being cited compeired, and being examined on the premisses, she did boldlie and constantlie aver that she hade noe other father to her child but her maried husband; she is continewed till further tryell, and the Minister of the towne appoynted to take paines on her till the next Pbric day.

At Invernes, 20 *August* 1673.

The Bretheren resolve to keep at Daviot the next dyet for visitatione of that church, and the minister of the parioche is appoynted to preach that day.

Bessie Dean in Invernes being cited, compeired, and being dilligentlie examined anent the father of her present youngest child, she asserted as befor, and told that she could never doe otherwise; she is dimitted till the Pbrie meet at Inv'nes, and the Minister appoynted to take paines on her till then.

Margaret Fraser, daughter to the deceased Mr. Alex^r ffraser, somtyme schoolmaster at Invernes, is referred from the Session of Inv'nes to the Pbrie in regard that she hath brought forth a male child and will not declare who is the father of her child, being cited, not compeiring, she is to be sumonded to the next meeting of Pbrie at Invernes.

At Daviot, 9 Septr. 1673.

After that the Mod^r hade told the end of the Presbyteries comeing to that place, he desyred the Minister remove, then he asked the gentlemen and elders present how they were satisfied with y^r Minister in doctrine, discipline, life, and conversatione. They answered that they were verie well satisfied with him in these and in all things that belonged to his ministeriall functione, and that they nor the rest of the parochiners hade not anything to object in the contrare if he and the Laird of Calder, Patrone, hade settled anent the right of Patronage.

The Minister was called in and the elders good report of him declared to him. He was exhorted to walk ansuerable to y^r report of him, and that the differ betwixt the Laird of Calder and the Bishope of Morray did noe way reflect on him.

[The Minister report well of the Elders, and 'they were exhorted to continue in well doeing in hopes to receave the crown of righteousnes.']

[The Session Book and penalties were taken possession of by the late Min^r Mr. Alex^r Fraser, and 'The Mod^r and remanent bretheren desyred the present Minister, and w^t him two or three of the elders, desyre the book and former accompts of the hands of Mr. Alex^r foresaid, and if he should deny the same, then they were desyred to pursue the actione before the Commisser.'

At Invernes, 1. *Octob.* 1673.

[Mr. Hendrie Baylie hade his populare sermon, text Math. 5. 8; he sustained his disputs, his questionarie tryels, and the tryell of the languages, and was approven in these and all wy^r passages of his tryells: Wherfor the clerk was desyred to writ a testificat to him remitting him to the Bishope to receave a licence to preach the gospell where he may haue a lawfull call.

Alex^r Rose and Alex^r Fraser, Bailies of Invernes, appeared and prayed the Pbrie to supply the now deceased Mr. James Sutherland's pulpit until they get another Minister. Their prayer granted, and the bretheren to preach from the youngest to the oldest, beginning with Mr. James Grant, Urquhart.

Bessie Dean still declares that her husband is the father of her child, and is referred to, and summond to appear before the Synode, 15 Oct. next.]

That day Margaret Fraser was cited and compeired and being enquired anent the father of her child ansuered with many asseverationes that she did not know who was the father of her child, but that on a certaine tyme their came a certaine person in to the shope wher she was in the twilight, and assaulted her, and begate the child on her, she not knowing who he was, from whence he came, nor where he went. Y^e Bretheren, not being satisfied with this her answer, after rebuke referred her to the Synode, and was charged *apud acta* to be p̃nt the same day with Bessie Dean.

The Minister of Dorres delared to the Presbyterie that their came latlie a young knavish fellow from Burgie to the Paroche of Dorres, who had lived lewdlie y^r during his abode their, to wit, for the space of ane half yeir and more; he was delated to haue fallen twise in fornica°ne, and did constantlie prophane the Lords sabbathes by drinking and dancing with harlots, and now and then stealling. He called himself $Alex^r$ Sutherland, but wee are informed that his name is Thomas Leith; he is removed from the s^d paroche of Dorres, and non of the parochiners knowes where he is gone to. The $Brey^{rn}$ haue referred the matter to the Synode, that the breyren of the Synode would make dilligent scrutinie for him in their respective bounds. He carryeth his mark about with him, to wit, to be scabbed in head all within the rimm of his bonnet, and black hared, without haveing noe testimoniall from the Parioch of Dorres.

['Margaret Downe, formerlie fugitive from the discipline of Inv'nes for the space of seven yeirs for her heynous fall in incest w^t her deceased husbands $broy^r$ son,' compears *in sacco*, confessed, and gaue evident signs of remorse, is referred to the Synod 'for advise how to receive satisfactione of her, and that because her fall was through ignorance of the notarietie of her guilt; after they fell she enquired for marriage as if they were not in forbidden degrees of affinitie, as the Minister at more length did proport.']

At Invernes, 5 *of November* 1673.

This being the first day after the Synode, Mr. Hugh Ros, expectant in divinitie, hade his homilie, text, Math. 5. 14, and was approven.

As also Mr. Alex^r Ros, sone of the deceist David Ros of Earlesmill, was admitted schoolmaster at Invernes, of the towne of Invernes, and for his tryalls hade the third ode of Horace and hade his oratione *de vanitate hum. scientiae*, and all oy^r tryalls usuall in the like case, and was fullie approven in every step of his tryalls by the Presbyterie and the magistrates and burgesses of Invernes, and was unanimouslie accepted of the Magistrates and town of Invernes to be their schoolmaster of the Grammar School.

That day Bessie Dean in Invernes was cited and compeired, and was stricklie examined who was the father of her present child, answered as before that she knew no other man to be father of her child, but her married husband. The Presbyterie nott hearing any scandalous conversa°ne or bad report of her since her husbands removall from the natione, haue theirfor appointed Mr. Alex^r Clerk, Minister of Invernes, to baptize her child.

Margaret Fraser compeired before the Synode, and being examined anent the father of her child, she still denying herself to haue knowne who was the father of her child, the Bishope and Synode not being satisfyed with her and her denyall, haue theirfor appoynted Mr. Alex^r Clerke, minister of Invernes, to proceed against her with processe of excommunicatione till the veric sentence (except she confes), and to beginne the next Lords day.

At Invernes, the 14 *of Janrij* /74.

That day the Minister of Inverness reported that he hade processed Margrat Fraser to the verie sentence. The Presbytrie desyred the s^d Minister to extract the s^d processe and give the same to Mr. Hugh Fraser, Minister of Kiltarlatic, to be revised, and the s^d Mr. Hugh is appoynted to give in his diligence to the Presbytrie of the formalitie and informalite of the s^d processe the next dyet.

At Invernes, 1 *April* 1674.

[Letter from the Bishope read, prorogating the meeting of Synod to the first Tuesday of May, 'upon severall grave and weightie considerations.']

The Bretheren of the Presbyterie are appoynted to bring in

a list of all the Papists duelling in y^r respective paroches to the Synode.

That day the Minister of Boleskine reported that Hugh Fraser, son to Thomas Fraser of Little Glendoe, had fallen in incest with Janet McGillivoir, qlks Janet had fallen formerlie in fornication with Jo^n Fraser of Gortleage, within the Paroche of Dorres, uncle, to wit, Mother's brother to the said Hugh fraser, yet notwithstanding of the hainousnes of their cryme nether of them will ansure nor satisfie the discipline of Boleskine. The Session thereof have referred them both to the Pbrie, and being both of them summoned to this dyet, they were cited and not compeiring are to be sumond to the next dyet.

That day the Minister of Boleskine regrated that Donald dow Mack conachie nan each in Glenlea within the Paroche of Boleskine compeired befor the Session of Boleskine, and boasted as also menaciouslie threatened the Minister with many opprobrious and barbarous malicious speeches. The bretheren being much weighted with this malicious fellow his carriage, and the cause of his out-breacking, to wit, because he hade desyred the s^d Donald his son satisfie the discipline of the Church for his fall in fornication, haue therfor appoynted two bretheren, Mr. James Fraser, and Mr. Hugh Fraser, Minister of Kiltarlatie, goe where Alex^r Chisholme, Baylie regallitie, is, and hold forth the carriage of the s^d Donald to him, that he would take such course with him as that he may be severelie punished to the terrour of others, and the s^d bretheren are appoynted to give ane account of y^r dilligence to the next dyet.

Forsamickle as the Bretheren are informed that y^r will be a greatt conventione of Papists in the Castell of Inv'nes where the Laird of Cotts duells for the tyme, and that from all corners about where papists are, and that at Easter next, have therfor appoynted Mr. James Fraser and Mr. Hugh Fraser goe and meet with Alex^r Chisolme, Shireff deput, and desyre him put the last and late strick act of counsell against papists in executione against them, or at lest that he use all possiblie dilligence for preventing their meeting, but especiallie on the said day, and the s^d bretheren are appoynted to give report of y^r dilligence to the next meeting.

At Elgine, 6 *May* 1674.

Conveened the Mod^r and remanent Bretheren of the Pbrie and they appoynt the next meeting of the Pbrie to hold at Inv'nes the 3 day of Junij ensueing. The Bishope, with consent of the Bretheren of the Province, haue appoynted a subsynode, consisting of some ministers forth of every Prbrie, with the Bishope, to hold at Inv'nes the s^d third of Junij, for visiting the affaires of the Church within the Pbrie of Inv'nes; and Mr. James Strachan of Thorntowne being appoynted to preach, whilk is to hold for the doctrine of that day.

At Inv'nes, 3 *Junij* 1674.

Conveened the Bishope and respective Bretheren of the severall Pbries within the province nominat and appoynted, and all the bretheren of the Pbrie of Invernes, except Mr. Alex^r Clerk, who was sick and bedfast.

The name of God was called upon.

That day Mr. James Strachan preached, text Gal. 1. 8.

The affaires of that day is set downe at large in the scrolls of the Synode.

At Inv'nes, 1 *Julij* 1674.

The Minister of Dorres reported that Margaret McHendrick is goeing about from Paroche to paroche begging, not haveing anything of her own, therfor doth not stand in the place of repentance; she is considered in regard of the scarcitie of the yeir, but especiallie among the Hylanders.

The Bretheren Commissioners sent to Alex^r Chisolme, Baylie regallitie, reported that Alex^r Chisolme promised (after examinatione) that he would punish Donald Dow McConachie nan each in Glenlea, according to his guilt in the cryme given in against him.

That day the Bretheren Commissioners from the Pbrie to Alex^r Chisolme reported that he promised to use the outermost of his endevour to stope any meeting of the papists at Ester next in the Castell of Inv'nes.

The Synodicall referres given at Elgin the 5 of May /74:—

[Among other refers are 'That the whole bretheren of the Pbrie attend the Bishope and bretheren of the Subsynode to hold at Inv'nes the 3 Junij, and that flagicious persons and turbulent obstinat papists be sumoned to that day, whilk was done.' 'To intimat the excommunicatione of Andrew Innes, boatman in Germouth, Margaret Richie, his wife, Jean Innes, y^r daughter, Jo^n Glass bucher in Elgine, Anna Stewart y^r, all excommunicated for dishaunting of ordinances and obstinacie in poperie.' 'To pay the bursar in divinitie betuixt and the third of Junij, and y^t each broy^r unpaid give the Mod^r six pens (pence) for defraying the expenses of one to be sent to the Chancellor.']

At Invernes, 22 July '74.

That day it was reported that Hugh McAllister vic ean roy [1] had convalesced, but that he was one of the Captains of the Wach, and therfor could not compeir befor the Pbr̄ie to vindicat himself in thir troublesome tymes wherin thieves and robbers haue turned insollent and resolute in wicked[ness].

[Among the subsynodical refers read to-day are that the bretheren process all the Papists who did not compear at the subsynod, and 'that Mr. Hugh Fraser, Minister of Kiltarlatie, excommunicat Sr Jo^n Byers of Cotts, Lillias Grant, his Ladie, and Robert Monroe, Seminarie priest, for obstinacie, defection, and apostacie from the doctrine and ordinances of the Church of Scotland. Mr. Hugh ffraser promised to obey the order.' Mr. Fraser was, no doubt, requested to attend to the matter, as Mr. Clerk, Minister of Inverness, was ill.]

At Inverness, 12 August '74.

Mr. Hugh Fraser promiseth to obey the ordinance anent excommunicating Sir Jo^n Byers of Cotts, Lillias Grant, his Ladie, and Robert Monroe, Seminarie priest, and that precislie the 23 August.

At Invernes, Sept. 9, 1674.

The exercise prescribed the former Pbr̄ie day was delayed till the next Pbr̄ie day, because that by the Bishopes appoyntment Mr. Gilbert Marshall, who is presented by the Lord

---

[1] Hugh was remitted by the kirk-session of Dores to the Presbytery for adultery.

Kintaile to the vacant charge of Invernes, had his edict served to this day, wherupon Mr. Alex^r, Mod^r, preached conforme to the ordinance, text Act 20. 28; the sermon being closed, the edict being the second tyme read, and being asked if their were any person or persons their present that had ought to object against the admissione of the said Mr. Gilbert Marshall at the most patent Kirk door, and therafter at the severall heritors, magistrates, and others then present, all of them answered negativelie, and earnestlie pressed his admissione, wherupon the Mod^r proceeded to the admissione by delivering to him the sacred Bible, the book of discipline, and the key of the Kirk door, as is usuall in such cases, seriouslie exhorting him to pietie, humilitie, fidellitie, and sedulitie in his calling, who with his whol remanent bretheren gave him the right hand of fellowshipe, and immediatlie therafter the heritours, magistrates, and elders present did unanimouslie embrace him by reaching forth y^r hands to him, declareing their acceptance of the said Mr. Gilbert for y^r Minister, promiseing obedience, faithfullnes, and assistance to him according to their severall stationes. Therafter the said Mod^r and remanent brethren passed to the Manse and Gleibe somtyme belonging to the late Mr. James Sutherland, and gaue the said Mr. Gilbert reall possessione in the same, and locall stipend belonging therto, dureing his ministrie and service at the said Kirk of Inv'nes, which the said Mr. Gilbert accepted, and tooke instrument ane or moe in Andrew McPhersone, Nottare publick, his hand, as the same at more length in itself doth proport.

That day Mr. Hugh Fraser, Minister of Kiltarlatie, reported that according to the ordinance of the subsynode, preached at Invernes the Lords day, being the 23 of August, text, 1 Tim. 1. 19, 20, and did excommunicat Sir Jo^n Byer of Cotts, Lilias Grant, his Ladie, and Robert Monroe, Seminarie priest, and that for defectione to, and obstinacie in, poperie.

At Invernes, Octob. 1, 1674.

Margaret Fraser (mentioned in the 2 Synodicall refer) was not excommunicat in regard that severall speciall friends belonging to her did earnestlie supplicat Mr. Alex^r Clerk, Mod^r, that he would not excomminicat her till they should meet with her, she being for the tyme in London, and they being of purpose to goe their to meet with her their, in goeing about their lawfull affairs; as also Mr. James Fraser, Minister of Wardlaw, reported that he had receaved a letter from the said Margaret bearing that she would do anything that he would persuade her in the affaire, and that she expected a lyne from him, whilk the said Mr. James promised to send w^t the first occasione, and that he would aquent the Presbytrie of her replie to him, and entreated that her excommunicatione might be suspended till then. The Bretheren judged this relevant.

Invernes, Novemb. 4, 1674.

No doctrin that day be reason that Mr. James Grant, q^o should exercise, and Master Michael Fraser, q^o should add, cum not till eleven a'cloak, who at there comeing were both sharplie rebucked, and Mr. Michael, according to the ordinance of the last Synod, was appoynted to compeare befor the Bishop and Bretheren of ye Subsynod to hold at Elgin the last tuesday of November ensueing for his long absence from his charge in Edinburgh.

Anent the Bretheren that were absent ye last Presbr̄ie, Mr. James Fraser, min^r at Kirkhill, declared that he was in Morray about his necessarie affaires, and could not keepe that day.

Mr. Roderick McKenzie declared that he was bedfast y^t day.

Mr. Hugh Fraser, Min^r at Croy, declared y^t he behoved in ye forenoone of that day to waite upon Mr. Andrew Massie, Subprinc^{ll} of the Kings Colledge, for some business of concernement, and so could not be present; however, he was rebuked for his preferreing his privat to his publict concernement.

The said day the Min^{rs} of Invernes reported that, although there was an order for excommunicateing Isobell Robertson in Kinmylies, that they were advised be the Bishope to delay the sentence, seeing they hed some hopes of gaineing her from popery, and to be ane hearer; and that they were takeing paines with her.

[Mr. James Fraser had written to Margaret Fraser in London, but no reply yet.]

That day George Cuthbert of Castlehill was delated to have spoken reproachfullie of three Bretheren of the Presbr̄ie, wiez

Mr. Thomas Houstoun, Mr. Rorie Mackenzie, and Mr. James Smith, that he should see them drunk at the time of the last Subsynod at Invernes, about the 4 of June last. The Presbrie officer is ordained to give him an litterall sumonds to appeare befor them the ensueing Presbrie day wch is to hold the 9 of Decem. next.

The Synodicall refers—

1. To mak intimatione of the excommunicatione of the Laird of Cotts, Lillias Grant, his Lady, and Robert Munro, excommunicated for obstinacy in popery, and dishaunteing of ordinances.

2. That the Mod^r mak enquirie concerneing the observatione of the 29 of Maij, and that the Presbrie book beare record that the samen is observed.

3. That the Burss Money due to ye Bursar of Divinity for the year 1674 be given to Thomas Fraser, Student in Philosophie.

Invernes, Janry. 6, 1675.

That day Mr. Gilbert Marshall reported that he preached at Dunlichity December 27, according to the Lord Bishope and Subsynods order, and rebucked the Min^r, Mr. Michael Fraser, for his long absence from his charge.

Sicklike, Mr. Hugh Fraser, Min^r at Kiltarlaty, reported that he preached at Kirkhill conforme to the Bishope and Subsynods order, and did intimat the Min^r, Mr. James Fraser, his suspension.

That day the Bretheren of the Presbrie appoynt the Min^{rs} of Invernes to tak notice of such Protestants as officiats as Clerk and fiscall to the Laird of Cotts, an excomunicat Papist, his courts in the Castle of Invernes, and to conveen y^m before there sessione, and thereafter if need be to the Presbrie, and to report there diligence.

The Presbytrie officer reported that he was at Castlehills house, bot that he was absent in Aberdeane, so that he could not fix an Sumonds on him. The Bretheren appoynts to sumond him to the nixt Presbrie day.

That day the Officer is ordayned (by order from the Lord Bishope and Subsynod at Elgin) to sumond Thomas Watson and Jo^n M^{c}pherson in Invernes to declare q^t they know anent

Mr. Wm Smith, Min^r at Duthell, his miscarriage in drunkness when the s^d Mr. W^m was in Invernes last.

Invernes, Feb. 3, 1675.

The Ministers of Invernes reported that according to ye Presbrie order they called befor ther Sessione Alex^r M^cintosh, Clerk, and Hugh Fraser, Fiscall, to the Laird of Cotts his Courts, and that both of them confessed that what they did officiat was through ignorance; craved God and the Inhabitants to whom they gaue offence pardone, and hereafter enacted themselves never to officiat under Cotts, or any other under Church censure. The Bretheren were satisfied with this diligence and procedour.

The Moderator and Bretheren appoynt Mr. Gilbert Marshall, and Mr. Hugh Fraser, Min^r at Kiltarlaty, to go to-morrow to Castle Stuart to speak to the Erle of Morray, and to complean to his Lo. as High Sireff, that Robert Munro, an excomunicat Papist, is seduceing seuerall unsettled ignorant people, and to entreat his Lo., according to the Laudable Acts of Parliament and Councell, to lay his restraint upon him in the future.

That day George Cuthbert of Castlehill, beeing ceited c'peared, and beeing challanged by the Moderator that he was heard to report that he saw Mr. Thomas Huistoune, Mr. Roderick Makenzie, and Mr. James Smith, drunk at the time of the last subsynod at Invernes, Answered that he was readie upon oath to depone that he saw nether of them drunk then or at any other time, bot that some told him, and he thought that it was through malice, that they saw some Ministers so, bot who these Min^rs were or those that told him so, upon his credit he forgot. The Bretheren removeing him, and haveing bot one witness that heard him vent such calumnies, they ordaine the Moderatour to write to the Bishope for his advice how to proceed any farder against ye s^d Castlehill, and to report his diligence the next ensueing Presbrie day.

The s^d day Thomas Watson and Jo^n Mackpherson beeing ceited compeared and were examined severallie as followeth:

Thomas Watson beeing enquired whether or no they saw Mr. Wm Smith, Minister at Duthell, drunk when he was in his company in Invernes last in John M^cpherson's house, answered

D

y^t beeing in y^e s^d house with Mr. W^m he observed him to call frequentlie for drink, more as did become a Minister of the Gospell, and thereby at last was in such a condition that he thought it unworthie to stay in his company, and removed himself; beeing enquired if ye s^d Mr. W^m left ye town that night, answered, not, but heard y^t he went to bed after his removall; being enquired if it was through drunkness that he went to bed, answered that he would not free him bot it was; being enquired if he heard that he rose agayne that night, answered he heard he did not.

Sicklik the s^d Jo^n M^{c}pherson compearing, was enquired as followeth, first, if he saw Mr. Wm Smith drunk the forsaid night in his house, answered y^t the s^d Mr. Wm. cam to his hous upon Saturday afternoone, accompanied w^t Thomas Watson and Jo^n Neilson, and told him y^t he was the ensueing Sabbath to preach at Calder in Mr. Donald's absence, who was to preach at Dyck y^t day, and y^t he called for more drink y^n was fitteing for one of his office on such a day; 2^{lio}, beeing enquired to be positive and to declare if he was drunkyn, answered that he thought shame to stay with him, and, to get him away, y^t he absented himselff from his company, and q^n he returned soon agayne that his servants told him y^t he was in bed; 3. beeing enquired if he rose agayne y^t night, answered negativelie: 4. beeing enquired if he saw Mr. William ye nixt day, answered, not, y^t he rode away befor he or bedfellow were up. 5. beeing enquired if Mr. W^m went to Calder and preacht according to his promiss to Mr. Donald, answered, not, but heard since y^t all the congregatione mette and stayed till after sermon time and had no Minister: 6. beeing enquired where went Mr. W^m to, y^t sabbath, if to any church, answered y^t he was certainly enformed y^t he went to no church, bot posted home and was mett by Connedge the Sireff in the mount betuixt the Parioches of Moy and Duthell, who took offence at his unministeriall travelling upon the Lords day; beeing lastly enquired if he had any more to say, answered negativelie. The Bretheren referrs both these declarationes in this matter to ye ensueing Synode.

The s^d day the Bretheren heareing that Collin Chisolme of Mountaitt [1] had sent for Robert Monro the excomunicat

---

[1] Mountaitt—Buntait, the Glen-Urquhart portion of the parish of Kiltarlity.

priest, and by him baptized his child, and y[t] the s[d] Collin and his spouse   Lawder, were fallen away to poperie; therefor they ordaine Mr. Hugh Fraser, Min[r] at Kiltarlatie, to process the s[d] Collin and his wife, and to report his diligence to the ensueing Presbrie.

Invernes, March 3, 1675.

Mr. Rorie Mackenzie beeing enquired where he was absent from y[e] last Pbrie, answered y[t] he was hindered by the torrent in the water of Nairne. Excused.

[Mr. Gilbert Marshall and Mr. Hugh Fraser reported that they had not seen Earl of Moray, as he had gone to Darnaway, but that they would see him on his return to Castle Stuart.]

The Moderator beeing enquired if he wrot to the Bishop anent George Cuthbert of Castlehill, answered he did, and that his advise is that if Castlehill did appeare judiciallie befor the Prebrie and denyed all such calumnies, if we could prove notheing against him by witnesses y[t] heard him speake against Ministers, that we should pass him untill we find more clearness to fix the guilt upon him, and then censure him accordinglie, bot in the meane tyme for forder cleareing of the three Bretheren, Mr. Thomas Huistown, Mr. Rorie M[c]Kenzie, and Mr. James Smith, the persons wronged, that an visitatione be kept at each of there Kirks in this moneth of March, and an exact triall be taken of there ministeriall deportement; and our Presbrie book to carrie our diligence at the ensueing Synod.

[The next meeting to be at Moy.]

The s[d] Mr. Hugh Fraser, Minister at Kiltarlatie, reported that he hath begun to process Collin Chisolme of Mountaitt, and his wife   Lawder; the Bretheren ordeaneth him to proceed, seeing there is a great defectione to Popery in these fields.

At Moy, y[e] 17 of March 1675.

The Min[r] beeing desyred to remove the Elders were posed one by one upon the following queries:—

1. They were enquired how they were satisfied with there Min[rs] doctrine, Answered that they were well satisfied y[r]with, and edified.

2. Beeing enquired if he was zealous and impartiall in discipline, Answered that he was, without respect of persons.

3. Beeing enquired if he was frequent in catechizeing, Answered that he used sometimes to catechize, bot wished he were more frequent.

4. Beeing enquired if he made conscience of visiting the sick in both his parishes, Answered he did q^n he was desired.

5. Beeing enquired how long since he celebrated the sacra^t of the Lords Supper, Answered two years ago. Beeing enquired how long befor y^t last time, Answered eight yeares befor: being enquired if at any time since his admissione did he celebrat the said sacrament in his other parish of Dalarossie, Answered, not.

6. Beeing enquired if he used to haunt aile houses to tipple or drink drunk therein, Answered not, bot lived ministeriallie and most soberly alwayes.

7. Beeing enquired if he prayed in any of their families q^n he lodged with y^m be night, Answered he did frequentlie.

8. Beeing asked if he prayed nightlie and daylie in his own familie, Answered to there certayne knowledge he did.

9. Beeing asked if they had a collector for the penalties, Answered they had, bot was illiterat and so could not keep a book.

10. Beeing enquired if he and they did lay a restraint upon pypeing violeing and danceing at Lickwaks, Answered not as yet.

11. Beeing enquired if he tymely inhibited any to receive servants or strangers from other parishes without testimonialls, Answered negativelie.

12. Beeing enquired if he had an register for discipline, baptisms, marriages, and collectiones for the poor, Answered that they knew of none, and y^t they regrate the want of the samen.

Mr. James Grant, the visitor, beeing enquired if he received the Session book to revise, Answered, not.

The Min^r, Mr. Rorie, was called in and the Moderator in name of the Bretheren exhorted him to continue in weledoeing, and blessed God for his diligence and ministeriall, painfull walkeing, and

1. He was desired to be more frequent in catechizeing his people.

2. To celebrat the sacrament of the Lords supper more frequentlie, especiallie once each yeare in either of his congregationes, and seeing that sacram^t was not celebrat in his time in the Parish of Dalarosie to begin there first this ensueing sumer.

3. He was rebucked because his Sessione book was not filled up, and he is ordained that the same may be filled up yearely whether he be visited or not; and to bring his book full to be revised at the first Presbrie y^t holds at Invernes, as he shall be answerable.

4. He and his elders are appoynted there nixt sessione day to choose an Collector that can read and write, y^t may keepe an formall account of y^r penalties and how the samen are distributed.

5. He is ordained, as he shall be answerable, to keepe the 29 day of Maij, preach y^{r}on, and advertish yearly his people to be present from pulpit that none may pretend ignorance, and seeing he hath two congregationes, to serve and preach ye s^d day be vice in each parish yeare about.

6. He is desired to discharge danceing, pypeing, and violeing at likwaks, and to punish ye guiltie with church censures.

Lastly, he is desired to discharge receiveing of serv^{ts} or strangers hereafter without testimonialls. All these things he promised to performe, and reforme and amend what he thought amiss.

The Elders beeing removed, and the Min^r beeing enquired anent them, declared that he was wele pleased with them all, onlie desired the Moderator to exhort them to keepe more frequent at sermon, y^t some of y^m upon the least impediment useth to do. The s^d Elders beeing called in, the Moderator gave them thanks for the countenance and concurrance they gave their minister; they were exhorted to continue in strengthening his hands and keepe more frequent with him at doctrine and discipline, wch all of them promised to performe.

At Boleskin, 30 March 1675.

Conveened the Moderator and remanent Bretheren of the Prebrie for visiteing that Congregatione, except Mr. Hugh Fraser, Min^r at Kiltarlaty, who excused his absence be his letter, seeing he was to celebrat the sacrament of the Lords supper the ensueing sabboth. The name of God was called upon.

The Min^r, Mr. Thomas Huistone, preached Luk. 19. 8.

The Moderator desired a list of the elders, q^{ch} was deliv^d, and were present as follows : wiz^t Thomas Fraser of Faraline, James Fraser of Meikle Garth, Hugh Fraser of Kinmonive, James Fraser of Ardachie, Alex^r Fraser of Dalcraige, Jo^n Fraser of Migovie, Wm Fraser, Tutor of Foyer, Hugh Fraser his sonn. Deacons, James Mackranold in Knockie, Don^d M^{c}phail in Meikle Garth, Hugh Fraser in Corthly; all present.

The Moderator declared to the Gentrie and Elders the reasone of the Bretherens comeing that day to visit that congregatione, viz. to try and know how the work of God was groweing and thriveing amongst them. To this end he enquired at the Min^r, Mr. Thomas Houistone, if this visitatione was tymouslie intimated to both his congregationes of Boleskin and Kilcummeing,[1] he declared, and also his elders that it was, as the bretheren might see by the numberous c'ventione of the people y^r present.

The Minister was removed, and the severall elders and deacons were posed, one by one, upon these queries following.

[The queries are of the usual nature. The elders are satisfied with the Min^{rs} life and doctrine and discipline. He celebrated the sacrament of the Lord's Supper at Boleskine three years ago, but at Kilcuming, 'to there knowledge, never.' 'Beeing enquired if there Min^r did haunt aile houses or was given to tippleing or drunkness, answered that they knew nothing of y^t in him, bot lived soberlie and rebucked others of his flock q^o were given to that vice.' 'Beeing asked if he lived upon his Manss, answered positively.' 'Beeing enquired if he preached as yet upon the 29 of May, answered negativelie.' 'Being enquired if he punished Sabboth breakeing and restrained abuses at Likewaks, answered he did.']

The Minister being called in . . .

1. He was desired to celebrat the sacrament of the Lords supper yearly once, and being enquired q^t was the reason that

---

[1] Kil-Chuimein, the old name of Fort Augustus.

he did never celebrat the s^d sacrament in Kilchuming, Answered that he had not an kirk to celebrat it in, except he should celebrat it in the open fields, y^t the Kirk was fallen, and though he used the law against the Heritors, yet none of them valued any procedour he used. The Bretheren referrs this case to the advise of ye Bishope and Synod, what shall such Bretheren do in reference to the celebratione of the Lords supper in such places as want an church to celebrat the same comelie and orderlie in.

The Bretheren exhorted him to preach each yeare upon the 29 of Maij, and to press and invite his parishoners from pulpit to there thankfullnesse and loyaltie upon the s^d day for his Majesties happie restoratione to his prerogatives, kingdomes, and people.

[The Min^r is well pleased with his elders. The session Book found formall. The Kirk officer approved.]

At Dores, March 31, 1675.

The Moderator desired a list of the Elders, w^h was given, and read as followeth: Wm Macintosh of Borlome, Paul M^{c}baine of Kinchyle, Do^d Fraser of Erchett, Jo^n Fraser of Erigie, Alex^r M^{c}bane of Drumond, Alex^r Fraser of Leatclone, Wm Fraser of Ruthven, James Fraser in Dundelchaige, Angus M^{c}intosh in Drumond, Malcome Mackintoshe in Dores, Lauchlan M^{c}baine in Chappel toune, Donald M^{c}baine in Cloine, Jo^n McCoill duj in Borlome, Jo^n M^{c}ean duj, y^r; all present.

[In answer to the usual queries, the elders stated that the Minister never catechised until three years ago; that he never celebrated the sacrament of the Lords Supper; that he never preached on 29 May; that he did not preach 'befor and afternoone in the long day of Summer;' that they were pleased with his life and doctrine; that he lived 'soberly and examplary'; and was zealous, impartial, and accurate in discipline. He also zealously punished sabbath-breaking, and 'pypeing, violeing, and danceing at Lykwaks.' He had a 'thesaurer' to collect and account for the penalties, but he 'was not learned, and no account was taken of him this while ago.'

The collections for the poor were distributed 'twice in each yeare, bot especially at Lambmess.'

' Beeing enquired if there Minʳ lived in his manse and neere the Kirk, answered not, bot two or three mylls off.']

The Minister being called in . . .

1. He was advised to examen and catechise all his congregatione at least once each yeare.

2. He is desired to give the Sacrament of the Lords supper to his people once this Summer, as he shall be answerable.

3. He is desired to preach hereafter yearely upon the 29 of Maij, as he shal be answerable, and was rebucked for neglecting this loyal dutie so long.

4. He is advised to preach in the long dayes of Summer in ye fore and afternoone to such as are neere the Kirk, within three myles.

5. He was with his Elders ordained to tak an account of the Colleactor, and to put up there glass windowes, and haue a treasurer that culd read and write and could keep an accurat book and accompt.

6. Being challenged and rebucked that he resided not in his manse, he answered that he culd not, for such reasones that he would comunicat to my Lord Bishope and venrable Synod; however, the Moderator pressed him to dwelle in his manse as he $wish^d$ to stope the mouthes of such that took occasione to speake of him for his non-residence there.

The Elders being removed, the Minʳ was enquired how he was satisfied with them, Answered that he was well satisfied in reference to discipline with them all. However, that seurall of the gentlemen had some delinquents that have not paid ther penalties to the Collector. The Elders beeing called in, ye Moderator shew them there Ministers good report of them all, and entreated them to continue in encourrageing and strengthening ther Minʳˢ hands, and to tak in these penalties y^t were unpayed, y^t their glass windowes may be filled up, and other places necessare of the fabrick of the Kirk repared.

[The Session book formal, but had no cover—'only in stormy weather they had few or no Sessiones.']

The Moderator and Bretheren regrated that they had not an school in the Parish of Dores. The Minʳ and Elders answered that seuerall gentlemen had Schooles in their own houses for educateing and traineing up of their children, and they were upon an feasable way, if this deare yeare were by, to conveene and stent themselves for an publict school for the comon good of the whole parish.

The Bretheren exhorts y^m to follow and cherish this good motione, as they wish that the knowledge of God may be upon the groweing hand among y^m, and y^r posterities to bless there actiones qⁿ they are gone.

At Daviot, Maij 11, 1675.

Conveened the Moderator and remanent Bretheren, except Mr. Thomas Huiston, and Mr. Hugh Fraser, Min^r at Croy, qho wer both excused be ther letters.

No visita°ne or doctrin that day in respect y^t ther cam no Elders or people present from neither of the paroches, except Donald McBain off Faily allenarly.

The name of the Lord being called uppon, the Bretheren present recomends to Mr. Gilbert Marshall and Mr. Hugh Fraser, qho are to keep ye Subsynod att Elgin the eight of Jun ensueing, to represent to my Lo. Bishop and ye Subsynod how wee are slighted be the s^{ds} parochiners in not conveining w^t us as they wer ordained, and to report y^m for their absence.

The Presbrie ordaines Mr. Gilbert Marshall and Mr. Hugh Fraser, Min^r of Kiltarlty, to speak to the Earle of Murray anent excomminicat preist and papists as it was formerly ordained.

The said day Collin Chisholm in Buntait, and Christan Lauder, his spouse, apostats to popery, being cited, compeired not, they wer ordained to be sumonded pro 3°.

The Synodical referrs—

First, that the Minr^si of Invernes deall effectually with Isobell Robertson to reclaim from popery.

2^{ly}. That ye Bretheren be diligent in obtaining a return from Marg^t Fraser in London anent ye child shee brought furth in Inverness.

.   .   .   .   .

4. That the 29 day off May be observed be ye Bretheren according to the Act off Parliament.

5^{tly}. That Mr. Rorie McKenzie mak search for a mother to the child hee baptised to Charles McKenzie.

The Presbrie ordaines the s^{ds} Mr. Rorie to wryt to Mr.

Alex^r Fordyce, Min^r att Rafford, anent the young woman in Burgy q^m ye s^{ds} Charles McKenzie giveth up to be ye mother of the s^{ds} child, and to report his diligence to the Presbrie and subsynod according to order, as he shall be answerable to both.

Invernes, 2 Jun. 1675.

The s^d day Mr. Gilbert Marshall declared to the Presbrie y^t he had taken paynes with Isobell Robertson, shee being within his division, but had not hopes to reclame her, but shee being baptised in the Popish Church and bred, desyred that the sentence should not proceed against her untill he had spoken to the Bishop and report his diligence to the Presbrie.

The s^d day Mr. James Fraser, Min^r at Kirkhill, declared he had wrytten to Margrett Fraser in London, with the Invernes Merchands, and at their returne should signifie her answer to the Presbrie.

The Bretheren being required if all of them did loyally keip the 29 day of May according to order, answered positively.

[Mr. Rorie Mackenzie had written the Min^r of Rafford as ordained, but had not received a reply yet.]

The s^d day Collin Schisome, and his spowse Christan Lauder fors^{ds}, being cited pro 3° and not compeiring, Mr. Hugh Fraser, their Min^r, is appoynted to process them from pulpitt, and to report his diligence.

Invernes, Jun. 30, 1675.

After calling uppon the name of God that day, no doctrine be reason y^t Mr. Thomas Huiston was valetudinarie. The Bretheren ordaines the doctrin to be as formerly, except Mr. Thomas, qho was diligent for prepareing his fflock to the sacrament of the Lo. Supper, and, being tender withall, should employ a Broy^r to supply his *vice*.

That day the Bishop directed ane letter to the Moderator and Presbrie desyreing them to confer with Mr. Colin Dalgleish, who had formerly fallen away from the Protestant religion to Poperie, and now being again enlightened by the Lo. Spirit to see his error and wandring, hath returned to the bosome of his mother church. Accordingly the Bretheren conferred with him severallie, and y^{r}after joyntly, and fand y^t the s^d Mr. Collin was truely weighted with his bakslyding, and protested in face of Presbŕie by the Lo. his assistance to continew a Protestant all the dayes of his lyffe, and to evidence ye same be a publict recanta°n when and wher the Bishop and Presbŕie should enjoyne him. The Bretheren, haveing found great satisfactione of him in privat and publict, hawe ordained the Moderator to wryt the same in ther name to the Bishop according to his Lordships desyre in his s^{ds} letter.

Invernes, Julij 28, 1675.

The s^d day the Moderator, present Bretheren, w^t the consent and assent of the absent Bretheren the preceding day, for forder encourrageing of Mr. Colline Dalgleish, have unanimously agreed that every broy^r provyd for supplying of his present necessity als much as ordinarly they give in a zear to the Bursar of divinity, and to bring in this to the next Presbŕie, and that besyd q^t they are to pay for this zeir to the present Bursar in Divinity, and the Moderator is desyred to wrytt to the seuerall absent Bretheren forthwith to bring in the s^d money to Mr. Colline, if no sooner, precisely to the next Presbŕie.

The s^d day Mr. Gilbert Marshall reports that its ye Bishop his advyse y^t Isobell Robertson fors^d being baptised and bred in the popish Church be referred to the Synod as zett before ye sentence of excomminicatione passt agst her.

Invernes, August 18, 1675.

The s^d day the Mod^r haveing enquyred iff the seuerall Brethren in ther respective congrega°ns did keip the day off fast and humilia°n, they answered positively.

Invernes, Sept. 8, '75.

The Presbŕie referreth to the advyce of the Bishop and Synod how to obtaine letters of Intercommuning agst excomunicat preists and papists.

The s^d day W^m M^{c}pherson, adulterer and y^{r}after fornicator in Invernes, haveing appeared severall yeares *in sacco*, evidenceing his publict remorse for his s^{ds} gross sinns, supplicated the Presbŕie to be absolved, and hee appeareing before them with teares and other signes off his repentance, is referred to the

Ministers of Invernes to be absolved, and to report ther diligence.

The Process against Collin Chisolme and Christan Lauder his wyff is goeing on.

The s^d day the Bretheren wer appoynted to bring in there Burse Money to the Synod to Mr. Georg Dunbar, Bursar in Divinity, qch they promised to doe in his owne presence without faill.

The s^d day the Moderator presented a letter from ye Bishope q^{r}in his desyre is that the Bretheren call before them Mr. Colline Dalgleish, and tack his abjura°n off poperie subscrived under his hand, and to registrat the same in the Presbrie Book *in futuram rei memoriam*, as also that the s^d Mr. Collin mack a publict recanta°n in the High Church of Invernes after sermon, the Minister preaching on a text to that purpose, and y^t he subscrive ther publictly before the whole congregation the Confession of Faith, and therafter returne to the ensueing Synod with a declara°n in Latin of his future resolution to adhere to ye reformed religion all the dayes of his lyff, and to abhoir ye false doctrine of the Church of Rome.

The s^d Mr. Collin being called, gawe in the followeing paper subscryved under his hand.

[Here follows a long Latin Renunciation, signed 'Colenus Dalglisius.']

Qch paper being redd in the audience of the Bretheren to ther great satisfaction, the Presbrie ordaines the Moderate, Mr. Alex^r Clerk, to preach, according to the B^p his desyre, in the High Church of Invernes, uppon a text fitt for ye occasion, and after sermon to call for Mr. Collin to the readers seatt, and cause him in audience of the whole congrega°ne to hawe a recantation of poperie, and show how hee was seduced and what kyndness the Lo. used for his reclameing to his Mother Church, and lastly cause him subscrive the Confession off Faith of the reformed Church off Chryst in Britain and Ireland, and this to be done the ensueing Lo. day, being ye tuelth day of Sep^{tr} 1675, and to report his diligence to the next Presbytrie.

Invernes, Octobris 6, 1675.

The s^d day the Moderator declared that according to the

Bish. and Presbytries order hee preached, text Luk. 15. 24, in reference to Mr. Collin Dalgleis, uppon y⁰ 12 day off Sep^tr last, q^rafter divine service, ye s^d Mr. Collin made ane publict recanta°n of Poperie, and subscrywed ye Confession of Faith, both to the great satisfaction of the beholders, and that y^rafter hee, with ye Magistrats and Elders, according to the Bishops desyre, gave him ye right hand of fellowship, and embraced and receaved him to the bosom of his reformed mother Church againe.

The Bretheren by his report receaved also great satisfaction, and desyres y^t Mr. Collin be present at the Synod in Elgin ye tuelff of Octr instant with his declaration, as the same is requyred also by my Lo. Bishop.

Mr. Hugh Fraser, Minister of Kiltarlaty, is goeing on with ye process against Collin Schisolme and Christan Lauder his spouse for ther apostacie to Poperie.

The s^d day Mr. James Fraser reported y^t hee had wrytin to Margratt Fraser in London according to the Bishop, Synod, and Presb̅ries order, and hath receaved no satisfactorie answer in reference to a father to her child brought furth in Invernes before shee fled away. Therfore ye Brethren referres this matter for advyce to ye Synod, if the delayed sentence of excommunication shall be pronounced against her, shee being now fugitive and without the kingdome.

That day ye Bretheren thinks fitt y^t in regard that the tuo Bretheren qho wer appoynted to keip att the Subsynod and did not keip y^t dyett, and thereby no diligence returned to the Presb̅rie from the Bishop and members of the subsynod anent the visita°n of Daviott, that the same be referred to the Bishop and venerable ensueing Synod for advyce and what course the Presbytrie is to tak with those whole parochiners qho absented themselves from the s^d appoynted visitation.

That day the Moderator earnestly requested all ye Bretheren to keep the ensueing Synod, and to bring in ther seuerall proportion off the Burse money then to be given to the Bursar, Mr. George Dunbar, ther Bursar for the zear 1675.

Att Elgine, 13 *Octr.* 1675.

The Moderator and remanent Bretheren haveing conveined, appoynted ther next meitting to hold att Daviott for the visiting of the s^d Church the 9th day off November ensueing being tuesday, wher Mr. Gilbert Marshall is ordained to preach, and the Minister off Daviott ordained to give his Session Book to Mr. James Smith, Min^r att Dorres, to be revised. The Moderator is to wryte to the Parishioners and Elders of both these Paroches to meitt there the s^d dyett, lest they pretend excuise as formerly.

At Daviot, the 9 of Novr. 1675.

Conveined the Moderator and Remanent Bretheren of the Presbytrie, except Mr. Thomas Huison, Mr. Hugh Fraser, Minister at Kiltarlatie, and Mr. James Grant. The name of God called upon. The said day no doctrine nor visitation of the affaires of that Church, in respect there was no convention of Gentlemen, Elders, or people, except Angus McIntosh of Daviot, Lachlane McIntosh of Aberarder, Duncan McPhail of Inverarnie, and Donald McBain of Phailie, who declared that the visitatione was intimate be their Minister two severall Lords days, but in respect of the shortnes of the day, and this day being the terme day of Mertimes, that they culd get none of the people to keep this diet, and so intreated the Presbytrie to prorogate their visitation to summer when the day is at the lenth, and that all the people will be most willing to keip any diet then, and especially if they meet in the Parish of Dunlechitie.

The Bretheren, taking this slighting of their meeting to consideration, haue thought fit that the matter, with the desyre of the present gentlemen, be referred for advice to My Lo. Bishoppe and the ensuing Subsynod, and recomends to the Bretheren that are Commissioners for the said Subsynod to report the Bishopes answer, etc., to our next Presbytrie.

The Moderator declaires that according to the last Synods order he caused Alexander Ross, Presbytrie Officer, to give literall Summonds to Mr. Roric Mackenzie, Minister at Moy, to compeir before the Lord Bishope and the Bretheren of the Presbytrie of Elgin the 3 of Novr instant. Mr. Roric McKenzie forsaid being pn̄t decleired that he was at Elgin the s^d day, and therupon produced ane letter from the Bishope and said Presbytrie, written and subscryved be Mr. Alexander Tod,

clerk *pro tempore*, desyring that the Presbytrie should carefully
and exactly examine upon oath the witnesses in that matter of
fact relating to Charles McKenzie his baptising of his child in
the Parish of Moy, and giving his band to Mr. Rorie McKenzie
for satisfying the Church discipline at Rafart; whereupon the
said Mr. Rorie brought Angus McIntosh who subscryved wittnes
to the band, and Alex^r Noble with whom the child was nursed,
to evidence upon oath what they knew in that affair, And
moreover reported that Alex^r Archibald, the other subscryved
wittness in the band, was in the Parish of Invernes.

The said Angus McIntosh and Alex^r Noble being solemnly
sworn, and the said Alex^r Noble being removed, The Moderator
asked at the said Angus McIntosh what he knew anent the
forsaid band, answered that Charles McKenzie, Son to the
Laird of Pluscarden, being in Rorie McKenzie's house in Moy,
send a bond to him to his own house, wherein he was insert as
a wittness, but not p̄nt when Charles did subscryve it, and that
he subscryved wittnes therto, which he repented therafter, seeing
he saw not the prin^{ll} [principal] subscryve it.

Next, according to his oath, he declared that the said Charles
came therafter to visit that child that was nursed in Alex^r
Nobles house, and stayed two nights in Mr. Rorie's house.

Thirdly he declared that the said Alex^r Noble told him that
the said Charles sent tuo dollars with the man that brought
the child to his house in part of fourtie merks that he and his
wife should have for nursing the said child a zeir.

4ly That the said Charles came therafter and conveyed the
said child away from the said Alex^r Noble before severall
wittnesses in the Kirktown of Moy, and brought the childs
foster Mother alongs with the child to the water of Nesse, and
at her returne she told him that she receaved from the said
Charles ane mark peice for her pains thither, beside the
fortie merks her husband received formerlie according to condescendence.

Sicklyke, the said Alex^r Noble compeired and being desyred
by the Moderator, according to his oath declared what he knew
anent the forsaid child, Answered that the said Charles
McKenzie sent a man called Thomas Dunbar, and a woman
called Isobell Callom, both in Both, with ane child to his house,

who brought him two dollars in hand, when he receaved the child, with a promise of more when he should see the father, whom they said was the said Charles McKenzie.

Next he declared that he went to Alves therafter, and he receaved two other dollars from the said Charles in his fathers stable, before he came away, and faithfully promised to give him the rest at his first coming to the Parish of Moy.

3dly He declared that the said Churles desired him to seeke baptisme to the said child, from Mr. Rorie McKenzie, qch he did, and the child was called George as the said Charles desired.

4^{ly} He declared that he receaved the rest of the 40 merks compleit in Mr. Rorie McKenzies own house, in presence of the said Mr. Rorie, his wiffe, and his family.

Lastly, he declared that after the child was a yeir old the said Charles came to Moy, with some others with him, and receaved the said child from him before seuerall wittnesses in the Kirk officers house, and that he sent his wiffe with the child a peece of the way the lenth of the boat of Bonah on the Watter of Nesse, and she received a merk peece for her paines, and at her return told that the child was conveyed by the said Charles and his Company to Strathglasse.

The Brethren referred to the Ministers of Invernes to try for the other wittnes, Alex^r Archibald, and to take his declara°n upon oath upon the premises, qch declara°n, with the forsaid declara°nes, the Moderator is to direct to the Lo. Bishoppe and ensueing Subsynod, at Elgin the 24 of Novr instant, and the said Mr. Rorie is ordained to keep there and to report his diligence to the Presbytrie at his returne.

At Invernes, Decr. 8, 1675.

The s^d day the Ministers of Invernes declared that they made search for Alex^r Archibald according to the last Presbytries desire, and that he is not either in the brough or landward of Invernes.

Also the Moderator declared that he sent ane extract to the Bishoppe and Subsynod of the Bretherens diligence in examining the Wittnesses anent Charles McKenzies bond and child.

The said day the Moderator and Brethren having ane order

from the Bishoppe that Mr. Alex^r Clark and Mr. Charles Ritchie, Students in divinity, be admitted to tryalls, and come on the exercise, they appointed Mr. Alex^r Clark to have for his homilie Text John 17. 3, and Mr. Charles Ritchie for his 1 Tim. 1. 15, at Invernes the 5 of Janr. 1676.

Att Invernes, the 5 of Janarie 1676.

[All present except Mr. Huiston, Mr. Hugh Fraser, Kiltarlitie, and Mr. Rorie McKenzie, 'heavilie sick.' Alex^r Clark, and Charles Ritchie had their homilies, as previously ordained, and ordered to exercise and act next day. Approven.]

That day Mr. Michael Fraser, Minister at Daviot, declared that my Lo. Bishope hath left to the Brethrens option to keep the visitation of Daviot or Dunlechetie before or after the ensewing Synod as they think fit.

The said day Mr. James Fraser, Minister at Wardlaw, heavily regrated that his hands are weakned in discipline in severall instances by Mr. Hugh Fraser, Minister of Kiltarlaty, in marrying delinquents belonging to the said Parish of Wardlaw without any testificat, but rather contrare to the said Mr. James his missives. He married two in process before the Presbytrie a while agoe, and a third latlie, called   Wrqhart, when the said Mr. James was absent in Murray about the 29 of Decr last. The Brethren referres to satisfie Mr. James for the said regrates untill the said Mr. Hugh be p̃nt, and the Moderator is ordained to write to him to be precisely p̃nt the next Presbytrie day.

The said day Mr. Robert Monroe, expectant, p̃nted to the Presbytrie ane supplication given in and subscryved be Mr. Thomas Huison, Minister at Boleskine, Mr. James Grant, Minister at Urquhart, and the heretors of Abertarfe and Glenmoristone, to be directed to the Bishope, Patron of Kilchuimen, and Mr. James Stewart, Chancellor of Morray, Patron of Glenmoristone, for their joynt and mutuall ratification, to haue the said Mr. Robert Monroe settled as Minister and their helper in the said bounds of Abertarfe and Glenmoriston, as the supplication in itself at more length beares.

The Bretheren taking the condition of the said bounds to their serious consideration referr the said supplication to my Lo. Bishoppe and Chancellor forsaid, and desyre that the

Moderator write to them both with the said Mr. Robert, and to report his diligence to the next presbytrie.

At Inverness, the 26 *Janr.* 1676.

[All present except Mr. Roric McKenzie 'who is sick,' and Mr. Hugh Fraser, Kiltarlitie, 'who is South about some Law affaires.']

The said day the Moderator pñted to the Presbytrie ane letter from the Bishoppe declareing that he did cordially homologate and ratific the supplication from the Minister and Heretors of Abertarfe and Glenmoriston to haue Mr. Robert Monroe, expectant, Minister and helper in the said bounds, and seeing the said Mr. Robert was now a great while a preacher in this province and elsewhere, and the people's necessity requiring heast in his tryalls, that the Brethren hereupon appoynt him to haue the exercise, with ane comon head, the languages, and questionary tryalls, and to cause Mr. Thomas Huison and Mr. James Grant to serve his edict in there respective bounds, that after diligence he may returne to his Lo. for ordination; and withall to register the said supplication in the Pbr̃ie books *ad futuram rej memoriam.*

The Brethren taking the Bishops said order to consideration appoint Mr. Robert Monroe to exercise Coll. 3. 18, and Mr. Alexr Clark, Student, to add, Feb. 9/76. As also the Bretheren appoint the Moderator to draw up the edict according to the Bishopps desire, and Mr. Thomas Huison and Mr. James Grant to read the same in Kilchuimen and Glenmoriston, and to report their diligence the 23 day of Februarie ensewing, being the last day of the said Mr. Roberts tryalls.

The said day the Moderator declared that he hath searched the Presbytrie books and cannot find the act anent suspending of Ministers that willfully thryce or oftener absents themselves from the Presbytrie without any excuse.

The Brethren calling to mynd that such ane Act was latlie emitted by the Lo. Bishoppe and Synod doe referr this matter as yet to the ensewing Synod that the said Act may be corroborate by their authoritie as a mean to cause the respective brethren to keep punctually hereafter, otherwise send their relevant excuse why they are absent.

9 Feb. 1676.

[Mr. Robert Monroe exercised Coll. 3. 18, and Mr. Alex^r Clark added. Approven.]

At Invernes, 23 *Feb.* '76.

Conveened the Mod^r and remanent Brethren, except Mr. Rorie McKenzie tender, Mr. Michael Fraser excused by his l̃re, and Mr. Hugh Fraser in the South. The name of God was called upon.

Mr. Robert Monroe had his comon head *De Justificatione*, and his theses, q^{ch} he delivered formerlie, were disputed, as also he had his questionary tryalls, and the languages, and what else is usuall in the lyke case, and he was unanimously approven in these and all the other steps of his tryalls.

Mr. Alex^r Clark, Student, is appoynted to haue the Controversie *De peccato originali* the 8 of March ensueing, and to direct his theses tymouslie to the brethren.

The said day Mr. Thomas Huison reported that Mr. Ro^t Monroes Edict was served at Kilchumen the 13 of Feb. last, and Mr. James Grant reported that the said edict was served at Glenmoriston the 20 Feb. The heretors and Elders of the said places were cited at the Church door, but none compeiring, the Ministers, Mr. Thomas and Mr. James forsaid, answered for them, showing that they were very willing to accept of the said Mr. Robert as their future Minister, according to their former supplication in all points.

The brethren, having taken the same to their consideration, have appointed the Moderator to write to the Bishoppe that his Lo. may give Mr. Ro^t ordinatione conforme to his former letter.

At Invernes, 8 *March* 1676.

[Mr. Robt Monro got ordination at Elgin on 2d March instant, and the Ministers of Boleskine and Urquhart, and the heritors and Elders of Abertarf and Glenmoriston, ordained by the Bishop to be present at Kilchuimen on the 12th current, 'where Mr. Thomas was to preach, and there and then to give collation and institution to the said Mr. Robert,' and to report.]

That day Mr. James Fraser, Minister at Wardlaw, regrated

that notwithstanding of the ordinance of the Presbytrie enjoyning Mr. Hugh Fraser, Minister of Kiltarlaty, to send Duncan M^{c}avis Relapse in adultery in the said Parish of Wardlaw, and Patrick Harper, fornicator there, both now receeding in the Parish of Kiltarlaty, yet the ordinance is not obeyed and hereby his hands are weakned still. [Here follow, in a different hand, the words 'Anent this see the margen.' And on the margin the following is written : ' This regrate was condemned by the Bishope and Synod in regard of ye Brother's absenc, which synodicall act I witness (signed), ALEX. CLERK, Moderator.]

The Bretheren referrs the decision of this matter untill Mr. Hugh come home and be heard.

The said day Mr. Gilbert Marshall, Minister at Invernes, reported that he was at the Earle of Morray as he was ordained be the Presbytrie, and signified to his Lo. Robert Monroe, the excommunicate pretended preist, his insolence in seducing souls within some bounds of the Sheireffdome of Invernes and Piie thereof, and that his Lo. respive [respective] answeir and pious resolution is that upon the advertisement and complaint of any of the Ministers of the said Presbytrie against the said excomunicate preist, he being found within any of their parishes, his Lo. getting certain notice, that he shall cause secure his persone that he may not mislead the people any longer.

At Invernes, March 22, 1676.

Mr. Thomas Huison and Mr. James Grant reported that according to the Bishops order they were at Kilchuimen upon the 12 of March, being the Lords day, and Mr. Thomas Huison did preach, text, and after sermone delivered to the said Mr. Robert Monroe the sacred bible, and the keys of the Churches doors, with the books of discipline, as is usuall in such cases, seriously exhorting him to humility, fidelity, and sedulity in his future ministeriall function, and immediatly therafter all the gentlemen and elders p̄nt did cordially and unanimously, by reaching furth of their hands, signifying and declaring by this their acceptance of the said Mr. Robert Monroe for their future Minister in these respective bounds of Abertarfe and Glenmoriston, promiseing obedience, faithfullnes, and assistance to him, according to their severall power and charge.

Sicklyke the said Mr. Thomas declared that he gave the said Mr. Robert reall possession and infeftment in the manse and gleib by delivering to him timber, stone, and earth, as is usuall in such cases.

The said day the Presbytrie referrs to the Synod for advice how to get letters of intercomuning against ye excomunicate preist and papists within their bounds, and especially David Bailly, excomunicate November 27, 1667, by Mr. Alex^r Clark, Minister at Invernes, and James Baily, excomunicate by Master James Sutherland, late Minister at Invernes, 21 of June 1668, and since married by Robert Monroe, excomunicate Preist, who also baptized a child to him begotten in fornication, as also the said Robert Monroe, Preist, John Bires of Cotts, Lilias Grant his Ladie, excomuncate the 23 day of Agust 1674, at Invernes by Mr. Hugh Fraser, Minister at Kiltarlatie.

The Synodicall referrs.

. . . .

5. That Mr. James Fraser, Minister at Kirkhill, once more write to Margaret Fraser, fugitive from the discipline of Invernes, to London, for her positive answeir who is the father of her child brought furth in Invernes before her removall.

Answer.—The said Mr. James declared that he could not get any sure bearer to London untill the Merchands of Invernes repair thither in May next, and that with them he will be pressing to her for ane satisfactory answeir, and thereafter shall report his diligence to the Synod and Prie.

6. The Moderator is to write to Abd. [Aberdeen] to the reverend Ministers thereoffe to try if Isobell Robertsone was borne of popish parents, baptised by a preist and educated in the Popish profession.

Answeir.—The Moderator declared that he wrote to the said Reverend Brethren of Abd. and that he received ane answeir from Mr. George Meldrum signifieing that James Robertsone sometymes of Cults, and Katherine Gordone his spouse, lived and died in the Reformed profession of this Church of Scotland, to qch he was wittnes at their severall departing out of this life, and that in their life tyme they caused baptize and educate all their children, and especially the said Isobell Robertson, in the Orthodox Religion, and that she never apostatized during her minority, and abode within the town and bounds of the Pbrie of Abd. untill she came to the Lord of Cotts family.

. . . . .

Mr. Michael Fraser is appointed to reside in his Parish of Daviot, and to build a chamber for himselfe to that effect.

The Brethren appoints the Supplication of Abertarf and Glenmoriston for Mr. Robert Monroe to be insert upon the succeeding page.

Meeting closed with prayer.

> Unto the Right Reverend Father in God Murdo Lo. Bishope of Morray undoubted Patrone of the Kirks of Boleskin and Abertarfe, and to the Reverend Mr. James Stewart, Chancillour of Murray, undoubted Patron of the Kirks of Urqhart and Glenmoriston, Wee the under-subscryving heretours, gentlemen, and Elders of Abertarfe and Glenmoriston, humblie supplicateth,

THAT Whereas upon mature and serious consideration we the said Ministers and respective Parishioners haue unanimously aggreed and condescended with Mr. Robert Monroe, Expectant, to serve hereafter *per vices* at Abertarfe and Glenmoriston with the benefice and office according as our said condescendence subscryved mutually be us at more length beares, and that we haue before our eyes the glorie of God, the propagation of his Gospell there, the peoples necessity of constant informa^{o}n and reformation, with repression of popry upon the growing hand neer these bounds, which wee cannot punctually wait on so frequently as wee would wish in respect of the distance of these places and the dangerous waters interjected betwixt them and our usuall residence in our other congregations : Heerfore wee humblie and cordially supplicat your Lo. and Mr. James Stewart, the other Patrone, to homologate and ratifie this our reasonable, mutuall, and just desire, that therupon your Lo. may passe ane order to the Moderator and Prie of Invernes for settling pntly and speedily the said Mr. Robert in the function of the Holy Ministrie there, seeing wee haue had divers tymes great satisfaction of his doctrine in the said congregations : And in answeiring this our lawfull desire as your Lo. will doe good and great service to your Master the Lord Jesus Christ, and be instrumentall to settle further illumination and knowledge in these dark and remote corners of your dioces, So you will move us allwayes in our severall statione to begg that the Lord may continue you long above us in your most holy function, and to remain, as wee still are,

Your Lo. most humble affectionat Servants and Supplicants.

  Sic subscribitur J. GRANT of Glenmoriston.

        Mr. JAMES GRANT, Minister at Urqhart.

Mr. T. HOUSTON, Minister at Boleskin.

Jo. FRASER of Little Glendo.

Jo. FRASER of Borlume.

M. FRASER of Culduthell.

ALEX^R. FRASER in Carngodie.

'I, Murdo, Bishoppe of Morray, haveing considered the above written Supplication, doe approve theroffe, and consents thereto so far as concerns me as Patrone of the Churches of Boleskin and Abertarffe. Given under my hand at Spynie the 19 day of Jar 1676 yeirs.

    Sic sub. MURDO, Bp. of Morray.'

'I, Master James Stewart, Chancellour of Morray, having considered the above written Supplication, doe approve theroffe, and consents therto so far as concerns me as Patrone of the Churches of Urqhart and Glenmoriston. Given under my hand at Kinmachen the 4 day of Februarie 1676 yeirs.

    Sic sub. Mr. JAMES STUART, Chancellor of Morray.'

Invernes, 24 May 1676.

That day the Moderator and Brethren received ane letter from Mr. George Balfoure, Min^r at Ardclach, showing off his sharp visita°n sicknes and weaknes of body through old adge, and yrfore by the advyse of some Brethren of both the Presbytries of Invernes and Forres hee did settle and condescend with Mr. Charles Ritchie to be his future helper, and yrfore supplicated ye Pbr̄y y^t his tryalls may be accellerated, and yrafter recomended to the Bishop for a license to preach and withall to shew his Lordship off the s^d condescendence. The Brethren, takeing the s^d reverend Broy^{rs} condition to considera°n, doe appoynt y^r next Presbytries meitting to hold ye 7th of June ensueing.

The Ministers of Invernes declare y^t Don^d Miller, trelaps in fornication, is fugitive to Assint, the Moderator is desired to wryt to the Min^r of Assint to send him back to satisfie the Kirk discipline.

7th June 1676.

[Mr. Charles Ritchie had his disputs uppon *De satisfactione Christi*, ye questionary tryalls, and the languages, and being removed was approven, and is appoynted to haue his popular sermon next day. All had kept the 29th of May.]

The Moderator declared y^t the Min^t off Assint, Mr. John Gray, is deposed by the Bishop and Synod of Caithnes, so y^t they could not gett Don^d Miller, fugitive from these bounds, as yett untill the place be settled with ane actuall minister.

June 21, '76.

The Bretheren appoynts the Moderator to wryt to the heretors of Daviott and Dunlechety to know what tyme they may conveniently keip the appoynted visita°n at Dunlechety, and to return ther answer to the next Presbry, lest the Brethren as formerly travell there in vayne.

Att Inverness, July 19, 1676.

The Moderator declared that he wrott to Lachlan M^cintoshe off Aberarder, and remanent heretors and Elderes of the United paroches off Dunlechety and Daviott, anent ye visita°n, as hee was ordained the last Presbry day, and y^t answer is, y^t seeing they are necessitat to abyd in the Glens to shelter and keep ther bestiall and goods ffrom the Lochabber and Glencoa Robbers, y^t it is impossible for either of the gentlemen, elders, or people, to keip the s^d visita°n untill att least y^r harvest be done, and then they will unanimous meit at Dunlechety any dyett the Presbry appoynts, and in the mean tyme, before the s^d visita°n meitt, y^t the heretors are willing to meitt with a select number from ye Presbry that a forsable way may be taken for a manse to ther min^r, qreby hee may bee incourraged to reside still amongst them.

The Brethren taking ye premisses to considera°n, to leave the s^ds heretors and parochiners excuisless, doe think fitt to delay the s^d visita°n as yett untill the 2^d dyett after there return from the ensueing Synod, and in the meantyme doe appoynt Mr. James Fraser, Min^r att Kirkhill, Mr. Rory McKenzie, Min^r at Moy, and Mr. Gilbert Marshall, Min^r at Invernes, and Mr. James Smith, Min^r att Dorres, to repair with Mr. Michael Fraser, Min^r off Daviott, to the towne and bounds of Gask, a mide place betuixt these United paroches, and to consult with ye s^{ds} heretors anent a speedy way to gett a manse built to the said Mr. Michael, y^t yrby hee may constantly reside with his flocke, and more carefully goe about his ministeriall function, and to report precisely y^r diligence herin to ye first dyet in October after the Synod, and in the mean tyme the Brethren appoynts Mr. Michael to reside in some place of his paroches as hee shall be answerable, and q^t regrates hee has or shall have for a place of residence to give the same in to the fors^d visita^{o}n.

Att Invernes, August 16, 1676.

The Brethren y^t wer^e appoynted to meitt at Gask with the heretors of Deviott and Dunlechety declared y^t they have not kept as yet, because the heretors did not appoynt a day. The Presb͞ry appoynts Mr. Michael Fraser to speak to these heretors, and to appoynt ye dyett, oyrwyse they will appoynt it themselffes at ther next Presb͞ry day.

Att Invernes, 13 *Septr.* 1676.

Mr. Michael Fraser declareth y^t the heretors of his united paroches referres ye appoyntment of ye meitting at Gask to the Presb͞ry, but intreats y^t the dyett be not this fourtnight to come, because in y^t tyme all of y^m will be busie about ther harvest.

The Brethren taking this to ther considera^{o}n appoynts ye s^d dyett to hold att Gask or Far upon the first Tuesday of October ensueing y^t they may report y^r diligence as s^{d}is to the Bishope, Synod, and Presb͞rie.

At Dunlichatj, Novr. 7th, 1676.

Conveened the Moderator and remanent Brethren, except Mr. Hugh Fraser directed by the Brethren of the Chapter Commissioner to my Lord Arch Bp. of Saint Andrewes, etc. The Lords name being called on, Master Gilbert Marshall preached, text 1 Thess. 5. 12.

[The Minister, Mr. Michael Fraser, approved, except that he had not celebrated the Lords supper since his entry to the Parish.]

The Gentlemen and Elders being enquired if there Minister resided in aither of his paroches, answered, not. The Minister replied that he had not a manse to lodge in. The heritors being asked why there was no manse in aither of the congregations, answered that they had y^r joynt thoughts for building ane in Daviot a good whyle ago, and that y^r conclusione is, which they were desired to intimat to the Presbytrie, that they are content to stent themselwes for buildeing of a sufficient manse in the sowme of three hundred mks in hand befor the work is began, as also to furnish upon there own expensses men and horses to lead all the timber to Daviot from Strathspey, or Invernes, beside the hewen work y^t is requisit to be in the house: this condescendence satisfied the minister, q^o was to build the manse himselff upon the recept of the money. The Bretheren exhorts both Min^r and heritors to fulfill there engagements herein, that the minister may dwell and reside among his people. Mr. James Smith, who visited the Sessione book, declared that the same was formall and orderly.

[The officer gives satisfaction.]

At Invernes, December 6, 1676.

The said day Mr. Gilbert Marshall, Minister at Invernes, produced a process led against Marjorie Leith, spouse to Patrick Gordone in Invernes, by the Session y^{r}of, conteaneing severall alledged scandalous guilts, as the process itselff at more length proprts. The same being raid, the Bretheren are not cleare as yet to give there decisive Judgement thereanent, and yrfor recomends to the s^d Mr. Gilbert Marshell to use all diligence scrutinie for cleareing the process fullie, and report his diligence to the Presbrie.

At Invernes, 4 Aprile 1677.

[Marjorie Leith's process referred to the ensuing Synod, by order of the Bishop.]

At Urquhart, June 5, 1677.

Conveened the Moderator and Remanent Bretheren except Mr. Hugh Fraser, Minister at Croy, absent thorow a paine in his legg. Gods name called upon.

Master Hugh Fraser, Min^r at Kiltarlatie, preached, text Ephes. 5. 15.

The Moderator declared the reason of this present visitatione, and enquired if the same was tymouslie intimated, the Minister and Elders answered it was, as the populous meeteing of the hearers did testifie.

The Moderator desired to give to the Clerk an list of the Elders and deacons, which was given in as followeth: Thomas Grant of Balmakaan, John Grant of Corriemonie, James Grant of Sheuglie, Patrick Grant in Inchbroome, Donald Cuming of Dailshangie, James Cuming his son, James Cuming in Pitkerrell, Farq^r Cuming in Garthalie, Wm Grant of Achmony, Alexander and Robt Grants in Carrogarre, Alex^r Grant in Balmakan, Duncan Grant in Divech, and Gregorie Grant, Pitkerrell, etc.

The Minister, Mr. James Grant, being removed, all these Elders severallie were enquired how they were satisfied with there Ministers doctrine, life, and conversatione, all of them gave him ane singullare applaus. Sicklik beeing enquired if he frequentlie catechised, visited the sick, and celebrated the Sacrament of the Lords supper, answered that he went about all these ministeriall duties painfully, and that he was prepareing for celebratceing the Lords supper, wch he could not do untill a period should be put to the harvest. Being asked if he prayed in families q^n he lodged with y^m out of his owne house, all answered positively. Being enquired if he preached on the 29 of May, answered he did yearely, and pressed all the parochiners to be present.

The Minister beeing called in, the Moderator blessed the Lord for the good applause he had of his Elders, and desired him to continu in weledoeing, and to celebrat the sacrament of the Lords Supper as soone as possible he could, which he promised to do.

The Elders beeing removed, and the Minister beeing enquired if they were faithfull in there trust, or if he had anything to admonish them of, he answered that they were most faithfull, and that there was notheing could encourrage him in his ministeriall office, bot they were all most cordiall to strengthen his hands.

The Elders beeing called in, the Moderator thanked God for

the sweet harmony that was betwixt them and there Minister, and beseeched them to continu in weledoeing.

The Minister beeing enquired if he had an decreite of plat, answered, not. The Bretheren appoynts him for his own present benefit and successors to provide for one tymously.

The Minister and Elders beeing enquired if they had an school, answered that they had none for the present, bot q^n the Laird of Grant cam to the cuntrey that they were to require his helpe and assistance how to get some victuall to mantean an Schoolmaster; they were exhorted to do the same, which should be good service done to God.

Such as visited the Sessione book declared that they had not a bound register, bot scrolls as yet; the Presbfie ordeans to get an new book and mak an exact register, wch they promised to do.

[The officer approved of.]

The s^d day Robert Cuming of Inchbryne, with some others of his rela°ns, did compeare before the Presbbrie for themselves and in name and behalf of William Cuming, Shiriff Clerk of Invernes, and George Cuming his Brother, merchand y^r, and gave in there supplicatione sheweing that forasmeikle as John Grant of Corrimony had built an new dask upon that divisione of the Church appropriated and set apart be consent of the whole session as his proper allocatione there, and one part of the s^d dask, to wit, the northerest corner therof, beeing sett upon an buriall stone belonging without controversie to there praedecessors, q^{r}fore it was there earnest desire and humble supplicatione that the said dask should be removed to the west the space of an foote of ground or more if needs be, and that alwayes without prejudice to the said dask or reflectione on the s^d John Grant q^n they burie y^r dead y^r, q^n Providence shall offer occasione. The s^d John Grant of Corriemony beeing called in, and beeing asked concerneing the premisses, acknowledged y^t it was such that they supplicated for y^{m}selves and there successors, and consented to the termes above specified, and seeing both parties were content the Presbytrey gave there approbatione to there mutuall decisione.

At Kiltarlaty, July 3, 1677.

The Moderator declared the reason why this visitatione was

appoynted, and especially to tak notice and inspectione if popery be upon the groweing hand in the over-paroch of Strathglass, and to this end asked if this visitatione was tymouslie intimated; both Min^r and Elders declared that it was, as the numberous auditores could evidence. The Moderator desired that a list of the Elders and deacons should be given to the Clerk, which was done and read as followeth: Thomas Fraser of Beufort, Hugh Fraser of Culbokie, Hugh Fraser of Glenvakie, Simeon Fraser of Bruiach, Hugh Fraser of Baldown, Thomas Fraser of Teanakyle, Hugh Fraser of Faneblaire, William Fraser of Bowblanie, Jo^n Fraser of Culmullin, Alex^r Fraser in Killachick. . . . Mr. Hugh Fraser of Eskidaile, Elders. [Then follows list of Deacons.]

[The Minister well reported of by the Elders, but he only once celebrated the Lords Supper since his entry to the Parish.]

[The Elders] being asked if popery was upon the groweing hand in the over parioch, answered that such as were popish enclyned were in the province of Ross where the Chisolme with is family and dependents were.

The Minister being asked q^t was the reason that he proceeded not to process Collin Chisolme and   Lawder, his spouse, according to the Presbries order, answered that the s^d Collin and wife is nether now in this parioch nor within this Presbrie or province, bot within the province of Ross, and at there removeall he desisted from processeing them, untill he should know the Presbries mind therein. The Bretheren referrs this for advice to the Synod, whether or no he is to proceed in processing the s^{ds} parties notwithstanding they are out of this parioch and out of the province, because he began to process them.

[The Elders well reported of by the Min^r; Register not bound; and the Minister and Elders promise 'to produce a good handsome book bound for there register betuixt this and the first Presbry day at Invernes.']

The Schoolmaster, Mr. John Monro, beeing removed, both minister and elders gave him a large applaus of his painefullness and diligent attendance on school and sessione, and also y^t he was of a Christian, civill, blameless conversatione; he beeing called in was desired to walk worthy of the good comendatione his Minister and elders gave of him.

The Minister regrated that some of the heritors did clame some divisiones of the Church as only proper to y^m and to none other, however did not plenish the samen nether in dasks or pewes. The Presbrie ordaine them to mak up this defect betuixt this day and some day that the Min^r and Elders shall condescend on, otherwayes to forfault and lose there aledged right.

The s^d Donald Roy, Shireff Officer forsaid, beeing sumoned to this dyet and beeing cited, compeared, and beeing desired to glorify God and confess his sin of adultery w^t Kathrin nic ean Tyre in Bruiach, notwithstanding of the many and frequent conferences his Minister had with him, and that two Bretheren were sent out to speak with him, yet he stood to an obstinat denyall, without any hope of confession, except the extraordinarie divyne hand of God work on him. Herefor the Bretheren advised his Minister, Mr. Hugh, to tak him diverse Lords dayes before the pulpit in presence of the whole congregatione, and to offer him the oath, and pray for him that God may open his obdured heart, to confess the truth, and if he continu obstinat, to tak his oath at last upon the head of the child as is the practise of this Kirk and Kingdome.

At Kirkhill, August 21, 1677.

Conveened the Moderator and Remanent Bretheren. The name of God was called upon. Mr. Hugh Fraser, Minister at Kiltarlaty, preached, text Col. 1. 28.

The Moderator enquired if this visitatione was tymously intimated to the congregatione. They answered it was as the numbrous multitud of the auditors in itselff did proport.

The Moderator desired that a list of the Elders and deacons should be given in to the Clerk, which was done accordingly and read as followeth—

Elders.—Thomas Fraser of Bewfort, Hugh Fraser of Struy, Hugh Fraser of Culbokie, Hugh Fraser of Belladrume, Alex^r Fraser of Moniack, James Fraser of Achnagairne, Mr. Simeon Fraser of Finisk, James Fraser in Dunballach, John Fraser in Inchberrie, Wm Fraser in Phoppachie, and James Fraser in Kirkhill.

Deacons.—Andrew Peirie, in Bunchrue, Donald Johnson in Inglishtoun, Alex^r Wright ther, Jo^n Macksorle in Kirktowne, Donald Macksorle in Lemnech, Finla McCoil oig in Inshberie, Donald M^{c}phaile in Home, Alex^r Smyth ther, etc.

The Min^r beeing removed, the Elders were enquired one by one how they were satisfied with there ministers doctrine, life, and conversatione, if he was a visitor of the sick, and if he frequently catechised his people, and celebrated yearely the sacrament of the Lords supper, and preached on the 29 of May, all ane by ane answered that they blessed God for him that he observed all these ministeriall duties, and was so panefull that they were affrayed that he should thereby shorten his own dayes in all likliehood.

The Minister beeing called in, the Moderator in name of all the Bretheren blessed the Lord for the affectionat joynt commendatione and applaus he had in all the steps of his ministeriall functione and carriage, from the whole gentlemen, elders, and deacons p$\bar{n}$t: he was brotherely exhorted to continu in his zeale within the Lords vineyard, who should give him his crown and reward at his second appearance.

The Elders beeing removed, the Minister was enquired q^t satisfactione he had of his Elders, and if there were anything q^{r}of he would have them admonished, Answered that he blessed God for the concurrence they gave him in all things that he layes to there charge, that they are able, consciencious men, as forward and zealous in discipline as he can desire, that all of them q^o are heritors brings in such delinquents as are within there bounds, and constraines them, nill they will they, to satisfie discipline, and that they are nether countenancers nor pleaders for any vicious person, bot kythes[1] impartiall to all suche.

The gentlemen and elders beeing called in, the Moderator in name of the Bretheren blessed God for the large applaus and singullare praise-worth commendatione that there minister hath given them, and, as they wish to be styled faithfull servants by Christ in the day q^{r}in he will mak up his juells, to continu still zealous and faithfull.

---

[1] Kythe, to show, to appear.

The Bretheren of Invernes that did visit the book declared that the book is most formall, and for panefullness and diligence of the Minister, Elders, and clerk in there severall stationes decerned therein, it deserves singullare commendatione.

Master Thomas Fraser, Schoolmaster, beeing removed, the Minister and Elders were enquired q^t satisfactione they had of him, q^t was his life and how he attended his charge, all of y^m professed that they were verie wele pleased with him; he beeing called in, the good report of his Min^r and Elders was made knowne to him, and was exhorted to walk exemplare in holieness before the young ones, and to continu worthie of the commendatione that was given of him. He beeing enquired q^t satisfactione he had for his paines and attendance from the Min^r, heretors, and Elders, answered that he was pleased and satisfied with them all.

[All well pleased with the officer.]

The Bretheren thinks fit that the next Presb̃rie day be an visitatione at Abertarff, and Mr. James Fraser, Minister at Kirkhill, to preach there, September nixt the 25, becaus the people then shall be all at home from the marcat of Invernes. Mr. Robert Monro is to give tymous advertisement, that the Bretheren may not mak an tedious jurney there in vaine, wch he promised to do.

The Moderator, Master Alex^r Clerk, declared that he had an discharge under Mr. William Annands hand for two hundred m̃ks, which he payed to him as heyre to Mr. John Annand, late Minister at Invernes, for meliorateing the manse now in the s^d Mr. Alex^r his possessione, q^{ch} he keeped from registrateing until he should get under the late Bp. of Morrayes hand q^t he received from the s^d Mr. John Annand, and seeing he hath both in his possessione that he desyres the Bretheren to homologat to the registratione of both; wch the Bretheren condescended to, and are as followeth verbatim from the principalls:—

'I, Master William Annand, lawfull son to the deceist Mr. John Annand, sometime Minister at Invernes, be thir p̃nts grant mee to haue received from Master Alexander Clerk, one of the p̃nt Min^{rs} thereat, the sowme of two hundred m̄ks money, and that in contentation of the like sowme payed be the s^d deceist Master John

Annand, be order of Presbrie, to an Reverend father in God, Murdo Lord Bishope of Morray, designed therein Minister at Invernes, for the melioratione of the s^d umq^{ll} Master John his Manse, as the act of Presbrie made thereanent at length beares, q^{r}of I grant the receipt in numerat money, and for me my aires exōrs and successors, exoners, quiteclames, and simpliciter discharges the s^d Mr. Alex^r Clerk, his airs, ex^{rs}, and successors, of the samen for ever, and binds and oblidges mee and my forsaids to warrand this my discharge to be good and sufficient to the effect underwritten to the s^d Mr. Alex^r Clerk and his forsaids at all hands and agst all mortall, as law will, Consenting thir p͠nts be insert and regr̄at in the Books of Councell and Session, Sireff or Commissar Books of Morray and Invernes, therein to remaine *ad futuram rej memoriam*, and constituts
My Prōss etc. In Witness q^{r}of I haue subscribed thir p͠nts writen be George Adamson, Writer in Elgin, the eighteenth day of Jarij 1666 yeares, befor thir witnes John Chalmer, Town Clerk of Elgin, and the s^d George Adamson, Writer hereof.

        sic sub.   Master William Annand.
                    J. Chalmer, Witnes.
                    G. Adamsone, Writer and Witnes.'

'I Murdo, Bp of Orkney, late of Morray, do by these presents attest that the above written act of ye Presbitery of Invernes, whereby they ordained that I should haue the above spec^t sowme from Master John Annand his aires, exors and successors, and I do acknowledge the recept of the said sowme accordingly, as I do testifie the samen under my hand at Invernes the 15 day of August 1677 yeares.   *sic sub.*   Murdo, Bp of Orknay.'

This visitatione was continewed to this 21 of August, in respect of the marcat of Invernes, wch held upon the 14, 15, and 16 dayes, at wch the Elders, nether people, could keepe with the Presbrie.

The meeting closed with prayer.

                  At Kilchumen[1] *in Abertarff,*
                      the 25 of Septr. 1677.

Conveened the Bretheren of the Presbrie, except Mr. Alex^r Clerk, Mod^r, q^o excused himselff, beeing ordered by the Magistrats to preach that day the electione sermone for chooseing

---

[1] Kilchumen, now Fort Augustus.

the Magistrats of Invernes, for wch he appoynted Mr. James Fraser, Minister at Kirkhill, to moderat in his absence. Also Mr. Rorie Mackenzie, Mr. Gilbert Marshell, Mr. Hugh Fraser, Minister at Croy, and Master Michael Fraser were absent. The name of the Lord was called upon.

Mr. James Fraser preached, text Eph. 5 cap. 8 v^s. After sermon he asked if this visitatione was tymously intimated, they answered positivelie.

The Min^r, Mr. Robert Monro, gave a list of his Elders, which were read as followeth :—

Elders of Abertarff.

John Fraser of Borlume, Alex^r Fraser y^r, Thomas Fraser of Ardochie, W^m M^cwyre there, Jo. Fraser of Little Glendo, Duncan Fraser of Murvalgan, Duncan M^cean in Inshnacardich, John Miller in Killchumen, Do^d Dow in Borlume, and Thomas M^cfarq^r vane in Ardochie.

Elders of Glenmoriston.

Jon M^cevin in Inver, John M^cferq^r in Livishie, W^m M^calester in Invervuick, James Grant ther, and Donald McWilliam in Livishie.

The Minister was removed, and the Elders were enquired concerning him as to his life, conversatione, doctrine, and discipline, they answered *una voce* that they were wele satisfied with him (except the Elders of Glenmoristonne regrated he did not keepe with them everie sabbath *per vices*), and also the s^d Elders reported that severalls of My Lord M^cdonalds familie[1] doeth of late come to the ordinances, and that others are expected, and that he doeth all that lieth in his power to suppress poperie.

The Minister was called in and approven for his ministeriall deportment, was exhorted to continu in weldoeing, and to studie the popish controversies whereby he would be enabled to convince gainsayers and reclame the astrayeing ignorant.

The Elders beeing removed, the Min^r was enquired q^t he had to say to them, answered, that he was wele satisfied with them; bot that for want of an edifice since the kirk fell, that they had no place to put delinquents in for publict repentance,

---

[1] Angus Macdonell of Glengarry, created Lord Macdonell and Arros by Charles II.

y^rfore he entreated the Bretheren to tak an serious course w^t the heritors for seting up and building a place for Gods worship.

The Elders were called in and commended and approven in all things q^rin they did favour and encurrage there minister, and they were exhorted to hold hand to discipline.

The Minister regrated that the Bridg was ruinous: the Elders were exhorted to use all diligence for setting up the s^d Bridge, and that because the water is interjacent betuixt the Kirk and ye people that resort the ordinances, which the people do regrate, bot that they are not able of themselves to set up that bridge without the assistance of the whole parioch afarr off as wele as neere at hand. Herefore they entreat the Presbṛie to writ to my Lord M^cdonald and his friends, who are inhabitants of ye remotest part of the parioch, to giv y^r help and concurrence. The Brethren promises to write to his Lordship q^n he returneth from Edinburgh.

The Moderator asked at the Elders p̄nt why they were not buildeing a kirk, they answered that they sent some gentlemen to the session of Boleskin in ther Easter Parioch to concurr with them joyntly in building the said edifice, seeing they are concerned as wele as they, and have not gott an satisfactorie answer with these commissioners.

The Presbṛie thinks fit that they send other two gentlemen to the fors^d sessione as yet the nixt Lords day, and the minister to bring a report of there diligence to the nixt Presbṛie.

The Minister regrated that there was not a ferric boat upon the water of Oviach[1] for transporteing of himselff and parishioners, to q^ch the gentlemen present replyed that Malcome Fraser of Culduthell did oblige himselff to uphold a boat there, so that the Parishioners would pay the boatman conforme to former condescendence, which the boatman sought not as yet, y^rfor the Mīn^r and Elders are desyred to keep y^r condescendence to Culduthell that he may keepe conditione with them.

The Min^r also regrated that there was not a boat to transport him to his charge upon the water of Glenmoristonne. Mr. James Fraser and Master Hugh Fraser promised to speak to the Laird of Glenmoristonne for the s^d boat, as also anent the most comodious place q^r the sermon may be heard each Lords day.

---

[1] River Oich.

The Officer beeing removed, and enquirie beeing made anent
him, it was declared both by Min^r and Elders that he was
deficient in his office; being called in he was rebucked by the
Moderator and ordayned to waite on his office more diligently
inder the paine of depositione.

[10*th Oct.* 1677. Meeting of Synod at Elgin. On 11th the
Presbytery met at Elgin. Mr. James Fraser, Minister of
Wardlaw, chosen Moderator by the Bishop.]

At Invernes the 7 *Novem.* '77.

[Among the refers from last meeting of Synod are:—]

2. 'That bretheren take narrow inspectione anent trafficking priests their preaching or saying mass in famillies or conventicles, and upon certaine informatione to transmit their names to the Bishope.

3. That persons inorderlie maried be delated to the civill magistrate that they may be punished conforme to the late Act of Counsell.

5. That each broy^r thrise every yeir preach against rebellion, chuseing texts for that subject, and that the sacrament be celebrat at Ester. That the king in publick prayer be designed in all his titles, and that Archbishopes particullarie be designed in publick prayers.'

William McPhersone in Inv^{ss}, adulterer, reported to haue gone away to Holland to be a souldier.

At Invernes, 5 *Decemb.* 1677.

Mr Roderick McKenzie beeing enquired concerneing his absence the day preceding, answered that he could not cross the water of Nairne, y^r beeing a great deluge that day and the day befor. That beeing a known truth, he was excused.

That day compeired Patrick Gordon, Burges of Invernes, before the Presbrie y^{r}off, presenting ane supplica^{o}n subscribed be him and Marjorie Leith, his spouse, bearing y^t Mr. Alex^r Clerk, ane of the Ministers of Innernes, did greivously reflect uppon him, his wyffe and family, and y^t publictly in a sermon preached be him on the Lords day in the High Church of Innernes, Octo^r 14, 1677, being the sabboth day immediately after yᵉ Synod as yᵉ Supplicaᵒn in itsclff doth proport, and is registrat verbatim as followeth :—

> Unto the very Reverend Modʳ and Bretheren off yᵉ Presbrie of Innernes, the humble Supplicaᵒn of Patrick Gordon, Burges of Innernes,

Most Humbly Sheweth and meaneth,—

That uppon the fourteenth day of Octoʳ, being yᵉ Lords day immediatly followeing yᵉ meiting of the Synod of Murray, Before qᶜʰ venerable, grave, and impartiall Judicatorie yᵉ sᵈ Marjorie compeired and was (as is knowne to your Reverend wysedomes) absolved of the lait scandall shee was charged for, with qᶜʰ tedious proces, by the means and procurement of the Supplicants implacable adversaries, shee was for yᵉ space of ane yeir compleitt keipt in a most drumly condition, and being by God's providence released of this heavie and unsupportable chaine, and thinking uppon nothing more then friendly to forgive her enemies, especiallie yᵉ Instruments of her troubles, for furthering and cherishing of qᶜʰ resoluᵒn shee repaired to the publict ordinance an the forsᵈ Sabbaoth, wher the followeing discourse was delyvered from pulpitt be Mr. Alexʳ Clerk before all yᵉ Congregaᵒn, and yᵗ so pressingly yᵗ since yᵗ day many grave and judicious persons declared they never heard yᵉ lyk delyvered from the chaire of verity, the discourse followes by qᶜʰ the preacher made it palpable yᵗ his intention was to effront and defame yᵉ supplicants, and in cleare termes spok thus :

Within thir few dayes I saw a lying letter wrytten be a subtill young man, and subscrybed by a simple old man, and red in my owne audience, qʳin wᵗ teares and sorrow he declares his wyffe to be both religious, holy, pious, just, and chast. As for her piety and sobriety God knowes it, and for her chastity all of you heares it. But its observable yᵗ notorious persons are alwayes defended by persons alyk guilty as themselffs, for wee find yᵗ qᵘ Absolom murdered his broyʳ Amon, Joab, a murderer lyk himselff, sent yᵉ widow of Tekoa with a number of subtill, devilish, lying tales to mak his peace with his father; even so shee was defended by persons alyke guilty with herselff. And uppon a tyme a Stranger asking for stabling att her house, a wyse man passing by answered yʳ is no stabling ther for horses, bot for men yʳ is stabling. But, iff hee had said right, yʳ is stabling for divells; and applyed thus : I desyre you all to refraine from that howse qᶜʰ is a plauge and a pest amongst us, for, Jezebell lyk, shee attyres herselff as iff shee wer not guilty, but for use of terror to y'one y^t hath sufferings y^t it is ane earles of everlasting suffering and vengeance; and I heard of a man made honest by Act of Parliament, but her shame and reproach shall never be wipped off. They talk shee is come off in coach, but black is ye coach off it; and att the close off his discourse hee desyred all ye people to chewe y^re cuide on what they heard. In his first prayer hee said, O Lord, however wicked and divellish persons may in this world have many to plead y^ro unjust causes, yet the day will come q^n none will be found to excuse them; and in his prayer after sermon thus: God bless our Magistratts and q^tever way they be weakened be the hands of men, give thou them grace, O Lord, and strength y^t that they may crush iniquity.

Your wysedomes may easily Judge the supplicants condition to be now worse than at first, beeing so publictly rendered odious in ye eyes and esteime of such as had charity for us, both in towne and countrey, and y^t at such high rate y^t severalls qho formerly profesd slender kyndnes for us began att last to wonder and pity us in this peice off our usage. Yo^r Reverend wysedomes may firmly believe the Supplicants to hawe no less than sadd and grieved hearts y^t they should be necessitat (and to speak from our hearts ingenuity, it is no les) to mak this sadd address, especiallie y^t cause and ground should be given them be ther Pastor qhom they never provocked y^rto, but rather honoured and loved him as ther father and ffaithfull ffriend, and accordingly not only intimacie and familiaritie betwext them, but a most intire and unfainzied correspondence never violat by the Supplicants, nor cause given the s^d Mr. Alex^r Clerk, y^r Pastor, to make the least breach y^roff. Howbeit hee hes taken offence, the ground q^roff hee never so much as once enquyred off the Supplicants, nether footed there floore or spoke to either of them (save once in his owne house nott called be him) thir bypast fyfteen moneths.

May it y^rfore please your wysedomes to consider of the abowe wrytten discourse, and ye scope and nature of it, and what wrong, shame, and loss ye Supplicants hawe sustained with ye former tedious proces. But worst of all this last unexpected peice of oppen and publict reproach, q^ch work from the beginning hath so borne downe the Supplicants y^t it hath crossed them in ther persons, wasted a considerable part of ther little interest, ecalypsed ther credit, destroyed ther lawfull calling uppon q^ch y^re lyvelihood depended; in a word, hath made a clear path to usher in to the supplicants and family both penury and want, iff not in danger to

be utterly ruined if not speidily repaired to ther credit, q^ch they
begg may be looked to and regairded by your Reverend wysedomes,
to q^m they most humblie make address for y^t effect. Almightie
God, grant your Reverend wysedomes a dowble portion off his
spirit y^t yee may be found faithfull labourers in his vyneyard, and
att last reap ye comfortable fruitts y^roff to your endless comfort
and joy, q^ch is the strong and ardent desyres off ye supplicants, q^ho
shall ever pray.   *Sic sub.*   PATRICKE GORDONNE.
                                      MARJORIE LEITH.

[The above supplication taken into consideration by the
Presbytry, who allowed the Supplicants to produce evidence of
the statements made by Mr. Clerk, who 'hath not been weill
advysed, presumeing to reflect uppon the leidges without any
ground, but much more against the late act of the Bishope and
Synod of Murray, q^rin the s^d Marjorie Leith was cleared off
all q^roff shee was formerly aspersed, and y^t without the contra-
diction off any one Minister in the Synod, the s^d Mr. Alex^r
Clerk beeing then present there, and by his taciturnity seemed
to consent.' After various steps, and consultation with the
Bishop, the following witnesses amongst others were on 1st
May '78 examined, viz.: Alex. Dunbar, Provost; Finlay
Fraser, Bailie; Robert Barber, Bailie; Alex^r Ross, Dean of
Guild; Wm Baillie, Commissar Deput; Wm Cumming, Sheriff
Clerk. The Presbytery found the 'lybell sufficiently proven.'
On 15th May the evidence was reported to a meeting of the
Bishop and Subsynod at Inverness, when the Presbytery's pro-
ceedings were approved of. The subsequent proceedings are
given in the Synod Register.]

Att Invernes, July 31, 1678.

That day Mr. Alex^r Clerk, Minister of Invernes, reported y^t
hee had received a letter from Mr. James Wallace, one of the
ministers off Orkney, who had given up the names of Alex^r
Beseck and Janet nein v^c Gillmichael, fugitives from Invernes,
to all the Ministers of Orkney, to be enquyred for, and promised
to give him ane account y^roff w^t the next occasion.

Att Invernes, 25 Septr. 1678.

That day the whole Bretheren regrated that Seminary tra-
fegueing preists are goeing up and downe through ther paroches

awouedly confidently and affrontedly, and w*t*all doe baptise children begotten of delinquents, and doe heavily regrate y*t* Straglass and y*e* paroch of Commir is so pestered w*t* poperie that a totall defection is feared there iff not speidily prevented.

It is regrated also that the Leidges doe converse familiarly w*t* excomminicat Papists and Preists, especiallie in the Towne off Invernes, as if they frie subjects, q*ch* regrate is referred to the Bishop and Synod of Murray for advyce.

[At the 'private censure' it was found that the Sacrament of the Lord's Supper had not yet been celebrated in Kiltarlity; that Mr. Michael Fraser, Daviot, did not yet reside within his own Parish, his manse not being yet built—he promised to build before the next Synodical Meeting; and that Mr. Rod*k* Mackenzie, Moy, did not reside at his kirk for want of a sufficient Manse. 'He is exhorted to build ane sufficient manse conforme to the Act of Parliament to y*t* effect, and himself to repaire hither *quam primum.*']

Att Invernes, Nov. 20, 1678.

That day the Moderator declared y*t* hee had received ane letter from my Lo. Bi. showeing y*t* Mr. Michael ffraser, Min*r* of Daviott, was suspended for a certaine tyme, and y*t* hee did wryte to Mr. Roderick M*c*Kenzie, minister at Moy, to repair to Daviott and there preach on ane Lords day, and to mak intima*o*n to the people off the s*d* paroch of the suspension of ther Min*r*, w*t* the continuance and reasons y*r*off, and this day y*e* s*d* Mr. Roderick declared y*t* hee had done conforme y*r*to.

As also y*e* Moderator declared y*t* y*e* Bish. desyred to supplie y*e* s*d* charg dureing y*e* s*d* vacancie. That day Mr. James Smith, Minister att Dorres, is ordained to preach att Dunlechity the Lord's day com 8 days.

[Among the Synodical refers are: 'To intimat y*t* persons goeing to superstitious wells are to be censured.'[1] That 'the

---

[1] The ancient custom of 'going to superstitious wells' early attracted the attention of the Synod; but the custom prevailed till far into the present century, and has not yet been entirely discontinued. On 26th April 1626 the Synod records: 'In respect it is surmized that many people hes gain this yeir to wells and chappellis in forme of pillgrimage from all quarters within this provinces theirfore y*e* Synod ordaines euerie brother to sumond a number of their

Bretheren of Invernes provyde a sallarie to y^{re} Presbytrie Clerk according to former practice in that place, viz. ane Dolleare from every Minister per annum;' 'y^t Bursars off Divinitie haue ther mantenance collected tymously, els ye Moderator to pay them.'

Att Invernes, Decr. 11, 1678.

That day the Moderator presented a letter wryten to him from my Lord Bish. w^t a bundell of printed procla^{o}ns ishued from the King and Councell, ordaineing to keep a solemn fast throughout the whole realme ye 18 day of December instant; and all the Bretheren are ordained to mak intima^{o}n yrof in y^r severall congrega^{o}ns the next Lo. day, and declare the reasones of ye same.

That day ye Moderator presented a letter directed to him from the Lo. Bishop desyreing y^t such Ministers as wer present at ye debate betwext Mr. Hugh Fraser, Min^r of Croy, and Mr. Michael Fraser, Minister of Daviott, should compeir before the Lo. Bish. and his assessors att the Subsynod ye 8 day of Janrij next ensueing, and Mr. Alex^r Clerk and Mr. Gilbert Marshall, Ministers of Invernes, and Mr. Andrew Fraser, Student in Divinity, are enjoyned *apud acta* to be present the s^d day. Also ye Moderator is to direct ane officer to summond the

---

parochiners to compeir oulklie [weekly] befoir y^o bishop and his bailzie, q^u hes obtained ane commission for repressing ye same, and that ye brethren of ye exerceis of Elgin begin this course the nixt oulk [week].' The Synod's minute of 4th October 1642 bears that 'The gryt abuse continuing in this province be ye frequent repaireing off persones of all rankes unto superstitious wells and chappells, especiallie to ye Chappel of Grace well nere the Water of Spey, and it being found ye Lords of his Majesties privie Councill had laitlie made and caused published some werie Lawdable Acts against these and ye lyk abuses, The saidis Acts being publicklie read in ye assemblie, after deliberatione, It is thought fitt zat Intimatione be maid of these Acts to such as are commissioners nominat within the same for repressing of these abuses in this Province, namely to the Shereffe [of] Murray, The Laird of Kilravock, The Laird of Brodie, The Provest and broughe of Elgine, That they be in readiness to concur w^t the Laird of Innes at ye tymes requisit for repressing off the said superstitione, and to this effect ordaines coppies of y^o saidis Acts to be sent to everie ane of them.' The Well of Grace was the most noted of the many holy wells within the province. On 1st November 1705 the Synod records: 'As to the reference concerning the Chapel and Well commonlie called the Chapel and Well of Grace, apoints ane address to be made to the Assembly for ane Act for suppressing of superstition used at that place; and appoints everie Min^r to suppress it as far as they can.'

absent Bretheren to attend y{e} s{d} meitting for beareing witnes in y{e} s{d} matter uppon oath.

Att Invernes, Febrij **19, 1679.**

That day Mr. James Smith reported y{t} hee had preached at Dunlechetie sabboth day was fourtnight, and declared to the s{d} paroch y{t} Mr. Michael Fraser, ther Minister, was suspended *de novo* att the last Subsynod, and yt hee is to continew under the s{d} censure till the next Synod, intimating unto the s{d} people the reasons and grounds off the same.

Att Invernes, March **5, 1679.**

That day, after Invocation of y{e} Lo. his name, y{e} Moderator [Rev. James Fraser] produced a letter directed to him be the Bishop of Murray, the tenor qreof is as followes:

'Ther being a proclama{on} emitted from y{e} King his Councill of late come to our hands, ordaineing and commanding all papists of q{tsoever} qualitie w{t}in this kingdome to mack ther address to the Arch Bishop and Bishopes of this diocess before some certaine dayes in the s{d} proclama{on} specified, to the end they may, after conference had w{t} y{e} Archbishopes and Bishopes, be either convinced or convicted. These are therefore requyring zou and y{e} other Bretheren of your Presbytrie (being called by you to meitt *pro re nata*) to send us tuext this and the 8 day of March preceisly particular lists of all the papists w{t}in each of ther paroches, and lett the list of each paroch be faithfully wrytten and sub{t} by the Minister of the samen, but w{t} this distinction y{t} you mark p'ticularly: 1. quho are excommunicat papists; 2{dly}, qho haweing professed the Protestant Religion ar become apostats; and 3{dly}, qho hawe been bred Papists from their infancie.'

The Moderator, conforme to the fors{d} ordinance off the Lo. Bishop, gawe tymous advertisement to each Brether, who accordingly conveened to this day.

The Ministers off Inverness being enquyred what Papists wer w{t}in ther charge gawe in a list as followes:

'Wee, undersubscribers, Ministers off Invernes, declare that these underwrytten Papists did apostatize from the Reformed Religion, and y{r}fore wer processed, and, continewing obstinat, they are by y{e} order of the late Bishope of Murray and Synod y{r}of excomunicat; ther names are David Bailzie of Dochfure, James Bailzie there, Johne Byars of Cotts and Lillias Grant his lady, resideing in the Castle of Invernes (Agnes Monro, Spouse to James Bailzie, qho is not yet excommunicat, but to be processed). This wee verifie to be of truth, at Inverness ye 5 of Martch 1679.

Sic sub. 'Mr. Alex^r Clk.
Mr. Gilbert Marshall.'

The s^d day Mr. James Grant, Min^r of Urq^{rt}, sent in a list of his papists as followes :

'I, Mr. James Grant, Min^r of Urq^t, doe testifie and declare y^t (blessed be God for it) ther are no Papists in this Paroch of Urq^{rt}, except Katherin McDonald, spouse to Jhon Grant of Coremony, qho was both borne and bred among Papists, and one Hector M'Lean, a young man baptized in our church but bred among Papists since his youth, but nether of these excommunicat; q^{ch} is verified under my hand att Kilmore in Urq^{rt}, 5 of March 1679.

Sic sub. 'Mr. James Grant.'

The Papists of Abertarff ar as followes :

'I, Mr. Robert Monro, Minister off Abertarf and Glenmoriston, doe testifie and declaire these Papists did apostatize from the reformed religion before my entrie, vizt, Allan M^{c}donald of Kieltrie, and Mary Chisolme his spouse, all his children, servants, and tenents; Donald McDonald of Culachie, his wyff, servants, and tenents; Allan McDonald of Culachie, his whole family (except Mary Fraser, his wyff); Ranald McDonald off Pitmean, his wyff, children, and tennents; all ye people of Carngoddy and Ochtera; Jhon McDonald in Lick, his wyff and whole familie; the tennents of Oberchalder, Alex^r Buj in Portclare, his wyff, and children.

'The Papists of Glenmoriston are, Alex^r McDonald in Achlean, his wyff, and whole familie; Allan McDonald in Innervuick, his whole family (except his wyffe); Archibald M^{c}conachie v^c Phadrick in Innervuick, but not his wyff nor family.

'The excomunicat are, both for Incest and Defection to Poperie, Johne Grant in Duldregin, and Katherin Fraser his wyff, and part of his family. This to be off truth I verify under my hand att Invernes, March 5, '79. 'Mr. R. Monro.'

'A list of such persons as hawe bein bred Protestants w^{t}in the Paroch off Kiltarlitie, and hawe made defection to popery, viz., Georg Monro in Commer, John McRorie v^c ean v^c Don^d v^c eachin, Margrat Monro his wyffe, there; Donald M^{c}allister v^{c}tijre and

Mary nein Thomas More his wyff, there; Ferq^r M^c W^m v^c ean, and Beatrix nein tyr his wyff, and John his son, there; Roderick McAlister v^c Rorie and Elspet nein Chlerich his wyffe, there; Donnean Due McHutcheon v^c ean Liea, there; William more M^{c}ean v^c William there; Hutcheon M^{c}ean Miller in Guisachan; Alex^r McHutcheon, Smith there; Donald McIver in Erchless; Alex^r Fraser of Kinneras; Simon Fraser in Kulmaskiak.

'These two followeing are excommunicat, viz., Roderick McIver in Maald, William McHucheon v^c William Roy in Commer. This to be of trueth is verified under my hand att Invernes, the 5 day of March 1679. *Sic sub.* 'HUGH FRASER.'

That day there being no other Papists in any Paroch w^{t}in this Presbytrie as each Minister had declared, ye Moderator enclosed the former lists, subscryved by each Min^r concerned, in a letter directed to the Lord Bishope.

[The above were the only lists given in.]

Att Invernes, April 2, 1679.

That day ye Moderator produced a letter sent him from ye Lord Bishope, approveing the formall procedour of the Presbytrie in giveing upp the list of ilk Papists w^{t}in y^r respective congrega^{o}ns.

Att Invernes, May 14, '79.

Alex^r Denoone, Burges off Invernes, being sumonded to this dyett for cohabiting w^t Isobell Robertson, alleadged to be marryed be a priest, being cited, not compeiring, to be sumonded pro 3°.

That day the Moderator presented the Synodicall Refers, q^{ch} being read wer recorded as followeth.

1st, That ye Collections for the Montrose Merchants be given to the severall Moderators and to be keeped by them untill further order.

2dly, To enquyre for Isobell Ferqhar, fugitive from Rothes, for adultery; for Alex^r Sympson and Margaret Reuch, adulterers in Belly; For Francis Wallace, adulterer in Raffort; Jhon Forbes, adulterer in Moy; Janett Gaderer in Kinneder for murdering her owne child; for Alex^r Besack and Janet Fraser, adulterers in Invernes.

3dly, Collection to be made for Glasgow, and the contribution for Christian Fullertowne, to be sent be the severall Moderators to Mr. James Horne or Mr. Hugh Ros for her use.

4^{ly}, That adulterers not sentenced w^t death by the civill Magistrat to be censured by the Church for the scandall, and to pay ther penalties according to Law.

5^{ly}, To enquyre for John Cuming, fugitive from Edenkeily, for suspected adultery.

6^{thy}, To pay the Bursar money.

7^{ly}, To cause sumond Mr. Jhon Monro, session Clerk of Kiltarlatie, Alex^r Fraser of Kinneras, and Hugh Fraser of Belladrum, and Mr. Hugh Fraser, Minister of Kiltarlatie, to compeir before the Lo. Bishop and Bretheren the 30 of Apryle 1679.

The Bretheren wer appoynted be the Moderator to notice the Refers of the Synod as every one was concerned.

That day the Moderator presented a letter sent him be the Bishope of Murray bearing 1. that y^r is ane order of Councill determining that all women of note qho goe to conventicles shall be fyned, and tho ther husbands pay ther fyne for them zett iff they outlive ther husbands the heir shall mak them repay it out of their joyntures: this to be modestly and prudently intimat to such women to prevent ther future danger. 2dly, That it is requyred be his Majesty his councill y^t all schoolmasters, chapplaines, and Paedagoiges shall appear before the Lo. Bishop, and tak the oath of alleadgeance, and declare ther acknowledgement and submission to the present government of Church and State as it is now established by Law, and if any shall refuse ther are to be proceided against, and also the gentlemen qho retaine them will be fyned at the councill. This ordinance is imparted to every Minister *apud acta* w^{t}in the Presbytrie, that betuext this and the first of June next each Schoolmaster, chaplaine, and paedagouge w^{t}in ther respective paroches may compeir before the Lo. Bishop and tak the s^d oath, That qho take it may report his certificat to us to be recorded in our Register, and compareing them w^t those y^t refuse wee may send the list of such recusants to the Lo. Bishope to be sent to the Councill. 3dly, The Bishop showes that y^r is a visita^{o}n of the Church of Alderne appoynted to be on the last Wednesday of Jun, y^rfore all ye Ministers of our Presbytrie are appoynted to compeire ther y^t day, together w^t ther Schoolm^rs, chaplaines, and paedagouges, because it will be easier for them to come there y^n goe to Spynie.

Att Invernes, July 23, 1676.

That day the Minister of Inverness declared that thay had conferred with Alex^r Denoone, and y^t hee had promised to giwe satisfactione to the discipline, and to produce under the hands of two witnesses to the presbytrie the next day when and where hee had bein married be Priest Dunbar.

Alex^r Besack and Janet Fraser, fugitives from Invernes, reported to be att Tung in Strathnaver, the Ministers of Invernes are ordained to wrytt to the Minister of the fors^d place to remitt them back againe, q^ch they promised to doe *quam primum.*

The ordinance concerneing Schoolm^rs, chaplaines, and Paedagouges is renewed *de novo,* and enjoyned to repair to the Bishope, and report ther testimony back to the Presbyterie.

Att Invernes, Augt. 27, 1679.

That day the Minister of Abertarff declared y^t Dowgall McConachie v^c conill, fornicator in Glenmoriston, did supplicat the Session ye last Sabboth to be receiwed before them, and offered to engadge himselff by cautionrie to satisfy the discipline of the Church, entreating to forbeare the proces before the Presbytrie, q^ch for advyce is referred to the Presbytrie. It is therefore judged expedient, because of the distance of ye place, and rudenes of ye people, to yeild to his humble demand, and ye Minister exhorted in his owne pastorall prudence to use all lenity and meikness to gain such.

That day the Minister of Dorres reported y^t Alex^r Bailzie in Borlum compeired before the Session of Dorres ye last Lo. Day, and did humbly supplicat ye Session to receive him to his repentance, and to forbeare processing of him before the Presbytrie, obleidgeing himselff w^t all submission to giwe due obedience in all poynts, q^ch demand the Minister and Session wer not frie to grant w^tout consulting with the Presbytrie yranent. The Presbytrie will not yeild to any such practice,

Therfore enjoyned the Minister to cause sumond once yett to the next dyett, w^t certification if hee obey not that the proces shall goe on in his contrar.

At Invernes, 1 *Oct.* 1679.

The Moderator haveing also enquyred iff the Bretheren in ther respective Paroches have celebrat the Sacrament of the Lords Supper since the last Synod, it is found y^t most of the Bretheren hawe not given it, and ther reason was y^t the frequent charges y^t ther people gott to be in armes against the M^{c}donalds obstructed ther friedom to that great work.

The s^d day, before the meitting closed, the Moderator thoght fitt to declare y^t Hugh Fraser of Belladrum, Alex^r Fraser of Kinneras, Mr. Hugh Fraser, Minister of Kiltarlatie, and Mr. Jhon Monro, Schoolmaster at Kiltarlatie, wer by the Bishop, his last missive to him, desyred to be sumonded to meitt him and his assessors at Alderne, att a visita°n, being the 25 of June 1679, and since that meitting did not hold, therefore did forbear any further summonding of y^m till further orders, q^{ch} is not given out as yett.

At Elgine, October 14, 1679.

[Among the Synodical refers read is, 'that the collection for the Glasgow people be given to the severall Moderators to be kept till furder order.']

At Invernesse, 3 *March* 1680.

That day, the name of God being called upon, Mr. Alex^r Cumming, Preacher of the Gospell, hade his popular sermon, text 1 Pet. 5. 8, *cum intuitu* to the Charges of Moy and Dalarossie, to q^{ch} he is presented by the Bp. of Murray, and the Moderator declared that he had prescribed the s^d Mr. Alex^r this task by order of the late Bp. of Murray, now of Galloway, and Calen,[1] by ye Mercie of God now Bp. of Murray, both whose letters he this day presented.

The young man being removed his labours were approven.

The s^d Mr. Alex^r Cuming is appoynted to have a comon

---

[1] *Calen*—Gaelic for Colin.

head yᵉ next dyet *de gratia universali*, and to have his theses in readines to be distributed yᵉ next day.

That day Mr. James Smith, Minister at Dorres, is ordered to repair to the Church of Moy, and yʳ to serve Mr. Alexʳ Cuming his edict, in order to his entrie to the sᵈ charge, and to giwe a full report of his diligence next meeting day.

[John Roy Fraser in Wardlaw, and Angus McAllan in Dalarossie, to be proceeded against for deserting their wives.]

At Invernesse, Aprill 7, 1680.

That day Mr. James Smith, Minʳ at Dorres, reported zᵗ, conform to zᵉ former ordinance, he hade gone to the Church of Moy in Stratherne, and preachd to yᵉ people yʳ, being on ane Lords day, March 14 last bypast, haveing caused read ane edict at yᵉ most patent kirk doore imediately befor entring publick worship, and after the close of divine service he declared publickly that the moderator and remanent breyren of the exercise of Invernes hade sent him there to shew them that Mr. Alexʳ Cuming, Student in divinitie, and preacher wᵗin the p'sbitrie of Cromdale, was presented to the Churches of Moy and Dallarassie, and hade past his tryalls to that effect befor the presbetrie of Invernes, and was approven in all the steps therof, as the edict read in the forenoone and now indorsed on the Kirk door did proport. Therfor charged yᵉ parishoners, or at least some Comissioners from yᵐ, to compeir befor yᵉ prbetrie qᶜʰ is to hold at Invernes the 12 day of May next, to declaire their willingnesse to accept or reject yᵉ sᵈ Mr. Alexʳ Cuming to be their future Minister.

That day Angus McAllan McIntoshe, in the parochin of Moy, compeired judicially for himselffe and as Comissioner from the rest of the parishoners of the two paroches of Moy and dallarassie, declareing that they were all well pleased wᵗ Mr. Alexʳ Cuming, and were content, and unanimously consented to have him to be their future minister; whereupon the Modʳ, wᵗ consent of the Bretheren, desired the Clerk to draw up a sufficient testimonie to yᵉ sᵈ Mr. Alexʳ of approbation to be given to our ordinarie the Bp. of Murray, along wᵗ the former adict, yᵗ he may receive colaᶜⁿ, institution, and imposition of hands from him, qᶜʰ testimonie was granted conforme, and subᵗ be the Modʳ and clerk.

At Invernesse, Julij 1680.

That day Mr. James Fraser, Moderator, presented a letter sent him from the Lord Bp̄ of Murray, injoining him to repair to Moy in Stratherne, and y^r to admitt Mr. Alex^r Cuming to be their future Minister and incumbent at ye united kirks of Moy and Dallarossie, which conforme upon the 23^d of May last, being ye Sabath day, haveing a frequent convention of the parishoners, Heretors, and elders pn̄t *nemine contradicente*, performing all the ceremonies requisite at such a solemne actione.

At Invernesse, August 4, 1680.

[All present 'except Mr. Hugh ffraser, minister at Croy, being at Aberdene, and Mr. Hugh ffraser, Minister at Kiltarlitie, who is in Inchgald.'[1]]

That day James Fraser in Duntelchake gave in a supplicatione and grievous complaint bearing y^t Duncan Shaw in Knocknikeall had reported in severall places and severall companies y^t he had struck his own wife w^t a joint stoole, wch was the occasion of her death, and at oy^r times y^t he had murthered and killed his wife, for q^{ch} he humbly pleads for a redresse. The s^d Duncan being sumoned to this dyet, citted, not compeiring, is to be sumond to ye next dyet pro 2do.

At Invernesse, Septr. 1, 1680.

That day Alex^r Rose, presbetrie officer, gave in ane execu°ne bearing that conforme to the former ordinance he hade sumoned Duncan Shaw in Knocknikeall, being cited, compeired for him Angus McBain, Messenger, and Jo^n M^{c}bain No^r publick, and produced ane advocation in the s^d Duncan Shaw his favours, as also the s^d Angus did take instrument in the s^d John M^{c}bain No^r publick his hand, where he hade produced ye s^d advocation judicially, and delivered a double y^{r}of in the Moderator his hand, the affairé is continued and referred to the Synod for advice.

That day Janet McIntoshe in Moy compeired befor the presbetrie and gave in a grevous complaint against Duncan M^{c}ean her husband, showeing that he hade violently and

---

[1] Inchgald—*Innsigall*, the Islands of the Strangers, applied to the Hebrides while in the possession of the Norse.

wickedly put her away from her house and his fellowship in the moneth of March last, and the Ministers, friends, and christiane neighbours hade dealt most seriously w^t him to accept of his wife into his fellowship again, yet could never prevaile with, nor perswade him to that effect, and he being formerly sumoned to compeire befor the p'sbitrie gave in some reasons why he would not accept of his maried wife, and being most convinceingly dealt w^t by the Mod^r and remanent breyren of ye exercise *in judicio*, and apart also, declared that he could give no reason except that he could not love her. This not satisfying the presbetrie he was exhorted to adhere under the pain of being processed, yet, notwithstanding all the paines taken upon him, continues obstinate and hard hearted, and will do no kynde of dutie to his said wife; y^{r}for Mr. Alex^r Cuming, Minister of the s^d parochin, is appointed to charge him three severall lords dayes from the pulpit imediately after the close of divine worship to adhere to his wife, and to give report y^{r}of to the next dyet, q^{ch} is to hold at Invernesse Septr. 29.

At Invernesse, Septr. 29, 1680.

That day Mr. Alex^r Cuming, Minister at Moy, reported y^t conforme to the former ordinance he hade given the first publick charge to duncan M^{c}ean to adhere to his wife. The s^d Duncan, after humble addresse and application to his Minister, promiseing obedience, is referred by the s^d Minister w^t consent of the Session to this dyet, citted, compeiring, being seriously spoken to by ye Moderator and remanent breyren, and the hazard and great danger that he would incurre in his person and portion by this his malicious and wilful desertion of his fors^d spouse, and the strictnes of the civill Law and ecclesiastick discipline against such, even to ye rigour of excomunication, he is thoroughly convinced, and, under a deep sense of his former obstinacie, is brought to a knowledge and confession of his sin, and hoped y^t God would incline his heart to adhere to his spouse, and supplicated a moneth's continuation, and suspending any process against him, q^{ch} the Presbetrie granted, and desired his Minister to be frequent and serious w^t him.

That day severall breyren of the presbetrie regrated y^t how soone they did pursue their delinquents many of them would rune to the preists and by y^m be maried or haue their children baptised, by this meanes discipline is slighted and contemned, and these turne cy^r fugitive or obstinate. Also it was the grall regrate and greivance of the breyren y^t swearing, drinking, and sabboth breaking was current and usuall to their great greife. Therfor desires the advise of the Synode how to goe to work for suppresseing the fors^d insolencies and greivous sinnes.

That day the Moderator enquyred of all ye breyren if the twentie ninth day of May, ye anniversarie solemne day of thanksgiving for y^r kings restoration, was keept; answered affirmative. 2. He enquired if the Synodicall referres were observed conforme to the former ordinance in their due methode and maner by all the breyren. Answered affirmative.

That day the Moderator enquired if the holy Eucharist or Sacrament of the Lords Supper was celebrate by each broy^r w^tin his respective charge, at least once a year. Some were found who hade given it, but ye remisseness and neglect of oy^rs is sadly rerated.

At Invernesse, October 27, 1680.

[Among the Synodical Refers read at this meeting were the following: 'That ye Schoolm^rs and chaplains repair to the Lord Bp. to be licenciat by him, oy^rwayes be suspended;'
'That the preists names be sent into ye Lord Bp. to be sent by him to the Councell.'

'To pay the Burses of divinity.'

'To haue in readines the contribution for the bridge of Invernes against the Synod.'

'To intimate and collect ye contributione for the harbor of Portsoy conform to ye act of Councell granted to that effect.'

'That every minister of ye Presbetrie give a Rex dollar to Mr. Robert Monro for to officiate as Clerk and whoever refuses to give this to him are ordained to officiat as clerk y^mselves.'

'To give the sacrament of ye Lords Supper once every year, oy^rwise the Minister to be suspended.']

That day compeired doncan McEan vic Conchy in ye parochin of Moy, who, alleadging some oy^r reasones of non-adhereance w^t his wife Isobell M^cquine, not insert here formerly, they and y̅ᵉ examinaᵒⁿ of yᵐ referred to his own session, and the Minister to give ane account to the presbetrie how soon the same is done.

At Invernesse, November 24, 1680.

Mr. Andrew Fraser (Student in divinity) delivered his comon head *de perseverantia sanctorum*. Approven.

The sᵈ day all our referres and ordinary discipline are supersided because our Bishop is in town (and present at yᵉ meitting) haveing come hither to compose the difference that was betwixt the Frasers and Mackintoshes, and some of our Ministers being concerned as assessors wᵗ him in yᵗ affair, were necessitate to waite upon him.

At Invernesse, December 22, 1680.

That day the Ministers of Invernesse reported that John McAndrew vain Invernesse did by oath in the face of the Congregaᵒn purge himselfe from suspected adultery wᵗ Katharein nin Donald vic Cay.

At Invernesse, January 12, 1681.

The referre concerning Duncan Mᶜean and his alledgeance agˢᵗ his wife referred as yet to the session of Dallarosie for furyʳ tryall, and yᵉ Minister to make report to yᵉ next dyet.

At Invernesse, April 6, 1681.

The referre concerneing Doncan Mᶜean and his wife continues as yet till she be cleared of the alleadged scandall of adulterie raised against her by Dugall Mᶜdugall in yᵉ paroche of Dallarosie.

That day the Modʳ inquired if all the Breyren hade carefully observed the synodicall referres, intimated and recorded the same in their own registers; answered affirmative.

The 3d Synodicall referre it is reported yᵗ preist O'Neil, resided in the Castle of Invernes from yᵉ 25 of Decʳ till Easter last, and preist Monro, resides still in Strathglasse, and preist Francis Mᶜdonald in Glengerey, Father Hugh Orein, anoyʳ preist, residing in the Chissolmes Country under the notion of a phisician—yᵉ account of all qᶜʰ is referred to yᵉ Bp. and Synod.

The 11th Referre concerneing ye sacrament of ye Lords supper, it is found y^t ye Ministers of Invernes, Daviot, and Wardlaw haue celebrated the same about and after Easter, but ye not giveing it at all, or but verie seldome, is verie much to be regrated, and consequently ye fors^d act be yearly renewed.

Att Daviot, May 10, 1681.

The s^d day conveened the Moderator, Mr. James Fraser, and with him Maister Hugh Fraser, Minister at Croy, and Mr. Alex^r Cuming, Minister at Moy, w^t Mr. Michell Fraser, Incumbent, and conform to the former appointment proceeded to the appretiation of the s^d Mans, and having mett w^t such Heretours as wer there present, we all went to the parish Church of Daviot, q^r after Invocation of ye Lords name, the Moderator enquired the Minister of the place if he had given timous intimation and advertisement to the parishoners of the s^d meeting, answered affirmative; as also the Heretors, elders, and Deacons present confirmed the same; the Moderator enquired further if he had brought w^t him Massones, Carpenters, Smiths, glaziers, and oy^r workmen usually called for apretiation of Manses, answered affirmatively; the which workmen being all present were deeply sworne one by one with uplifted hands, to deale uprightlie and honestly in ye s^d appretiation according to their skill and knowledge. All this being done, with consent of the Heretors present, *nemine contradicente*, the Moderator tooke instrument in Hector Fraser, Notar publicks, hand, and ye s^d workmen were immediately thereafter directed to the s^d Mans, w^t the s^d Notar as Clerk, to appretiat the samen; and seeing the day was much spent we have superceeded the designation of the Gleab of Daviot till a new occasion. The next meeting to hold at Invernes June 8. The meeting closed w^t prayer.

At Invernes, June 8, 1681.

The said day the Moderator presented the referrs of the Synod of Murray, holden at Invernes Aprile 19, and being read Judicially were all recorded as followeth :

1. That such as haue not given in their contribution for the Montrose Marchants at their first presbiteriall meeting may

collect ye same and send it Allex^r Falconer the Bishops Sone q^m prim^m.

2. The contribution for Portsoy harbor collected to ye next Synod.

3. That such as haue not given the Sacrament of the Lords Supper the last halfe yeare goe about the samen or the next Synod under the Certificat contained in the last Act.

4. That no widow or widower receave the benefit of mariage unless they have confirmed the testament of the defunct, or secured the doing of the same as accords of Law.

5. That Ministers absent from prin^{ll} meetings without excuse in write, and these found relevant, are to be censured.

10. That the Bursar of divinity be payed *quam primum*.

Att Invernes, 13 *July* 1681.

David McKglashen, Saboth braker in the parochin of Croy, being disobedient to the disciplin y^r, being summoned to ye dyet, Cited, compearing, denyed the fact, yet the s^d scandall being proven legally against him, is appointed to satisfie ye Church disciplin there *sub periculo*.

The last solemn fast appointed to be keept by publick authoritie for the reasons in the proclamation insert was punctually keept by all the Brethren July 6, 1681.

Att Invernes, Septr. 21, 1681.

Janet Nindonald, an confest adulteress w^t James fraser in Kiltarlity, stands to her former confession, and is going on in the profession of her repentance. The s^d James standing to his former deniall, both of them referred to this dyet, ye s^d Janet being cited, compeareing, declared seriously as before. The s^d James fraser cited, compeared, being strictly examined, both confronted, circumstances urged, stands most obduredly and obstinatly to his deniall as before. They are dismist. The Minister enjoined to take great paines on y^m, and if he continues obstinat his oath to be taken publickly before the congregation with one hand upon the child's head, and the other hand upon the Bible, which is the usuall practice in such cases.[1]

---

[1] The result of this order was that Fraser confessed being the father of the child, as reported to the Presbytery on 19th April 1682.

[Reported that the only Ministers that dispensed the Lords Supper in terms of last Synodical refers, were those of Croy, Inverness, Daviot, Moy. The remissness of the others is 'mater of regreet.']

At Inverness, Novr. 9. 1682.

The s^d day the Moderator presented the Synodicall refers, and being read were recorded in our Register as followes :—

1. The whole Bretheren are to give up a list of the Papists and oy^r separatists in their respective Parishes to the Bp this October [*i.e.* October 1682, the Synod having met on the 12th of that month].

2. To mind the Acts of Councell for the severall contributiones.

At Inverness, March 22, 1682.

The said day Mr. Donald Forbes presented a Letter subscribed by all the Heretores and elders of Kiltarlity requireing earnestlie that the Presbrie would send them a Minister to preach and keep Session w^t them, seing they wanted Sermon since 1st of January last, by the recusance of their own Paster. The prebrie haue granted y^r request and appoints the Moderator [Rev. Jas. Fraser, Wardlaw] to be w^t them the Lords day come eight dayes, if Mr. James Grant keep not w^t them next Saboth as he promised.

At Invernesse, Aprile 19, 1682.

That day the Moderator declared that he had preacht att Kiltarlitie conform to the former ordinance, and keept session y^r, where the present desolation of the said parish under their vacancy is very much regrated, sin and ignorance abounding, popery increasing in the upper parish more than ever by the incessant paines of the traffiquing priests, and the resetting of them among some of the Gentrie there who do too much encurrage them.

The Moderator desyred the Bretheren to attend the Bishop and Synod ensueing, which is to hold at Elgin 25 instant, and to bring w^t them their severall proportiones of the divinitie Bursers money for this halfe year.

At Elgin, Aprile 25, 1682.

Conveened the Bretheren of the Exercise of Invernes, such as were p̃nt at the Sinod and resolveing to appoint their next meeting day. The Moderator declared that the Bishop was resolved to enter his visitations in our Prebr̃ie next month, and the first visitation to hold at Croy, May 15. Therefore desired all the Brethren to be present, time and place fors^d, to attend the Bishop and meeteing.

At Croy, May 15, 1682.

Conveened the Lo. Bishop, w^t Mr. Alex^r Tod and Master Berald Innes, out of the pr̃by of Elgin, Mr. Donald M^{c}kpherson Moderator of the Pr̃by of Forres, and Mr. William Falconer, Mr. Hector McKenzie, Moderator of the Presbitry of Abernethy, w^t the Bretheren of the Exercise at Inverness, and after Invocation of the Lords Name, Mr. Michel Fraser, Minister of Daviot, preacht, Text John 17. 18, 19.

After Sermon the Lo. Bishop and Bretheren haveing conveened for visitation of the said Church, The names of the Elders of the said Parochin was delivered to the Clerk as followes :

Elders.—Alex^r Ross of Clava, younger ; John Dallas of Cantra, Hugh Fraser of Daltullich, Alex^r Ross of Holme [Holme-Rose], Robert Shaw of Wester Leyes, John Baly of Leyes Cruii, John McKillvray of Midleyes, Lewes Tulloch in Cantra.

Deacons.—Kenneth McKintoshie, Deacon ; Donald McKintoshie, William Ross, older ; William Ross, younger ; John Dow Ross, John McKpherson, Alex^r McKlean, William McKay.

The Session Booke of Croy was delivered to Mr Michael Fraser, Min^r of Devy,[1] to be revised—was found formall.

The Elders being solemnly posed w^t uplifted hands to declare truth wherein they should be enquired anent the Minister, if he was diligent in catechising, exemplar in conversation, preacht to their edification, visiting the sick, administring the Sackrament, and impartiall in the exercise of disciplin, and other Ministeriall duties ; in all these he received approbation,

---

[1] Devy (Jevy), the Gaelic pronunciation of Daviot.

and good estimation, from all the Elders and Deacons, being severally inquired.

The Minister being inquired if he had satisfaction and concurrence of the Elders, declared affirmatively.

The Lo. Bishop inquired if they had a Schoolm^r in the Parochin for educating children and readeing the holy Scriptur. The Min^r replied y^t they had no fixed sallary for one, it was therefor strongly recommended to take speedy comenceing for settling one and providing mantinance conform to ye Act of Parl.

It was inquired if the officer, Donald Davison, was dutifull in his office, sober and christian in his conversation, got approbation from all both Minister and Elders.

The Minister was inquired if there were any Mortification, he replyed there were none. And if he had Tables, Cloaths, and Cups for celebration of the Lords Supper; he replied y^r was a Communion Table; other necessaries were borrowed.

The Fabrick of the Church being considered, and some defect ruin found in thack and windowes, was recommended to the Minister and Elders to looke carefully to its reparation.

It was also recommended to ye Minister and Elders to look to the improvement of the Common Good, and q^n delinquents were obstinat and refractory in paying penalties to have immediat recourse to the Authority of the Commissary.

The Minister complained of some abuse and indignities he and his wife had suffered of Donald McKandrew vain in Croy, saying that he had wrot a testament falsly, and was bribed to that effect. The s^d Donald being conveened before the Commissary, and the s^d calumny judiciall proven against him, was fined, and recommended to the Session of Croy back, to satisfy in sacco, and proveing obstinat, is cited and compeareing, is injoined be the Lo. Bishop to satisfy the disciplin conform to ye ordinance, also to be procest befor the Presby.

The meeting closed wth prayer.

At Daviot, May 16, 1682.

The Lo. Bishop and Bretherin haveing conveened for visitation of the s^d Church, the name of God being invocated, Mr. Hugh fraser, Min^r at Croy preacht. Text, Collos 2. ult.

The session booke was called for, and not being filled up, it was ordained, under pain of censer, to be written and closed against the next ensueing Synod at Elgin October 11.

The list of the Elders and Deacons of the United Parochins off Daviot and Dunlechety are as followes:—

Lachlin McKintosh of Obcrarder, Ferq^r McKillvray of Dounmaglash, Alex^r McKintoshie of Farr, Eun McKpherson of Fluchity, Robert Shaw of Tordarroch, John McKintosh in Elrig, Angus McKphail in Inverarny, William McKilvray in Lergs, Donald M^{c}kbean of Falzie, elder and younger, Doncan M^{c}kphail, Lachlin M^{c}kherson Easter urchol, William Cumming, James McKintoshie, Lachlan McKivirrich, John McKbean in Lergs.

Deacons.—Alex^r McKay, Finlay McKillimichell, Doncan McKbean in Gask, John McKilmichel, Doncan McKjames, William McKgeorge.

The Elders present were solemnly required w^t uplifted hands to answer in truth q^{r}in they were to be inquired concerning their Minister behaviour personall or pastorall, if he preached soundly and plainly to their edification, catechised frequently, administered the sacrement of ye Lo. Supper, visited the sick, and behaved as a faithfull Min^r of ye Gospell, in all points of his duty; being severally inquired they gave him a good testimony, and declared that they had nothing to say against him but his frequent absence and avocation about his affaires, q^r the Lo. Bishop admonished him of seriously and enjoined him to amend and help.

The Minister being inquired if the Elders did encurrage him by their concurrance and assistance in disciplin, he declared they did.

In regard the Church was found ruinous, wanting thack in severall places, the windowes not glassed, the Lo. Bishop seriously recommended to their care to have this helped with all convenient speed.

The Bishop inquired if they had necessaries for the celebra^{o}n of the Lords Supper, the Minister replied that they had not o^t [aught] a long time before nor since his entry: they are seriously exhorted to provid such necessaries as are meet for y^t sacred action w^t all convenient speed.

It was inquired if there was a Schoolm^r in the Parochin, ye Minister answered y^t they could not nor had any becaus there was no incurragement for one nor no mediat centricall place q^r they could fix a schoole to the satisfaction of all concerned.

The Bishop inquired if they keept a Register of Baptisms and mariage, the Minister answered he did.

It was inquired if the officers of the two Churches of Daviot and Dunlechity caried soberly and christianly as they ought, and faithfull in their duty, they haue good testimony from ye Minister and Elders of both parishes.

The meeting clos^d w^t prayer.

At Kirkhill, May 17, 1682.

The Lo. Bishop and remanent conveened for visitation of the said Church, and after invocation of the Lords name, Master Gilbert Marshall, Min^r at Invernes, preacht, Text 2 Cor. 15. 20.

The session booke being called for, it was delivered to Master Gilbert Marshall to revise, who found it a compleit Register and formall, being filled up to this same very day; also the register of Baptism and Mariage, with the bill-booke of Mortality of ye said Parochin since the present incumbant's entry.[1]

The List of the Elders and Deacons of the Parochin of Wardlaw were delivered to the Clerk as followes :—

Elders.—Thomas Fraser of Strachin, Thomas Fraser of Beufort, Hugh Fraser of Struy, Hugh Fraser of Belladrum, elder, Hugh Fraser of Belladrum, younger, Alex^r Fraser, Barron of Moniack, James Fraser, younger thereof, James Fraser of Achnigarn, John Fraser in Inshbary, Master Simon Fraser of Finask, James Fraser of Dunballach.

Deacons.—John Wright in Englishtoun, Collector; Finlay McKeanroy there, John McKsoirle in Kirketowne, Donald

---

[1] 'The Bill of Mortality for the Parish of Wardlaw' (Kirkhill) was, in 1884, discovered in a private house in the parish, and is now in the General Register House, Edinburgh. It extends from 1663 to 1709, and contains, not only entries of deaths in the parish and neighbourhood, but also memoranda of other events which the learned author of the 'Wardlaw MS.' found of interest during his long incumbency of the parish.

McKsoirle in Lemineeh, Finlay M'Koniloig, in Inshbary, Andrew Peery in Rindony, Donald McKphail in Holme, John McKonildonich there, Thomas McKean vickonil in Craggag, James McKvarran in Drumcharduy, John Clerke there, William Barron in Drumreach, Andrew McKonilvickandrew in Moniak, James Spense in Achnigarn, John fraser in Kingilly, Thomas McKean vore in Grome, Finlay McKonil vick robby there, John fraser in fingask, Alex^r Smith in Donaldstoun, Donald McKthomas there, Alex^r McKandrew oig in Lovat, Alex^r McKonil vick robby there.

The Lord Bishop required these Elders and Deacons w^t uplifted hands to answer upon oath wherein they were to be enquired anent their Min^r Life and Conversation, personall and pastorall, his doctrin, visitation of the sick, catechising, administration of the sacrament every yeare, and what else concerned his sacred office; they all gave him an ample testimony and approbation being severally enquired.

The Minister being called in was enquired if he had all necessary concurrance and assistance from the Elders and Gentlemen in the exercise of disciplin, declared that he had as great incurragement from one and all of them jointly as a Minister could require in all things, and their orderly, sober, examplar life and conversa^{o}n q^h adorned all.

The Lord Bishop inquired if they had a schoole, and a fixed sallary for a Schoolmaster. The Minister replied y^t there was a chalder of victuall stated for him, and Decreet thereupon, w^t 20 libs out of our box, and also the Baptism and Mariage money, and a p^t [present] schoolemaster serving who besides his attendance of the Schoole, was precentor and clerk, and read the Scriptures publickly every Lords Day in the Irish betuixt the second and third bell.

The Schoolm^r, Mr. Thomas Fraser, being removed, the Minister was inquired if he was carefull and dilligent in his charge, sober and christian in his conversation, receaved approbation and good testimony from both Minister and Elders in q^t concerned his office.

The Officer, Donald McKandrew, being removed, was found faithfull and honest in his trust, and got the approbation of Min^r and Elders.

The Lord Bishop inquired the Minister if he had necessaries for the celebration of the sacrament of the Lo. Sup., replied that he had a very good large table, two good towells, a Basin also, but y^t he borrowed silver cups yearely.

The fabrick of the Church was found compleit in thack, glass windowes, Lofts, dasks, church bible, pulpit cloath, and an excellent Bell and bellhouse. The Bishop gaue them ample commenda°n and incurragement, exhorting them to persist in well doing, Minister and Elders mutually assisting and strengthening each oy^r to ye end.

The Meeting closed w^t prayer.

At Petty, May 19, 1682.

The Lo. Bishop and Remanent Bretheren conveened for visita°n of the s^d Church, where after invocation of the Lord's name, Mr. James Fraser, Minister at Wardlaw, preacht. Text, 1 Corinth. 4. 1.

The Session booke being called for was recommended to Mr. Hugh Fraser, Parson of Croy, to be revised, and found formall, is approved.

The List of the Elders aud Deacons of the Parochin of Petty, being citted, was delivered to the Clerk as follows :—

Elders.—Donald McKqueen of Corribroch, John Cuthbert of Altirlies, David Denune, Chamberlan ; Duncan McKqueen, Rachkmore ; Hugh Dallas of Brachly, Hector McKintosh in Breachly, John Denune in Connadge, Doncan Cuthbert in Altirlie, Hugh Ross in Altirly, James Lieth in Mid Coule.

Deacons.—Malcolm McKintosh in Conadge, Donald McKlean in balnichric, John McKay in Torcingnawn, William fraser in Fermott, Lachlin McKrory in Altirly, Martin McKintoshie in Fleemintoun, John McKintosh in Dallichield.

The said Elders and Deacons being required w^t uplifted hands and solemn oath to declare truth wherein they should be inquired anent their Ministers conversation, personall or pastorall : they all gaue him good name and approbation ; onely they did regreit that he now becomming so weak and infirm through ald age, and could not attend the catechising, or goe at all to visit the sick, that [they] had need of a helper for the better advancing the glory of God and the interest of the Gospell, and good of soules in the place.

The Minister being enquired if the Elders were assisting and concurring w^t him in the exercise of Disciplin, he declared affirmatively, that they carried to his mind. Y^e Bishop did seriously exhort them to be examplar in life and conversation to oy^{rs}, and see God honoured and his worship promoved.

The Bishop inquired whether they had a schoole and a fixt Schoolem^r, they replied that they had, and his incurragement suteable; and a flourishing schoole. The Schoolm^r, Mr. George McKqueen, being removed, the Min^r and Elders being inquired if he caried dilligently in his charge and christianly in his life, they declared he did, and was a great help to their Minister.

The Minister was inquired if he had all necessaries requisit for the Celebration of ye sacrament of the Lo. Supper, declared that he had a Table onely, other things he borrowed.

The officer being removed, the Bishop inquired anent his life and conversation, and dilligence in his office, he is commended of all and approven.

The Fabrick of the Church is compleit and plenishit dayly with Lofts and dasks and other things necessary.

The Lord Bishop did seriously recommend to ye Minister that in regard of his great infirmity through old age, he was not able to catechise or visit the sick, y^t he would therefore have his serious thoughts of providing a sufficient well qualified man for assisting him in the work of the Ministery, and that he would concurr w^t him; this being so absolutely necessary was recommended to the Breyren of the Exercise of Inverness to be active in it with convenient speed.

The Meeting closed w^t prayer.

At Invernes, July 5, 1682.

That day, after Invocation of the Lords name, The Moderator presented a Letter direct to him from the Lo. Bishop recommending Mr. Thomas Fraser, preacher of the Gospell, to pass trialls before us in order to the Church of Dorris now vacant through the recusancie of Mr. James Smith,[1] late incumbent

---

[1] Smith had refused to take the Test.

there, and also enjoining y^t the said Mr. Thomas trialls should be accelerat w^t all possible speed; he had this day his exegesis *De Primatu Petri*, and delivered his theses to be disputed next day.

That day the Moderator presented the Synodicall referrs q^h being read judicially were recorded as follows:

. . . . . .

4. To mind a contribution to Mr. Robert Munro (Minister of Abertarff) in regard of his present straites and indigencies.

5. That each Minister absent from the Synod shall send in his letter of excuse twelve fs. (shillings) Scots to the Clerk of the Synod.

6. To mind the Bursar of Divinity his money.

No disciplin this day in regard of many Bretheren's absence, and our severall vacancies by not takeing of the Test.

The Bretheren to acelerat Mr. Tho. Frasers triall conforme to the Bishop's order, haue appointed the 12 instant to meet again at Invernes and the s^d Mr. Thomas to haue his popular sermon, Text, Rev. 3. 19.

The Meeting closes w^t prayer.

At Inverness, July 12, 1682.

Mr. Thomas Fraser had his popular Sermon, Text, Revel. 3. 19, and also sustained the Disputes, Questionary trialls, and Languages, *cum intuitu ad loc.*, and being removed was approven in all the steps of his trialls, and is forthwith recommended to the Bishop by our unanimous testimonie to gett collation and ordination to the Church of Dorris.

The process of William Fraser in Gusachan, John Fraser there, and other delinquents within the parochin of Kiltarlity sists in regard of the desolation and vacancie of the place.[1]

At Invernes, Sepr. 20, 1682.

That day Mr. Hugh Fraser, Minister at Kiltarlity, being recusant formerly, not haveing taken the Test, and now sitting w^t his Bretheren, haveing fulfilled the Law, and taken the s^d Test, he is earnestly exhorted to advert to that charge which

---

[1] Kiltarlity was vacant for several months through the minister having refused to take the Test. See next minute.

lay vacant and desolat this long time, and to renue the process against the severall delinquants of the s^d Parochin, and to report dilligence to the p̄rbrie again the next day.

That day Mr. Gilbert Marshall, Minister at Invernes, supplicated the Presb̄rie for supplying Mr. Alexander Clerk's place who hath been sick this while bygone. The p̄rbry considering the necessitie of supply the populus charge of Invernes, by reason of their Ministers present condition, haue ordained Mr. James Smith, Minister at Dorris, to preach at Invernes sunday eight dayes, and Mr. Hugh Fraser, Minister at Croy, the Lords day thereafter.

At Inverness, Nov. 15, 1682.

[Mr. Michael Fraser absent, 'who is not yet returned from England.']

That day the Parson of Petty sent his Letter to the Prb̄ry haveing inclosed in it an Edickt subscribed by the Bp. of Murray for apprising the Mans in Petty, and desireing that the Mod^r, w^t any oy^r Brother of the exercise, should repaire thither the next weeke upon any convenient day they thought fitt. The Mod^r, w^t Mr. Gilbert Marshall, are to be there, God willing, next Wednsday ; y^rfore ye edickt to be served to y^t day.

That day the Moderator presented a Letter direct to him from the Bp. of Murray, of the dait at Elgin Octobr. 12, 1682, anent ye settling of a stipend and stated Benefice for Mr. Alex^r Cumming, Min^r of Moy. The Mod^r delivered the said Letter to the incumbent, desiring him to draw the Heretores to a meeting in any mediat place where he and some other Bretheren might wait upon them for an amicable setlement.

The said day the Moderator presented the Senodicall referrs w^h were read and recorded as followeth :

. . . . . .

3. To give up to the Bishop the Names of Seminary Priestes and such as mary and baptise w^t them, the obstinat to be processt, and, to the end y^t Letters of intercommuning may be obtained against the excomminicat, the Bretheren at their next meeting not to faile to send to the Bishop 14 Sh. scots from every Broy^r for the expense of the s^d Letters of intercommuning.

4. That each Brother mind the Bishops advice in reference to their grave decent and ministeriall habit.

At Inverness, Feb. 14, 1683.

Janet Prot, Adulteress in Petty, going on in the profession of her repentance, as is reported to us by Mr. Alex^r Denune, Preacher of the Goepell, who is now by the Bishop's ordinance placed helper in Petty by reason of the extreame weakness and age of Mr. Alex^r Fraser, the present Incumbent. [Denune had recently been licensed by the Bishop, having completed his trials before the Presbytery on 4 October 1682.]

That day the Moderator declared that since the last meeting day he had receaved a letter express from his ordainer, the Bishop of Murray, enjoining him to repair to the Church of Dorris upon an convenient day and there to institut Mr. Thomas Fraser, Minister of Dorris, haveing formerly receaved ordination and collation from our Bishop to that charge; the which Institution and admission the s^d Moderator expeded after Divin service (and sermon had to y^t effect) in the Church of Dorris the last Lords day being 11 instant, w^t all the ceremonies requisit in such a solem act, before the Congregation without any objection or opposition made by any of the Heretors or Parishioners against the s^d Mr. Thomas his Institution, but on the contrare such Heretors and Elders as were present gave him a cordiall reception.

At Invernes, Apryle 4, 1683.

That day Master Thomas Fraser, Minister at Doris, heavily regrated to the Breyrane of the Exercise that he was extreamly discurraged and his hands weakned in the s^d charge by Mr. James Smith, his Predicessor, who yet liveing in the manse close by the Church, doeth not only himself and famiely Dishant [dishaunt] the ordinance, to the great scandall of the gospell, but also inhibits others whom he may imped from comeing to the ordinances, and also baptises children w^{t}in the s^d paroch clandistinly unknowne to the Incumbent; q^{ch} grievance is to be redressed only by the Bishop and Synod.

That day Master Alex^r Denune, preacher at Pettie, p̃nted the apriseing of the s^d Manse in Mundo to be recorded in our register at the earnest desyre of Mr. Alex^r fraser, parson of Pettie, the tenor q^{r}of is as follows :—

'At the Manse of the Kirk of Pettie ye twentieth day of November 1682 years; the q^{ch} day Master James fraser of Phoppachie, Minister of Wardlaw, Moderator of ye Presbytery of Inverness, and Master Gilbert Marshall, Minister at Inverness, two of ye ministers of the Presbytery of Inverness (w^{t}in the q^{ch} ye manse underwryten of ye s^d Kirke of Pettie belonging to Mr. Alex^r Fraser, Minister y^{r}of, is situat and built) authorised nominat and appointed be the Bp. of Murray and the s^d Presbytery of Inverness for attending and seing the s^d Kirk of Pettie to be appretiat and comprised, and haveing taken along with us honest and judicious tradesmen such as masons, wrights, carpenters, and smiths, and oy^r workmen, who being all solemnly sworne, viz. William Henrie and Andrew Ross, Massons, burgeses of Invernesse, Robert Fraser *alias* Gow, Smith in Dallyeild [Dalziel], William McGilandrice, Smith in Conadge, Andrew Munro, Wright in Culernie, and Finlay Forbes, Wright in Pettie, and the Edict emitted to the effect above wrytten being duelie and orderly intimated, published, and served to this day, as the Edict, intimation, and execution in themselves respective at more lenth bears, the s^d Andrew Munro and Finlay Forbes, wrights, haveing seen and considered the whole timber and timberworke of the hall, chamber, pantrie, kitchin, and remanent houses and roomes of the s^d Manse, and well advised y^{r}anent, they both w^t once, but [without] variance, have aprised and aprises the samen to be worth the soume of ane hundreth and twentie m̄rks, six shillings, four pennies scots money.

'Sic subscribitur

    'De mandato dictor/   ANDREI MONRO and
        FINLAY FORBES, etc.,

                'D. DENOONE, No̅ris pub.'

'The s^d William Henrie and Andrew Ross, Massons, haveing also seen and considered the whol stone work and mason worke of the s^d Manse, being weel advised y^{r}anent, they both, w^t one voice but variance or discrepance, have aprised and aprises the samen to be worth the soume of four hundreth and twentie m̄rks money fors^d, and the s^d Robert fraser *alias* Gow and W^m McGillandrice, Smiths, above named haveing seen and considered the whol iron work of the s^d manse and hadhouse y^{r}of, w^t the locks, keys, iron bands, windows, stenchels, and remanent Smith worke pertaineing y^{r}to, and being weel advised y^ranent, they both, with one advice and voice but variance, have aprised and aprises the samen to be worth the sowme of threttie mks Scots money, *sic subit^r* W^M Henderson, mason. A. R., mason,

'De mandato dictor Roberti fraser and Gulielmi McGillandrice scribere nescien ut aserv^t etc   Da. Denoone N̄or Pūb.

' And the s^d hail workmen abow-nominat haveing seen and considered the hail glasen work and windows of the s^d manse and house y^rof, and being well adwised y^ranent, they all, w^t one voice but variance, aprysed and aprises the samen to be worth five mks five shilling four pennys money fors^d, the whol sowms respective abowrytten at q^ch the s^d manse was aprysed being all calculat extending to five hundreth seventie six merks twelve shillings money fors^d. In testimony q^rof and the truth of the hail premiss thir presents are sub^t by the s^d Mr. James fraser and Mr. Gilbert Marshall, and ye s^ds hail workmen and tradesmen abownamed, and also be David Denune, Notar publick, Clk to the s^d apryseing, day, moneth, year of God and place abowrytten.

      ' D. Denoone n.p. Clk to the premiss.
     Mr. J. Fraser, Moderator.

      At Invernesse, May 23, 1683.

No report of the delinquents in Petty because it hath pleased the Lord to remove from this Life our very reverend and pious brother, Mr. Alex^r ffraser, late Min^r y^r.

      At Inernesse, Septr 26, 1683.

The s^d day the Mod^r enqrd if all the breyren hade received ye act and proclamation appointing a solemne day of thanksgiving to be kept on the 9th of Septr instant for the happy discovery of the late horrid plot[1] against his sacred Mātie, his royal highnesse, and the established government, and if they read the same the second day of September conforme to the will of the s^d act and proclamation. All the breyren answered they hade gone about the same carefully and seriously.

The s^d day the Mod^r desired the breyren of the exercise would be asisting to supply the Church of Invernesse since it hath pleased the Lord to remove his reverend dear grave colleague,

---

[1] The Rye House Plot.

Mr. Alex^r Clerk, by death, q^{ch} they all promised to doe unlesse the vacancie were speedily supplyed. That day Mr. Thomas ffraser, Min^r of Dorres, heavily regrated to the Bretheren of the Exercise that notwithstanding of the former greivance given in against Mr. James Smith, late Minister there, he continues still to weaken his hands by baptizeing children clandestinly, some of q^{ch} doe belong to persons disobedient to the discipline, dishanting all ordinances, and violently possessing the gleib and manse belonging to the s^d Mr. Thomas, q^{ch} greivance was referred to the Bishop and Synod for redresse.

The s^d day Mr. James ffraser presented the Synodicall referrs which he could not sooner purchase from the Clerk of the Synod, q^{ch} were read and insert as after followes

. . . . . .

3. That each Minister send in with ye first convenience a dayes collection to the Moderator of Forres or Elgin for Alex^r Man, a hopeful student.

4. That Mr. Alex^r Cuming, Minister at Moy, use legall diligence against his heretors for securing his stipend as he will be answerable.

At Elgine, October 17, 1683.

Conveeined the Moderator and remanent brethren of the exercise of Invernesse, such as were present at the Synod, and appointed their next meitting day to be at Invernesse Novr 7, and appointed Mr. Angus M^{c}bean, Student in divinity (being orderly presented by the Laird of Strichen to be one of the Ministers of Invernesse, and recomended by My Lord Bp. of Murray to the breyren of the exercise to passe his tryalls in order therto) to have the exercise and addition, text, 1 Thes. 1. 8.

At Invernesse, November 7, 1683.

That day, after invocation of the lord's name, conforme to the former ordinance, Mr. Angus M^{c}bean delivered his exercise and addition, text, 1 Thes. 1. 8. as a part of his tryalls in order to his entrie to the ministrie at Invernesse, and being removed was approven, and is appointed to haue his comon head the next meitting day, *de concursu prejvio*, and to defend ye theses y^{r}on, q^{ch} theses he is to send tymously to the breyren.

At Invernesse, Nov^r*. 28, 1683.*

That day after invocation of the name of God Mr. Angus M^{c}bean delivered his comon head *de concursu prejvio* and y^{r}after defended the theses, being removed was fully approven, and these being the tryalls only appointed him by My Lord Bp., considering the great necessitie of his speedie admission to the vacancie at Invernesse, Therfor the Brethren of the exercise gaue the s^d Mr. Angus a full and ample recomandation to the Bp. of Murray that he might receive his Edict, be ordained, and his admission accelerat to the s^d place.

At Invernesse, December 19, 1683.

This being the day appointed by My Lord Bp. for giveing institution to Mr. Angus McBean to the vacancie of the Church of Invernesse, he being lawfully presented by the Laird of Strechein, and his Edict being duely served, and he ordained, and the people tymously advertised to be present the s^d day at his institution, Therfor the Moderator [Mr. Gilbert Marshall] proceeded to his admission by delivering him the sacred bible, ye book of discipline, and the keyes of the Churches doores, with oy^r solemnities used in such cases, exhorting him to humilitie, pietie, and diligence, who, with the remanent breyren, gave him the right hand of fellowship, and y^{r}after all the Magistrates, heretores, and elders, with unanimous consent, received him to be one of their ministers, promiseing obedience, faithfulnes, and assistance to him according to their severall stations; thereafter the s^d Moderator and remanent brethren passed to the Manse and Gleib belonging to the late Mr. Alex^r Clerk, and gaue the s^d Mr. Angus M^{c}bean real possession in the same and locall stipend belonging y^{r}to dureing his lifetime and service at the s^d Kirk of Invernesse, q^{ch} the s^d Mr. Angus accepted, and tooke instrument one or moe in Jo^n M^{c}bean, Notar publick, his hand, as the same in itselffe at more length beares. Thereafter the bretheren supersided the disciplin because of the paucity of their nember, and stormines of the weather.

At Invernesse, Feb. 6, 1684.

[Mr. Alex. Denune, who had been presented by the Bishop to the 'united churches of Pettie and Brachalie,' had his popular sermon and ordained to haue a comon head next meeting *de potestate clavium*].

At Invernesse, Aprill 2, 1684.

The s^d day Mr. Thomas Houston, Minister of Boleskine, regretted by his letter to the breyren of the Exercise, that all persons of all ranks indifferently buried their dead within his church, not only his own parochiners but some oy^rs of the neighbouring paroches, so that severall coffines were hardly under ground, which was like to be very dangerous and noisome to the hearers of the word within the s^d church, and y^rfor earnestly intreated the advice of his breyren how to cary y^ranent; which the breyren referred to my Lord Bisp. and the ensueing Synod.

The s^d day some of the breyren declared that they were severals times importuned to preach funerall sermons when persons were buried who hade left no monument of their charitie to the poor, or oy^r necessarie works, notwithstanding of their ability, Therefor they desired that my Lord Bp. and the ensueing Sinod might be consulted y^ranent, whether or no such persons should haue the honour of a funerall sermon.

The s^d day the Moderator inquired whether or no the breyren hade given the sacrament of the Lords supper to their people this year, severalls of the breyren answered they hade given the same; and the rest told that they were impeded by the greatnes of the stormie winter and oy^r inevitable impediments, but they resolved with the first conveniency to goe about the same and were prepareing their people in order thereto.

At Elgin, 23 *April* 1684.

Mr. Hugh Fraser, Minister of Kiltarlitie, intreated y^t Mr. Donald Forbes, his Schoolmaster, should haue the exercise ye s^d day (4th June next) Considering y^t he hade begune his tryalls alredie conforme to my Lord Bp.'s order, and he undertooke to advertise ye s^d Mr. Donald and y^t he should haue the exercise and adition, Text, 1 Thes. 1c. and 9v.

Invernes, June 4*th* (1684).

[Among the refers from the Synod was the following:—' 5. To mynd ye melioration of ye Manss of Inverness.']

The s^d day in obedience to the 5th referr concerneing ye mellioration of one of the Manss of Invernes, sometymes posest by ye late deccast rev^d Mr. Alex^r Clerk, ye Breyren haue apointed and referred to the Mod^r and Mr. Michael ffraser, Minister of Deviot, to goe upon some convenient day befor ye next meeting, and to bring w^t them a competent number of skilfull workmen, chosen by ye mutuall consent of Master Angus MackBaine, now Minister at Invernes, and Jean ffraser, relict to ye s^d umq^l Mr. Alex^r Clerk, and to apretiat the s^d melioration.

The s^d day ye Mod^r inquired if ye Brethrine hade receaved tymous advertisement, and had solemnly keept ye publicke day of Humiliatione appointed by Authoritie upon ye twenty eight of May: They all answered Affirmatively.

Therafter he inquired if all ye Bretheren hade solemnlie keept ye publique day of thanksgiveing upon the Twentie ninth of May. They all answered Affirmativlie.

At Invernes, Jullij 2d, 1684.

Donald Bain, suspected Adulterer w^t ye s^d Agnes Makenzie, continewing in his denyall is ordained to purge himselfe by his oath befor ye Congregation of Invernes, w^t his hand on ye childs head, and in presence of ye fors^d Agnes, and yet ye Ministers are apointed to be at pains w^t him to sie if it be possible to bring him to any acknowledgment.

The s^d day the Mod^r declared y^t befor Mr. Michael fraser went South (to Edinburgh) he and the s^d Mr. Michael brought workmen chosen as was ordained for apretiating ye melioration of ye Mans of Invernes by Master Alex^r Clerk, and y^t they hade orderly proceeded in ye same, and ye workmen being deeply sworn did apretiat ye samen to ye sowme of ane hundreth [merks] Scots money, q^{ch} appretiation ye Mod^r p̃nted subscr^t by a Nottar publique, and ye s^d aprysers, containing ye particulars of ye apretiation, and Lykwayes he p̃nted ane oy^r discharge (by and attour ye late apretiation) of Two hundred m̃rks payed be Mr. Alex. Clerk, late Min^r at Invernes, to ye executors of Mr. John Annand, sometyme Minister y^r, and payd by ye s^d Mr. John Annand to ye Right rever^d Fay^r in God Lord Bishop of Orkney, y^n Minister at Invernes, qch Discharge was sub^t by

Master William Annand, Ex^r to ye s^d Master John, and homologate by ye s^d Lord Bp. of Orkney, and was founded on on ane act of apretiation apointed by ye Presbitery of Invernes in ye tyme y^t ye s^d Lord Bishop of Orkney was minister at Invernes, and since confirmed by the Bretherine of yis exercise and ratefyd in ye Sinod of Murray as yis book bears.

And now it is ye earnest desyr of Jean ffraser, relict and executrix to Mr. Alex^r Clerk, y^t ye s^d Two hundred m̃rks be repayed to her by ye entrant conforme to yese former practises and acts fors^d, and lykwayes yis hundred m̃rks now apretiat.

The Mod^r and Bretherine y^{r}for haveing riply and seriously considered ye peapers, acts and whol tract of ye affair, and seeing it was put upon y^m by my Lord Bishop and Synod to put a close to the s^d mater, w^t unanimous consent Did ordaine and by yir presents Ordaines and Decernes Master Angus MacBain, now Min^r at Invernes (befor his entrie to ye s^d Mans), to pay to ye s^d Relict and executrix of ye s^d Master Alex^r Clerk, the s^d soume of Three hundred m̃rks scots money, and Lykwayes ordains y^t in all tyme comeing ye Intrant be oblidged to pay ye same, and y^t ye s^d Mans be allwayes affected w^t ye s^d soume unless ye parish pay of and releave ye samen, and referrs yis y^r sentance and Decreit to my Lord Bishop of Murray to be aproved, and y^t he may referr ye same to ye Lords of his Maj^{ties} Councell and Session y^t y^r authority may be interpond y^{r}unto for ye pay^t y^{r}of, and haue ordained yir p̃nts to be insert and registrat in this Book to that effect.

At Invernes, November 19, 1684.

[Among the Synodical refers read this day were] :—

2. To intimat from pulpit in the respective congrega^{o}nes within the Dyocess ane act of Synod intimating that no persons be receaved in ony parish without a sufficient testimony under certificat to the receavers of theiss befor the presbiterie.

3. The former act of Synod for restraining of extravagancies of penny brydalls renewed.[1]

---

[1] The following acts of the Synod (Moray) may be noted. On 25th Feb. 1640—' In respect off ye gryt disorders yat haw fallen out in dyverse parts off ye land by drunkennes and tuilzieing at pennie brydalls, Thairfor it is ordained that thair be no pennie brydalls maid on ye Sabbothe.' On 27th Oct. 1640—'Mr.

5. That the Mod^r of each presbiterie collect from everie Minister 20 shilling scots at the first meeting, to be sent to the Bp. for Mr. James Cook; lykewayes, that at the same tyme some charity may be expected for Gilbert Andersone in Keith, newly cutt of the gravell.

Johne Martiall [Minister of Dundurcos, now united with Rothes] being founde to hawe maid a marriage on the thursday, and w^t ye same persones keiped a pennie brydiall on ye nixt Sabbothe day, hawing a minstrell playing to y^o Churche and frome ye same befoir them, is sharplie and grawlie rebucked in ye faice of ye Synod.' The following resolutions regarding penny weddings and lykewakes were passed at a meeting of Sub-Synod held 8th June 1675:—'The qlk day the L. Bp. and Brethren of the Subsynod convenied for the tym, takeing into y^r grave and serious consideration the great disorders, with the scandalous Lascivious and unchristiane cariages of the comonaltie, for the most pairt at pennie Brydells, by y^r frequent resort and great confluence ordinarlie at such occasions, for removing of q^{ch} evills, and suppressing q^{ch} disorders, y^e L. Bp. w^t Breyren foresaid thought fitt and expedient to constitut these following articles to be observed g$\bar{r}$ally in tym coming:

'1. That the usuall excessive number be limited to and restrained to eight persons allenarlie on each side of the maried persons.

'2. That all piping, fidling, and dancing w^{t}out doores of all q^{m}soever resorting these meetings be restrained and discharged.

'3. That all obscene Lascivious and promiscuous dancing within doores be discharged.

'4. That the two dollars consigned at the contract of the maried persons (q^{ch} is also ordained to be deposited not onlie as pledges of performing y^r intended purposes of mariage but also of ye civile and sober deportment of all y^{es} that shall countenance y^r mariage feast) remaine in the Session Clarke's hands untile the Lords day after the mariage, y^t in caise of contravening one or oy^r of the foresaid articles be anie q^{m}soever, then and in y^t caise, the foresaid two dollars shall be confiscated to the comon good of the parishe Church, and this by and attour the publicke censur to be imposed upon the transgressors of the fors^{ds} articles.

'In lykmanner, the L. Bp. and Brey^{rn} foresaid being informed off and deeplie weighted with the superstitious and heathnish customes practised at Lykewakes in manie places within this diocie, at q^{ch} tym sin and scandell does greatlie abound, to the dishonor of the great Lord and offence of sober christians, for redressing q^{r}off, and that the deportment and cariages of such who resort y^{es} Lykwakes may be as becometh Christianitie, the L. Bp. and Brey^{rn} fors^d ordains that the ordinarie cruding [crowding] multitude of profane and Idle persones be debarred, and that none frequent or countenance these meetings but those of the defuncts nearest relations or those y^t may be usefull for christiane Counsell and comfort to the mourners and afflicted, discharging stricklie all light and Lascivious exercises, sports, Lyksongs, fidling, and dancing, and y^t anie present at such occasions behave y^{m}selves gravely, christianlie, civilly, and soberlie, spending the tym in reading the scriptures and conferences upon mortalitie; ordaining this Act to be publicklie read throughout the diocie.'

At Invernes, March 11, 1685.

The which day the Mod^r declared that he had receaved a letter from my Lord Bp. ordaining him and the Bretherine of the Exercise to goe to the Church of Dalarosie for setling severall Debaits y^t did aryse concerneing Dasks in the s^d Church, y^{r}for the next meeting is to hold at Dalarosie Apryl the 9th, and the Min^r of the place appointed to preach the s^d day and Mod^r apointed to advertise him tymously y^{r}of.

At Dalarasie, Apryl, 1685.

Conveened the Moderator [Mr. Gilbert Marshall, Inverness] Mr. Angus McBean [Inverness] and Mr. Alex^r Cuning [Moy and Dalarossie], all the rest being absent by reason of the tempestuous weather and the great speats of ye waters.

No doctrine the s^d day because the people wer not able to cross the waters till towards night.

After Invoca°ne of the name of God, the Mod^r and Bretherin p̄nt haveing heard and considered the severall debeats concerning sundrie dasks in the s^d church did at length with a great of pains [*sic*] freindly agree all the persons concerned to all their contentments.

At Invernes, Jullij 8th, 1685.

The which day the Mod^r inquired the reason of the bretherins absence from the last meeting of the exercise [held 10th June, the only Ministers present being those of Inverness, Kirkhill, Dores, and Petty]. Mr. Hugh Fraser of Kiltarlitie replied that he was not returned from the South, and the rest could not wait upon the dyet considering the great stirrs that was in the Countrie in respect of the prepara°ne to his Majties host.

At Invernes, August 26, 1685.

The which day the Mod^r asked the Bretherin then p̄nt [all present except Croy, Moy, Daviot, and Boleskine] par̄lie [particularlie] if they hade observed the day of thanksgiving August the 13 for the happie and successful supression of the rebellion in both Kingdoms. All answered affirmativelie.

At Invernes, Julij 14, 1686.

Mr. Michael fraser hade his comon head *De infalibilitate ecclesiae.*

This day the Mod^r receaved a letter from my Lord Bp. recommending Mr. Robert Cuming, expectant in the Ministrie, to the ordinarie steps of his tryalls *cum intuitu ad locis,* haveing receaved ane presentation to the United Churches of Urq^{rt} and Glenmoristone now vacand throw the translation of Mr. James Grant to Abernethie, y^{r}for the Mod^r and Breyren appointed the s^d Ma^r Robert to undergoe his questionarie trials, and trial of the Languages, the next meeting day, q^{ch} is to hold at Invernes August ye 11th.

At Invernes, August 11*th*, 1686.

After invocation of the name of God, conforme to the former ordinance Mr. Robt Cuming, sustained his q^{rie} tryalls and tryall of the Languages, being removed, was aproven, and is enjoined to have exercise and adition, text, 1 Thes. 1. cap. and 14, the next meeting day, q^{ch} is to hold at Invernes the 8th day of September, and lykwayes they apointed him to haue his comon head *de libero arbitrio* against the meeting y^{r}after, and to distribute his Theses ye s^d 8 day of Sept^r.

The s^d day Mr. Robt Monro protested that Mr. Robt Cuming's presenta°ne should be but [without] prejudice to his collation to the Church of Glenmoriston, q^{ch} the Mod^r and Breyrine referred to my Lord Bishop and Sinod to determine.

At Invernes, Septr. 8*th*, 1686.

[Mr. Robt Cuming had exercise and distributed his Theses.]

At Invernes, Septr. 22, 1686.

[Mr. Robert Cuming had his comon head and sustained the disputes, was aproved, recommended to the Bishop ' y^t he might receave his Edict, and to be orderly ordained and colated to these churches to q^{ch} he has been p̄nted.']

At Invernes, Novr. 3, 1686.

The said Mr. Hugh [Fraser, Kiltarlitie] declared by his letter that in obedience to my Lord Bishop of Murray his order he had gon to the Church of Urquhart on the 24 of October last, being the Lord's day, and did give institution to Mr. Robert Cuming to be Minister there conform to his presenta°ne and Colation, And that with all solemnities use and wont in such caices.

The Moderator inquired the Bretheren if they hade solemnly keept the 14 day of October, being his majesty's Birth day. They all answered affirmitively.

Lykewayes he inquired if they hade publickly read the proclamation against Leasing-makers. They all lykewayes answered affirmitively.

[Among the refers from the Synod was the following]:— That Mr. Alex^r Cuming, Min^r at Moy and Dalarasie, is apointed to keep and meit with the Bretherin of the exercise of Abernethie, and to carrie on and proceed in his disciplin befor the said exercise untill the next Synod in order to a futur disjunction of the s^d Mr. Alex^r from the Exercise of Inverness, and Annexation of the said Mr. Alex^r to the said Exercise of Abernethie, if the samen shall be found expedient at the nixt Synod.

At Inverness, December 2d, 1686.

The reason why the Bretheren did not meet untill this day was because the Bretheren did atend the Funeralls of the Right Reverend Father in God Colin late Lord Bishop of Murray, whom God called out of this Life November 11, 1686, to the enjoyment of eternall hapines, whose Funerals were honourably and solemnly celibrat with great greef at Elgin, Novemb. 22.

At Inverness, March 2d, 1687.

[Mr. Thomas Fraser, Dores, had a common head *De peccato veniali et mortali*, Text Rom. cap. 6, v. 23. Approved.]

April 27th, 1687.

Mr. Angus M^{c}bean had the exercise and addition, Text, 1 Thes. cap. 2. ver. 14. Approved.

[At next meeting (June 1st) Mr. Macbean is 'absent without excuse.' On 6th July he is absent 'now the 2^d tym without any excuse.'

At this meeting Mr. Alex^r Denoon, Pettie, had a Common head *De Transubstantione*. Text, 1 Cor. cap. 11. v. 28.]

At Inverness, August 3*d*, 1687.

[Mr. Angus Macbean absent without any excuse.]

The said day John Grant in Glenmoriston, a papist excomunicat 20 yeares ago for ane incestuous mariage, he being irregularly maried be a popish priest to his uncle's wife, and now she being dead, and the said John haveing forsaken the errores of the popish Church and returned and imbraced the Orthodox Religion, did humbly suplicat to be receaved to the publick profession of his Repentance for his guilt and scandall, to the end he might be relaxed from the dreadfull sentence of excomunication and receaved again into his mother Church; which suplication the Moderator and Bretheren having taken to their serious consideration appointed two of the Bretheren to go and speak privatly to the said John and to search further [*sic*] or not he was weighted with his guilt and sincerely resolved to forsake his former errores. Thereafter the two Bretheren returning, declared that they had confered with him and found him in all appearance both weighted with his guilt and fully resolved all the dayes of his life hereafter to continue in the protestant Religion.

Therfor the Moderator and Bretheren thought fitt to call the said John befor them, who compeired *in sacco* and acknowledged his guilt, and after many grave, weightie, and serious exhortationes, he was remitted back to satisfie the disciplin of the Session of the United Parochins of Urquhart and Glenmoriston.

The said day the Moderator and Bretheren haveing taken to their serious Consideration the absence of Mr. Angus Macbean, one of the Ministers of Inverness, three severall dayes without any excuse, and being lykewayes informed that the said Mr. Angus did disown the Government of the Church of Scotland as it is now established by Law, by Archbishops, Bishops, and Presbiters. Therfor they did appoint the Moderator [Mr. Marshall, Inverness] and Mr. Michael Fraser, Minister at Daviot, to go and speake with the said Mr. Angus, and to enquire what was the Reasones of his absenting himselfe, and his disowning the Government as they were informed, and to give a Report of their diligence to the next meeting.

At Inverness, September 7th, 1687.

[Mr. Robert Cuming, Minister of Urquhart] reported by his said letter that John Grant who was excomunicated for his incestuous mariage, was humbly and orderly going on in the publick profession of his repentance.

The said day the Moderator and Mr. Michael Fraser being inquired what answer they hade receaved from Mr. Angus Mackbean anent his willfull deserting the meeting of his Bretheren, and his avowed disowning of the Government; the said Mr. Michael Fraser Reported that Mr. Angus Mackbean declared plainly that he hade no freedom to keep Synods or presbitries any mor, and that it was over the belly of conviction that he entered into the Ministrie under Bishops, and that his convictions were returning with greater force upon his conscience, he could not overcome them, and that he was convinced that Presbitrie was the only Government that God owned in these nations: and that when he inquired the said Mr. Angus what he thought anent all the Murderes, Rebelliones, and assasina°nes of the west countrey people, he answered that it was enough for the Moderat partie of these people to hold their tongue anent thes things; and that his full resolution was, which he could not win over, to make all the satisfaction he could to the Presbyterian partie, to preach for them and in their favoures for his too much appearing against them: and that he could not promeiss, tho he should be dispensed with by Bishop and Presbitrie, from keeping their meetings iff preaching in this Town not to give ground of misconstruction to these that owned our Government established by Law. All which Report the Moderator attested.

Lykewayes the Moderator declared that Mr. Angus Mackbean, both in his publick Lectores and sermones, did so reflect upon the Government of our Church, and was like to make such a schism at Inverness as could not be endured by any affected to the present Government, and therefor that he hade called some of his nearest Bretheren, to witt, Mr. James Fraser, Min^r at Wardlaw, Mr. Michael Fraser, Min^r at Daviot, and Mr. Thomas Fraser, Min^r at Doores, and that by their speciall advice and consent hade caused sumond the said Mr. Angus to compear at this meeting to answer for his reproachfull doctrin, and, conform to the Synodicall Referr, to give a further accompt of his absence, with which declaration and proceedor all the Bretheren mett this day were very well pleased, and did aprove the same in every point.

The said Mr. Angus not apearing, the Magistrates and other persons who were charged as witnesses of his doctrin interposed themselves with the Moderator and remanent Bretheren, that all process should be delayed till the nixt Meeting, and that they should use their endeavour to persuad the said Mr. Angus to be mor orderly and to meet with his bretheren and satisfie them, which if he would not do they resolved to leav him to himselfe if he would not follow their advice. The Bretheren of the presbitrie thought it fit by reason of the present circumstances to empower ye Moderator to call a select Number of his nearest bretheren whenever necessity required, in order to the expeding of all that ' may contribut for the peace and unity and standing of the present Government within this precinct.

The meeting clos'd with prayer.

At Inverness, October 5, 1687.

Conveened the Moderator and Remanent Bretheren except Mr. Angus M^cbean.

Mr. Robert [Cuming] reported that John Grant in Glenmoriston, excomunicated for his incestuous mariag, is humbly and orderly going on in the publick proffession of his Repentance, and that the said John was earnestly suplicating to be relaxed from the sentence of excomunica^{o}n. The Moderator and bretheren takeing his circumstances to their serious consideration, he being a gentleman of good accompt in his own Countrey, and liveing near by Glengarie, the Inhabitants of q^{ch} countrey are for the most part all papists, and are useing many endeavours to make the said John relaps into his former apostacie, and not being willing in the least to discurrage him, Therfor they referred him to my Lord Bishop of Murray and the ensueing Synod.

The said day Mr. Angus Macbean having yet willfully absented himselfe, and neither the Magistrates nor his other freends haveing in the least prevailed with him, and the mater being of such weight and of so dangerous consequence, the Moderator and Bretheren have referred it to My Lord Bishop and Synod of Murray.

The said day the Moderator enquired if all the Bretheren hade orderly read at the tymes appointed the Act against Leasing makers. They all answered affirmitively.

Lykewayes he put all the Bretheren in mynd to observe solemnly the 14 day of this instant October, being the Kings Birthday.

At Elgin, October 19, 1687.

The said day conveined the Moderator and remnant bretheren then present at the Sinod, and appointed their next meeting to hold at Inverness the 7 of December next. The reason y^t they delayed to meet till y^t day was that both the Bretheren of the Sinod and of this exercise resolve to use all brotherly, prudent, and tender methods for reclaiming Mr. Angus Mackbane, one of the Ministers of Inverness, to his duty. And the Sinod lykewayes hath appointed four Reverend Brethcren to go to Inverness in their name to conferr with him in the intervall, and to carry with them a serious and brotherly letter directed from the Sinod to him. And in case these brethren should not prevaile with him, conform to our Right Revd Ordinar his speciall advice and direction, severall Ministers from each Exercise of the Sinod are to go to Inverness at the fors^d dyet to be assistants to the Moderator and Brethren in that affair.

The Brethren appointed Mr. Hugh ffraser, Minister at Kiltarlitie, to haue a sermon y^t day to that purpose, it being a matter of so great weight.

At Inverness, Decr. 7, 1687.

The said day conveined the Moderator and brethren of the Exercise, but none of the Brethren appointed by the Sinod, nor any lyne from them. Having incalled the Holy Name of God, there was no sermon this day in respect that the Moderator declar'd y^t Mr. Angus Mackbane, lately one of the Ministers of Inverness, had the next and imediat Lord's Day after the Sinod last by past, being the 23^d of October last, solemnly in his sermon in the forenoone, in the Church of

Inverness, dissowned the Church Goverment established be Law, and publickly demitted his charge of the Ministry under the present Goverment, and willfully deserted his flock, And at that same tyme did publickly exhort and entreat all men whatsoever to abstaine from speaking to him any more in that affair. The Report of which all the Brethren judged to be the reason of the absence of the Brethren appointed for their assistance, and the sermon being prepared for the intention of the meetting, the Brethren thought fitt to referr it to ane other occasion, since Mr. Mackbane had willfully deserted his charge, and the Brethren appointed did not come.

The said day the Brethren being informed that Mr. Mackbane, the verie next Lord's day after his willfull desertion of his charge, had gone to Ross, and there, in a meetting house, had preachd to the Schismaticks; and the Lords Day after that did return to Inverness, and preach y^r at a conventicle, and so began his schisme in one of the most loyall, orderly, and regular cities in the Nation—Therfore the Brethren desyr'd the Moderator to write to our Ordinary the Bishop of Murray, now lying tender at Glasgow, and to acquaint his Lo/ with the whole affair, and to intreat his advice and direction how to carry herein.

The said day Mr. Robert Cuming, Min^r at Urchart, Reported that John Grant in Glenmoriston, conforme to the Ordinance of the Sinod of Murray, was solemnly and publickly relax'd from the weighty sentence of excomunication; and therfore the Moderator appointed that all the Brethren should make publick intimation thereof in their severall congregationes, and likewayes referred the same to the Sinod that the same might be publickly intimat by all the Brethren.

The said day Mr. Donald Forbes, Schoolmaster at Kiltarlitie and probationer in Divinitie, was appointed to haue a comon head, the next meetting day, *De Schismate*, seeing Mr. Thomas Huistown, who had been formerlie appointed to haue the exercise, was old, infirm, and weak, and not able to travell in the Winter season. The next meeting appointed to be at Inverness January 14, and Mr. James Fraser, Min^r at Kirkhill, is appointed to supplie the vacancie at Inverness first, and the Brethren to succeed.

I

At Inverness, February 1, 1688.

Convein'd the Moderator and Brethren, except Mr. Michael Fraser who was chosen and elect by the Chapter to go to Edinburgh, in obedience to the commands of my Lord Arch Bishop of St. Andrews His Grace. Having incalled the name of God, the said day Mr. Donald Forbes had a comon head *De Schismate*, Text Rom. 16 ch. 17 v. Being removed and his labours considered, he was approven.

The said day the Moderator reported that conforme to the ordinance of presbitrie September 7, 1687, he had advised with severalls of his nearest brethren; and that he, with their advice and consent, had impowered Mr. Michael Fraser, Min^r at Daviot, to intreat my Lord St. Andrews His Grace (our Diocess being now vacant) to use all ordinar means for suppressing the schisme begun at Inverness, which all the Brethren approved, and desired the Moderator to write south again to the s^d Mr. Michael to the same effect.

The said day the Moderator enquired all the Brethren if they had read the proclamation against Leasing-making conform to the order of Councell: they all answered affirmatively.

At Inverness, March 7, 1688.

The said day the Moderator enquired if all the Brethren had solemnised the day of Thanksgiving for her Majesties being with child, conforme to the Act of Counsel published theranent. They all answered affirmatively. The said day the Moderator reported that conforme to the ordinance of the Brethren, he had again written to Mr. Michael Fraser, and Likewayes received ane return from him showing him to be actively going about the affair entrusted to him, and that 'gainst next meetting they might expect a more full return.

At Inverness, March 27, 1688.

The said day the Moderator reported that the reason of changing the day of this meeting was ane letter he had received from Our Ordinary William, Lord Bishop of Murray, who was consecrat at St. Andrews March 11, and had appointed ane Sinod to hold at Elgin the first Tuesday of Aprill next.

The said day the Moderator reported that he had received a

letter from Mr. Michael Fraser, yet at South, wherin was inclosed The Act of Deposition of Mr. Angus M^cbane, lately one of the Ministers of Inverness; and likewayes ane letter for Our Ordinary, my Lord Bishop of Murray, ordaining the same to be intimat in the Church of Inverness on ane Lords Day in the forenoon, after divine service : which ordinance was obeyed and performed by Mr. Hugh Fraser, Min^r at Killtarlitie, March 11. And it was thought fitt by the Moderator and Bretheren that the said Act should be here insert and registrat, As after followes :

'At Edinr., February 27, 1688.
' The whilk Day, in pn̄t of The Most Revd Father in God, Arthur, Lord Arch Bishop of St. Andrews, primat and Metropolitan of all Scotland, and of the Right Reverend Father in God, William, Elect Lord Bishop of Murray, Doctor Alex^r Monro, Prin^{ll} of the Colledge of Edin^r, Doctor John Strachan, Professor of Divinity there, Dr John Robinson, Moderator of the Exercise at Edin^r, Dr William Gairnes, one of the Ministers of that Citie, Mr. Andrew Burnet, Min^r y^r, Mr. Michael Fraser, Min^r at Daviot, and Mr. John Mackenzie, Min^r at Kirkliston, Compeired personally Mr. Angus M^cbeane sometyme one of the Min^{rs} at Inverness (as being cited to the s^d day) And being interrogated by the s^d Lord Arch-Bishop, Praeses of the meetting, How long he had been in Holy Orders, Answered four years or y^rby, and that he received Episcopall Ordination : being also inquired whether he had deserted the station and Ministry of the Church q^{ch} had been assigned him, and whether he had affected a Schisme and separation from the said Nationall Church, and whether he was under the Oath of Canonicall Obedience, Answered He could not gainsay it, and that he had interrupted his Obedience since October last bypast. And being further posed, Whether he designed and was willing to returne to his duty again (the Armes of the Church being still open and ready to receive him upon his Repentance) He declared he had no mind to doe so. Whereupon, the matter being taken to serious consideration by the s^d meeting, without any dissent, the said Mr. Angus M^cbean, for his Perjurie, Schisme, and Contumacie, was Judicially by the s^d Lord Arch Bishop (in the vertue of his Metropoliticall capacitie) deposed from the Exercise of any part of the pastorall office, and depryved of all benefices that might accrue to him q^rby, since the tyme of his willfull desertion,

wherunto he acquiesced, with certification that if he should transgress y^rin, the sentence of Excomunication should pass against him; and further, it was appointed that this present sentence of Deposition and Deprivation should be publickly intimat from the pulpit of Inverness, on ane Lords Day after divine service, in the forenoon, by Mr. Hugh Fraser, Min^r at Killtarlity, for vindicating the Churches authority, and Terrour of such Backslyders.

'*Sic subscribitur*—By Order and Warrant off

'WILL: Elect Morravien.'

[Among the Synodical Refers read at this meeting were]:

3. That conforme to instructions given be our Ordinary to the Sinod (to take inspection into and cognosce upon the behaviour and disorderly walking alleadged against Mr. Angus M^cbane, Min^r at Inverness) and the resolu^ons of the Sinod y^ranent, there are appointed to conferr with the s^d Mr. Angus M^cbane, betwixt and the 2^d day of November next ensueing, these Brethren, vizt Mr. Samuel Tulloch, Mr. Michael Cuming, Mr. George Innes, and Mr. David Cuming, who are to carry and present to the s^d Mr. Angus ane earnest and affectionat Letter appointed to be directed, in the name of the Sinod, be Mr. Alex^r Ker, Moderator therof, and to use all y^r endeavours to recover and persuade the s^d Mr. Angus to return to his dutie.

4. That in case the said Mr. Angus listen not to the s^ds Brethren then the first Wednesday of December next is appointed for severall Brethren to meet at Inverness, and to joyne with the Brethren of the s^d Exercise there to consider and cognosce upon what may be laid to the charge of the s^d Mr. Angus, viz., Out of the Exercise of Strathbogie, Mr. William Chalmer and Mr. Alex^r Rose. Out of the Exercise of Elgin, Mr. Beroald Innes and Mr. James Cook. Out of Forres Mr. William Falconer, Mr. William Law, and Mr. George Dunbar. And out of Abernethie Mr. Hector McKenzie and Mr. James Grant.

At Inverness, May 2, 1688.

Conveined the Moderator and remanent brethren, and haveing incalled the holy name of God, the Moderator preached a Sermon, Text 2 Cor. 5. 20.

The reason why the Exercise was continued and the said sermon preached was because Mr. Hector Mackenzie, Min^r at Kingousie (being orderly presented by Kenneth Earle of Seafort, undoubted patron of the Church of Inverness, and his Edict duely served conform to the appointment of my Lord Bishop of Murray), was this day admitted and institute one of the Min^{rs} of Inverness, with all the solemnities usuall in such cases, as the Instrument of his admission and Institution in itselffe at more length bears.

[Among the Refers from the Synod read are]:

2. That the Relaxa^{o}n and absolution of John Grant in Glenmoriston (for Incest and Defection to Poprie) from the sentence of Excomunication be intimat.

3. That at Baptiseing of Infants the parents make confession of y^r Faith by owning and acknowledging the Apostles Creed, As also that after prayer the Lords prayer be subjoyned, and after praises the doxologie be sung, and all the Brethren to be particularly enquired thereanent at the p̄rbrie censure.

5. That the sentence of suspension formerly pronounced against the said Mr. Robert Monro, for his accession to ane Mock-marriage, at Inverness in Novr last 1687 years is continued untill the first Lords day of May next ensueing, as also in respect of two other unorderly marriages, confessed be the s^d Mr. Robert Monro, he is ordained to appear publickly in the Church of Inverness upon the s^{ds} first Lords day of May next, or any Lords day y^{r}after in the forenoone, and at the close of divine service before the pulpit in face of the Congregation, to make humble and solemn acknowledgement of his offence anent the s^d mock marriage and his other scandalls that accompany'd his miscarriages, Craving God pardon, and all whom he might y^{r}by haue offended. Wherupon Mr. Gilbert Marshall, after grave and serious admonitions, is to tender to the s^d Mr. Robert Absolution from the s^{ds} scandalls.

6. That the s^d Mr. Robert is under certification that in case he comitt any such misdemeanours hereafter, he shall be depryved and deposed simpliciter.

7. That Mr. Thomas Huistone, the next Sunday next after the said Mr. Robert Monro his absolu^{o}n as said is, go to the Church of Abertarff, and after divine service y^r to be performed

be the s^d Mr. Thomas, he give publick intima°n to the Congregation of the said Mr. Robert his absolu°n and reposition to his former charges and exercise of his offices in the ministrie as formerly.

8. That all former Acts anent irregular marriages are ratisfied and renewed, and that no Min^r take upon hand to celebrat the office of marriage w^tout orderly proclama°nes on three severall Lords dayes (unless ane Licence from the Ordinary allow) w^t certifica°n the contraveener shall be censured w^t suspension for the first, and depriva°n and deposition for the second tyme he shall be found in such irregularity.

9. That the sentence of Deprivation and Deposition pronounced be my Lord Arch Bishop of St. Andrews, the Bishop of Morray, and others their assessors, conveined at Edin^r the 27 of Februar 1688 yeares, against Mr. Angus Mackbean sometyme Min^r at Inverness, be not only registrat and insert in the Sinod register of Murray but also in the books and Registers of the Exercise of Inverness y^r to remaine *in futuram rei memoriam*.

At Inverness, June 6, 1688.

The said day Mr. Gilbert Marshall, Moderator, declared that on the first Lords day of May last, he had absolved Mr. Robert Monro publickly in the Church of Inverness, and that the said Mr. Robert had given satisfaction to the Synodicall Referr in all points.

Lykewise Mr. Thomas Huistown, Min^r at Boleskine, reported that on the second Lords day of May he preached in the Church of Abertarffe, and after divine service made publick intima°n to the Congregation of the said Mr. Robert his absolution and Reposition to his former charge and exercise of his office in the ministrie as formerlie.

At Inverness, July 4, 1688.

The said day the Moderator inquired all the Brethren whether they had observed the day of Thanksgiving on the 28 of June for the birth of the Prince of Scotland. All answered that they had all solemnly observed the same.

At Inverness, September 5, 1688.

Conveined the Moderator [Mr. Marshall] and Mr. James Fraser, Minister at Kirkhill, all the rest absent, some by reason of the great stirrs that were in the Countrey anent the late rebellion and bloodshed in Lochaber, and others necessarily w'drawn as their excuses did carry, and therefore this meetting was adjourned to the 19 of Septr next. The Exercise and place of meetting to continue as formerlie, and the breyren tymouslie to be advertised y^{r}of.

At Inverness, September 19th, 1688.

Conveined the Moderator and remanent Brethren (except Mr. Hugh Fraser, Min^r of Croy, who was tender and not able to travell, excused by his Letter) and having incalled the holy name of God, Mr. Michael Fraser had the Exercise and Addition, Text, 1 Thes. 3 ch. 6 and 7 v., being removed and his doctrine considered, was approven.

The s^d day the Moderator inquired all the Brethren present if they had publickly read on the Lords day after divine service the publick proclama^{o}n emitted by the Counsell anent the severall seditious Books and Libells y^{r}in mentioned. All answered affirmatively.

Lykewise the Moderator inquired the Brethren if they read from pulpit the Act against Leasing-making at the severall tymes appointed be the s^d acts. All answered affirmatively.

The s^d day the Moderator desyred such of the Brethren as had not payed the Bursar of divinity to bring the s^d money with them precisely at the Sinod, q^{ch} they promised to do.

The next meetting is appointed to be at Elgin w^t my Lord Bishop and Sinod of Murray the first Tuesday of October next, q^{ch} meeting the Moderator seriously exhorted the Brethren carefully to attend.[1]

---

[1] This is the last minute of the Presbytery under Episcopacy. A considerable number of leaves at the end of the volume have been cut out. They were probably not written upon. The next volume commences in 1702. The majority of the brethren of the Presbytery adhered to Episcopacy at the Revolution, but still retained their charges; and the probability is that for many years the Presbyterian clergy of the Presbytery did not hold regular meetings or keep any record of their proceedings.

RECORDS OF THE PRESBYTERY OF DINGWALL.

At Dingll, 19 *June* 1649.

Convened Mr. Do^d Fraser, Moderator, Mr. Robert Monro, Mr. Ferq^r McLennan, Mr. George Monro, Mr. Don^d Ma^{c}crae, and Ranaild M^{c}ranaild, Ruling Elder from Kilmorack.

The name of God incalled.

Mr. Dod. Ma^{c}crae appointed Clerk of ye Pr̄ie ontill Mr. Jon M^{c}crae, qho is ordinare clerk, return from Edinburgh. That day there wes no doctrine, because Mr. Dod. Fraser, who sould handle a comon head, wes not prepared, be reason y^t he wes all the tyme at the Commission at Chanrie and at Alderne, and be ye Comission directed to the Kirk of Lochbruime.

'The References of the Commission at Alderne to ye Pr̄ie of Ding^{ll}.

'The Errata of ye pbrie and Session Recorded to be Registrat yrin and subscribed vith the Clerks hand.

'The kirks to be visited with all c'nvenient dilligence, Preaching to be in ye afternoone, for ye cause of God and against ye enemies y^{r}off, and the Registers y^{r}off to be marked be the Presbytrie.

'The Covenant to be insert in ye Presbyterie and Session Books.

'Dilligence to be vsed for the plantation of Schoolles.

'The Act of ye Generall Assemblie to be observed for choosing Elders.

'Not to neglect testimonialls about termes.

'Mr. Jo^n M^{c}crae ordained to be more painfull to reforme the evil menners of Ding^{ll}, to be[1] ye residents to refraine from goeing to wells on the Lordes day.

---

[1] *To be*: *i.e.* to compel.

'Mr. Thomas Ross to delyver to y⁰ Pbrie all the records of the kirk he hed and the presbyterie to requyre the same.

'Maister Robert Monro to be more frequent in catechising.

'Mr. Ferqʳ MᶜLennan to forbear his oft repaire to yᵉ hielands, to be moir cairfull in executing publick orders from the Church, to be moir forward for the cause of God, to keep companie with the brethren rayʳ then with Mr. Murdo Mackenzie, late Minister of Dinguall.[1]

'Mr. Doᵈ Mᶜcrae to be moir cairfull for yᵉ soulles of Killchreist, and diligent in catechising.

'No exaction of oathes of persones suspected of witchcraft.

'Mr. Murdo Mackenzie, late Minister of Ding^ll, ordained befoir he be absolved to acknowledge, not onlie in word but also in wreitt under his owen hand, his manifold prevaricatione, and particularlie the equitie of yᵉ sentence pronounced be the Gen^ll Assemblie and yeir Comissiō at Alderne, and to acknowledge the reasones of his appeal to be but calumnies and lies, and the prie to report their dilligence to the Gen^ll Assemblie with the Commissione to the same.'

'(signed)   Mr. David Dumbar, Clk. Comm.'

'The Comissione of the Genll Assemblie haveing long debated yᵉ processe of Mr. Doᵈ Ross, Minister of Lochbruime, particullarlie anent the scandell of fornicatione with Christian buy, finds much imprudence in not goeing solemnlie and wyslie about his own cleiring qhen this scandell brak out, and find manie presumptiones albeit not a cleir probation that the scandell is not zet removed.[2]

'Lykwayes finds be the lybell given in be Coline Mᶜkenzie of Tarbeit yᵗ his cariag in manie churches wes not ministeriall, as in particulare in giveing way to sell wyne in his house, and in keeping companie with some gentlemen drinking wyne upon the sabbath.

'In keeping ane adulteress in his house efter yᵉ odious fact known.

---

[1] Mr. Murdo Mackenzie was deposed about 1639 for not submitting to the Acts of the famous Glasgow General Assembly of 1638, which declared against Episcopacy and for Presbyterianism, and thus brought about what is commonly known in Scotland as the Second Reformation. In 1648 the Assembly declared him 'uncapable for ever of the ministry, with a recommendation to the Presbytery to proceed against him with excommunication.' The Presbytery's proceedings against him frequently appear in subsequent Minutes.

[2] See Minute of 11th Sept. 1650.

'That upon ye desyre of few elderes upon pretence of avoiding inconvenience he sould marie divers people in a Bairne [barn] for the qlk he hed bene suspended from Sept. 19, 1648 till yis day.

'The Comissione taking ye premisses to yeir c'sidera^on, for purgeing of the scandell, haue appointed Mr. George Monro, Minister at Vrqhairt, to goe to Lochbruime and preach yer the 24 of June instant, being ye sabbath, and with him Mr. Alex^r Mackenzie, Minister at Lochcarron, Johne Baine of Tullich, and Andro Monro, portioner of Culkairnie, and in face of the congregation, efter sermon, the said Mr. do^d. to purge himselfe be his solemne oath of the alleadged fornica^on with Christen boy, the woman being requyred to be present, and to c'fess humblie his miscarriage above mentioned.

'Efter which he is ordained to be reponed to the function of his ministrie in all thinges as befoir his suspension, and yis to be reported to the clerk of the Comissione imediatlie efter his reponeing, and that the Prie of Ding^ll, with ye whole prowince of Ross, vse all c'venient dilligence to transplant the s^d Mr. Do^d wherever the Lord sall open a doore for the better employment of his talent: and the Prie and Prowinciall Assemblie to be onserable for their dilligence heiranent when they sall be requyred.'

  '(signed)   Mr. David Dumbar, Clk. com.'

The Bretheren of the Prie taking to yer c'dera^on the reference of the commission anent Mr. Murdo Ma^ckenzie, late Minister of Ding^ll, and being informed y^t he is sick (as his lre directed to the comission did proport) ordained Mr. ferq^r McLennan, and Mr. Dod M^ccrae, to goe and visitt him and report their dilligence heiranent ye next day.

That day Mr. John Ma^ccrae noiated and chosen Comissioner, and Andro Monro portioner of Culkairnic, Ruling Elder, for ye ensueing Grall Assemblie.

Ordained ye hieland kirks to be visited at Lambmass and to begin at the Kirk of Kintaill.

Ordained the Kirk of Kiltearne to be visited ye 3 July nixtcome, and the Minister to preach on his ordinarie.

Mr. George Monro and Mr. Alex^r Ma^ckenzie ordained to go to Lochbruime according to ye ordinance of ye comissio at Alderne, and report yeir dilligence y^rin at Kilterne the nixt day.

The Brethren reported the thanksgiving for the wictorie at Balvenie observed.¹

The action closed with a blessing.

At Kilterne, Julie 3, 1649.

Convened Mr. Do^d fraser, Moderator, Mr. ferq^r MacLennan, Mr. George Monro, Mr. Robert Monro, and Mr. Dod M^ccrac, Ministers, and Elderes of the said kirk, Hector Dowglass of Balconie, ferqhair Monro of Teahnaird, Mr. Johne Monro of Swairdell, Hew Monro in Katuell, Johne Roy in Teanaird, Hew Monro in Fowlles, and Hew Monro of Teamerchies.

The name of God incalled.

Mr. Robert Monro, Minister of Kilterne, preached 125 Psal. 1. 5.

The Session Book being requyred nothing presented bot scroilles, Therefor he is ordained to fill up his book, and send it to Mr. ferq^r McLennan and Mr. George Monro, qho are appointed to visit the same, and report their dilligence the next day.

The Minister removed, and the Elderes enquyred and sworne, deponed, that to ther knowledge he preached sound doctorines, and to the tymes, that he is edifieing, frie of Malignancie² in preaching and cariage; and being particularlie enquyred if he did entertaine Malignantes in his house befoir the day of Balvenie, declared that his grandson and Do^d baine (a chirurgian) did frequent his house befoir the s^d day, bot that Mr. Robert wes diverting them from y^r malignant courses according to his power: siklyke declares that Biguous³ and some otheres, being drank, came to his house an Saturday at night,

---

¹ After the execution of Charles I., the Royalists of the North rose under Thomas Mackenzie of Pluscardine (Lord Seaforth's brother) and Mackay, Lord Reay, in support of Charles II. They entered Inverness on 22nd Feb. 1649, expelled the garrison, and demolished the town walls. On 8th May following they were defeated at Balvenie in the parish of Mortlach by Leslie's horse.

² The 'Malignants' opposed the Solemn League and Covenant of 1643, which they considered unconstitutional and rebellious, and were, generally speaking, the supporters of the King and the followers of Montrose. They did not necessarily disapprove of the more moderate Covenant of 1638. As a rule they, like Montrose, adhered to it.

³ Mackay of Bighouse.

bot y^t Mr. Robert came not nier yem, and y^t therfoir they brak his bairne [barn], strick his man, and tak meat and drink according to y^r own pleasure, and y^t the morrow, being Sunday, y^t he preached expreslie against yeir courses.

And being posed what they knew of his cariage toward the malignants efter ye day of Balvenie, ansered that he entertained none to yer knowledge bot his grandson, and y^t the most qlk they heard him express wes thus, That he wes sorrie for ye miscarriage of these malignants, q^{ho} had procured yer own fall;[1] yet y^t he rejoiced y^t God had scattered his enimies.

That he lectures and preaches befoir and efter noon, y^t he attends his charge and meddles not with civil affairs, that he keeps familie worship at home and presses the same upon the people, y^t he visits ye sick qhen requyred, and y^t he is a good disciplinator.

The Elderes being removed and the Minister called, and being enquyred, declares that they are faithfull in delating delinquents bot slak in executing discipline, that they are of good c'sa°n [conversation] and that some of them observe familie worship.

The Elderes being called are ordained to be more assistant to ye Minister in putting discipline in execution.

The Minister declared resident, y^t he labours no land bot his gleeb, and being posed anent the provision of his kirk, declares y^t he has agreed with the heritors for 5c.m.[2] and 3 chaulders of wictuall: forder declares y^t he knew not how much his predecessor had, bot that Mr. David Monro, his predecessor, told him y^t their wes a c'descendence betwixt him and ye heritors, as those y^t wer pressent this day c'fessed the same; yet that they wer not oblidged to giue the same vnto anie other: and the brethren being informed that the c'discendence wes registrate they ordaine Mr. Robert to seek for ye extract y^{r}off.

And ye Brethrein, for forder cleiring of the matter, enquyred the heritors whither their wes anie private pac°n [paction]

---

[1] By their rise under Mackenzie of Pluscardine and Lord Reay, and their defeat at Balvenie.

[2] 500 merks.

betwixt them and yer Minister, deponed that ther wes no such thing.

The Minister and Elderes declared y^t Wednesday is appointed for weiklie catechising, ordained to be moir painfull in catechiseing, and declareing y^t the c'munion wes not administrate since his entrie, because of ye troubles, he is ordained to haue a formall table for the co'munion and to administrat ye same with all obsaruences.

Mr. Jon Monro declared Thesaurer, and declared honest be ye Minister and elderes. No clerk therfoir ordained to help ye same.

And being enquyred what progress they made for planta^{o}n of a schooles, ansered y^t they wer to c'tribut for ane schoolle with Alines;[1] the forder tryall of yis c'tinnewed intill the visita^{o}n of Alines.

Angus Pyper, kirk officer, declared faithfull in his calling.

Declares that ther are colle^{o}nes sabbathlie, ordaines the collectiones to be taken up according to the Act of ye gr̄all Assemblie.

Declares that ther is none y^t resort to excomunicat p'sones.

Mr. ferq^r Ma^{c}Lennan and Mr. Do^d M^{c}crae enquyred anent their visiting Mr. Murdo McKenzie, declares y^t Mr. Murdo is bedfast.

Mr. George Monro enquyred anent the reference of Mr. do^d ross, declared y^t he, Mr. Alex^r. McKenzie, and ye guid man of Tullich went to Lochbruime and reponed Mr. do^d ross according to ye ordinance of ye com̄ission.

The Kirk of Kilmorack to be visited yis day 15 dayes, and ye Minister preach on his ordinarie matter.

The ac^{o}n [action] closed with pray^r.

At *Kilmoraik, the* 17 *Julie* 1649.

Conveined Mr. ferq^r McLennan, Mr. George Monro, Mr. Johne Monro, Mr. do^d M^{c}crae, and Mr. do^d Fraser, Ministers, and Alex^r Chissolm of Comar, Hew fraser, fiar of Struy, Jon fraser of Clunwakkie, Allan M^{c}ronaild of Teachknock, Allex^r fraser of Little Struy, Jon McCulloch, Ranaild McRanaild,

---

[1] Alness.

Thomas fraser, W^m fraser, Allex^r M^candro, Jon Smith, David Tailzor, Johne M^cfinlay, Hutcheon McWilliam, Elders of the said Kirk.

The name of God incalled.

Mr. ferq^r McLennan, who wes late Mod^r, appointed to moderate this metting.

The Session book being presented, and nothing to visited y^rin, because it was wisited be the comission at Alderne latlie.

The Provision of the Kirk declared be the Minister to be sex hundreth and twentie merks be decreitt of platt and thrie hundreth merks of augmentation: c'descended upon be the heritors: q^{lk} c'descendence is denyed be all the heritors y^t wer present except Allex^r Chissolme of Comar[1] who acknowledged y^t the condiscendence wes, and also his own willingnes to pay c'forme.

Declares y^t he had sufficient gleib and manse.

That he keiped weiklie catechising.

Declares that he presses a schooll; ordained to urge the same moir and moir, and report his dilligence to ye prie.

That y^r is no excomūnicat person within ye Paroch.

Alex^r fraser of Little Struy, Thesaurer for ye Wester pairt of the Paroch, and Alex^r M^ceandowie, ye east, both declared honest and faithfull.

The Minister removed.

The Elders deponed that his doctrine is sound and edifieing to y^r knowledge, that he keiped familie worship in his own house, that he presses ye same upon the people, that he preacheth in ye afternoone at Kilmorack, y^t he preacheth morning to the tymes, y^t he is no tryster in civill business, that he visits the sick when requyred, that he is painefull in discipline and ministeriall in c'versa^on and lyfe, and gives a good report of him in all thingis belonging to his calling.

The Elderes removed,

The Minister called and declared the Elderes faithfull and cairfull in y^r calling; ordained the Minister, with some elderes, to goe about ye Paroch and presse familie worship upon ye people, and report his dilligence to ye presbyterie.

---

[1] The Chisholm.

At Vrqhairt, 31 Julie 1649.

Convened Mr. Dod. fraser, moderator, Mr. ferq^r McLennan, Mr. George Monro, Mr. Johne Monro, and Mr. Dod MacCrae, Ministers, and Murdo Mackenzie of Little findon, Jon fraser in Kinkel, Jon Monro ther, Andro Monro in Milchaith, dod. baine ther, dod. McAllister vic finlay in Kinkell, finlay McAllister vic finlay ther, Finlay dodson [Donaldson] in Milchaich, doncane oig M^{c}finlay in Kinkel, dod M^{c}rorie yer, Johne M^{c}finlay gowe, and ferq^r M^{c}ean waine in Culbokie, Elders.

The name of God incalled.

The Minister, Mr. George Monro, preached the 4 Johne.

A ltre [letter] from Mr. Robert Monro, proporting him sicklie and unable to keip our meitting.

No thing presented bot scroilles, and being enquyred why he did not present a book, ansered y^t he wes to get a new book; ordained to doe the same with all dilligence, and report theiroff to be made to the Prie.

The Minister removed,

The Elderes being sworne, deponed that he preacheth befoir and efter noone, That Tuesday is appointed for weiklie catechising bot y^t he hed not entered zit, That he attends his charge, y^t he lives ministeriallie, y^t he keips familie worship in his house, and presses the same upon ye people, That he visits the sick, and y^t y^r is a zeir since the Comunion wes given.

The Elderes removed,

The Minister called, and being enquyred why he did not administer the Comunion yis zeir bygone, ansered y^t be reason of ye troubles he hed not c'venient tyme; he is theirfoir ordained to prepare the people, and give the sacrament with all dilligence.

And being enquyred c'cerneing ye Elderes, declared yem faithfull delaters, bot slack in executing discipline.

The Elders called,

They are ordained to be more cairfull to execut discipline.

Because of frequent prophanation of ye Lordes day in yis paroich by aquavitey bearers,[1] ordained that those with whom

---

[1] This was the famous whisky district of Ferintosh.

such merchants are on the Saterday at night dismisse yem not vntill monday morning vnder y⁰ paine of censure, and the session to proceid against the c'traveiners with the censures of y⁰ Church.

Ordaines y^t fishers on the Lords day in zairs ebbe or anie other way be severelie censured.

Ordaines that tuo Elderes be appointed be y⁰ Session to goe alonges and try q^{ho} within y⁰ Paroich resorts to supplicatione wells, especiallie on the sett day, and delate them to the Session q^{r}be they may be censured conforme.

The Minister declared the Provision of the Kirk to be sex hundreth merks and the wicarage, and declareing y^t he tabled his ac°n befoir y⁰ Comission for planta°n of Kirks, he is ordained to present the same.

Ordaines the Kirk theking [thatching] to be helped, the pulpit repaired, a new table for y⁰ Comunion provyded and all other things necessarie for y⁰ decencie of y⁰ same.

The brethren finding y^t their hes not bene a compt of penalties exacted this tyme bygone, ordaines the same to be done with all dilligence.

Ordaines vniformitie of penalties throwout the whole prie and that the single fornicator pay 4 m.[1] at lest.

And the Minister and Elderes declaring that they were goeing about to seik for a man to be scholmaister and clerk to y⁰ Session, they are ordained to goe an with dilligence and mak report of y⁰ same to y⁰ Prie.

Jon McWilliam, Kirk Officer, declared faithfull, saife onlie slak in executing the orders of y⁰ Session, especiallie in poinding; ordaines him to amend yis vnder paine of censure.

The Collec°nes for y⁰ poore found to haue beine distributed.

Dod. M^{c}ean vic finlay excomunicate declared to be obedient in giving satisfac°ne.

[Here follow cases of discipline; ordained 'to mak repentance *in sacco.*']

The Brethrein taking y⁰ long vacancie of Contain to their c'sidera°n, and c'sidering y^t they had received no anser from y⁰ Prie of Invernes annent Mr. Duncane M^{c}cullach his transplanta-

---

[1] 4 merks.

tion to yᵉ sᵈ kirk, and heiring yᵗ the P̃rie of Invernes wes to visit yᵉ Kirk of Vrqʳᵗ [in Inverness-shire] qher yᵉ sᵈ Mr. Duncane is serueing for yᵉ tyme, upon tuisday nixt, ordained Mr. dod fraser to repair thither the said day for requyreing ther absolut anser in the mater of yᵉ said transplantation.

Siklyk, c'sidering ye ordanance of yᵉ Com̃issiõ of yᵉ grãll assemblie for visitaᵒn of yᵉ kirks of Ross, Southerland, and Catnes, meitt at Alderne, the   day of   recomending to yᵉ P̃rie of Invernes and Dingˡˡ to meitt togidder to sie how yᵉ kirks of Kiltarlitie and Kilmorack might be better accomodat as they are for the tyme, and whither a third paroich might be erected in yᵉ bounds of yᵉ sᵈ paroiches; and being informed yᵗ yᵉ P̃rie of Invernes wes to meitt at Kiltarlitie the eight of Agust nixt, ordained all the brethrein to meitt ther yᵉ sᵈ day with the P̃rie of Invernes, to the purpose forsaid.

Ordaines the Kirk of Vrray to be visited on thursday nixt, and the Minister to preach on his ordinarie text.

The Brethrein taking to yʳ c'sideraᵒn the scandell of alleadged adulterie of Elspett Baine, ordaines Mr. ferqʳ MacLennan to preach at Dingˡˡ yᵉ nixt Sabbath, and to try if Elspet Baine wes within yᵉ bounds and if anie light might be had on yᵉ sᵈ mater.

The meitting closed with prayer.

At Vrray, 2do August 1649.

Conveened Mr. Dod fraser, Modʳ, Mr. ferqʳ McLennan, Mr. George Monro, Mr. Joⁿ. Monro, and Mr. Dod Macrae.

The name of God incalled:

The Minister preached 4 Sal. 2. 2.

Becaus of the incapacitie of Elderes [1] the Brethren c'tinew their m'dgement for remedieing the same vntill resoluᵒn hade be their Comissioner from the grãll assembly, and the minister ordeined to act qᵗ in him lyes in the matter of discipline.

The Ministʳ enquyred c'cerning the prowision of the Kirk, declaires the same to be five hundreth threescoir ten merks be decreit of Platt, qʳoff the viccarage is overvalued to two hundreth merks; as also declaires yᵗ when Mr. Joⁿ Mckenzie,

---

[1] That is, through Malignancy.

now Minister at Tarbat, entered Minister to the Kirk of Vrray, the heretors of Vrray, secluding Kilchreist, c'descended to give two chalders victuall, threttie two schillings st'ling of augmenta^{o}n for bettering the provision of the said kirk, qlk c'descendence as he heares was acted in a provinciall Synod c'forme q^{r}unto his predecessor, Mr. Jo^n McKenzie, was payed, zet the greatest number of the heretors payes not him becaus he is not able to produce the said Condescendence; which the Brethrein tacking to c'sideration they ordeined y^t Mr. Jo^n McKenzie sould be spocken and enquyred c'cerning the matter efter his returne from the South.

The Minister declaires y^t he hes sufficient gleib and manse, according as was designed to his predecessors.

The Brethren, c'sidering how difficult it is for ministers in the low countrie to serve at Strachonan, thinks it fitt y^t for accomoda^{o}n these bounds be visited how soone they may c'veniently.

Mr. Ferq^r McLennan and Mr. Dod. M^{c}rae ordained to preach at Strachonnan, as is incumbent to them.

Duncan M^{c}alister vic conill dowy, relapser in adulterie, being referred from the Session to this meitting, called, not compeirand, bot his father compeiring in his name and declairing that his guids were stollen from him and that he was upon the persuit of them. The Brethren finding the same to be true, c'tinewes the proces till the visita^{o}n of the hielands be past. To be resolved anent the tyme of which visita^{o}n the Presbyterie of Invernes at Kiltarlitie to haue [a sederunt] at Kilmorack.

The Meiting closed with prayer.

At Kilmorack, 8 *Aug. post meridiem.*

Conveined Mr. dod Fraser, Mod^r, Mr. Ferq^r Ma^{c}lennan, Mr. George Monro, Mr. Do^d M^{c}rae, and Mr. Jo^n Monro.

The name of God incalled.

The Brethren tacking to their c'sideration the expediencie of visiting the hiland kirks, and the ordinance made theranent formerly, appoynts to tacke journey (God willing) upon Monday nixt, and to visit the kirk of Kintaill upon the Wednesday, the Kirk of Lochalsh upon the Thursday, and the Kirk of Lochcarrin upon the Fryday immediately following and ordaines Mr. Do^d Ma^{c}rac to adv'tise them c'forme, and to writt to Mr. Alex^r M^{c}kenzie, Minister at Lochcarrin, requiring him in the Presbyteries name to adv'tise Mr. Rorie M^{c}kenzie at Garlich, and Mr. Do^d Ross at Lochbroome, to meete with them at Lochcarrin the said fryday for appoyting dyats for visiting their Kirks.

Maister Rorie MacLeod appoynted to be readdie to exercise the first Presbyterie day at Dingwall.

The meiting closed with a blessing.

At Kintaill, 15 *Aug*. 1649.

That day c'veined Mr. Do^d Fraser, Mod^r, Mr. ferq^r McLennan, Mr. George Monro, Mr. Ferq^r M^{c}rae, Mr. Jo^n Monro, and Mr. Do^d Macrae, Clk.

The name of God incalled.

The Minister preached Col. 3. 9.

No elders or people present, except some few that were not c'siderable.

The minister enquired whither he hade made intima^{o}n of the visita^{o}n to the people and q^t wes the reasone they did not c'veene, ansered that he made intima^{o}n, and y^t he heard the reasone of their absence was y^t they were on the persuit of guids that were stollen and tacken away from the severall corners of the countrie.

The Minister, enquired why the Kirk thacking wes not repaired, ansered y^t the troubles of the tymes wes the caus theroff.

And being enquired c'cerning the provision of the Kirk, ansered y^t it wes the third pairt of the viccarage extending to ane hundreth libs, and y^t he hade so much land as extended to three hundreth libs, and y^t he hade the same by way of c'descendence with the superior, as all his predecessors since the first reforma^{o}n hade the same.

And being enquired whither he had gleib or manse, ansered he hade neither of these.

No pulpit, no collectiones for the poore, no desks.

> Referres of the Presbyterie at this visita^{o}n to the minister and Session.

1. That the Kirk be repaired, a pulpit made, a suitable stoole for public repentance erected, the Kirk floore pavemented, the beames of the couples filed, no burialls to be within the Kirk, the Kirk zaird dycks to be bigged, the windowes to be brodded and glasend, the Kirk to be plenissed with desks, and their diligence in the premisses to be reported to the nixt ensueing provinciall.

2. That the minister seeke for gleib and manse and provision to his Kirk, and that he urge the Presbyterie for designa°n efter resoluti°n hade theranent with their Comissioner from the grāll assembly.

That he provyd a session book well bound, and that the same be filled and sent to the Presbyterie before the fyfteene day of September nixt.[1]

That there be a collector and collec°nes for the poore, a thesaurer, and a kirk box.

That prophainers of the sabbaoth, especially by beiring burdens and fisching, be severely censured.

That ane week day be keeped for catechising, baptism, and mariage.

That familie worship be pressed upon the people, and the severall families visited to that effect.

That the people be catechised and prepared for the Communion, zett not to administer the same without advyse q^{r}be malignants their receiving of it before dew satisfaction given may be the better prevented.

That trelapsers in fornica°n, adulterers, and incestuous persons, be brought before the Presbyterie before they be received on repentance, and sicklyke before they be absolved.

That a schoole be urged, and report of diligence heirin be made to the provinciall.

That swearing, drunckennes, and cursing be censured according to the Act of parllament.

That absents from the Kirk on dayes of publick worship be censured.

That the Minister have a list of the Malignants within his

---

[1] See Minute of 17th Aug. 1649.

paroch, and the severall degrees of their guilt, to be given to the Presbyterie q^n it sall be required.

That testimonialls be sought at termes.

That Do^d M^{c}conchie vic finlay dowy be sent to the session of Lochalsh, to anser for his adulteries committed in that paroch.

Ordaines all the saids references to be insert in the session booke, and intima°n to be made of them the nixt sabbaoth.

The meiting closed with a blessing.

At Lochalsh, 16 *Aug.* 1649.

Conveened Mr. Do^d Fraser, Mod^r, Mr. ferq^r M^{c}rae, Mr. ferq^r M^{ac}Lennan, Mr. Do^d McLennan, Jo^n Monro, and Mr. Do^d M^{c}rae, clk of the Presbyterie of Ding^{ll}.

The name of God incalled.

The minister preached Math. 9. 3.

No elders in capacitie.

Nothing found in this Kirk but the bare walls.

The tryall of the scrolls of the Session of Kintaill being c'tinewed till this day, Mr. ferq^r McLennan and Mr. Jo^n Monro appoynted to visit them, and give in their report tomorrow at Lochcarron.[1]

Mr. George Monro and Mr. Jo^n Monro appoynted to visite the scrolls of the session of Lochalsh, and to macke their report tomorrow at Lochcarrin.

The Minister enquired anent gleebe and manse, declares y^t there is neither gleebe nor manse designed.

And being enquired anent the provision of his Kirk declaires the same to be five hundreth merks, and y^t only be way of c'descendence with the superior.

The Presbyterie inquiring of the minister if he hade made intima°n of the visita°n, and q^t was the reasone of the people not conveening, anscred he did macke intima°n bot knew not q^t was the reasone of the peoples absence.

The brethren, hearing y^t ane Christine neine ean vic Kenneth, incestuows within the Ile of Sky, did reside in Lochalsh, ordained y^t she sould be removed and not suffered to abyd in

---

[1] See Minute of the 17th Aug.

the countrey vntill she proported a testimoniall from Mr. Archibald Ma^{c}queen, minister at [place blank in register.]¹

Jo^n buy, Kirk officer, declaired be the Minister faithfull and painfull.

Referres to Session and Minister.

That the Minister raise letres of horning, and charge the parochiners to roofe and thech the Kirk, and his diligence to be reported to the nixt ensueing provinciall vnder payne of censure.

That pulpit be made, a stoole of publick repentance erected, the Kirke floore pavemented, y^t no burialls be within the Kirk, the kirkzaird dyck be bigged, and windowes brodd and glassened, the Kirk plenissed with desks, and report to be made anent all these particulars to the nixt ensueing provinciall.

The Visitation of ye Kirk of Lochcarron.

At Lochcarrin, 17 Augt. 1649.

Conveined Mr. Do^d fraser, Mod^r, Mr. do^d McLennan, Mr. George Monro, Mr. ferq^r McLennan, Mr. Alex^r McKenzie, and Mr. do^d M^{c}cra, Clerk of ye Prie of Dingwall.

The name of God incalled.

Mr. Alex^r McKenzie, Minister yer, preached, Rom. v. 10.

No elderes, in capacitie be reason of Malignancie.

Ordaines that the Kirk thacking be helped.

A formall stoole of repentance found, bot ney^r pulpit nor dasks.

Ordaines a pulpit and dasks to be made, the windowes to be glassened, the kirk zaird dyck bigged, the Kirk floore to be pavemented, the beames of ye couples to be filled, and y^t no burialls be within ye Kirk.

The late Elderes being present declares that the minister did urge the subscription of the League and Covenant first and last, bot that yey refused the same both the tymes for fear of yer Superiors; Qlk the Brethren taking to yer c'sidera^{o}n, continewes proceiding against them till resolu^{o}n had from the grall assemblie.

---

¹ Mr. Archibald Macqueen was minister of Snizort, but his parish was evidently not known to the Presbytery of Dingwall !

The Minister enquired if he did keip a week day for catechising, Baptisme, and mariage, ansered y^t he did appoint Thursday for y^t effect. The Prie ordaines the s^d day to be keiped, and the people to be prepared for ye Comunio^n bot not to administrate ye same vntill the Prie's advyse be had.

Ordaines the Minister to present the Sumonds of Walua°n for prowyding his Kirk, and mak report of his dilligence to ye nixt ensueing Prowinciall.

Ordaines him to urge ye Prie for designa°n of Gleib and Manse efter resolu°n had from the grall assemblie.

Doncane M^{c}do^d vic Wurchie declared collector of ye penalties. No collectiones for ye poore, and no kirk box—q^{r}foir ordaines to haue both.

The Minister ordained to vrge a school, and mak report of his dilligence to ye next Provinciall.

[Cases of discipline: Greadich nein ean vic Conchie Ryach, 'being declared fugitive, ordained to be summarlie excumunicat the nixt sabbaoth for her incest, adulterie, and severall fornicatione, and mak report of ye same to ye prie, and to adwertise ye rest of ye hieland ministers to mak intima°n theiroff.']

The report of the Scroilles of Session of the Kirk of Kintall.

Mr. ferq^r McLennan and Mr. Johne Monro reported y^t they are informall, manie of ye errata not mended. No mention of the Thanksgiving for the wictorie at Balvenie.

The Report of the Scroills of ye Kirk of Lochalsh.

The said Scroilles being visited be Mr. George and Mr. Johne Monros, their report y^t he mended the former errata much, bot made no mention of ye Sederunts.

Report of the Scroilles of ye Kirk of Lochcarrin made be Mr. ferq^r McLennan and Mr. Johne Monro.

No mention of keiping the Thanksgiving for ye wictorie at Balvenie notwithstanding intima°n y^{r}off insert; zet the late Elderes declared y^t the same was keiped. No satisfaction appointed to fornicators, ney^r c'fessing nor c'peiring.

No mention of anie penalties of delinquents.

A Session ordaineing Banishment.

Ordaines Mr. Allex^r McKenzie, Minister at Lochcarrin, to observe the directiones of ye Comission at Alderne for remedieing the former errata.

The visitation of Gairloch and Lochbruime c'tinewed be the way long not rydable and inabilitie of brethren to goe afoote, and because of our Comissioners home coming of, when the Brethren expects forder information and new directiones from ye Genrl Assemblie, and because ther could no certain dyat be appointed for visiting these Kirks in regard of ye Ministers ther absence.

Ordaines Mr. George Monro and Mr. Jo^n Monro to visit Mr. Murdo Makenzie, late Minister at Ding^{ll}, and report his c'dition for ye tyme to ye prie the first day of Meitting.

Ordaines the nixt prie day to hold at Ding^{ll} ye 28 August 1649, and the Ministers of ye hieland Kirks ordained to sumnond the delinquents unto y^o said day.

Mr. ferq^r McLennan ordained to adwertise Mr. Rorie M^{c}cleoud to exercise y^t day according to the former appointment.

The Meitting closed with prayer.

At Dingwall, 28 *Aug.* 1649.

Conveined Mr. do^d fraser, mod^r, Mr. Robert Monro, Mr. ferq^r m^{c}Lennan, Mr. George Monro, Mr. Jo^n M^{c}crae, Mr. Johne Monro and Mr. do^d McCrae, Ministers, and Neill Beton, ruling Elder from Alnes.

The name of God incalled.

Mr. Rorie McCleoud haveing exercised, Act. lc. 9, 10, 11 v^s.

Removed, his doctrine tryed and approven.

Mr. Johne McCrae haveing directed the declara^{o}nes of the grall assemblie, and the reasones of ye fast appointed be the grall assemblie to be keiped upon y^o last sabbaoth of yis instant to all the Brethren seuerallie, and enquyreing if they had receaved yem, all acknowledged the reset of them, and declared y^t they red the declara^{o}n and intimat the fast ye last sabbaoth.

The Summe of the Reasones of ye said fast.

1. The c'tineuance and increase of sin and prophanitie, especiallie of ye sin of Witchcraft.

2. Secondlie, The interruption of ye Lordes work in England and Ireland and sore oppression of his people, by prevaleing partie of Sectaries in ye one, and Malignantes in ye other.

3. The King his not granting ye just and necessarie of yis Kirk and Kindome for secureing of Religion, and his making peace with the Irish Rebells.

Wee are to entreat ye Lord to delyver ye king from ye snare of Malignant counsells, and to enclyne his heart to giue satisfaction in yese thinges y^t c'cerne Religion y^t he may be estableished on his throne.

To pray for stedfastnes to this land, especiallie to yose qho haue the charge of publick affaires, y^t in ye middest of so manie snares and tenta°ns, they may keip ther integritie and not declyne to ye Right or to ye left.

That the Lord would strengthen those who suffer for his cause in England and Ireland, and break ye yock of yer oppressors, and carie on his work amongst them unto the praise of his own name, comfort of his people, and shame of his enemies.

That he would regaird ye necessitie of the poore by giveing a fair and seasonable harvest, and bestow upon his people a plentifull measure of ye fruits of ye earth, for preventing ye famine threatened and feared, and enabling the kingdome to beare necessarie burdens without repyneing.

Mr. Thomas presented ane Act of the genṝll Assemblie for opening of his mouth, the tenour wheroff followeth:

' *Edinb.* 24 *Julie* 1649 *post merid.*
' *Sess.* 23.

'The Assemblie haveing considdered the deposition of Mr. Tho. Ross, who was deposed about a year since, and haveing heard the s^d Mr. Thomas himselfe give evidences of his sence of sorrow for his miscarriage, As also Considdering the testimonies from the prēbie, Synod, and Commission for visitation of Ross, concerning this satisfaction given to them, doe y^rfore refer him to the p̄ṝie of Dingwall, and doe heirby ordayne them with all diligence to open his mouth, and to put him in a capacitie for the Ministrie q^r it may please God to giue him a law^{ll} call.

'*Sic subscribitr.*,

'H. Ker.'

The ansers y^{r}of c'tinewed untill ye nixt day in regaird the tyme wes farre spent be reason of ye manie referres; and the Commissioner his dilligence as it to be enquyred.

Mr. John M^{c}cra, Comissioner, haueing dlyvered in Prie thrie Actes of the grall Assemblie c'cerneing y^e [   ] of receaveing the Engagers.[1] Seven actes of Parliament anent ye poore, and one Act of Redresse, and haueing sent fyve declara^{o}nes, fyve reasones of the fast, fyve actes anent ye poore, one act annent the receaueing of the Engagers for ye Ministeres of ye hieland Kirks, and Mrs. [Messrs.] George and John Monroes declareing they receaved them, and directed ye same to y^o severall ministeres, all ordained to mak use of yem with all dilligence.

Suchlyk, declareing y^r wes a Comission appointed be ye grall assemblie for visiting ye Province of Ross, to meitt at Chanrie the last tuesday of September nixt, ordained all ye Brethren to mak intima^{o}n of the same, and advertise yer elderes to be present ther.

Sicklyk, reportes that Mr. Thomas Ross delyuered one hundreth merks and himselfe fourtie and fyve pounds to Patrick Dickson for James Murray his restes, and promises to report a full discharge upon the resett of tueentie and sex merks. His dilligence approven.

Allex^r Baine of Knockbaine, c'peiring and acknowledging a sense of his errour for his accesse to ye late Rebellion by his goeing to Invernes,[2] and supplicating the Prie to tak his repentance and receave him—his anser continewed to ye nixt day.

---

[1] The Engagers were those who had taken part in the Duke of Hamilton's 'Engagement' in 1648—their purpose being to reconquer England for Charles I. Hamilton led an army into England, but was defeated by Cromwell at Preston. The General Assembly opposed the Engagement, and after its collapse the famous Act of Classes was passed enacting penalties against the Engagers, and excluding them from office and Church privileges.

[2] The rising for Charles II., under Mackenzie of Pluscardin and Lord Reay, which came to an end at the Battle of Balvenie. During its progress, the 'rebels' took Inverness (February 1649), and demolished its walls and fortifications.

Ordaines ane lre to be wreitten and directed with yᶜ Kirk Officer of Lochalsh for advertiseing y° ministeres of Lochcarrin, Lochalsh, and Kintaill, of yᵉ dyat of yᵉ Comission for visita°n of yᵉ Prowince, and ordaines Mr. John Maᶜcrae to adwertise y° minister of Garloch, and ferqʳ Mᶜlennan yᵉ minister of Lochbruime.

The nixt meitting appointed to be 11 Sept.

The meitting closᵈ with prayr.

At Dingwall, 11 *Sept.* 1649.

The exercise c'tinewed because of the many referrs, and many ingadgers to come in before the Presbyterie.

Maister Ferqʳ Mᶜlennan and Mr. George Monro enquired c'cerning their diligence anent the revising of Mr. Rob. Monro his Session booke, reports they revised it, and gaue in the observationes following:

1. Delinquents ordained to be jogged.¹
2. Intima°n of one fast, and yᵉ reasons not specified.
3. Sessiones intermitted, and yᵉ reason not insert.
4. Intima°n of the Thanksgiveing for y° wictorie at Balvenie, bot no mention of yᵉ keiping of it.
5. Elderes elected not c'forme to the order.

Ordaines the errata to be helped according to the directiones of the Comission at Alderne.

This day a formall session booke wes sent to the Presbyterie be Mr. Ferqʳ Maᶜrae, Minister at Kintaill, according to the ordinance of the visita°n at his kirk, which wes delivered to Mr. Ferqʳ Mᶜlennan and Mr. George Monro to be visited, and they ordained to macke report of ther diligence the nixt day.

Catherine nein rorie vic ean vic conichie Riach, within the Paroch of Lochcarrin, reported from the minister to haue been excomunicat according to the ordinance at the visita°n of Lochcarrin, ordaines the Brethren to macke intima°n thereof in their severall Kirks.

All the brethren reports that they keiped the fast.

The opeining of Mr. Thomas Ros his mouth c'tinued, vntill

---

¹ That is, put into the jougs.

he deliver the evidences of the Kirk of Alnes to the Presbyterie according to the ordinance of the commission of visita°n at Chanrie the   day of

Margaret Monro in Culcraiggie delated for charming and referred be the Session of Alnes to the Presbyterie, called, compeired and acknowledged the turning of the seive and the sheir, and being enquired how she learned the same declared y^t it was from Shihag Vrq^{rt} in Delines, and that the said Shihag, her two sonnes, William Clunes and Finlay riach, were p͡ut q^n she learned it; ordained to compeir againe before the Presbyterie q^{n}ever she sould be required, for which Neill Beaton inacted himselfe cautioner. And Mr. Jon Monro advettised to caus the Presbyterie of Tayne to tacke course with the said Shihag and her sonnes, seeing they reside within that Presbyterie.

The Presbyterie c'sidering the expediencie of the planta°n of schooles and the Act of Parliament made theranent, thought fitt that the vnderwritten persones sould be required be the ministeres of the severall paroches q^r they reside, to meete with the Presbyterie the nixt day for tacking course for erection and planta°n of schooles within the Presbyterie c'forme to the tenor of the Act of Parliament: for which effect the persones following were nominat and ordained to be required, viz., Robt Monro of Obstill, Hew Fraser of Eskadaill, Hector Douglas of Balkney, Androw Monro, portioner of Culcairne, Do^d Finlaysone, portioner thereoff, Hew Monro of Teaninich, Hew Monro of Foiris, Androw Monro in Teanuar,[1] Hew Monro in Keatuall, Jo^n Monro in Newtowne, Jo^n Monro in Kinkell, Mr. Jo^n Monro of Swardill, Ferq^r Monro of Teanaird, and Neill Beaton in Culcraigie.

Mr. Jo^n Ma^{c}rae was this day no͡'at and appoynted Comissioner for the Presbyterie for repairing to the Presbyterie of Invernes to require their anser in the matter of Mr. Duncan M^{c}culloch his transporta°n from Vrq^t to Contin, giving him full power to reasone and anser q^t sall be propounded in name of the Presbyterie.

That day a number of Ingadgers from severall paroches com-

---

[1] Teanuar: Tigh-nuar—Gaelic name of Novar.

peired before the Presbyterie upon their hearing of the act of gⁱall assembly intimated by their severall ministeres, offering themselves to tryall and declairing their willingnes to give satisfaction according to their guilt, and desire to be received: which the Brethren tacking to c'serat°n proceided in tryall of them as follows.

The names of the Ingadgers compeiring the said day from the Paroch of Alnes:

Joⁿ Maᶜkenzie of Davachcairne compeiring as said is, and exhorted to be ingenuous in his c'fession, acknowledged he was classed before for complyance with James Grahame¹ and yᵗ he did c'tribut by giving men and meanes to the vnlawfull ingadgment against Englande, being forced to it by qʳtering, and that he was at the casting downe of the walls of Invernes in the late Rebellion.

[Dod Monro, Robt Monro, and 'Hew Monro sonne to Teannich,' confessed being in the 'Ingadgment against England.']

Ingadgers within the Paroch of Kilterne:

Joⁿ Monro in Culnaskeah confessed that he was a Lieuctenent in the vnlawˡˡ ingadgment against England. David Monro in Keatuall c'fessed that he was ane ensagne bearer in the vnlawˡˡ ingadgment, and accessarie also to the late insurrection in the north.

Joⁿ Monro of Ardully c'fessed yᵗ he was in the unlawfull ingadgement against England, and accessorie to the late rebellion, bot yᵗ he had office in neither of them, and that he knew not the intention of the Insurrection vntill he came to Keassack.

[Several others confessed they were common soldiers in the Ingadgment and rebellion.]

Ingadgers within the Paroch of Dingwall:

Alexʳ Bayne of Knockbayne c'fessed yᵗ he subscrived the remonstrance,² and was censured for the same, yᵗ he contribut

---

¹ The Marquis of Montrose.
² In June 1646 the General Assembly excommunicated the Earl of Seaforth for contriving a 'perfidious Band' under the name of 'an humble Remonstrance,' against the National Covenant and the League and Covenant of the Three Kingdoms. It consisted of several articles, one of which invited the King to come to Scotland. It was extensively subscribed in Ross-shire.

to the vnlaw[ll] ingadgment in men and meanes being forced and compelled thairto, and that he chanced to be in the late insurrection and rebellion bot knew not their intention vntill he came to Keassack, and y[t] he forsooke them befoir the walls of Invernes were cast down.

[Jo[n] Bayne his brother made similar confession.]

Ingadgers compeiring from the Paroch of Fottertie :

Jo[n] Ma[c]kenzie in Davochcairne c'fessed he was accessorie to James Grahames rebellion in Seaforts company, y[t] he was to receive the office of a lievetennant in the vnlaw[ll] ingadgment, and that he was in the late rebellion and at Invernes.

[Several others confessed to being 'at both Invernes and Balveinie '—and others confessed having been ' at Invernes bot not at Balvenie.']

Ingadgers from the Parish of Urray :

Maister Coline Ma[c]kenzie of Kinnock, and Duncan M[c]alister vic conell dowy, confessed.

Parish of Urquhart :

Neill Monro of Findon confessed he was a member of a Comittee y[t] was for the vnlaw[ll] ingadgement, and y[t] his contributing men and meanes to it was be compulsion, and y[t] he was at Invernes in the late Insurrection, bot stayed not.

The classing and enjoyning censure to the said Ingadgers c'tinued till farther tryall and advysement, and they are sumoned *apud acta* to compeir before the Presbyterie againe q[n]ever they sould be advertised by their severall ministers.

That day Jo[n] Monro of Lemlair compeiring before the Presbyterie acknowledging his error, and, professing great greife and sorrow for his accession to the vnlawf[ll] ingadgement and the late rebellion in the North, and c'sidering y[t] according to the act of the g[r]all assembly none above the degree of a leivetenant guiltie as he was, can be received on repentance vntill they haue their recourse to the g[r]all assembly or their comissioners, Therefore supplicated the Presbyterie to grant him a certificat of his cariage before the vnlaw[ll] ingadgment and since his coming off the late rebellion, to be proported to the Comission of the g[r]all assembly, to which he intended to haue his recourse with all c'venient diligence for receiving such censure as they would be pleased to enjoyne : Quhich being c'sidered by the Presbyterie, his desyre was thought relevant, and granted.

Sicklyke, Captaine Androw Monro acknowledging his accesse to the vnlaw^{ll} ingadgment for England, and professing his greife for the same, and supplicating the Presbyterie for a certificate of the Lyke tenor upon the same ground, and the same effect, his desyre thought relevant, and granted.

The Brethren c'sidering y^t many of the malignants and Ingadgers were not come in zet, appoynted y^t the acts of gr̄all assembly sould be intimated againe, and y^t a list be given of such as sall not compeir be their severall ministeres, q^{r}be they may be processed.

At Ding. 18 Septemb. 1649.

Mr. Jo^n M^{c}rae absent, being direct comissioner to the Presbyterie of Invernes for receiving their anser in the matter of Mr. Duncan M^{c}culloch his transportation. Mr. Do^d M^{c}rae did give in a list of Ingadgers within the Parochins of Vrray and Kilchreist, c'teining the persones following:

Rorie Mackenzie of Davachmoluagg, Kenneth McKenzie his servant, W^m M^{c}conill vayne vic ean vreick, Duncan M^{c}conill vic ean riach, James M^{c}vic rob in Wester Farburne, Hector McKenzie of Farburne, Rorie McKenzie fier of farburne, Jo^n buy M^{c}finlay gowne, Thomas begg M^{c}chlachar, Thomas Moir M^{c}chlachar, Jo^n Keil [Caol] M^{c}coule, Jo^n M^{c}conill dowy vic W^m, Jo^n M^{c}ean vic conill vic Thomas, Duncan M^{c}fcrq^r voir, Jo^n riach M^{c}W^m vic conill roy, Jo^n roy Mc Jock, Kenneth Kaird, Do^d M^{c}finlay tailezeor, Do^n M^{c}ean greasich, Alex^r Bayne of Tarradaill, Thomas Roy M^{c}conill vaine, Captaine Bayne, Brahan.[1] Of the which persones compeired the said day the persones following:

Hector McKenzie of farburne, c'fessed y^t his men vere readdie to goe with Seafort on the vunlawfull ingadgement, and went with his sonne to Inv'ness and Balveinie on the late rebellione.

Alex^r Bayne of Tarradaill compeired, c'fessed only his subscribing the remonstrance, and that he c'tribute for the vnlawfull ingadgement through compulsion.

---

[1] And many others, the list containing seventy-six in all.

A list of ingadgers given in be Mr. Robt Monro, Minist^r at Kilterne, c'teining the p'sones following:

Wm Smith his sonne, Andrew Logan, Do^d Bayne, Jo^n M^{c}ranald, Jo^n dow cordiner, Jo^n Miller, Do^d Gardiner, do^d McJaspart, Hector frankman. . . . Robt Monro, Lemlair his sonne.[1]

List of Ingadgeres within Vrq^{rt} and loggie:

[List of fifteen given in—of whom six compeared—some of whom confessed that they were at Inverness, others that they were at Balvenie, and others that they were at Inverness and Balvenie.

[Several Ingadgers from the Paroch of Alness appeared, and confessed they were 'with James Graham and in the late Insurrection'—some at Inverness, others at Balvenie.]

Alex^r McKenzie of Coule, compeiring from the Paroch of Contin, c'fessed only his subscriving of the remonstrance and y^t he wes privie to the late Insurrection, bot wes against it in judgement.

Alex^r McKenzie, sonne to Mr. Murdo McKenzie, late Minister at Dingw^{ll}, compeiring from the Paroch of fottertie, c'fessed he wes at Keassock in James Grahames rebellion, and went over the ferrie to James Grahame his camp, and that he wes at Invernes and Balvenie in the late rebellion.

The censuring and classing c'tinewed as before, and farther tryall and sumonding of pairties not compeiring as zet referred to the severall ministers.

Mr. ferq^r reported y^t he caused sumoned Mr. Murdo McKenzie, late Minist^r at Dingw^{ll}, according to the formere ordinance, and a letre p̄nted [presented] from Mr. Murdo himselfe proporting the c'tinuance of his infirmitie, and his willingnes to obey when health sould serve him. The l̄re ordained to be keeped and the processe c'tinewed.

Androw Monro, portioner of Culcairne, Do^d finlasone portioner theroff, Hew Monro of Teahninich, Hew Monro of Foiris, Androw Monro in teanuar, Hew Monro in Keatuall, Jo^n Monro in newtovne, Jo^n Monro in Kinkell, Ferq^r Monro of Teanairdich, and Mr. Jo^n Monro of Suardell, all formerly

---

[1] And others, the list numbering twenty-two in all.

nōat comissioners for planta°n of Schooles, compeiring and required be the Presbyterie to meete among themselves for thinking upon and setting doune a course for planta°n of Schooles; having met and resolved accordingly, reported to the Presbyterie they thought y^t twell libs out of the thousand merks rent might suffice, bot c'tinewed the absolute determina°n of anything vntill they met with the rest of the members nōiat by the Presbyterie, Viz. Robt Monro of Obstill, Hector Douglas of Balkiny, and Thomas Fraser of Eskidaill, who were necessitated to be absent this day, for attending the comission of revalua°n of rents.

Continewes the referres of Highland kirks to the nixt day becaus the day was farre spent.

The Brethren reports y^t their severall Parishiners desires a c'tinua°n of the execu°n of the act of Parliament anent the maintenance of the poore, vntill the end of harvest.

A supplica°n given in be the burgh of Ding^ll for a pairt of the vacant stipend of Contin for putting up of their brigg. The anser c'tinued.

Siclyke a Supplica°n given in be the Parisheneres of Alness and other gentlemen, for a supply out of the said vacant stipend for upputting the bridge of Alness. The brethren did allocat two hundreth merks of the said stipend of crop 1 m. vi^c fortie nyne [1649] for that purpose.

Siclyke, Mr. Coline McKenzie, late Minister at Contin, his c'dition being c'sidered and tacken to heart by the brethren, Because of his good behaviour and indigence, allocates to him the said vacant stipend for cropt 1 m vi^c fortie eight yeires: ordeining him withall to repair the manse upon his receipt theiroff.

Mr. ferq^r McLennan reports he did wreitt to Mr. Do^d Ros, bot received no anser as zet.

At Dingwall, 9 Octob. 1649.

Mr. Ferq^r exercised Act 1. 12, removed, his doctrine tryed and allowed. Mr. Jo^n Ma^cra, adder, absent, excused be ane ltre proporting he was attending ane child of his owne at the poynt of death, proporting also y^t he hade repaired to Invernes the last twesday to the Presbyterie, and y^t they c'tinewed their absolute ans^r anent Mr. Duncan M^cculloch his transporta°n, vntill thursday come eight dayes.

Mr. Jo^n M^cra appoynted to exercise, and Mr. Robt Monro to adde the nixt day.

That day (c'forme to ane ordinance of the Comission of the gr̃all assembly for visiting the Kirks of Ros at Alderne the   day of   last) there was ane declara°n drawen up to be subscribed be Mr. Murdo Ma^cKenzie, late Minister at Ding^ll, bearing his acknowledgement of the equitie and justice of the procedours and sentences of the respective Judicatories of the Kirk against him for his privious trafficking with the malignants, and acknowledging the reasones of his appela°n from the sentence of the Presbyterie of Dingwall against him to haue bene bot calumnies and lies, which declaration was ordeined to be directed to him, and Mr. George Monro and Mr. Colline Ma^cKenzie to goe alongis to be witness^s to his subscribing it, and report their diligence thereanent the nixt day.

Continewes the referrs to the Hielands vntill the ministers of these parochens come to the Provinciall.

Considering that the Comissioners for planta°n of schooles haue not set dovne as zet any solid course for planta°n of schooles, The ministers of the severall parochins q^r they reside ordeined to adv'tise them to be p̃nt in Presbyterie the nixt day, and bring with them the act of parliament theranent.

Conforme to the Act of the gr̃all Assembly ordeining Mr. Thomas Ros his mouth to be opened, The Presbyterie declaires him capable of the benefit of the said act in all poynts.

[A number of Ingadgers appeared and confessed being in the late rebellion, amongst whom is Captaine Alex^r Bayne who 'c'fessed he wes with James Grahame at Inv'nes and on the late Insurrection at Inv'nes and Balvenie.']

Ordaines Mr. Jo^n M^crae to repair to the Presbyterie of Inv'nes thursday come eight dayes to receive their vttermost anser anent Mr. Duncan M^cculloch his transporta°n.

It is ordeined that a list of poore boyes having the Irish language be given in to the Presbyterie the nixt day for election of one to be trained up at Schooles on the Presbyteries charges, providing alwayes that ther parentes be not able to susteene them nor disaffected to the publick. The benefit of giving in of which list is for this vice c'ferred upon the Parochin of Alnes.

The meiting closed with prayer.

At Ding., 23 Octob. 1649.

That day compeired Mr. Do^d fraser, Mod^r, Mr. George Monro, Mr. Jo^n Monro, Mr. Do^d M^{c}ra, Mr. ferq^r McLennan, Mr. Jo^n M^{c}ra, clk ; Robt Monro of Obstill, and Neill Beaton in Culcraggie, ruling elderes.

The name of God incalled.

Mr. Jo^n Ma^{c}ra exercised Act 1. 15-22.

Mr. Robt Monro, adder, absent, excused by his lre proporting his infirmitie.

Mr. Jo^n Monro to exercise, and Mr. George Monro to adde the first day of meitting efter the Provinviall.

That day the referres of the Comission of grall assembly for visiting the Kirks of Ros, to the severall Presbyteries presented, and delivered to the Presbyterie, togither with a warrant from the said Comission for sumonding the ministers of the hilands with literall sumonds to the nixt meiting of the Comission in Maij.

Mr. George Monro and Mr. Coline Ma^{c}Kenzie enquired c'cerning their diligence in repairing to Mr. Murdo Ma^{c}Kenzie to see him subscribe the declara^{o}n drawen up the last day, reported z^t he refused to subscribe the same, aleadging z^t it wes more rigid as the Comission gaue warrant, which being c'sidered be the Presbyterie, ordaines z^t a lre be written to Mr. Murdo requiring him to come dovne to the Presbyterie to the nixt meiting to be resolved of his doubts, and to give satisfaction to the ordinances of the Kirk, with certifica^{o}n he sould be excomunicated in caise of failze, and appoyntes z^t the draught of the declara^{o}n formerly drawen up sould be brought and pñted to the Provinciall to advise with them theranent.

The classing and censuring of the malignants c'tinewed be the Presbyterie vntill they be advysed with the Provinciall.

Mr. M^{c}ra reporting he wes not able to repair the day appoynted to Inv'nes, ordained to goe the nixt Presbyterie day.

Wm Reid, late Schollmaister at Kincardin, compeiring before the Presbyterie and shewing his desire and willingnes to enter Schoolemaister at Vrq^t, bringing with him ane testimoniall subscribed be Mr. Hector Monro, late Minist. at Kincardin, testificing of his literature, good educa°n and cariage, recomended to Mr. George Monro to receive Schoolemaister at Vrq^t.

None of the Comissioners nōiat for planta°n of Schooles compeiring, being severall wayes taken up. The matter c'tinewed vntill they might with more c'venience.

Two Irish boyes being brought before the Presbyterie be Mr. Jo^n Monro, Minister at Alnes, one of them called Jo^n Monro, sonne to Hutchone Monro, wes elected and pñted to the Presbyteries bursse, and appoynts Mr. Jo^n Monro to have a care to see him enter to the schoole without any delay.

All the Brethren being severally tryed and examined, approven, except y^t Mr. George Monro wes found to haue preached notte for a long tyme at Loggie, and y^t Mr. Ferq^r McLennan preached none at all at Strachonnan, both ordeined to help this fault vnder payne of censure.

The nixt day of meiting to be appoynted at the Provinciall.
The meiting closed with prayer.

At Dingwall, the 20 of Novr. 1649.

The exercise was continewed because of the shortnes of the day and multiplicitie of particulars to be ordered the s^d day.

Mr. Jo^n M^{c}crae reported y^t he went to Invernes according to the former ordinance, and y^t the Prebie promised to conclude that particular at y^r next meiting at Aldearne, and to send y^r last answere w^h Mr. Duncan M^{c}culloch himselfe imediatelie after the s^d meiting.

That day Mr. Jo^n M^{c}crae, by consent of the whole breyren of the Prēbie, is chosen Moderator, and Mr. Jo^n Monro clk. for the next provinciall assemblie.

That day the prēbie haueing advysed w^h the provinciall anent the draught to be subscryved be Mr. Murdo McKenzie, doe appoynt Mr. Do^d fraser and Mr. Jo^n Munro to repaire to the s^d Mr. Murdo w^h the declara°n appoynted formerlie to be sub^t by him, and to requyre his subscription y^{r}to, w^h certification if he refuse the same to be sentenced w^h excomunica°n sumarlie.

Compeired Rorie McKenzie of Davachmoluag and confessed his accession to Ja. Grahames rebellion, and that he was in readines to goe to the late vnlaw^ll ingagement as Major, and his accession to the late rebellion in the north, asserting his reall greife for the same, and his earnest desyre to be received to the Covenant and satisfac°n for his s^d miscarieages; c'tinewed till his minister make furder tryall of his cariage, wch is recomended to him accordinglie.

Compeired Rorie McKenzie yor of farburne and Confesses his accession to Ja. Grahames rebellion and to the late rebellion in the north, reporting his being reallie grieved for the same and desyring to be received to the Covenant and satisfac°n for his s^d miscariages who is continewed till his minister make furder tryall of his cariage wch is recomended to him accordinglie.

The maner how one Irish boy shall be mantained continewed till the next day.

Compeired Tho. fraser in Crochell and confesses that he was desyrous to haue had a charge in the late vnlaw^ll ingagem^t bot not his actuall ingagem^t w^h the rest that went to England, reporting his earnest desyre to be received to the Covenant and satisfac°n, his answere is continewed to the next prēbie day, and his minister appoynted to make furder tryall of his cariage.

The references from the Comission of the g̃rall assemblie appoynted for visiting the Kirk of Ross are appoynted to be insert in the prēbie book, and all the breyren to take extracts y^roff and to report ther diligence of performance of q^t is recomended in the s^d references, q^rin they are p^ticularlie concerned against the next day.

The classing of the severall malignants according to the severall maners of satisfac°n to be injoyned to each of them c'tinewed till the next day.

Mr. Do^d M^ccrae supplicated for ane act of transporta°n for such reasones as the s^d supplica°n did at lenth proport, bot the breyren suspend y^r giveing answere y^rto vntill they sie him haue ane orderlie call to ane other congregation.

[Letter from Mr. George Gray, Minister at Dornoch, requesting Florence Munro adulteress, who had fled from Dornoch to

Kiltearn, to be sent back. Mr. Robt. in Kiltearn ordered to use all diligence.]

Meiting closed with prayer.

At Dingwall, the 11 of Decr. 1649.

Mr. Do^d fraser and Mr Jo^n Munro report that they repaired to the hight of Strachonnan q^r Mr. Murdo McKenzie was p̄nted vnto him the declara^{o}n appoynted be the Kirk to be sub^t be him, who promised to be heir this day himselfe, health serving, or oyrways his vther answere, who being cited, c'peired not, bot sent his l̄re and a declara^{o}n drawn vp be himselfe vnder his owne hand, wch being red and considdered, The breyren in one voyce doe declaire that they ar not satisfied wth the draught of his s^d declara^{o}n, And therfore haue drawn vp y^r owne declara^{o}n over againe, And appoyntes the same to be directed to him againe by his sone Allex^r, wth a l̄re requyring his subscription y^{r}to but anie furder altera^{o}n or c'tinewa^{o}n to be at vs the next prēbie day, with certifica^{o}n if he fayle to be sentenced with excomunication sumarlie.

The breyren declaire that they ar not as yet throchlie resolved about •the maner of mantaining the Irish boy vntill they deale furder wth y^r Sessiones, wch is accordingly recomended to be performed with diligence vnto the severall breyren.

Mr. Dod fraser reportes he learned nothing of Tho. fraser in Crochell his furder accession to anie malignant courses then he declared himselfe before the presbyterie the last day, and y^t he had vsed all the tryall possiblie he culd for furder information.

followes the references of the Comission of the grāll assemblie appoynted for visiting the Kirk of Ross.

'That the nationall covenant of this Kingdome w^h the solemne league and covenant of the thrie Kingdomes w^h the renova^{o}n y^{r}off and subscrip^{on} y^{r}to be insert and regrat in all regres of presbyteries and sessiones repiue [respectively].

'That the trayning of boyes haueing the Irish language at Schooles be carefullie performed, and y^r respue regres [respective registers] bear record of diligence y^{r}anent.

'That bursars students of divinitie be carefullie educated and mantained be the whole province.

'That all the people in everie congregaᵒn grāllie be requyred as well as the elders to be pnt at visitaᵒnes of kirks, and posed grallie if the people haue anie thing to object against ministers cariage in yʳ pastorall charge.

'That Session bookes be tymously delyvered and examined at visitaᵒn of Kirkes.

'That adulterers and incestuous p'sones yʳ names be sent south to the civill Magr̄at.

'That the Prēbrie of Tayne admitt not Mr. Neil Mᶜleod, Schoolemʳ at Tarbat, trelapse in fornicaᵒn and deposed be the Comission, to anie charge till he give evident singes [signs] of his repentance and good cariage.

'That no oathes be taken or sought in the mater of witchcraft or suspicion of danger yʳby from yʳ neighbours, and yᵗ the persones suspecting to haue reciued wrong be witchcraft doe not seik anie cure anie way from the suspected witch, and whosoever c'traveines to be procest till they satisfie in sackcloath and till they giue evident singes of yʳ repentance.

'That the act anent beggers be intimat in everie paroch kirk, and be put in pn̄t execution betwixt this and the first lords day of Noʳ next.

'That Schooles be erected in everie paroch, and diligence yʳanent be reported to the next provinciall of Ross betwixt this and the next visitaᵒn at Chanr̄ie.

'That the prēbrie of Chanr̄ie prosecute the plantaᵒn and provision of the Kirk of Chanr̄ie betwixt his and Noʳ next and to giue an accompt of yʳ diligence to the provinciall and next visitaᵒn at Chanrie.

'That Mr. Murdo MᶜKenzie not able to come to the prēbrie of Dingwall be dealt wʰ by some breyren of the prēbrie and requyred to acknowledge his offences and subscryve the band conceiued be the Comission at Ald. [Auldearn] 1647, and satisfie in publick qⁿ he is able in bodie.

'That all Minʳᵉˢ within the p'vince preach poʳfully against witchcraft and devillish practises of yᵗ sort.

'That prēbrie take compt of everie broyʳ how he spends the saboth day in lecturing and preaching, and yʳ everie session book mention textes of lecture and sermone.

'That the prēbrie of Chanr̄ie haue care of planting a schoole at Kilmuir West.

'That the prēbrie of Tayne inquyre furder and try concerning the scandalous carriage of Mr. Jo^n McKenzie, and to injoyne him repentance for his former miscariage and for q^t shall be furder fund against him.

'That the prēbrie of Dingwall be carefull of the cariage of Mr. Robt. Munro, Min^r at Kiltearn, and to be diligent in vseing all meanes q^{r}by he may haue a helper becaus of his infirmitie.

'The furder tryall of Mr. George Munro, minister at Rosemarkie, is referred to a comission to sit at Aldcarne *ad hunc actum* only the first tuesday of No^r next, or, in cace impedim^{ts} fall in, at anie oy^r tyme the Mode^r sall appoynt, witnesses y^{r}anent to be cited be the prēbrie of Chūnr̄ie, and y^t the s^d prēbrie haue a care of the s^d Mr. George his charge.

'That the prēbrie of Tayne settle the difference betwixt Mr. Wm Ross and Mr. Hector Munro, and to be c'ptable [accountable] to the next Comission at Chanr̄ie y^{r}anent.

'The next meiting of this Comission to be at Chanr̄ie the 1 twysday of May next.

'That the prēbrie of Dingwall summond the M^{rs} [ministers] at Lochcarron, Lochailsh, Gerloch, and Kintayle, repiue with y^r rueling Elders to be at the next Comission at Chanr̄ie.

'That all the Min^{rs} and rueling elders within Cathnes and Suy^{r}land be requyred to be pnt at the next visita^{o}n at Chanrie.

'That the severall prēbries be carefull y^t the errata and remedies be insert in y^r regres.

'*Sic subscribitur*,

'J. Young, C̄lk. Com.'

[Classing of Malignants continued. Kenneth McKenzie of Scatwell, Kenneth McKenzie of Assint, and Roric McKenzie of Tollie, compeired, and confessed their accession to Ja. Grahame's rebellion and the late rebellion in the North, and having contributed men and means—their great grief. Continued till furder tryall made of their cariage. Scatwell 'subscryved the remonstrance of Seafort.']

Mr. do^d M^{c}crae, vrging his transporta^{o}n, is continewed, and Mr. George Munro appoynted to speak to the parocheners of Vrray for seing to y^r pastors maintenance, pressing his removeall cheifelie becaus he cannot liue among them, and Mr. Do^d himselfe is appoynted to vse all diligence according to the laws of the kingdome for provyding of his kirk.

Dingwall, 25 of Decr. 1649.

Mr. Do^d fraser delyvered the comon head *de propaga°ne peccati originalis*, his text was 1 Cor. 15. 22, who being remowed, and his doctrine tryed, was approwen.

Mr. George Munro is appoynted to exercise, and Mr. Dod fraser to ad, the next day.

A lre was p̄nted from Mr. Jo^n Munro importing at lenth relefant reasones of his necessitat voyage to Strathnaver, who is excused accordinglie.

Mr. Murdo McKenzie, being cited, not c'pciring, his sone Alex^r did pūte a declaration subscryved be the s^d Mr. Murdo at Keanlochbeancharan the 18 of De^r 1649, bot did not returne the principall draught directed be the prēbrie to him q^rbe they might be collationed the one with the oy^r, notithstanding he was desyred in the prebr̄ies lr̄e to returne the same, Therefore the breyren appoyntes the s^d Mr. Murdo to be excomunicat the next Lords day imediatlie after the insueing prebr̄iall meiting vnles he subscryve and sent to the s^d meiting the declara°n drawn vp according to the ordinances of the judicatories of the Kirk, and ordaynes the severall breyren to make intima°n heiroff out of pulpitt in ther severall c'grega°nes.

The mantenance for the Irish boy c'tinewed till Mr. Jo^n Munro his returne by whom the s^d boy was p̄nted.

That day was p̄nted a lr̄e from the severalls of the Malignantes importing that they culd not be heir this day in reguard they were appoynted to attend the Comittie of revalua°n, Ordayned y^rfore the severall breyren to advertise them to compeir the next day.

The said Mr. George reportes y^t he spake to the heritors of Wrray who promised to send a satisfactorie answere to the desyre of the prēbrie vnder ther hands, bot the prēbrie not receiveing the same doe renew the ordinance for Mr. George his going to speake them as formerlie.

A lr̄e was p̄nted from the Chancellor, of the dait at Ed^r 7 of November 1649, requyring the Breyren to haue y^r recourse to the comission appoynted for plantation of Kirks for provyding ther severall Kirks according to the Act of Par̄lt latelie granted in favors of the Kirk, ordaynes the severall breyren to vse and report y^r dilligence heiranent with all conveniencie.

The meiting closed with prayer.

Dingwall, the 8 *of* Ja^{rij} 1650.

That day the principall draught sent to Mr. Murdo McKenzie of the declaration to be sub^t be him was p̄nted be allex^r McKenzie, his sone, subscryved wh the s^d Mr. Murdo his owne hand at Keanlochbeancharan the 5 of Ja^{rij} 1650, bot in reguard y^r were no witnesses to the s^d subscrip^{on} ordaynes Mr. George Munro and Mr. Coline McKenzie to repaire to the s^d Mr. Murdo, and to sie the s^d Murdo subscryve the said declara^{o}n, and they to subscryve witnesses y^{r}vnto, and to report y^r diligence y^{r}anent the next day.

The breyren report that they made intimation to the Malignants to c'peir befor the p̄rbie this day q^{r}of a great number haueing come, being cited, compeired, ar all appoynted to make satisfac^{o}n as followes, viz.

Thos of the gentrie, or y^t haue bein elders vnder the degrie of a lifetent [lieutenant] that were promoters off or actuallie in anie two of the vnlaw^{ll} and malignant courses, ar ordayned to sitt in sackcloth vpon a furme befor the pulpit during the tyme of divyne service.

And thos that were on mae courses to stand in sackcloth as s^d is.

Thos that were assisters onlie be c'straint and being prest y^{r}to to one or mae of the s^{ds} vnlaw^{ll} courses, to be called out of y^r dasks and to signifie ther detestation to the sd^s coureses.

Thos of the gentrie vnder the degrie fors^d y^t had accession only to the late insurrect^n in the North, or were only on comitties for carieing on the vnlaw^{ll} ingagemt, to stand in y^r owne habite before the pulpitt during the tyme of divyne service.

All the rest of the comones to stand in the bodie of the Kirk in y^r owne habites as s^d is.

The severall breyren ar appoynted to receive all y^r malignants vnder the degrie of a lifetent, according to the abouewritten classes, and to bring in the lists of y^r names as they are receiūed according to the sd^s classes, to be insert in the p̄rbrie book, and this to be done with all diligence.

The said Mr. George [Munro] declaires that in reguard the heritors of the paroch of Vrray were attending the Comittie of revalua^on he suld not meit with y^m, yrfore renewes the ordinance of his speaking to them q^n they come home.

Recciued two lřes from the paroch of Gerloch, one from Mr. Rorie McKenyie, Minister y^r, importing that he had made intima^on to the Lard of gerloch to c'peir before the presbyterie this day bot withall testifieing that he was very infirme and vnable to come, and the oy^r lře was from Gerloch himselfe importing the same and withall that he would health serving be heir the next day.

[Letters from 'Mr. Dod. Clk in Lochailsh,' 'Mr. ferq^r McCrae in Kintayle,' and 'Mr. Allex^r McKenyie in Lochcarron,' in regard to cases of discipline referred from Sessions to the Presbytery.]

Compeired Jo^n McKenyie of Aplecross who confest his accession to the late rebellion in the north, professing his greife for the same, and desyring to be receiued to the Covenant and satisfac^on, is c'tinewed till farder tryall, and appoynted to be heir the next day.

Dingwall, 22 Jarij. 1650.

Mr. George Munro and Mr. Coline McKenyie report that in reguard of the greatnes of the storme after ther going gettward to Mr. Murdo McKenyie they were forced to reteire : Therfore renewes the ordinance of y^r going ther, and to report y^r diligence the next day.

Mr. George Munro reports y^t he spoke to the heretors of Vrray who promised to be heir this day, who being cited and some of y^m c'peiring, being inquyred anent the provision of the Kirk of Vrray, doe promise to make thankfull pay^t of y^r pñt proportiones, and advyse y^t Mr. Do^d M^ccrae vse diligence with the Comission for plantation of Kirks for getting a competent stipend to his kirk, and y^t they shall give c'tent in qtsoever shall be the said Comission be modified to him. Qw^ch the prēbrie appoynts the s^d Do^d to goe about with all diligence.

[Several malignants from parish of Dingwall—among them 'Allex^r Bayne Ranaldson '—appear confessing malignancy and 'recommended to Mr. Jo^n Macrae to be received according to the act of classes.']

Compeired Keneth McKenyie of Gerloch, confessed his

accession to Ja. Grahame's rebellion, and to the late rebellion in the north, professing his greife for the same and desyreing to be receiued to the covenant and satisfac^on, who is c'tinewed till furder tryall and is ordayned to be heir the next day.

Compeired Kenneth McKenyie y^r, who c'fest his accession to the late insurrection in the North, who is remitted to the Session of Gerloch to be furder tryed and receiued according to the maner prescryved in the act of classes.

The breyren being inquyred of y^r diligence anent provyding of the poore doe report y^t they are going on according to the act of parlt. bot find manie difficulties in, y^rfor ar appoynted to vse all possible diligence y^ranent with all conviniencie.

Mr. Jo^n M^ccrae regrates that he cannot prevaile in the mater of planting of a schoole in Dingwall, y^rfore ordaynes Mr George Munro to speak Andrew Minro, Clk of the Comission for planta^on and provision of Schooles, to this effect, and to report his diligence against the next day, and Mr. Jo^n himselfe to sumond the Magistrats and heritors of Dingwall to c'peir the next day for the effect fors^d.

Ordaynes the breyren to meit on Monday before the prēbrie day.

At Dingwall, the 4 of Feby. [1650] *being Monday.*

That day Keneth McKenyie of Gerloch, Keneth McKenyie of Assint, Rorie McKenyie of Davachmolŭag, Keneth McKenzie of Scatwell, Rorie McKenyie of Farbŭrne, their accession to the severall courses of rebellion, being tryed they ar fund by y^r owne confessiones and the best informa^on y^t the breyren after exact tryall culd find, to be guiltie as followes: Keneth McKenyie of Gerloch fund accessorie to Ja. Grahame's rebellion and the late insurrection in the North.

Kenneth McKenyie of Assint fund accessorie to Ja. Grahame's rebellion, c'tributed men and meanes to thes q^rtered vpon towards the vnlaw^ll ingagemt and access^one to the late insurrec^on in the north.

Rorie McKenyie of Davachmolŭag fund accessorie to the same, guiltie as Assint.

Keneth McKenyie of Scatwell sub^t the remonstrance, and accessorie to the late rebellion in the North.

Roric MᶜKenyie of Farburne followed Seafort in Ja. Grahame's rebellion, being his domestick servant, and accessorie to the late insurrection in the north.

Therfore the breyren, considdering the forsᵈ persones severall guiltes, and yᵗ all of them were eminentlie active in the late rebellion in the north, being vrgers and seducers yʳto, plotters and pryme promovers yʳoff, doe yʳfore ordayne them to repaire forthwith to the comission of yᵉ g̃rall assemblie sitting at Edinʳ in this p͠nt month of febʳⁱʲ, to make satisfacᵒⁿ as yʳ they shall be appoynted, with certificaᵒⁿ, if they faile, to be imediatelie processed. And ordayned yᵐ to be sumoned to the morne fifteine dayes to receiue sentence according to the abovewritten ordinance.

P͠nted a l͠re from the breyren of the prēbrie of Chanrie desyring some of oʳ number for yʳ assistance in expeding some affaires of importance qʳin they ar c'cerned themselfes, being bot few in number for the tyme, most pᵗ of the breyren being in the south, Therfore Mr. George Munro, Mr. Joⁿ Mᶜcrae, and Mr. Doᵈ fraser ar ordayned to repaire to them the 20 of febʸ, according to yʳ desyre for the effect forsᵈ.

The meiting closed with prayer.

Dingwall, the 5 of Feby. 1650.

That day conveined Mr. Joⁿ Mᶜcrae, Moderator, Mr. George Munro, Mr. ferqʳ MᶜLennan, Mr. Doᵈ fraser, and Mr. Joⁿ Munro, Clk.

The name of God incalled.

No exercise in reguard of the exerciser's [Mr. Doᵈ Mᶜcrae] absence from whom was p͠nted a l͠re importeing his being tormented with the worme and desyring to be excused.

Mr. George and Mr. Coline report that Mr. Murdo MᶜKenyie did obleidge himselfe to be at the prēbrie the next day precisely vnder payne of excomunication, who is c'tinewed till the sᵈ day.

The Moderator reportes yᵗ he sent a doublie of the act of classes to Mr. Roᵗ in Kiltearne, for his information.

The breyren report that they haue not all yʳ malignantes as yet, who are yʳfore appoynted to vse diligence in the receiueing them, and to bring in the listes of them, classed, with all c'veniencie.

Mr. George Munro reported y{t} Andrew Munro, clk. of the Comission for planta{on} and provision of schooles, is not in health, so y{t} he culd not be heir this day to meit with the heritors anent the schoole of Dingwall, and of the heritors themselfes c'peired Tulloch and Knockbayne who did represent y{r} difficultie of mantayning a schoolem{r} be themselfes vnles the paroch of foddertie did joyne with them, who ar y{rfore} advysed to speak to the heritors of the s{d} paroch for y{t} effect. And withall appoyntes Mr. George and Mr. Jo{n} Munro to desyre the former comissioners for provision of schooles to be heir the next day for takeing course heirwith, as shall be fund most convenient, and the s{d} breyren to report y{r} diligence the next day.

A lre was pñted from the Comission of the grall assembly appoynting Jo{n} Munro of Lemlayre to c'peir before them at Edin{r} at the sitting of the s{d} Comission in Maij next, for his accession to the late vnlaw{ll} ingagement, w{ch} is appoynted to be intimate to the s{d} Lemlair in due tyme to be performed be him with certification, if he fayle, to be processed.

Mr. George Munro reportes that Do{d} M{c}ean vic finlay, excomunicat in his paroch, is now absolued. Appoyntes the severall breyren to make intima{on} heiroff in ther severall congregationes and to report y{r} diligence heirin the next day.

Dingwall, febrij 19 1650.

That was cited Keneth M{c}Kenyie of Gerloch, Keneth M{c}Kenyie of Assint, Rorie M{c}Kenyie of Davachmoluag, Keneth M{c}Kenyie of Scatwell, Rorie M{c}Kenyie of farburne, who compeiring ar appoynted to repaire forthwith to the Comission of the grall assemblie to be receiued be them to satisfac{on} for y{r} malignancie, with certifica{on}, if they fayle, to be imediately processed. And appoyntes the severall breyren within whose paroches they reside to process them who make not y{r} address according to the former ordinance, and Mr. Jo{n} M{c}crae appoynted to process Assint in case of faylie in reguard y{r} is no minister in Contin q{r} he dwells.

That day c'peired Mr. Ro{t} Munro and Mr. Jo{n} Dallas from the presbytrie of Taine, desyring the assistance of this presbytrie for tryall of the scandall of the alleadged adulterie of Mr. Jo{n} M{c}Kenzie and Elizabeth Bayne [Bayne Tulloch's Daughter] and desyring Tulloch, and his familie, tennants, and cotters, with Ranald Bayne and such oy^rs as within this presbytrie can give anie clearing in the scandall fors^d, to be cited before vs to that effect.

[Here follows the evidence of Tulloch, his wife, etc., regarding the alledged scandal.]

That day was p̄nted a supplication be Keneth McKenyie of Gerloch, and Keneth McKenyie of Assint, beareing y^t by the lawes of the Kingdome horning and cap^on is obtayned against them for Seaforts debts, so y^t personallie they cannot repair to Edin^r vnbeine incarcerat, and y^rfore they petition the prēbrie y^t ther process be suspended till they obtayne the Comission of grāll assemblies answer anent y^r satisfaction. Wheruppon the prēbrie assignes them this day six weeks to report y^r last diligence, and bringing to the prēbrie a satisfactorie anser from the Comission, with certification if they fayle to be y^rafter immediatlie pro-cessed. And the Clk. is appoynted to giue them ane extract of y^r severall guilts, and of the ordinance fors^d.

Compeired Mr. Murdo McKenzie, and in prēbrie subscryved the former declara^on, who is appoynted forthwith to goe on in his repentance as conforme to the former act of prēbrie he was injoyned, bot in reguard of the vacancie of Tarbat and Chanrie, to wch he was formerlie appoynted to repair, he is now appoynted to goe to Tayne, for Tarbat, and Rosmarkie for Chanrie, onlie the Kirk of Kilernan is diseused with because y^r is no minister y^r, and the s^d Mr. Murdo is appoynted to begin his repentance at Tayne, and to bring a certificat from the severall sessiones q^r he come, of the performance of the satisfac^on injoyned to him.

Mr. ferq^r McLennan is appoynted to preach at Contin, and to intimat the act anent the receiuing of malignantes.

[Brethren report that they have not yet received all the malignants and ordained to do so and bring in 'the rolls of them.']

Mr. George and Mr. Jo^n Munro report that the Comissioners for provision of Schooles ther answere was that they culd c'clud nothing furder till they did sie whether the Par̄lt would allow y^r bookes of revalua^on of the shyres of Ross and Invernes, in wch ane modifica^on and alloca^on was made for schooles in everie paroch of the Shyre, wch they conceive will be competent if allowed.

Compeired Tho. M^cnaoise, who, haveing confest his malicious impreca°nes against the ministrie, is appoynted to satisfie *in sacco* in all the Kirks of the Prēbrie, and to report a testimonie from the severall Sessiones of his performance of the tenor of the former ordinance vnder payne of process.

Compeired Hew Ros from the paroch of Kilmorack, shewing his willingnes to be schoolem^r at the s^d Kilmorack, and the Prēbrie being certified of his good educa^on and c'versation, and finding vpon tryall his abilitie for instructing of children, and fitting them for gramar schooles, doe y^rfore admitt him to the s^d charge, recomending him to Mr. Do^d fraser to be receiued and incouraged for y^t effect.

Dingwall, the 5 of March 1650.

That day the comon head was c'tinewed till the next day in reguard of the mulitude of affaires that day to be expeded.

Mr. ferq^r McLennan being inquyred whither Scatwell had repaired South, declaires that he did not, nor was within the bounds of the prēbrie, who p̄nted a l̄re from the s^d Scatwell bearing relefant reasones of his necessarie absence out of the bounds, and impossibilitie of repairing South vntil he sie how God will dispose of his eldest sone being heavilie diseased of a high feaver, and supplicating y^rfore that his process may be suspended vntill his child recouer or be called, promising y^rafter to repaire to the Comission with all diligence, wch the breyren haueing taken to y^r c'sidera^on did grant.

Mr. Do^d M^ccrae reportes that he began to process Davachmoluag and Farburne.

[Evidence regarding Mr. John McKenzie and Elspet Bayne.]

[Mr. Do^d Fraser gave in a list of his malignants as they were received. M^r. ferq^r McLennan reports his having preached at Contin, and presents a list of malignants there, being all commons. They all confess and are ordained to repaire to Foddertie to be received be the s^d Mr. Ferq^r according to y^r classes.]

Dingwall, 19 *of March* 1650.

Mr. Do^d M^{c}crae delivered the comon head *de perfec^{one} scripturaru.*

Mr. Ferq^r McLennan is appoynted to exercise, and Mr. Do^d M^{c}crae to add, the next day.

Compeired Keneth McKenyie of Scatwell, Rorie McKenyie of Davachmoluag, and Rorie McKenyie of Farburne, supplicating y^t in reguard the Comission of the gr̄all assemblie is not sitting that y^r process may be suspended till the insueing q^{r}terly meiting of the Comission in May, at wch tyme they inact y^{m}selfes to repair to the s^d comission, and bring ane satisfactorie answer to y^r prebr̄ie of y^r satisfac^{on} according to the appoyntment of the Comission, whose desyre was granted, and they appoynted to perforem the promises with the certifica^{on} before expressed.

The Breyren haueing inquyred after the cariage of Jo^n McKenyie of Ord and Keneth McKenyie in Brakanord and finding them to haue bein actuielie accessorie to Ja. Grahame's rebellion and the late insurrection in the North, and being as Capt^s vpon the heads of the c'paines at Balveinie, doe y^{r}fore refer y^m to the Comission of the gr̄all assemblie at Edin^r in May insueing, appoynting y^m to repair thither to the s^d dyett, and to report to vs y^r diligence and the commissiones anser anent y^r satisfac^{on} with all possible c'veniencie after the sitting of the s^d comission, with certifica^{on} to be processed in cace of faylie.

[Evidence in Elspet Bayne's case.]

[Mr. Robt. in Kiltearne and Mr. Jo^n Munro gave in the lists of their malignants ' as they were receiued according to the order of classing. The booking y^{r}of is c'tinewed till the rest of the listes come in.']

The breyren heiring y^t Alex^r McKenzie sone to Mr. Murdo McKenyie was without, and being desyrous to know of his fay^{rs} proceiding in reference to his satisfac^{on}, caused cite the s^d Allex^r, who c'peiring and being inquyred anent his fay^r, did pr̄nt a lr̄e from the s^d Murdo importing y^t Knockbayne had obtayned Cap^{on} against him for wrongous claimes, and desyring y^t a protec^{on} might be obtayned to him from Knockbayne, and y^t y^n he would vse all diligence for expeding of his satisfac^{on}, wch the breyren taking to y^r considera^{on} they appoynt Mr. George Munro and Mr. Ferq^r McLennan to repaire to Knockbayne to try whither he will grant the s^d protec^{on}, and to report y^r diligence the next day.

And withall knowing y^t some breyren of the severall neighbor prebr̃ies ar latelie come from the south, appoyntes Mr. Do^d fraser to repair to the prebr̃ie of Invernes, Mr. George Munro to the prebr̃ie of Chanrie, and Mr. Jo^n Munro to the prebr̃ie of Tayne to be advysed anent the p^{t}iculars following, viz.

1. What course to take with Mr. Murdo McKenyie in case Knockbayne refuse him a protec^{on}.

2. Anent an answer to the Chancellor's lr̃e.

3. Anent some scandalous cariages and expressiones of some of the members of the armie in our bounds.

Qwherof the s^d breyren are to report y^r diligence the next day.

Girsell McKenzie receiued her contribution from all the breyren except Contin and the hiland kirks.

The Irish boy his proportion for his mantenance sent to him from the whole breyren, except Contin and the hiland kirks.

Compeired certaines of the heritors of Contin, pñting a supplica^{on} for y^{m}selfes and the remament heritors, desyring the vacant stipends y^r to be imployed on publick works within y^t paroch, whose anser is suspended till the sds vacand stipends be c'pleitly vplift, and to that effect appoynts Coline McKenzie of Tarvie, Collector of the same, giveing him full po^r to vplift the same and grant discharges y^{r}vppon, with all expedition, who hes inacted himselfe to delyver the same to the prebr̃ie q^{n}soever it is collected, and appoynts the extract heiroff to be given vnto him for his warrand.

Appoyntes Mr. Jo^n M^{c}crae to furnish a post to goe to the hiland kirks with the Comissiones Sumondes to be dulie execute be him, and the breyren to give expence to the s^d post for y^t effect, and the diligence heirin to be reported the next day.

Mr. Jo^n M^{c}crae did pñt a bill of greivance against Allex^r McLauchlan, servant to Mr. Murdo McKenzie, importing his being oppressed with the (said) Allex^r so y^t he culd not peaceably injoy his gleib for him more y^n thir severall yeirs bygone, with severall blasphemous oathes to the dishonor of God, and expressiones and cariages to the contempt and effront of the s^d Mr. Jo^n, as the s^d bill did at more lenth proport; appoyntes yrfore the s^d Allex^r to be sumoned to the next day.

Dingwall, 9 *Apryle* 1650.

[Explained that no meeting on 2^d April on account *inter alia* of Alex. McKenzie of Coule's funeral.]

That day Knockbayne being cited, c'peired, and did grant under his hand a protection to Mr. Murdo McKenzie vntill the 14 of May insueing, for expeding of his repentance. Therfore renewes the ordinance for his present repairing to make satisfac^{on} as was formerlie appoynted, with certifica^{on} as was before exprest.

The Breyren sent to advyse with the neighbor presbytries report that it was advysed.

1. That the anser of the Chancellors lr̃e be c'tinewed till the sitting of the Comission for planta^{on} of Kirks.

2. That Mr. Murdo suld be sentenced in cace of not going on in his repentance, tho Knockbayne refused a protec^{on}.

3. That we suld proceid in tryall of the cariage of the members of the armie in our severall Sessiones vntill y^r be clearnes fund of anie miscariage, to be recommended to the officers vnder whose c'mand they ar that course may be taken by them for purging the armie of anie y^t is grosly scandalous.

Mr. Ferq^r McLennan appoynted to speake to Tarvie that he goe activelie and with all c'veniencie about the vplifting of the vacand stipends of Contin, or y^t he will be denuded of his Collectorship, and to report his diligence heirin the next day.

Mr. Jo^n M^{c}crae reportes that he sent a post with the Commissiones summondes to the hiland Kirks.

Cited and c'peired Allex^r McLauchlan who declaired as he was p^{t}icularlie inquyred anent Mr. Jo^n M^{c}crae his bill as followes :—

That he had my Lord Seaforts warrand for intromitting with the s^d Mr. Jo^n his gleib, and that by ane assigna^{on} from Jo^n M^{c}allister, who was formerlie servitor to Mr. Murdo McKenyie, That the ploughes q^{r}with he laboured the s^d Mr. Jo^{ns} gleib belonged to Mr. Murdo and his sone. That he had the oates y^t he sowed in the said gleib out of Mr. Murdo's barnes in Pitglassie.

That he interrupted the s^d Mr. Jo^{nes} servant from sowing the gleib by takeing the sheet from him.

That he took God's name frequentlie in vayne.

Bot in reguard the s^d Allex^r denyed pt of the s^d Mr. Jo^n his bill, witnesses being cited sworne in p̄nce of the p̄rie according to order, they deponed severallie as followes :

[Evidence that Alex^r struck Mr. John's man, and impeded Mr. John himself from hindering his (Alex^{rs}) man from sowing the gleib—that he put his hand on his dirk and declared 'that he would doe his owne turne, lett judicatories doe q^t they list.' 'That he did shake Mr. John's man out of the sheit violentlie,' and that he ' uttered severall outrageous speaches.']

Qwerfore the s^d Allex^r for his c'temptes and oathes is appoynted to satisfie in sackcloth in the paroches of Vrq^t, Alnes, and Dingwall, and y^r to be receiued be Mr. Ferq^r McLennan, and Mr. Jo^n M^{c}crae to serue his vice in Foddertie the day he bees receiued, and the s^d Alex^r to performe the tennor of the premisses with all c'veniencie vnder payn of process.

And appoyntes Mr. Jo^n Munro to writt a l̄re to the Committie of Warr of the Shyre for vseing of such courses as they c'ceive most c'venient for helping the s^d Mr. Jo^n to the profit and peaceable possession of his gleib in tyme c'ming.

Receiued a l̄re from the Moderator of the Comission of the grāll assemblie, advysing the continewa^{on} of Assint and Gerlochs process till ye next qrterly meiting in May.

The severall breyren report y^t Tho. M^{c}noaise satisfied in ther severall Kirks for his malicious imprecationes against the Ministrie.

The breyren report y^r making vse of the declara^{ones} of Estate and Kirk against Ja. Grahame's declara^{on} by reading and explaining the same in ther severall c'grega^{o}nes.

The breyren, c'siddering that the neighbor presbyteries had received ane ordinance and reasones for keiping of a solemne fast wch as yet ar not come to our hands, doe y^{r}fore ordayne the next adjacent to the neighbor prēbries to gett doubles of the s^{ds} reasones to be comunicat to the rest of the breyren of this prēbrie, and appoyntes the s^d fast to be intimat the insueing Lord's day, and to be celebrat the next Lord's day y^rafter, and the breyren to report y^r diligence heirin the next day.

Cited and compeired Finlay M^cconchie vic finlay, and Shiack nein finlay vic george his wyfe, both in the Paroch of Vrq^t, c'fessing ye consulting with a witch for getting the profite of y^r drink, formerlie taken away from y^m as they alleadge, and making vse of a charme to y^t effect, and professing y^t it took effect to y^r mynd, Continewes the s^ds persones to the next day, who are sumd^t *apud acta* to c'peir the s^d day: and appoynts Shiack nein Do^d in Tavrie, whom they alleadge to haue had a hand in c'tryving the s^d charme, to be sumoned to the next day pro 2°, the principall c'tryver of the same being dead.

[Mr. Ferq^r McLennan to repair to Strathconan, and to search anent authors of the murder committed there.]

Dingwall, the 16 *of Apryle* 1650.

That day c'veined, Mr. Jo^n M^ccrae, Mod^r, Mr. Donald Fraser, Mr. George Munro, Mr. Do^d M^ccrae, and Mr. Jo^n Munro, clk.

The name of God incalled.

No exercise y^t day because of the exerciser's infirmitie.

[Evidence regarding Elspet Bayne.]

That day haueing inquyred anent Mr. Murdo McKenzie his repairing according to the ordinance for making of satisfac^on, Compeired his sone, pñting ane vndaited l^re bearing attestationes of his great infirmitie, wch being c'siddered, and finding in the same apparent c'tradic^ones, secounded by his owne sone's declaration, and c'siddering that y^r ar yet four sabothes in the tyme granted by the protec^on to him, doe y^rfore (being desyrous to gaine him) appoynt the s^d Mr. Murdo to performe his satisfac^on before the daite of the s^d protec^on expire, with certifica^on to be imediatelie sentenced upon c'traveining heiroff.

The breyren report that they haue gotten clearing of some enormities in certayne members of ye armie, and y^t they ar going on with y^r sessiones for furder tryall, wch is furder recomended to be performed with diligence.

Pñted a l^re from Mr. Rorie McKenzie at Gerloch, with the executiones of the Commissiones sumonds.

Mr. George Munro reportes that Allex^r McLauchlane came

not to him till the forenoones sermon was almost ended, at wch tyme he culd not be receiued to satisfac^on, who being cited c'peired and show y^t he culd not win sooner over Connan throch the porters [1] absence, y^rfore renewes the ordinance anent his satisfac^on as formerly.

The breyren report y^t they made intima^on of the fast the last Lord's day, and that they receiued doubles of the reasones, wch are thes y^t followes, viz. :

The seven former reasones of the fast appoynted to be celebrat the last saboth of Agust 1649.

And added withall that the Lord would breid a good correspondencie betwixt the king and the Comissioners.

Shiak nein Don, in Tavrie, charmer, to be sumoned pro 3°.

The breyren being informed of Ja. Grahame's landing in Cathnes with forces, and comeing forward for furder supplie for caricing one his former bloodie rebellious and perfidious courses, and considdering the act of the grãll [assembly] for receiueing of malignantes to publick satisfac^on, to import y^t all who formerlie were vpon the rebellious and malignant insurrec^ones in the land, and professing y^r repentance of the same and desyre to be receiued to satisfac^on, that if anie such suld furder promove anie rebellious course against God's work and people, they suld exc'municat. They doe y^rfore, for preventing anie associationes, considera^ones, or correspondencie with the s^d excomunicat, bloodie traytor or his forces, Ordayne all the breyren to make intima^on out of y^r severall pulpits that anie who shall associat or correspond with the s^d Rebell or his forces shall be sentenced with exc'munica^on sumarlie, and the seuerall breyren ar appoynted to performe accordinglie in cace anie breach fors^d shall happen to be comitted.

The meiting closed with prayer.

[The following docquet is here written with reference to the Register :]

'At Chanrie, June 5. post mered. Sess. 3.

'Adulterers c'peiring before the prēbrie remitted to the session without expressing censure, and malignant c'fessing not ordained to satisfie—frequent want of exercise and addit^on. The Coven^t not

---

[1] Ferrymen.

insert in the regis^re as was ordained—extennuation of accession to the vnlaw^ll ingagemt—designa^on of persones be y^r lands and styles without mentioning ther names; March 5, 1650, ane verie informall act. Apryle 9, 1650, ane informall act concerning the gleib of Tulloch. (Signed) J. Young, Clk. Com.'

The Wisitation of Kilterne.
14 *Maij* 1650.

All the Brethren present, wiz. Mr. Jo^n Maccrae, Mod^r, Mr. George Monro, Mr. Jo^n Monro, Mr. ferq^r Maclennan, Mr. Robert Monro, Mr. Dod Fraser, and Mr. Dod Mackcrae, and Robert Monro of Obstill, Hector Dowglass of Balconie, ferq^r Monro of Teahuaird, Mr Jo^n Monro of Sordell, Robert Monro of Baillchladdich, and Jo^n roy in Teahinord, Elders.

The name of God incalled.

Mr. Robert Monro preached, Isaiah 28. 16.

[Mr. Jo^n Monro chosen Mod^r, and Mr. ferq^r McLennan, clerk.]

[Reports as to Minister, Elders, and people, including ' that the Covenant was renewed.' 'That diligence is vsed for provision of the Kirk, that the gleib is c'petent and the Minister resident, the comunion not given since ye Ministeres entrie, bot prepara^on made for it. That yer is a table for ye comunion, bot no other furniture for it. That yer is a Treasurer for ye c'tribution of ye poore, and y^t ye s^d contribu^ones are distribute once in yeire.'

'And finding that it is expedient for the Minister to haue ane Helper in respect of his knowen infirmities, Therefore recomended to the Minister and Elderes to prowide for ane helper with all possible dilligence.']

The said day a lrē presented from Mr. Murdo McKenzie, late Minister at Dingwall, shewing y^t his sick and infirmitie did increase, which the Prēbrie haueing c'sidered, and finding the c'trare be informa^on and examina^on, and y^t the said lrē did not c'taine anie attesta^ones bot bare allega^ones, thought it not expedient to c'tinew ye sentence, Therfoir ordaines Mr. George Monro to goe on in pronounceing of ye same.

Mr. George Monro reporting y^t Allex^r McLauchlane did not repaire to ye Kirk of Vrq^rt for making his repentance c'forme into ye former ordinance, Therefore ordaines Mr. ferq^r McLennan, within whois paroch he resides, to processe him.

At Dingwall, Maij 28, 1650.

Mr. George Monro produced a Certificate of Mr. Murdo Mackenzie his repentance at Rosemarkie, Maij 19, and the Prēbrie appointed the said Mr. George, in caice of his not c'tinewing in making his repentance c'forme to ye former ordinance, to goe on in pronuncing ye sentence.

Hector McKenzie of Assin c'peiring, did supplicat the Prēbrie to receave him to satisfac^on and repentance for his accession to ye Insurrec^on in accompaineing ye Laird of Pluscarden to Balvenie. The Presbyterie, c'sidering ye said Hector wes young and not accessorie to anie other of ye Rebellious courses, ordaines him to mak his repentance be rysing out of his dask and making publick acknowledgement of his guilt at ye Kirk of foddertie, and Mr. ferq^r Ma^cLennan to receaue and cause him subscryve the declara^on of ye gerāll assemblie for abjureing ye said Insurrec^on.

The dilligence of ye Minister and Parochiners of Kiltearne being enquyred annent a helper, ther is no report from them, saife only y^t the Minister being present protested y^t he sould not be vrged with ane helper vntill ye next wisita^on of his kirk, at which tyme if he should be fund not to haue vsed incumbent and c'venient dilligence, Then he would be willing to accept of anie qhom ye Pbrie would appoint.

The Brethrein report y^t they keiped the Thanksgiveing for ye wictorie at Carbisdell abtained against James Grahame, and others, enemies to ye cause and people of God, his adherentes.

That day a lr̄e receaued from ye Comission of the Kirk importing ther sending of threittein psalme bookes of ye new paraphrase at sextein shellings ye peice, q^roff eight onlie wer receaued:[1] requyreing also the pryce of ye s^d books, of other publick papers, with tua zeirs annuitie of 20 S^s, to be sent south with our Commissioner to ye ensuing grāll assemblie. Qlk the Brethrein are appointed to provyde accordinglie.

---

[1] This is the first appearance of the 'Scottish Metrical Psalms,' which are still used in the Scottish churches. The version was, however, the work of an Englishman—Francis Rous, one of the Sectaries of Oliver Cromwell. 'I think at least we shall get a new Psalter,' writes Mr. Robert Baillie, on 14th Sept. 1649. 'I have furthered that work ever with my best wishes; but the scruple now arises of it in my mind, the first author of my translation, Mr. Rous, my

Ordaines the severall Brethren to intimate the processe of such malignants as did not repaire into yᵉ Comission of yᵉ Kirk according to yᵉ former ordinance of Pbr̄ie.

At Dingwall, 18 *June* 1650.

The Brethrein taking to yer c'sideraᵒⁿ yᵉ deposition of Mr. ferqʳ MᶜLennan, late Clerk, they did nōiat and chose Mr. Dod Mᶜcra Clerk for this vice.

The Exercise and addiᵒⁿ c'tinewed in respect of the multiplicitie of affaires, and especiallie of a few in number and the directing and provyding of a comissioner for yᵉ gr̄all assemblie.

Mr. George Monro Minister at Urquhairt reported ·yᵗ he made intimaᵒⁿ of Mr. ferqʳ MᶜLennan's deposiᵒⁿ the last Lords day according to yᵉ ordinance of yᵉ Comission of yᵉ gr̄all assemblie, as also yᵗ yᵉ sᵈ Mr. ferqʳ being present, did acknowledge yᵉ equitie of yᵉ sentence pronunced against him.

That day the Brethrein c'sidering howsoever Mr. Alexʳ Mackenzie, in Lochcarrin, and Mr. Dod Ross, Minister at Lochbroome, was ordained to be pn̄t in yᵉ Pbr̄ie this day to receaue informᵒⁿ annent the receaueing of malignants: and to lay a solid course for carrieing public papers to them, yᵗ zet they haue vilipended yᵉ sᵈ ordinance. Therfoir ordaines to advʳtise yem to keip yᵉ Pbr̄ie yᵉ next day vnder yᵉ paine of censure.

The Brethrein reports yᵗ they did intimate processe of excomunicaᵒⁿ to all the malignants yᵗ did slight repaireing to yᵉ Comission of yᵉ gr̄all assemblie according to yᵉ ordinance.

Mr. Jon Monro reports yᵗ Allexʳ MᶜLauchlin satisfies one Lord's day at Alness.

Mr. ferqʳ MaᶜLennzn reports yᵗ Hector Mᶜkenzie of Assin satisfied for his malignancie according to yᵉ ordinance.

The forder tryall of Thomas Fraser of Croichell c'tinewed

---

good friend, has complied with the sectaries, and a member of their republic. How a Psalter of his framing, albeit with much variation, shall be received by our church, I do not well know; yet it is needful we should have one, and a better in haste we cannot have. The Assembly has referred it to the commission to cause print it after the last revision, and to put it in practice.'—*Baillie's Letters.*

vntill our meitting with y̅ᵉ P̅rie of Invernes at Kirkhill upon the 27 of yis instant being Wednesday.

All ye Brethrein ordained to mak vse of the new psalmes.

All yᵉ Brethrein ordained to haue in readines yᵉ pryce of yᵒ psalme books, with ther twa zeirs annuitie of the 20s. and foure lib. 3s. and 8d. resting to vmqˡˡ James Murray, to be directed with our Comissioner to yᵉ g̅rall assemblie.

That day Mr. Dod fraser reported yᵗ Keneth McKenzie of Covill satisfied for his malignancie in the Kirk of Contin, and yᵗ he absolued him according to yᵉ appointment of the Comission of yᵉ g̅rall assemblie.

Mr. Joⁿ Monro reported yᵗ Rorie McKenzie of Redcastle satisfied for his malignancie in yᵉ Kirk of Killurnain, and yᵗ he receaved him according to ye ordinance of ye Comission of yᵉ g̅rall [assembly].

Siklyk the said Mr. Joⁿ reported yᵗ Mr. Murdo McKenzie, late Minister at Dingˡˡ, satisfied for his malignance ane Lords day in yᵉ Kirk of Alnes, and another in yᵉ Kirk of Killairnain, according to yᵉ ordinance of yᵉ Comission of yᵉ g̅rall assemblie.

Mr. George Monro, Minister at Vrqʳᵗ, ordained to preach the first Lord's day at Dingˡˡ and ther to absolue Mr. Murdo McKenzie late Minister at Dingˡˡ, and Alexʳ MacLauchlane upon evidence of repentance.

Mr. Coline McKenzie, late Minister at Contain, ordained to mak his repentance yᵉ first Lord's day at Dingˡˡ, Mr. George to mak report: and the subsequent Lord's day in yᵉ Kirk of Contain, and to yᵗ effect Mr. Doᵈ Mᶜcra ordained to preach at Contain and to receave and absolue him upon his evidencing repentance.

Mr. Joⁿ Monro ordained to preach at Kilterne yᵉ first Lords day to receaue Mr. David Monro, and Mr. Robert Monro ordained to preach in yᵉ Kirk of Alnes.

That day Mr. Joⁿ Monro, Minister at Alnes, was chosen Comissioner for yᵉ g̅rall assemblie, and Robᵗ Monro of Obsteill Ruling Elder and Comissioner for yᵒ same.

That day yᵉ Brethren c'sidering yᵒ great difficultie yey had to gett payᵗ of yᵉ wacant stipend of Contain They recomend to Mr. Joⁿ Monro, yer Comissioner, to bring home l̅res of horneing against yᵉ Parochiners ther.

At Dingwall, 2 *Julie* 1650.

That day Mr. Allex^r McKenzie, Minister at Lochcarrin, and Mr. Do^d Ross, Minister at Lochbroome, c'peired not according to ye former ordinance. Qlk ye brethren taking to yer c'sidera^{on}, and not being sure that they receaued advertisement, They ordaine lfall summondes to be directed to them to c'peir ye nixt Pbr̃ic day, to heir themselves sentenced in caice they receaued advertisement, or excused in caice they produce relevant reasons for ther not c'peirance, As lykwyse ye Brethrein c'sidering y^t they may pretend the want of helpe and books upon ye text prescryved, they ordaine yem to choise y^r own text, and to be prepared to teach at ther coming.

Mr. George Monro report y^t Mr. Murdo McKenzie and Allex^r McLauchlain satisfied according to the former ordinance, and y^t he absolued them.

Siklyk reports y^t Mr. Coline Ma^{c}Kenzie and Mr. ferq^r McLennan satisfied according to ye former ordinance in ye Kirk of Ding^{ll}.

Mr. Do^d M^{c}cra reports y^t Mr. Coline McKenzie satisfied in ye Kirk of Contain, and y^t he absolued him according to ye former ordinance.

Mr. Jo^n Monro reports y^t Mr. David Monro satisfied in ye Kirk of Kiltearne according to the ordinance.

That day a lr̃e presented vnder Mr. Robert Dowglass's hand, requyreing present pay^t to be made of ye 2 zeirs anuitie and the pryce of all bygon papers and books, in obedience wheroff euerie Broy^r is ordained to direct fyue lĩb with Mr. Jo^n Monro our Comissioner, and he ordained to bring home unto us all bygon books and papers y^t are not come to ye Pbr̃ie, and to be comptable for ye m̃oey y^t he receaues at his returne.

At Dingwall, Julie 16, 1650.

Mr. Alex^r McKenzie and Mr. Dod Ross being enquyred why they did not keip the last presbyterie day according the ordinance, declared y^t the advertisement came to ther hands so late as it wes not possible for yem to keip the s^d day ; qlk ye Pbr̃ie, efter tryall, finding true, they excuse them.

Ordaines Mr. Allex^r McKenzie and Mr. Dod Ross to send lists of yer malignants and sumond them to c'peir befor ye Pbr̃ie ye nixt day.

As also Mr. Allex^r ordained to adwertise the ministers of Kintaill and Lochalshe, and Mr. Dod Ross to adwertise y^o Minister of Garloch to y^t effect.

The Pbrie c'sidering Mr. Dod Ross his reporting that yer is a numerouse multitude of delinquents within his paroch, qho notwithstanding of his dilligence against yem c'tinewed disobedient, Therfoir the Brethrein haueing a mynd to wisit that kirk, c'tinewes the taking course against ye s^d delinquentes vntill the said wisita^on, qlk the Brethren resolue to goe about with all dilligence, efter yer Commissioner his returne from the Grall Assemblie.

The Mod^r enquyreing the Brethren if they receaued the Reasones of the fast appoynted be the Comission of ye grall assemblie of ye daite 21 June 1650 (directed be him to them severallie qhen they came to his hands to be intimated to yem) all reportes y^t they did receaue and intimate ye same.

The Reasones of ye said fast being these that followes.

1. The great danger y^t ye land and work of Reforma°n are lyable into by ye approach of ye sectarian forces.[1]

2. The present distressed estate of ye people of God in Ingland and Irland through ye tirranie of y^t partie.

3. The hazard wee are in from ye Malignant Partie, besyds ye danger from y^o sectaries.

4. The securitie, ignorance, prophanitie and formalitie y^t the land lyes in with small conscience of our solemne wowes, unthankfullnes for former mercies, and abounding of sorcerie in manie parts of yis kingdome.

To pray

5. That God would keip us from ye danger of y^t proud partie of sectaries, and delyver the neighbour kingdomes from ther tirranie.

6. That he would purge ye land from prophanitie and malignancie and all other sinnes, stirre up all sortes to yer dutie, and direct and blesse yem in ye performancie of it.

---

[1] Cromwell and his followers. Upon the death of Charles I. the Scots proclaimed Charles II. king. This brought about the war between them and Cromwell, in course of which they were defeated at Dunbar (3rd Sept. 1650), and almost annihilated at Worcester (3rd Sept. 1651). After Worcester the Sectaries ruled Scotland till the Restoration in 1660.

7. That he would shew mercie to our king, and bless the Commissioners labours with him for Religion and y⁰ peoples good.

8. That the Lord would gratiouslie c'tenance yᵉ ensueing gr̄all assemblie.

Ordaines Mr. Dod fraser to repaire to yᵉ Presbyterie of Invernes the nixt Thursday for renewing the Pbr̄ies desyre in urgeing Mr. Duncane Mᶜculloch his Transplantaᵒⁿ.

At Dingll., 30 *Julie* 1650.

Conveined Mr. Johne Maᶜcra, Modʳ, Mr. Dod Mᶜcra, Clerk, Mr. Robert Monro, Mr. Dod fraser; Mr. George Monro absent.

The name of God incalled.

The exercise c'tinewed in respect much of yᵉ tyme wes spent in attending yᵉ Adder, and the lr̄e of yᵉ Pbr̄ie of Edinbrugh came to our hands requyreing all possible dilligence to be vsed in collecting of our proportiones of the Levie mōey.

A lr̄e receaued from Mr. Dod Ross shewing yᵗ he had sumoned the malignants within his paroch to c'peir befoir yᵉ Pbr̄ie yis day, and proporting yᵗ in regaird ther wes a great multitude of malignants in these hielands bounds, who wer for yᵉ most pairt poore commones, pretending impossibilitie throw povertie to repaire to yᵉ Pbr̄ie. Qlk the Brethrein takeing to yʳ c'sideraᵒⁿ doe ordaines the Ministeres of yᵉ hielandes to put such of yer people as wer tennentes or commones to yer repentance at home, bot to sumond such as wer Elderes, heritors, taksmen, or caried office in anie of yᵉ Rebelliones courses, to c'peir befoir the Pbr̄ie, and yᵗ lr̄es be direct to yᵉ severall brethrein to yᵗ effect, Togidder also with doubles of yᵉ Act of Classing, to yᵉ end yey may be informed to receaue them to yer repentance according to yer guilt.

All the Brethrein reports that they keiped the fast.

Mr. Doᵈ fraser report yᵗ yᵉ Pbr̄ie of Invernes yer anser annent the Transplantation of Mr. Duncane Mᶜculloch wes that they give ane absolute anser, and grant him ane Act of Transplantaᵒⁿ vpon his producᵒⁿ of execuᵒⁿ of Sumonds of waluaᵒⁿ and lr̄es of horneing for provision of his kirk.

The Modʳ enquyreing if ye Brethrein receaued the warneing of yᵉ Comission of yᵉ gr̄all (assembly) of yᵉ daite at Edʳ 25

[June] 1650, qlk he direct unto them, declared that they receaued them, and made vse of yͤ same the last Lord's day.

The Modͬ enquyreing if yey hade receaued his lȓes vrging a present dilligence for collecting yͤ Levie mōey, Declares that they receaued the same and accordinglie wer useing dilligence, bot hade great difficulties to get yͤ same. And efter c'sideraᵒn of yͤ difficulties of yͤ severall Brethrein and remedies qhich the Pbȓie were resoluing upon for resoluing of yes difficulties: Ordaines the Brethrein to haue yͤ same in readdines yͤ nixt: as also lȓes to be directed to the Brethrein in yͤ highlands to yᵗ effect.

That day a desyre presented from yͤ Pbȓie of Invernes for vnderstanding of Rorie MaᶜKenzie of Dowchmiluack and Rorie MᶜKenzie fiar of fairburne yer guilt in reference to yͤ Rebellious courses prosecute be yem against kirk and kingdome, and of yer carriage since yͤ last Insurrecᵒn, being referred be yͤ Comission of yͤ gȓall assemblie to them to be censured c'forme. The c'sideraᵒn heiroff c'tinewed vntill yͤ nixt day, and thay ordained to be sumond to c'peir yͤ sᵈ day for forder tryall of yer carriage.

Allexͬ Mᶜgorrie and his wyfe within yͤ Paroich of Kilmoraik being referred to yͤ Pbȓie to be censured for prophanaᵒn of yͤ sabbaoth by stealling imediatelie efter the receaueing of yͤ sacrament, cited, not c'peiring, ordained to be sumond pro 2ᵈᵒ.[1]

The meitting closed with prayer.

At Ding., 14 *August* 1650.

Mr. George Monro his absence the last day being occasion of a necessitie urging him to attend the Comittie of Warre at Invernes, excused.

The Brethren c'sidering the necessitie of their using diligence in provyding their proportiones of the levie mōey not as zet provyded for, ordeins all to meete Twesday nixt and bring the same with them to be delivered to the Modͬ, and to be sent south with all c'venient diligence, and each of them to pay sixtene shillings by and attour their proportiones to be given

---

[1] MᶜGorrie and his wife (Agnes Nien Donald vic Vurrich) appeared before the Presbytery on 28th August, when he was found guilty and 'ordained to make his repentance in the Kirk of Urray on three several Lord's Days, and on three several Lord's Days in the Kirk of Kilmorack.' The wife was found not guilty.

to a bearer; And c'sidering the vacancie of Contin and Fottertie, They appoynt a warrant to be given to Mr. Coline MaᶜKenzie for seeking and uplifting the proportiones of the said Kirks from the heritors of them respūe [respectively].

The Pbr̄ie c'sidering z^t they were often troubled in seeking and finding out bearers for carieing directiones from them to the brethren in the hielands, Mr. Dod Ros, Minīst at Lochbroome, Mr. Alexʳ MaᶜKenzie, Minister at Lochcarrin, and Mr. Rorie MaᶜKenzie, Minister at Gerloch, being pn̄t, did at the desyre of the Pbr̄ie nōiat, and appoynt factors for themselves to that effect, as followes, vizt., The said Mr. Dod Ros did nōiat Joⁿ Ros, meason in Dingwall; the said Mr. Alexʳ. Do^d Mᶜcurchie, merchant; and the said Mr. Rorie, Mr. Murdo MaᶜKenzie late Minister at Suddie, factors for them respūe; which the saids persones did vndergoe and inact themselves to doe duetie accordinglie.

Executiones of sumonds against the Malignants in the hilands c'forme to the last dayes ordinance having returned this day, William Maᶜean vic William, and Ferqʳ MᶜConill vic hutcheon, elderes in Kintaill, were called, bot compeired not, ordeined to be sumoned pro 2do.

Siclyke, Murdo Mathewsone, Elder in Lochalsh, Murdo Mᶜalister, Joⁿ oig Mᶜ vic ean, Angus Mᶜean vic conill, Finlay MᶜConill vic finlay, Finlay and Alexʳ MᶜConchie vic ririe, Elderes in Lochcarrin, called, not compeirand, ordeined to be sumond pro 2do.

All the Ministeres of the saids parochins, and Mr. Rorie MaᶜKenzie at Gerloch, appointed to vse diligence in receiving all the comons in their respective c'gregationnes c'forme to the ordinance the last day, and to macke report theroff to the Pbr̄ie, and Mr. Alexʳ MaᶜKenzie to advertise Mr. ferqʳ Maᶜra and Mr. Dod MaᶜLennan theiroff.

Mr. Dod Ros, Minister at Lochbroome, reporting y^t he hade alreadie received his elders to repentance before the c'grega^{on} for their accession to the rebellion, and pretending he was warranted therto be the Pbr̄ies lr̄e sent to him, the Brethren suspends the examination theroff to the nixt day, and appoynts Mr. Dod to send the Pbr̄ies lr̄e for clearing of the matter.

The Brethren, c'sidering the c'di^{on} of the Kirks of Lochbroom and Gerloch, and the expediencie of visiting them (not being visited the last zeir with the rest) appoynts all the brethren to meete at Lochbroome for visiting the Kirk theroff the 10 day of Sepr nixt, and at Gerloch fryday therafter, and the ministers to macke intima^{on} heiroff to their Parochiners respūe, requyreing them to be p̄nt, and they to preach on their ordinarie texts.

[Mr. Dod Fraser reports that Thos. Chisholm could not be found to be served with a summons; and Mr. George Munro, Mr. Alexr. Mackenzie, Mr. Dod Ross, and Mr. Rorie McKenzie report having kept the fast.]

The Mod^r having immediately after his homecoming from the g̃rall assembly adv'tised the brethren severally to intimat and keepe the fast appoynted by the said assembly for the reasones of the former fast, and for praying for a good successe to our army against sectarian forces, and being this day enquired c'cerning their diligence therin, all the Brethren within the countrie reports they did intimat and keep the same. The Brethren of the Hilands ordeined to vse all possible diligence therin in lyke manner.

Mr. Do^d Fraser appoynted to goe to the Pb̃rie of Invernes as zet to urge a positive ans^r c'cerning Mr. Duncan McCulloch his transporta^{on}.

The Brethren of the hilands reports they haue made use of the warnings from the Comission of the former g̃rall of the dat at Ed^r 25 Jun. 1650 in their severall c'grega^{ones}.

The charge of the Schoole off Alnes being vacand, and Mr. Do^d Monro being called to it, willing to accept of the same, and compeiring before the Pb̃rie to receive their approba^{on} for his entrie therto, they doe approve the same and recomends him to the session of Alnes for that effect.

At Dingwall, 20 Augt. 1650.

In regard y^t Mr. Joⁿ Monro regrated y^t he could not get accession to his manse of Alnes, notwithstanding his admission to ye Kirk moire yen a zeir bygone, Qlks the Brethren taking to yer c'sidera^{on} they ordaine Mr. Thomas Ross to be sumond to remove from the said Manse, with certifica^{on} as is c'tained in ye Act of ye g̃rall assemblie to y^t effect.

That day compeired Rorie Mackenzie of Dawchmiluack and

Rorie Mackenzie fiar of fairburne, according to the former ordinance, and ye Brethren efter tryall finding no miscarriage in yem since the last Insurrec^{on}, doe therfoir appoint the same to be testified to ye Pbrie of Invernes, togidder with ane extract of ther guilt, according to yer desyre.

The Pbrie homologates the ordinance of the Prowinciall holden at Chanrie Maij 1, 1650, appoints twentie lib of ye vacant stipend of Contain to be given to Wm Petrie to help to sustain him at Schooles: and they ordaine Kenneth Mackenzie of Cowll to pay the same out of his part of the said stipend of ye croipe 1650.

That day Mr. ferq^r McCra, Mr. Alex^r McKenzie, Mr. Rorie McKenzie, Mr. Do^d Ross, Mr. Jo^n M^{c}cra, Mr. George Monro, Mr. Do^d fraser, Mr. Do^d M^{c}cra, and Mr. Jo^n Monro yer proportion of ye levie mōeys being ane hundreth merks ilk one, exhibites and delyueres to Mr. Jo^n Munro Moderator.

At Dingwall, 28 Agust. 1650.

No dilligence from Mr. Do^d Ross annent the Pbrie's letter, qlk he wes ordained to send this day, qlk the Pbrie c'tinewed vntill ye visita^{o}n of his kirk.

Johne Monro of Lumlaire presented ane Testimoniall bearing y^t he had made satisfac^{o}n for his malignant courses according to ye ordinance of the Comission of the Kirk, qlk certificate wes subscryved be Mr. Jo^n Annan to whom he wes recomended to y^t effect.

Thomas Chisolme being sumoned to yis day, cited, c'peired not, ordained Mr. Dod fraser to processe him.

Mr. Dod fraser reportes that the Pbrie of Invernes would not give ther anser annent Mr. Duncan McCulloch his transplanta^{o}n, because the said Mr. Duncan wes absent and sick for the tyme. Therfoir the Pbrie c'tinewes all forder dealling in y^t busienes vntill yer returne from the wisita^{o}n of the hieland kirks.

Hector Monro in Kilterne, c'peiring, c'fessed that he wes a captain with George Monro at Sterling, and since in service with him in Irland, qlk the Pbrie taking to yer c'sidera^{o}n, togidder with his supplica^{o}n desyreing to be receaued on his repentance. They referre him to the Commission of ye grāll assemblie.

The Visitation of the Kirk of Lochbroome.

At Lochbroome, 10 *Sepr.* 1650.
Sess. 1.

Quhilk day and place (c'forme to the ordinance off the Presbyterie at Dingwall 14 August last, c'cerning the visiting of the Kirk of Lochbroome) conveened Mr. Jo^n Monro Mod^r, Mr. Dod Fraser, and Mr. Jo^n Maccra.

Mr. Robt. Monro absent through infirmitie and weaknes, being vnable to travell.

Mr. George Monro and Mr. Dod Ma^{c}cra absent without excuse.

Elders pñt.

Murdo M^{c}evir, Hector Ma^{c}Kenzie, Rorie McKenzie, Alex^r Mackenzie, Murdo MacLennan, Alex^r McLennan, and Jo^n Fraser.

The name of God being incalled by the Moderator, Mr. Jo^n M^{c}cra was chosen clerke.

Mr. Dod Ros, Minister of the Paroch (having lectured on Math. 23. 38, *et seq.* and preached on Heb. 11. 24) removed, and the forenamed elders sworne, tryed, and examined c'cerning his carriage. The Brethren finds (upon inquirie made be the Mod^r) by their declara^{o}n that lawfull intima^{o}n was made of the visita^{o}n. That the subject of his lecture and sermon was his ordinarie. That his usuall doctrine was edificative. That he lectures and preaches vsually once on the Lords day, and urged a c'scionable keeping of it. That they knew no fault in his personall cariage. That he visited the sicke when he wes required.

Moreover, it is found be the saids Elders declara^{on}, That he preaches not in the efternoone of the Lords day. That he keepes not a day in the weeke for catechising or any publick exercise (for both which the peoples long distance from the Kirk wes alleadged as the caus), That he catechised none this twell month, That he vsed no particular visita^{o}n of his Paroch, That he tooke a relapser in fornica^{o}n to be his nurse before she satisfied the Kirke. That they knew nothing c'cerning his vsing family worship except y^t Rorie Mackenzie and Hector McKenzie declared y^t themselves being one night in his house he hade no evening prayer.

Such as were pñt of the people and c'grega°n (being few) called, sworne, enquired, and examined, declaired grãlly that they were well pleased with his cariage, and y^t they knew nothing qrin it was requisite he sould be admonished.

The Elderes being removed, and the minister called and examined c'cerning their cariage, declaires, That they were faithfull in keeping session, delating delinquents, and assisting to censure them. That as they had declaired to him, they vsed family exercise and publick prayers: concerning which themselves being examined, acknowledges y^t they used no publick prayers, and denyed y^t they declaired the lyke to him.

The Minister and elders being called and examined joyntly, its found y^t the kirk hath no provision bot the modifica°n of the Platt 1618, bot z^t there are sumonds of augmenta^{on} raised and executed against pairties having interest at the Ministers instance (as he declaires himselfe). In prosequuting q^{r}off he is appoynted to vse diligence.

That he have neither gleib nor manse, for remedieing of which he is ordained in lyke manner to use diligence.

That the sacrament of the Lords supper hath not bene administrat thir seven zeirs, the cause q^{r}off the minister alleadged to haue bene the troubles of the countrie, his c'tinewing for a long tyme under suspension, and the people their accession to the rebellion.

That the act of the grãll assembly against buriing in kirks is not observed, for remeid y^{r}off the minister is ordained peremptorily to processe the c'traveeners, and the elders exhorted to c'tribut and be assisting to the hindering it in tyme coming.

Murdo Ma^{c}Ewir, one of the Elders, presumptuously avowing his resolu°n to bury in the Kirk, deposed from the office of eldership, and sumoned *apud acta* to compeir before the Pbrie at Dingwall the 24 day of Sepr instant, to receive farther censure.

[The Minister being found to be Clerk of Session, he is ordained to have another as clerk.—No collection for the Poore ordained to have collection.—The Treasurer and Kirk Officer faithful.]

Its recomended to the Minister and Elderes y^t they be cairfull no strangers be received to the Paroch without testimonialls.

At Lochbroome, 11 *Sept.* 1650.
Sess. 2 *ante-meridiem.*

[Cases of Discipline—one Finlay M^{c}curchie vic finlay being censured for perjury.]

Same date.
Sess. 3, *die mercurij a meridie.*

Marg^t Dow sumoned for sorcerie by burieing a lamb vnder the threshold, called, compeirand, acknowledged the fact alleadged, affirming she did it only in simplicitie be the information of a poore woman that came to her house as a preventative against the death of the rest of her bestiall.

Marie neine vic neill sumoned for having a pocke of hearbs in her milk, called, compeirand, acknowledged she used it, bot in simplicity as a preventative against the tacking away the substance of her milknes, being informed of it be a woman that came from Lewise, as she alleadged.

Sicklyke, Marie neine Donill roy sumoned for the lyke called, not compeirand, bot Marie neine ferq^r her mother compeiring c'fessed y^t her daughter used it to her owne knowledge for the effect c'fessed be the other, being informed be Christine neine ean vic gillichallum in Loggie.

All the forenamed persones compeiring and c'fessing those practises being sharply rebuked be the Mod^r for these devilish and unwarrantable practices, both they and such as did not compeire were remitted to the Session to be put to publick repentance vntill they acknowledge their error and disclaime all such lyke practices.

Christine buy sumoned for 4 lapse in fornica^{o}n, and for slandering the minister by alleadging he was father to one of her bastard children, called, not compairand, ordeined to be processed with excomunica^{o}n, and any that sall entertaine her or any other fugitive to be delated to the Pbrie to be censured.

[Several persons found guilty of profanation of the Sabbath by fishing on that day, and remitted to the Session to be put to repentance.]

It being found z^t there is little or no ordour or course taken with delinquents and transgressors within Cogaich, its earnestly recomended to the session y^t this be remedied in tyme coming.

It being found y^t all the malignants are not as zet received to repentance, for their accession to the rebellion, the Ministers ordained to use diligence in putting and receiving them to repentance, and when they are received to renew the league and covenant, and to send a list of them all to the Pbr̃ie with a specifica°n of the severall degrees of their guilt, and manner and tyme of their satisfaction.

It is found be production of the Pbr̃ies lr̃e to Mr. Dod Ros, the Minister, y^t he hade not warrant from the Pbr̃ie (as he alleadged in Pbr̃ie at Ding. 14 August) to receiue elders that had accession to the rebellion to repentance without their compeiring first before the Pbr̃ie. Its found lykwyse z^t there are escaps and informalities of diverse sorts in his session booke, formerly observed and remarked as errata be the comission of the grãll assembly for visiting the Kirk of Ros, and not as zet helped by him according to the remedies prescrived be the said Comission. His escaps in this and all others his escaps found be the visitors, are referred by them (being bot few) to the c'sideration of the Pbr̃ie, and for that effect they ordeine Mr. Dod. to send the Kirk officer (Don^d Urquhart) to the Pbr̃ie the 24 of Sepr. instant y^t he may report to him from the Pbr̃ie q^t they sall determine theranent.

At Ding., 24 Sepr. 1650.

Mr. Do^d Fraser declairing he hade not fastened a process on Thomas Chissolme in regaird he promised to come to the Pbr̃ie this day. The said Thomas called, not compeirand, Mr. Do^d is ordained to goe on with the processe.

Its recomended to the said Mr. Dod. to adw'tise the Pbr̃ie hou soone Mr. Duncan M^{c}culloch recovered from his sicknes, q^{r}be they may appoynt comissioners to urge ane absolute anser from the Pbr̃ie of Invernes anent his transporta°n.

Alex^r McKenzie called, not compeirand for his tacking God's name in vaine, ordeines y^t he be sumond literally.

Mr. Jo^n Monro reports the manse of Alnes is not as zet comprysed, bot y^t it is to be comprysed tomorrow.

Mr. Jo^n Monro ordeined to preach in the Kirk of Fottertie, and to require the Parochinars to thinke upon and follow some speedie course for planta°n of the said Kirk with a minister.

Kenneth MacKenzie of Scatuall being formerly appoynted be the Pbṙie to be processed for his not repairing to the Comission of the grāll assembly to be admitted to repentance for his accession to the rebellion c'forme to the ordinance at Ding. 4 feb. last by past, did this day give in to the Pbṙie ane supplic°ⁿ beiring yᵗ he hade directed South a suplica°ⁿ to be p̄nted to the Comission of the Kirk or grāll assembly for granting him the favour to be received to repentance at home, and yᵗ he was informed yᵗ his desyre was p̄nted and granted, and that he expected that his brother Tarbat (who was on his voyage coming North) hade it in his company. Therfore supplicating the Pbṙie to c'tinew the processing of him vntill his brother's coming, and in caice he would not bring his reference, yᵗ they would be pleased to c'tinew him to the Provinciall or the nixt quarterly meiting of the Comission of the grāll assembly in Noʳ. Quhich the brethren tacking to their c'sidera°ⁿ, they c'tinew his processe till the Provinciall, appoynting him in the meantyme, if his brother come ere yᵗ tyme and bring a reference of him, yᵗ he present the same to the Pbṙie.

The Referrs of the Visita°ⁿ of Lochbroome.

Mr. George Monro being enquired c'cerning the reasone of his absence from the said visita°ⁿ ansered yᵗ he was sicke and directed a l̄re of excuse to Mr. Dod Maᶜcra to be brought thair, the examina°ⁿ and tryall qroff is, c'tinewed to the nixt day in regard of the said Mr. Dod his absence.

Murdo Mᶜewir called, not compeirand, ordeines to be sumoned pro 2ᵈᵒ.

The Kirk Officer of Lochbroome, not come to the Pbṙie as and for the effect the visitors appoynted.

The whole proceedors of the visita°ⁿ of Lochbroome being read *in pleno Pbṙio*, and Mr. Dod. Ros his escaps being c'sidered, the Brethren c'sidering he was absent himselfe and yᵗ the Kirk officer came not (according to the visitor's ordinance) for acquainting him with the Pbṙies determination, and c'ceiving the caus and reasone of his not coming to be the storme and great inundation of waters; they c'tinue the determining anything c'cerning these escaps and him vntill the nixt day.

At Dingwall ye 8 October 1650.

Mr. Dod Fraser reported y^t he made the first intimation of Thomas Chissolme his processe, and the said Mr. Dod appointed to proceid.

That day Mr. Joⁿ M^ccra and Mr. Dod fraser appointed to goe to the Pbrie of Invernes the first day of yer meiting to urge Mr. Duncane M^cculloch his transplanta°n, and to mak report of yer dilligence ye first Pbrie day.

Mr. Coline Ma^cKenzie, late Minister at Contain, reports y^t he delyvered the hundreth merk of levie möey for ye Parochin of Contain to Mr. Joⁿ M^ccra.

As also Mr. ferq^r McLennan did delyver one hundreth merk for ye Paroich of Foddertie to ye s^d Mr. Johne.

Allex^r Mackenzie being sumoned to this day, cited, c'peiring, c'fessing that haueing fallen in c'test with his minister he swore, Be God, y^t he would ray^r hazaird his person then lose eight pennies worth of his credit. Allex^r McKenzie being removed, The Brethren taking the said c'fession into yer c'sideration, They ordaine ye Moderator to rebuke him sharplie, with certifica°n if he did the lyke in tymecoming y^t he sall be moir seuerelie censured.

That day Mr. Joⁿ Monro c'plained y^t Johne Ross, Messenger, had arested the Manse of Alnes, with all ye pendicles therof, being warranted upon a pretended act of ane assemblie, to obstruct his possession of the same : Wlk the Brethren taking to y^r c'sidera°n they ordaine the s^d Mr. Joⁿ to purchase ane sumond from the Mod^r of ye Pro.

Dingwall, 5 November 1650.

That day conveined Mr. Joⁿ Munro Moderator, Mr. George Munro, Mr. Joⁿ McKra, Mr. Donald McKra, Mr. Donald fraser, Mr. Allex^r McKenzie, Mr. Donald Ros, according as it was appointed att Chanorie after the provinciall assemblie.

The name of God incalled.

No exercise in regaird the breyren was the last weike att Chanorie att the provinciall assemblie, and was necessitate to meitt this day with ovr brethren in the highland, that so they might the soonere repaire to there charges att home.

The said day Mr. George Monro and Mr. Donald fraser was

listed for election of the moderator, and the said Mr. George was chosen moderator.

The said day Mr. Jo^n McKra and Mr. Donald fraser was listed for election of the clarke, and the said Mr. Donald was chosen clarke.

Ordaines Mr. Jo^n Munro and Mr. Donald McKra to repaire to Invernes the first p̄rie day and to receive the finall anser of the p̄rie annent Mr. Duncan M^{c}culloch his transportation.

The said day Mr. Alex^r McKenzie was gravelie admonished for not preaching the last sabboth att Fodertie as he injoyned by the brethren the last weik att Chanorie, and ordaines heir-after to preach in one of the waikand [vacant] Kirks when he wold come dovne to the lowland, and not to slight the ordin-ance of the p̄rie vnder the paine of suspension.

Ordaines Mr. Jo^n Monro to delyver the comon head this day fyfteene dayes.

The qlk day the brethren taking to there consideration the diligence of the wisitors of the Kirk of Lochbrŭne, and finding Mr. Dod Ros, minister yratt, guiltie of diverse escapes in the discharge of his ministeriall function, as in perticulare y^t he did receive a woman scandalous throgh relapsing in fornication to be his nurse without putting her to publick repentance.

That being inquired whether his elders had wsed familie exercise ansered they did as they declared to him, wheras they ney^r wsed the samen nor declared so much to him by there ovne confession.

That being tryed concerning his peoples accession to the laite insurrection did deny there accession yrto, wntill Mr. Allex^r McKenzie, minister att Lochcarrin, did testifie that it was his parochiners of Lochbrune y^t raised his prochiners, for which being rebuked and ordained be the P̄rie to direct such of them as were elders or heritours to the p̄rie before he did receive them to repentance yet he did receive them att home, pretending he was warranted yrto by a letter from the p̄rie, qras the letter by production of it before the wisitors did evidence the contrarie.

That he was found slacke and remisse in processing Christan buy who haud sklandered himselfe formerlie with alleadged fornication with herselfe.

That he did not remeid the errata found formerlie in his session buike by the Comission for wisitation of Ros.

Therfore after mature deliberation finds him to have deserved suspension, and accordinglie doth suspend him from his ministeriall function, and all exercise y^rof, wntill the last sabboth of December next, and ordaines Mr. Allex^r McKenzie, minister at Lochcarrin, to intimate the said suspension the next sabboth, with certification if the said Mr. Dod Ros be found in any of the premisses culpable heirafter, or any othere neglects or scandalls coincident, shal be deposed.

Dingwall, 19 *November* 1650.

Mr. Joⁿ Munro and Mr. Dod McKra declared y^t they culd not repaire to Invernes the last p̄rie day, conforme to the former ordinance, in regaird y^t they were necessitate to meitt with the rest of the province att Kirkmichael, y^rfore ordaines them to repaire the next day conforme to the former ordinance.

Ordaines ane letter to be directed to our brethren in the highland to send there proportion of the bursers money to Mr. Rorie McKenzie, Student of theologie.

The said day Mr. Joⁿ Munro declared y^t he did repaire to Fodertie conforme to the ordinance att Dingwall, and y^t he preached there and keiped session, and y^t the parochiners promised to give in ane list this day, and accordinglie the laird of Tarbat p̄nted ane list subscribed onlie by himselfe, qlk the p̄rie taking to there consideration ordaines him to p̄nt the list the next day subscribed by all the heritors and elders of the Paroch.

Mr. Joⁿ Munro declared y^t he received Mr. ferq^r McLennan for his accession to malignancie according to the ordinance of the Comission of the generll assemblie.

Mr. Joⁿ Munro declared y^t he received Kenneth McKenzie of Scatuell for his accession to the remonstrance, wnlawfull Ingagment, and lait insurrection.

The said day Joⁿ McKenzie of Ord and Kenneth McKenzie in Knockboigter [Knockbaxter] did compeire, as they did severall dyets before, supplicating to be received to there publick repentance for there accession to the severall rebellions, y^rfore ordaines them to make there repentance for there accession to James Grahame's rebellion, unlawfull Ingagment, and laite Insurrection in the North, in the Kirk of Dingwall, in there ovne habite, the next sabboth, and to be received and to subscribe the declaration.

Ordaines Mr. Jo^n McKra to give the benefite of marriage to those within the paroch of Fodertie y^t shall be proclaimed and frie from scandall.

Ordaines the parochiners of Foddertie to pay the stipend of the crope 1650 to Mr. ferq^r McLennan.

Ordaines Mr. Dod fraser to preach att Foddertie the next p̃rie day.

Ordaines the Brethren to keipe the provinciall meitting this day fyfteine dayes att Chanorie, conforme to the ordinance of the last provinciall assemblie, and to bring with them the bursers money y^t is appointed to the Student of divinitie.

Dingwall, 17 *December* 1650.

No exercise in regaird y^t Mr. Coline McKenzie, who suld exercise, was necessalie withdraven in advancing the p̃nt levie in absence Do^d McKenzie of Loggie, whose affaires in the low land is intrusted to the said Mr. Coline McKenzie, y^{r}fore continues the exercise as before.

Mr. Jo^n Munro and Mr. Dod McKra declared y^t conforme to the ordinance they did repaire to Invernes, and y^t the Pb̃rie of Invernes adheres to there former anser annent Mr. Duncan M^{c}culloch his transportation, and that they promised to advertise the P̃rie of Dingwall when they will wisite the said Mr. Duncan his kirke.

That day Jo^n McKenzie of Davichkairne, Comissioner from the paroch of Fodertie, compeired, and, in regaird he had not a subscribed comission, ordaines the parochiners of Foddertie to send a Comissioner the next day with a subscribed comission.

Mr. Jo^n McKra declared y^t Jo^n McKenzie of Ord and Kenneth Mackenzie on Knockbaxter did satisfie conforme to the severall rebellions, and was received.

[Mr. Wm Dunuin appointed bursar.]

The brethren declaires y^t the warning of the Comission of the 24 of October was reade, qlk was directed be the Moderator since the last meitting to the brethren, he having received the samen since the last p̃rie day.

That day the Intimation of Mr. Dod Ros his suspension was exhibited.

Dingwall, 31 December 1650.

[No exercise in regard 'Mr. Colin McKenzie who should exercise was attending Reidcastle, who was at the point of death.']

The heritours and Elders of the parochin of Foddertie having given in to the P̃rie a supplication desyring that Mr. Dod fraser, one of the list formerlie given in, suld be transported from his p̃nt charge to the charge of the Kirke of Fodertie, The P̃rie, considering that the said Mr. Dod was formerlie desyrous of transportation, and conceiving a conveniencie in it, did inquirie the said Mr. Dod concerning his ovne mynd and thought of it, who declairing his unwillingnes to imbrace it, qrvpon his reasons being inquired, he promised to give them in the next day peremptorilie.

[Mr. Dod McKra reports that he preached at Foddertie. Mr. Jo^n McKra to preach at Contain, keipe session, and receiue ane list for the said Kirk, on the next P̃rie day.

Letter received from Mr. Jo^n Munro 'y^t he came getward to keipe the p̃rie, bot y^t his horse fell under him, and y^t he was not able to ryde.']

The brethren, taking to there consideration the desolation of Lochbrune, throch Mr. Dod Ros his suspension, Therfore ordaines Mr. Rorie McKenzie, minister att Gerloch, to repair to Lochbrune the first sabboth after these are come to his hand, and to repone Mr. Dod. Ros, and this to doe as he shal be anserable, and ordaines him to report his diligence to the P̃rie with all convenient diligence.

Dingwall, 14. Jar. 1651.

Mr. Dod fraser his reasones against his transportation to Foddertie being sought conforme to the former ordinance, and his ovne promise, did give in nothing bot a protestation y^t the p̃rie suld not proceid any farther in it untill his parochiners were heard, and, being inquired if he had nothing to say against it himselfe, replyed he desyred no more to be written or booked for the tyme, which the P̃rie taking to there consideration appointes sumonds to be directed to be served att the Kirk of Kilmorack upon a Sabboth day, warning all the parochiners of Kilmorack y{t} if they had any reason to alleadge against the said transportation they compeire before the prie this day fyfteine dayes by themselves or Comissioners from them to represent there reasones to the Prie, to be considered by them, with certification if they compeir not as said is, the Prie will proceide in the matter as they may be anserable.

[Since last meeting the Mod{r} received from the Com{n} of the grāll assembly and sent to the brethren a letter ordaining a fast for the reasons : 1st, 'The sinnes of the Royall familie'; and 2{d}, 'The Contempt of the Gospell.' The brethren report having kept the fast.]

The said day there was ane letter of the Comission of the grāll assemblie of the 14 of December received desyring to send ministers out of the respective bounds to attend the people y{t} suld be levied out of the samen, as also an act ordaining that none suld complye with Sectaries, and to make Intimation yrof, and accordinglie the brethren are injoyned to make intimation yrof the next sabboth.

The said day there was received anothere act of the Comission of the grāll assemblie against the lait rebellion in the North, and the meaning of the Comission of the Kirke of the Remonstrance of the Westland.[1]

Ordaines Rorie M{c}Kenzie of Corie to be sumond to the next day to try his accession to the severall rebellions in the north.

Dingwall, 28 Jar. 1651.

Sumonds directed to the Parochiners of Kilmorack, conforme to the former ordinance, returned duelie executed and indorsed, as the same att more length beares. The said parochiners called, compeired, Hew Fraser younger of Belladrum, and Ronald MacRonald Elder, in name of the Session and by wertue of a sessionall act as they alleadged, having no warrand to produce for there alleadgeance, nor any reason to give in

---

[1] Remonstrance against Charles II. by the Covenanters of Ayr, Renfrew, Galloway, Wigtown, and Dumfries. The Remonstrants protested against the admission of Malignants to public office, and declared that their pretended repentance was a profanation of the Divine ordinances. By their conduct they greatly helped Cromwell in the subjugation of Scotland.

against the transportation, for which pñded [pretended] ane impossibilitie to meitt with pairties having interest, the tyme being so short, which being considered be the brethren, they appoynt to compeire the next day peremptorlie with a formall Comission, and give in there reasons if they had any, with certification if they faile heirin they suld haue no furthere hearing or place to give them in, and they sumond *apud acta* for y^t effect.

[Mr. Jo^n McKra reports that he preached at Contin, that the people adhere to their former list. Heritors and Elders ordained to compeir the next Pr̄ie day.]

The brethren declared y^t they did intimate the act against complying with sectaries conforme to the ordinance.

The said day Rorie McKenzie of Corie being cited, compeired, and being accused for his accession to the severall rebellions y^t hes beine in the north contrare to the Covenant, confessed onlie y^t he was att Invernes with my lord in the tyme of the first rebellion for 6 dayes, and y^t he went to Assin. Continues him yrfore to further tryall, and ordaines Mr. Jo^n McKra to wreitt to Mr. Do^d Ros, minister att Lochbrune, to try what he knowes of the said Rorie McKenzie his accession to anie of the rebellions.

Ordaines the Moderator to wreitt to Mr. James McKenzie, expectant, to come to preach at Fodertie.

Dingwall, 11 *Feb*. 1651.

The parochiners of Kilmorack called, compeired, Thomas fraser of Eskadle, and Ronald McRonald, claid with a comission from the session and heritors giving Hew Fraser of Belladrum and them two joyntlie, or to any one of them, full power to speake and give in reasons against the said transportation and doe therin all things requisite in name of the parochiners requiring a continuation to the next day to give reasons against the said transportation, promising peremptorlie to continew the giving them in no longer, which the pr̄ie taking to ther consideration yeilded to there said desyre, considdering y^t some of the priñll heritors, and elders as was made knowne to the pr̄ie, were necessarlie withdrawne from giving there concurrence to the rest.

Mr. Dod McKra declared y^t he did repaire to Containe conforme to the ordinance, preached, made intimation, and keiped session, and this day compeired the Elders from the said paroch of Contain, to wit, Hew McKenzie and Dod McNeil, declaring y^t the heritours was not in the countrie, being imployed in the highland annent the pñt levie, y^{r}fore the Prie ordaines the heritours to adhere to the last list, and to nominate one of the said list for the said Kirk of Containe, and to compeire the next prie day eithere by themselves or there Comissioners for y^t effect.

Mr. Jo^n McKra declared y^t he wreitt to Mr. Dod Ros, bot received no anser as yet.

That day there was ane letter received from Mr. Rorie McKenzie shewing y^t Mr. Dod Ros was reponed conforme to ye ordinance.

Dingwall, 25 Febr. 1651.

Mr. Jo^n Munro excused for his absence, being necessarilie withdrawn to Straneyver, as his letter did proporte.

Hew fraser of Belladrum and Thomas fraser of Eskadle, Comissioners from the paroch of Kilmorack, compeired and did give certaine reasones against the said transportation of there minister, with a protestation that they suld haue pover to adde to them heirafter, which the brethren taking to there consideration, with othere reasones given for the said transportation, and considering the paucitie of the number pñt. they continued the determining anything in the matter wntill the next day, at which tyme it is granted to the parochiners of Kilmorak to adde to there reasons according to there protestation.

The reasones of the parochiners of Kilmorak against the transportatione are these:

1. We knov no priviledge the paroch of Fodertie hes above the paroch of Kilmorak to wrge ovr Minister with ane transportation.

2. To interrupe what is alreadie begune of the lords worke amongst ws is fearfull, pastor and people going about there deveres joyallie in ane street (?) harmonie to prosecute the same.

3. The experience we haue of his abilitie for the charge, and the not knowing of few or any so fitting for it that we can come be, doth fullie persuade us that the transporting of [him] were the onlie meane to advance and inlarge the Kingdome of Satan both in the height of this Paroch and the most remote places of the next adjacent paroch, which we are confident no honest man fearing God will enterpryse or seike after, neithere countenance such as intends the same, bot rathere (by interpoining there authoritie) obviate the same and prove assisting to ws, that therby the Kingdome of Christ may daylie more and more advanced and inlarged amongst us.

4. Considering the wastnes of the paroch, and withall it being populous, ovr ministers acquaintance both with the bounds and people, the conformitie which now (by the grace of God and his labours) that ovr people is brought to, and the prosperitie of the worke of God amongst ws, It is evident that he may doe more guid where he is then to be transported to Fodertie, It being alvayes easier to find ministers to lesser then greater charges, no reasonable man can deny bot that it is more expedient and necessarie for Gods glorie and his churches weill that largest and most populous parochines suld be plenished with the ablest and most fitting men.

Continews the former ordinance annent the Kirk of Containe in regaird of the heritors absence, being imployed annent the p̅n̅t levie, and the kirk officiere of Containe is ordained to sumond the heritours of Containe to compeire before the p̅r̅ie when they shall come home, to nominate one of the last list given in for the Kirk of Contain.

That day there was ane letter received from Mr. Dod Ros proporting severall enormities of his people, as also some diligence annent Rorie McKenzie of Corie, showing y^t he was informed y^t the said Rorie McKenzie had accession to the lait rebellion y^t was in the north in 1649, y^{r}fore ordaines the said Rorie to be sumond to the next day.

Ordaines Mr. George Munro, Mr. Jo^n McKra, Mr. Dod McKra, to speake the gentlemen and heritours of the name of McKenzie annent the forsaid enormities within the paroch of Lochbrune.

Dingwall, 11 *March* 1651.

A letter sent to the p̃rie from Hew fraser of Belladrum and Thomas fraser of Eskadle, comissioners for Kilmorake, shewing their compeirance before the p̃rie was impeded by there being necessarlie withdravin be imployment in the publick, and y^t they culd not send any reasones to be added to there former reasons in regaird they had not seine the reasons of the parochiners of Fodertie, which the brethren taking to there consideration, and finding they did not make wse of the P̃ries granting there former protestation so farre as to adde to there former reasones this day, and conceiving the same to be a dilator, they haue resolved not to grant any such lyke protestation heirafter, and y^{r}fore they haue appointed and ordained them to compeire the next day peremptorilie to receiue the reasons of the paroch of Fodertie, and with all conveniencie to give in there anser to the same, y^t the matter may be determined be the p̃rie, with certificatione if they compeire not for y^t effect the p̃rie shall proceide to determine in it, and they appoint Mr. Dod fraser to warne them to this effect by making publick intimation of this ordinance.

Continues the former ordinance annent the Kirk of Containe, for the former reasons.

The said day it was declared y^t Rorie McKenzie of Corie was in Keipach, y^{r}fore ordaines him to be sumoned to the next day if he comes home.

Mr. George Munro and the brethren appointed with him to speake the name of McKenzie, declared y^t they were not come from the highland as yet, y^{r}fore ordaines them to speake to them conforme to the former ordinance when they come from the highland.

Ordaines Mr. Dod fraser to preach att Fodertie or the next p̃rie day.

The said Allex^r Munro and David Munro did supplicate the P̃rie to be received for there accession to the laite wnlavfull ingagment, the said Allex^r confessing y^t he was lievtennent Coll. and the said David y^t he was captaine in the said ingagement, qlk the p̃rie taking to there consideration, referres them to the Comission of the g̃rall assemblie.

Dingwall, 20 *March* 1651.

This day the brethren did meitt, being advertyse be the Moderator, he having received ane letter from the laird of Tarbat desyring that the p̄rie suld mcitt to nominate ane minister for my lord of Kintail his regiment, and the laird Tarbat compeiring, and giving ane list of two ministers y^t were not within there respective bounds, as the letter of the Comission of the Kirk desyred, y^{r}fore the p̄rie ordaines Mr. Jo^n McKra to repaire to the moderator of the province to the end he may be pleasit to appoint ane meitting of the province to nominate ministers for the severall regiments, and this to be done with diligence.

The said day there was ane letter receiued from the Maister of Lovat desyring Mr. Dod fraser to be nominate for his regiment, qlk the p̄rie taking to there consideration continews the anser y^{r}of till the province meitt.

The said day Rorie McKenzie of Corie being cited, compeired, and being accused for his accession to James Grahame's his rebellion and laite insurrection, confessed, and was ordained to make his repentance in his ovne habite in the Kirk of Dingwall.

Dingwall, 8 *Aprill* 1651.

No exercise in regaird y^t Mr. Dod McKra, who suld exercise, was not in health, and declared y^t he was not able to delyver the exercise altho prepared for it; y^{r}fore continues the exercise as befor, and ordaines Mr. Jo^n McKra to exercise the next day, if Mr. Dod McKra shall march with my Lord of Kintaill his regiment according as he was appointed by the meitting at Kirkmichael.

No meitting since the 20 of March in regaird y^t the brethren keiped the severall meittings att Kirkmichael.

Hew Fraser of Belladrum and Thomas fraser of Eskadle being cited compeired for receiving the reasons of the parochiners of Fodertie, and the reasons having gone by his hand who had them, namelie, Mr. Jo^n Munro, he is appointed to send them with the first to Mr. Dod fraser, and he giving them to the parochiners, they appointed to repaire with them to the p̄rie the next day.

The said day Mr. Coline McKenzie declared y^t the Kirk officere of Containe did sumond the heritours of Containe conforme to the ordinance of the p̃rie the 25 of februare, and in regaird y^t they have not compeired this day, and that the most pairt of them consents to the last list y^t was given, as also the p̃rie finds y^t Mr. James McKenzie, who is one of the list, is impeded by the p̃rie of Tayne, Therfore referres the consideration y^{r}of to the next provinciall assemblie.

Mr. George Munro and Mr. Jo^n McKra declared y^t they spoken the gentlemen of the name of McKenzie annent the enormities within Mr. Dod Ros his paroch according as his letter did beare, and y^t they did find them willing to concurre to punish these delinquents y^t are in there bounds, y^{r}fore ordaines Mr. George Munro, Mr. Jo^n McKra, and Mr. Dod McKra to meitt at Logie the next fryday, and to wreitt ane letter to the officers of the Regiment, to cause the said delinquents to compeir before them the said day, if they be come dovne to the countrie, if not Mr. Dod Ros to sumnond them before the p̃rie.

Mr. Jo^n McKra declared y^t Rorie McKenzie of Corie did satisfie for his accession to the severall rebellions, according as he was injoyned by the p̃rie the last day.

The said Hector Munro of Coul did supplicate the p̃rie, humblie acknowledging his accession to the laite wnlavfull ingagment, and desiring to be received to his publick repentance, qlk the p̃rie taking to there consideration, in regiard y^t he had beine before active in God's cause, and since the said ingegment hes carried himselfe as a man abhoreing all malignant courses, as it was made known to the p̃rie, and now being of intention to march to the p̃nt expedition for the defence of religion, king, and countrie, y^{r}fore the p̃rie hes ordained him to make his repentance the next saboth in his ovne habite in the Kirk of Alnes.

Mr. Dod fraser declared y^t he did preach at fodertie conforme to the ordinance of the p̃rie March 11.

The brethren declared y^t the solemne warning was read conforme to the ordinance of the Comission of the grāll assemblie qlk came to the Moderator since the last p̃rie day and y^{r}after was directed to the severall breyren.

That day there was ane letter received of the Comission of the Kirk of the daite of the 20 of March ordaining a fast to be keiped the next sabboth after the receipt y^{r}of, Therfore the p̄rie ordaines the fast to be intimated the next Sabboth and keiped the sabboth y^rafter.

The causes q^rof are these :
We neid not to search farre in the causes of humiliation, y^r is none who lookes wpon the p̄nt pousture of the Kingdome, the sad judgments y^t are incumbent, and the fulnes y^rof notvithstanding of all y^t is come upon ws, bot will find them palpable.

1. Our continuing in the guiltines of our sinnes formerlie mourned for, though the lord's hand hes beine stretched out against us, the same seids of evill flowing afresh, even while the lord is pleading against ws.

2. Our grāll securitie and wniversall wnprofittablenes, wnanserable unto the lord's whethere of goodnes or severitie, so y^t we are ney^r bettered by the one nor the othere, q^rby if mercie prevent not our wounds may become wncuirable.

3. The prophanitie of many in the land, even of those who are employed in armes, who makes unfaithfullnes in levies, oppression, and wiolence in quartering, to the hazard of the worke and scandall of the gospell.

4. The slovnes and negligence against the enemie of truth, and of the peace of this kingdome, and ye governments notvithstanding of the pressure of the troubles y^mselves, cryes and groanes of the people and frequent exhortations and remonstrances of this kirk, as it cannot be looked upon bot as a great token of wrath from the lord upon us, so must we acknowledge it to be a great p^t of guiltines y^t now after so many monthes q^rin God hath wonderfullie given us a breathing in this p^t of the land, y^t yet little or nothing is done against the enemie.

5. The selfines of the tyme so y^t many in the 3 kingdomes, and even members of this same kingdome, as particularlie those of ye cheife citie be suffering, yet the most p^t of the land is secuire and tenacious and selfie in particulare interest, as if the publick were not concerned.

6. The rising of great differences of Judgments wpon the wncleannes of some annent the publick resolutiones, q^rby the work of God and delyverance of his Kirk and kingdome is obstructed.

7. The extreme distres of our brethren and desolation of the land besouth forth, of our cheife citie, the cruell and barbarous

wsage of our brethren y^t are prisoners, ye feare of famine, the manie scattered congregationes whose pastors are driven away and necessarlie detained from them, the hazard of there soules y^t are wnder the feitt of the enemie, the falling avay of some in there privous wayes, and the sad distress of some of ovr brethren and fellow covenanters in Ingland and Ireland.

8. That the lord in his iŭst displeasure against ovr manifold sinnes goes not forth with ovr armies, bot gives up the most considerable pts of the land and ovr strongholds y^{r}in wnto the hands of the enemie.

1. We are y^{r}fore in all humilitie and earnestnes to pray y^t God would poure ovt the spirit of repentance wpon all sorts, y^t we fast not to strife and debaite bot there may be ane imptiall searching of the sinnes which haue provoked God, and a sincere turning from them wnto the Lord, and y^t he wald forgive the iniquities of all rankes in the land, and turne from his feirce wrath which is burning against the same.

2. That God wald be pleasit to stirre up the spirits of people for there dewties to doe in there placcs as he calls them, y^t magistrats may be faithfull in there place, studying the publick good, and be furnished with counsell unto the end y^t officers and souldiers may be sanctified and fitted with faithfullnes, abilitie, and courage for y^r places, y^t all who wsed repentance in turning from there former malignant wayes may be established by grace to walke so as the gospell may not suffer by there miscarriages.

3. That God wald delyvere his kingdome from the p̃nt enemies, and restore the whole land to the former beautie of injoying the libertie and puritie of ordinances, and y^t he wald guard his people from these snares, and reclaime any y^t are fallen y^{r}in.

4. That God wald make his people willing, and stirre them wp for the defence of there brethren, and blesse and gathere there armies togethere, and may sanctifie them to be holie wnto and instrumentall for the delyverie of his distressed land, and y^t the lord wald judge those who haue unjustlie invaded his kingdome, and spoiled, and trampled, and trod dovne God's sacred ordinances, and murdered so many of God's dear people.

5. That the lord, who is one, wald give his people and

servants one heart and one way to serve him in his worke with one consent against all the enemies of his kingdome, and y^t he wald remove the groving offences of the times.

6. That God wald looke wpon the royall familie and blesse the King, and y^t he may be keiped frie both from the snares and dangers of the tymes, and in due tyme restore him to his right, sett him on the throne of all his 3 kingdomes, made ane instrument for the good of the worke and people of God, and terrible to all the enemies within the samen.

7. That the lord wald mercifullie remember ovr distressed brethren in ovr chiefe citie, and y^t desolate p^t of the land, and to bring the scattered congregationes to publick and frie wse of the ordinances, and to lift up the standard of the gospell in all the 3 kingdomes.

8. That till the delyverance come the lord's people may glorifie him in patient bearing of the crosse, without grudging and murmuring, till he plead there cause and bring them forth to the light.

Ordaines the brethren to meitt here this day fyfteene dayes.

The meitting closed with prayer.

Dingwall, 22 Aprill 1651.

The reasons of the paroch of Fodertie not being sent to the parochiners of Kilmoracke for want of occasion, bot brought this day to the p̅r̅ie, they were this day delyvered *in pb̅r̅io* to Mr. Dod fraser to be brought to his parochiners, and they appointed to compere before the p̅r̅ie with the same reasones and ther anser to them the next day peremptorlie.

The reasons are these :

1. It hath beine Mr. Donald's owne [desire ?][1] heirtofore to be transported, and accordinglie by Act of the lait comission of the grāll assemblie for wisiting the Church of ros he is declared transportable and the p̅r̅ie appo[inted to][1] transport him actuallie whenever he had a lawfull call, and nov he hes a fair and lawfull call to the Kirk of Fodertie.

2. Qras the said Act of Comission grounded upon Mr. Donald's abilities, and it is speciallie provyded by Act of the Grāll assemblie y^t places of noblemens residence be planted

[1] Words illegible—ink faded.

with able men considering y^t the favour granted to noblemen be y^t act is not grounded, as we conceive, upon there titles bot upon the considerablenes of there condition in othere respects. Therefore for as much as Sir Jo^n McKenzie of Tarbit, a man in many respects right considerable in there pairts, hes his ordinarie residence in the paroch of Fodertie, it may be humblie conceived y^t the p̄rie granting and passing a formall act for his transportation will be a reall homologating with the said Act of Assemblie.

3. A maine reason of Mr. Donald's former desyre to be transported and (as may appeare) of the said Act of Comission was the distance of his present charge from the p̄rie seate, the large extent of bounds of it, and the necessitie of serving ordinarlie att diverse places, which, together with diverse othere incomodities, being considered, with reference to his weake bodie, the burden y^{r}of will clearlie appeare to be insupportable to him, and to inferre and carie along with it not onlie great prejudice to his health, bot also the shortening of his life to the making of him altogethere unusefull for the church of God, all which difficulties and inconveniencies may be removed and prevented by his transportation, the paroch of Fodertie, being both compact of itselfe and adjacent to the p̄rie seat.

4. The most pairt of the parochiners of Fodertie having in tymes bygone miscarried by following severall courses no wayes agrieable to the statutes and ordinances of Kirke and state, all such like miscarriages and ovtbreakings may be prevented and remedied by this transportation having one wpon the watch-tower to forsie and forvarne of the like dangers.

5. Considering ovr Saviours saying, y^t a prophet is not despised bot in his ovne countrey, and y^t native countreymen anywhere may be thought, yea in effect may prove, too favourable in conniving att or reproving of men's escapes, this transportation may be humblie conceived to be verie expedient, the said Mr. Dod being a stranger to ws, and a native countreyman where he has his present charge.

6. The said Act of Comission may prove a way, and open a dorre (if not tymelie prevented), for the said Mr. Donalds his removeall out of his p̄rie, yea out of this province, and perhaps to ane Inglish congregation, all which severallie, much more

probablie will carie alongs with them great prejudice, as is apparent from the great scarcitie of Irish preachers throghovt the kingdome, and from the greater and ordinarie neid y̌ᵗ this province, and more especiallie this p̄rie, have to drave men to them for supplieing of, rathere as to let any from them, for adding unto the too many vacancies yᵗ are among them alreadie.

So that the expediancie of the said transportation as *māias bonum ecclesie* being cleirlie evidenced (as we conceive) by the premisses, and fortified with the authoritie of the grāll assemblie, as may appeare from the first reasone grounded upon ane act of Comission alreadie approven of by the grāll assemblie, by the second grounded imediatelie upon ane act of assemblie, we trust that your w/, taking the same to your consideration, togethere with the daylie increasing groūth of sinne amongst ws, through the wacancie of our Church, calling for remeid att your hands by this transportation, you wilbe pleased, without any furthere delay, to proceid in it, and put it to a poynt and closure, in confidence qʳof, as we referre the matter to your consideration, so we commend you and your proceiders in it unto the lord, and your w/ anser we crave and expect.

The brethren declared yᵗ the fast was keiped conforme to the ordinance, as also that they received the Remonstrance of the Comission of the Kirk to King and state, and the anser of the Comission to the Quere from the parliament.

The said day the brethren being severallie removed, tryed, and examined, were approven in there life and doctrine, and Mr. Donald McKra to haue a care of Kilichrist, in Strathorin, and Mr. Joⁿ McKra was ordained to repaire his kirk, reside and labour, to have ane schoole, and to cause his people to repaire to the Presbyteriall meittings.

Dingwall, 13 *Maij* 1651.

This day being the first day of our meitting after the provinciall assemblie, according as it was concluded by the brethren att Chanorie after the said provinciall assemblie.

Conveined Mr. George Munro, Moderator, Mr. Robert Munro, Mr. Joⁿ McKra, Mr. Joⁿ Munro, Mr. Donald McKra, Mr. Donald Fraser.

The said day Mr. Joⁿ Munro and Mr. Joⁿ McKra was listed

for the election of the moderator, and the said Mr. Jo^n Munro was chosen.

Ordaines Mr. Donald Fraser to continue clarke till the next provinciall assemblie.

Mr. Donald Fraser, Minister at Kilmorack, being inquired concerning his diligence in delyvering the reasons of the parochiners of Fottertie for transportation to the parochinars of Kilmorack, and in requiring them to compeire before pr̄ie this day with the said reasons, and there anser to them conforme to the ordinance thereannent, at Dingwall, Aprill 22, 1651, reported he did obey the said ordinance in all points, Whereupon the said parochinars of Kilmorack being called, and none of them compeiring, there was ane missive letter presented to the pr̄ie from the Maister of lovat, Hew Fraser of Belladrum, Thomas Fraser of Eskadle, and Ronald McRonald in Kilmorack, sheving they culd not keipe the meitting be reason they were called South, and desyreing the Pr̄ie not to proceid in the said Transportation withovt there presence. The Pr̄ie tacking the same to there consideration, and considering that notvithstanding of there ovne absence they might haue comitted the matter to others who stayed att home, or sent to the pr̄ie in wreitt what they had to obiect to the reasons of the parochiners of fottertie, they constructed there said letter to be nothing bot a delator, yet finding Mr. Dod fraser (whose transportation was sought) scrupolous in the matter, and as yet wnresolved, and promising to give to the pr̄ie in wreitt the next day peremptorlie what he had to say, they continue to fall upon the discussing of the reasons to the said day, giving withall way to such as are att home of the heritors and elders of Kilmorack to alleadge what they haue to say against the reasons of fottertie, with certification whethere they would compeire or not the pr̄ie wald proceid in the matter withovt farder delay.

That day there was received 12 copies of a short exhortation and warning from the Comission of the grãll assemblie, ordaines to make wse of them, and to report there diligence the next prie day.

Ordaines the brethren conforme to the ordinance of the last provinciall assemblie to wse diligence in setting doven a solid course for the Irish boy his maintenance, and to make report the next day.

Ordaines Mr. Robert Munro to preach att Fottertie or the next prie day.

Ordaines Mr. Robert Munro and Mr. Jo^n McKra to conferre with Mr. ferq^r M^{c}lennan and Mr. Dod McKra, and Mr. Dod fraser to conferre with Mr. Murdo McKenzie to take a more full notice of there recentment for there former miscarriages, and ordains the said brethren to make report the next day, and the said Mr. ferq^r and Mr. Murdo to declare themselves the next day before the prie for there miscarriages.

Ordaines the brethren to wse diligence to try if Mr. Rorie M^{c}cleod had any accession to malignancic or malignant courses, and to make report y^{r}of the next prie day.

Dingwall, 27 Maij 1651.

The said day Mr. George Munro handled ane comon head *de Transubstantione,* his text was Math. 26. 25.

Mr. Donald fraser, being inquired concerning his ovne mynd and resolution annent his transportation to fottertie, and required to give in wreitt what he had to say according to his former promise, declared y^t he culd not find himselfe resolved to embrace the call he had to fottertie. And Thomas Fraser in Beulie compeiring before the prie alleadging a Comission (bot producing none) from the Session of Kilmorack, desyred the Prie suld not proceide furthere in the matter of the said Transportation, be reasone of ye superiors and cheife heritors of the paroch there absence, which being tacking to consideration be the prie, they conceive all of them to be wsing dilaters, yet considering the nearnes of the provinciall meitting to hold at Dingwall the   day of   they waive the matter to be advysed with the said meitting, and in regaird Mr. Dod did not give in reasons of his willingnes to imbrace the call this day, they appoint and ordaine him to give them in the next prie day peremptorlie, without farder delay.

The brethren declared y^t wse was made of the warning of the Comission conforme to the ordinance the last day.

The brethren declared that they have wsed diligence for the Irish boyes maintenance, yet in regaird of the heritours absence, being called to the present expedition, as also the land being pressed with diverse impositions, they culd not proceid to take such a settled course as was expected for the said maintenance, yet they promised to doe there best to maintaine the said boy heerafter as they have done hitherto untill it please the lord to remove the present troubles of the Kingdome, y^t so the said maintenance may be stented wpon the land according as it is ordained.

The said day Mr. Robert Munro and Mr. Jo^n McKra declared y^t they conferred with Mr. ferq^r McLennan, as also Mr. Dod McKra and Mr. Dod fraser declared y^t they did conferre with Mr. Murdo, conforme to the former ordinance, and y^t they did find them humbled for there former miscarriages, and resolved heirafter to walke more circumspectlie as the Lord wald inable them, as also the said Mr. ferq^r and Mr. Murdo declared themselves att length before the pr̃ie, acknowledging there former miscarriages and there griefe and sorrov for the same.

The brethren being weill pleasit with the report of the forsaid brethren, as also with the said Mr. ferq^r and Mr. Murdo there declaration, y^{r}fore recomends the said Mr. ferq^r and Mr. Murdo to the next provinciall meitting y^t is to be keipe att Dingwall the   day of June next.

This day the brethren declared y^t conforme to the former ordinance they wsed diligence in trying if Mr. Rorie M^{c}cleod had any accession to malignancie, and y^t after due tryall they culd find no accession to any malignant courses, y^{r}fore ordaines ane testificate to be given to him.

The said day Jo^n Bayne of Tulloch did supplicate the pr̃ie in name of the parochiners of Contin that they might haue the benefite of the last list given in by them with Mr. Dod Ros and Mr. James McKenzie, qlk the pr̃ie tacking to there consideration, ordaines Mr. Jo^n McKra to repaire to Contain, there to preach, keipe session, and to desyre the elderes to nominate one of the said list, and he to produce ane act therupon the next pr̃ie day.

Ordaines the brethren to keipe the provinciall wisitation att Dingwall the   day of June next.

Dingwall, 8 *Julie* 1651.

Mr. Dod fraser, minister at Kilmorack, having given in to the Pr̃ie this day reasons against his transportation to fottertie,

The Prie considering y^t the discussing of them and of the othere reasons given in formerlie by the parochiners of fottertic and Kilmorack required a more full tyme then culd be spaired this day in regaird y^t we are to send avay ovr Comissioner for the grall assemblie, they continued the discussing of them to the next day.

The reasons are these :

1. As a minister suld not be thrust upon a people or paroch against there Will, so a minister suld not be wrged against his will to embrace a charge not being p'suaded in conscience he hes a lawfull call, from any reason that is given in be the parochiners of fottertie.

2. Hovsoever the Comission of the grall assemblie for wisiting the province of Ros declared me transportable, yet there act must be still wnderstood so as God's glorie may be required in the first place, and no act of grall assemblie be infringed, bot in this intended transportation, if it be proceided in, both are evidentlie wronged as shall appeare by those reasones following, first, It is known that the Station wherin I remane in that condition as what in respect of my father's weaknes who is nov ane infirme and aged man, and in regaird of the largenes of the bounds wherein my fathere and I are ministers att, that if I be transported my infirme fathere, not being able to attend devties requisite at all tymes, throgh my Removing great prejudice may arise, which without any neglect of devtie incumbent to me may be prevented, and devties p'formed, there being bot the breidth of the water betuix both the Kirks, as also what desolation may follow in these farre distant bounds of both paroches may be easilie knoven, and how farre soules coft [purchased] by the blood of Christ may suffer wrong and perish, may be easilie judged.

3. It was nevere the purpose of the grall assemblie, whose acts regulates Comitties appointed by them, to make men's condition worse by there transportation, bot to better them, as appeares directlie by the acts of ye grall assemblie, bot in this intended Transportation my condition shall be made worse, ney^r being designed Manse and Glebe nor modified provision by authoritie of parliament or any othere wayes which cannot be sufficient without ane act of parliament.

4. I was declared transportable by the Comission of the grāl assemblie in regaird of the wastnes of the bounds of my paroch (besides othere reasones knowen to them), qlk is not taken avay in this intended transportation in respect the paroch of Contain is intercected betuix the paroch of fottertie, and pairt of it qlk is in Strachonin, as also pairt of it marches with Stragairve.

The said day Mr. Jo^n McKra declared that conforme to the former ordinance the last prīe day that he did repaire to Containe, and there preached and keiped session, and that the people did wnanimouslie call Mr. Dod Ros to be there minister, and therewpon produced ane act of Session purporting there willingnes to embrace the said Mr. Dod to be there minister, as also the said Mr. Jo^n declared that the parochiners desyred the prīe to interpone there authoritie for transporting of the said Mr. Dod with all convenient diligence to be admitted to the forsaid charge of Contain, qlk the prīe tacking to there consideration, and withall considering that the said Mr. Dod is declared transportable by the Commission of the grāll assemblie, and he willing to embrace the said charge, Therfore ordaines ane edict to be served the next sabboth att Contain, and the said Mr. Dod Ros to preach there the said day, and the execution of the said edict to be sent heire this day fovrteine dayes.

The said day Mr. Ferq^r McKra being cited (being sumonded to this day conforme to the ordinance of the provinciall wisitation att Dingwall the   day of June) compeired not bot a letter was receiued from him proporting his inabilitie to travell this length, as also regraiting his prīt condition that he wes put ovt of the house of the Ile of Dounan,[1] qrin he dvelt since he had not a designed gleibe, etc: as also there was ane letter receiued from Symon McKenzie, laird of Lochsline,[2] purporting that he was not able to keipe this meitting according as he was advertised (conforme to the ordinance of the

---

[1] The Castle of Eilean Donan in Kintail of which he is said to have been constable. He really appears only to have been allowed to live in it, as he had no glebe and manse of his own.

[2] Simon MacKenzie of Lochslinn, near Tain, father of the famous Sir George MacKenzie, Lord Advocate to Charles the Second—'the Bloody MacKenzie.'

Provinciall wisitation att Dingwall the   day of June) in regaird of his imployment in the present expedition, qlk the p̄rie tacking to there consideration, as also the assessors appointed by the said provinciall wisitation not coming as they were appointed, y^{r}fore continues to proceide in the said matter wntill the said Mr. ferq^r be able to travell.

The said day Mr. Dod McKra was chosen Comissioner to the g̅rall assemblie, and Hew Fraser of Struy as Ruling Elder, giving them full pover to repaire to the said g̅rall assemblie, and there to proceide and conclude with the rest of the Members of y^t assemblie according to the word of God and acts of the reformed Church of Scotland.

Ordaines Mr. Dod Ros to make intimation to his parochiners of Lochbruine to compeir here this day fyfteine dayes if they have anything to object against his transportation to Contain.

The brethren did not meitt heire presbyteriallie this last month in regaird that we keiped the severall meittings with the rest of the province the first att Dingwall and the second at Alnes.

Ordaines the brethren to meitt heire this day fyftein dayes.

Ordaines Mr. Dod Ros to preach att Contain and Mr. Allex^r McKenzie att fottertie.

The brethren declared that the fast was keiped conforme to the ordinance of the provinciall meitting att Dingwall, qlk ordinance annent the said fast was received att the said meitting, ordaining the said fast to be keiped the 19 of June and the Lords day y^{r}after.

The reasons qrof are these :

1. We are to bevaile the great stupiditie and prophanitie which everiewhere abounds in all the land, so as there are werie fev who are sensible of there sinnes or sorrovfull for there chastisment wherewith God hath chastised ws, or who stand in the gape to make the hedge y^t the fierce wrath of God doe not overturne the remanent pairt of this land, ney^r doe they so profitt by the rod as to turne to him y^t smiteth them.

2. Though manie in the army and g̅nallie throghout all the land haue professed there repentance for there former

malignant courses, and haue beine received into ecclesiasticall societie, yet those who were in that course ought constantlie to remember there evill wayes and be ashamed, and mourne after the lord for the same.

3. We are to wrestle earnestlie with the lord y^t, laying aside his fierce wrath, he wald be gratiouslie pleasit to blesse ovr king, restore him to the possession of his just rights, and sanctifie him to be the instrument of God for the promoving of the work of reformation in Ingland and Ireland, and preserving it in Scotland, thae the lord wald be pleasit to assist him particularlie in the conduct of the armie, and to blesse all y^t have charge wnder him with faithfullnes, covrage, and authoritie, and sanctifie and strengthen the souldiers to doe there devties effectuallie and obedientlie.

4. That wee, sieing this blasphemous enemie infesting the land is a most wiolent enemie to the work of reformation and wnion of the Kirks of the thre kingdomes in religious worshipe and government according to the Solemne league and Covenant, y^t the trulie godlie in all the 3 Kingdomes are wnder the wiolence of his p'secution, the lord wald poure abundance of the spirit of grace and supplication, and stirre wp the spirit of all the godlie in the 3 kingdomes to wrestle with god for a delyverance att his tyme from this ovr comon and traiterous enemie.

5. That god wald gratiouslie unite the heart of those who are concerned and in hazard by the p̄nt enemie to act joyntlie in there stations for the cause of God and against the enemie with one heart and mynd, and remove all jealousie and heart burning from amongst them.

6. That as God hath gotten honour in making many of all rankes who were opposit to the worke of reformation to acknowledge there guiltines, and to submit to discipline, so he wald gratiouslie please to make them manifest the realitie of there repentance by there sincere and effectuall actings against the enemie, and constant guid carriage in all tyme coming.

7. That the lord wald provyde for the necessare preservation of the lives of his people from svord and feared famine, y^t the lord wald mercifullie lead ovt ovr armie, inable everie one y^{r}in to keipe themselves from everie wicked thing, covere there

head in the day of battell, teach their hands to warre and there fingers to fight, and make them have guid successe y^t the enemie may flie and fall before, and y^t the lord wald gratiouslie please by there meanes to delyvere ovr brethren y^t are wnder the foot of the enemie, and preserve the remanent of this oppressed kirk and kingdome from the wnjust wiolence of the cursed and cruell adversaries.

The meitting closed with prayer.

Dingwall, 22 Jullie 1651.

Conveined Mr. Jo^n Munro Mod^r, Mr. George Munro, Mr. Jo^n McKra, Mr. Dod fraser.

Continues the discussing of Mr Dod. fraser his reasons against his transportation to the next day, in regaird of the paucitie of the number.

The said day the execution of the Edict y^t was ordained to be served att Contain was exhibited, the tenor q^rof followes :

Mr. Jo^n Munro, Mod^r of the prie of Dingwall, and remanent members y^rof, to ovr lovit Hew $M^cKenzie$, Exr heirof, speciallie constituted, greiting, forsameikle as Mr. Dod Ros, minister att Lochbrune, declared transportable by ws, is nov cald entered in the ministrie att the Kirk and paroch of Contain nov wacant in ovr hands by deposition of Mr. Colin $M^cKenzie$, late minister y^rof. Therefore, These are requyring yov upon sight of this ovr Edict ye passe to the paroch kirk of Contan wpon ane lords day, before noone, in tyme of divyne service, and lawlie warne by publick proclamation of this ovr Edict all and sundrie the parochiners of Contain or anie pretending to haue interest in the said paroch, to compeire before the brethren of the prie of dingwall to the effect, if they or any of them knov anything in life or doctrine of the said Mr. Dod wherfore he may not be minister off the said paroch of Contain, that they propone and elect the same, with certification to them y^t oyrvayes [otherwayes] we will proceide in plantation of the said Kirk with the said Mr. Dod in conscience and devtie according to Gods word and order of the Kirk prescribed yrannent. The qlk to doe we comitt to yov conjunctlie and severallie ovr full power by this ovr edict, delyvering the same to yov duelie execut and indorst att ovr presbiteriall meiting. Given att Dingwall the 3 of Julie 1651 yeires.

The forsaid Edict was read be hew McKenzie in achiltie (according as his subscription y^{r}to did beare witnes) upon the 13 day of Julie 1651, att the Kirk of Contain, in tyme of divyne service, before thire Witnes, Coline McKenzie of Tarvie, Hector McKenzie of farburne, Murdo McKenzie of Achiltie, and diverse others.

This day the parochiners of Contin being cited to compeire if they had any thing to object against the said Mr. Dod, conforme to the Edict served y^{r}annent, and none compeiring to object against the said Mr. Dod his admission to the said Kirk, the brethren continues to appoint ane dyet for his admission to the next p̄rie day, in regaird of the paucitie of the number.

This day there was ane letter received from Mr. Donald Ros shewing y^t, conforme to the ordinance of the p̄rie the last day, Intimation was made to the parochiners of Lochbrune to compeire this day if they had anything to object against the said Mr. Dod his transportation, and accordinglie they being called, and none compeiring, the p̄rie resolves to proceid as before.

The said day it was declared y^t Mr. Dod Ros preached Att Contain, and Mr. Allex^r McKenzie att fottertie, conforme to the former ordinance.

Dingwall, 6 Agust 1651.

The said day the p̄rie tacking to there consideration the matter of Mr. Dod fraser his transportation to fottertie and having tacken a wiew of the severall reasons formerlie given in *pro et contra*, respective, they find some of the difficulties and inconveniences proponed in Mr. Dod fraser his third reason concerning the provision, gleib, and manse of the Kirk of fottertie to be reall, and conceiving y^t the same might happilie be removed be the heritours of fottertie, and hearing y^t S^r Jo^n McKenzie of Tarbat, the chiefe heritour, was already on the way coming home from the South, They thought fitt to continew the furthere discussing of the matter att this tyme, in expectation of the Laird Sir John McKenzie his coming, and his giving satisfaction in y^t particulare against the next day.

Ordaines the brethren to meitt the 19 day of Agust att Contain to admitt Mr. Dod Ros to the Kirke of Contain, and ordaines Mr. Jo^n Munro, Mod^r, to preach there y^t day.

The said day the Mod{e^r} did pñt ane letter of the Comission of the Gñall assemblie (qlk came laitlie to his hands) of the dait of the 24 of Maij 1651 yeires, informing the place and dyet of the next gñall assemblie, as also ordaining the pr̄ie to tacke notice if there were any of there number y{^t} were contrare to the gñall resolutions of the kingdome etc., as also ane act y{^r}upon ordaining such to be censured and the manner of it, qlk the brethren tacking to there consideration, the brethren are ordained to wse diligence in obedience to the forsaid lettere, and to make report y{^r}of the next day.

Ordaines Mr. Dod Ros to wse diligence annent what was recomended to him at the wisitation of his kirk, and to exhibite his diligence the next day att Contain.

The said day Mr. Jo{^n} M{^c}Kra regraited that he was crossed and hindered be Allex{^r} M{^c}Kenzie from the peaceable possession of his gleibe, y{^r}fore ordaines him to be sumond to the next day.

Contan, 19 *Agust* 1651.

Conveined Mr. Jon. Munro, Mod{^r}, Mr. Geo. Munro, Mr. Jo{^n} M{^c}Kra, Mr. Dod M{^c}Kra, Mr. Dod Ros, Mr. Roric M{^c}Kenzie.

The said day the brethren did meitt conforme to the ordinance the last day att Dingwall for admitting of Mr. Dod Ros to this Kirk, and finding y{^t} the people did not meitt according as they were advertised, as also the Notar not coming whose presence was necessare for the worke, y{^r}fore continues the same till Thursday come aught dayes, the 28 of this instant, and resolves to meitt the said day for the effect forsaid.

This day the pr̄ie tacking to there consideration the reasons given in *pro et contra* annent Mr. Dod fraser his transportation, and especiallie the inconveniences and difficulties proponed in Mr. Dod his third reason, and Sir Jo{^n} M{^c}Kenzie of Tarbat being present and wrging them to proceid in the matter of the said transportation, the pr̄ie did represent the said difficulties to the said Sir Jo{^n} sheving him y{^t}, although the reasons given in for the said transportation suld happilie be fovnd and judged to dovne weigh the reasons given in to the contrare, in other respects, yet in respect of the said difficulties and inconveniences Mr. Dod culd not be wrged to yeild to the transportation wnles these difficulties were removed, considering it

P

wald put him in a worse condition as he is in for the pñt, having a sufficient gleib and manse, and (as he alleadges himselfe) his pñt provision being worth a thousand marks per annum. To which the said Sr John ansered as follows, viz.:— y^t if the pñt gleib y^t was att fottertie wald not be found be the p̃rie to be a full gleib or any othere way incommodious for the minister, he wald give way to the p̃rie to designe a full gleib beside the Kirk; and, wntill he might have way be lav to cause the heritours build a sufficient manse conforme to the act of parliament, y^t he wald give him a werie sufficient manse to dvell in, and as for the provision of fottertie y^t it had fyve chalders wictuall and two hundreth marks alreadie, of which the laite minister was in possession, and, besid this, some tacks of some teynds in the paroch already expired and run ovt, which would make up beyond a chalder of wictuall to him; in consideration of all which he conceived his condition wald be bettered and not made worse by the said transportation. The P̃ric taking all to there consideration, finding it requisite to knov more particularlie the way hov the said chalder of wictuall of augmentation might be had, and S^r Jo^n promising to give them a further cleiring in it the next day, they continued the matter upon y^t consideration to this day fyfteine dayes.

The brethren declared y^t they had wsed diligence, conforme to the former ordinance, to try if any within there paroches was contrare to the publick resolutions of the kingdome, and y^t they culd not find certaine knowledge of any.

The said day Mr. Dod Ros declared y^t conforme to the former ordinance he did cause sumond to this day * * and Murdo McIver for burying within the Kirk of Lochbrune, all of which p'sons being cited, and not compeired, they are ordained to be sumond pro 2do.

The said Mr. Dod McKra having returned from the gñall assemblie, and his diligence being required after, the brethren findes themselfes satisfied y^{r}with, withall the said Mr. Dod did pñt reasons of a solemne and publick humiliation to be keiped upon the last Sabboth of agust, y^{r}fore ordaines the brethren to intimate the samen the next sabboth and keipe it the next sabboth y^{r}after.

The reasons yrof are these following.

1. Albeit the lord be evidentlie p'seving his controversie for the abounding of sinne in the land, yet no man sayth what have I done, bot everie man following his ovne way as the horse rusheth into the battell.

2. Tho in the midst of wrath the lord doth remember mercie towards ws, and stretcheth forth his arme still with the offer of reconciliation throgh Christ in the preaching of the gospell, yet the offer of his grace is not seriouslie imbraced.

3. The holie ordinance of God nov in so long a tyme continued with ws in puritie and plentie are neglected and dishaunted by many, sleigtlie and p'functoriouslie made wse of by others.

4. The wniversall evill of preferring ovr ovne things of ch. [Christ's.]

5. Ovr obstinate continuing in those evills qlk we must have palpablie read in the rod, qrby the lord hath beine scourging ws, such as covetousnes, etc.

6. As if continuance in sinne wnder judgment were too little we grov worse wnder afliction, fighting with God in the furnace, blasphemie, etc.

7. As for these thingis, and many things els which the prudence and faithfullnes of Ministers will easily lead them to observe, we ought to be humblie before the lord and poure spirits before him; So we are particularlie to pray and request y^t the lord wald be pleasit to give pardon to ovr king, states, airmie, ministerie, and people of all rankes, y^t the lord wald looke wpon the lov condition of the land, how justlie soever smitten by him yet most wnjustlie invaded by a blasphemous and p'fidious enemie.

8. That as he hes made judgment begin att his ovne house, he wald make the enemies drink of the dregs of the cup, heale ovr backslydings, make wp our begun rentings, save us from the spirit of separation, prosper ovr wndertakings, and yet be pleasit to goe ovt with ovr airmie and relieve his borne dovne truth and oppressed people in the 3 kingdomes, y^t truth may triumph over errour, Gods people may after there sad dayes injoy peace and truth, and our king, now in covenant with God and ws, may be restored wnto and settled in his due right,

for the good of religion in the thre kingdomes, in Scotland, England, and Ireland, according to the covenant.

Contain, 28 Agust 1651.

Conveined Mr. Jo^n Munro, Mod^r, Mr. George Munro, Mr. Jo^n McKra, Mr. Dod McKra, Mr. Dod Ros, Mr. Rorie McKenzie, Mr. Dod fraser.

After the incalling of Gods name, The said day Mr. Jo^n Munro preached 1 Thess. 4. 2.

The said day Mr. Dod Ros was admitted minister att Contan, and gott institution in all points conforme to the practise of this Kirk.

Dingwall, 2 September 1651.

The p̃rie requiring of S^r Jo^n McKenzie a farther cleiring of the way hov the chalder of augmentation might be had to fottertie, all the cleiring he gave them was werball assurance y^t certaine lands within the paroch, viz. the lands of Tollie and Dunglust, had no tacks of there teynds, or if they had they were null, being given *a non potestatem*. The p̃rie considering the matter (att the best) to be but disputable, and proponing to S^r Jo^n it was hard to wrge Mr. Dod to quite ane certaine for ane wncertaine thing, especiallie att such tymes as lawes were not potent in, he replyes if he culd get the rest of the heritours to contribute with him he wald make wp ane hundreth merks of money to be payed to him yeirly wntill he got way to evict these teynds, for which effect he sought continuation to the next day, for dealing with the rest of the heritours. Which the P̃rie tacking to there consideration, and judging his forvardnes and willingnes for advauncing the plantation of the church commendable, granted his desyre, and continued the matter to the next day.

Mr. Dod Ros declared y^t he went not to Lochbrune since the 19 of Agust, when he gave in diligence annent the delinquents in Lochbrune, yrfore ordaines him to summond them to the next day.

Ordaines Mr. Rorie McKenzie to repaire to Lochbrune, there to preach, and to declare the Kirk wacant, to represent to them the necessitie of provyding the Kirk with a qualified pastor, and to exhort them to be instant with the lord that he wald provyde a pastor for them according to his ovne heart; and he is ordained to report his diligence to the next provinciall assemblie.

Dingwall, 16 *Septr*. 1651.

This day S^r Joⁿ McKenzie of Tarbat being imployed in the publick and therethrough absent from the p̄rie, and not able to give in any diligence annent his dealing with the rest of the heritours of fottertie for contributing to the advauncement of the plantation of the Kirk according to his wndertacking the last day, be reason yrof, and of the paucitie of the number present, the p̄rie continues the discussing of the reasons, and determining of the matter of Mr. Dod fraser his transportation to the next day.

Mr. Robert Munro sent ane letter sheving y^t he was necessitate to goe to Stranaver to speake my lord Rea, continues the consideration yrof till his ovne coming.

The brethren declared y^t the warning and exhortation of the Comission of the Gñall assemblie conveined at Forfar 9 Agust 1651, was read conforme to the ordinance of the said Comission, qlk warning came to the Moderator since the last p̄rie day, and he yrafter sent the same to the brethren.

Dingwall, 30 *Sept* 1651.

This day Sr Jon. McKenzie of Tarbat compeiring and wrging the P̄rie to proceide withovt furder delay in the matter of Mr. Dod fraser his transportation, being inquired concerning his diligence in dealing with the rest of heritours for contributing to make wp a hundreth marks of augmentation to the minister according as he had formerlie promised, ansered he had not occasion to meit with all the heritours, bot y^t he would oblidge himselfe to make it good, and what els he offered concerning the gleibe and manse, so y^t they would make him sure of Mr. Dod fraser. Whereupon the P̄rie falling upon the consideration giuen in *pro et contra* annent the said transportation, and considering them severallie after p'ticulare examination of them and colla°ning them togethere, they judge the reasons of the parochiners of Fottertie for the said transportation of greaver weight then the reasons given in against it, notwithstanding yrof, be reason of the said Mr. Dod wnvillingnes to yeild to the said transportation, they thought fitt not to determine anything in the matter yrof wntill Mr. Dod were dealt with, imbracing it willinglie, who being accordinglie dealt with both in publick and private, yet continued still wnvilling, which being represented to S^r Jo^n McKenzie, commissionere for the paroch of fottertie, condescended y^t the p̃rie suld continue the determining any thing in it wntill he wald try whethere himselfe and the rest of the parochiners might find anothere more speedie and faire way for planting the Kirk ; qrvpon the p̃rie continued the matter to the next day.

Mr. Jo^n McKra to wreitt ane letter to Culcoie y^t he may cause her [Marie Do^d wic wurchie, Lochbrune, mother of an illegitimate child whose father she refused to reveal] give obedience, seing he is maister of the ground qron she resydes.

Dingwall, 14 *October* 1651.

This day report coming from S^r Jo^n McKenzie of Tarbat y^t he was sicke, and by reason yrof not able to be advysed with the rest of the parochiners annent any othere (besydes Mr. Dod fraser his transportation) for plantation of the kirk of fottertie. The P̃rie considering this and the nearnes of the provinciall assemblie to be holden att Tayne the last Tuesday of this instant, The p̃rie thought fitt to continue the matter to be advysed with the said provinciall, and to waive it for this tyme wntill anothere dyate.

The delinquents of Lochbrune, wiz Jo^n McIver etc. cited and not compeired ordaines ane letter to be directed to Symon McKenzie, laird of Lochsline, to the end he may interpone himselfe to cause them to give obedience.[1]

In regaird y^t Mr. Jo^n McKra his regrate this day that Allex^r McKenzie continues to crosse and molest him in the peaceable possession of his gleibe (notwithstanding of his former promise to the p̃rie) yrfore the p̃rie referres both to the consideration of the provinciall assemblie to be holden att Tayne.

Mr. Jo^n McKra declared that he had spoken with Culcoie

---

[1] The delinquents were cited three times before this, without response. Lochslin was a brother of Colin, first Earl of Seaforth and the father of Sir George Mackenzie of Rosehaugh, Lord Advocate to Charles II.

and that he promised to cause Marie nein dod wic wurchie to give obedience.

Dingwall, 18 *Novemb.* 1651.

This day being the first day of our meiting efter the provinciall assemblie as it was concluded be the Brethran at Tayne after the said provinciall assemblie.

Conveined the said day Mr. Jo^n Monro, Mr. Jon McKra, Mr. George Munro, Mr. Donald fraser, Mr. Donald McCra, and Mr. Donald Ross.

[Mr. Andrew Munro Expectant preached, and 'Mr. Rorie McCloid exhibited a testimonial of his doctrine, lyf and conversatione from the presbyterie of Dornach.']

The Brethren taking to there consideratione the vaicancie of the Kirk of Lochbroome, and haveing the occasione of the said Mr. Rorie, Ordaines ane letter in name of the presbyterie to be wryt to the laird of Lochsline to cause conveine the parochiners of Lochbroome, to heire the said Mr. Rorie McCloide preach in the said Kirk.

As also ordaines literall sumonds to be sent to Lochsline to werefie quhat he alledged in his letter sent to the presbyterie of Dingwall against Mr. ferq^r M^{c}cra, minister at Kintaile.

Allex^r McKenzie in Koldine compeiring c'forme to his former promise, qho is c'tent that thaire [be] a present perambula°ne of that Mr. Johne M^{c}cra callis his gleibe.

Mr. Colline Kinneddie being to goe of the countrey protests for a certificate of his lyf and conversatione dureing the tyme he remained in the cuntrey; qlk, after tryall, was granted.

Continewes the referres of the provinciall to this presbyterie to the nixt presbyteriall meiting, in respect of the sheortness of the day, and perambula°ne of Mr. Jo^n McKra his gleib.

Recomends Wm Reid to be supplied in the sowme of 40 pounds out of the vacand stipend of fottertie, conforme to the equitie of his supplicatione.

9 *Decemb.* 1651.

All the Brethren conveined the said day except Mr. Johne Monro quho is excused, being ordained be the moderator of the province to be p̄nte at Tayne with the provinciall book the said day.

The name of God being incalled. No exercise in respect of the shortness of the day, the deepness of the way, and the slowness of the cuming of the Brethren.

[Mr. Do^d McKra reports his inabilitie to preach at fottertie—ordained to do so and keep session, 'comforme to Tarbats letter of desyre.']

Conforme to the former ordinance Lochsline conveined the people of Lochbroome twa severall lords days, and did heire Mr. Rory McCloid preach, rendring thanks to the brethren for haveing a christian caire of them, protesting in the meanetyme that they could give ane anser in the accepta^{o}ne of any minister, till the heritours and wthers haveing entrest wer spocken in the planta^{o}ne yrof.

As also Lochsline c'fesses be his letter to haue recciwed ane citatione, quho in his letter promises to give obedience wppon ye brethrens nixt advertisement.

Ordaines that Lochsline be cited to the nixt presbiteriall day, and that he be desyred to deale with the parochiners of Lochbroome c'cerneing the planta^{o}ne of the Kirk thaireof.

Ordaines Allex^r McKenzie to be present the nixt presbiteriall day to haue the brethrens judgement of the perambula^{o}ne of the gleibe.

The said day Mr. George Monro, Minister at Urquhart, presented to the Brethren ane powar wryten and sub^{iut} be Mr. Murdo McKenzie and be Allex^r McKenzie his sonne, willing to refer all clames and questiones, both civile and Ecclesiastick, betwixt them and Mr. Jo^n M^{c}cra, to tua ministers and tua ruleing Elders.

Mr. Jo^n M^{c}cra declaires he sal be willing to the same quhan Mr. Murdo McKenzie sall appoynt peremptorely quhan and quhaire the samyne may be acted.

Ordaines the Brethren to meit this day eight dayes or sooner as the moderator adwertises them at Loggie.

Loggie, 16 *Deceb.* 1651.

All the Brethren present except Mr. Rob Mo'ro, Minister at Kilterne.

The meiting was private in regaird of the enemie.[1]

---

[1] The English.

Efter incalling of the name of God

The Brethren taking to thaire considera°ne the pitiefull esteate and conditione of thair distreassed deposed Brethren, and finding the stipends of vacande kirks within the presbiterie to be employed to no better or chairitable use then in helpeing theise indigent distressed brethren, Ordaines ane warrand to be wrytten and sub^{iut} be the clerk of the presbiterie to the laird of Tarbatt, in name of the moderator and remanent brethren of the pbr̄ie of Dingwell, to ansere Mr. Rorie M^{c}cloid, supplicant and expectant, in the sowme of ane hundreth merks mo^{ey}, of his proportione of the stipend of Fottertie of the cropt 1651 yeires.

And Sicklyk ordaines ane warrand to be wryten be the Clerk to anser Mr. ferq^r McLennan, sometyme Minister at Fottertie,[1] in the number of threttie foure bolls wictualls of the readdiest pay within the parochen of fottertie of the cropt 1651, and the said Mr. ferq^{re} to give those quho ansers him ane discharge in our name conforme to our act granted in his favours for the recept of the forsaid number of bolls, and to retaine a note wnder the said Mr. ferq^{rs} hand of the personnes that hes payit him, and quhat eich man hes payed.

Ordaines also that Mr. Hector Monro, sometyme minister at Kincardin,[2] have, as ane supplie for himselfe and his poore indigent familie, the sowme of ane hundreth merks mo^{ey} fro Mr. Thomas McKenzie of Inverlaoll, for his proportione of the stipend of Lochbroome nov vacande, Togidder with the sowme of twentie pounds mo^{ey} out of Coigach, of the stipend of Lochbroome, With the number of eight bolls wictuall out of the stipend of fottertie, being in use to be payed be Mr. Keneth McKenzie of Scatuall.

Ordaines the Brethren to meite this day fyfteine dayis at Urray, and that all and everie be diligent in laboreing to wnderstand quhat thaire brethren of wther presbiteries and diocesses does for the tyme.

The meiting closed with thanksgiveing.

---

[1] Deposed for Malignancy in 1650. Restored to the ministry in 1655, and afterwards settled in Lochbroom.

[2] Deposed probably about same time. He was succeeded by Mr. Thomas Ross who was deprived of the living after the Restoration, when Mr. Monro was restored to the charge.

No meiteing at Urray the day appoynted in respect of ane conventione of the Inglishes at Urray the said day.

Urquhart, 13 *Janrij* 1652.

The said day conveined at Urquhart Mr. George Monro, Mr. Donald McCra, and Mr. Donald Ross be ane advertisement from ye Moderator.

absents Mr. Jo^n Monro.
Mr. Jo^n M^{c}cra.
Mr. Donald fraser.

Ordaines the nixt meiteing to hold at Containe this day fyfteine dayis.

Receaved ane letter from Mr. Jo^n Monro for himselfe and for Mr. Andro Monro, expectant, quho wer necessitate to goe off the Countrey for certane causes qlk they wold state nixt meiting.

Mr. Donald fraser excused be his letter, and the cause his stay being found relevant.

Mr. Jo^n M^{c}cra excused, being bedfast eight dayes agoe.

No exercise the s^d day in respect of the absents.

Contane, 27 *Janij* 1652.

The said day compeired Mr. George Monro, Mr. Do McCra, Moderator, and Mr. Donald Ross, Clerk, and Mr. Do fraser.

Mr. Jo^n M^{c}cra excused, being bedfast.

Mr. Jo^n Monro excused, being in Cathnes.

Mr. Rob. Monro being in Straver (Strathnaver).

The said day Mr. Murdo McKenzie, sometyme Minister at Dingwall, compeired, protesting his willingness and earnest desyre to live peaceablie with all men and especiallie with a minister, and that meanly for that effect he came to the cuntrey heireing of this dayis appoyntment, to sie be quhat meanes the questione betwixt him and Mr. Jo^n M^{c}cra, Minister at Dingwell, might be taken away in ane peaceable brotherly manner, be certane selected friendes without delay, dureing his being in the cuntrey: wtherwayes, the brethren to beare witness of his willingnes and compeirance wndesired to that effect.

Urquhart, 9 *Marcij* 1652.

The said day compeired all the Brethren except Mr. Jo^n

M°cra quho is excused be his letter, proporting the necessitie of his goeing to Kintaile.

The said day Jo^n Monro of Lemlaire, and Hector Dowglass, Commissioners from Kilterne, seeking and earnestlie intreating for a minister to Kilterne, in respect of the vacancie yreof through Mr. Robert Monro his being this longtyme agoe in Stranaver.

Ordaines the saids Commissioners to be at Dingwell this day 15 dayis to receawe ane anser of thair Supplicatione.

Ordaines ane letter to be wryt and directed to Mr. Robert Monro, Minister at Kilterne, to repaire to ye presbyterie of Dingwell ye 23 of Marc^{ij} for to giue ane reassone of the deserting of his functione, with certifica^{one} that in cace he obey not we sall proceide as we sal be ansereable.

Ordaines y^t Mr. Hector Monro, sometyme Minister at Kincarden, get ye act granted in his favors as a supplie for his sustenta°ne out of ye vacande Kirk extracted out of the presbiterie books, and the samyne to be subscryved be the clerk of our presb̄rie.

Dingwell, 23 Marcij 1652.

Conforme to the former ordinance Mr. Robert Monro hes wryt ane anser of the brethrens letter showing his inabilitie to travell both in respect of the seassone and of his owne tenderness, as he attests in his letter, and theirwithall promising with the grace of God to repaire home with all possible diligence, especiallie and peremptorely or the last of Maij nixt.

Mr. Jo^n Monro is appoynted to preach at Kiltearne Sunday come eight dayis, and to bring a report to the nixt presbyterie day of his diligence, concerneing thair desyre, and this is granted as a satisfactione in a manner to thair commissioners sent to the presbiterie suiteing and earnestlie desyreing a minister to be sent to them to preach on ane Sabboth: q^{r}by they my^t be resoluit concerneing thair owen Ministers deserting of them to Stranawer.

Ordaines Mr. Donald Ross, minister at Contane, to produce the decreit of the platt of the kirk of Lochbroome the nixt presbyteriall day.

6 Apryll 1652.

Ordaines the Moderator of the presbiterie of Dingwall, Mr. Joⁿ M^ccra, Mr. Joⁿ Monro, and Mr. George Monro, to meite at Roskeene 13 of this instant, conforme to the Moderator of the provinces desyre be his letter.

Ordaines litterall summonds to be directed to Mr. Allex^r Ma^cKenzie of Lochcarron to compeire at Dingwell this day 15 dayis for baptizing ane child of Mr. Allex^r MacKenzie of Culcowie gottin in fornicatione within ane wther parochin, but [*i.e.* without] repentance.

Dingwell, 20 *Apryll* 1652.

The said day c'veined all the Brethren.

Conforme to the former ordinance Mr. Andro Monro preached populare doctrine, Rom. 8. 1-2.

Efter the name of God was called,

The said Mr. Andro being removed, his doctrine examined and tryed, was approwen.

It is granted to the said Mr. Andro Monro to preach q^rever he is lawfullie imployit within the presbiterie of Dingwall, being required either be minister or elders quhare the kirk is vacande.

Dingwell, 11 *Maij* 1652.

The said day Mr. Robert Monro, Mimister at Kilterne, his dimissione being presented, qre the accepta^{one} thairof is continewed to the nixt day in respect of the absence of some brethren.

Allex^r McKenzie in Kildine[1] being cited for calling his minister[2] kneve and a lyare, and abuseing him with uther speaches, compeired not, ordaines to summond him *pro secundo*.

Dingwell, 29 *Maij* 1652.

Continewes the consideration of Mr. Ro. Monro his dimissione in regaird of the absence of some brethren quhose presence is necessarie.

The said day Allex^r McKenzie compeired in obedience to the

---

[1] Son of Mr. Murdo Mackenzie, the deposed minister of Dingwall.

[2] Rev. John Macrae, minister of Dingwall.

ordenance, quho confessed to call Mr. Jo^n M^{c}cra a lyare, zit refuses the calling of him a kneve, and submitting of himselfe to Culcowie and Ronald Bayne, Notar, quho were present at the tyme, and hard quhat past betwixt the said Mr. Jo^n and Allex^r McKenzie, Ordaines that they be cited against this day 15 dayis, to declaire the truth in ye premisses.

In reference to the petitione of the parochiners of Lochbroome suiteing for ane minister, referres the anser thairof to the tyme ane Minister of the presbiterie goe thaire to heire of ane list giwen be the heritors, elders, and parochiners thairof.

Dingwell, 2 Junij 1652.

The said day efter Incalling ye name of God,

Conveined all the Brethren except Mr. George Monro quhose mciteing the said day beifore the appoynted day wes be reassone of ane letter sent to the moderator of ye presbiterie from the moderator of ye province, for appoynteing of ane day of generall mciteing of ye most of the province to heire of his diligence in his Commissione in the south, quho was to meite at Tayne the nynt day of this moneth, and to this effect that a Commissioner or tua my^t be elected for to keep the said meiting at Tayne, hes mett this day to keep correspondence, Quhairefore ordaines Mr. Jo^n Monro and Mr. Donald fraser to keep the said meiting day and place forsaid.

The said day Mr. Jo^n Monro and Mr. Do^d fraser being listed for Moderators, It is concluded that Mr. Donnald fraser be Moderator, and sicklyk ordaines that Mr. Dod Ross continewe clerk at this tyme, since the book is not filled up.

Ordaines Mr. Murdo McKenzie, sometyme Minister at Suddie,[1] get ane chalder of wictuall of the vacand stipend of fottertie as a supplie to his indigent familie, from such as ar resting within ye parochin of fottertie of ye cropt 1651 zeirs,

---

[1] Deposed for Malignancy, along with Mr. Colin Mackenzie, Minister of Contin, on 22nd May 1647. See *Proc. of Commission of General Assembly* (Scot. Hist. Society), vol. i. p. 265. One of the charges against the Mackenzies is 'preaching and praying before the Earle of Seafort, after they knew him to be excommunicat, and of eating and drinking with him, and the said Mr. Murdo himself said grace to him, and Mr. Colin heard it said by the said excommunicat's chaplane, and so communicat in worship with an excommunicat person.'

viz. 6 bolls from William Dingwell of Usie, ten firlots from Gilis Bayne in Knockbaxter, and 7 bolls 2 f. from ye guidman of Tulloch, and incace that any of the forsaids hes payit others, that the said Mr. Murdo have his recourse to get the whole from Tulloch conforme to his rest of ye said cropt.

Endis the meiting w^h a blessing.

Dingwall, 15 *Junij* 1652.

The said [day] conveined the Brethren, except Mr. Donald Ross, the cause of quhose absence is continewed to his coming.

Efter incalling the name of God,

No exercise, the meiting being appoynted occasionallie, for receaweing report from ye meiting of correspondence at Tayne the nynt of this instant moneth, and for certain poynts of discipline referred to this day.

Ordaines quhat may be collected in the severall paroches within this presbiterie to be brought to the nixt day for David Wallace, Supplicant, recommended be the g̃rall assemblie.

Mr. Robert Monro his dimissione, efter due consideratione admitted, the Kirk of Kilterne, declared vacand, and Mr. Johne Monro appoynted to preach and mak intimation of the vacancie thairof.

All the Brethren ar appoynted to vse diligence in summonding Captane Hector McKenzie and finlay Roy, trumpeter, if they may be found in any of thair parochins.

Ordaines Allex^r McKenzie to be sumond to this day 15 dayis, to heire probation hard against him for his slandering of Mr. Jo^n M^{c}cra in calling him knev and lyar, and to continewe Ronald Bayne to the said day, and ordaines ane letter to be directed to the sessione of Killernan to receave Culcowies depositione, and that Culcowie be acquented tymely to keep the forsaid sessione, in regaird his manifold imployments and distance from ye presbiterie, and the sessione to send ws the depositione the said day.

In reference to the Commissions l̃re Ordaines l̃res to be directed to the ministers of the hilands to send thair proportione against this day 15 dayes for the Commissioner for the generall assemblie.

Dingwell, 29 *Junij* 1652.

Mr. Dod Ross excused for absence last day in respect of his employment in Lochbroome.

Ordaines Mr. Allex^r McKenzie in Lochcarron to exercise this day sex weeks, and Mr. Rorie in Garloch to add, keeping the meiting on ane Wednesday in respect of thair distance.

Ordaines to giue David Wallace his collectione to Donald Glasse in Dingwell conforme to this warrand.

No report from Mr. Jo^n Monro anent Kilterne in respect of his absence.

Ordaines Mr. Jo^n M^{c}cra to giue sumonds to the Kirk officer of Fottertie, or ony wther Kirk officer in quhose parochines Captane Hector McKenzie or Finlay Roy comes, to compeire befoire the presbiterie of Dingwell.

Ordaines this depositione sent wnder the Clerk of Killernan's hand, to be sub^{uit} be ye minister y^{r}of and Culcowie, and that Allex^r Clerk be summond to this day 15 dayes, qreby Allex^r Clerk, in respect to his knowledge as he affirmes he knowes not this Allex^r Clerk.

Ordaines Allex^r McKenzie to compeire this day 15 dayis either to admitt or to repell the testimonie of Allex^r Clerk in so far as concernes Mr. Jo^n M^{c}cra and the said Allex^r McKenzie, w^t certifica^{oune} if he compeire not day and place forsaid, we sall admitt Allex^r Clerk as witness.

Mr. Jo^n M^{c}cra reports that he hes wrytin to the ministers in the hielands, qreas none compeired except Lochcarron, qrefore ordaines that they be advertised againe, q^{r}be thair contribu^{o}ne for ye Commissioner of ye gr̄all assemblie may be heire or this day 15 days, and that Mr. Murdo McKenzie wryte to his broy^r Mr. Rorie both concerneing his contributione and of the ordenance in exerciseing heire this day 40 days.

Ordaines everie brother to pay thaire proportione to the Co'missioner of the gr̄all assemblie.

Mr. George Monro is elected and choosen Commissioner, q^{r}fore it is statute that all have payment to the Co. this day 15 days.

Dingwell, 13 *July* 1652.

Efter Incalling the name of God,
Compeired all the Brethren.

The exercise is continewed to this day 15 dayis in respect of the diligence that must be vsed in ordering thinges necessare of our Commissione to the Commissioner of the grāll assemblie, and for wther weochtie effaires to be agitated this day.

Conforme to the ordenance of supplie to Wm. [*sic.* David?] Wallace, the samyne wes given be everic brother to his powar to Do^d Glasse in Dingwall.

Mr. Johne Monro his diligence anent the planta°ne of Kilterne approwen, albeit the same took no effect, q^rfore recommends to the said Mr. Jo^n to travell zit with the parochiners of Kilterne, and that Mr. George Monro, our commissioner, be advysed heareanent in the South.

Ordaines M. Jo^n M^ccra to cause summond Captaine Hector McKenzie and Finlay roy to this day 15 dayis, and to give directione to the Kirk officer of fottertie to keep the presbiteriall meiting, and to declaire ye enormities that ar in ye parochin, w^t certificatione if he compeire not anoy^r Kirk officer salbe choosen to supplie his place and to discharge a duety in his calling.

Ordaines Allex^r Clerk, Servitour to Culcowies brother, to be summond, and Allex^r McKenzie summond *apud acta* to this day 15 dayis.

The said day Ronald McRonald in Teachuick was elected and choosen ruleing elder w^t Mr. George Monro to the grāll assemblie for ye prēbie of Dingwell.

Ordaines Mr. George Monro to censor all that had interest in heiring or approweing of the charme vsed for recovereing Donald Glasse in Kilkell of his sickness, for thaire consulting and charmeing, according to the Acts of the grāll assemblie.

Dingwell, 27 Julij 1652.

The said day Allex^r Clerk cited, called, compeired as witness to quhat Allex^r McKenzie in Kildinne did speake against Mr. Jo^n M^ccra, minister at Dingwell, quho being sworne deponed that reallie he hard Allex^r McKenzie call M^r Jo^n a lyar, bot determinatelie he knewe not quhidder he called him a knave or not, bot his best thought it was said.

Ordaines Allex^r McKenzie to compeire this day 15 dayes, and to this effect to be summond

And that Ronald Bayne, Notare, be summond to yᵉ nixt meiteing to beare witness in quhat he hard Allexʳ McKenzie utter against Mr. Joⁿ Mᶜcra.

Ordaines that all be east the Kirk of Fottertie¹ repaire to the Kirk of Dingwell, and all be west yᵉ kirk of fottertie to resorte to the Kirk of Contane, and to be plyable to the ordenances of the saids kirks, and that yᵉ kirk officer goe wᵗ them to the saids kirks to mak them knowen.

Ordaines ane letter to be wryten be Mr. Joⁿ Mᶜcra to Mr. Wm. Lauder concerning finlay Roy, Trumpeter, fornicator within the parochin of fottertie.

Dingwell, 11 *August* 1652.

Allexʳ McKenzie cited, called, compeired not, ordaines to be summond againe to the nixt meiting,

and that Ronald Bayne be cited to the said day to beare witness betwixt Mr. Joⁿ Mᶜcra and Allexʳ McKenzie.

Mr. Allexʳ McKenzie at Lochcarron being accused for baptizeing ane childe gottin in fornicatione to Culcowie elder without anie warrand from presbiterie or Sessione, The said Mr. Allexʳ declaired yᵗ Culcowie affirmed that thair was no minister at yᵉ kirk in quhose parochin the childe was gottin, and yᵗ Mr. Allexʳ McKenzie of Culcowie obliest himself be his band to satisfie the ordenance of the kirk quheneuer he wer required, qlk band Lochcarron hes, Quho is ordained to exhibite the said band to the presbiterie the next meiting day, and continewes the censor of the said Mr. Allexʳ of Lochcarron till our brethren absente nowe be p͞nte.

Ding., *August* 31, 1652.

Efter Incalling the name of God,

All the brethren p͞nt except Mr. Dod Mᶜcra.

No exercise in respect of the exercisers lawfull abstractioune with the Erle of Seafort quho came laitly to the meiteing.

Ordaines the former Brethren to exercise and add ye next day.

Allexʳ McKenzie not being lawfullie be the kirk officer ordained to be summond to yᵉ nixt meiting to heire his censure, and the

---

¹ Vacant for the time.

executiounes of the cita^{n}e to be literallie exhibited with the witnesses.

It is statuted that Mr. Allex^r McKenzie of Lochcarron exhibite and produce Culcowies band he haid of him in satisfactioune for his fornica^o^{n}e w^t Isabell Hosack.

It is appoynted that Mr. Jo^n Monro repaire to Kilterne to preach, keep sessione, and exact of the parochiners a list of ministers to be represented the nixt p̄rie day as ane anser to Andro Monro and Robert Monro, Commissioners from Kilterne, and to this effect ordaines Mr. Andro Monro, expectant, to preach the said day at Alnes qlls Mr. Jo^n Monro is at Kilterne.

Allex^r McKenzie in Kildune compeired and charged *apud acta* to compeire this day 15 days to heire himselfe sentenced for his irreverentiall words against his minister.

The said day Mr. Rorie McKenzie, expectant, presented testimoniall from Elgine, approwen be ye p̄rie of Cha'rie, declaireing of the lyf, conversa^{o}une, and doctrine of ye said Mr. Rorie, q^{r}upon libertie is granted to him to preach within this p̄rie quhan he is callit lawfullie be ony minister within ye presbiterie, and ordaines him to preach at fottertie ye next Lords day.

The said day Mr. George Monro, Commissioner, exhibited his diligence in presenting ye acts of ye grāll assemblie, with ane ordenance of a solemne fast to be observed tuo severall lords dayes immediatelie efter the intimatione of the said fast the nixt lords day.

Causes of a fast to be appoynted be ye generall assemblie to be keiped in all ye c'gregationes of this land, to be keeped ye 2 and 3 Sabbothes of Septemb. 1652.

Albeit our sadd conditione of itself cry aloud to mourneing, it being our deutie to stir wp the lords people to tak on him in this day of his displeasour, we find it incumbent to all the land, and charges in it uppon them as they wold have the lord to turne away from his fearce wrath so hoate perscheweing and burneing ws wp, that they wold scarch and try y^r wayis and murnefullie befoire ye lord, and at this tyme ly in ye dust, for all these provoca^o^{n}es w^h ar ye chiefe causes of all the evills that ar come wpon ws.

1. Besydes manie sinnes heirtofoire mentioned in former causes of fasts, we ar to mourne for the land destroying sinne,

The contempt of the gospell, qlk the comprehensone of so manie oy^r sinnes set doune be ye commissione of the assemblie 1650, a sinne so odious in ye sight of God, that neglecting so gryte a salua°ne and slichting the bloode of ye covenant, we cannot escape ye vengeance of ye gospell.

2. Becaus the sadd dispensatione we haue mett w^t and the wonderfull work wrought amongst us ar neiy^r exed (?) nor improwen be ws, our wound is greivous that we hawe not greived, the lord hes smitten ws, bot we refused to retarie, zea none taking ye lord for thair partie nor accepting ye punishment of ye iniquitie, we revolt more and more, this is a lamentatione and salbe for a lamentatione.

3. Becaus of Covenant bracking, especiallie in this our day of our calamitie and tryall, committed oppinly in ye midds of all the land, and ye schameless dispyseing of ye oathe of God so often and so solemly sworne be ws, nor thinking to escape by iniquitie lyes y^{re} refuge, thus ye lord is mocked and his name prophaned, for which he will not hold ws guiltless.

4. Becaus of Zions breach which seemes wnreparable, shee is brocken breach uppon breach, hir vaile is torne, hir headge brocken downe, hir pretious thing defyled, blasted, exposed to foxes and beares, and q^{ll} it is thus with hir, hir louers forget hir, hir children still contending in ye fornace, notwithstanding of ye gryte contraversie ye lord hath w^t the wholl land.

5. Becaus of ye fowle dep'tor from ye true doctrine of C.[1] receawed in yis kirk, and separa°ne from ye communion and government y^{r}of, y^t some ministers and some wy^r wnsteable soules hes turned asyde wnto, contrarie to ye solemne covenant and wowes, to ye hiest contempt of ye name of God and gryt scandell of ye gospell.

6. Becaus of gryte oppositione made to ye work of God be ye royall familie, and manie eminent families of ye blood, oppressione, ignorance of God, wnbeleiffe, wncleanenesse, covetousnes, falshood, decept, hypocrisie, and wy^r grosse iniquities that hes abounded among all rankes of ye land, both in ye preceiding and p͞nt genera°nes.

7. Becaus of ye manie sinnes of ye ministers, the work hes

---

[1] Christ.

not bene strenthned, nor those quho hes bene driven away soucht for, for we have not worked for soules, bot done dueties by commissione, nor the thingis of God, for theise we aught to mourne and requeist ye Lord through Jesus C. that he would pardone all these abominationes, subdue ws by his spirit, that we may fall in love w^t Chryst, be obedient to ye gospell, y^t seeing many things we may observe them and regard the works of ye lord and opera^{o}ne of his hands, yat he wald heale our backslydings, repaire our breaches, reclame ye seduced, and tak away all our iniquities, furnishe ye contrarie w^t ye king, nobles, ministers and ye people, comfort our prisoners, and y^t he wald be pleased to stay amongst ws and preserve vnwiolable ye liberties of his house, and help ws for his names sack, becaus we are brought werie low, and y^t remediing ye distressed esteate of Gods people in these lands, wald carie on ye work of reforma^{o}ne to the w^c we ar ingadged by covenant, and wald build his Zion, and appeire in his glorie.

Closes ye meiting w^t prayer.

Dingwell, 14 *Sept*. 1652.

Conforme to the ordinance, Mr. Jo^n Monro repaired to the Kirk of Kilterne, quho keeped Sessione and willed them to list quhan they wald, quho unanimously, except Fowlis, did nominate Mr. Andro Monro; as also Robert Monro compeired as commissioner from Kilterne, protesting that ye pbrie wald labour with all diligence to put the said Mr. Andro Monro in capacitie for ye call forsaid.

Ordaines Mr. Donald fraser to keep the meiting of ye parochiners of Kilterne on fryday nixt, being ye 17 of Septemb. yre; the said Mr. Do^d, w^t Mr. Jo^n Monro, ar appoynted to confer with the heritors of Kilterne, and especiallie w^t Foulis, for ye planta^{o}ne of the said Kirk, and to mak report to ye pbrie the nixt meiting day.

The said Mr. Andro Monro being asked be the brethren and be the Commissioner of Kilterne if his mind goes to accepting the said call, q^{re} the said Mr. Andro zields himselfe to the dispositione of ye brethren in the said call, so that he sie the parochiners of Kilterne goeing unanimously to the accepta^{o}ne of him to the said charge.

Ordaines Allex^r McKenzie in Kildine to mak his repentance publickly Sonday come eight dayis in ye Kirk of Dingwell, being for a pairt on ane stoole opposite to the pulpit, for speaking irreverentlie to Mr. Jo^n M^{c}cra, being his ordinarie minister, in calling him ane lyar and ane kneve, and to this effect ordaines Mr. Donald Ross to preach the said day at Dingwell, and to report his diligence in ye obedience of ye said Allex^r McKenzie, and Ordaines Mr. Jo^n M^{c}cra to preach the said day at Contain, and Mr. Donald Ross to receive the said Allex^r.

Mr. Rorie McKenzie, Expectant, declared that he taught at fottertie Sunday was eight dayes.

The Brethren declaires that the first day of the fast was keeped, and ar to keep the nixt lords day for ye second.

Ordaines the brethren to use all diligence in the contributione for Glasgowe with all sort of people in y^r c'gregationes.

Ends the meiting w^t prayer.

Dingwell, 29 Sept. 1652.

Mr. Don^d fraser reports that Fowlis refused to give his anser till the Kirk wer provyded first in a stipend, as also Mr. Jo^n Monro reports that ye Laird of Fowlis refuses to woyce to ye accepta^{o}ne of ony minister, bot such as wer approwen be ye godlie in ye west cuntrey, nor any adheiring to the grāll assemblie or approweing the samyne wald be receaued be him; qrefore continewes to be resoluit with the province in this poynt.

Mr. Jo^n M^{c}cra and Mr. Donald Ross were willing to obey the ordenance of pbr̄ie, wer not that they receawed ane letter beareing the manner of ane appella^{o}ne to the province of Ross, qlk being considered be the brethren, finds the appella^{o}ne not valide, in respect of the insufficiencie of ye reasonnes, as also in respect the same was not delyvered to the Moderator tymeously conforme to the acts of ye grāll assemblie, and y^{r}foire ordaines ye said Allex^r McKenzie to be procest be Mr. Donald Ross at Dingwell for the first day, and Mr. Donald to report his diligence heirin the nixt pbr̄ie day. And Mr. Johne M^{c}cra to preach at Containe q^{lls} Mr. Donald is at Dingwell.

Mr. Rorie McKenzie, expectant, be ane ordenance of the

pbrie, and at the dasyre of some of the heritors of Fottertie, is licentiate to preach at the Kirk of Fottertie, being vacande, and no dilligence used be the parochiners of Fottertie in the planta°ne of thaire Kirk.

Ordaines Mr. Jo^n M^{c}cra and Mr. Donald Ross to travell with the heritors thaireof, qrbe some of their number may compeire the nixt pbrie day.

The Brethren report that ye fast was keiped.

Ordaines ewerie brother to use all possible diligence in the contributione for Glasgowe.

Continewes the processe of Lochsline and Mr. ferq^r M^{c}cra, in regaird of Mr. ferq^r his inabilitie to travell.

Dingwell, 12 Octob. 1652.

Mr. Rorie McKenzie, Minister at Garloch, is continewed to exercise to the nixt occasione, and ordained to preach Sonday come eight dayis at Kilterne, if he be in health.

Mr. Jo^n M^{c}cra being sick and not able to preach at Containe conforme to the ordinance, qrfoire Mr. Donald Ross shawed that he could not goe the said day to Dingwell, in respect of ane conventione of Nobles quho appoynted to be at Containe the said day.

Mr. Johne M^{c}cra haueing spocken the laird of Tarbat and Dawachmaluack in ye matter of the Kirk of Fottertie, quhose promise was to keep our meiting ye next presbiterie day.

The brethren reports them to use all diligence anent the contributione for Glasgowie, quho comes bot slowe speide, zit exhorted to use diligence.

Ordaines the brethren to use diligence for bringing thair contributione for the Irishe students mentenance against the nixt presbyterie day.

The said day the brethren pñte wer severallie removed, tryed, and examined, were weill reported off, and approwen in lyf and doctrine.

Compeired the said day the laird of Tarbat in name of the rest of ye parochiners of Fotterie, shaweing it to be the parochiners desyre that the presbiterie sould concurr with them to sic if Mr. Allan McLennan could be moved to accept of that charge, and to that effect desyred ane letter wer wryt be the pbṝie to the said Mr. Allane, and accordinglie it was done, and the Laird of Tarbat ordained to mak report of the anser of the said letter to the nixt presbiteriall meiting.

Dingwell, 9. Novemb. 1652.

This day being the first day of our meiting efter the provinciall assemblie according as it was concluded be the brethren at Tayne efter the said provinciall assemblie,

Conveined all the brethren, except Mr. John Monro, Moderator. [Mr. John Monro was 'detained at Dornoch be the Commissioners of the Kirk, he being one of the members thairof.']

Continewes Allex^r McKenzie in Kildine to the nixt presbiteriall day, to the end that Mr. Johne Monro, Moderator of the province, be present to informe ws in the determina°ne of the province anent the agriement betwixt the said Allex^r and Mr. Johne M^{c}cra.

Ordaines Mr. Johne M^{c}cra to speak the Laird of Tarbat in reference to our letter sent to Mr. Allan McLennan his coming to the Kirk of Fottertie.

The brethren ar ordained to vse diligence in the contributione for the distreassed people off Glasgowe, and in speciall such as ar present of the brethren in the hielands or they leave the cuntrey, and that they acqueint Mr. Ferq^r M^{c}cra and Mr. Donald McLennan of this ordenance, leist they pretend ignorance heirof.

Ordaines diligence to be used in the contributione allotted to the bursers of divinitie, and the Irishe boyes, leist they be stayed from thair studies for want yreof.

The said day Mr. Allex^r McKenzie, Minister at Lochcarron, was gravely rebuked for baptizing of a child gottin in fornicatione be Mr. Allex^r McKenzie of Culcowie uppon Cristaine Hosack within the Parochin of Suddie, without ordors from the presbiterie of Chanonrie or of the elders of the parochin of Suddie, notwithstanding of the vacancie of the said Kirk for the tyme.

Dingwell, 23 Novemb. 1652.

Continewes Allex^r McKenzie in Kildine his particulare to the nixt pbṝie day.

Mr. Joⁿ M^ccra being inquired concerneing his diligence w^t Tarbat, declaires he haid occasione to meit w^t him in reference to the pbr̃ie letter to Mr. Allan McLennan.

Ordaines ane letter to be wryten be the Brethren to Mr. Allan, quho is in the cuntrey for the pñte, to knowe of his anser to our former letter concerneing the kirk of Fottertie.

Ordaines the Brethren to use thair best diligence in collecting of the contributione for Glasgowe, and the students off divinitie against the nixt meiteing day.

Ordaines the Laird of Tarbat to anser Mr. Murdo McKenzie, some tyme minister at Suddie, the sowme of ane hundreth four pounds of the stipend of Fottertie of the cropt 1651, with ane chalder of wictuall of the forsaid stipend of the cropt 1652, and that of ye readdiest pay yreof, in respect of his indigencie, and quho is recomended be ye grãll assemblie to be cared for.

Siclyk that Tarbat anser Wm Reid, student, iij bolls wictuall.

Continewes ane anser to Mr. Joⁿ M^ccra his desyre of transporta^one to the nixt pbr̃ie day, till we receave the desyre of the parochiners of Kintaile in seeking the said Mr. Joⁿ to the charge thairof, and to testimonie of thaire willingnes in his acceptatione.

Ordaines Mr. ferq^r McLennan, sometyme Minister at Fottertie, to be supplied out of ye foresaid parochin in the number of xx bolls wictuall of the readdiest pay y^rof of ye cropt 1652 zeires.

It is appoynted that Mr. Jon M^ccra cause summond Joⁿ Bayne of Tulloch, Ronald Bayne, Notare, Allex^r Bayne of Knockbayne, etc., to ye next pbr̃ie day to declaire quhat they knowe of the designatione of the gleib of Dingwell of old in Mr. Johne McKenzie's tyme.

Mr. John Monro choosen Moderator, and the clerk continewed.

Closes the meiting w^t prayer.

Dingwell, 21 *Decemb.* 1652.

Ordaines ane letter to be wrytin to the laird of Tarbat, and to the rest of the heritors of the parochin of Fottertie, and the plantatione of the kirk thairof, and that in respect Mr. Allan M⸰Lennan, quho was once or twyse wrytin wnto, is in the cuntrey for the present.

Ordaines the brethren to use diligence concerneing the contributione to Glasgowe.

The Brethren promises pay^t to the students of divinitie or they depart of the towne.

Dingwell, 4 *Janij* 1653.

No doctrine the said day in respect of the weather, and Mr. Donald fraser's necessarie absence, quho is excused be his letter and the sloweness of the conventione of the brethren.

Conforme to the ordenance of the brethren at Dingwall, 23 Novemb. 1652, Johne Bayne of Tulloch compeired, quho declaired ingenuously in pb̅rie that the gleib of Dingwell was mett and measured be the brethren of the kirk of Ross, such as Mr. George Monro in Chanrie, Mr. Jo^n Malcome, Allex^r M⸰Kenzie at Containe, Mr. Robert Ross at Alnes, Mr. Robert Monro at Urquhart, Thomas Pape at Cullicudden, and divers wyrs in Mr. Jo^n M⸰Kenzie his tyme.

Sicklyke Jo^n Kaird, burges of Dingwell, and Jo^n M⸰Zlassich, quho in theas dayis was kirk officer to Mr. Jo^n M⸰Kenzie, Minister at Dingwall, deponed solemnly that the gleib nowe in Mr. Jo^n M⸰cra his possessione was the gleib be designation mett and measured be the abovewrytin brethren.

Ordaines Mr. Jo^n M⸰cra his designation of the gleib of Dingwell to be insert and registrate in the presbyterie booke.

In respect the court day is keeped on the pb̅riall meiting day, and some of the brethren hes particulars to be present attending the court. It is ordained that the pb̅rie day be altered for a tyme, and that Thursday be keeped, and Thursday come fyftene dayis be keeped at Dingwell.

Dingwell, 3 *Feb.* 1653.

Ordaines the brethren to use diligence in paying their contributione to the Irishe student.

Commissioners from Lochbroome compeiring and desyreing ane minister to be sent to them to preach, use discipline, and to give the benefite of baptisme and marriage to such as ar honest men, appoynts Mr. Donald Ross to repaire to Lochbroome to the effect forsaid, and to receave of the delinquents the ordinarie contributiones for the students of divinitie and humanitie, Commissioners charges, and quhat els is incumbent to them as is in wyere paroches.

Dingwell, 18 *Feb.* 1653.

The brethren all present except Mr. Do^d Ross, quho is in Lochbroome conforme to former ordenance.

No doctrine the said day in respect of the slownes of ye brethrens coming through tempest and invundatione of waters, and the clerks absence.

The said day the Commissioners for y^o contributione of Glasgowe presented thair Commissione for receaving of the samyne, quhaire the Brethren presented payment of thair contributione and receaved discharges conforme.

It is granted the said day to Mr. Murdo McKenzie, sometyme Minister at Suddie, to be supplied in his livelihoode in quhat is not disponed of the vacande stipend of Fottertie, and that ane act be wrytin heirwppon, and to extract the said act, and that it be subs^{uit} be the moderator and clerk.

Dingwell, 3 *March* 1653.

Conveined all the brethren.

No additione in regard the adder (Mr. Dod Ross) was storme stayed in Lochbroome.

Ordaines that the minister of Lochalse and Gerloch be advertised concerneing thair contributione to the bursers.

Dingwell, 17 *Marcij* 1653.

The parochiners of Kilterne regraiteing thair sadd conditione, sinne abounding, and no discipline, Ordaines them to be supplied once in the moneth be the severall brethren of the pbrie of Dingwell to preach and exercise discipline, *ordine Catologi*.

Referres Mr. Jon M^{c}cra his anser to Mr. Murdo McKenzie his bill to the provinciall.

Ordaines Mr. Hector Monro, sometyme minister at Kincardin, to be supplied out of the parochin of Kilterne be Hector Dowglas and wy^r Heritors within the said parochin, except Fowles and Lemlaire, and that they pay the supplicant quhat they wer in use to pay formerlie to the minister of Kilterne, and that the clerk of the pbr̄ie extract the act, and give it wnder his hand to the said Mr. Hector Monro.

The brethren of the pbr̄ie being desyred be Mr. Jo^n M^{c}cra to trye by quhat meanes the Gleib of Dingwell was put out of the ministers possessione, and in particular that a commissione be sent from the pbr̄ie to Jo^n Bayne of Tulloch, nowe in the bed of infirmitie, for taking his declara^{o}ne anent the said gleib, and if he knowe of any transactiones betwixt the Erle of Seafort and Mr. Murdo McKenzie, and becaus it is wncertaine bot the said Jo^n Bayne may dye befoire the nixt pbr̄ie day, that the brethren meit at Dingwell Monday nixt, being the 21 March, and the said Mr. Murdo to be summond to compeire the said day and place forsaid, to anser for the old pbr̄ie booke he had in his custodie.

Dingwell, 21 *Marcij* 1653.

Conforme to the former ordenance Mr. Murdo McKenzie being lawfullie sumnoned, cited, compeired not. Ordaines he be sumnoned pro 2do to the nixt pbr̄ie day.

Mr. Johne M^{c}cra being demanded why Mr. Murdo was not summond to sie if he haid ony thing to object against Johne Bayne of Tulloch: anseред that Jo^n Bayne was in the way of recoverie, and hopes he may be weile personallie to keepe the nixt pbr̄ie day.

Ordaines ane letter to be wrytin to certaine of the parochiners of Dingwell to be pn̄te the nixt pbr̄ie day for inquireing of them some things for the kirk of Dingwell.

Dingwell, 7 *Appr*. 1653.

Conforme to the former ordenance Mr. Murdo Mackenzie being lawfullie summond be Jo^n Dingwell, in presence of Do^d M^{c}finlay and Anguse Betoune, was called, compeired not, ordaines to be sumond pro 3°.

Or the brethren closed Mr. Murdo directed ane man of his to declaire his intentione in cuming conforme to the sumonds giwen him, haid not sicknes interweined.

Sicklyk, compeired Wm Dingwell, Ronald Dingwell, bailzie,

Donald Dingwell, Allex^r M^{c}conill duj, Allex^r McRonald, James Kempt, all burgesses w^{t}in the brough of Dingwell, according to the desyre of the pbr̃ies letter, to giue informatione so farre as they knowe of the esteate of the gleibe of Dingwell, quho declaired the haugh of Kildine (as they haid be report) was designed for ane gleib in Mr. Johne McKenzies tyme, and that it was reputed as a gleib, bot that they knewe not whidder Mr. Jo^n possest it long, nor quhat way. The brethren desyreing them to call all things in this matter to mynd against the nixt day of meiting, and to be readdie to declaire quhat they knewe in it as led witnesses, and particularly whidder they did wnderstand any thing of a transactione, reported to have bene made be Mr. Murdo McKenzie by taking Usie in contenta^{o}ne of it from the heritor, all being continewed *apud acta* for that purpose, ordaines that literall sumonds be directed to Tulloch, Towie, and Knockbayne, to the effect forsaid, and Mr. Murdo to be summond to compeire the said day to sie if he can object ony thing against the forsaids.

Receawed the said day ane letter from the Commissioners of ye church, with reasones of a fast to be observed w^t all conveniencie, which is appoynted to be kept.

[Space left for the reasons, but same not filled in.

Unfilled space also for ' Act of Mr. Jo^n M^{c}cra his designa^{o}ne of Gleib.']

21 *Appryll* 1653.

Conforme to ordenance compeired Mr. Murdo McKenzie, sometyme minister at Dingwell, and did exhibit and delyver the old pbr̃ie booke being at the beginning thairoff of the daite 12 Novemb 1633 zeires, and ending at the daite 18 Octob. 1637. The wholl consisting of 20 leaves wrytin, q^{re} it is ordained that the clerk of ye pbr̃ie wryte the recept thairof and giue a note of ye recept of ye same to Mr. Murdo McKenzie.

Mr. Murdo McKenzie refuses to anser the brethren in reference to the witnesses laid for tryall of the haugh qlk is called the gleib of Dingwell, bot desyres the pbr̃ie to goe on the best they can in tryall thaireof.

And for the better tryall of the forsaid gleib, compeired

Ronald Bayne, Notare, quho confessed that he hard be comone report that it was in excambioune that Mr. Murdo past the gleib of Dingwell to the heritor.

Jo^n Kaird confessed the lyke, and forder that he hard that Mr. Murdo McKenzie receawed some bolls of wictuall zeirly for the said gleib dureing his seruice at the Kirk of Dingwell.

Donald Dingwell confesses the samyne to be constantlie reported.

Wm Dingwell, and Ronald Bayne, bailzie, confesses in lyk maner the same.

Keneth McKenzie in Brackanord deponed that he hard his wmqll father say that Mr. Murdo hade the land of Usie partlie for the said gleibe.

In respect that Jo^n Bayne of Tulloch his tendernes, being bedfast, it is ordained that Mr. Jo^n Monro, Mr. George Monro, and Mr. Donald Ross travell to Tulloch for to try of him quhat he knowes of the said gleib.

Dingwell, 19 *Maij* 1653.

Being the first day of our meiteing efter the Provinciall, as it was c'cluded be the brethren at Chanrie efter the said provinciail assemblie.

Conveined Mr. Jo^n Monro, Moderator, Mr. George Monro, Mr. Dod frasere, Mr. Don^d M^{c}cra, Mr. Donald Ross.

Mr. Donald Fraser chosen Moderator.

It is statute that such as hes not payit the students of divinitie, and ye Irishe boyis to vse diligence in paying the samyne, and yat ane particular letter be wryten to Mr. ferq^{re} McLennan, to send ye saids c'tributiones eiy^r be taking them of the delinquents of Lochbroome conforme to the trust put wppon him, and his wndertaking to our broy^r Mr. Dod Ross, sent them be ws at ye desyre of certaine parochiners y^{r}of, or else to pay ye samyne of ye deuties of ye kirktounes, qlk is in his possessione be wertue of our po^r, and that ane letter be wrytin to Mr. Dod Clerk, Minister at Lochalsh, for his part of ye saids co'tributiones, lest the students be hindered from y^r studies.

Referres the particular referred be ye province anent Mr. Jo^n M^{c}cra and Mr. Murdo McKenzie to the tyme yat Mr. Jo^n M^{c}cra be present.

[Mr. Jo^n M^{c}cra's absence was excused, 'haveing obteined live to goe to Kintaile.']

The brethren appointed to speak Tulloch reports that Jo^n Bayne faithfullie deponed in thair presence that Mr. Murdo McKenzie made vse of him, and of Rorie McKenzie of Knockbaxter to deale w^t Seafort in yat transactione of ye hawgh and Usie, and yat Seafort consented thairto. It is recommended to the brethren to be diligent to y^{ro} po^{ro} in vseing weekly catechising and familie exercise.

It is appoynted that Mr. Jo^n M^{c}cra, Mr. Donald M^{c}cra, Mr. George Munro, and Mr. Donald Ross keepe at Loggie Weaster 22 Maij for rectifieing and filling wp the pbr̄ie booke against the meiteing of correspondence.

The said day compeired Mr. Andrew Monro, exhortant, desyreing a testificate of his lyfe and doctrine dureing his abode with ws, qlk the brethren ordaines to be giwen to the said Mr. Andrew, and to be sub^{vit} be the Moderator and clerk, and that Mr. Andrew mark himselff in the pr̄ie booke that he tak no charge elsquhaire without acquenting the pbr̄ie of dingwell.

Recomends to the seuerall brethren within the pbr̄ie to search if thaire hes beene ony with child quho hes absented themselves as fugitives, or remaines in ye cuntrey without a child, being formerlie with childe, qrby the murder of a child within the parochin of Urray may be tryed.

Alnes, 21 *Junij* 1653.

Ordaines ane wy^r letter to be wrytin to the Minister of Lochalsh and to Mr. ferq^{re} McLennan for the co'tributiones granted to the students of divinitie and Irishe boyis.

It is appoynted that Mr. Murdo McKenzie in Usie compeire this day fyfteine dayis at Dingwell, to anser the poynts of his bill against Mr. Jo^n M^{c}cra, minister at Dingwell. And that the witnesses formerlie summond for cleireing quhat they knowe of the beneficc of the Kirk of Dingwell be sumond *de novo* against the said day.

Ordaines Mr. Donald M^{c}cra to be diligent in searching c'cerneing the child murdered in his parochin of Urray.

Ordaines ane letter to be wrytin to ye ministers of Lochcarron, Garloch, and Lochalsh, to come or send heire thair co'tributione for the c'missioner appoyted to ye grāll assemblie.

Dingwell, 7 *Julij* 1653.

Ordaines diligence to be vsed be such as hes not payit thair c'tribu°ne to the students of divinitie and Irishe boyis.

Conforme to the Sumonds giwen, compeired allex^r Bayne of Knockbayne quho deponed that umq^{ll} George Erle of Seafort caused him drawe up a procuratorie to his brother Simon McKenzie to perschewe Mr. Murdo McKenzie for the deuties of Usie in respect that Mr. Jo^n M^{c}cra evicted the rychts he gawe his Lp [Lordship] of ye haugh of Kildine in contenta^{ne} of Vsie, or else to debar Mr. Murdo from Vsie.

Rorie McKenzie, from Towie, compeireing deponed that he hard it constantlie reported that thair was a transactione betwixt Seafort and Mr. Murdo. Donald Kempt and Jo^n McKenzie in Vsie deponed the samyne.

It is ordained that Tulloch be cited to this day fyftene dayis to give presbyteriallie a more cleire declara°ne of the said transactione.

It is appoynted that Mr. Jo^n Monro get ane extract of the reference of the provinciall relateing to Mr. Murdo McKenzie and Mr. Jo^n M^{c}cra from ye clerk of ye province to ye nixt pb̄rie day, seing Mr. Murdo McKenzie protests for the samyne befoire he give his ans^r, and Mr. Murdo is sum̄ond *apud acta* to the said day.

Mr. Donald M^{c}cra declaires his diligence in tryall of ye murder of the child w^{t}in his parochin, zit could find no furder tryall then one, Kenneth M^{c}eane v^c conill Zlass, quho confessed that he wrought once such a plaid as was found about the deade childe to Agnes neine Ronald woire in Ord, zit y^{r}after denyed the samyne, acknowledging himselff in so saying to be a lyar: qrefoire ordaines Mr. Donald to try forder in the particular.

Mr. Donald fraser is nominate and appoynted as Commissioner at the grāll assemblie, and that all the p̄nte brotheren haue thair co'tribu°ne Monday nixt to be delyvered at Loggie Wester tymely, and that Mr. ferq^r McLennan pay for Lochbroome, and Mr. Jo^n Monro, Mr. Johne M^{c}cra, and Mr. Donald

Ross pay for the vacant Kirks of Kilterne and fottertie *pro rata*.

George Monro of Teanowar[1] is nominate and choosen ruleing elder for the general assemblie.

It is appoynted yat Mr. Allex^r McKenzie, minister at Lochcarrone, Garloch, and Lochalsh [*sic*] repaire to the pbrie, and, co'forme to former ordenances, exercise and add, and that they send thair proportione of ye co'tributione to the Comissioner of ye grall assemblie, students of divinitie and Irishe boyis, wnder the paine of suspensione, and that within a month in cace they faile in performance in ye premisses.

The brethren taking to thair consideratione the necessitie and penurie of Robert Munro, son to wmq^{ll} Mr. David [Don^d ?] quho supplicates some thing for his livelyhoode, ordaines Jo^n Monro of Lemlaire to pay his proportione of the stipend of Kilterne to the said supplicant.

Dingwell, 21 *July* 1653.

All the brethren p̃nte except Mr. Donald Ross quho was appoynted to goe to Lochbroome to give the benefits of baptisme and marrage y^{re} at the desyre of the parochiners yreof.

Mr. Murdo McKenzie cited, compeired, as for ans^r to the reference promised to pass from his bill giwen against Mr. Jo^n M^{c}cra, and to subscryve ye samyne, so that Mr. Jo^n M^{c}cra doe ye lyke.

Alnes, 10 *August* 1653.

Mr. Murdo McKenzie compeired and presbyteriallie consented to tak up his bill giwen in to the pbrie of Dingwell against Mr. Jo^n M^{c}cra, and so pass from ye same: as also Mr. Jo^n M^{c}cra promised never to mak use of the said bill heirefter directlie or indirectlie.

Ordaineing the papers giwen in be Mr. Murdo McKenzie to be keeped till the samyne be seene be the province.

Dingwell, 25 *August* 1653.

Mr. Donald fraser, comissioner, reported the maner of the

---

[1] Teanowar—Tigh-nuar, the Gaelic name of Novar.

bracking wp of the grall assemblie, and recomends to the brethren severallie to mak the best vse in publick and private of theise sadd dispensations.[1]

Dingwell, 15 Sept. 1653.
[No business minuted except two cases of discipline.]

Dingwell, 6 Octob. 1653.
[Mr. Jo^n M^{c}cra excused for his absence the previous day, 'being in Kintaile and stayed through the inundatione of watters.' Mr. John Monro excused 'being bedfast.']

18 Octob. 1653.
At the desyre of the Moderator the brethren mett at Dingwell, q^{re} the governor of Inverness derected ane letter to the pbrie for tryall quhat mortifica°nes hes formalie bene allotted for mantenance of Schooles in all paroches.

Quhaire Mr. Jo^n Monro and Mr. fraser comissionate to goe to Invernes to ans^r the governors letter, and to be informed in the maner of our procedors in erecting of Schooles.

Dingwell, 21 Octob. 1653.
The Commissioners appoynted for Invernes reports that schooles ar ordained to be kept conforme to the Act of parliament in ye severall congregationes, and thairfoire ordaines the brethren to intimate the said ordenance in thair several congregationes, to wnderstand, if they consented thairto, or for the better accomoda°ne a conjunctione of paroches be made for acting the work.

The brethren being severallie removed, and tryed in lyf and doctrine, are approwen.

At Dingwell, 17 Novemb. 1653.
[No business, except discipline.]

---

[1] The General Assembly met on 20th July, but the members were immediately turned out of doors by the English under Colonel Cotterell, and marched out of Edinburgh. There was not another Assembly until after the Restoration.

Dingwell, 8 Decemb. 1653.

Conveined all the brethren, except Mr. George Monro, quho is excused, being bedfast.

The said day Mr. Johne M^{c}cra is choosen Moderator.

Ordaines Mr. Jo^n M^{c}cra, Mod^r, to repaire to Invernes c'cerncing the schooles within the pb$\bar{r}$ie of Dingwell.

Mr. Dod Ross excused, being stormestayed in Lochbroome.

The said day the Irishe bursar c'peired, and efter tryall and examina°ne is found wnsufficient for the place bestowed on him, declaires the burse to be vacand, Ordaineing that with all diligence ane wy^r be found to the said place against this day 15 dayis.

Dingwell, 22 Deceb. 1653.

Mr. Jo^n M^{c}cra declaires he went gateward to Invernes, conforme to the ordenance of the brethren, zit was forced to reteire himselff in respect of ye storminess of the weather, and wnderstanding of the Governor's sicknes, to quhom thaire was no access.

In respect the Irishe students place was declaired vacant, and the diligence of the brethren in supplieing the place inquired, compeired ane youth called Hew Monro, sonne to Allex^r Monro, wmq^{ll} Minister at Stranaver, quho hes past ane zeire of his cours of philosophie, and wndertaking to prosecute his studies, being of gud expecta°ne, nominates and admittis him to the benefite allotted for the Irishe boy. Inacting himself to exercise his talent be the advyse of the brethren of y^e pb$\bar{r}$ie of Dingwell, and that he withdrewe not himself to ony wy^r pb$\bar{r}$ie without licence sought and obtained of the forsaid brethren.

Dingwell, 29 Decemb. 1653.

Pro re nata conveined Mr. Jo^n Monro, Mr. George Monro, Mr. Donald M^{c}cra, moderator for the tyme, and Mr. Donald Ross.

The name of God incalled.

The said day ferq^{re} Monro and Andrew Monro, c'missioners from the parochiners of Kilterne, exhibitcing y^{re} comissione cub^{vit} desyreing the c'currence of y^e pb$\bar{r}$ie in the planta°ne of the Kirk of Kilterne

Ordaines Mr. Joⁿ Monro to repaire to Sutherland as Comissioner from the pbr̃ie to speake and invite Mr. Thomas Hogg, student of divinitie, to repaire to the Kirk of Kilterne, and to preach thair on anie Lords day, and that ane letter be wrytin and sub^{ult} from ws with Mr. Joⁿ Monro to that effect.

Closes w^t prayer.

Dingwell, 26 Janij 1654.

Mr. Joⁿ M^ccra reportes that he spoke the Governour of Invernes concerneing the establishing of Schooles, whose anser was that he could doe nought in the bessines till he mett with Fowles.

No report this day from Mr. Joⁿ Monro, c'cerneing Mr. Tho. Hogg.

The said day a letter was presented from ye pbr̃ie of Dornoch sub^{vit} be Mr. George gray, desyreing and intreateing ws to desist from suteing Mr. Thomas Hogg.

Ordaines ane anser to be wrytin to the said letter, but [without] prejudice to our sute.

Ane Supplica°ne was presented be Knockbayne from the Parochiners of Fottertie, desyreing one of our number to preach and keep sessione to tak course for the planta°ne of the Kirk thaireof.

The pbr̃ie ordaines the supplica°ne to be ansered, and one to be numinate the nixt pbr̃ie day.

At Dingwell, 9 feb. 1654.

Mr. Joⁿ Monro reports yat he acted conforme to his comissione in goeing to Sutherland, and that he acted also powerfullie as he could with Mr. Thomas Hogg for to come to Kilterne of quhom he hade a promise, quho conforme hes come and preached tua severate Lord's dayis at Kilterne, qre the wholl people vnanimously wer satisfied, hopeing and protesting for ye c'currence of the pbr̃ie for his planta°ne with them with all possible diligence, as is represented be Andro Monro of Culcairne and ferq^{re} Monro of Teanoard commissioners from ye said paroche snb^{uit} be the heritors, elders, and commonnes, as the Comissione at lenth beares.

The said day the pbr̃ie sends thair Call conjunctlie w^t the parochiners of Kilterne for Mr. Thomas Hogg to be heire at the pbrie this day 15 dayis, and that a letter to this effect be wrytin to him sub^{vit} be the moderatour.

23 feb. 1654.   *At Dingwell.*

The said day Mr. Thomas Hogg be the desyre of the pbrie and parochiners of Kilterne c'peired, quho is injoyned to handle the controverted head of *paedobaptismo* in reference to his actuall planta°ne at the Kirk of Kilterne, to be delyvered this day 20 dayis. And the said Mr. Thomas, being inquired wppon the former act, declaires that wpon the conditiones forsaids he will be present with ws to delyver the said comonne head, or to give his definitive anser concerneing obtempering or not obtempering the former call, with the reasones for ye same.

Ordaines ewerie brother to bring in thaire contribu°ne for the Irishe boy the nixt pbrie day.

Dingwell, 16 *Marcij* 1654.

Conveined all the brethren.

Efter incalling the name of God.

No doctrine the said day in respect of Mr. Thomas Hogg's absence.

Ordaines the former brethren to exercise and add this day 15 dayis, in cace Mr. Thomas beis not present.

Mr. Donald M^cra excused for his last dayis absence, being impeded and molested be the Englishe garisone.

Donald McZowne in Auchnafoile [in Urquhart] adulterer, repudiating his maried wyfe, compeired with his maried [wife], quho is ordained to satisfie for his adulterie, and to adhere to his maried wyf, Recommending to Wm Dingwell, one of the bailzies of Dingwell, to put the said Donald in ward till he find cautioner wnder the paine of ane hundreth pounds to doe duetie to his lawfull wyf.

The said day the brethren, taking to their considera°ne the conditione of Mr. Murdo McKenzie, sometyme Minister of Suddie, and the indigencie of his wyfe and children, conforme to the recommenda°ne to us from the grāll assemblie and provinciall in favors of him and wy^rs of his qualitie, we appoynt and ordaine that he be ansered of the wholl stipend of fottertie nowe vacant, and y^t of the cropt J m. vi. c. and fiftie zeires, and tha ane act heirwppon be extracted to him be the clerk.

Closes the meiting with prayer.

Dingwell, 30 *Marcij* 1654.

Donald McZowne in Auchnafoile hes found cautioner to accept and cohabite with his maried wyf, as Mr. Donald M^{c}cra reports.

Dingwell, 20 *Maij* 1654.

Conveined all the brethren.

Being the first day of our meiteing efter the provinciall, continewes the electioune of the moderator till the nixt day. No exercise, the meiteing of that day being for establisheing of our nixt meiteing, becaus the meiteing was not appoynted at the provinciall.

Continewes the exercise as before to this day 15 dayis.

[No meeting again till 5th Sept.]

Alnes, 5 *Sept*. 1654.

All the brethren of the Pbr̄ie of Dingwell present.

Mr. Jo^n Dallass, Assess. from Tayne.

Mr. Gilbert Andersonne Assess. from Chanrie.

The name of God incalled.

No exercise that day in respect Mr. Thomas Hogg was not in readdiness conforme to former ordenance, being necessarie employit be ye Erle of Sutherland.

The wholl parochiners of Kilterne compeireing the said day protests that thaire is not a call presented be the commissioners of Golspie or Pbr̄ie of Sutherland to the said Mr. Thomas Hogg, and thairfore no ground to be a lett to the pbr̄ie of Dingwell in proceding in reference to Mr. Thomas Hogg's admissioune to the parochin of Kilterne, and desyres this thair protesta°ne to be insert in our registers.

Quhilk efter serious considera°ne, and dealeing with the Commissioners of Golspie and Pbr̄ie of Sutherland for cleirnes in the matter of the said call, and finding no call, Thairefore judgeing the parochiners of Kilterne to haue full interest in the said Mr. Thomas through the fullnes and formalitie of thair procedours, and requires Mr. Thomas to enter his tryalls as is set downe in former ordenance, finding the said Mr. Thomas to have nothing to say in the formalitie of Kilterne be his owne confessione, and so to delyver theses on the commone head eight dayis befoire the meiteing qlk is to hold at Dingwell this day 15 dayes.

Closes with prayer.

Dingwell, 19 *Sept.* 1654.

Conveined all the brethren of the Pb̄rie.

The name of God incalled.

Mr. Thomas Hogg compeired, zit delyvered no doctrine in respect of ane call sent to him the said day from ye parochin of Golspie, and the pb̄rie of Sutherland willing him to halt for a tyme, qlk hes bene ane interruptione on a sudden, and a steepe to hinder his willingnes in obedience to the former ordenance, qlk excuse was not approwen be ye brethren. Quhairefore ordaines that the said Mr. Thomas delyver the comone head this day 15 dayis at Dingwell.

Receiwed the said day ane letter from ye Erle of Sutherland willing the brethren to desist from admitting Mr. Thomas Hogg to the Kirk of Kilterne, or to ony wyther charge w'in the diosce of Ross, in respect his lps [Lordship's] interest in the said Mr. Thomas.

The brethren ordaines ane letter in anser to the Erle of Sutherland to be wrytin with Mr. George Gray, quho brought the said letter.

Mr. George Gray, haveing nothing for the pb̄rie bot the delyuerie of ane letter, not contenting himselfe with ane letter, bot with obediencie to ye Erle of Sutherland, protests, notwithstanding of the former declarator, as not haveing commissione, bot as ane of the number of the pb̄rie of Sutherland, that thaire be no forder procedors in reference to Mr. Thomas Hoggs tryells or planta°ne at all, qlk he desyred to be insert in our records.

Appoynts the burss qlk is for the Irishe boy, to be giwen to Robert Monro, sonne to Mr. George Monro at Urquhart.

Dingwell, 26 *Sept.* 1654.

Convened all the brethren.

The name of God incalled.

Mr. Thomas Hogg delyuered the comone head, 1 Cor. 7. 14, quhose travells in giveing of theses convenientlie, and doctrine conforme, ar approwen.

The said day Rorie McKenzie of Dawachmaluack and Jo^n McKenzie of Dawahcarne, being commissioners from the Kirk of fottertie, chosen wppon ye 24 Sept. in presence of Mr. Jo^n M^{c}cra, quho preached ye said day at fottertie, quhose concurrence the heritors and elders desyrit to be represented to the pbrie in wryting to Mr. Andro Monro, expectant, to the end they mig^t heire him preach.

The brethren ordaines ane letter to be wrytin to the said Mr. Andro to the effect forsaid.

Dingwell, 4 Octob. 1654.

Mr. Jo^n Monro exercised, Mr. Tho. Hogg added, Act 6. 11, quha ar approwen. Ordaines Mr. Thomas hogg to exercise, and Mr. Donald Ross to add, 10 Octo. at Dingwell.

Ordaines Mr. John Monro to preach at Kilterne the nixt Lords day being the 8 of this instant, and serve ane edict the said day, intimateing the planta^one thaireof be Mr. tho. hogg, and that all haveing entresst compeire to declaire if ony thay [have which] may be lawfullie objected in the contrare, at Kilterne 17 Octob.

Dingwell, 10 Octob. 1654.

Mr. Thomas hogg exercised, Act 6. 12, 13, quho is approwen.

Ordaines Mr. Thomas hogg to hawe a populare sermon this day eight dayis at Kilterne, that the brethren may heire him, and knowe the approba^{o}ne of the people of the parochin, and to anser such questiones as salbe proponed be the brethren, 17 Octo.

Mr. Jo^n Monro reports his diligence in preaching at Kilterne, and served ane edict the said day.

Kilterne, 17 Octob. 1654.

Mr. Thomas hogg preached a populare sermone Math. 9. 6, both in Englishe and Irishe, quhose travells are approwen, and ansered such questiones as was proponed be the brethren.

The edict served at Kilterne, execute and indorsate, was presented, and the people being inquired if ony they hade to oppone against Mr. Thomas hogg, ansered negatively, being weile pleased with him.

The said day Rorie McKrishe is constitute Kirk officer at Kilmorack conjunct w^t the former kirkofficer in respect of the spatiousenes of the parochen.

Kilterne, 24 *Octob.* 1654.

All the brethren convened.

Mr. Joⁿ Monro preached, 1 Timoth. 1.

Mr. Thomas Hogge was lawfullie admitted to the charge of the ministerie at Kilterne, qre the heritors and elders thairof were all present.

Closes w^t prayer.

Dingwell, 21 *Novemb.* 1654.

Conveined all the brethren, except Mr. Joⁿ M^ccra quho is bedfast.

No exercise in respect of the weatheir, and not cuming tymely.

Ordaines the brethren to praepaire them to stay a night in the towne for filling wp thair pb̄rie booke.

Recommends to the brethren diligence in paying the students of divinitie.

Continewes the divisione of the thrie chalders wituall allotted be the province to the supplicants to the nixt meiteing of the brethren.

Dingwell, Decemb. 12, 1654.

The said day convened all the brethren.

The name of God incalled.

No exercise the said day, in respect the exerciser was abstracted be quartering on, and wther causes known to the brethren, quho is excused.

The said day Mr. Joⁿ Monro is chusen Moderator.

Ordaines zit diligence to be vsed be such as hes not pay^d Mr. Thomas Ross, student in divinitie.

The brethren not being fullie resoluit for the tyme that Mr. Murdo McKenzies sonne, to o^r knowledge, is ane object for bestoweing on him quhat is ordained to be bestowed to poore supplicants, till forder tryall of the indigencie of his father, qrefore desyres to tak notice of his fathers abilitie to the nixt day of meiting.

Dingwell, 2 Jany. 1655.

All present, except Mr. Donald Fraser, quho is bedfast.

The brethren, efter notice taken of W^m McKenzie his supplica°ne given in to the Synodall at Tayne the last day of Octob. 1654, and referring the distribu°ne of three chalders wictuall out of the vacant stipend of Fottertie to the discretione of the pbr̄ie of Dingwell, hes found that the said W^m McKenzie is not for the present of ony part or portionne of the forsaid wictuall, in regard Mr. Murdo McKenzie, sometyme Minister at Dingwell, quho is father to the said W^m, is powerfull to sustaine at Colledge, without any support of anie wther in this manner at the present till he be considered heirefter of the superplus of the forsaid stipend, qlk is referred for a tyme with a proviso.

Ordaines the three chalders wictuall to be equallie devyded betwixt Jo^n McKenzie, sonne to wmq^{ll} Mr. W^m McKenzie, Minister at Tarbat, and Allex^r Ross, supplicants, in respect we knowe perfectlie them to be altogidder indigent and objects of the said contributione.

The said day Rorie McKenzie of Dawahmaluck hes inacted himself to purchase to the Pbr̄ie the consent of the heritors of Fottertie in fawors of thease supplicants for the contributione granted, with certificatione if he obtaine not the said consent he salbe anserable for thric chalders wictuall.

Dingwell, 23 Janry 1655.

Conveined all the brethren, except Mr. George Monro, bedfast.

[No business recorded except discipline.]

Dingwell, 13 Feb. 1655.

Referres the unbaptized lass of 15 yeires, fathered on Captane Hector McKenzie, to be catechized and instructed in the artickles of the faith, and to be brought before the Pbr̄ie the nixt Pria^{ll} meiteing.

Dingwell, Marcij 6, 1655.

The unbaptized lass compeired, and promiseing to reside in the parochin of Contane, Referres to Mr. Donald Ross to instruct hir, and, efter knoweledge, to giue hir the benefite.

It is recommended to the brethren to think wppon and report the nixt day thair best thoughts concerneing quhat particular evidences of repentance ar to be required of delinquents is necessaire befoire the benefite of absolution be granted to them.

Mr. Ferq^{re} McLennan his supplica°ne for a recomenda°ne of his lyf and conversa°ne since his depositione continued to the nixt meiteing day.

Dingwell, 27 *Mar.* 1655.

Continues the brethrens thoughts concerneing the evidences of repentance to the nixt day.

M^r ferq^{re} McLennan haveing giving in a supplic°ne to the Pbrie desyreing thair Testimoniall of his cariage since the tyme of thaire last testimoniall granted to him, w^t a recomenda°ne to the provinciall in reference to the oppining of his mouth, The Brethren taking the samyne to thair considera°ne, and considering he did not reside ordinarlie amongst them since that tyme, bot some certaine space at divers tymes, they hawe, efter tryall of the brethren, found that dureing his resorting amongest them he hes caried himself humble, modestlie, and as it became a man wnder censour, in so far as they knewe, and that according to the best informa°ne they could hawe wppon tryall he did carie himselff in lyk manner dureing his residence elseq^{re}, qlk they recommend to the provinciall to tak to thair considera°ne, as thair wisdome sall think expedient.

Dingwell, 17 *Appryll* 1655.

Ordaines that the brethren search diligentlie at the provinciall w^c of the brethren of the province hes the booke of discipline, q^{r}be thair may be ane inspectione taken thaireof, to be advysed with to the forder informa°ne anent the evidences of repentance.

The brethren, severallie removed and tryed, ar approwen in lyf, doctrine, and conversa°ne.

Alnes, 15 *Maij* 1655.

All the brethren of the Pbrie present.
Assessors to the meiteing.
Mr. George Monro at Rosemarkie.
Mr. Johne Dallass at Tayne.
Mr. David Ross at Loggie.
Mr. Rob. Monro at Roskeene.
Mr. Andro Ross at Tarbat.

The brethren, considering the laudable acts of the assemblie of this Kirk 1619, in rela°ne to the receaweing in to the felloweshipe of the Kirke such personnes as fall in publick scandall, and the shoort cuming of many, if not of all among ws, in putting the samyne in executione, at leist in the full rigour of it, Doe heirefoire recommend to the speciall care of the severall brethren hencefoirth to observe the tennor of the said acts in receaweing all sorts of delinquents in thair respective places; particularly that everie brother may have some experience and warrand in y^r awin consciences, that such personnes sall have some meassor of knoweledge of thaire sinne, and apprehensione of mercie in Chryst, nixt to be found forsaking his former sinnes, also and keything[1] his hatred of it and all wy^r knowen sinnes also both in himself and wy^{re} [others] and that thaire be seene evidences of his desyre of grace in seeking God by prayer, and so everie way manifest a reaall purpose and some beginning of change and reforma°ne of lyfe, privatelie and publicklie, befoire both sessione and congrega°ne.

The Pbrie recommends not only weekly catechiseing, and owersceing the familie exercises, bot also that ilk Minister give ane accompt of his diligence in the same to the Pbrie, that transgressors yreof may be judged in cace they act not conforme to the act of ye generall assemblie, 30 August 1645.

Ordaines the meiteing to be at Dingwell this dayis xx dayis.

Sicklyke recommends to the brethren to tak a generall [*sic*] w^t swearers, drunkards, railers of the lyf and conversa°ne of ministers and elders, Sabboth brackers, and quhat els breeds scandell either to the professione or personnes.

---

[1] Kythe, to make known, to show.

Dingwell, 5 Junij 1655.

Convened the brethren except Mr. Jo^n Monro and Mr. tho hogge, Mr. Jo^n Monro excused. Referres Mr. tho. till he be present.

The said day Mr. Wm Lawder, minister at Awoch, presented ane letter directed to him be the Erle of Seafort comissionateing him to deale w^t the Pbr̃ie of Dingwell for Mr. Donald M^{c}cra, Minister at Wrray, his transporta°ne to ye Kirk of Kintaile, since his fay^r is most willing to demit in favors of ye said Mr. Donald, and the people most desyrous to have the said Mr. Donald to be thair minister, since thair pñte minister is both old and weake, and not able to discharge the deutie required. The anser qreof is continued to the nixt Pbr̃ie day, in respect of the absent brethren.

Dingwell, 26 Junij 1655.

All the brethren present, except Mr. Thomas hogg, quhose lr̃e of excuse is suspended till he be present.

The said day ane letter from Seafort was exhibited relateing Mr. Donald M^{c}cra his transporta°ne to the Kirk of Kintaile.

The brethren ordaines a formall course to be vsed in the procedore, and to that effect that the minister of Kintaile call his sessione, and that the minister of Kintaile mak his will appeire to the brethren be his letter, and that a call be the Sessioners and people, and incace it heis Mr. ferq$^{re's}$ will that he call Mr. Allex^r McKenzie at Lochcarron to keepe sessioune with him and his people, that the procedor may goe on the more ordourly, and that a letter be wrytin to Mr. ferq^{re} and Mr. Allex^r McKenzie to this effect.

[Agnes neine   Kilmorack, confessing incest, ' is ordained to be excommunicat be her ordinaire pastor the lords day come eight dayis.']

It is ordained that the severall brethren intimate to thair congrega°nes that they desist of the superstitious abuses vsed on St Johnes day by burneing torches through thair cornes, and fyres in thair townes, and thaire-efter fixing thair staicks in thair Kaileyeards.

Alnes, 17 *Julij* 1655.

C'peired the said day Mr. Wm Lawder, Mr. Pat. Durham, Mr. George Monro at Rosmarkie, Mr. David Ros, Mr. Androw Ros, Assessors, with the whole brethren of Dingwell except Mr. Donald M^cra, quho is excused, obtaineing licence to goe to Kintaile, quho sould add ye said day.

Continewes the ordenance concerneing the transporta°ne of Mr. Dod. M^cra to the nixt meiteing 7 August.

Ordaines Mr. tho. hogg to repaire to the Kirk of fottertie to keepe Sessionne and to learne the will of theas in the planta°ne of ye kirke yreof.

Dingwell, 7 *Aug.* 1655.

The said day Mr. Colline McKenzie at Killernan, and Mr. Wm Lawder compeired as Commissioners for the Erle of Seafort and parochiners of Kintaile concerneing Mr. Donald M^cra his transporta°ne from Wrray to Kintaile.

The brethren doe find it expedient, befoire the giweing of thair anser to the Commissioners, that they in a Christiane prudencie sould by Mr. George Monro appoynted by ws to repaire the nixt lords day to the Kirk of Urray, and efter divine service to sound the peoples mynds in reference to the said Mr. Do^d his transporta°ne, in a discreit way informe ourselves of thair mynds thairannent for better inabling ourselves to ansere the saids commissioners the nixt day, and that this be no sett stopp of discipline against the said transporta°ne, or our giveing ansere the said day.

Mr. Thomas Hogge reports his goeing to fottertie, quho preached y^r and moderated in Sessionne, qre the people wer desyrous to heire Mr. Jo^n McKillicane preache one day amongst them.

The brethren appoynts Mr. Thomas hogg to repaire to Morray with thaire letter to invite Mr. Jo^n McKillican to come and preach at fottertie, conforme to the desyre of the parochiners yreof.

At Roskeine, 28 *August* 1655.

Mr. George Monro, Moderator, Mr. Jo^n Monro, Mr. Thomas Hogg, Mr. Jo^n M^cra, Mr. Donald M^cra, and Mr. Donald

Fraser, brethren of the Pbrie of Dingwell. Mr. Gilbert Andersoune, Mr. George Monro, and Mr. Wm Lawder, Assessors for correspondence with the said Pbrie from the Pbrie of Chanrie, and Mr. David Ros, Mr. Jo^n Dallass, and Mr. Andro Ros, Assessors for correspondence from the Pbrie of Tayne, and diverse wy^r brethren of the Province of Ros, namely, Mr. Robert Monro, minister at Roskaene, Mr. Hector Monro at Eddertayne, Mr. Wm Ross at Ferne, Mr. Thomas Ros at Kincarden, Mr. James M^cculloch at Kilmuire, Mr. James McKenzie at Nig, Mr. Coline McKenzie at Killernan, Mr. George Dunbar at Suddie, Mr. Charles Pape at Cullicudden, and Mr. Robert W^msoune at Kirkmicheal, did meit day and place foresaid, and taking to consideratione the many addresses made be Mr. ferq^re McLennan, late Minister at fottertie, to severall Judicatories of the Kirk, in reference to the oppineing [opening] of his mouth, though they did not conceave themselves a competent Judicatorie for such a purpose according to the acts and ordinarie practice of the Church, zit taking to heart the gryte neide and exigence of the planta°ne of vacand Churches, especiallie in the Hielands, the evidences of the said Mr. ferq^re, his sincere remorse and humilitie in reference to the particular causes of his depositioune, and of his Christian carriage as became a man under censure, and becaus of the improbabilitie of a superior Judicatorie competent to be hade with such convenient diligence as the present exigence of faithfull preachers calleth for:[1] Thairefoire the said Pbrie of Dingwell, with thair said assessors, togidder with theas wy^r fornamed brethren of the province thaire advyse and concurrance, did conclude (without prejudice of, and with submissioune to any superior Judicatorie competent) to proceide *cum periculo* in the said matter, and accordingly they did all unanimously oppon the said Mr. ferq^re his mouth, and declaire him in a capacitie for the ministerie wppon a lawfull call, and that in reference to the Kirk of Lochbroome first, he haweing a lawfull call thairto.

Dingwell, 4 *Sept.* 1655.

No exercise the said day, the meiteing being *pro re nata.*

---

[1] There was no General Assembly since Cromwell broke up the Assembly of 1653, and none till after his death.

Absents Mr. Jo^n Monro, Mr. Do. M^{c}cra, Mr. Do. Fraser.
The name of God incalled.

Mr. Thomas Hogg reports conforme to his commissioune, that he went tua severall tymes to Mr. Jo^n McKillican to call him to preach at fottertie, quho in obedience to the Pbr̃ies letter preached at fottertie 2 Sept.

The said day Donald Kaird, Commissioner from fottertie, compeired, quha declaires that the parochiners yrof vnanimously doe call the said Mr. Jo^n McKillican to be thair pastor, and desyreing the Pbr̃ie to concur with them in calling the said Mr. Jo^n to goe about ane expedient deutie, according to the custome of this church, in reference to his spedie planta^{o}ne to the Kirk of fottertie.

The Pbr̃ie ordaines that the desyre of the parochiners of fottertie be ansered.

Mr. George Monro suspends his anser in his diligence conforme to his commissioune with the Parochiners of Wrray, to Mr. Dod M^{c}cra and the rest of the absent brethren be present.

Dingwell, 25 Sept. 1655.

The anser of the letter directed be the Pbr̃ie returned from Mr. Jo^n McKillican, bearing that divers difficulties and perplexities made him unable to give a peremptorie anser for the tyme. The Pbr̃ie taking the same to consideration thought meit to renue thair former desyre of his repaireing to the Pbr̃ie the nixt day, and for that effect to wryt and send a second letter.

Dingwell, 23 Octob. 1655.

No anser receiwed from Mr. John McKillican, the considera^{o}ne qreof is continewed wntill Mr. Thomas Hogg returne from Morray.

Mr. George Monro reports from the parochiners of Wrray that they admire [wonder] that thair minister sould be taken from them without acquenting them thairof, and that they wald send commissioners to the Pbr̃ie the nixt Pbr̃ie day.

Mr. Colline McKenzie, minister at Killernan, appeireing as Commissioner for the parochiners of Kintaile, did wrge ane anser from the Pbrie to thair proceidings in Mr. Donald M°cra his transporta°ne to Kintaile. : The Brethren continewes to proceide in rela°ne to the said transporta°ne wntill thair full number be pñte, in regaird of the importance of the matter, and paucitie of thair number, with which the commissioner did acquiesce, desyreing yat Mr. Dod M°cra sould be acquented of the next meiteing.

Dingwell, 13 *Novemb*. 1655.

All present except Mr. Thomas hogg.

Ordaines ane edict to be served the nixt lords day in the Kirk of Wrray.

Continewes Mr. Thomas Hoggs diligence conserneing Mr. Joⁿ McKillican, to Mr. Thomas hogg be pñte.

Ordaineing the ministers to repaire to the Pbrie with thair delinquents quhen they sand ony to give ane full informa°ne to the brethren of the manner of thair offence, and for the better informa°ne of themselves.

Duncan McMurchie v^c Cwile in the parochin of Garloch regraitcing his wyf to haue deserted him, being referred to the Pbrie from the Sessione of Garloch, compeired befoire the brethren, and being asked in the cause of ye desertioune declaired be his owne confessioune himselff to be impotent for a certane space efter his mariage, bot thairefter finding himselff potent, was repudiate be his wyf, and deserted him and went to hir parents.

Agnes Kempt in Garloch, being maried wppon the said Duncan, compeired, professing hir unwillingnes from the beginning to marie the said Duncan, bot moved and threatned be the superior of the land, acknowledging hirsclff to be free from any carnall dealing with the said Duncan ewer to this tyme.

Ordaineing some of the brethren, such as Mr. George Monro, Mr. Donald M°cra, with certain wther frends mett with the forsaids at Loggie to sie quhat they can work wppon these maried persons to agree them and advyse them in thair Christiane deutie towards wthers [each other], and thair diligence to be schewen the nixt Pbrie day, and that theis people be cited to compeire day and place forsaid.

Dingwell, 4 Decemb. 1655.

All the brethren present.
The name of God incalled.
No exercise in respect of the shoortnes of the day and the Impossibilitie of goeing or rydeing in the way.

Ordaines the former brethren to delyver the exercise the nixt day.

Mr. Thomas Hogge diligence in his Commissioune in dealeing w^t Mr. Jo^n McKillican approwen, quho reported that he was in Morray tua severall tymes acting in his commissioune, quho is ordained to prosecute his diligence.

Conforme to the ordenance ane edict was served at the Kirk off Urray 25 Novemb. 1655, duely execute and indorsate be Jo^n Glass, Officer and clerk to the Sessioune of Urray.

Ordaines Mr. Colline McKenzie and Mr. Wm Lawder to give in thair reasonnes for the wrged transporta^{o}ne, and that the parochiners of Wrray compeire the said day to heare theas reassonnes.

Donald McKenzie of Loggie compeiring for Agnes Kempt in Garloch takes wppon them to qualifie and prowe the mariage past and solemnized betwixt Agnes Kempt and Duncan McWurchie v^c cwile to be wnlawfull and never with consent, quha protests a day to be granted for calling his wytnesses, qlk was granted.

Dingwell, 8 Janry. 1656.

The said day appeired Mr. Jo^n McKillican conforme to his promise he wryte and anser to o^r letter in reference to the planta^{o}ne of the Kirk of Fottertie.

Quhaire he is injoyned to handle the contraverted heade *De potestate clauium* the 17 Jan^{ry} 1656.

Conforme to former ordenance, Mr. Colline McKenzie and Mr. Wm Lawder, commissioners for the wrged transportatione of Mr. Donald M^{c}cra from Wrray to Kintaile, presented reassonnes for the samyne.

Ordaines that the Parochiners of Urray anser theas reassonnes the 17 Janry. nixt come, and especiallie Seafort, quho is concerned in both paroches of Urray and Kintaile, quho is to be in the cuntrey shoortlie.

Compeired Daniell McKenzie of Loggie, Allex^r McKenzie in Auchlanachan, Donald M^cgillichean in Kinkell, and Duncan M^cerichie v^c Cwile quha was maried wppon the said Agnes Kemp, testifieing and deponeing that neither consent nor mutuall deutie to thair knoweledge hes bene performed either befoire or efter mariage be the said Agnes, bot only constrained thairto be the Superiour of the land and hir parents.

Ordaines Mr. Donald Ross to wryte ane letter to Mr. ferquhere McLennan to be p̄nte 17 Jan^r 1656 to anser the petitioune of Lochbroome.

Dingwell, 17 *Janry*. 1656.

Compeired all the Brethren.

The name of God incalled.

Mr. Jo^n McKillican, conforme to the ordenance of Pb̄rie, gaue in his theases, and handled the comone head enjoyned him, and ansered such as impugned the theases, quho is approwen.

Ordaines the said Mr. Jo^n to exercise wppon the ordinarie matter of exercise 24 Janry.

Compeired the said day Mr. ferq^re McLennan, qre the Call of the parochiners of Lochbroome was exhibited and reade be ye brethren.

Quhaire they ordaine ane letter to be wrytin to theas of Lochbroome in reference to the call given be them to the said Mr. ferq^re to incurage him, wtherwayis that Mr. ferq^re salbe disposed on be the Pb̄rie in cace they act not heirin as effeires within fyfteine.

Receawed ane letter from Seafort c'cerneing the wrged transporta°ne, promiseing with all conveniencie to plant the Kirk of Wrray elsweile as Kintaile, to quhose letter ane anser was wrytin and sub^vit.

The said day ane supplica°ne was presented, wrgeing a transplanta°ne of Mr. George Monro in Urq^t to the paroch of Snysard.

Continewes the supplica°ne of the parochiners of Snysard to the nixt pb̄rie day.

Dingwell, 24 *Janry*. 1656.

Mr. Jo^n McKillican exercised, Act 7. v^s 17, quhose travell is approwen.

Ordaines Mr. Jo^n McKillican to lectour in a popular manner and give some specimen of his Irishe, Collos. 3. 1, this day 15 dayis.

The said day receawed ane Returne to o^r former letter, from Seafort, by the former Commissioners, Mr. Colline and Mr. W^m.

Continewed Mr. George Monro Supplica°ne in reference to the Call from Snysard the nixt day of meiteing.

Dingwell, 7 Feb. 1656.

Mr. Joⁿ McKillican taught conforme to ye former appoyntment, Coll. 3. 1, a populare sermon, quho is approwen.

It is appoynted that Mr. Joⁿ McKillican preach at Fottertie the nixt lords day, to the end the people may heire him, and that ane edict be fixed at the Church doore yreof the said day, reade and execute duely, and that the said Mr. Johne lector wppon Math. 28, and give some specimen of his Irishe the nixt pbr̄ie day at Dingwell, being 14 feb.

Continewes wy^r referres to the nixt Pbr̄ie day at Dingwell.

And that some of the brethren speake the erle of Seafort on that day to mak ws knowe his intentioune.

Dingwell, 14 feb. 1656.

Mr. Joⁿ McKillican lectured Micha 7, 5, 6, 7, approwen.

The brethren all present, and wnderstanding of Seafort his willingness in the planta°ne of ye Kirk of Wrray, doe vnanimously consent to Mr. Donald M^ccra his Transporta°ne from the church of Wrray to the Church of Kintaile.

And to that effect doe ordaine ane edict to be served at Kintaile for Mr. Donald M^ccra his admissioune with all diligence. And that Mr. Allex^r McKenzie repaire to the Church of Kintaile with the edict, and cause execute the same in reference to Mr. Donald M^ccra his admissioune, and that the same be returned w^tin a moneth.

Appoynts the brethren to meit at Fottertie 26 Feb. to admitt Mr. Joⁿ McKillican.

Fottertie, 26 feb. 1656.

Conveined all the brethren.
The name of God incalled.
Mr. George, Moderator, preached.

Conforme to the ordenance, receaued the Edict duely execute and indorsate, and hes found no contradictioune in the contrare, qrefoire gave presenta°ne and admissioune to Mr. Jo^n McKillican to the charge and ministeriall functioune of Fottertie.

Ordaines the nixt meiting to hold at Dingwell 18 Marc^{ij}.

Ordaines Mr. Donald M^{c}cra to preach at Wrquhart the nixt lord's day, and ane edict to be served at the Kirk yreof intimateing Mr. George Monro his transporta°ne to Snysart; and Mr. George Monro to preach the said day at Urray.

Closes the meiteing with prayer.

Dingwell, 18 *Marcij* 1656.

That day ane letter was receawed from Mr. ferq^{re} McLennan, schaweing that the edict conforme to the ordenance of the Pbr̄ie was served at Lochbroome, and the executione of the edict was presented that day. Quhaire Mr. Donald Ross was ordained to repair to Lochbroome, and to admit Mr. ferq^{re} McLennan to the Kirk of Lochbroome.

The said day receaued ane letter from Mr. Allex^r McKenzie reporteing his diligence anent the edict he serveit at Kintaile; continewes the samyne to the nixt day till the clerks cuming with such papers as concernes the foresaid particular.

Receaved the said day the executione of ye edict from Wrq^t returned, and the people called and not compeired, nor none cumming to prosecute the call, continewes it to the nixt day.

Dingwell, 15 *Appryll* 1656.

Conveined all the brethren except Mr. Donald Ross, quho is in Lochbroome be appoyntment of the Pbr̄ie for to admit Mr. ferq^{re} McLennan to the charge thairof.

The referres of Lochbroome and Kintaile referred to the Clerks cuming.

The said day Mr. George Monro is transported to the Church of Snysard and Rasay within the Province of Skye, and ordaines Mr. Thomas Hogg to repair to the Church of Wrq^t the nixt lords day and intimate the Kirk thairof to be vacant.

19 *Maij* 1656, *At Fottertie.*

Conveined all the brethren—*pro re nata*—Efter prayer—

Conforme to the former ordenance Mr. Thomas went to the Church of Wrquhart, and intimated the vacancie of the Kirk y^reof.

Ordaines Mr. George Monro his act of transporta°ne to be extracted be the Clerk of the Pbr̄ie.

Closes the meiteing with prayer.

Dingwell, 3 Junij 1656.

Conveined all the brethren.

The name of God incalled.

Mr. Donald Fraser handled the contraverted head whidder the infants of beleivers not considderat by explicite covenant within a particular church may be baptized.

The said day Mr. Jo^n M^ccra is choosene Moderator.

It is statute and ordained that the wholl brethren meit at Containe the tent day of this instant, for the visita°ne of the Kirk of Lochcarron and Appelcross, and that Mr. Allex^r McKenzie[1] be wrytin to that he may conveine his people the 13 day of this moneth, lest ony excuse be pretended.

Mr. Donald Ross reports his diligence in admitting Mr. ferq^re McLennan, Minister at Lochbroome, 6 Appryll 1656, the parochiners thairof being present, without ony opposi°ne.

Dingwell, 24 Junij 1656.

No exercise in respect the causes of the fast and acts of the Synode wer to be coppied and wrytin.

In rela°ne to Mr. Donald M^ccra his transporta°ne and admissioune to the Church of Kintaile, appeired Mr. Wm Lawder, Commissioner appoynted formerlie for the Erle of Seafort and congrega°ne of Kintaile, and desyred conforme to the former act ordo^r for the said Mr. Donald M^ccra his admissioune to the charge thaireof, and to that effect presented ane letter wnder Mr. ferq^re M^ccra his hand schawing his willingnes in the accepta°ne of the said Mr. Donald as his helper, fellowe labourer, and conjunct minister with him in the said Charge, Thairefore the Pbr̄ie consents and condiscends that Mr. Allex^r McKenzie, Minister at Lochcarron, repaire to the Kirk of Kintaile the third lords day of July nixtocome, and admitt the said Mr. Don^d to the charge thairof.

---

[1] Minister of Lochcarron.

Dingwell, 29 *Julij* 1656.

No exercise in respect of the laite and slowe meiteing, the brethren not being fullie advertised of the dyate, and the adders absence.

The reasoune of this interwall was the appointement of the brethren at Kincarden and Roskeine, and the intimaᵒne and keeping of the fast.

No report as zit from Kintaile in reference to Mr. Doᵈ Mᶜcra his admissioune, neither ony anseʳ from Mr. Allexʳ MᶜKenzie or Applecross of the l̄res sent to them for tryeing the Idolaters, if ony be in Appilcross or in the adjacent partes yreof.

Ordaines certaine brethren to speak the Erle Seafort of oʳ goeing to Appilcross 4 Sept. to the end his lp. countenance our goeing thair, and that Mr. James MᶜKenzie be aduerteised to be in readiness to goe the lenth the said day wᵗ the rest of the brethren.

Ordaines ane letter to be wrytin to Mr. Allexʳ MᶜKenzie, Mr. Rorie MᶜKenzie, of the necessitie of thair meiteing with thair Brethren at Appilcross the said day, and in the meantyme that they keep the Pb̄rie this day 20 day at Dingwell.

Ordaines Mr. ferqʳ MᶜLennan in Lochbroome to be acquented oʳ nixt dayis meiteing, that he with his delinquents referred to the Pb̄rie may appeire the said day.

Conforme to ordenance the brethren declaires that the fast was observed.

Ordaines the brethren quho hes not payit thair contributioune to Robert Monro, quho is Ireshe student (be consent of the Pb̄rie), pay all thair pairt yreof with all diligence as they salbe anserable to the Pb̄rie.

21 *August* 1656, *Dingwell*.

The said day conveined all the brethren, except Mr. Donald fraser, quho is excused be his letter.

The name of God incalled.

Ordaines the brethren to be more tymeous in meiteing.

Receawed the said day ane l̄re from Applecross declaireing his diligence and concurrence in discipline with the Minister, and especiallie in restraineing the abuses formerlie vsed in the worshipe of God in a superstiteous manner.

It is appoynted that Mr. Allex^r McKenzie (quho is present at this meiteing conforme to ordenance) adverteis the people of Appilcross[1] to be present at the Kirk thaireof conforme to the former ordenance the 4 Sep., and all the brethren to meit, conforme to the act, at Contan.

Appoynts Mr. Donald Ross to adverteise the ministers of Lochbroome and Garloch to keepe at Appilcross ye 4 Sept. peremptorly, and Mr. Allex^r McKenzie to acquent Mr. Donald M^{c}cra at Kintaile, wnder the paine of censour in cace they keepe not the said day and meiteing, and to censor the said Mr. Dod Ross and Mr. Allex^r in case they aduerteise not thaire brethren.

Ordaines Mr. Jo^n McKillican to aduerteise Mr. Donald fraser to keepe day and place forsaid, with certifica^{c}ne as said is.

At Appilcross, 5 Septemb. 1656.

Conveined Mr. Jo^n M^{c}cra, Moderator, Mr. Jo^n Monro, Mr. Thomas Hogg, Mr. Jo^n McKillican, Mr. Donald fraser, Mr. Donald M^{c}cra, Mr. Rorie McKenzie, Mr. Allex^r McKenzie, and Mr. Donald Ross.

The name of God incalled.

Mr. Jo^n M^{c}cra haid doctrine.

Mr. Jo^n Monro reports that he adverteised Mr. James McKenzie, and receaweing his anser schaweing the impossibilitie of his cumming in respect of his wyfes seeknes, and wthers of his familie.

Mr. ferq^{ro} McLennan being tymeously adverteised could not keep the meiteing in respect of his tenderness in taking phisick, as his letter beares, bot if possible he may travell to keepe with the brethren at Garloche.

The minister being inquired be his brethren of the maine enormities of the parochin of Lochcarrone and Appilcross, declaires some of his parochiners to be superstitious, especiallie in sacrificeing at certaine tymes at the Loch of Mourie,[2]

---

[1] There was no minister at Applecross at this time, nor, indeed, until 1731. The district was served by the minister of Lochcarron. There was a parish at Applecross during Roman Catholic times, but after the Reformation it, for a time, ceased to exist. The parish was re-erected in 1726.

[2] Loch Maolrubha—St. Maelrue's Loch—now Loch Maree. Maolrubha crossed from Ireland to Scotland in 671 A.D., and two years later founded the church of Aporcrosan, now Applecross (in Gaelic, A'Chomaraich—the Sanc-

especiallie the men of Auchnascallach, quho hes bene sumond, cited, bot not compeireing, executiones lawfullie giwen be Tho. Rorie [blank], Kirkofficer of Lochcarron, quhose names ar as followes: Donald M^{c}conill chile, Murdo M^{c}ferq^{re} v^c conill oire, W^m M^{c}conill oire, Gillipadrick M^{c}rorie, Duncan M^{c}conill wayne v^c conill buj, Allex^r M^{c}finlay vic conill duj, Donald M^{c}eane roy v^c chenich, Johne M^{c}conill reach, Murdo M^{c}eane roy, Murdo M^{c}eane woire v^c eane zlaiss, Finlay McGillifudricke.

Ordaines the kirkofficier to charge theas againe to compeire at Dingwell the third Wednesday of October nixtocome, and that thair minister compeire the said day at Dingwell, and that he preach at the vacand kirk of Wrquhart the ensucing lords day he is in the cuntrey.

The said day the Pbrie of Dingwell, according to the appoyntment of Synode for searcheing and censureing such principalls and superstitious practizes as sould be discovered thaire, haveing mett at Appilcross, and finding amongst wy^r abominable and heathinishe practizes that the people in that place were accustomed to sacrifice bulls at a certaine tyme wppon the 25 of August, w^c day is dedicate as they conceave to St. Mourie, as they call him,[1] and that thair wer frequent approaches to some ruinous chappells and circulateing of them, and that future events in reference especiallie to lyf and death in taking of jurneys was expect to be manifested by a holl of a round stone, qrein they tryed the entreing of thair heade, w^c if could doe, to witt, be able to put in thaire heade, they expect thair returneing to that place, and faileing, they conceaved it ominous; and withall thair adoreing of wells, and wther superstitious monuments and stones tedious to rehearse, hawe appoynted as followes: That quhosoeuer sall be found to commit such abhominationes, especiallie sacrifices of ony kynd

---

tuary). From that centre he evangelised the portion of the Highlands now embraced roughly in the counties of Ross and Cromarty. Next to Columba, Maolrubha was the most famous of the early missionaries to the Highlands.

[1] St. Maolrubha (see footnote, p. 279). The brethren had evidently no idea that Mourie was the same as Maolrubha—if they ever heard of that saint. Even the late learned Rev. Dr. John Kennedy of Dingwall, in referring to this minute, wrote: 'Whether this Mourie was a heathen deity, a Popish saint, or one of Columba's missionaries, it may be impossible to determine.'—*The Days of the Fathers in Ross-shire*, second edition, p. 6.

or at ony tyme, sall publickly appeire and be rebuked in sackcloath sex severall lords dayis in sex severall churches, viz. Lochcarron, Appilcross, Contane, Fottertie, Dingwell, and last in Garloch paroch church, and that they may wppon the delatione of the Sessioune and minister of that paroche he sall cause sumond the guiltie persoune to compeire befoire the Pbṝie to be convinced, rebuked, and yreto be injoyned his censo^{rc}, and with all that the Justice sould be acquent to doe y^{re} deuties in suppressing of the forsaid wickedness, and the forsaid censure in reference to thaire sacrificeing to be made vse of incace of convict and appeireing and evidences of remors be found: and, faileing, that they be censureing w^t excomunica°ne.

Ordaines the minister to exercise himselff w^t his people in such manner as at his cumming to Appilcross once in the fyve or sex weekes, at each lords day of his cumming, he stay thrie dayis amongst his people in catechiseing a pairt of them each day, and that he labor to c'vince the people of thair former error by evidenceing the hand of God against such abhomina°nes as hes beine practised formerlie.

Appoynts Mr. Allex^r McKenzie to informe the Presbiterie of any strangers that resorts to theas feilds as formerlie they hawe to thair former heathinishe practises, that a course may be takin for thair restraint.

The said day the said Mr. Allex^r reports that, conforme to the ordenance of the Pbṝie, he went to the Church of Kintaile and admitted Mr. Donald M^{c}cra to the charge thaireof, qre it is appoynted that the act of transporta°ne and the admissioune be insert in the Pbṝie book.

Jo^n M^{c}rory in Glencannich, Adulterer w^{t}in Kilmorack, being declaired penitent be his ordinarie pastor, compeired, confessing his sinne of adulterie, is referred to be receaved at Kilmorack.

Closes with thanksgiveing.

Kenlochewe, 9 Sept. 1656.

The brethren all present except Mr. Jo^n M^{c}cra, Mr. Donald Fraser, and Mr. Donald M^{c}cra.

Ordaines Mr. Allex^r McKenzie, minister at Lochcarron, to cause summond Murdo M^{c}conill v^c Wurchie v^c conill v^c allister in Torritan, and Donald Smyth in Appilcross for sacrificeing at Appilcross, to compeire at Dingwell the third Wednesday of October, with the men of Auchnaseallach.

The brethren taking to thair considera°ne the abhomin°nes within the parochin of Garloch in sacrificeing of beasts wpon ye 25 August, as also in poureing of milk wpon hills as abla°nes, quhose names ar not particularly signified as zit, referres to the diligence of the minister to mak search of theas persounes and Summond them as said is in the former ordenance and act at Appilcross, 5 Sept. 1656, and with all that by his private diligence he have searchers and tryers in euerie corner of the cuntrey, especiallie about the Lochmourie, of the most faithfull, honest men he can find, and that such as ar his elders be particularly poseit concerneing former practises, in quhat they knowe of theas poore ones quho are called Mourie his derilans,[1] and ownes theas titles, quho receawes the sacrifices and offerings wpon the accompt of Mourie his poore ones, and that at leist some of theas be sumond to compeire befoire the Pbr̃ie the forsaid day wntill the rest be discovered, and that such as haue boats about the loch transport themselves or wthers to the Ile of Mourie, quharein ar monuments of idolatrie, without warrand from the superiour and minister towards lawfull ends, and if the minister knowes alreaddie ony guiltie that they be cited to the nixt pbr̃ie day, and all contraveiners y^{r}efter as occasioune offers in all tyme cuming.

The brethren heireing be report that Minrie [Mourie] hes his monuments and remembrances in severall paroches within the province, bot more particularly in the paroches of Lochcarron, Lochalsh, Kintaile, Contan and Fottertie and Lochbroome, It is appoynted that the brethren of the congregationes haue a correspondence in trying and curbeing all such w^{t}in thair severall congrega°nes, and for thease that cummes from forren cuntreyis that the ministers of Garloch

---

[1] The Rev. Dr. Kennedy (*Days of the Fathers in Ross-shire*) reads this word *deviles*, and Sir Arthur Mitchell (*The Past in the Present*) makes it *devilans*. The word is, however, plainly *derilans*. In the vocabulary appended to Kirke's Bible, *deireoil* is given as Gaelic for *afflicted*. *Derilans* would thus mean the afflicted ones, the poor ones, the insane. To this day the mentally afflicted are taken to St. Mourie's Isle, Loch Maree, to be cured.

and Lochcarron informe themselves of the names of theas and the places of thair residence, and informe y͞e Pb͞rie yreof, that notice may be giwen to theas concerned.

Recommends to the ministers of Lochcarrone and Lochalsh diligence in catechiseing as said is in y͞e act at Appilcross, 5 Sep., and that they be cairefull in thair visita°ne of the sicke, and that the act of Synode be observed anent baptisme of children, and that they [be] cairfull to keepe provincialls and pb͞ries as they ar advertised, according to the acts of Synods.

Closes with prayer.

At Dingwell, 14 *feb.* 1656.[1]

That day the Pb͞rie of Dingwell taking to thair considera°ne the call giwen to Mr. Donald M°c͞ra, minister at Wrray, by the congrega°ne of Kintaile with consent of Mr. Donald[2] M°c͞ra, p͞nte minister at Kintaile, nowe adged and infirme, and so wnable to doe deutie as formerlie (or as is necessarie) to embrace or exerce the office and functioune of the ministerie at the said Kirk as thaire lawfull or actuall minister, and thairefoire desyreing the Pb͞rie to grant ane act of Transporta°ne, for that effect presenting also wnto thair cleire reasounes and evident demonstra°nes of the necessitie and expediencie of the said transporta°ne, by thair Commissioners, as thair wrytin call and reassounes thaireof at gryte lenth proports. After mature and long delibera°ne of the praemiss the Pb͞rie, with ane unanimous consent, did condiscend to the forsaid call and desyre of Transporta°ne, and by the tennour heirof doe grant ane act of Transporta°ne, inacting and ordaineing that Mr. Donald M°c͞ra, being so lawfullie called by the congrega°ne of Kintaile, is p͞ntlie in full right and capacitie of Transporta°ne from Urray to Kintaile, without ony impediment or obstacle, and without all reclameing and gainesaying of the Pb͞rie, Ordaineing also that the same be put in execu°ne with all convenient diligence. And yrefoire ordaines ane edict to be served for that effect at the Kirk of Kintaile, that none pretend ignorance, appoynteing Mr. Allex͞r M°Kenzie, Minister at Lochcarron, to preach at the Kirk of Kintaile, and sie the said edict returned and indorsed within a moneth.

---

[1] This and the next minute not engrossed according to the order of their dates.
[2] Should be Farquhar.

At Dingwell, 24 *Junij* 1656.

Notwithstanding of the Act of Pbṝie 14 feb. 1656, anent Mr. Do^d M^{c}cra his transporta°ne to Kintaile, and the edict giwen and served according to that act, zit wppon certane scruples and emergent difficulties, the full settilment of the transporta°ne and admissioune according to the forsaid act and edict being hidderto delayed, The desyre of the congregatioune off Kintaile was this day renued by thair commissioner, earnestlie seeking the executioune of the presbiteroes former act and ordenance, and to y^t purpose wes pṝnted to the Pbṝie a letter from Mr. ferq^{re} M^{c}cra, Minister at Kintaile, nowe adged and infirme, proporting his willingnes and earnest desyre to accept Mr. Donald M^{c}cra as a fellow-laborer and conjunct actuall minister with him in the charge and functioune of the ministerie at Kintaile, Thairefoire the Pbṝie be the tennour heireof doe renue and ratifie the former act, and further consents and condiscends to Mr. ferq^{re}'^{s} desyre, that is, that he and Mr. Dond. M^{c}cra be actuall conjunct ministers at Kintaile, both haveing interest and right to office and benefice (except in so farr as for the pṝte mantenance they may mutuallie condiscend in a proportionable way) so that the longest liver of them is and remaines actuall minister of Kintaile, and further it is ordained that ane act of presentatione and admissione heirwppon be drawin wp in name and favors of Mr. Do^d M^{c}cra to the forsaid office and benefice, without prejudice to Mr. ferq^{re} his pṝte or future ryght, if be providence he sall survive the said Mr Donald; but that efter his death, if the said Mr. Do^d survive, this pṝte act of presenta°ne and admissione followeing thairwpon salbe sufficient wnto him for his due ryght to the office and benefice forsaid, dureing all the dayis of his lyfe, without all oppositione or gainesaying in the contrarie, excepting only the Pbṝies liberties at his desyre to renue the samyne. And finallie it is ordained, that the said act of admissioune and pnta°ne be drawin wp in the tennour forsaid and sub^{vit} be the clerk. Also it is appoynted that Mr. Allex^r McKenzie goe to the Kirk of Kintaile and admitt the said Mr. Donald according to the ordinarie solemnitie, and by delyuering to him the act of admissioune and letter of pnta°ne wppon ye tuentieth day of Julij nixtocome, or at leist immediatelie wpon the nixt lords day yreafter.

'To all and sundrie quhom it may concerne, Be it knowen that for as much as wnto ws, Moderator and remanent members of the pbrie of Dingwell, thair hes bene presented ane earnest desyre and formall call from y⁰ congregatione of Kintaile with the express consent of Mr. ferq^{ro} M^{c}cra, p͠nte minister of Kintaile, nowe adged and infirme, that we wald grant ane act of Transporta°ne in favors of Mr. Donald M^{c}cra, minister at Wrray, to be thair p͠nte actuall minister, or at leist conjunct minister with the forsaid Mr. ferq^{re} nowe adged and infirme, and that the forsaid call and desyre, efter long and mature delibera°ne, hath bene found be ws relevand, necessarie, and expedient, Thairfoire we haue granted and assented to the forsaid call and desyre, and made ane authentick act of transporta°ne for the finall and full accomplisheing and satisfieing of the samyne, as the said act at more length proports; And furthermore we, as wndoubted patrones by Act of Parliament of the forsaid Kirk of Kintaile, doe by the tennour heirof lawfullie present and actuallie admitt the abovenamed Mr. Donald M^{c}cra to the functioune of the ministerie at Kintaile, and to the benefice thaireof, and to the fruits, rents, parsonage, wicarage, profites, provents, emoluments, and casualties, and all wther deuties belonginge or that may belong thairwnto; and to the manse, gleib, and kirklands of the samyne, and all priviledges and liberties belonging yrwnto, or that by lawe may belong thairwnto, Giveing for this effect our full po^r to Mr. Allex^r McKenzie, Minister of Lochcarron, to pass to the Kirk of Kintaile wpon the tuentieth day of Julij in this instant zeire of God 1656 zeires, and thair to enter and admitt the said Mr. Donald M^{c}cra into the office of the ministerie at Kintaile, and benefice belonging thairto, and to all that belong or be law may belong thairwnto, he investing him thairwnto by the ordinarie rites and solemnities, and by delyuering wnto him this our present act of admissione and letter of presenta°ne, Provydeing alwayis that this act of admissione and letter of presenta°ne be conceaved as to a conjunct ministrie with Mr. ferq^{ro} M^{c}cra, and without all prejudice to the said Mr. ferq^{ro} his p͠nte and future ryght to the forsaid office and benefice incace by providence he survive the said Mr. Donald, but that the longest liuer of the tua is and remaines actuall minister of Kintaile, with full and just ryght and title to the office and benefice, and that if the said Mr. Donald sall by providence suruive the said Mr. ferq^{ro}, Then and in that case this present act of admissioune and letter of presentatioune salbe sufficient wnto him for his due ryght to the said office and benefice, and to all things belonging or that lawfullie may belong thairwnto, for all the dayes of his lyfe, without all oppo⁻ᵒⁿᵉ, exceptioune, or gainesaying in the contrarie, excepting only the pbr̄ies libertie to renue this letter of presentaᵒne simplie in his owne name. Wherefoire we humblie require the honoˡ Judges and commissioners for ministraᵒne of Justice in this natioune, wppon sight of this our Act of admissioune and letter of presentaᵒne, to interpone thaire poʳ and Judiciall decreit wppon a simple charge of ten dayes allennarely,¹ for causeing the said Mr. Donald, his factors and serwants in his name, be thankfullie ansered, obeyed, and payed of all and sundrie fruits, rents, tenthes, and emoluments belonging or that may belong by lawe wnto the benefice of the forsaide ministerie of Kintaile, and that of this instant cropt and zeire of God 1656, and zeirely and termely in tyme cumming dureing his lyfetime and seruice at the said Kirk, conforme to his pr̄īte admissioune yreunto, and the collaᵒne and institutioune to be granted and takin thairewppon in competent forme as effeires. Giwen in our pbr̄ie at Dingwell, and appoynted to be subᵘⁱᵗ in name of the Pbr̄ie, 24 Junij 1656, by Mr. Donald Ross, Clerk to the said pbr̄ie.

Sic subscribitur,
MR. DONALD ROSS, minister at
Contane, Cke. Pbrij.

Dingwell, Sept. 23, 1656.

The said day Mr. Murdo McKenzie, sometyme minister at Suddie, gawe in a supplicatioune for the oppening of his mouth, and proposed some abstractiounes qlk he asserted was the cause he supplicated not soonere, wntill thease wer removed, and the brethren taking the same to thair consideraᵒune, and finding that by thease abstractiounes he meaned the miscariage that was alledged of him in Tayne by demneing and drinking, and that all that he produced for his vindicaᵒune from it wes a testimoniall from David Ross in Tayne, in quhose house he was that night, thought not the said testimoniall a sufficient vindicatioune, in respect it was bot in a priuate manner, and from a partic coincident in the samyne guilt, and becaus it seemed to reflexe wpon the Sessioune of Tayne, quho did putt to censoure thease quho wer less guiltie, as they thought.

Johne Mᶜfinlay vᶜ chenich, adulterer with a sojours wyf

---
¹ Only.

within the parochin of Kilmorack, referres him to the Sessioune thaireof to give obedience.

Neile Munro of findoune, desyreing a minister to keepe Sessioune at Wrquhart with them the lords day come aucht dayis, appoynts Mr. Johne Munro to keepe the said day in obedience to his desyre.

Dingwell, 15 Octob. 1656.

The said day Mr. Murdo McKenzie in Knockbaxter presented ane wy^r testimoniall wnder Mr. Johne Dallass hand, qlk the presbiterie conceaved not evident, and apprehended it could not be receaved better then befoire the provinciall. To qlk it is referred.

Mr. Jo^n Munro declares that in obedience to the former ordenance he went to the Church of Urquhart and did heare Mr. David Monro, expectant, preach 5 Oct. 1656.

The Brethren haueing receaved ane letter from Mr. Allex^r McKenzie, minister at Lochcarron, purporting his infirmitie, Referres ane anser to his owin cumming to the cuntrey.

In respect that none of the hyland ministers compeired not conforme to the ordenance of the presbiterie, referres thair sensoure to the province.

The sacrificers within the parochin of Lochcarron and within the land of Auchnasellach, being all alwfullie sumond be the Kirk officer of Lochcarron, conforme to the ordenance of the pbr̃ie, called, compeired not, ordaines literall Summonds to [be] sent to them be pbr̃ie, with the Kirk officer of Lochcarron, to compeire at Chanr̃ie the last tuysday of Octob, befoire the Synode of Ross, and that ane letter be wrytin to the guidman of Culcowie, within quhose lands they are in, to Interpone his authoritie in making thease Idolatrous people repaire to the Synode according to the ordenance of the brethren. And that ane wther letter be wrytin to Mr. Colline McKenzie, minister at Killernan, to sollist Culcowie to giue his assistance in the premiss.

Ordaines ane letter to be wrytin at desyre of the Commissioners of Wrquhart to Mr. W^m fraser, minister at Inverness, to repaire to the Kirk of Urquhart, and to preach on ane lords day, that the people may heire him.

Ordaines such brethren as hes not payit thair proportiounc to Robert Monro, Burser, to pay the samyne with all conveniencie as they salbe anserable to the Synode.

The brethren being severallie reproved, tryed, and examined, wer weile reported in lyf and doctrine.

At Dingll, 18 Nor. 1656.

Mr. Joⁿ Makillican having represented to the brethren the insufficiencie of the pñt Gleib appointed for the M^r at Fottertie, wch being pondered, it was ordained that ane edict sould be served the next ensueing Lords day that tymous warning might be giwen and parties c'cerned of the Brethren's Intentione to designe a sufficient and compleit Gleib for the vse of the pñt M^r and his successors, this day 20 dayes, being the 9 of Dec^r.

Att Dingll, Der. 9, 1656.

The Mod^r haveing inquired qt dilligence had been vsed in reference to the former ordinance annent the serving of ane edict annent the designa°ne of a Gleib at Fottertie, The said edict was found to be duly served and indorsit, execu°ne's y^{re}of being pñted, the pñt day being apointed for the designa°ne, and finding no appearance of any oppositione, haveing lykwayes the adwise of Sir George McKenzie of Tarbat, heritor of the gleib to be designed, and consent of James M^cdod [Macdonald] pñt possessor, they resolved to goe about the business, which efter prayer they did effectuallie, goeing to the place appointed of ther orderlie walking, and legall steps and [¹] descriptione lykwayes of the Gleib and its marches.

Dingwell, Penult Decr. 1656.

The said day Mr. John Monro made report of his obtempering the pbries desyre by preaching and keeping Sess. at Vrqht the day appointed, the result yrof was ane letter sent to Mr. W^m fraser intreating to exercise them whither he conceived he might fastly loused from his pñt charge, hovever this might have been [¹] to be ane formall progress in calling a M^r to that place, yet it was thought expedient to wait for ye result of ye forsaid dilligence.

---

¹ Ink faded.

That day was pñted a supplica°ne in name of Jo{^{n}} Mackra, student in humanitie, for a part of y{^{e}} wacand stipend of Wrray, to his better mentenance at the Pbrie Schooles. The supplicant was referred to obtaine the heritors consent, wch being pñted, the petitioune vas to be considered.

Att Fottartie, March 25, 1657.

The said day the Brethren, Masters Johne Munro, Johne M{^{c}}cra, Don{^{d}} Fraser, Johne M{^{c}}Kilican, Don{^{d}} Ross, Thomas Hog, being met together prayer was made.

There had beene no exercise becaus the time was conceived short enough for goeing about intimelie the executione of there intentioune at yt time, to witt, the designa°ne of a Glebe. Mr. Johne M{^{c}}ra presented a supplicatione in name of Johne M{^{c}}cra. The Brethren referred anie anser till Mr. Donald M{^{c}}ra suld be present in person, when, with consent of the heretours, they ar to grant his petitioune as sallbe thought expedient.

That day Johne Munro of Limlaire reneued his petitioune in behalfe of Christiane Munro, relict to the late deceist Mr. George Munro, and anser was continued till the full number of hands of the heritours concerned should be at the condescendence, which being presented lacked many subscriptiones mainlie requisite; Thereafter the Brethren having ane intentione to goe about the designatione, which was done warrantablie thereafter according to the law of the natione and practice of the Church in such cases, as the designatione subscrived by the Brethren's hand, containing the bounds and marches thereof, can evidence. The nixt dyett being appointed to be at Ding{^{ll}}.

At Dinguall, June 2, 1657.

Mr. Johne Munro, upon certain consideratones mouing him, amongst others the incompletione of his present provisions, intreated the Brethren for ane Act of Transportabilitie.

Some of the brethren informing the meeting that there wer specious grounds to hope the occasione of his motione might be remoued, ane anser was continued till the nixt meeting.

That day Christiane Munros supplicatione was reneued, together with the consents of the heritours represented, and her desyre granted therin, and withall the Brethren being privie to and having compassione on the supplicants low conditione, and considering how of the s^d stipend of fiftie sex appointed to be disposed of in anser to the supplicatione forsaid, that some part was alloted to Mr. Murdoich McKenzie, they conceiued it there duetie in charitie that the part alloted to Mr. Murdoich being as yet onuptaken, should contineue with her, and for satisfactione to the s^d Mr. Murdoich, that, with the consent of the heretours, Farburns proportione of the yeire fiftie seven be added to Couls out of 56, q^{ch} make an 100 merks, of yis Couls proportione, being 26 merks, is all q^{ch} is excepted of the stipend 56 indisponed of to ye s^d relict.

The Commissioners from Wrq^{rt} appearing by there applicatione to the Presr̃ie, did seeme to passe from there applicatione, and prest concurrence of the Presr̃ie as formerlie.

The Brethren, taking there desire to consideratione, found ane impediment then q^{ch} appeared not formerlie, which occasioned yet more a retreiting from progress in y^t business, for one of y^r number gave in some scruples as reasones of his dissent against the sending a Commissionere from the Presbr̃ie, and protested for libertie to add as convenientlie he might and conceived duetie thereafter.

1. Of these were given in the s^d day tuo following, first—private correspondence and condescendence of the s^d Mr. William[1] with the parochiners by letter and promise, possiblie before the presbr̃ies call was obtained, and so preposterous, before the ordinarie way of learning the Lords mind was known.

2. The said Mr. William his professing of ane intention willfullie to desert the parochin q^{r}in he is for the time, notwithstanding of all satisfactione offered by them to him, especiallie his present dispositione being compared with his severall transplantationes before, in some of which, (as is supposed) his way was neither orderlie nor himself patient therin. These being pondered, and y^t others were promised, the Brethren conceived it duetie not to proceed untill the nixt Presbyteric day, when the member informer is required to haue in readinesse all the known exceptions he hath, ore then they

---

[1] Mr. William Fraser. See Minute of 15th October 1656.

not to be relevant for obstructing the progresse of the fors^d businesse after.

Mr. Murdoich McKenzie requireing a testificatt, receiued no anser untill the nixt meeting, appointed to be this day twentie dayes.

Dinguall, June 23, 1657.

The appointment anent burials in Kirks is reported by the brethren to be obtempered.

That day compeared Commissioners from Wrq^{rt}, with ane letter from Mr. William Fraser, q^rin (as it appeared) hauing perused them, he alleadged the reasons were aspersions and detractiones and calumnies, wishing the brother to disoun them, otherwayes he would studie his own reparatione, which the brother refused, apprehending it duetie not to disown that which he conceived to be truth, which the brethren signified in ther returne to him by a letter qrin they desired him to doe as he thought expedient.

That day the brother fors^d gaue in some other additionall reasons, first the sinnfullnesse of emptieing Invernes (in case Mr. William be a qualified man) of a Minister, together with the disadvantadge may be sustained by transporting of such a man (it being as is supposed) not onlie out of such ane eminent place of itselfe, but where there is comonlie repairing and residing a confluence of strangers and intelligent countrey gentlemen.

2. Secondlie, the disconformitie of y^t transplantatione with severall acts of assem.

3. 3^dlie. The nonharmonious concurrence of the parochiners to that transplantatione, in that severalls of note and qualitie concerned in the place being strangers to and dissenting from the calling of the s^d Mr. Will.

4. 4^{lie}, the said Mr. Will was observant of keeping presbyteriall meetings while he was in this province before, tegether with the dissatisfactione he gave to the samen, and especiallie to the presbrie of Chanrie (as may be seen in retentes qⁿ he transplanted himselfe to Invernes.)

It was judged requisite that the Presrie sould be satisfied, and these exceptions discussed ; And it was apprehended yt uthers more weightie might be after added, as should be found expedient, therefore as yet they proceeded not in that business.

A testimonie was giuen to Mr. Murdoich McKenzie, as no known cleare guilt was to be layed to his charge discovered to the presbrie.

At Dingwell, Jul. 28. 1657.

That day the Brethren ordinarlie conveening were mett, except the clerke, whose excuse of his infirmitie was sent. The Moderator not coming preciselie at teun o'clocke, tho shortlie efter, the rest of the brethren for the most part would not stay anie longer then the peremptorie houre appointed.

The nixt meeting they resolved should hold that day fourthnight.

At Dingwall, Aug. 11, 1657.

That day a letter was appointed to be wreittin from the Presrie to Mr. Donald Ross to direct it to the Highland ministers, relateing to there negligence in obtempering the act of the Synod anent there monthlie meeting at Kainlochew, and there corresponding with the Presbrie.

At Dinguall, Septemb. 1, 1657.

That day Mr. George Munro, Minister at Rosemarkine, presented a letter from the Presbrie of Chanrie anent the transporting of Mr. Johne Munro, minister at Alnes, to the Kirk of Killicuddin, some gentlemen being present from the fors^d parochine for that effect.

But the brethren considering that after inquirie these gentlemen had no commissione, and some of the brethren being absent, continued the anser to the next dyett.

In the meanetyme Mr. John M^{c}ra was appointed to returne ane anser to the Presbyterie of Chanrie's letter, with Mr. George Munro fors^d.

There was ane appointment y^t day that the brethren of the Highlands sould be acquented againe to repaire to the presrie according to the act of Synod, to exercise and concurr with y^r brethren as sall be required and injoined.

That day the brethren considering how Mr. Donald Ross had severall times regrated, and as yet did, the bad incouragement he had in the parochine of Conton, by reason y^t he was not at all duelie satisfied of y^t small provisione which he had in the place, as also of the peoples want of accommoda°ne, by reason of wantinge bridges vpon the waters, and dasks in the church to sit.

The nixt dyet was appoynted to be at Conton y^t day twentie dayes, to comone with the parochiners in the fors^d particulars, and Mr. Donald Ross was appointed to make intima°ne to them and the people for there convoca°ne to the s^d day, q^n Mr. Johne McKilican was appointed to preach, and in case of his necessarie abstractione, which he feared, Mr. Johne Munro was appointed to be advertised tymeouslie to undergoe y^t dutie.

[No meeting at Contin on 23 Sept. as some of the heritors from home.]

At Conton, Octob. 6, 1657.

That day these concerned in the parochine of Conton, as Coul and some others, being present, who being inquired of anent the discouragement of their minister, by reasone of unsatisfactorie deliverie of his provisione, made it evidentlie appeare y^t the blame should be transferred wpon Mr. Don^d Ross, whose remissnesse and unfittnesse to take ane effectual course for uplifting the samen onlie occasioned ane ondutifullnesse to him, and likewayes promised to be assisting to him to make his due provisione forthcuming. As for anie disadvantage ore hinderance the people might haue by want of bridges and seats in the church [Minute stops here, being incomplete].

At Dingwall, Octob. 20, 1657.

That day conveined all the brethren ordinarie conveeners, except Mr. Tho. Hog.

Prayer was made. The reasone of Mr. Thomas Hog his absence was his waitting my Lo. Seafort, who representing the Parochine of Urray in calling of Mr. Geo. Cuming, then at Elgine, had gone from Invernes thitherwards, but upon the 16 of the instant month, and upon supplica°ne to the Presbr̄ie for one of there number [Record destroyed].

The s^d day compeared Mr. Coline McKenzie, desiring the transplantatione of Mr. Johne Munro to the Kirk of Kilcuddin.

Likwayes Mr. Johne Munro required ane anser to ane petitione formerlie given in by him anent his transplantabilitie.

In the meantime compeared also F[   ] and George Munro, in Alness, Commissioners from the parochine therof, for retentione of the s^d Mr. Johne with his present charge, and to imped the intended transplantatione.

Thereafter compeared from the parochine of Kilcuddin, Ardullie, Kinbeachie, and Charles M^cleane, commissioners, pressing the transplantatione of the s^d Mr. Johne.

The Presr̄ie, after solid consideratione, hauing heard both parties, Judgeing it requisit, ordained ane edict to be served at the Church of Alnes the nixt Lords day, intimating the desire and diligence of the parochiners of Kilcuddin to have the s^d Mr. Johne transplanted from Alnes and settled with themselves, that in case the parochiners of Alnes haue anie laūfull objectiones against the progresse of the s^d businesse they may haue seasonable advertisement to give in ther reasons the nixt pbr̄ie day, being the tent of Novēm., with certifica°ne to them if they faill to doe as s^d is the Presbr̄ie sall proceed in the due and orderlie steps as is requisit in such cases.

As also Mr. Johne Munro desired y^t ane act of transplantabilitie might be insert in the Edict, which was agreed.

That day the brethren present being severallie removed and tryed, Mr. Donald Ross was exhorted to be painfull and diligent in wisiting and examining the people.

Mr. Johne McKillican to indevour to pray in the Irishe language, and to own a portione of Strachonin for a part of his parochine, which he profest he could not condescend on, not knowing the samen to be annexed to the parochine of Fottartie at his entrie to the ministrie. This matter was referred to the consideratione of the Synod at Chanrie Oct. 27.

The rest of the Brethren exhorted to be painfull and diligent.

Dinguel, November 10, 1657.

It pleased the Brethren to choose and constit y^t Mr. Thomas Hogge be Moderator of the Presbyterie, and Mr. John McKillican clark.

The execution of the edict served at Alnes relative to Mr. John Monros transportabilitie was returned to the Presbytrie.

The Laird of foulis, zounger, and the goodman of Assin, Commissioners from the parochin of Alnes, compeared, and intreated no act shuld be givin that day for declairing ther minister transportable, But that the Presbytrie shuld be pleased to appoint ther nixt days meeting to be at Alnes, wher they engaged in the names of the rest, that rational satisfaction shuld be given for the pleasant commodious settling of Mr. John amongst them, else they suld woluntarlie condescend to his transporta°n.

The Commissioners beeing removed, the presbytrie considered ye mater, and thought it convenient the desir shuld be granted, wherfor the nixt days meeting was appointed to be Alnes.

Rorie McKenzie of Davauchmaluack, and the Goodman of Farbourn, younger, Commissioners from the Parochin of Urray, compeared and requested the Presbyteries concurrence for calling of Mr. Georg Cuming to enter on such parts of his qualifica°ns befor them as was requisit, that with al possible diligence he might be planted actual minister among them.

Those gentlemen being removed the Brethren thought fit to appoint Mr. John McKillican to go alongs with them whenever they pleased.

Alnes, November 24, 1657.

The heritors, gentlemen, and parochiners of Alnes compeared befor the Presbytrie, and after some debats and reasonings ther was ane harmonious condescendens for Mr. John Monros accommodation at that place, and not onlie for him but also for his successors after him serveing ther.

Neil Monro of Findon, and some other gentlemen, commissioners from Wrquhart, compeared, and intreated one suld be given them to preach the nixt Lords day that a call might be dravin vp for Mr. Robert Rosse—the Brethren, taking this to consideration, appointed Mr. John McKillican to preach at Wrquhart the nixt day.

The Brethren inquired what diligence was used in the matter of Urray, the Commissioner reported if the people and presbytrie were striving and serious that Mr. Georg Cuming might be engaged and gained.

Dinguel, December 15, 1657.

Noe exercise this day because of the exerciser's (Mr. John Munro) bodilie infirmitie and weaknes.

No addition, because the adder, Mr. Donald Rosse, was not prepared, for which the Brethren thought fit to give him an admoniti^{o}n be way of reproofe.

There was ane heavie and a sad regrait made by Mr. Farquhar M^{c}ra of Kintail in a letter sent to the Presby, upon the wnnatural, wnchristian, and unministerial carriag of his sone Mr. Donald, in depriveing him of his livelehood by wnjust, obscure, and wnlawful ways, as his letter doth more fullie declair; the Brethren, seriouslie considreing the matter, ordained a letter (containeing a somance) shuld be written to Mr. Donald for presenting himself the nixt day befor the presbitrie.

The Brethren inquired what was doen at Urquhart, the report was that ye parochiners wnanimouslie subscrived a Cal for Mr. Robert Rosse, and besought the Presbytrie, because none of them culd be present, to appoint on of ther number with a cal to goe alongs with ther commissioners on such a day [   ] to invite him. The Brethren appointed Mr. John McKillican to goe with the cal for Mr. Robert.

Dinguel, 29 *December* 1657.

Mr. Donald Rosse added, and the brethren was much dissatisfied with his method, matter, and weaknes, and desyred he should be reprehended with a premonire.

Mr. George M^{c}uloch is to add.

Mr. Donald M^{c}ra was this day present in presby; and the Mod^r inquired what was the reason of his cruell and wnhumane dealing with his father, his replie was y^t he had as great reason if not mor to complaine on his father, but for the tyme he would forbear reflex^{o}n and recrimination, onlie he desired to have two of the Brethren to whom he would communicat his mind in privat—which was granted him.

These brethren (when returned) culd not learn by what he informed the certaine ground of the controversie, but suspected ther was foul play among them, and therfor the presbytrie thought it necessarie a visitation shuld be at Kintail, haveing the concurrence and assistance of the Sinod alongs with them, and in the meantyme ordained that Mr. Don^d shuld restore his livelehood to his father againe, especiallie the wiccarage, which Mr. Do^d promised to performe.

Dinguel, Jan. 19, 1658.[1]

Mr. Thomas Hogg, Mod^r.
Mr. Georg M^{c}uloch exercised vpon Acts 7. 35, and
Mr. George Cuming added—the Brethren were weil satisfied with both, and desired the Mod^r to encourage them.

Mr. Georg Cuming is to exercise the nixt day; and Mr. John M^{c}cra is appointed to add because he was spared the last day for his bodilie infirmitie. But Mr. John began to controle the presbitries apointment, and entred in a needlesse strife, and becam untractable, and would not by ani fair means or entreatie wndertak his duetie. Wherfore the Presbytrie was forced to remove him, and when the thoughts of all the Brethren round about were inquired (he being removed) of his carriage, all thought he greatlie miscaried, and deservd a sharpe censure. Mr. John beeing called for, the Mod^r signified the Presb. mind to him, and rebuked him for his litigiousnes, needlese contention, and wntractablenesse. But he remaneing and insisting in his former stubbournesse and wilfulnes, would not accept of, nor wndergoe the censur, But declaired by way of protesta^{o}n ag^t it, and desired his declara^{o}n (as he tearmed it) to be insert. The Brethren though it necessar that no such thing shuld be insert in ther scroles wntil he gauc it in writ wnder his ovn hand, and gaue him continuation to the nixt day, at which tym he promised to present it.

Ther was a letter directed to the presby. from the Erle of Seafort intreating the accelera^{o}n of Mr. Georg Cumming his trials, that with al diligence he might be admitted actuall minister at Urray; Which desir was grantd.

Mr. George M^{c}culloch is appointed to haue a common head wpon Universal redemption, and to give his theses the nixt day.

Februar 15, 1658.[2]

[The Mod^r and remanent Brethren present.]
Mr. Georg Cuming exercised on Acts 7. 37, and was approwin.

---

[1] The portions of this and next Minute through which the lines are drawn are, in the original, deleted in different ink. On the margin are written, in a different hand, the words, 'Shamelesse lying.' The Minutes are written by Mr. John M'Killican.

[2] See footnote to Minute of 19th January 1658.

Mr. John M^ccra added vpon the same words, and the Brethren were not a little dissatisfied with his wearieing tediousnes, misapplica°n of scripture, want of edifica^tion in severall farr off sought passages savouring of much bitternes and disaffection, and for something that the Brethren judged wnsound, viz. that the mane and principal qualifica°n of a minister as such was knovledg. For these things the brethren desired the Mod^r to give him an admonition.

Mr. Georg Cumming is appointed to haue a disput on the perseverance of the sancts and to hav his thesee in readines ag^t the nixt day.

The Mod^r presented an appella°n received from Mr. John M^ccra to the nixt ensueing Provincial, and the Brethren finding it to be extrajudicial (no word being of it the day before) unecessar, and unexpedient, dealt with Mr. John, both in privat and publick, to tak up his paper, but he would not, But gave in a second paper, how to tearm it we knew not, but he called it himselfe a supplica°n for inserting his appella°n, and for receaveing an extract of a processe wnder the clark's hand. The Brethren finding his deportment unbeseeming a supplicant, and much mor a minister of the Gospel that desired to live in peace with his brethren, Judged it convenient no anser shuld be givin him til the Sinod; and that the authentick papers shuld be onlie keept (without trans^riveing them) to the provincial.

Februar. 23, 1658.

The Brethren ordained Mr. Do^d Rosse to writ a letter to the high-land Ministers to inquire why ye Sinods ordinance was neglected.

March 2, 1658.

Rorie McKenzie of Tollie, beeing referred from the session of Dinguel to the presbyterie for drunkenesse, but the fact culd not be judicial provin; wherefor the Mod^r in the nam of the presbyterie exhorted the supposed delinquent that he shuld watch ag^t that evil, and seek the lord to guard him ag^t that tempta°n.

March 9, 1658.

Mr. John McKillican sought the Brethrens advise, what shuld be doen with a young man falling in incest and not coming to the years of discretion. The finding the matter difficult referred it to the Sinod.

Mr. George Cuming is to preach in Irish the next day.

March 16, 1658.

The Brethren ordained Mr. John McKillican to drav vp an edict to be served at Urray by Mr. Rosse the nixt Lords day in relation to Mr. Cumings planta°n.

Mr. George M^cculoch is licensed to preach publicklie when and whereever he is lawfullie called.

Coul McKenzie and Garloch, Commissioners from Urq^{rt}, compeired, and intreated the Presbyterie shuld goe alongis with them to invit Mr. Fraser of Invernes to be ther minister. The anser is referred to the nixt day.

Mr. George Cuming is to be admitted to the Church of Urray on the last day of March.

March, Penult., 1658.

The Commissioners of Urquhart compeired and desired to know why the presbyterie did not concurr willinglie and cordialie with them in calling Mr. Wm Fraser, and the Brethren told they had some exceptiones ag^t it, and desired that the Mod^r shuld deliver these exceptiones to Coul McKenzie, who was on of the Commissioners.

On of the Brethren inquired of Coul if he had ani assurance of Mr. W^m, and he told that Mr. W^m promised to com.

The Master of Lovat and young Furbourn, with others of the parochin of Urray, compeared and desyred the Presbytrie shuld not proceed in Mr. Cumings plantation till they shuld have a hearing of his Erish. The Presbyterie offered a hearing to them on the morrow, But this would not please their fancie wnlesse they shuld hear him on a Lords day. The Brethren conceiving that their drift was rather to hinder his admission then to receive ani satisfaction of his qualifica°ns, they granted their demand to shonne contention, and so Mr. George's admission was prorogated.

The Presb.' resolved to go on *cum periculo* with Mr. Cumings admission on the 13 of April, after his preaching at Urray. But Mr. John M^{c}cra stickled ag^t the resolution, and becam pertenacious and werre loquacious, that some of the Brethren wer forced to say y^t that part of the ministrie was bitternes to them, and wished a destruction of the presbi. and to be anext to other preb.[1]

Urray, April 13, 1658.

Al the Brethren, except Mr. Thomas hogg and Mr. John M^{c}cra, conveened, and desired the lords presence by prayer.

After sermon preached by Mr. John Munro,

Mr. George Cuming was admitted without anie let or protesta°n, and receaved by al concerned in the parochin of Urray who were present.

Coul McKenzie and others of the Parochiners of Urqhart compeired and professed they would no further prosecut their calling of Mr. Fraser to be their minister, but the presbytrie would be pleased to send on of their number to preach to them the nixt lords day. It pleased the Brethren to appoint Mr. John McKillican to preach at Urquhart.

[At the end of the Minute of 13th April 1658, which also closes the volume, is written by the hand which wrote the marginal remarks on the previous Minutes:—'Maister Johne Macgillican was clk. to thir lying Records.' No further Minutes are recorded until 1663—after the Restoration, and the establishment of Episcopacy.]

---

[1] The portion deleted is so deleted in the original. On the margin is written, 'The spirit of lieing and malice.'

At Dinguall, May 19, 1663.[1]

The brethren of the Presbyterie haveing at the last synod appoynted this day to be the first dyet of their meitings, conveened all, except Mr. Robt Ross, who sent ane ltre of excuse.

At Dinguall, 9 *June* 1663.

Mr. John Mackenzie signifieing to the prebr̃ie that he wanted accomoda°n for residence at his chairge, the prebr̃ie appoints Mr. Donald Fraser, Moderator, to writ to Mr. John MacKillican[2] to make the house q^{r}in he dwelled readd for Mr. John Mackenzie against Lamb-messe.

At Ding. 1663, *upon Julie* 21.

A meiting of the chapter haveing avocated the brethren from keeping the day appointed, this day conveened Mrs John Macra, Mod^r, John McKenzie, Do^d fraser, Robt Rosse, George Cumine, Donald Rosse.

Master John Macra, Schoolm^r of Dinguall, is constitute Clerk to the Prebr̃ie.

In reference to the ordainance of the prebr̃ie anent writing to Mr. John McKillican to give assurance to Mr. John McKenzie whither he would quit the hous of Inchrorie to Mr. John Mackenzie at Lamb-masse, Mr. Don^d Rosse to whom the lr̃e directed to Mr. MacKillican wes delyvered, reports he sent to him with William Miller, and hearing that the lr̃e miscaried he

---

[1] This Minute, which is the first of a new volume, is also the first under the Episcopacy established by Charles II.

[2] Mr. MacKillican, Minister of Fodderty, refused to conform to Episcopacy, and was deposed in May 1663 for 'absenting himself from the Diocesan meeting, not answering the citation, and preaching, praying, and reasoning against prelatical government.' Along with Mr. Thomas Hogg, of Kiltearn, who had also been deposed for his opposition to Episcopacy, he continued for years to hold conventicles in Easter Ross. They both consequently suffered fines, and imprisonment in various prisons, including the Bass. Mr. John MacKenzie was Mr. MacKillican's successor in Fodderty.

went himselfe personallie to Mr. MacKillican and made knowen to him the prïe's desyre requiring ane answere, whose answere wes, that he received not their lře to q^ch tyme he would delay his answere; which the Prebřie finding to be bot a shift, especiallie considering that MacKillican himselfe begged as a favour of Mr. John McKenzie to suffer him to keep the house till Lambmesse; The Mod^r in name of the Prebřie is appointed to writ to the Bishop and Tarbet, shewing the state of things.

A Petition given in be Agnes MacKenzie for divorce from John Dinguall her husband, having fallen in adulterie with anoy^r woman, considered, and the matter being proven be extracts out of the session book of Kilmorack, her Petition is granted, and her condition referred from the Prebřie to the Comiss^rs.

Kathrine, Spous to Donald McAllister in the parioch of Wīq^rt, brought in her appeal to the Prebřie from the Session of Wīq^rt for appointing her to stand two Lords dayes *in sacco* and to mak profession of her rep. [repentance] for asserting that those things that looked lyk sorcerie q^ch were found after she flitted in the hous out of q^ch she flitted were put there be Isobell MacKenzie, spouse to Andrew Fraser, Chamberlane of Ferintosh; And the prebřie considdering the slander and censure, she is remitted to satisfie accordinglie, provyding that if she give sufficient evidence of her rep. the first day, y^t she shal be urged no more.

The Mi^r of Dinguall representing to the Prebřie that he could not get the toūnes men moved to build the kirk yard dyk, both the Baillies ordained to be sumoned to the nixt prebřie.

The Prebřie homologates the act of the session of Dinguall anent the stent they laid upon the parioch for maintenance of the poore within it.

The Prebřie ordaines that the vacand Kirk of Kiltearn and Alnes[1] be served be the bretheren of the prebřie *per vices* so oft as they can, and Mr. Robt Rosse to begin at Kiltern Sunday com eight dayes.

---

[1] Kiltearn was vacant through the deposition of Mr. Thomas Hogg, who refused to conform to Episcopacy. Alness was vacant through the death of Mr. John Monro in 1662.

At Dinguall, 11 *August* 1663.

The Baillies of Dinguall cited, not compeiring, to be sumoned pro 2ᵈᵒ.

Enquirie made if Mr. Robt Rosse obeyed the ordinance anent preaching at Kiltern, it is found that he did; Mr. Donald Fraser ordained to go the nixt day to Kiltern and Mr. George Cumin the sabath following to Alnes.

A letre being sent to Mr. Donald Macra, Miʳ of Lochelshe, complaining on Mr. Rorie MᶜKenzie, Miʳ of Gerloch, for denying him marriage upon the bare alleadgence of a young man, that he had a promise of marriage of the woman—The Modʳ is appointed to writ to Mr. Rorie that he send with all dilligence to the young man to mak out his allegations, or to find surtie to doe so within a convenient tyme, which if he doe not that he goe on in the mariage.

Joⁿ Maconil oig in the Parish of Wrray cohabiting in adulterie with Agnes nic ean chile, and both relapsers in adulterie, being referred to the Prebrie, cited, and not compearing, it is ordained yᵗ the Modʳ writ to Farburn in whose land they reside to cause separet them and satisfie.

At Dinguall, 1 *Septemb.* 1663.

The Baillies of Dinguall cited, compeiring, being enquired why they did not caus build the Kirk yard dyk answered they culd not without consent of yʳ tounes counsel, the result of qᶜʰ yʳanent they promised to bring to the nixt prebrie.

At Dinguall, 22 *Septr.* 1663.

The Baillies of Dinguall cited compeiring gives in the answere of the tounes counsell, viz. That they are content to build the Kirkyard dyk March nixt (considering they could not doe it sooner be reason of the season of the year) upon condition that neither Miʳ nor toune meddle with the grasse of the Kirkyard untill it be desyded whether has best right.

Joⁿ Maconil vic ferqʳ and Marie nien khenich ghlaise, both trelapsers in fornica: being referred from the session of Kilmorack in order to enter yʳ repent: cited and compeiring, confessed, and after exortaᵒne were remitted to the Session to satisfie *in sacco*, and in the meantyme, forasmuch as the woman alleadges a promise of mariage of the man, q^{ch} he deneyes, they are desyred q^n charged to come to the pbr̃ie, and the woman to bring her broy^r alongs, who wes (as she sayes) present q^n that promise wes made to her.

At Dingual, 13 Octob. 1663.

That day conveened Messrs John Macra, Mod^r, Donald Rosse, Donald Fraser, Robt Rosse, George Cumin ; Mr. John Mackenzie absent sent ane lr̃e of excuse q^{ch} wes accepted.

The name of God incalled.

No doctrine be reason of the brethrens late cuming, all except Mr. John Macra, and Mr. Donald Fraser, the doctrine continued as formerlie.

Whereas it wes condescended to, upon a prebr̃ie day be al the bretheren, that everie broy^r cuming late should give in a sex pens to be given to the poore, Mrs Donald Rosse, Robt Rosse, George Cumin, who came behind tyme today being desyred to pay, refused.

Mr. Robt Rosse pretexts that he is willing to pay his 6 ps. provyding the uthers pay theirs.

Mrs John Macra and Donald Fraser declares that they think them censurable who refuses, and doe refer the mater to the Bishop's determina°n.

Mr. Robt Rosse protests that two bretherens opinion be not enough to mak acts without the major part of the prebr̃ie. Mr. John Macra protests that it be q^n the Mod^r with the minor part is right and the major part guiltie.[1]

At Dingual, 3 Novr. 1663.

The Mod^r urged that according to the Bishops ordainance the vacand Kirks of Alnes and Kiltearn should be supplied, but the most of the brethern declyned becaus of the winter season.

Hector Mackenzie, referred from Urray for drunknes and disobedience, to the Session, cited, and not compeiring, to be summond pro 2do.

---

[1] At several meetings before this complaint was made of the 'lateness' of members, and the 'exercise' was, in consequence, repeatedly 'continued.'

Lykwise Finlay Buy referred from the Session of Urray for drunkness and beating of his moy^r, cited, compeiring, and being rebuked, is remitted to the Session to satisfie *in sacco*.

Jon Maconie vic ferq^r and Marie nien khenich ghlaishe, and y^r witnesses viz, Do^d M^{c}eachan and Alex^r MacKenich, ordained to be sumoned to the nixt prebrie, with certifica^{o}n in case the parties compeir not probation shal be laid and the prebrie decern accordinglie.

At Dingual, Nov. 24, 1663.

The bretheren being informed that the parochiners of Kiltern and Alnes exclaimes ag^t them for not supplieing y^r vacancies according to the Bishops desyre, The Prebrie appoints y^t Mr. Robt Rosse preach Sunday come eight dayes at Alnes and Mr. Donald fraser that day 15 dayes at Kiltern, Bot Mr. Donald protesting ag^t y^r appointment, and chooseing ray^r to submitt to censure then to obey, be reason of the winter weather, the greatnes of his owne chairge, and the vast distance of the places, Mr. George Cumine is ordained to goe to Kiltern to preach the s^d day.

It coming to the prebries hearing That Mr. Thomas Hog exercises part of the ministerial function in some families within his late parioch of Kiltern, appoints him to be sumond to the nixt prebrie.[1]

John Maconie vic ferq^r and Marie nien Kenich glaish, with Donald Maceach, and Alex^r Mackenich glaish, witnesses, not compeiring efter citations, except John Maconil vic ferq^r, and the prebrie not being able to say anie thing ag^t him, dimits him.

Hector McKenzie, not compeiring, to be Sum^d pro 3°.

At Dingual, 22 Decr. 1663.

The Mod^r being enquired concerning his diligence in sumonding Mr. Thom. Hog conforme to the former ordainance, answered that he could not get intelligence q^r he wes that he might fix a sumonds on him, and that haveing meat with the deane (q^n he wrat to the Bishop anent him) he desyred him to wait on the Bishops answere.

---

[1] See footnote, p. 301, *supra*.

Hector Mackenzie cited, and not compeiring, the prēbrie ordaines Mr. George Cumin, his Mi^r, to speak Fairburn and the rest of the s^d Hectors friends to deale with as powerfullie as they could.

At Dingual, 12 Jan. 1664.

Mr. George Cumin reports that he spok Hector Mackenzies friends who promised that they should tak some course with him.

The Bretheren ordained to bring the 50 shil. each man for the divinitie burser ag^t the nixt day.

At Dingual, 9 Feb. 1664.

The Bretheren for the most part declynes to pay the burse to Mr. John M^{c}kenzie this yeir, pretending they payed him at once for both this yeir and the last.

The bretheren ordained to bring in money for Doctor Sibats books peremptorilie the nixt day.

At Dingwall, 1 March 1664.

Mr. John Macra, Schoolm^r of Dinguall, ordained to haue a privat tryal before the Prēbrie against the nixt day, text Matt. 11. 28.

At Dinguall, 5 April 1664.

No presbyteriall meiting this day 15 dayes becaus Mr. John Macra, Moderator, and Mr. John Mackenzie, arch-deacon, were both necessarilie withdrawn, the one to Kintaill, the other to Rosse.

No public exercise in reguard the bretheren had much adoe, and also because of a privat tryal q^{ch} Mr. John Macra, younger, had before them, Matt. 11. 28.

Murdo Buy referred from the Session of Urray for disobedience to the Session, cited and compeiring, and finding suretie to satisfie, is remitted.

Hector Mackenzie, referred from the session of Urray for habitual drunknes and unrulines cited and compeiring, confessing nothing, continued till the nixt day.

The nixt meiting of Prēbrie to be appointed at the provincial meiting.

At Dingwal, November 15, 1664.[1]

[Mr. John Macra, Student in divinity, preached *de Judice controversiarum* and was approved. He resigned the Clerkship to the Presbytery, and Mr. John Gordown was appointed Clerk he 'being the youngest Minister.' Mr. John Mackenzie, Archdeacon, absent on account of sickness, and at his request Mr. Don^d Ross appointed to preach at Foderty next Lord's day. Hector Mackenzie not compeiring, was summoned pro 3°.]

At Dingual, Decr. 7, 1664.

[Hector Mackenzie not cited, as his residence uncertain. Mr. George Cumine 'to make search for him and to fasten a sumonds on him compeir against the nixt day.'

Mr. Donald Ross did not preach at Fodderty, having been engaged in Strathconan. His excuse found relevant, and he is ordained to preach at Fodderty next Sunday.]

Dinguall, Decr. 27, 1664.

[Mr. Donald Ross who ought to haue added, absent. His censure continued until he be present.]

'Hector Mackenzie, who wes ordained to be summond to this day pro 3do, wes not summoned because the officer could get no informatione of his residence. Wherefor the Presbyterie ordaines Mr. George Cumine to fasten a Summonds on him q^{r}ever he can be apprehended.

That day the Moderator reports that he had received a letter from the Bishop to be intimated to the Presbyterie, appointing tuo of ther number to be at Chanery the fyft of Januarie next, anent some publick concernment. The Presbyterie taking this to ther consideratione did ordain Mr. Donald Fraser and Mr. John Kordown to be present at the said meeting.

The Bishop did signify in the said letter that he as Patron of the Kirk of Vrq^{rt} had given a presentatione to Mr. Donald Fraser, present incumbent at Kilmorack, to be Minister at Vrq^{rt}, therfor required the Presbyterie to send on of ther number to Vrq^{rt} the first of Ja^{ry} to serve his edict; Wherfor the Presbyterie appoints Mr. George Cumine to be at Vrq^{rt} for that effect.

---

[1] No Minute is recorded between 5th April and 15th November 1664.

The Bishop did signify in the said letter that tuo of ther number should be at Chanry the fyfteenth day of Ja^{rij} next for Mr. Donald Fraser his ordinatione; Therfor the Presbyterie appoints Mr. George Cumine and Mr. Walter Rosse to that effect.

Dingwall, Janry. 24, 1665.

[Both the Moderator and Mr. John McCray, Student in divinity (who was to haue preached a popular sermon) absent, having been called to Chanry by the Earl of Seaforth.]

The said day Mr. Donald Fraser declared that he had excomunicated Donald M^{c}ean vic ean glash in his Parish of Vrq^{rt}; Therfor desyred the Presbyterie in ther respective congregations should intimate the same.

Dingwall, March 4, 1665.

[Mr. Johne M^{c}cra, Student, had a popular sermon on Col. 3. 1. The Presbyterie declared they were satisfied with it.]

The Presbyterie appoints Mr. John Kordoun to give a Testimony to Mr. John McCray, Student in Divinity, to be presented to the Bishop, bearing the Presbyteries approbatione of all the ordinary steps of his tryalls; q^{ch} accordingly wes done.

The said day the Moderator presented a supplicatione in behalf of the distrest men of Portpatrick, some whereof were captives with the Turks, and others of them totaly ruined in fortune. The Presbyterie taking this to their consideratione it wes ordained that they should make intimatione thereof to ther respective people, and to haue ther proportions ready against the next Synod.

That day the Moderator reports that the Bishop appointed him to speak the Presbyterie to use all possible diligence to celebrate the Holy Sacrament of the Lords Supper against the next Synod, q^{ch} they promised to doe.

That day Mr. George Cummine delivered five pounds as his proportione of the money due by him to the Bursar in divinity.

[Hector McKenzie not appearing, Mr. George Cumine ordained to advise with the Bishop what to do concerning him.]

Dingwall, March 28, 1665.

That day Mr. Donald Fraser gave fyve pounds money as the proportione due to the Bursar in divinity from the Session of Vrquhart.

The said day the Brethern being enquired what diligence they had used in providing ther proportione of money due to the Bursar in divinity, they that were deficient promised to haue it in readines against the ensuing Synod.

That day the Moderator produced ane order of his Majesties Secret Councell of Scotland in reference to William McKy, Merchand in Dumbarton, a sufferer under the late vsurpatione and rebellione, recomending him to the charity of the severall parishes of this kingdome.

The Bretheren taking this to ther consideratione, were ordained to make intimatione of the same to the severall congregationes, and to give ane accompt of ther diligence against the ensueing Synod.

Dingwall, April 11, 1665.

That day Mr. Murdoch McKenzie, Min^r at Lochbroome, regrates that he is constrained to leave his Ministry for want of maintenance, and therfor did desyre to be advysed with the Presbyterie what course to take heeranent. The Bretheren taking this to ther consideratione thought fitt to referr the samen to the Bishop and ensuing Synod.

The said day the said Mr. Murdoch regrates that he hes not a convenient meeting place for preaching, the Kirk of Lochbroom being unthatched, the Bretheren did advise him to advise with the Bishop and Synod thereanent.

Dingwall, May 30, 1665.

[Mr. Walter Ross excused his absence from the last meeting (11 April) as he was at the funeral of Balnagown's Brother. Mr. Don^d Ross made the same excuse. The Brethren reported that they had all preached on 29th May.]

That day William M^{c}cleod and Christian nien Alister beg, referred from the session of Foderty to the Presbyterie in reference the said Christian had brought furth a child, alleadging the said William to be the father of it, both compeiring, and being enquired he (as before) denyed the same, the woman adhereing to her former confessione : The Presbyterie, taking this to their serious consideratione, ordained the said William M^ccleod to clear himself of the said scandall by oath befor the congregation.

The said day ane order presented by the Moderator, sent to the Presbyterie from the Bishop, requiring his Majesties proclamatione for a publick fast to be keeped the second Wednesday of June in behalf of the Royal Navy, and for a blessed successe to the intended warr against the United Provinces,[1] to be intimated by the Bretheren to ther severall congregationes the Lord's day preceding the said Wednesday, and which the Bretheren that were present promised to doe.

Dingwall, June 20, 1665.

[The Bretheren reported that they had all kept the fast ordained last meeting.]

The said day Mr. Johne McKenzie, Archdeacon, advysed with the Presbyterie in reference to a woman in his Parish whose husband being caried to Barbados after the battell of Woster, and married ther for certainty, whether the said woman might haue the benefitt of marriage with another man ; The Presbyterie, taking this to ther serious consideratione, ordained the said Mr. John to advyse with the Bishop heeranent.

That day Donald don M^cleich, referred from the sessione of Vrq^{rt} for disobedience and deforceing the officer, sumoned to this day, and compeiring, wes ordained to be imprisoned till he shuld furnish surety to give obedience to the said sessione, and to satisfy discipline for his former disobedience.

Dingwall, July 11, 1665.

The said day the Moderator presented a letter to the Presbyterie from the Bishop, ordaining the Presbyterie to receive Mr. John McKenzie, Student in divinity, to pass his tryalls in reference to the Ministry of Kilmorack. The Presbyterie, taking this to their consideratione, ordained the said Mr. John

---

[1] This, the Dutch War, had actually been declared on 22nd February 1665. The proclamation was evidently issued before the declaration.

to haue the additione against the next day, and Mr. Donald Fraser the exercise. That day Mr. George Cumine being enquired what diligence he had used in advising with the Bishop in reference to Hector McKenzie, declared that he had spoken the Bishop thereanent, who desyred him to get Hector McKenzie his processe with the first convenience, Wherfor the Presbyterie ordains Mr. John Gordown, Clerk, to have it in readiness against the next day.

That day Mr. George Cumine gave fyve pounds money as the proportione of money payable by the Sessione of Urray to the Bursar in divinity for anno 1664.

That day the Moderator presented a Proclamatione from his Majestie commanding a Publick thanksgiving to be kept for the glorious victory obtained by the Royall Navy over the fleet of the United Provinces;[1] The Bretheren taking this to ther consideratione, did ordaine to make intimatione of the samen in ther severall congregationes, and to keep the same.

Dingwall, August 1, 1665.
[Mr. Donald Fraser exercised, and Mr. John McKenzie, Student in divinity, added on Rom. 3, 7, 8. Both approved. Mackenzie ordained to exercise, and Cumine to add, next day. The Clerk delivered Hector Mackenzie's Process to Cumine. The Bretheren declared that the thanskgiving had been kept.]

That day the Moderator presented a letter sent from the Bishop to the Presbyterie, ordaining one of ther number to be sent to Foderty the next Lords day to make intimation to the Heritors and others of the Parish of Foderty of a visitatione of the Church and Parish y^{re}of, that they might be present the said day, being the nynth of August. The Bretheren taking this to ther consideratione, ordains Mr. Donald Rosse to be at Foderty the said day, and to make intimatione therof.

At Foderty, August 9, 1665.
That day conveened with the Bishop all the Presbytery of

---

[1] This victory was won off the coast of Suffolk on 3rd June. The tables were soon turned, and before the end of the war the Dutch fleet sailed up the Thames, destroying shipping and other property ; and 'the roar of foreign guns was heard for the first and last time by the citizens of London.'

Dingwall, the Archdeacon excepted, Messrs James and William McKenzies, Assessors from the Presbyterie of Tain. After preayer, acted as follows:

That day Mr. Jo^n M^ccra preached.

That day Mr. Donald Rosse being enquired if he had preached at Foderty, and instructed the visitatione of the said Church, according to the Bishops and Presbyteries order, declared he had used diligence therin.

That day none of the Heritors, fewars, woodsetters, nor elders compeired, except David Monro, Alex^r Dinguall, Gilbert Beth, Duncan McPhaile, Donald Mathesone, and Donald Tailer, elders.

That day the Minister, Mr. John McKenzie, wes not present, nor no excuse sent from him.

That day the Reverend father the Bishop called for the Session books, the list of penalties, collectiones, Baptismes, and Marriages from the Clerk, who declared that he had all thes, though not to hand.

That day the said Reverend father enquiring whether the Holy Sacrament of the Lords Supper wes celebrated in the said Parish, and whether the people were frequently examined, and if ther wes frequent preaching; To the first it was answered that the sacrament was not given in the said Parish thes twelve yeers bygone: That the people were not wholly examined, But Mr. Roderick McKenzie sone to the said Archdeacon did sometymes preach, and catechise.

The Bishop and his said assessors, taking to ther consideratione how the said meeting wes slighted by the Heretors and gentlemen of the said Parish, notwithstanding the said visitatione wes intimated according to order: It wes concluded that ther should be a meeting for the forsaid effect at Chanry the 30 day of August next, which Mr. Roderick McKenzie was ordained to intimat the next Lords day to the said Heretors and others concerned, with certificatione if they did not compeer, that the Bishop and his said Assessors would proceed according to law, in the Plantatione of the said Church.

Dingwall, Sept. 5, 1665.

The said day the Moderator presented ane order sent from

the Bishop to the Presbyterie, ordaining a day of Publick fast and humiliatione to be keeped in the severall congregationes for the rageing of the plague of pestilence in England, and for preventing it in Scotland, and the said day to be keeped the 13 of Septr next; which the Bretheren taking to ther consideratione promised to do.

Dingwall, Septr 13, 1665.

That day convened with the Moderator none exceptc Mrs Donald Fraser and John Gordown.

After prayer acted as followes:

That day Mr. John McKenzie had ane exigeses *de voluntate Dei*, and disputs thereanent, a questionary tryall, and a tryall in the Greek language, wherein (being removed) he wes approven.

Dingwall, November 21, 1665.

The said day Mr. Walter Rosse reported that Mr. Johne McKillican as yet had not required baptism to his child, twentie dayes and more being expired; Therefore required that the Presbyterie would fasten a summonds on him according to the Bishops and Synods appointment; The Presbyterie taking this to ther consideratione, ordained the Clerk to issue Summonds to that effect, and the said Mr. John to be summoned to the next day pro 2^c.

That day compeered John Monro in the Parish of Alnes, complaining on Helen Fraser in the said Parish of Alnes, that whereas he had been contracted with her and been proclaimed before the Congregatione of Alnes, and that the said Helen had sworn before honest witnesses that she should never do good to any other man so long as he wes alive: Notwithstanding of all this (upon what accompt he knew not) the said Helen hed broken promise to him and violated Church orders, and incurred the failzie usual in such cases; Therfor requested the Presbyterie to take the premises to ther consideratione, and to give him redresse. The Presbyterie, taking this to ther consideratione, thought good to referr the said supplicant to the Sessione of Alnes, to doe in it as they find most convenient, the business being better knowen to them then to the Presbyterie.

That day Mr. John Gordown advysed with the Presbyterie

in reference to a woman in the Parish of Kilterne called Janet Nienan, whose husband hes bein abroad these fyfteen yeers and upward, and married abroad which hes been certified by severalls that have come from Barbados wher the said person is, whether the said woman (having caried herself civily free of Church censure during the said tyme) may haue the benefit of marriage with another man: The Presbyterie taking this to ther serious consideratione ordained the said Mr. Johne to advise with the Bishop thereanent.

Dingwall, Janij 2, 1666.

[Mr. Donald Rosse rebuked as he was not prepared to add.]

That day Mr. Walter Rosse reports that he had caused Summond Mr. John McKillican for not requiring baptism to his child according to the Presbyteries order, who declared that he had receiued the benefitt of baptism already to his child from Mr. Andrew Monro, Minister at Thursay in Caitnes: The said Mr. John being cited and not compeiring Mr. Walter is ordained by the Presbyterie to advise with the Bishop theranent.

Dingwall, Janij. 23, 1666.

That day Mr. Donald Rosse had a common head, *De notis ecclesiae*, who being removed, the Moderator enquiring the Bretherns Judgement anent what Mr. Donald Rosse had delivered upon the said subject, Judged him to have been very confused, and ordained him to mend it.

Dingwall, Feb. 11, 1666.

[No doctrine, as Mr. Don[d] Rosse absent he having 'alleadged that he wes impeded from his own house by the water.']

Dingwall, March 6, 1666.

That day Rorie McKenzie of Dochmoluak compeering, desyred ane answer to his former supplicatione, requiring that Mathew Robertsone of Dochcarty sould be ordained to make satisfactione for slandering the said Rory with alleadged miscariage with Mathew Robertsones wife. The Bretheren considering that by the witnesses led in the said mater ther wes nothing but suspicion and Jealousie, and the said Mathew

Robertsone being called and inquired concerning the said particular, did openly profess that he wes in no wayes jealous of the said Rory McKenzie and his wife, and if any words did escape him upon which others might put such a construction he was heartily sorry for it, and wes content to acknowledge so much to Rory McKenzie of Dochmoluak, and crave pardon for the same. Which the Brethern taking to ther consideratione, and the Bishop referring it to them (as the Moderator reported), they haue, according to the Bishops appointment, ordained the said Mathew Robertsone to acknowledge so much befor the Presbyterie to the party, and to crave him pardone in any thing he hes given him offence; The which being done by the said Mathew Robertsone, Rory McKenzie of Dochmoluak did acquiesce to it without ony furder prosecutione of it.

Dingwall, April 10, 1666.

That day the Bretheren being severallie removed, and the Moderator enquiring anent ther personall and ministeriall deportment, all present wer found diligent in preaching and catechising, save that Strathconan wes much neglected; Wherfor the Bretheren concerned, viz.: Mr. George Cumine and Mr. Donald Rosse, ordained to take pains upon the people of the said place.

That day the Moderator admonished Mr. Donald . Rosse for giving marriage and Baptisme to severall persons without testimonialls.

Dingwall, June 19, 1666.

That day the Moderator enquiring if the 29 of May had been keeped as a Day of Thanksgiving for the King's restoratione and coronatione, the Bretheren present declared they had.

Dingwall, July 31, 1666.

That day the Moderator reports that ther is one in his parish of Dingwall called Katerin Rosse, who hes brought furth a child to Donald Bain in Dingwall, as she alleadges, both being referred by the session of Dingwall to the Presbyterie for further clearnes, the said Donald being called and not compeering wes ordained to be summoned against the next day.

The said Katerin being called and compeering, adhered to her former confessione, wes ordained to be present the next day.

That day the Moderator enquiring the Bretheren if the 18 of July, injoyned to be keeped by his Majestie for imploring the Lords blessing and concurrence to the Royall Navy against the fleet of the United Provinces, wes observed, the Brethren declared it wes.

That day the Bretheren were ordained to have the Bursers money in readines against the ensuing Synod.

The said day Mrs Donald Fraser, Walter Rosse, Donald Rosse, George Cumine, Donalds M^{c}craes,[1] yor and elder, Rory McKenzie, Alex^r McKenzie, and John Gordoun declared that they had satisfied Mr. John Rosse Bursar in divinity, in his proportione for the last half year.

That day Mr. John Bain, Student in divinity, declared that he had applied himself to the forsaid study, desyred that he might be admitted to give a tryall or specimen of his endeavours. The Prēby taking this to ther consideratione ordained him to haue a homilie on Matt. 11. 28 against the next day.

Dingwall, August 21, 1666.

The said day Mr. Johne Bain had a Homily on Matt. 11. 28, and being removed, the Presbyterie were satisfied with him as a beginner, and hoped that betime he might doe good in the Church of God, and desyred him to acquaint himselfe with the controversies that he might the better enable himselfe for the Ministry.

That day compeered Donald Bain, Sumoned to this day pro 2° for alleadged fornicatione with Katerin Rosse, both in the Parish of Dingwall, and being enquired anent the same adhered to his former denyall; The said Katerin not being present both were ordained to be sumoned against the next day.

Dingwall, August 28, 1666.

The said day assembled with the Right Reverend father in God, John Bishop of Rosse, the Presbyterie of Dingwall; M^{rs}

---

[1] *Sic*, but should be *Johns* M^{c}craes.

George Monro and James Houstone, assessors from the Presbyterie of Chanry.

After prayer acted as followes:

That day Mr. Walter Rosse had a popular sermon on 2 Tim. 2. 15.

That day the said Reverend father, with his forsaid assessors, did appoint Mr. John M^{c}cray to give Institutione to Mr. Johne McKenzie the   day of   who wes to be transplanted from Kilmorack to be Minister at Foderty.

The said day compeered Donald Kempe, indweller in Dingwall, supplicating the said Reverend father and his assessors, that whereas his wife Jonet Vrq^{rt} had fallen in that heinous sin of adulterie with one Johne Kaird a vagrant, and had brought furth a child to him ; That the said Reverend Father would be pleased either to speak the Comiss^{rs} of Rosse, or els to write to the Comiss^{rs} of Ed^r for a divorce from the said Jonet Vrq^{rt}; The said Revd Father and his assessors taking this to ther consideratione, and that the said Donald Kemp, supplicant, had deported himself soberly without ony known publick scandal, and finding the said supplicatione to be of verity, The said Reverend father granted his supplicatione to him.

The meeting closed with prayer.

Dingwall, Septr. 11, 1666.

The said day compeered Donald Bain and Kater Rosse both Sumond to this day, who being confronted she alleadged as befor, the said Donald denying as befor, q^{r}upon he declared himself willing to give his oath. The Presbyterie taking this to ther consideratione, ordained the said Donald to clear himself by oath publickly befor the congregatione of Ding^{ll}.

The said day Mr. Walter Rosse reportes that Grudach Nickillandris, ane excommunicate woman, came to the sessione of Alnes (since her last supplicating the Presbyterie) offering all kynd of obedience to ther Church discipline, and supplicating that she might be relaxed from the fearful sentence of excommunicatione under which she lay ; The Presbyterie remitts her to the Bishop and ensueing Synod.

That day the Moderator enquiring if all the Bretheren had keeped the fift of Septr as a day of publict thanksgiving for the glorious victory obtained by the Royall navy over the fleet of the United provinces, all the Bretheren declared they had.

That day all the Bretheren being severally removed and inquiry made by the Moderator what were each ones deportment, both in ther personall and pastorall functione, all were found to be exemplary in ther personall carriages, and diligent in pastorall functione.

Dingwall, October 16, 1666.

[Letter read from the Bishop ordaining the Presbyterie to receive Mr. John M⁽c⁾cra, Student in divinity, to pass his tryalls befor them. The said Mr. John ordained to add the next day.]

Dingwall, Nov. 6, 1666.

[Mr. John M⁽c⁾cra, Student, added on Rom. 4. 5. 6.—approven —ordained to exercise next day. The Prēsby ordaines Mr. John Bain, Student, to haue ane Exigesis *De Notis Ecclesiae*, and to haue it in readines whenever he should be required.]

Dingwall, Nov. 26, 1666.

[That day Mr. John M⁽c⁾cra, Student in divinity, exercised, and Mr. John Gordoun added, on Rom. 4. 6, 7, 8,—approven. The said Mr. John M⁽c⁾cra ordained to haue a comon head *De fide Justificante*, and to emitt theses thereanent against the next day.]

Dingwall, Decr. 17, 1666.

[Mr. John M⁽c⁾cra, Student, 'had a common head *De fide Justificante*, and disputes thereon.' He is ordained to haue a popular Sermon on Mat. 7. 14, 15, next day.]

Janry 29, 1667.

[John M⁽c⁾cra, Student in divinity, had a popular sermon on Mat. 7. 14, 15—approven. He was 'ordained to haue a questionary tryall, and a tryall in the Languages, against the next day.']

Dingwall, Feb. 19, 1667.

['Mr. John M⁽c⁾cra, Probationer in divinity, had a questionary tryall and a tryall in the Greek.'

'That day the Presbyterie ordained a testimoniall to be given Mr. John M^{c}cra, Student in divinity, bearing the Presbyteries approbatione of him in all the steps of his tryalls.']

That day the Moderator declared that the Bishop wrot a letter to be intimated to the Presbyterie, specifying that the Bretheren in ther respective congregationes should mak intimatione of a collectione for Alex^r Ogilvy, Student in Philosophy, to be sent to Chanry against the midst of March.

Dingwall, April 2, 1667.

[The Bretheren intimated that they had used diligence in the collection for Alex^r Ogilvy. Mr. Walter Rosse intimated that he 'had relaxed Grudach Nickgillanders from the sentence of (ex)communicatione, and therefor desyred that the Bretheren might mak intimatione thereof in ther respective congregationes.']

Dingwall, May 16, 1667.

That day no exercise. Mr. John Bain, Student in divinity, having ane exigesis *de Notis Ecclesiae*, and disputs theranent, which the Bretheren taking to ther consideratione, judged him to be somewhat confused in both, and advised him to acquaint himself better with the theological controversies that he might the better enable himself for the ministry.

Dingwall, June 1667.

That day no exercise, because Mr. Jo^n Bain, Student in divinity, had a popular sermon on Jon. 3. 16, who being removed, and the Bretheren taking to ther consideratione what he had delivered upon the said subject, thought fitt to advise him to acquaint himself better with the study of divinity.

[Meetings held on 2 July, 23 July, and 13 August, but no business of interest, except that on 23 July 'Mr. Charles Alexander, Schoolmaster of Dingwall, was ordained be the Prebrie to haue ane exegesis *de justitia originali* the next day'; and that on 13 August he delivered his exegesis, 'and lykewise sustained the thesis, and wes recomended for his pains and dilligence.']

At Dingwall, Septr. 3, 1667.

The Bretheren being removed severallie, and the judgement of the rest being required of everie one, They were all weill reported of and commended, and Mr. John Gordon [Kiltearn] declareing how he wes much hindered in the exercise of his ministerie by some disloyall and disaffected persons, namelie, Mr. Thom. Hog and Mr. John Mackillican, their frequenting severall places and families in his parioch, he wes enjoined by the Prebrie to report his condition to the Bishop at the Synod.

At Dingwall, 31 Decemb. 1667.

No ministeriall meeting untill this day in respect of severall other subsynodicall meetings indicted by the bishop, vherin the Moderatour and most pairt of the Brethren wer taken up.

The Brethren wer ordained to collect some charitie from their respective congregations for ane captaine Wm Murray, a distressed gentleman, against the nixt prebrie day.

Dingwall, 21 Janrij 1668.

Mr. Charles $Alex^r$ having formerly past some privat tryalls vas received on the publict tryalls, and accordingly enjoyned to adde the nixt day, but the moderator declaring that hee could not bee present the s^d day for to exercise, the said Mr. Charles was therefor ordained to haue a popular sermon on Tit. 2 and ii. vse [verse] again this day twenti days.

Mr. Donald Rosse his excuse thes three last days in respect of the greatnes of the waters and his not knowing the prbriall meetings vas irrelevant, and therfor was rebuked for his leasines, and ordained to bee mor observant.

The Brethren delyvered ther charitie for Captain William Murray collected out of ther resptve parishes.

Dingual, Febi. ii. 1668.

[Charles $Alex^r$ preached, and the Brethren are satisfied. He is ordained to add next day.]

Dingual, 3 March 1668.

[No exercise, by reason that the day vas far spent and the Brethen wer late in coming.]

[On 14 April Chas. Alex^r exercised, and on 19 May he had a common head *de certitudine salutis*. Approved.]

At Dingwall, Jun. ult. 1668.

[The Bretheren declared that they had kept the 29th of May as a day of thanksgiving for the Restoration.]

That day compeered Jo^n Dingwall in the Paroch of Fodertie, alleadging David Monro in the said Paroch to have said that he wes not baptised; the said David being sumoned to this day, compeered, and being asked anent the said allegatione, declared that he said he knew not whether he wes baptised or not. Which the Presbyterie taking to ther consideratione, and finding it to be spokin *animo malitioso*, judged him censurable, and so to be publickly rebuked after sermon in his own desk.

At Dinguall, Julij 21, 1668.

That day no exercise, Mr. John M^{c}cra, younger [of Kilmorack], who sould haue exercised, being employed in the visitatione of the Highland Churches.

At Dingwall, Septr. ij. 1668.

The forsaid persons, viz. Keneth Euay, Kenneth McKenzie, Duncan McKenzie, and Jo^n M^{c}ean vic Alister, referred from the Session of Contan, summoned to this day pro 2°, not compeering, to be summoned pro 3°: Withall the Presbyterie ordains Mr. Donald Rosse to speak the Lady Seaforth, on whose land they dwell, that she may cause her Chamberland make y^m yeeld obedience.

That day Mr. Walter Rosee ordained to try whether Mr. Jo^n McKillican had advertised severalls in the Paroch of Alnes to com and hear him on a Lords day in the Minister his absence, and to make report thereof to the Bishop and ensuing Synod.

Dingwall, Decr. 15, 1668.

That day a letter sent from the Bishop to the Presbyterie ordaining the Brethren to preach an Christs nativitie day, which wes intimated them. The Moderator [Mr. Don^d Fraser] undertakes to acquaint Mr. George Cumine [absent]. Mr.

John M^{c}cra, Mi^r at Dinguall, undertakes to acquaint Mr. John McKenzie and Mr. John M^{c}ra, younger [both also absent].

Dinguall, 26 *of Janry.* 1669.
Mr. John McKenzie [Archdeacon] had a Common head *de Dej Scientia*, who, being removed, was approven.

Dingwall, June 24, 1669.
Compeered Angus McDonald in the Parish of Kilmorack, who being fyned by the Session of Kilmorack in twentie pounds for giving a house to Agnes Nick killichoan contrary to the ordinance of Sessione, desyreing that the Presbyterie would free him of the said penaltie, seeing (as he said) he wes not in knowledge of that act of Sessione, he not being in the countrey when it wes made. The Presbyterie, taking this to ther consideratione, remitts him to the session, ordaining him to haue the penaltie modified by the sessione in readiness against the visitatione at Kilmorack.

Compeered a boy of about ten or twelve years desyreing the benefitt of Baptisme, which wes granted, and Mr. John McKenzie ordained to baptise him.

Dingwall, 12 *April* 1670.
Mr. John Gordone and Mr. Walter Rosse regrated that severall persons of their parishes did frequent Mr. John McKilican his house on the Sabboth day, to whom the said Mr. John used to preach; the consideratione q^{r}of is referred to the nixt Synod.

At Dingwall, 29 *Nov.* 1670.
Mr. William Fraser, Student in Divinitie, was ordained to haue a comon head *de perseverantia sanctorum*, 20 Dec^r.

At Dingwall, Ja^{rij} 11, 1671.
That day Mr. Valter Ros, Clerk to the Synod, delivered to the Bretheren ane list of the fugitives from the severall parishes of the Dyocess of Ross, and the Moderator desyred publique intimation to be made thereof in there severall congregationes, to the end all such might be found out and punished.

That day according to the act passed be my Lord Bishop (in Synod in favours of Mr. Allex^r fearne admitted then burser) sex of the bretheren were appointed to pay to him there severall proportiones of the burse yeirly during his localitie.

That day the bretheren, taking to consideration Mr. Donald Ross his need of ane helper for dischargeing his ministeriall duety, did ordaine him to repaire to my Lord Bishop to be advised with him hereanent.

At Dingwall, the last of Jan^{rij}, 1671.

Mr. John Gordon delivered the comon head (*de praedestinatione*) and gave full satisfaction to the bretheren, finding his opinion orthodoxe and conforme to the Judgement of the more learned and sound Divines.

That day the bretheren declared that they hade made publique intima°ne in there severall congregationes, of the names of such as were contained in the list of fugitives delivered to them the former day.

At Dingwall, 21 Feby. 1671.

[Mr. Donald Ross reports 'that the Bishop promised to furnish him with ane helper.']

At Dingwall, Apryle 11, 1671.

['The Scrols of the Presbyterie of Kennlochiu were visited, which tooke up so much tyme as that there could be no exercise.']

Dingwall, 13 June 1671.

The Brethren were ordained to make publique intimatione to there severall congregationes of the act passed in Synod against Middesummer fires.

At Dingwall, 24 July 1671.

Mr. George Cuming desired that it might be [word illegible] wher he was forced to pay his present Manss^s to his predecessor min^r, so that he conceaved it lawfull that compensa°ne be given to him according to law and his expenss^s from those bound and concerned to make a Manss to the Minist, according to law; and the Presbyterie appoints the s^d Mr. George to use diligence with the Parishioners to gett compensa°ne, either freindly or legallie, and to report his diligence to the Prēbrie how soon he may.

That day Thomas Fraser being referred from the Session of Alnes for keeping of Conventicles and dishaunting the publique ordinances, and for disobedience, called, and not compeiring, was appointed to be Sumoned pro 2°.

15 August 1671.

That day Thomas Fraser being cited, and not compeiring, as ordained to be sumoned pro 3°.

5 Septr. 1671.

Thomas Fraser being literally sumoned, cited, and not compeiring, was declared contumatious, and yrefore referred to the Bishop.

17 *Oct.* 1671.

That day Do^d M^{c}quien in Dingwall compeired, referred from Dingwall Session for alleadging y^t Mr. John M^{c}cra, Minister at Dingwall, did violentlie beat his daughter, and did so terrifie and chace her y^t he almost drave hir to the sea to drowne hir iff her father the said Don^d had not come to hir speeddie release, all q^{ch} the said Don^d denyed, and Mr. John M^{c}cra undertooke to prove the nixt day.

Dingwall, November 14, 1671.

The meeting is ordained to keep yet at Loggy[1] in order to Struy younger, who being under a civill restraint, could not com to Dingwall.

Dingwall, Decr. 19, 1671.

In regard that the meeting appointed to hold at Loggy did not keep, Mr. M^{c}cray, younger, reports that he sent tuo elderes to speak Struy younger, but as yet they made no report.

---

[1] Conan. The members of Presbytery appear to have been accommodating to such as were under civil restraint, that is, against whom warrants of imprisonment (in all probability for debt) had been issued. On 19th July and 9th August 1670 they met at Loggie to try John Kaird for adultery, he 'being under a civil restraint, so that he could not come safely to the Presbyteries ordinary place of meeting.'

Compeered William Glass, referred from the Sessione of Urq^t for disobedience, who being ordained to find surety to give obedience, Donald Monro in the said Parochin entered surety for him.

Janur. 9, 1672.

Compeered Henry Bain, late Bailzie in Dingwall, petitioning the Presbyterie to give him redresse of a slander of murder cast on him by Donald Monro at the Milne of Bridge end and his wife, which wes continued till the next day, and the said donald and his wife to be sumond to the said day.

Compeered Donald Monro, Petitioner, intreating the Presbyterie to turn over that slander cast upon Henry Bain by his wife, on her authors. Continued to next day.

Jany 30, 1672.

The referr anent Henry Bain his Petition continued till the next day.

Feb. 20, 1672.

Henry Bain his Petitione continued to the next day.

Mr. George Cumine regrates that ther is ane excomunicate person in his parochin whose company is to much frequented. Wherfor he is ordained to censure such as correspond with him.

March 12, 1672.

Compeered Henry Bain and Katharin Monro, sumoned to this day, but were continued to the next in regard of the Clerk's absence, who had the whole processe, as also in regard of the absence of other Bretheren.

April 2, 1672.

Compeered Katharin Monro, who confessed the Bill, and being removed, the Presbyterie, taking the whole processe to consideratione, ordained her to appear in publick *in sacco* tuo Lords dayes, and she remitted to the Sessione to cause her satisfy.

Dingwall, May 14, 1672.

That day Mr. Don^d Fraser, Mod^r of the Prēbrie of Dingwall, delated and regrated how that Agnes mor nin vick ean glaish, now in the Parish of fottertie, had publicklie on the high way and in presence of ane brother, Mr. John Gordowne, scolded, lyed, menaced, cursed and used imprecations ag^t him, and it being nottour that the said Agnes is *malae famae* in the matter of witchcraft, the presbyterie ordained to sumoned hir to the next day.

June 5, 1672.

Mr. Walter Rosse is appointed to have a comon head *de creatione hominis.*

[The Bretheren reported that they had preached on the 29th May.]

That day no returne from the Highland Min^{rs}, and notwithstanding that they wer acquainted and written too to keep this day with the prēbrie at Dingwall, yet non came nor anie word from them except from Mr. Rorie McKenzie off Gerloch, who wrott a letter off excuse q^{ch} was not judged relevant at that tyme, bot is continewed till his coming, and another letter from Mr. Murdoch McKenzie, who declared he could not meet for fear off caption. Therefore the prēbrie appoints to writt to the Highland Min^{rs} to come and meet with the Prēbrie at Dingwall the tenth day of Julie next.

Agnes more nin vic ean glaish sum^d, cited, and not compearing, to be Sum^d pro 2°.

25 *June* 1672.

['The above agnes not compearing, to be summoned pro 3°'].

10 *Julie* 1672.

Conveened the Mod^r and the brethren, with Mr. Rorie McKenzie, Min^r of Gerloch.

The Prēbrie considering that though the Min^{rs} off the Highlands was reanexed to the Prēbrie of Dingwall, by appoyntment and ordinance of the Bishop and Synod, and that now they had written to y^m and acquainted them to meet with y^m tuo severall diets, and yet none of them came, They appoynt and ordaine y^t they be ye third tyme written too, to come (as they will be answerable to the Bishop and Synod).

That day Mr. John M^{c}cra, younger, declared that he was readdie to processe young Struy [on 25th June he was instructed 'to processe him with excommunication], bot that he came to him and desired continewation, and that the Prēbrie wold be pleased to meet him some convenient place without Dingwall, to which he could not come for fear of caption and arrest, and that he wold endeavour to give them satisfaction. Therfore the Prēbrie appoynted Mr. Don^d fraser, Mr. George Cuming and Mr. John M^{c}cra, younger, to meet at Loggie Wester anie day they pleased, twixt this and the nixt Prēbrie day, and cite Struy before them and report ther dilligence to the nixt day.

That day Agnes More nin ean glaish compeared, and being inquired why shee menaced and threatned that she wold mak Mr. Do^d fraser repent the sending hir goodson out off the countrey, and why shee used imprecations ag^t the said Mr. Do^d fraser, Shee answered that shee repented to haue so said, and confessed hir ignorance and follie in doing, and therefore shee was ordained to be publicklie rebuked by hir Min^r after sermon for the same.

That day John M^{c}doir, referred from Kiltearne for drunknes and tuilzing on the Lords day, declared that he did nothing bot qhat he did in his owne defence, that himselfe being sober was persewed to his owne house and assaulted by Andrew Morrich, being drunk, and the Prēbrie, finding the same to be truth, absolved him.

6 August 1672.

[Mr. James McLennan, expectant in divinitie, found of 'good report and competent abilities to looke towards the functione off the ministrie,' and appointed 'to give a *specimen ingenij* by delivering a comon head *de Sabbatho* the next prēbrie day.

Meeting with young Struy at Loggie on 22^d July, when he declared his readiness to obey church censure.]

26 August 1672.

That day Mr. James McLennan delivered ane exegesis or Comon head *de Sabbatho*, and sustained a disputt on the theses off the same subject, after q^{ch} being removed the br̄en present declared that they had abundant [satisfaction?] off him, and incourradged him to go on in his studies, and to be readdie to accept off another tryall, when the Prēbrie wold enjoyne the same.

Dingwall, 12 Septr. 1672.

The Prēbrie referrs to the Bishop and Synod to consider on the disobedience off the Highland Miñ[rs] in not attending the meetings off the Prēbrie at Dingwall, notwithstanding that they were so oft written too.

Dingwall, December 2, 1672.

The Presbyterie ordains Mr. Rory M[c]Kenzie, Student in divinity, to haue ane exigesis *de Paedobaptismo* against this day sex weeks, and to emitt Theses therupon.

In regard that Mr. John M[c]Kenzie refuses to serve the people of Main in Strathconan because the benefice is takin from him, The Bishop is to be spokin to theranent with all conveniencie.

Mr. John M[c]Kenzie regrates that ther wes not a competent gleib at Fodertie, therfor requires the Brethren according to the Bishop his order to meett at Fodertie the last of December for designing a Gleib out of the Kirk Lands next adjacent to the Kirk.

Dingwall, December ult., 1672.

[The meeting at Fodertie not kept, in regard the principal Heretor of the parish wes absent.]

Dingwall, Janry. 21, 1673.

The next meeting is appoynted to be at Fodertie the eleventh day of Feb[ry] next, and the Clerk is ordained to give warrand to serve edict against the said day, that non concerned may pretend ignorance.

Fodertie, Feby. 17, 1673.

Conveened with the Moderator [Mr. Don[d] Fraser], M[rs] George Cumine, Jon M[c]cra, younger, and Mr. John Gordoun.

The last meeting appointed to be the 11 of ffebruary did not hold in regard the weather wes so boysterous.

Conveened lykwise of the Heretors, The Lord Tarbat, Mathew Robertsone of Dochcartie, Kenneth M[c]Kenzie, younger of Dachmaluak, John M[c]Kenzie of Dochcairne, and Alex[r] Dingwall of

Urie, and Thomas Fraser, Notar Publick, and having gone the length of Tollie as the neerest Lands to the Church of Fodertie (as is alleadged) designed as followes.

[Space for designation left blank.]

Dingwall, Maij 13, 1673.

That day ane act of Privie Counsell against conventicles being read, was ordained to be intimated publicklie to the severall congregationes of this Prebrie.

June 3, 1673.

The Clerke of the Prebrie is appointed to wreitt a letter to the Highland Bren of this Prebrie, desiring them to meet at Dinguall this day sex weekes, and that Mr. Alex^r McKenzie, Min^r of Lochcarron, come prepared to preach a populare sermon on Coll. 3. v. 2.

The Minister of Kilmorack did regrate that Thomas Chissolme, younger, with his sonn, Donald M^{c}ivur, Thomas M^{c}hutcheon moir, with some others of his parishe, did not onlie dishaunt publict ordinances, but moreover did freqnent the fellowshipe of a preist, which the Bren considering adwised him to deal with them in privat about ther offensive cariage, and if he should find them to be refractorie, to cause warn them to the Presbrie.

That day Mr. John McKenzie, minister of fottertie, did promise according to ordinance of Synod to discharge ministeriall dutie to that part of Strathconan q^{ch} belongs to the parishe of Fottertie, untill a way be found and condescended on for establishing his mantenance.

Jun. 24, 1673.

The Clerk shoues that he did wreitt a letter to the Highland Bren of this Presbrie, as was appointed at the last meeting.

The Minister of Kilmorack reports that these dishaunters of religious ordinances delated by him to the last meeting would not compeare before sessione, wherfore he is ordained to cause warn them to compeare the next Presb. meeting.

That day compeared Alex^r McKenzie of Touvie, being referred from the Session of Dinguall, and complained on Donald Munro in Dinguall and his wiff, affirming that they, flitting from ane house of his, did take a great quantitie of the earth of the house with them, and did cross-cut all the couples thereof; which cariage appearing unwarrantable and superstitious, did hinder the tenant's entrie who had agreed to duell in the s^d house. Donald Munro and his wiff cited, compearing, and inquired whether they had either done ore caused doe these things, answered that they removing from the house in q^{ch} they latlie duelled did sueep a little quantitie of earth haueing some corn in it, and take it with them to be meat to their foules, but simplie denyed that they cutted, ore caused cutt, the couples of the house; which the Brēn taking to their considering continued for further tryell, ordaining Touvie that if he knew anie witnesses who might give further clearenesse about these things, he would tell their names to the Kirk officer of Dinguall, that they might be warned to the nixt meeting.

That day it being found that Mr. Don^d Rosse had baptized a child to a man y^t was a fugitive from discipline, and that he had also married a man and a woman upon ane insufficient testimonie, the matter was referred to the Bishope and the Synode nixt to meet.

Jul. 15, 1673.

[None of the Highland Ministers appear, except Mr. Murdo McKenzie, Minister of Lochbroom. The Clerk ordained to write them to attend the Presbytery meeting on 5th Augt.

The Kilmorack popish dishaunters had not been cited, and the Minister again ordered to cite them for next meeting.

None appeared to prove the charge ag^t Donald Munro and his wife.]

5th August 1673.

[None of the Highland Ministers appeared notwithstanding the Clerk's letters to them.

The Kilmorack 'Popishe Dishaunters were not cited in reguard that they were dwelling at their sheallings, and therefore it is ordained that they be summonded at their dwelling places to compeare to the nixt meeting.'

The Brēn haueing considered the abuse q^{ch} Mr. Donald Ross and his sonn sustained by his Kirke Officer, ordaines to summone him to compeare at the nixt meeting.]

Augt. 26, 1673.

[Mr. William Fraser, Student in divinitie, handled a Common head *de gratia universali*. No report as to the Kilmorack papists, Mr. M^{c}cra being absent. No report of the wrong done Mr. Don^d Ross by his Kirk officer, Mr. Ross being absent.]

The Brēn c'sidering the desolate c'ditione of the parish of Dingual by the removal of their late Minister, Mr. John M^{c}cra, ordained Mr. John Gordone to preach at Dinguall the Sabboth comes eight days.

Oct. 14, 1673.

Mr. John M^{c}cra reports that some of these suspected papists in his parishe were sicke, and others not at home, and therefore he was ordained to cause warn them to the nixt meeting.

That day compeared James Cattanach, Kirke Officer of Contane, and being inquired whether he did strikk Mr. Do^d Rosse as was alleadged and comonly spoken, answered, that being highlie prowoked by Mr. Donald Rosse his son, he did strikk him, and y^t Mr. Donald interveening to defend his sonn, his hatt fell off his head, but simplie denied that he did strik him; which presumptuous cariage the Brēn taking to their consideratione, discharged the s^d James Cattanach from exercising the dutie of a Kirk Officer, and ordained him to stand *in sacco* 3 Lords dayes before the Congregation of Contan, and on the third to be sharplie rebooked, and his dischargement from being Kirk Officer declared by a minister afterward to be appointed to preach in Contan y^t day.

Novr. 4, 1673.

Mr. John M^{c}cra reports that he had caused personallie warn Don^d M^{c}ivur, Thomas Chissolm, and John Chissolm, his son, William M^{c}hutchson in Innerchannich, as being suspect of poperie and dishaunters of publict ordinances; who being cited, and not compearing, are ordained to be warned pro 2do.

John McPhatricke and Alex^r McKonil vic allister, referred from the Sessione of Vrquhart for breach of Sabboth, warned, cited, and not compearing, is ordained to be warned pro 2do to the nixt meeting.

Nov. 25, 1673.

That day compeared John McPhatricke, referred from the

Session of Urquhart, quo being found guiltie of breach of Sabboth by buying oxen and trawailing with them through three parishes on the Sabboth, is remitted and ordained to satisfie in these parishes.

That day it was ordained that the act made by the last Synod against wagabond beggars should be intimated out of pulpite to the severall congregationes of this presbyterie.

The Bishope sent a letter desireing to surrogate Bernard M°Kenzie, Student of Ph'hie, to the burse q^ch Mr. Rorie M°Kenzie, late Schoolmaster of Dingwall, had.

Dinguall, December 16, 1673.

The Popishe dishaunters of ordinances referred from the Sessione of Kilmoracke, warned, cited, and not compearing, and their minister morover regrating that these formerlie mentioned with severall others in that Parishe, did keep frequent meetings with a priest called Robert Munroe, he is ordained to advise with the Bishope theranent.

It is reported that the Act of Synod against wagabond beggars was intimated.

Dinguall, Feb. 17, 1674.

The Moderator is appointed to exercise, and Mr. George Cuming to add, at the nixt meeting; and Mr. George Dunbar is likwise appointed to be readie to haue ane oratione, and to give ane exigesis of these words of Boethius in his booke *de Consolatione Philosophiæ*.

> 'To triplicis mediam naturae cuncta moventem
> Connectens animam, per consona membra resolvis.'

and that as a specimen of his abilities to teach the grammare school of Dinguall unto q^ch he was latelie presented.

Mr. John M°cra reports that he spake to the Bishope anent these popishe dishaunters of ordinances in the Parishe of Kilmoracke, who adwised him to processe them with excommunicatione, and to speake to the civile magistrate to exercise his dutie therein.

The Presbrie appoints Mr. John M°cra, now Minister of Dinguall, to preach in Kilmoracke betwixt this and the nixt meeting, and to declare that congregatione wacant.

Dinguall, Mar. 10, 1674.

That day Mr. George Dunbar hade ane oratione in Latine, with ane exigesis on the poesie formerlie mentioned, in both q^{ch} he did acquit himselfe to the full satisfactione of the hearers.

The Bishope sent a letter desireing that anie of the Br̃en of this presbr̃ie who knew anie papists to be in their parishes, should send a list of their names to him; and the Br̃en pñt being inquired if there were anie such in their parishes, answered that they knew of none except such as are in the parishe of Kilmoracke whose names are given up to the Bishope alreadie.

July 21, 1674.

The officer haveing neglected to Sumoned the persons suspected of poperie w^tin the parish of Kilmorack, hee is ordained to use diligence, and summond y^m pro 3° ag^t the next day of meeting.

John M^cfinaly vic conil donich, referr from the session of Contan for disorderly baptizing of Infants, beeing sumonded, cited, and not compeiring, hee is ordained to be sumonded pro 2°.

August 18, 1674.

[The Kilmorack papists cited, not compearing, are declared contumacious, and referred to the Bishop aud next ensuing Synod. John M^cfinlay vic conil donich, not compearing to be cited pro 3°.]

Sept. 10, 1674.

John M^cfinlay vic conil donich beeing sumonded, and cited, compeired; and beeing accused for disorderly baptizing of infants, hee c'fessed his fault, alledging y^t q^t hee did was done through ignorance, and after the sinfullnes of his scandalous usurpa°n was held out to him hee was remitted to the session to satisfie *in sacco.*

December 29, 1674.

[Mr. John McKenzie, Student in divinity, delivered a Comon head *de universali redemptione.* Approven.]

Anne McLey, convicted of charming, referred from the

Session of Dingwall, being summoned and cited, compeired, and after the sinfullnes of her offence was declared to her, shee was remitted to the Sessione to satisfie *in sacco*, and upon evidence of remorse, to be absolved.

Dingwall, 14 *Dec.* 1675.

That day Donald Loban and Katrin Robertson, both from the paroch off Urquat, who had compeered severall other days before the Presbitrie seeking for a divorce be reason of the said Donald Loban's impotencie, as was asserted by the woman and freely confessed by himself after a twelwmoneth's cohabitation, they were desyred to haw ther recourse to the comishars for a divorce.

July 11, 1676.

That day William Dingwall, Baylie of Dingwall, compeared before the Presbyterie in behalf of the towne of Dingwall, supplicating the Brethren of the Presbyterie for a contributione to help the repairing of the kirk street of the said towne, to q^{ch} request the Moderator and the rest of the Bretheren assented, and promised each of them ther respective contributions therto.

Sept. 19, 1676.

[The Highland Bretheren, who were ordained to attend to-day, all absent except Mr. Don^d M^{c}ra.]

That day in reguard that the Bretheren in the Highland were so frequently absent from the presbyteriall meetings, the Bretheren of the Presbyterie reports them to the Bishop and Synod.

Nov. 28, 1676.

That day Maister Collin Douglesse (who obtained libertie from the Bishop to enter on tryalls at the preceeding Synod) delivered a comon head *de Lumine interno*.

Feb. 13, 1677.

That day compeired Donald McLey from the parochin of Contane, giving in greivance that notwithstanding of the severall endeawours he had made to cause his wife adhear to him according to the Presbyteries appointment, yet that she still contineus refractorie, q'rfor the Presbitrie recommends him to the commissars.

April 12, 1677.
That day the Minister of Containe having represented to the Bretheren Mr. Donald Rosse his disorderly administra°n of baptisme and mariages without his knowledge, they referred him to the Bishop and ensuing Synod.

May 22, 1677.
That day Cattir M^{c}finlay v^c ean v^c conill in the parochin of Containe, compeired befor the moderator and the rest of the bretheren, regrateing that her husband, Donald McLey, did not adheare to her, and that he at severall tymes did abuse her most inhumanly, qrfore the Presbyterie ordaines them both to be sumoned to the nixt Presbyterie day.

June 19, 1677.
That day Cattir nien finlay v^c ean v^c conil and Donald McLey in the Parochin of Containe, being sumoned, cited, and not compeiring, is ordained to be sumoned pro 2do.

At Dingwall, July 5*th*, 1677.
That day the brethren conveined with the Moderator except the brethren in the heighlands who should haw come to that dyat.

That day Cattir nien finlay v^c ean v^{c}conil and her husband, Donald McLey, in the paroch of Containe, being sumond, cited, and compeired, confessed their intoward cariage toward ane another, and after they were bitterly rebuked for the same, they are ordained to behaue better in tyme to come.

29 *Janr.* 1678.
[All the brethren had preached on 25th December except Mr. George Cumine ' who wes tender for the tyme.']

25*th of Feb.* 1678.
Finlay M^{c}ean chile, and Katrine nic coil voire, both c'peiring from the Presbyterie [*sic*, ought to be ' Session '] of Containe, and confessing that, notwithstanding they had been married thir twelve moneths agoe, yet they never knew one anoy^r lyk

man and wife, and that by reason of the s^d finlay's acknowledged impotencie, and both desyrcing they might be divorced, at least that they might be recomended to the judge ordinar, The prebrie does recomend them to the nixt ensueing Synod.

April 11, 1678.

[' Mr. Donald Macra in Lochels, Mr. Allex^r Mackenzie, Mir̃ of Locharon, Mr. Rorie McKenzie, Mir̃ of Gerloch, and Mr. Murdo McKenzie, Mir̃ of Lochbroom,' absent, ' who sent not so much as a letter of excuse for y^r absence.']

Mr. Walter Ros, conforme to the Bishop of Ros his order, declaired that he sumoned Jo^n Mackillican [1] to the Prẽbrie for calumniating and slandering him; the said Jo^n Mackillican cited, and not c'pearing, is to be charged pro 2°.

At Dingwall, April the last day, 1678.

That day conveened with the Moderator, Mr. George Cuming, Mr. Walter Ross, Mr. Jo^n Gordowne, Mr. William Fraser. After prayer acted as followes.

That day no exercise in regard that this meeting was appointed (to interveene betuixt and the Presbyterie day formerlie appoynted by the Modcrator and the bretheren for delivering the exercise), and that for dispatcheing of Mr. Roderick Mackenzie, Chanter, south as Commissioner from the Synod of Ross to the Primate, in order to the processe deduced ag^t Mr. Thomas Vrq^{rt}, late Minister at Cromartie, and therefore the exercise is established as formerlie.

That day appoynts that the Moderator, with Mr. George Cuming, Mr. Walter Ross, Mr. William Fraser, and Mr. John Gordowne, do meet at Chanr̃ie and concur with the rest of ther brethren off the Presbiteries of Chanr̃ie and Tayne for sending ther Comissioner South for the affair foresaid.

Dingwall, 4 *June* 1678.

That day the Moderator inquired the brethren present if they had preacht upon the twentieth and nynth day of May last, and had observed and solemnized the same in commemora-

---

[1] Son of Mr. John Mackillican, minister of Contin.

tion of his Maties happie restauration. They all answered that they did so.

That day the Moderator presented ane letter from the Right Reverend Father the Bishop, desireing that the Moderator, with a select number of the bretheren, should repair to Chanrie to put a finall period to Mr. Thomas Vrq^{rt} his process, and therfore the Moderator and the rest of the brethren appoynted (y^t with the said Mod^r) Mr. John M^{c}cra, Mr. George Cuming, Mr. William Fraser, and Mr. Walter Ross, should tomorrow (being the fift day of June) meet at Chanrie w^t the rest of the Miñ^{rs} off the prebries off Chanrie and Tayne to that effect.

That day Hugh Fraser [young Struy] cited and not compearing, to be sumonded pro 3°, and seeing y^t the said Hugh Fraser hes so oft troubled the Presbiterie, and was formerlie declaired contumax, and somtymes promises to give obedience to the presbiterie and session and yet turnes refractorie and disobedient, the Moderator and the bren desired Mr. William Fraser to advise with the R. Reverend Fay^r the Bp qhat shall be done with the said Hugh Fraser.

That day Mr. Walter Ross declared y^t John McKillican (Son to Mr. John McKillican) has given satisfaction for his misbehaviour and miscarriage to him according to the prebries [ordinance] given to the said Mr. Walter theranent.

Dingwall, 2d Julie 1678.

That day Mr. William Fraser declared that he had advised with the R. R. Bp. concerning Hugh Fraser, and that he was desired to admitt Hugh Fraser to the publick profession of repentance, and therefore his processe before the prebrie is sisted at this tyme.

That day compeared Agnes nin dod. oig vic finlay, from the parish of Contan desireing that she might be suffered to marrie Murdoch M^{c}allan with whom she was contracted, and that because ther could be no further stop in hir way, since their was proofe that Alister M^{c}W^m vic ean vic conel hir former husband who went to France was dead by drowning, and to that effect compeared John M^c ean vic ryrie, who deponed upon oath that he saw the said Alex^r M^{c}W^m vic ean dead, as also Mr. John Gordowne declared y^t the same was told him by others y{t} came from France; qlke the Prebrie considering desyred Mr. John M{c}Kenzie, Mir̃ at Contan, to give hir the benefit off marriage with the said Murdoch M{z}Allan.

6 August 1678.

That day Mr. Roderick Mackenzie, Minister at Gerloch, by his letter to the prebrie, declared that he had sumonded by his officer to this prebrie day, Hector MacKenzie in Mellan, in the Parish of Gerloch, as also John, Murdoch, and Duncan M{c}Kenzies, sons to the said Hector, as also Kenneth M{c}Kenneth, his grandson, for sacrificing a bull in ane heathnish manner in the iland of St. Ruffus, comonlie called Ellan Moury in Lochew [1] for the recovering of the health of Cirstane Mackenzie, spouse to the said Hector Mackenzie, who was formerlie sick and valetudinarie, who being all cited, and not compearing, ar to be all sumoned againe pro 2°.

Compeared John M{c}conel vick ean oig in Attadell, in the Parish of Lochcarron, complaining that Marie nin dod. vick James *alias* Crookshank his spouse had run away fugitive with another man called donald M{c}ean vick ryrie, and intreated the Prebrie, seeing that the said Marie had deserted him, and wold not adher to him, that they wold be pleased to grant him a recomendation to the Comiss{rs} of Ross as Judges competent to prosecute and obtaine a divorce from the said Marie nin do{d} vick James; Qlk the Prebrie taking to ther consideration, and finding that qhat the said John M{c}conel vic ean oig had asserted was also attested by a letter from Mr. Alex{r} M{c}Kenzie, Mir̃ of Lochcarron, they granted him a letter off recomendacion, and desired the clerk off the prebrie to writt the same and subscrive it as ther clerk for the said effect.

3 Septr. 1678.

[The Mellan Sacrificers not compearing, to be cited to the next meeting, pro 3°].

That day Mr. John Gordowne complained y{t} ane Mr James Vrq{rt}, a deposed and intercommuned minister,[2] did keep con-

---

[1] Loch Maree. But the head of Loch Maree is still called Kinlochewe—the Head of Lochewe.

[2] Mr. Urquhart had been minister of Kinloss, to which he was restored after the Revolution.

venticles at the Laird of Foulis his house, and that the said
Mr. James did baptise diverse childeren in the parish of
Kilterne, such as a child to the Laird of Foulis, to Hector
Munro of Drummond, to John Beatowne in Culniskea, to
Alex^r Munro, Smith in Foulis, and to Hector Sutherland,
Milne Knave[1] in Catwell, and to diverse others, who all delayed and postponed to baptize ther children (though the said
Mr. John Gordowne had diverse tymes desired and required
them to baptise ther children) till they could get the occasion
of a deposed disloyall person, such as the said Mr. James
Vrquhart, as also regrated y^t Mr. Walter Denūne keept conventicles in Culbin, with Lemlairs relict, notwithstanding y^t
the said Mr. Walter was prohibit be the Earle of Seaforth by
a letter sent to him;[2] Qlk the Presbiterie taking to ther consideration, thought fitt that a letter be sent to the Bishop of
Ross complaining off these disorders, to the end y^t he might
acquaint his son the Bishop of Galloway (being now in this
countrey) therewith, and y^t ther names be presented to the
Councell, y^t such disorderlie courses might be suppressed, and
withall appoynted Mr. John M^{c}cra and Mr. John Gordowne
tomorrow (being the fourth of Sept^r.) to complaine Mr. Walter
Denune his keeping of seditious conventicles, and represent the
same to the Earle of Seaforth, who was to be at Dingwall tomorrow, to take some course for suppressing the said Mr.
Denunes insolencie and disorderlie walking.

Compeared John M^{c}ean vic Thomas and Marjorie nin william,
from the Parish off Vrray, who both intreated and mutuallie
desired to be recomended by the Moderator and Brēn to the
Comiss^{rs} to obtaine a divorce in regard that it was mutuallie
confest both by the man and the woman y^t the s^d John M^{c}ean
vic Thomas was impotent and not able to discharge the dutie
off ane husband to the s^d Marjorie notw^{t}standing of ther being
married thir some years bygone together, and therefore the
Presbyterie recomended them to Comiss^r to that effect.

---

[1] Knave, a male servant. Milne Knave, the miller's servant, who enjoyed the mill dues known as knaveship.

[2] See Scott's *Fasti. Eccl. Scot.*, vol. iii. part i. p. 335, for an account of Mr. Denoon's persecution and eventful career. After the Revolution he became minister of Golspie.

That day Mr. John Mackenzie, Mod^r, presented ane letter from the R. Reverend Bishop (together with ane copie off ane Act off Councell) desireing to uplift a contribution for the bulwarks off Peterhead and Stonhyve, qlk was read publicklie in the prēbrie, and ane copie delivered to everie Min^r, and desired to bring ther contribution to the nixt Prebr̄ie day and deliver the same to the Md^r.

1st Octobr. 1678.

[No diligence from the Minister of Gairloch as to the Sacrificers, and their process continued.]

Mr. John M^{c}cra declared that he had spoken My Lord Seaforth anent Mr. Walter Denune, and y^t the said Earle promised that he wold acquaint the Councell anent him, as also Mr. Walter Ross declaired y^t he delivered the prebries letter to the Bp of Ross in presence of the Bishop of Galloway, who promised to acquaint the Councell with thes disorders (according as they wer appoynted the last meeting day.)

The Mod^r inquired the Br̄en anent the contribution appoynted to be uplifted for Peterhead and Stonhyve—they all promist to bring it in to the Synod and deliver it to the Mod^r y^{r}at.

Alex^r M^{c}lean *alias* Bayne, adulterer with Anne Ninickgillivichell, Sumnonded to this day, compeared *in sacco*, and being earnestlie exhorted to repent, confest his guilt and was remitted to testifie his repentance publicklie before the Congregation at Vrqhart, from whence he was referred to this diet.

That day it was delated y^t the said Alex^r McLean had spoken blasphemie, to wit, That C. Jesus was a sinner all the tyme he lived on earth, and that the same had been proven agst the said Alex^r M^{c}lean by one witness before the Session of Vrqhart, the extract off q^{ch} process Mr. Don^d Fraser was appoynted to send to the prebr̄ie the next day, and his son Mr. Alex^r Fraser (who was present) ordained to acquaint his father, Mr. Don^d Fraser, to that effect; yet the said Alex^r M^{c}lean, being posed y^{r}upon before the prēbr̄ie, he utterlie refused y^t ever he had spoken anie such thing, bot John Glass in Brahan, who was sum̄ded to the prebr̄ie as a witness agst the said Alex^r in the said matter off blasphemie, was excepted ag^t be the said Alex^r, and declared y^t he wold give in reasons the nixt prebrie day why the said John Glass could not be admitted agst him, and so they wer sumded *apud acta* (both the said Alex^r Bayne and John Glass) to compeare the next day.

April 8, 1679.

This day compeered Alex^r McLean, and John Glasse who wes led witnesse against Alex^r McLean in that processe deduced against him. It being notourlie known that the said Alex^r M^clean wes an habituall drunkard, and latelie in the Parish of Urray, at which tyme he uttered some unbesecming expressions. Therefor the Presbyterie appoynts him to repair to the Session of Urray, and to satisfie the Church discipline ther.

Compeered Robert Catanach in the Parish of Alnes supplicating the Presbyterie that redresse might be given him of a slander cast on him be W^m M^cmiller in the parish of Kilterne; the said William avowing and asserting stronglie that he wes father to the said Robert. The said W^m M^cmiller being called, not compeering, is ordained to be sumoned pro 2° to the next day.

May, 1, 1679.

Compeered W^m M^cmiller complained on be Robert Catanach and being enquired anent the slander cast on Robert Catanach be him alleadging the s^d Robert to be begottin be him in fornication three and thrtteie yeers agoe, confest the same and not being able to qualifie the same otherwise then be his owne allegatione, the Presbyterie taking the premisses to consideratione, doe ordain the s^d William M^cmiller to satisfie as a fornicator and a slanderer both in the parishes of Alnes and Kilterne.

Sept. 2, 1679.

That day compeired befor the Preby John McCurchie in the Parish of Dingwall, regrateing the undutifull and unchristian carriage of Isobell Gow his married wife, and representing y^t notwithstanding of the frequent endeavors used by the session of Dingwall for makeing the s^d Isabell Gow adhere to and cohabite w^t him, she did willfullie insist to desert his company and refused to cohabit w^t him. And in regard that Mr. John

M^{c}cra, Miñ^r at Dingwall, declared y^t they were referred from the Session to the Prebr̄y, the fors^d Isabell being sumonded was cited, and compeired, and beeing asked why shee refused to live w^t her husband, shee answered that shee had conceived such ane aversion for him ever since the time of the solemniza°n of y^r marriage, y^t shee could not obtaine of herselfe to love him or live with him. And beeing further asked (after the sinfull- nesse of her s^d confessed aversion was represented to her) if shee had resolved and would promise for the future to cohabite and live w^t her husband, shee would neiy^r make any satisfactorie declara°n of her inten°ns nor give any assurance or promise (as the Prēbry required of her) y^t shee would in aftertimes behave according to her dutie, and live w^t her husband. And there- fore the Prebr̄y judged it meet y^t the fors^d John McCurchies request to recomend him to the Judge ordinarie for obtaineing a divorce, and appoynted y^r clerk to give the extract of this y^r act to the s^d John McCurchie after ten days were expired if hee should be advertised by M . John M^{c}cra that the fors^d Isabell Gow would not (within that time) condescend to live w^t her husband, as the Presbyterie exhorted her to doe.

[Dingwall, Jan. 6, 1680.

Mr. George Monro, Student in Divinitie, had a common head *de anima.* Approven.]

Dingwall, Feb. 3, 1680.

That day the Moderator produced a Comission directed to him by the R. R. Bishop for visiting the Kirk of Dingwall in order to the reparation y^{r}of, and enjoyning him and the rest of the bretheren of the Prēbrie to appoynt a day and nominate some of y^r number to meet to y^t effect, q^{r}upon they appoynted Mr. John M^{c}ra, Mr. John Gordon, Mr. John McKenzie, Min^r at Contan, and Mr. William fraser, to meet at Dingwall upon the 12 day of Februarie 1680, and ordered Mr. John McRa, Min^r at Dingwall to call wrights and masons and to give intimation of the diet to the heretors of the Parish of Dingwall and oy^{rs} concerned.

At Dingwall, Feb. 12, 1680.

Conveened, with Mr. John McKenzie, Moderator of the

Presbyterie of Dingwall, Mr. John M‹Ra, Mr. John Gordon, Mr. John M'Kenzie, Minister at Contan, and Mr. W^m fraser, together with the town and heritors of the Parish of Dingwall, and after prayer,

The Moderator haveing declared that the meeting was appoynted in order to the settling of a way for the repara°n of the Church of Dingwall, did produce the Comission directed to him by the Bp. for the effect fors^d, q^{ch}beeing read by the Clerk of the Prebry, the Moderator fors^d exhorted the heretors of the Parish of Dingwall, and the representatives of the brugh of Dingwall there present to fall upō a speedie course for repairing the ruinous fabrick of y^r Church; q^{r}upon, after advice taken, they condescended upon the termes following, That is to say,

Donald Bayne of Tulloch and Alex^r McKenzie of Tollie (beeing the heretors of the landwart pairt of the parish) did undertake for their share to build the north side of the Church of Dingwall from corner to corner, and the eastern door upon the south side of the same w^t a window above it, together w^t the equall halfe of the whole roofe, they getting the equall halfe of q^t materialls are alreadie prepared for the work.

And the Brugh of Dingwall, with the territories y^{r}of, did undertake to put up the rest of the Church sufficiently and decently, and all the fors^d parties concerned did promise and engage to begin the reparation of the s^d Church in the latter end of the next ensueing spring, and to goe one w^t the work w^t all convenient diligence.

The meeting closed with prayer.

March 2, 1680.

Donald Roy, Donald M^{c}finlay vic ean and Do^d McDonald vic ean, referred from the Session of Urq^{rt} for profana°n of the Lord's day and useing charmes, beeing sum̄ded and cited, compeired and after confession of y^r sin, the hainousnesse q^{r}of was held forth to them, they were remitted to the Session fors^d to satisfie *in sacco*.

Aprile 6, 1680.

[Alex^r McCurchie from Urquhart confesses profanation of the Lord's day and charming, and remitted to the Session to satisfy *in sacco*.]

July 6, 1680.

Alex^r M'ean vic gillireich, guiltie of adulterie with Ann nin William vic yoke, q^{ch} Ann was guiltie also of using charmes and superstitious ceremonies such as witches are s^d to use, to the end that she might render the s^d Alex^r impotent to his own wiffe; both these persons being referred from the Session of Urray and cited, compeared *in sacco*, and the evill of these their abhominable sinns being gravelie held furth to them, they were remitted to the s^d Sessione to enter the evidencing of their repentance; and the woman was ordained not onlie to undergoe Church discipline in Vrray but also in other parishes adjacent, viz., to stand *in sacco* one Lords day before the congregatione of Kilmorack, and 2^d at Contane, and a 3^d at Urqr^t.

Andrew McAndrew, referred from the sessione of Urq^{rt} for striking a man on the Lords day in the Church in time of divine service, compeared, and being gravelie reproved for y^t his sinn, was remitted to ths s^d sessione to satisfie the discipline thereof.

Dingwall, May 3, 1681.

The Minister of Kiltern regrated that there were frequent Conventicles in his parishe to the dividing of his congregatione, and weakening of his ministrie in that place, q^{ch} the Bren referred to the consideratione of the Bishope and the next ensueing Synod.

That day some of the Bren regrated that their Churches were werie ruinous, that they had not gotten free manses, but such as themselves had bought and builded on their oun expensis, and that a considerable part of their stipends in use to be payed formerlie was detained from them since thair entrie to the ministrie, q^{ch} also was referred to the consideratione of the Bishop and the next ensueing Synod.[1]

---

[1] This is the last Minute in volume ii. of the Records.

At Dingual, the 7th day of July 1681.[1]

The 7 of July being appointed at the last Synod to meet on it presbiteriallie, al the brethren in the Low countrie belonging to the Presbiterie of Dingual, viz. Mr. Jo^n Mackenzie, minister of fodertie, and archdeacon of Ros, the Moderator, Mr. Donald fraser, minister of Urq^{rt}, Mr. George Cumin, minister of Urray, Mr. Walter Ross, minister at Alnes, Mr. Jo^n Gordon, minister of Kilterne, Mr. William fraser, Minister of Kilmorack, Mr. Jo^n McKenzie, minister of Contane, and Mr. Jo^n M^{c}cra, Minister of Dingual, did meet, and after prayer acted as follows:—

The rest of the ministers of that Presbiterie, viz. Mr. Donald Macra, Min^r of Kintail, Mr. Donald Macra, min^r of Lochels, Mr. Rorie McKenzie, Min^r of Gerloch, and Mr. Murdo McKenzie, Min^r of Lochbroome (Lochcarron being vacand through the decease of Mr. Alex^r Mackenzie) were absent be consent of y^r distance.

That day Hugh Fraser of Struy being referred from the Session of Kilmorack for disobedience, and summoned *pro tertio*, cited, and not compearing, is continued be ordour from the Bishop untill the bretheren who were appointed at the Synod to goe to Straglaish to confer with the Papists there, should speake to him, and to give in their report to the nixt Synod.

6 *Sept.* 1681.

Mr. Jo^n Gordon, Mi^r of Kiltern, did regrait and complaine to the Presbiterie that Mr. Jo^n Mackillican keeped ane conventicle at Ketual the 28 of August last by past—which the brethren referred to the Bishop and ensueing Synod.

3 *Oct.* 1681.

Mr. Jo^n Gordon did complaine to the Presbitric that Mr. Walter Denune, a vagrant preacher, did keep a conventicle at Ketual the first of Octob. last, which the Moderator and remanent brethren refer to the Bishop and ensueing Synod.

13 *Decr.* 1681.

That day the Moderatour delyvered a letter to be read be the Clerk in presence of the Brethren sent from the Bishop

---

[1] The first Minute of Volume iii.

anent the Test, together with the Councells explanation, and his Majesties approba°n y^rof. The tenor of which Letter sent from the Bishop follows :

'REVERED BRETHEREN,—You have had under your consideration for some good tyme the oath q^{ch} the King and Parliament have judged necessarie to require of all who have now, or who hereafter shal haue, any publict trust, office, or imployment, in this Church or Kingdome. The designe of which oath is verie distinctly expressed in the act, viz. to cut off al hope from papists and other dissenters of being hereafter imployed in anie office of publict trust; which designe being good, and nothing unlawful contained in the oath, I cannot conjecture why anie man who is a true Protestant and loyal subject should refuse to take this oath, being enjoined be lawful authoritie. It is now high tyme to be at ane end of your resolutione in this mater, and in case you should inclyne to refuse, which I hope none of you will, I would haue you remember that they cannot be anie light or frivolous pretenses or exceptions that will ether satisfie your owne consciences or vindicat you from the slighting or contempt of the comands of that authoritie which yourselves acknowledge to be the highest under God, without whose countermand you ought not to withdraw your readie obedience. And that you may yeeld it in this case with safe and comfortable consciences I earnestly advise not to put rigid meanings upon anie clause of the oath (as I have perceaved some haue been too apt to doe) but to think, as in al dutie you should, that the meaning of the King and parliant in al the parts of it, was no other then what may consist with the Law of God, the Law of the Kingdom, and sound reason; and if al the articles of the oath (as I judge they are) be capable of a sense agreeable with these, and not contrarie to anie of them, I see not why anie honest man who is a protestant may not take it. Therefor I beseech you use no longer delay in tacking up your final resolutions to obey, which will prove a more effectual meane for preserving religion then anie thing we can hope may follow your refusal. I shal be here, God willing, to attend you till the first of Januarie ensueing, and so praying God to give you counsel what you ought to doe in this and whatever else is incumbent to you, I continue,

'Your most affectionat brother,

'*Sic subscribitur*,   ALEX^R. ROSSEN.

'Chanorie, November 1681.'

Al the brethren of the presbitrie concluded to meet at Chanorie Thursday the 28 of December current, to close y^r resolutione anent the Test.

5 *Sept.* 1682.

That day Mr. George Cumin declared that David Monro, of Killichoan,[1] and Do^d his broy^r (as he was informed) did profane ye Kirk of Killichrist by putting some oxen and encloseing y^m y^{r}in over night, and he haveing written to y^m to y^t effect they returned him answere to doe y^m the to suffer [2] y^m to vindicat themselves from y^t aspersion before ye Prēbrie of Dingual, to whose censure, if they should be found guiltie, they were willing to submitt, and ye s^d David and Do^d having this day compeared before the prēbrie to y^t effect, and being interrogat be the Moderator whether they had comitted such profanation, they answered y^t they did not put anie of y^r cattel into ye church, but y^t some beasts of theirs y^t were feeding about ye Kirkyard, becaus they could not gett y^m keeped within a fold, did stragle into ye church, which had neiy^r doore nor roofe, q^{r}upon ye Mod^r offering to proove that they did drive y^m into ye Kirk, as was reported, and closed ye doore upon y^m, he summoned them *apud acta* be the Prēbrie ye first tuesday of October, and Mr. George Cumin was appoynted to Summond witnesses to y^t day.

Janet Monro referred from ye Paroch of Contin, compeared before ye presbrie, and did complaine on her husband Do^d macdunichie vic ol vane for not adhereing to her, nor giveing her anie part of his meanes for her sustainance, and ye said Don^d being sumoned to this day to give a reasone of his non adherence cited and not compearing is appointed to be cited pro 2°.

3 *Oct.* 1682.

Don^d and David Monros compearing, did stand to y^r formal deneyal, and Mr. George Cumin having sumonded as witnesse ag^t them Thomas Mac ean vic Gillereach and Dod. mac ean chile, who being cited and compearing, The Mod^r enquired if they had anie exceptiones against these witnesses, they answered negatively, q^{r}upon ye Mod^r haveing [3] the nature of

---

[1] In Kiltearn.   [2] *Sic.*   [3] Blank in the record.

ane oath and haveing swore ye wittnesses, all were removed except ye s^d Thomas deponed as followes, viz, That ye s^d David and Do^d comeing from Innernes marcat in August last, haveing a certaine number of oxen and bulls, and after they had put y^m in a fold, and ye beasts did break ye fold, they offered to put y^m within ye Kirk, and that he and his neighbour did inhibit them to doe so, but yet, notwithstanding y^t, upon ye morrow, after ye s^d David and Do^d were away, they found ye marks of ye beasts within ye Kirk, and a cart and a beir q^ch was brought from y^r houses at ye kirk doore, but he refused to depone y^t he sawe y^m drive or send y^m into ye Kirk. He being removed, and ye s^d Don^d mac ean chile being called in, deponed ye same with his fellow *ut supra*. The prēbrie, takeing ye matter to y^r c'sidera°ne, with all ye circumstances, appointed ye said David and Donald Munros to goe on a Lords day once betwixt that and ye nixt presbrīe to ye Kirk of Killichrist, q^n Maister George Cumin was to preach y^r, and after sermon, in presence of ye congrega°ne, Mr. George should give y^m a publict rebuke, and y^t they should humblie acknowledge and c'fess y^r fault for offering to profane such a place.

Don^d mac ean vic al vane sum^d, cited, and compearing, and being enquired why he did not adhere to his wife Janet Munro, he deneyed his non-adhereing to his wife, and affirmed y^t his wife fled from him to her fay^r without his c'sent, and promised to prove kind to her from hence, q^rupon her fay^r, who was p̄nt, was advised to send his wife to the said Donald.

March 7, 1683.

Mr. Rory McKenzie, Deacon, had a popular Sermon on 1 Tim. 1. 8.

April 3, 1683.

Compeared Donald Og m^eean dui, suspect of adultery with Mary Nien Dul vic ean vore, she confessing the same formerly, he denying, notwithstanding of the variety of presumptions proven be severall witnesses against him, is appointed to stand *in sacco* and afterwards to clear himself be oath.

The Presbyterie considering that the Bretheren in the Highlands doe neither com nor send to the Presbyterie, and in regard that referrs from them canot be closed without ther own presence, The Presbyterie referrs them to the Bishop and Synod ensueing.

Compeered Arthur Ssoiles in Obstell, supplicating the Presbyterie for a contributione to the repairing of the bruse [1] of Alnes. The usefulness of the work considdered, the Bren promise sexteen pounds scotts, payable the next Presbyterie day.

Mr. Philip M^{c}cra, Student in divinity, being recommended be the Bishop to the Presbyterie, is ordained to haue ane exegesis *de satisfactione Christi* against the next day.

April 1, 1684.

Jean Bayne for the time in the paroch of Dingwall being lately brought to bed of a child as she alledged to Thomas Watson a Souldier of Suddey's Company, being referred from the Session of Dingwall for examina°n, was called and compearing, after tryall alledged the s^d Thomas was ffay^r to her child, She is ordained to be present the nixt dyet being May 6.

May 6, '84.

Jean Bayne being called, compeared, and adhereing to her former declara°n, was y^{r}upon asked why she hade defamed Mr. John Gordon, Mī^r at Kilterne, giveing him out to be ye fay^r of her child, and denyed she ever spoke any such thing.

Some of ye Brethren upon her denyall replyed they were informed she hade said to severall women in Dingwall, y^t Mr. Gordon was ffay^r to her last Birth; and y^t she spoke so partarly to Kath. Monro her midwiffe, q^{ch} she stiffely refuseing, the s^d Kath: was y^{r}upon pñtly called, and compearing, being askt anent the premisses, declared y^t q^{ll} the s^d Jean was yet in her pangs she asked her q° was ffay^r to her child, and y^t she answered Mr John Gordon, and for further verifica°n hereof the s^d Kath: appeared to the testimonie of severall oy^r women q° were y^n and y^r present, q^n she urged her as said is, namely Agnes Dingwall, Agnes and Elspet Bayns, all in Dingwall. But notwithstanding, the s^d Jean still adhered to her former declara°n.

Q^{r}upon the s^d Mr. John Gordon craved y^t the s^d Kath. Munro

---

[1] Brew-house.

should be reputed the author of ye s^d slander, untill she found anoy^r, and accordingly pleaded she should be sum^d *apud acta* to compeir ye nixt dyet to make good her alleadgance, q^ch was accordingly done.

The officer is enjoyned to sñd all Kath: Monros witnesses to the nixt dyet, being June the third.

June 3, '84.

Jeane Bayne and Kath: Monro being called compeared, both adhered to y^r former respective declara^ons.

Kath: Monros witnesses being called, compeared, and being all deeply sworn anent the premisses, the rest being removed, Agnes Bayne declared, by the oath she made y^t she was present q^n ye said Jean Bayne was in travell and delivered, and y^t the s^d Kath: Monro charged the s^d Jean upon oath to declare q^o was fay^r to her child, and y^t the s^d Jean answered as she should make account to God in ye great day, she knew no oy^r ffay^r but the s^d Thomas Watson, notw^tstanding the s^d Kath: (as ye s^d Jean did then insinuat) wold have her saying oy^rwise.

Agnes Dingwell declared she was not present at the delivery, and y^rfore she was not in bona fide to say, she heard Jean Bayne averring Mr. John Gordon to be ye fay^r of her child at y^t time and in y^t place, but y^t she heard her alleadge no less elseq^r and at oy^r times.

Elspet Baine declared y^t the s^d Jean Baine answered upon oath to ye s^d Kath: y^t Thomas Watson was fay^r to her child, and further said she never heard ye s^d Jean affirme the s^d Mr. Gordon was ffay^r to her child, either y^n or y^r or at any oy^r time or place, only she heard by report he was ffay^r, but not from herself.

Jean Baine being againe called and askt whether or no she was able to depone upon oath y^t Mr. John Gordon was not fay^r to her child, answered she could not only vindicat him by oath, but also all oy^rs of his character from ever offering to be anyways base w^t her.

Kath: Monro haveing succumbed in proba^on by the former witnesse is againe called, and being askt whether or no she hade oy^r witnesses could prove the truth of her former declara^on, answered she hade, and being desyred to name y^m, spoke of

Doᵈ Whyte and his wiffe, Isabell Anderson, Agnes Bayne, daughter to Baylie Bayne, elder, all in Dingwall, who being all called, only Isabell Anderson, Agnes Bayne, and Doᵈ Whites wiffe compeared, and being all deeply sworn,

Isabell Anderson, the rest being removed, declared by the oath she made, yᵗ the sᵈ Jean Bayne said in her shope yᵗ Mr. Gordon was ffayʳ to her child.

Agnes Bayne declared yᵗ the sᵈ Jean Bayne sᵈ to herselfe yᵗ the sᵈ Mr. Gordon was fayʳ to her child, and desired her to goe to Kath. Monro, Midwiffe, and cause her conceale qᵗ she hade formerly revealed to her anent Mr. Gordon.

Doᵈ Whites wiffe declared she never heard her say any thing anent Mr. Gordon.

This processe suspended to the nixt dyet, being Jully 1.

Jully 1, '84.

The Moderator and remanent Brēn, takeing to consideraᵒn whether or no they should proceed to censure Kath. Monro and Jean Bayne for yʳ falsifications in the slander alleadged by yᵐ agᵗ Mr. Gordon, resolved it was not fit to proceed to any present censure untill Mr. Gordon were brought to the utmost tryall anent yᵗ slander, qᶜʰ they judged could not be done by yᵐ in the absence of yʳ Ordinary, or at least wᵗout a license from him; qʳfore being for the present deprived of both, they suspend all future proceeding in yᵗ affair till Providence send yʳ Bp. amongst yᵐ, or yᵗ he declare his pleasure yʳ anent. And least in the mean tyme the said Jean should make her escape and leave the sᵈ Mr. Gordon under the slander, they recomend to the sᵈ Mr. John to affoord her maintenance a peck of vict¹ weekly, qᶜʰ at the Brens desire the sᵈ Mr. John Gordon aggreed to.

Dingwall, Sepr. 16, '84.

The meeting this day held be order of Synod, because of Mr. John Gordon's proposeing before the Bp at the last Synod to bring witnesses to prove agᵗ Kath Monro, qᵐ he formerly charged as his accuser in the slander above menᵒned, yᵗ she promised in name and behalf of yᵉ Laird of Fowlis to give fyve

---

¹ Victual : meaning grain, or meal.

hundred merks to Jean Bayne so she should affirme Mr. Gordon to be ffather to her child, qlk witnesses, together w^t the said Kath. were called as follows.

Kath. Monro being first called, comp. and being askt whether she acknowledge y^t Mr. Gordon charged her w^t at the last Synod, viz., y^t she promised in name and behalf of the Laird of ffowlis to give Jean Bayne fyve hundred m̃ks so she should affirme Mr. Gordon to be fay^r to her last Birth : the s^d Kath. denyed : whereupon the witnesses adduced by the s^d Mr. Gordon to prove his s^d charge are all called, and compeared, and the s^d Kath. being askt whither or no she hade any just excep^{on} ag^t any or all of these witnesses, answered negatively : the Witnesses y^{r}fore (qose names are as follows, Alex^r McAndra, Don^d White, Agnes Dingwall, Elspet Bayne, all in Dingwall) being deeply sworn one by one, anent the premisses, were all com̃anded to remove, and after delibera^{on}, are againe cited by course, and first

Alex^r McAndra in Dingwall being called, compeared, and being desired to tell the truth according to his knowledge and according to the oath he gave, in the matter aleadged by Mr. Gordon before the Bp and Synod, answered by the oath he tooke, y^t he never heard the s^d Kath. Monro speake or promise the like to the s^d Jean Bayne ; q^{r}upon he is desired to remove.

Do^d White in Dingwall being also called to the effect fors^d, deponed as said is, and being removed, Agnes Dingwall is called and comp., deponed in manner above specified, and removing,

Elspet Bayne is called and comp. deponed as said is.

The nixt meeting to be held at Kilterne, 23 Septr current, q^r all the Br̃en of this Pbr̃ie w^t a select number out of ye pr̃bies of Tayne and Chanonrie are to hold a visita^{o}n at the Bp's desire as his Com̃ission given y^{r}anent doth more fully bear.

The meeting closed w^t prayer.

At Kiltearn, Septr. 23, '84.

Conveened w^t the Moderator all the Br̃en of the exercise at Dingwall, together w^t the Remanent Members of ye visita^{o}n above spec^t, as they are nominate in the above-mentioned Comission, except Mr. Do^d ffraser, Mr̃ at Wrquhart, Andrew Ross, Min^r at Tarbat, and Rorie McKenzie, Chanter of Ross.

The Moderator preached in the English language on first Pet. 3. 16, and in Irish, Jam. 3. 1.

After Prayer,

The Commission for holding the visitat°n being publictly read, The Mī^r of y^t paroch was desired to give account of his Elders, q^{ch} were only three, qōse names are as follows, Wm Urquhart, Do^d Ross, and Do^d ffinlayson, Elder.

The Mī^r being removed, Wm Urquhart was called and being examined whether or no he could give any account of the originall of y^t scandall charged upon his paroch Mī^r, declared as follows, y^t Jean Bayne was charged to compeare before y^r session touching a suspicion of her being w^t child, and being askt if she was w^t child, acknowledged she was, and being further interrogat q° was the fay^r y^rof refused to tell, and, being more hotly put to it, ask^t q^t was y^r concern, she was able to free herself from all men in y^t paroch, q^rupon she was yⁿ dismissed, and a little after craved a testifica°n of her honest behaviour dureing her abode amongst y^m, q^{ch} she obtained.

But the s^d Wm Urquhart being further examined if she was put to oath answered negative, only (s^d he) the Mī^r presented the Bible to her, and no more.

Donald Finlayson, Elder, being called to the effect fores^d, declared he knew nothing in the affair.

Don^d Ross being called, declared *ut supra*.

Don^d Finlayson, yō^r, Clerk to ye Session, being askt why he gave her a testificat untill she were further tryed, answered, he gave it her at ye Minister's desire.

Mr. Andrew Ross, Mī^r at Contan, Clerk to ye s^d visita°n, being desired by the Moderator to get a list of ye heritors of y^t paroch, hade account of y^m from Hugh Munro of Swardale and oy^{rs} as follow :

Sir John Monro Elder of ffowlis, Hector Monro of Drummond,
    Wm Monro of Teanaird, Hugh Monro of Swardale, Hector Monro of Kilterne, Wm Monro, Portioner of Keatwall, Ro^t Monro of Clyne, Ro^t Monro of Lemlair, Robt Polson of Clyne, David Monro of Kilchoan, Hugh Monro of Tearibban, Alex^r McKenzie for Balconie ; all present except Sir John Monro of ffowls.

and being all akst if they hade any informa^en to give anent the scandall charged upon y^r M$^{\bar{i}r}$, answered y^t for y^r pts [parts] they hade nothing to say, but referred the evidence of y^e matter to such witnesses as were personallie summoned to give y^r declara°ns anent the s^d scandall; q^{ch} witnesses are as follows, Kath. nin doil vic horish, woman-servant, and Ronald M^{c}indoir and John M^{c}phail, men-servants to the s^d Mr. John Gordon; Muirach Reildach, Kath. nien ullay ic ulliam, James. Logan, Christian nien doil ic allen in the paroch of Kilterne, Agnes Bayne, Elspit Bayne and Agnes Dingwall, in Dingwall, and Donald Deisse, Beddall to the s^d Mr. Gordon.

M^r. Gordon being askt whither he could except ag^t any or all these witnesses, answered he excepted ag^t Kath. nin doil vic horish because of her nonage, being but sexteen years old as herselfe declared; ag^t Murach Reildach as Minor, because clade w^t a husband; ag^t Christian nine doil ic allen as no sufficient witness in a matter criminall because a woman; ag^t Agnes Bayne because a whore and a scold; ag^t Agnes Bayne and Elspet Dingwall as no fit witness in a matter criminall, being women; ag^t James Logan, because a thiefe as he alledged; ag^t Donald Deisse because a lyar and a talebearer. No exception ag^t Ronald M^{c}indoir or John M^{c}phail, who being y^{r}fore called and deeply sworn to declare q^t they knew anent the s^d scandal, John McPhail (the oy^r being removed) declared y^t by night or by day, hour or moment, he never could observe any unseemly behaviour betwixt the s^d Mr. Jo^n Gordon and the s^d Jean Bayne: being hereupon removed, Renold McIndoir is called to the effect fors^d and deponed as s^d is.

The members of the visita°n, takeing to considera°n whether Mr. Gordons exceptions were relevant, yea or no, Mr. John M^{c}ra, Thesaurer, declared he thought not the minoritie of women because married, or of women under one and twentie or y^t women in g$\bar{r}$all could not be sustained witness in Criminall maters, relevant except°^{ns}, nor any oy^r aledged by Mr. Gordon except he made good his allega°ns by cleare and evident proofe; Mr. Thomas Fraser, Chancelour, was of the same mind, and y^{r}fore the matter was to be examined at the nixt meeting at Dingwall, being Novr 4, 1684, and this meeting to close. But y^t the Heritors pleaded y^t Jean Bayne, q° was principall accuser, should be allowed audience before the visita°n.

To q^ch the Moderator, subdean, and oy^rs of the Bren answered it was ag^t the rules of discipline and law to admitt a person as accusser q^o hade alreadie judiciallie assoiled the s^d Mr. Gordon and y^t it was more than they could answer for to y^r Ordinary, haveing no Commission to y^t effect. But oy^rs of the Bren replyed it was reasonable to admitt her for satisfac^on to ye gentlemen y^n and y^r present; q^ch, together with the gentlemens won importunitie, prevailed, but still the Moderator urged it was to no purpose, for anything she could said ag^t Mr. Gordon could have no weight, seeing she hade alreadie vindicated him *in sacco*. But, notwithstanding, they still pleaded to admitt her, and y^rfore being called, and askt q^t she hade to say, answered she hade nothing to say but y^t Mr. Gordon was fay^r to her child, q^ch she asserted w^t all imaginable confidence, and desired some one or two of the Bren to retire w^t her, and she should convince y^m of ye truth hereof by some secret token twixt her and the s^d Mr. Gordon.

Q^rupon Mr. Thomas Fraser, Chancelour, and Mr. George Cuming, Min^r of Urray, were enjoyned to goe apart w^t her, and learn q^t this meant, q^o made account upon y^r returne y^t anything she said wold not prove or inferre guilt, but the thing they concealed as being unworthie of audience.

Mr. John Gordon is desired by the Moderator to provide ag^t the nixt dyet to make good his exceptions ag^t the witnesses led and adduced ag^t him, oy^rwise yey wold receave y^r declara^ons, q^ch he accorded to.

Dingwall, Novr. 4, 1684.

This day y^r was nothing to be done except to examine the relevancie of Mr. Gordons exceptions ag^t the witnesses adduced at Kilterne, q^ch being required, Mr. Gordon reponed y^r could be nothing done w^tout a stated accuser, and such could not be found.

Therefore the Bren taking to considera^on y^t the Moderator hade alreadie written to the Bp to know his mind anent the visita^ons progresse at Kilterne, and y^t he hade not as yet receaved a return, they thought fit to suspend all further processe till the Bp's homecoming, and ordained ye nixt meeting to be keept at Dingwall the first twesday of Dec^r, and ordained Mr. Walter Ross to acquant Mr. W^m McKenzie and Mr. James Houston of the pbries resolution anent the premisses.

This day John Beaton of Coulnaskie undertook to prove ag^t Mr. Gordon y^t he s^d out of pulpit y^t some of the parochiners of Kilterne did suborn persons to belye him in the matter of Jean Bayne, q^{ch} he promised to make good by witnesses the nixt day.

Mr. John Gordon at the Bren̄s desire promised to keep his man-servant to the nixt meeting if it should hold twixt and Candlemas.

Mr. George Cuming appointed be order of Pr̄ie to preach at Urquhart ye next Sabbaoth.

Dingwall, Decr. 2, 1684.

The Moderator recomends to the Bren̄ to observe the feast of our Saviours nativitie.

Jarij 6, 1685

[The Bretheren had observed the feast of the Nativitie.]

This day the Elders of the paroch of Urquhart haveing supplicated the Pr̄ie to have y^r vacancie supplied, the Bren̄ resolved that it should be supplied by the Thesaurer qose Charge thei thought it was, and y^{r}fore should be served either by himself or his vicar.

March 3, '85.

This day the Moderator made account of a letter receaved from the Bp anent Mr Gordon's processe, in q^{ch} the Bp desired Jean Bayne should be sum^d to compear before this seat, and askt whether or no she should adhere to the Synods sentence, if not y^t she should be processed. The Moderator haveing y^{r}fore caused summond her to this dyet, and she being called and compearing, was askt as s^d is, but she obstinately refuseing to adhere to the Synods sentence, was told she should be processed according to the Bp's order. But the Bren̄ referred ye matter to further considera°n.

April 7, 1685.

This day the Bren̄ takeing to considera°n y^t Jean Bayne obstinately refused to submitt to the Synods sentence, advised q° should processe her, But the Moderator advertised he wrote for further advice to the Bp, and y^{r}fore the matter was delayed to the nixt meeting, being May 5, 1685.

May 5, 1685.

There being a standing statute for perpetuall solemnization of the 29 of May, in comemora°n of our late Soveraigne Charles the 2ᵈ of blessed memorie his birth and restoration, the Moderator recomended to the Bren to observe yᵒ sᵈ anniversary as formerly.

Jully 7, 85.

That day Jannet Fraser in the paroch of Dingwall, and servᵗ in Tulloch's familie, was conveened before the Pbrie on presump°n of her being big wᵗ child, and destroying yrof, of qᶜʰ presump°n yᵉ Mīnʳ of yᵉ sᵈ paroch produced written evidences upon the disposition of severall persons examined by him to yᵗ effect, as the sᵈ evidences in yʳselves doe bear; But the Bren finding yᵗ cryms of yᵗ nature were above yʳ cognizance and decision, determined to represent yᵉ case to the civil Judge, qᶻʰ was accordingly done, the clerk wᵗ the desire of the Pbrie haveing wrote a letter to Sir Rorie MᶜKenzie of Findon, Shereff Deput of Ross to yᵗ effect; The sᵈ Jannet being sent also to him accompanied wᵗ the Kirk Officers of Dingwall and Urquhart.

August 4, '85.

Hector Mᶜlean [in contin quadrulapse in fornication, and last with marion nin Archie] called, comp. and being sharply rebuked, is remitted.

The Minr of Contan haveing advertised the Bren yᵗ the sᵈ Hector hade a purpose to marry shortly, advised whether or no he should shorten the ordinary dyets of pennance appointed to such delinquents, It was resolved yᵗ seeing he was a person habituated to yᵗ sin, and yᵗ marriage (nixt to the grace of God) was the best remedie to provide agst his further falling, he should stand three or four days, and if yⁿ he gave any reasonable evidence of his remorse, he should be absolved.

There being a proclama°n issued by his Majestie Privie Counsell to celebrate a thanksgiveing through this kingdome for the late defeat of the Kings enemies,[1] upon the 13 of

---

[1] The defeat of the Duke of Monmouth at Sedgemoor on 6th July

August current, being Thursday, The Moderator notw'tstanding ye s^d proclama°ne was not come to his hand, advertised ye B̄ren to intimate to y^r respective congregations y^t the s^d thanksgiveing was to observed the fors^d thursday.

Dingwall, Novr. 10, 1685.

This day the B̄ren mett be vertue of the Bps and Synods order to examine the witnesses adduced in Mr. John Gordons processe, and accordingly Mr. John M^cra and Mr. Walter Ross, to q^m it was recomended to examine the witnesses led in the Paroch of Kilterne on some stated occasion preceeding this meeting, being askt whether or no they were carefull of this trust, Mr. Walter Ross answered it was not possible for him to attend it ye day appointed, because the waters interjected twixt his and Kiltern paroch were unpassable.

Mr. John M^cra answered he went to the s^d paroch and examined the witnesses, q^ose names are as follows, vizt, Kath. nin ulay vic ulliam, Christian ni vic allan, and being further askt q^t y^r depositions were, answered y^t Christian ni vic Allan deponed she was never witnesse to any of Mr. John Gordons and Jean Baines converse, and y^t she was never to her knowledge in one house or town w^t y^m both together, except q^n the visita°n held at Kiltern, but y^t she heard Kath. nin doil vic horish say, y^t she saw the s^d Mr. John Gordon and the s^d Jean Bayne miscarry.

Kath. nin ullay vic ulliam deponed she never saw them together but at ye visita°n at Kiltern, and y^t the s^d Jean Bayne told her y^t her child was begot in the paroch of Dingwall by a Souldier.

The Moderator haveing enquired whether y^r was any account from Mr. Arthur Suy^rland anent Kath. nin doil vic horish, Mr. John M^cra told he receaved a letter from him importing his diligence in searching for her, q^ch letter is delivered to the Clerk to be given up to the Bp and sub-synod.

That day the Moderator haveing enquyred of the B̄ren how they should proceed ag^t the s^d Kath. nin doil vic horish in her absence, and they being in recent memorie y^t it was the Bp's will y^t Mr. Gordon's witnesses to prove her a thiefe should be receaved whether she were present or no, after search made for her, y^rfore they thought fit to examine the witnesses adduced by Mr. Gordon, whose names are as follows: John McCurchie, a married man of age fourtie year, Mary Chisholm, ane unmarried woman of age 30 year, and Mary nin doil uyre, ane unmarried woman, about 40, q° being all deeply sworn, and the two women w^t Mr. Gordon being removed,

John McCurchie deponed, y^t the s^d Kath. nin doil vic horish was wont w^t false keys to open the s^d Mr. Gordons cellars and amberies and steal part of everything belonging him and dispone y^rof at her pleasure, and y^t at her goeing away she stole a white plaid from him.

Mary Chisholme deponed she was in certaine knowledge y^t the s^d Kath. stole ten elns of white plaid and ane half stone of cheese at her way goeing out of Mr. Gordon's house, as also some cheese at diverse times from herself, and y^t about Whitsunday last she proffered ye said white plaid to Mr. Gordon and his wiffe, but being afraid to come in y^r presence went away w^t againe, threatening she should either steal a Cow or ane herse from y^m in compensa°n of her wages, which she aleadged was owing by the s^d Mr. Gordon; and the s^d Mary Chisholm further declared y^t she heard it s^d y^t the said Kath. nin doil vic horish made use of false keys to steal Mr. Gordons goods, but y^t she was in no certaine knowledge yrof.

Mary nin doil uyre deponed she was in certaine knowledge of her stealing small linnens, some cheese, and ane white plaid from ye s^d Mr. Gordon and his wiffe.

Thereafter the Br̄en proceeded to examine the relevancie of Mr. Gordons exceptions ag^t Agnes Bayne, and Mr. Gordon being askt if he called his witnesses to this effect, answered he did. Their names are as followes, viz., Don^d Ross and Gilbert Robertson, both in the Paroch of Kilterne, and Jannet nin ean vic ulliam, the latter absent; the oy^r two comp. viz., Don^d Ross and Gilbert Robertson, the former a married person about fourtie, the latter unmarried about one and twentie years.

Agnes Bayne being called and askt if she hade any exceptions ag^t these two, answered negatively; they yrfore being deeply sworn, all the parties and witnesses being removed, except Don^d Ross, the s^d Donald deponed he heard the s^d Agnes Bayne threaten she should be fit side w^t Mr. Gordon.

Gilbert Robertson being called deponed as follows, y^t one a certaine time he heard the s^d Agnes Bayne say she should be fit side w^t Mr. Gordon, and on anoy^r time the week before Synod last partlarly, he heard her swear y^t after nixt Sabbaoth he should never fill the pulpit.

The Br̄en referred the relevancie of yese objections to the Subsynod, and accordingly summond the s^d Agnes Baine *apud acta* to be pn̄t at the Subsynod.

5 Janr. 1686.

The Right R. Bishop and Synod having recommended to the Presbyterie the examina°n of Mr. John Gordon's process ag^t Malcome M^{c}gillicharich in Kinardie in the paroche of Dingwell, importing that some persons had promist ten bolls of beare to the said Malcome for fastening Jean Baynes allegation upon the said Mr. John Gordowne, as also the processe agst Agnes Bayne in Dingwell, bearing that she threatened that she wold cause shoot the s^d Mr. John Gordowne through the head with a pair of balls, Mr. John Gordowne being present stands to his allegations.

Malcome McGillicharrich being called, compeared, and being inquired whether he had said that some persons offered him ten bolls beare as is aforesaid, he answered negative; qrupon Mr. John Gordowne leads in the witnesses afterwritten, viz. Rod. Bayne, Tutor of Tulloch, Cristan nin Tir and Helen nin ferq^r in Milninch. The witnesses called, compeared, except Cristan nin Tir fors^d, and, no exception made agst y^m, wer deeplie sworne and admitted, both parties removed.

The said Rorie Bayne, a married man about the age of 50 years, deponed that he heard the s^d Malcome Mackgillicharrich say as is libelled.

The s^d Helen nin ferq^r, a married woman about 40 years of age, deponed negative.

Lykwyse, The said Agnes Bayne being called, compeared, and being Inquired whether she spoke as is lybelled, denyed.

The said Mr. John Gordowne, to prove his lybell agst the said Agnes Bayne, leads thes following persons as witnesses, viz., the said Rorie Bayne, Katherin Ross his spouse, Agnes nin vic onil in Dochcartie. The Witnesses called, compeared, and no exception made agst y^m. They wer sworne and admitted, and both parties removed.

The said Rod. Bayne being inquired if he heard Agnes Bayne say as is libelled, answered positive.

Katherin Ross, a married woman of the age of 36 years, being inquired, deponed positive.

Agnes nin Conel, about the age of 32 years, being inquired, deponed positivlie.

Cristin nin Tir not present, is to be sumded to the nixt day.

That day Agnes nin Dod vicay, referred from Contan, who brought a child a whyle ago and fathered the same on Keneth McCurchie in Dingwell, who then acknowledged the same and satisfied the discipline of the Church, yet now it is found out that the said Keneth was not indeed the father of it bot one John M^cfinlay duj in Contan, who was married to the s^d Agnes hir sister, and that the said Kenneth owned the said child out of his relation to the said John M^cfinlay duj being his vncle, and to clock y^t Incest. The said Agnes being present, was inquyred who was the reall father of her child answered, That Donald Chisolm in Contan was the father of it, and neither the said John M^cfinlay duj nor the said Kenneth McCurchie. The said Donald Chisholme called, compeared, and being inquired, denyed the same, and did instantlie prove that the said Agnes nin Dod vicay did confess before the Session of Contan, that ther was scandalous converse betwixt hir and the s^d John M^cfinlay duj.

That day Keneth McCurchie, referred from Dingwell, called, and not compearing, to be cited pro 2°, and the s^d Agnes nin vicay sumded *apud acta* to compeare the nixt meeting day.

John M^cW^m voir, referred from Vrq^rt, who had been severall dayes formerlie before the Presbiterie for not cohabiting with Agnes nin Tarlich vic Alister his spouse, called, compeared and confest y^t he was impotent and could not performe conjugall duties; q^rupon the Presbiterie recommended the said Agnes, who was also present, to procure a divorce before the Commissars as Judges competent.

[No account of 'Katherin nin Do^d vic horish for q^m Mr. James McKenzie, subdeane, promist at the last subsynod to make search for hir in his paroche of Nigg, and to send hir to the Presbiterie.']

Dingwall, 2 Febr. 1686.

That day Cirstan nin Tir, spouse to Malcome McGillicharrich in Kinardie, called, compeared, and being inquired if she heard the said Malcome McGillicharrich at anie tyme say y^t ther was ten bolls of beare promist him be some person for causing Jeane Bayne to father the child brought forth by hir on Mr. John Gordowne, shee being admitted and sworne, and no exceptions made agst hir, deponed negativlie.

2 March 1686.

Kenneth M^ccurchie, from Ding^{ll}, and Agnes nin dod vicay, from Contan, sumded, cited, and compearing, the said Keneth being inquired, declared y^t he was not father to the child brought forth by the said Agnes, bot that he tooke that guilt upon himselfe for his relation to and at the persuasion of John Du in Contan, who was the true fay^r of it. The presbiterie therefor appoynted the said Keneth M^ccurchie to stand in sack cloath in the Church of Contan untill signes of repentance should be seen in him.

Donald Chisolme in Contan regrated to the Presbiterie that the said Agnes nin do^d vicay had impudentlie and felslie slandered him by alledging that he was father to the child that she brought to John Du in Contan. The Presbiterie, after search, finding that the said Donald Chisolme was wronged by hir, absolved him, and censured the s^d Agnes.

Dingll., 6 April 1686.

Mr. Donald Forbes preacht a populare Sermon, Heb. 12. 12, and was approven, and the Brethren considering that the said Mr. Donald Forbess had past all the ordinarie steps off tryall as Expectant, and had given sufficient proofe of his abilities for the ministrie, and had given abundant satisfaction to the Bren in all the forsaids steps, did therefore recommend him to the R. R. Bishop for a license to preach the Gospell, and appoynted the Clerk of the Presbiterie to draw up a recomenda^on to be sub^t be the Mod^r and the said Clerk to y^t effect.

[The following were the 'steps of tryall' passed by Mr. Forbes: On 5th Janry. 1686, he 'had a Comon head *de satisfactione Christi* and delivered the same, for q^ch he was approven and was appoynted maintaine disputs yrupon the nixt presbiterie day.' On 2d Feb. he 'maintained disputs upon the theses *de satisfactione Christi*, and was approven,' and was 'appoynted to exercise the nixt day of meeting on Rom. 9. ch. 15. 16 v^ses.' On the 2d March he exercised accordingly, and was approven, and appointed to have deliver a popular sermon on the 6th April, when the above minute was passed.)

4 *May* 1686.

[The Synod had not kept its last intended meeting 'because the Bishop went to attend the Parliament.' The 29th of May to be observed.]

6 *July* 1686.

That day Mr. John Gordowne complained that John M^ccalich in the Paroche of Kilterne suffered two off his children contemptuouslie to die with[out] Baptisme, and is therefore to be sumõned to the nixt day for his contempt of the sacra^t.

[M^ccalich was cited to severall subsequent meetings, but not appearing, he was, on 14th April 1687, referred to the Bishop and Synod. He declares himself a Conventicler. See Minute, 2d Aug. '87.]

7 *Septr.* 1686.

Mr. John McKenzie [the Moderator and Arch-deacon] absent because he was commissioned by the R. R. Bishop to goe to Mr. John McKilligin in Alnes, to prohibte him to keep conventicles in this diocess.

18 *Oct.* 1686.

That day conveened, with Mr. John Mackenzie, Moderator, Mrs John M^ccra, Geo. Cuming, William Fraser, Andrew Ross, Walter Ross, John Gordowne, with M^rs Do^d M^ccra, Min^r of Lochailsh, Mr. Donald M^ccra, Min^r of Kintaile, Mr. Roderick Mackenzie, Min^r of Gerloch, Mr. Alex^r M^eKenzie, Min^r of Lochcarron, Mr. John McKenzia, Min^r of Lochbroome.

[The Brethren had all preached on 14th October, the Kings Birth day.]

[Finlay M^cean vuy, Sum^d from Kintail for not cohabiting with Duesh his wife, 'confest that he was impotent and not able to do his wife the dutie of ane husband. Therefore the said Duesh desired a recomendation to the Comiss^{rs} to prosecute a divorce, q^{ch} was granted.']

That day Mr. Wm Fraser complained that Ewen McHucheon vic ewn (who had fallen in adulterie with Margret nin homas in his paroche of Kilmorack) profest himself a Papist to shun the censure of the Church, was referred to the Bishop and Synod nixt.

1 Feb. 1687.

Marie nien Dhonchie roy, referred from the Session of Lochbroom, for a recomendation to the Commiss^{rs} in order to the obtaining a divorce from her husband Kenneth McCurchie, who refused to adhere, and in the mean time had fallen in adulterie, compeared and was continued in regard that the s^d Kenneth, being sum^d and cited, did not comppear, and is appoynted to be sum^d pro 2°.

March 1, 1687.

Donald McLey in Strachonnan sum^d, cited, and not compearing, is to be sum^d pro 3°, and Mr. George Cuming was appoynted to make a representa°n to the s^d Donald his liveing in habituall adulterie, to the Justices of Peace for y^r concurrence.

April 14, 1687.

Mr. George Cuming declared that (as the Brethren had recomended to him) hee had represent to the Justices of peace, particularly to the Laird of Coul, the s^d Donald McLeay his liveing in habituall adulterie.

The Brethren considering that though their supplying the Parish of Contan was someq^t troublesome to them, yet nevertheless, diverse of the parishinoers did repine verie much that they were left so long unprovided of a settled minister, they judged it fit to haue the desolate condition of the s^d parish of Contan represented to the R. R. Bishop and Synod.

6 Decr. 1687.

There was no doctrine delivered that day, Mr. John M^ccra, late Schoolmaster of Dingwall (who was appointed to exercise), haveing gone to Aberdene in order to attend the profession of Theologie.

Feb. 7, 1687.

The Min^r of Wrq^{rt} reported y^t he had begun to pray publictlie for Donald McLennan.

[Donald McLennan was suspected of 'being guiltie with Jonat Fraser.' On 6 Dec. 1687 he appeared before the Presby. at the Bishop's request (he having failed to appear at previous meetings of the Synod and Presbytery), and denied guilt, 'q^{r}upon he was then ordained to compeare before the session of Urq^{rt} q^r that scandal had been raised on him and Jonat Fraser, and that in order to further examination and getting clearnenesse in that matter: and the min^r of Urq^{r}t was ordained to take his oath before the congregation after his compearance and examination before the Sessione.' On 3d January 1688 'the Min^r of Wrq^{rt} reported that Donald McLennan had not compeared before the Session of Wrq^{rt} as was ordained, the reason q^{r}of could not be known till Mr. Walter Ross came, in whose Paroch the s^d Donald resides.' On 7th Feb. the Minister reported that McLennan had appeared 'as was ordained, and haveing been seriouslie exhorted to deal ingenuouslie, did still adhere to his innocencie: q^{r}upon since clearing him of the scandal under q^{ch} he lay but his oath, he was ordained to be readie to give his oath before the congregation of Wrq^{rt} Sabboth come eight dayes thereafter.' Then follows the above report as to public prayers for him. These had their effect, for on 7th March, the Minister having reported that McLennan 'had confessed before the Session guilt with Jonat Fraser, and therefore had referred and caused summoned him to compeare before the pñt meeting, the said Donald compeared *in sacco*, confessing that he was guiltie with the said Janet, yet denying he was father of the child lately brought furth by hir: being seriously exhorted to glorifie God in the true and full confession of his sin, was remitted to the Session to satisfie Church discipline.]

Aug. 2, 1687.

The Minister of Kiltern informing that John M^chalich awoues himselfe to be a conventicler, the Bren thought it not their concern to follow him further untill they adwise with the Bp and Synod.

4 Oct. 1687.

Mr. John M^ccra, Schoolmaster of Dingwall, is ordained to haue a Common head *de libero arbitrio* at the first meeting of the Prēbrie efter the nixt Synod.[1]

---

[1] The last Minute recorded in volume iii. is dated 13th Oct. 1687. The next volume begins in 1716. In the interval there was not a sufficient number of Presbyterian ministers within the bounds to constitute a meeting, and, other Northern presbyteries being in the same position, an attempt was made by Mr. William Stewart, minister of Kiltearn, Mr. Hugh Anderson, minister of Cromarty, Mr. William Mackay, minister of Dornoch, and Mr. Walker Denune, minister of Golspie, to carry on the work of the Church, by getting themselves formed into the 'Presbytery of Ross.' That Presbytery did not long survive. Its records, beginning 25th July 1693, and ending 12th November 1701, contain some interesting reading.

APPENDIX

The following are the Engagers in Kiltearn whose names are omitted on page 157 :—

'David Monro c'fessed only that he was in the unlawfull ingadgement against England, bot that he hade no office.

'Robt Monro sonne to Lemlair c'fessed lykewyse that he was in the unlaw^{ll} ingadgement against England, bot had no charge.

'Hutcheon Monro c'fessed he was a com'on sojour both in the unlawfull ingadgement and the late rebellion.

'Andrew Logan, Do^d Monro, W^m M^{c}allan, Do^d M^{c}nicoll, Do^d M^{c}conill vic Jaspairt, c'fessed y^t they were com'on souldiers in the unlaw^{ll} ingadgement.'

The persons omitted from the Fodderty list (p. 158) are :—

'Murdo M^{c}conill oir, Do^d McJames vic Robt, James dow, Do^d M^{c}ean vic thomas, Gillandries M^{c}ean dowy, c'fessed there accesse to the late rebellion by being at both Inv'nes and Balvenie.

'Do^d M^{c}conill oir, Gilbert Boyth, Andrew M^{c}conchie vic andrew, Duncan M^{c}conill vic conchie vic andrew, Jo^n M^{c}thomas vic alister, W^m M^{c}alist^r vic William vic Finlay, Murdo Vrq^{rt}, Do^d M^{c}conill voir, Thomas Ross, Jo^n M^c W^m vic thomas, Do^d M^{c}gillighlaish, Jo^n M^{c}conill vic andrew, W^m M^{c}george, Alex^r M^{c}gilliriach, Alister Graisich, Alex^r Dowyn, Do^d M^{c}allist^r vic finlay brembner, David M^{c}ean vic gilliphatrick, and Duncan M^{c}phoid c'fessed they were at Invernes, bot not at Balvenie.'

The following is the complete list of Engagers within the parishes of Urray and Kilchrist (p. 159) :—

'M^r Do^d M^{c}rae did give in a list of ingadgers within the parochins of vrray and kilchreist, c'teining the persones following : Rorie Ma^{c}kenzie of Davachmoluagg, Kenneth M^{c}kenzie his ser-servant, W^m M^{c}finlay, W^m M^{c}conill vayne vic ean vreick, Duncan

M^{c}conill vic ean riach, James M^{c}vic rob in Wester Farburne, Hector M^{c}kenzie of Farburne, Rorie M^{c}kenzie fier of farburne, Rorie begg M^{c}eachin, Do^d M^{c}alister vic gillandries, Jo^n buy M^{c}finlay gowne, Thomas begg M^{c}chlachar. Thomas moir M^{c}chlachar, Jo^n M^c Wm Mersall, Jo^n M^{c}ridler in mid farburne ; Jo^n keil M^{c}coule, Jo^n M^{c}conill dowy vic W^m, Jo^n M^{c}conill vic ean, Do^d M^{c}conill riach, Jo^n Vrq^{rt}, Alister M^{c}ghowin, Wm Moir, Duncan Greisone, Do^d M^{c}soirle, in bellvraid ; Jo^n M^{c}ean vic conill vic thomais, Do^d M^{c}finlay na loigh, Alister M^{c}conill vic ean, Jo^n M^{c}alister vic conill dowy, Do^d M^{c}ean roy, in teahnafile ; Duncan M^{c}ferq^r voir, Do^d M^{c}ritchie, Do^d W^m roy, Do^d M^{c}tormoid, Duncan M^{c}anteir, Jo^n riach M^c W^m vic conill roy, Jo^n M^{c}gillimichaell, in kinchuldruim ; Jo^n M^{c}kenzie of oird, Kenneth M^{c}ean dowy, Andrew besack, in oird ; Andrew McJames ghow, Alex^r M^{c}conill ghow, Jo^n roy M^{c}jock, Jo^n M^{c}conill vic gillichalm, Jo^n M^{c}rorie vic Mathon, in Achnasole ; Finlay M^{c}rorie vic Mathon, Alex^r M^{c}conchie, Kenneth kaird, Do^d M^{c}rorie vic Mathon, Do^d M^{c}conill roy vic curchie, in arkon ; Do^d M^{c}alister vic conill dowy, Kenneth and Duncan his brethren, Finlay McJames gow thair ; Do^d M^{c}conchie vic Kenneth, W^m roy McGeorge, Jo^n M^{c}conchie vic ean vreick, Do^d M^{c}finlay taielzeor, Kenneth M^{c}conchie, Do^d M^{c}alister vic coule, in moy ; Do^d bayne M^{c}george, Do^d M^{c}cay vic thomas, James M^{c}W^m vic andrew, Alex^r M^{c}conill vic ean dowy, James Grant, in Brahan ; Captaine Bayne thair ; Alex^r McGeorge in Vrray ; W^m M^{c}chaptin, Rorie M^{c}jock, W^m M^{c}jock, Jo^n M^{c}ean vic cuyan, Do^d his brother, Alex^r M^{c}ghowin, in Rih-dun ; W^m M^{c}ritchie, Jo^n M^{c}thomas dowyne, Murdo M^{c}ritchie, in ardnacraisk ; Do^d M^{c}ean greasich, Alex^r Bayne of Tarradaill, Thomas roy M^{c}conill vaine, Jo^n M^{c}toirmoid, Do^d M^{c}ean vic cathie in Tarradaill.'

The following are the persons omitted from the list of the Kiltearn Engagers (p. 160) :—

'Alex^r M^{c}ean vic George, Hector M^{c}reacan, George M^{c}conill monro, W^m M^{c}ean vic gillimichaell, Jo^n Bayne in Dargon, Jo^n M^{c}alister roy, Do^d M^{c}finlay vic alister dowy, Alister roy M^{c}cay, Hector Monro, Wm Vrq^{rt}, W^m M^{c}W^m vic cay, David M^{c}alister.'

The Engagers from Urquhart and Logie (p. 160) are :—

'Patrick Skinner, Do^d roy, Alex^r M^{c}ritchie, W^m M^{c}thomas, in Vrq^{rt} ; Do^d Glasse, Thomas Glasse, Jo^n bayne M^{c}ritchie, Jo^n Mc Andrew vic ritchie, Do^d oig M^{c}ritchie, in Gerloch Kinkell ; Finlay M^{c}nakaird, Kenneth M^{c}curchie, Do^d roy M^{c}thomas, Hutcheon

M^crob^t, Joⁿ Fraser, Andrew greasich, in Loggies; of which compeired Do^d M^critchie, c'fessed only he wes at Inv'nes, Patrick Skinner, that he wes at Balvenie, Do^d M^cW^m, that he wes at Inv'nes, Do^d Glasse at Inv'nes and Balvenie, Joⁿ bayne M^critchie at Inv'nes and Balvenie, Do^d oig M^critchie, *idem*.'

'Ingaders compeiring this day from the Paroch of Alnes [See p. 160].

'Gillicalm M^cean c'fessed he wes with James Graham [Montrose] and in the late Insurrection at Inv'nes; Hector Monro y^t he wes on the vnlawfull ingadgement; W^m bulgich, W^m roy, Do^d Monro, Duncan M^cgillichalme, Finlay M^cchattich, Joⁿ M^cconill roy, *idem*; Ranald M^cconchie vic Ranald, at Balvenie; Do^d M^ckeallie, the ingadgement.'

Engagers omitted, p. 162.

'Alex^r roy in Inschrorie within the Paroch of Kilmorack, compeiring and examined anent his accession to the rebellion, c'fessed he wes on the late Insurrection against Inv'nes.'

'Ingadgers compeiring from Vrray.

'Kenneth M^cean vic eachin c'fessed his going to Invernes; W^m M^cfinlay at Inv'nes and Balvenie; W^m M^cconnill vaine, Inv'nes and Balvenie; Duncan M^cconill vic ean riach, Keassack, Inv'nes and Balvenie; James M^cvic rob, Inv'nes and Balvenie; Do^d M^calister vic gillandries, Inv'nes; Joⁿ buy M^cfinlay dowyie, Inv'nes; Thomas begg and Thomas moir M^cchlacher, at Inv'nes and Balvenie; Joⁿ Mersall, at Inv'nes; Joⁿ Ma^cridler, at Inv'nes and Balvenie; Joⁿ M^ccoule, Kessack, Inv'nes and Balvenie; Joⁿ dow M^cW^m, Kessack and Inv'nes; Joⁿ M^cconill vic eau, Inv'nes; Do^d M^cconill riach, Kessack, Inv'nes and Balvenie; Joⁿ Vrq^{rt}, Inv'nes and Balvenie; Alister M^cghowin and Wm Moir at Inv'nes and Balvenie.

'Captaine Alex^r Bayne c'fessed he wes with James Grahame at Inv'nes, and on the late Insurrection at Inv'nes and Balvenie.

'Alex^r McKenzie in Cuiltaldod, within the paroch of fottertie, c'fessed his being at Kessack first and last, and seemed truely penitent.'

Malignants in Dingwall (p. 171).

'Compeired Alex^r Bayne Ranaldson, Do^d McKenzie, Joⁿ clk [clerk], Joⁿ Elder, Do^d M^ccurchie, Do^d glass, Alex^r elder, W^m Mc Do^d vic rorie, Hector Taylor, all within the paroch of Dingwall, who did c'fess ther accession to the late rebellion in the north, all professing y^r greefe for the same, and petitioning to be received to the Covenant and satisfaction, who all ar recommended to Mr. Jo^n Macrae to be received according to the act of classes, and before he receive y^m to make all the tryall he can anent ther furder accession to former malignant courses and cariages.'

The names of the malignants contained in the lists given in by Mr. Donald Fraser and Mr. Farquhar Maclennan on 5th March 1650 (p. 176), and in the lists submitted by the minister of Kiltearn and Mr. John Munro on the 19th of that month (p. 177) were never recorded in the Minutes.

INDEX

ABERCHALDER, xxxi, 91.
Abertarff, vi, vii, xvi, xxxiv, 65, 67, 70, 80, 82; list of papists in, 91.
Act of classes, 173, 370.
Adamson, George, writer in Elgin, 81.
Adultery, xvii, xviii, xxxi, 2, 39, 41, 59, 68, 78, 84, 92, 100, 102, 145, 149, 151, 165, 174, 281, 286, 303, 317, 338, 340, 344, 364.
Agnes nin Dod. vicay, xlii, 361, 362.
—— nin ean chile, 303.
—— nin vic onil, 360, 361.
—— nin Tarlich vic Alister, 361.
—— nin Ronald woire, 255.
—— more nin ean glaish, xl, 325-327.
—— nick Killichoan, 322.
—— nin dod. oig vic finlay, xliv, 337.
Alexander, Charles, schoolmaster of Dingwall, xlviii, 319-321.
—— graisich, 367.
—— M'Conchie vic ririe, 191.
—— M'conill vic ean, 368.
—— M'conill vic ean dowy, 368.
—— M'conill ghow, 368.
—— M'ean vic gillireich, xli, 344.
—— M'ean vic George, 368.
—— M'Finlay vic conill duj, 280.
—— M'Konil vic Allister, 331.
—— M'Konil vick robby, 108.
—— roy, in Inschrorie, 369.
—— roy M'Cay, 368.
—— M'William vic ean vic conal, xliv, 337.
Alness (Alines), vi, vii, ix, xlvii, 141, 156, 157, 192, 197, 199, 210, 269, 294, 302 and n, 304, 305, 313, 321, 341; 'engagers' in, 157, 369; contribution for Alness brew-house, 349; bridge of, 161.
Alves, 64.
Andersone, Gilbert, xlv, 121, 261, 270.
Anderson or Whyte, Isabell, 351.
Andrew greasich, in Loggie, 369.
—— M'conchie vic Andrew, 367.
—— M'James ghow, 368.
—— M'Konilvickandrew, 108.

Angus M'ean vic conill, 191.
Annan, John, 80, 119, 193.
—— William, 80, 81, 120.
Anne nin William vic yoke, 344.
—— ninickgillivichell, 340.
Applecross, vi, xxx, xxxvii, xxxviii, 277, 278, 279 and n, 280, 281.
Aquavita merchants, 143 and n.
Archibald, Alex., 63, 64.
—— M'Conachie vᶜ Phadrick, 91.
Ardullie, 294.
Assynt, xxxi, 205, 294.
Auchnaseallach, 280, 282, 287.
Auldearn, 2, 93, 136, 137, 142, 152, 155, 167, 168.
Ault Sulua, Boleskine, 25, 27.

BAILLIE, ALEX., in Borlum, 94.
—— David, of Dochfour, xxxvi, 69, 90.
—— Hendrie, 39, 40.
—— James, a papist, xxxvi, 69, 90.
—— John, of Leyes Cruii, 104.
—— William, 87.
Bain or Bayne, Agnes, 349, 350, 351, 354, 359-361.
—— Alex., of Knockbaine, 154, 157, 248, 253, 255.
—— —— of Tarradaill, 159.
—— captain Alex., 159, 162, 368, 369.
—— Donald, xxxii, 119, 139, 143, 160, 315-317, 343.
—— Elizabeth, 145, 174, 176, 177, 181, 349-353.
—— Gilis, in Knockbaxter, 238.
—— Henry, bailzie in Dingwall, xlii, 325.
—— Jean, 349-356, 358, 362.
—— John, 158, 368.
—— —— of Tulloch, 138, 141, 174, 175, 218, 238, 248, 249, 251-254.
—— —— student of divinity, 316, 318, 319.
—— Roderick, 360, 361.
—— Ronald, 175.
—— —— notar, 237, 238, 241, 248, 253.

Bain, Ronald, bailie, 253.
Balconie, 353.
Balfoure, George, at Ardclach, 71.
Balnagown, 309.
Balvenie, battle of, viii, 139 and *n*, 140 *n*, 151, 154 *n*, 156, 158, 162, 367, 369.
Barber, Robert, 87.
Barron, William, in Drumreach, 108.
Bayne. *See* Bain.
Beaton (Betoune), Angus, 251.
—— John, in Culniskea, 339, 356.
—— Neill, 152, 156, 163.
Beggars, act of synod against, 332.
Beseck, Alex., xxxii, 87, 92, 94.
—— Andrew, in Oird, 368.
Beth, Gilbert, 312.
Bighouse. *See* Mackay of Bighouse.
Blasphemy, 340.
Boat of Bonah, 64.
Boleskine, v, xvii, li, 4, 23, 25, 26, 53, 83.
Bona, vi.
Both, 63.
Boy or Buy, Alex., 91.
—— Christian, 137, 138, 196, 200.
—— Finlay, 305.
—— John, 150.
—— Murdo, 306.
Boyth, Gilbert, 367.
Brahan, English garrison in, ix, xxvii.
Brembner, Dod. M'Allister vic Finlay, 367.
Brodie, laird of, 89.
Bulgich, William, in Alness, 369.
Bulls, the sacrifice of, 280, 338.
Burnet, Andrew, minister in Edinburgh, 131.
Byers, sir John, of Coats, xxxi, xxxv, 43, 45, 46, 48, 49, 69, 91.
—— lady. *See* Grant, Lilias.

CAIRD (KAIRD), DONALD, 271.
—— John, 249, 253, 317, 324 *n*.
—— Kenneth, 159, 368.
Calder, laird of, 35, 37, 38, 40.
Callom, Isabell, 63.
Carbisdale, defeat of Montrose at, 184.
Carngoddy, 91.
Castlehill. *See* Cuthbert, George.
Castle Stuart, 49.
Catherine nin rorie vic ean vic conichie Riach, 151, 155.
Cattanach, James, 331.
—— Robert, xlii, 341.
Cattir, M'Finlay v^c ean v^c conill, 335.
Chalmer, John, town clerk of Elgin, 81.
—— William, 132.

Chambers, Christian, 3, 4, 5.
Chanonrie, xlvii, 167, 168, 175, 200, 247, 270, 292, 308, 312, 336, 337, 347.
Charles II., viii, x, xiii, xxii, xxiii, 99, 357.
Charms, xli, 156, 196, 240, 333, 344.
Child murder, xxx, 92, 254, 255.
Chisholme (Schisome), Alex., xxx, 3, 4, 6, 43, 44.
—— —— of Comar, 141, 142 and *n*.
—— —— Colin, of Buntait, a papist, xxxvi, 50 and *n*, 57, 58, 60, 61, 77.
—— —— Donald, xlii, 361, 362.
—— —— John, 329, 331.
—— —— Mary, 91, 359.
—— —— Thomas, 192, 193, 197, 199, 329, 331.
Chlerich, Elspet, 92.
Christian nin doil vic allen, 354, 358.
—— nin Alister beg, 309.
—— neine ean vic gillichallum, 196.
—— neine ean vic Kenneth, 149.
Church collections, xlv, xlvi.
Clerk, Alexander, xlii, 2, 15, 16 and *n*, 17, 19, 20, 26, 36, 42, 44, 46, 60, 65-67, 69, 80, 81, 84-87, 89, 91, 112, 116, 119, 239, 240.
—— Donald, in Lochalsh, 171, 253.
—— John, 108.
Cloggie, William, 25, 26.
Clunes, William, 156.
Coats, laird of. *See* Byers, sir John.
Cogaich, 196, 233.
Commir, 88.
Connan, 182.
Contin, vi, viii-x, xxxi, xxxviii, 161, 174, 178, 179, 186, 191, 199, 203, 205-209, 218, 220, 221-228, 234, 241, 246, 277, 281, 282, 292, 293, 364.
Conventicles, xiii, xiv, 93, 301 *n*, 324, 329, 338, 339, 344, 345, 363, 366.
Cook, James, 121, 132.
Cotterell, colonel, 257 *n*.
Covenant of 1638, vii, viii.
Cristan nin Tir, 360-362.
Cromwell's soldiers in the north, ix.
Crookshank, Marie, 338.
Croy, vi, xxii, xxx, li. 16, 103, 104.
Culbin, 339.
Culcowie. *See* M'Kenzie, Alex.
Culduthell. *See* Fraser, Malcom.
Culloden, holy well at, xxxix.
Cumming, Alex., 95-98, 101, 112, 116, 122, 124.
—— David, 132.
—— Donald, of Dailshangie, 75.
—— Farqr., in Garthalie, 75.

INDEX

Cumming, George, 76, 293, 295, 297-301, 304-308, 311, 315, 321, 323, 325, 336, 337, 345, 355, 356.
—— James, 75.
—— —— in Pitkerrell, 75.
—— John, 93.
—— Michael, 132.
—— Robert, of Inchbryne, 76.
—— —— of Urquhart, 123-125, 127, 129.
—— William, sheriff-clerk of Inverness, 76, 87, 106.
Cuthbert, Alexander, 22.
—— Doncan, in Altirlie, 109.
—— George, of Castlehill, 47-49, 51.
—— John, 31-35 and *n*, 39, 109.

DALAROSSIE, vi, 52, 95, 97, 122.
Dalgleish, Colin, his abjuration of popery, xxxvi, 58, 59, 60, 61.
Dallas, Hugh, of Brachly, 109.
—— John, 104, 174, 261, 267, 270, 287.
Dancing at lykewakes, 52-55; at penny weddings, 121 *n*.
David M'ean vic gilliphatrick, 367.
Daviot, vi, xvi, xvii, xxii, li, 19, 32, 35, 37, 57, 61, 62, 65, 72-74, 101, 103, 104 and *n*, 105, 106; parish registers of, 107.
Davison, Donald, 105.
—— Isobell, 32.
Dean, Bessie, 39, 40, 42.
Declarations of Estate and Kirk, 180.
Deisse, Donald, 354.
Denune or Denoone, Alex., 92, 94, 113, 117, 124.
—— David, 109, 114, 115.
—— John, in Connadge, 109.
—— Walter, 339 and *n*, 340, 345.
—— William, 202.
Derilans, 282 and *n*.
Dickson, Patrick, 154.
Dingwall, 248-255, 302, 303, 343; persecution of malignants in, viii.
—— bridge, ix.
—— Agnes, 349, 350, 352, 354.
—— Alex., 312, 328.
—— Donald, 252, 253.
—— John, xlii, 251, 302, 321.
—— Ronald, 251.
—— William, 238, 251, 253, 260, 334.
Donald bayne M'George, 368.
—— dow Mack conachie nan each, xviii, 43, 44.
—— M'Alister vic coule, in Moy, 368.
—— M'Alister vic gillandries, 368, 369.
—— M'Alister v^c tyre, 91.

Donald M'Alister vic Finlay, 143.
—— M'Alister vic conill dowy, 146, 149, 158, 368.
—— M'Cay vic thomas, 368.
—— M'Conchie vic Kenneth, 368.
—— M'Conill roy vic curchie, 368.
—— M'Conill voir, 367.
—— M'Conill chile, 280.
—— M'Conill riach, 368, 369.
—— M'Conill vic Jaspairt, 367.
—— M'Donald vic ean, 343.
—— Macdunichie vic ol vane, 347-8.
—— M'Ean chile, 347, 348.
—— M'ean greasich, 159, 368.
—— M'ean roy, 368.
—— M'ean vic cathie, 368.
—— M'ean vic cayan, 368.
—— M'ean vic finlay, 144, 174.
—— M'ean vic ryrie, 338.
—— M'ean vic Thomas, 367.
—— M'ean vic ean glash, 308.
—— M'ean roy v^c chenich, 280.
—— M'ean na loigh, 368.
—— M'finlay vic alister dowy, 368.
—— M'finlay vic ean, 343.
—— M'James vic Robt, 367.
—— M'rorie vic Mathon, 368.
—— M'Thomas vic Andrew, 28.
—— og M'ean dui, 348.
—— oig M'ritchie, 369.
—— Roy, 368.
—— Roy M'Thomas, 368.
—— William roy, 368.
Donaldson (Dodson), Finlay, in Milchaich, 143.
Dores, vi, xvi, xviii, xxi, xxx, li, 55, 94, 110, 113.
Douglas, Collin, 334.
—— Hector, of Balconie, 139, 156, 161, 183, 235.
—— Robert, 187.
Dow, Donald, in Borlume, 82.
—— John, 160.
—— Margaret, 196.
Dowgall M'Conachie vic conill, 94.
Downe, Margaret, 41.
Dowyn, Alex., 367.
Dress of the clergy, xix, xx, 11 and *n*.
Drummond, Donald, of Drummond, 24.
Drunkenness, xxiv, xxv, 48-50, 99, 139, 341.
Duff, James, notar publick, 26, 27.
Dugald Macconachie vic Conill, xxxiv.
Dunbar, battle of, x, 188 *n*.
—— a priest, 94.
—— Alex. 22, 87.
—— David, 137, 138.
—— George, xlviii, 60, 61, 132, 270, 332, 333.

374   INVERNESS AND DINGWALL RECORDS

Dunbar, John, 2.
—— Patrick, 1, 25, 26.
—— Thomas, 63.
Duncan M'Alister vic conill dowy, xviii, 368.
—— M'Conill vic conchie vic Andrew, 367.
—— M'Conill vic ean riach, 159, 368, 369.
—— M'conill wayne v⁰ conill buj, 280.
—— M'ean vic Conchy, 99.
—— Duc M'Hutcheon v⁰ can Liea, 92.
—— M'Do^d vic wurchie, 151.
—— M'ferq^r voir, 368.
—— M'Murchie vic Cuile, xliii, 272-274.
—— oig M'Finlay, 143.
Dundee, viscount, xix.
Dunglust, 228.
Dunlichity, vi, xviii, xxv, xxxi, 1, 19, 20, 32-35, 37, 62, 65, 72, 73, 106.
Durham, Patrick, 269.

EDDERTAYNE, 270.
Education and maintenance of Irish students, xlv, 162, 164-166, 169, 177, 178, 216-218, 246, 247, 249, 253-256, 258, 260, 262, 278.
Eileandonan castle, 220 and n.
Elder, John, 369.
—— Alexander, 369.
'Engagers,' viii; lists of, 154 and n, 156-162, 367.
Episcopacy, xiii-xv, xix.
Erchet, the goodwife of, 21.
Euay, Keneth, 321.
Ewen M'Hucheon vic ewn, xxxiii, 364.

FALCONER, ALEX., 102.
—— Colin, bishop of Moray, 95, 112, 113, 116, 117; funerals of, 124.
—— William, 104, 132.
Farr, xxxi. *See* Mackintosh, Alex.
Fasts, xi, xxii, xxiii, 152, 153, 180, 182, 188, 192, 204, 210-213, 221, 226, 242, 313.
Fearne, Alex., 323.
Feast of the Nativity, observance of the, 356.
Ferintosh whisky, xxv.
Ferne, 270.
Ferquhar, Isobell, 92.
—— M'Conill vic Hutcheon, 191.
—— M'ean waine, 143.
—— M'William v⁰ ean, 92.
Finane, St., image of, xxxvi, 1.
Finlay M'Coil oig, 79.
—— M'conchie vic Finlay, xli, 181, 196.

Finlay, M'Conchie vic ririe, 191.
—— M'Conill vic Finlay, 191.
—— M'Conill vick robby, 108.
—— M'Ean chile, 335.
—— M'ean vuy, 364.
—— M'James gow, 368.
—— M'Koniloig, 108.
—— M'rorie vic Mathon, 368.
—— riach, 156.
Finlayson, Donald, 156, 160, 353.
Fodderty, vi, viii, x, xii, xxi, xxxviii, xlviii, 174, 176, 191, 197, 199-203, 206, 208, 209, 213-219, 224-229, 233 and n, 240, 273, 276, 281, 282, 288, 294, 301 n, 309, 311, 317, 328; 'engagers' in the parish of, 158, 367.
Forbes, Donald, 103, 118, 129, 130, 362.
—— Finlay, 114.
—— John, 92.
Fordyce, Alex., minister at Rafford, 58.
Fornication, xxxi-xxxiv, 39, 41, 43, 59, 68, 72, 137, 138, 144, 151, 196, 200, 236, 241, 242, 303, 309, 315, 316, 349, 350, 365.
Fort Augustus, 54, 55, 65-67, 81 and n.
Foulis, laird of, 244, 245, 251, 294, 339, 351.
Frankman, Hector, 160.
Fraser, Alexander, xxxvi, 2, 12, 14-16, 19-26, 28, 29, 31, 35, 38-40, 55, 71, 77, 78, 82, 92, 93, 95, 100, 107, 113-115, 141, 142, 340.
—— Dow, 26.
—— Andrew, 27, 89, 302.
—— Donald, xi, xx, 24, 28, 55, 136, 139, 141, 145-147, 199, 203, 208, 209, 213, 215, 216, 218, 223, 234, 237, 244 *passim*.
—— Duncan, of Murvalgan, 82.
—— Finlay, 87.
—— Hector, of Dundelchak, 8.
—— notary publick, 101.
—— Helen, 313.
—— Hugh, 43.
—— —— notary publick, 24, 28.
—— —— of Baldown, 77.
—— —— of Belladrum, 78, 93, 95, 107, 204-206, 208, 209, 216.
—— —— in Corthly, 54.
—— —— of Croy, 2, 5, 6, 8, 16 and n, 21, 22, 24, 31, 37, 47, 57, 74, 82, 89, 97, 101, 105, 109, 112, 135.
—— —— of Culbokie, 77, 78.
—— —— of Dalcraige, 25, 54.
—— —— of Daltullich, 104.
—— —— of Daviot, 104.
—— —— in Drummond, 25.
—— —— of Eskadaill, 77, 156.

INDEX 375

Fraser, Hugh, of Faneblaire, 77.
—— —— of Glenvakie, 77.
—— —— of Kinmonive, 54.
—— —— of Kiltarlity, 3, 4, 8, 12, 15, 16, 21, 22, 26, 30-32, 36, 37, 42, 43, 45, 46, 48, 49, 51, 53, 57, 61, 62, 65-69, 75, 77, 78, 93, 95, 97, 111, 118, 122, 123, 128, 131, 132.
—— —— of Leadclune, 28.
—— —— of Struy, 78, 107, 141, 221, 324, 326, 327, 337, 345.
—— James, 2, 4, 5, 15, 16, 36, 43.
—— —— fornicator, xxxii, 102.
—— —— tutor of Foyer, 25-27.
—— —— of Achnagairne, 78, 107.
—— —— of Ardachie, 54.
—— —— of Borlum, 82.
—— —— Barron of Moniack, 107.
—— —— of Dulcrage, 24.
—— —— in Dunballach, 78, 107.
—— —— in Dunchea, 28.
—— —— in Dundelchaige, 55, 97.
—— —— of Meikle Garth, 24, 54.
—— James, of Phoppachie, minister of Wardlaw, ix, xxii, 14, 23, 29, 47, 48, 58, 65, 67, 69, 73, 78, 80, 82, 84, 90, 97, 101, 103, 109, 114, 126, 129, 135; unpublished writings of, xxix.
—— Janet, 92, 94, 357, 365.
—— Jean, 119, 120.
—— John, 194, 369.
—— —— of Borlum, 71.
—— —— of Clunwakkie, 141.
—— —— of Culmullin, 77.
—— —— of Erigie, 8, 55.
—— —— in Fingask, 108.
—— —— of Gortleage, 43.
—— —— in Gusachan, 111.
—— —— in Inchberrie, 78, 107.
—— —— in Kingilly, 108, 143.
—— —— of Little Glendo, 71, 82.
—— —— of Migovie, 28, 54.
—— Katherin, 91.
—— Margaret, xxxi, 39, 41, 42, 46, 47, 57, 58, 61, 69, 91.
—— Michael, 32, 33, 35-38, 47, 48, 65, 67, 70, 71, 73, 74, 82, 83, 88-90, 101, 104, 112, 119, 123, 125, 126, 130, 131.
—— Philip, 22.
—— Robert, 114.
—— Simon, of Briuach, 77.
—— —— of Finask, 78, 107.
—— —— in Kulmaskiak, 92.
—— Tavish, of Little Garth, 25.
—— Thomas, 48, 142, 324, 354, 355.
—— —— notary public, 329.
—— —— schoolmaster, 1, 80, 108.

Fraser, Thomas, of Ardochie, 82.
—— —— of Beufort, 77, 78, 107.
—— —— in Beulie, 217.
—— —— in Crochell, 165, 166, 185.
—— —— of Dorres, 110, 111, 113, 116, 124, 126.
—— —— in Dunchea, 28.
—— —— of Eskadaill, 161, 205, 206, 208, 209, 216.
—— —— of Faraline, 25, 54.
—— —— of Strachin, 107.
—— —— of Teanakyle, 77.
—— William, 25, 142, 287, 288, 290, 291, 299, 300, 322, 331, 336, 342.
—— —— tutor of Foyer, 54.
—— —— of Bowblanie, 77.
—— —— in Fermott, 109.
—— —— in Gusachan, 111.
—— —— at Kiltarlatie, 26.
—— —— in Phoppachie, 78.
—— —— of Ruthven, 55.
Frasers and Mackintoshes, quarrels between, 100.
Fullertowne, Christian, 93.

GADERER, JANETT, 92.
Gairloch, vi, xxxviii, 152, 168, 171, 188, 192, 272, 279, 281, 282.
—— laird of. *See* M'Kenzie, Kenneth.
Gairnes, William, minister in Edinburgh, 131.
Gardiner, Donald, 160.
Gask, 73.
Geillie More, 25, 27.
General assembly, dissolution of the, 257 and *n*.
Gillandries M'ean dowy, 367.
Gillicalm M'ean, 369.
Glasgow, contribution for, 245, 246, 248, 250.
Glasse, Donald, 239, 240, 368, 369.
—— John, 45, 273, 340, 341.
—— Thomas, 368.
—— William, 325.
Glencoe robbers, 72.
Glengarie papists, 127.
Glenlia, xviii.
Glenmoriston, vi, vii, xvi, xxxiv-li, 65-67, 70, 82, 83, 123; list of papists in, 91.
Glenshiel, vi.
Glen Urquhart, xxi.
Golspie, 261.
Gordon, John, xxi, xliv, 307, 308, 311, 313, 320, 322, 323, 326, 336-339, 342, 345, 349-352, 354-356, 358-363.
—— Katherine, 2, 69.
—— Patrick, xlii, 74, 84-87.
Gorten na Keirach, 25, 27.

Gow or M'Curchie, Isobell, 341, 342.
Grahame, James. *See* Montrose, marquis of.
Grant, laird of, 30.
—— Alexander, 25, 26.
—— —— in Carrogarre, 75.
—— —— in Balmakan, 75.
—— Duncan, in Divech, 75.
—— Gregorie, in Pitkerrell, 75.
—— James, 32-34, 36, 39, 40, 47, 52, 62, 65-68, 71, 75, 91, 103, 123, 132.
—— —— in Brahan, 368.
—— —— in Invervuick, 82.
—— —— of Sheuglie, 75.
—— John, of Glenmoriston, an excommunicated papist, xxxv, 125-127, 129, 133.
—— —— of Corrimony, 36, 75, 76, 91.
—— —— in Duldregin, 91.
—— Lachlan, 1, 25, 26.
—— Lilias, (lady Byers), xxxv, 45, 46, 48, 69, 91.
—— Patrick, in Inchbroome, 75.
—— Robert, in Carrogarre, 75.
—— Thomas, of Balmakaan, 75.
—— William, of Achmony, 75.
Gray, George, at Dornoch, 165, 259, 262.
—— John, of Assint, 72.
Greisone, Duncan, 368.
Grudach Nickillandris, 317, 319.
Guthrie, John, bishop of Moray, vii.

Hamilton, Duke of, viii.
Harper, Patrick, 68.
Hay, James, 3-7, 31.
—— William, bishop of Moray, 130, 131, 135.
Hector M'Reacan, 368.
Helen nin ferq^r, 360.
Henrie, William, 114.
Hepburne, John, 22.
Highland dress among the clergy, xix, xx.
Holy wells, xxxviii, xxxix, 88 and *n*, 136, 144, 280.
Hogg, Thomas, xii-xiv, xx, 259-264, 269, 271, 273, 276, 289, 293, 294, 297, 301 *n*, 305, 320.
Horne, James, 93.
Hosack, Isabell or Cristaine, 242, 247.
Houston, James, 317, 355.
—— John, 25, 26.
—— Thomas, xv, xxvi, 2-4, 6, 11, 12, 21, 24-28, 48, 49, 51, 54, 57, 58, 62, 65-68, 71, 118, 129, 133, 134.
Hugh M'Allister vic ean roy, xviii, 45 and *n*.

Hutcheon M'Robt, 369.
—— George, schoolmaster, 1, 14.

Idolatrous Practices, xxxvi-xxxix, 1, 279, 282.
Impotency, cases of, xliii, 6-8, 272, 334-336, 339, 361, 364.
Incest, cases of, 41, 43, 125, 149, 151, 299, 361.
Inchgald, 97 and *n*.
Inchrorie, 301.
Innerchannich, 331.
Innes, laird of, 89.
—— Andrew, 45.
—— Berald, 104, 132.
—— George, 132.
—— Jean, 45.
Inverness, English garrison in, ix; taken by rebels, 154 *n*, 157-159, 162; bridge of, 99.
—— castle, xxxiv, 100.

James Dow, 367.
—— M'vic Rob, 159, 368, 369.
—— M'W^m vic Andrew, 368.
Janet nin An, xliv, 310, 314.
—— nin Donald, 102.
—— nein vic Gillmichael, xxxii, 87.
—— nin ean vic ulliam, 359.
John M'Alister roy, 368.
—— M'Alister vic conill dowy, 368.
—— bayne M'Ritchie, 369.
—— buy M'finlay gowne, 159.
—— M'Andrew vic Ritchie, 368.
—— Keil M'coule, 159.
—— M'conchie vic ean vreick, 368.
—— M'Conill roy, 369.
—— M'conill reach, 280.
—— M'ean vic Alister, 321.
—— M'ean vic ryrie, xliv, 337.
—— M'conel vick ean oig, 338.
—— M'conill vic Andrew, 367.
—— M'conill vic ean, 368, 369.
—— M'conill vic conill vic Thomas, 159.
—— M'conill vic gillichalm, 368.
—— M'conill dowy vic W^m, 159, 368.
—— M'finlay vic conill donich, 333.
—— M'finlay duj, 361, 362.
—— M'finlay v^c chenich, 286.
—— M'ean vic conill vic Thomais, 368.
—— M'ean vic cuyan, 368.
—— M'ean vic Thomas, 339.
—— M'ean vic Conil Doniet, xxxi.
—— buy M'Finlay dowyie, 369.
—— buy M'Finlay gowne, 368.
—— —— gowe, 143.
—— Maconie vic Ferq^r, 303, 305.
—— M'Konildonich, 108.

John Maconil oig, 303.
—— riach M'W^m vic conill roy, 368.
—— M'Rorie v^c ean v^c Don^d v^c eachin, 91.
—— M'rorie vic Mathon, 368.
—— oig M'vic ean, 191.
—— riach M'W^m vic conill roy, 159.
—— Roy M'Jock, 159, 368.
—— M'Thomas dowyne, 368.
—— M'Thomas vic Alister, 367.
—— M'W^m vic Thomas, 367.
—— dow M'W^m, 369.
—— M'William voir, 361.
Johnson, Donald, in Inglishtoun, 79.

KAINLOCHEW, 292.
Kaird. *See* Caird.
Katherine nin Donald vic Cay, 100.
—— nic coil voire, 335.
—— nin Donald vic Horish, 354, 358, 359, 361.
—— nic ean Tyre, 78.
—— nien ullay vic ulliam, 354, 358.
Keanlochbeancharan, 169, 170.
Keassack, 157, 158, 160.
Kempt, Agnes, in Garloch, xliii, 272-274.
—— Donald, xliii, 255, 317.
—— James, 252.
Kennedy, Colline, 231.
Kenneth M'Alister vic conill dowy, 368.
—— M'ean dowy, 368.
—— M'eane v^c conill zlass, 255.
—— M'ean vic eachin, 369.
—— M'Kenneth, 338.
Kennlochiu presbytery, 323.
Ker, Alexander, 132.
—— H., 154.
Ketual, 345.
Kilchrist, raid of, xxxvii, 215; 'engagers' in the parish of, 159, 367; profanation of Kilchrist church, xxxi, 347.
—— heritor of Urray, 146.
Kilcumming. *See* Fort Augustus.
Kildine haugh, 252, 255.
Kilernan, 175, 186, 238, 239, 287.
Killicuddin, 292-294.
Kilmorack, vi, xlvii, 141, 142, 145, 146, 204-206, 208, 213, 216-219, 281, 302, 303, 310, 317, 330-332, 345, 369.
Kilmuir, 167, 270.
Kilravock, laird of, 89 *n*.
Kiltarlity, vi, xvi, l, 12, 13, 77, 103, 111 and *n*, 145.
Kiltearn, vi-viii, xii, xiii, xlvii, 138, 183, 235, 238-240, 244, 250, 256, 258, 260-264, 302 and *n*, 303-305,

327, 341; 'engagers' in the parish of, 157, 160, 367, 368.
Kinbeachie, 294.
Kincardin, 233, 235, 270, 278.
Kinneddie. *See* Kennedy.
Kintail, vi, xvi, xviii, xxxviii, 138, 146-148, 151, 168, 188, 209, 248, 268, 269, 271-278, 282-285, 296.
Kirk-burial, xvii, 118, 150, 195, 226.
Kirkhill or Wardlaw, vi, xix, xxi, xxix, 28, 101, 107 and *n*, 186; parish registers of, 107 and *n*.
Kirkmichael, 201, 209, 270.
Knockbayne, 174, 177-179.

LAUDER, CHRISTAN, a papist, 51, 57, 58, 60, 61, 77.
—— William, 241, 269, 270, 273.
Law, William, 132.
Leasing-makers, 124, 128, 130, 135.
Leith, James, 109.
—— Marjorie, 74, 84-87.
—— Thomas, 41.
Lemlair. *See* Munro, John.
Loban, Donald, 334.
Lochaber, rebellion in, 135; robbers in, xix, 5, 72.
Lochalsh, vi, viii, xvi, xxxviii, 146, 149, 151, 168, 188, 282.
Lochbroom, vi, xvi, xxi, xxxviii, 136, 138, 141, 152, 191, 192, 194, 198, 200, 203, 207, 221, 224, 226, 228, 230-232, 233 *n*, 235, 237, 239, 249, 253, 255, 270, 274, 276, 277, 282, 309.
Lochcarron, vi, viii, xvi, xxxviii, 146, 147, 150, 151, 168, 277, 279-282, 287, 345.
Lochend of Lochness, 15.
Loch Maree, xxxvii, xxxviii, 279 and *n*, 282, 338 *n*.
Lochslin. *See* Mackenzie, Simon.
Logan, Andrew, 160, 367.
—— James, 354.
Logie, 210, 232, 272, 324 and *n*; 'engagers' in the parish of, 160, 368.
—— Wester, vi, ix, 254, 255.
Lovat, lord, 31.
—— master of, xi, 209, 216, 299.
Luggcroft, 25.
Lykewakes, xxiv, 52-55, 121 *n*.

M'ALISTER, DAVID, 368.
—— John, 179.
—— Kathrine, 302.
—— Murdo, 191.
—— Wm., in Invervuick, 82.
M'Allan, Murdoch, xliv, 337, 338.
—— William, 367.

M'Andrew, Alex., 108, 142, 352.
—— Andrew, xxv, 344.
—— Donald, 105, 108.
—— John, 100.
M'Avis, Duncan, 68.
M'Bain or M'Bean, Alex., of Drumond, 55.
—— Angus, xiii, xiv, 8, 97, 116-120, 122, 124-129; deposition of, 131, 134.
—— Donald, 28, 38, 55.
—— —— of Faily, 19, 57, 106.
—— Doncan, in Gask, 106.
—— John, in Lergs, 106.
—— —— notary public, 97, 117.
—— Lachlan, 8, 55.
—— Paul, of Kynkyle, 8, 55.
M'Calich, John, 363.
M'Chaptin, Wm., 368.
M'Chattich, Finlay, 369.
M'Chlachar, Thomas Begg, 159, 368, 369.
—— —— Moir, 159, 368, 369.
M'Coill, John, in Borlome, 55.
M'Conchie, Kenneth, 368.
M'Conill, Alex., 252.
M'Coule, John, 368, 369.
M'Culbert, Wm., 18.
MacCulloch, Duncan, xvi, xxi, 2, 6, 12, 14, 16 and *n*, 144, 156, 162, 164, 189, 192, 193, 197, 199, 202.
—— George, 296, 297, 299.
—— James, at Kilmuir, 270.
—— John, 141.
M'Curchie, Alex., 343.
—— Donald, 191, 369.
—— John, 341, 342, 359.
—— Kenneth, 361, 362, 364, 368.
M'Doir, John, xxv, 327.
Macdonald, lord, (Glengarry), xxxvi, 82 and *n*, 83.
—— Alex., in Achlean, a papist, 91.
—— Allan, of Culachie, 91.
—— —— of Kyltrie, xxxvi, 91.
—— —— in Innervuick, 91.
—— Angus, 322.
—— Donald, of Culachie, xxxvi, 91.
—— Francis, a Roman catholic priest, xxxv, 100.
—— James, 288.
—— John, in Lick, 91.
—— Katherin, 91.
—— Ranald, of Pitmean, xxxvi, 91.
M'dugall, Dugall, 100.
M'eachan, Donald, 305.
M'Ean, Duncan, 82, 97, 98, 100.
—— John, 55.
M'eandowie, Alex., 142.
M'evin, Jon., 82.

M'Ferq^r., Duncan, 159.
—— John, 82.
M'finlay, Donald, 159, 251, 368.
—— John, 142.
—— William, 367, 369.
M'George, Alex., in Urray, 368.
—— William, 106, 367.
M'ghowin, Alister, 368, 369.
M'Gilandrice, William, 114.
M'gillichalme, Duncan, 369.
M'Gillicharrich, Malcome, 360, 362.
M'gillichean, Donald, in Kinkell, 274.
M'Gillifudricke, Finlay, 280.
M'Gillighlaish, Donald, 367.
M'gillimichaell, John, in Kinchuldruim, 368.
M'Gilliriach, Alex., 367.
M'Gillivrey, Donald, tutor of Dunmaglass, 19.
—— Ferq^r., of Donmaglass, 106.
—— Janet, 43.
—— John, of Midleyes, 104.
—— Martin, of Aberchalder, xxv, 33, 34.
—— Wm., of Largs, 19, 38, 106.
M'glashen, David, sabboth braker, 102.
M'Gorrie, Alex., 190 and *n*.
—— Agnes (nien Donald vic Vurrich), 190 *n*.
M'halich, John, 366.
M'Hendrick, Margaret, 44.
M'Hutcheon, Alex., 92.
M'indoir, Ronald, 354.
M'Inroy (M'Keanroy), Finlay, 107.
M'intyre, Beatrix, 92.
—— (M'Anteir), Duncan, 368.
M'Iver, Donald, 92, 329, 331.
—— John, 230.
—— Murdo, 194, 195, 198, 226.
—— Roderick, in Maald, 92.
M'James, Doncan, 106.
M'Jaspert, Donald, 160.
Mackay of Bighouse, riotous proceedings of, 139 and *n*.
—— Alex., 106.
—— John, in Toreingnawn, 109.
—— William, 104.
—— merchant in Dumbarton, xlv, 309.
M'Keallie, Donald, 369.
MacKenich, Alex., 305.
MacKenzie of Kintail, xxxvi.
—— Agnes, xxxii, 119, 302.
—— Alex., minister at Lochcarron, 138, 141, 147, 150, 152, 166, 169, 171, 177-181, 185, 187, 188, 191, 193, 194, 197, 199, 221, 224, 225, 236, 238, 239, 256, *passim*; death of, 345.
—— —— in Auchlanachan, 274, 276.

INDEX

MacKenzie, Alex., of Balconie, 353.
—— —— of Coule, 160, 290, 293, 299, 300.
—— —— in Cuiltaldod, 369.
—— —— of Culcowie, 230, 236, 238, 241, 242, 247, 287.
—— —— of Tollie, 343.
—— —— of Touvie, 329.
—— Bernard, 332.
—— Charles, xxxiii, 57, 58, 63, 64.
—— Cirstane, xxxviii, 338.
—— Colin, x, xxvi, 161-163, 186, 187, 199, 202, 203, 209, 223, 237 n, 270-271, 273, 287, 293.
—— —— at Killernan, 269.
—— —— of Kinnock, 158.
—— —— of Tarbeit, 137.
—— —— of Tarvie, 178, 179, 191, 224.
—— Donald, 369.
—— —— of Loggie, 202, 273, 274.
—— Duncan, 321, 338.
—— sir George, of Tarbat, 288.
—— Girsell, 178.
—— Hector, 104, 132, 133, 194, 304-308, 311.
—— —— of Assynt, 180, 184, 185.
—— —— of Farburne, 159, 224, 290, 295, 299, 303, 306, 368.
—— —— in Mellan, xxxviii, 338.
—— captain Hector, 238-240.
—— Hew, 206, 223, 224.
—— Isobell, 302.
—— James, 205, 210, 218, 270, 278, 279, 312.
—— John, xliv, xlvi, 131, 145, 146, 168, 174, 176, 248, 249, 301 and n, 302, 304, 306, 310, 311, 313, 322, 333, 338, 342, 345, 363.
—— —— of Applecross, 171.
—— —— of Davochcairne, 157, 158, 202, 263, 328.
—— —— of Ord, 177, 201, 202, 368.
—— —— in Usie, 255.
—— sir John of Tarbat, x, 198, 201, 209, 214, 224-226, 228-230, 232, 233, 246-248, 328.
—— Kenneth, 159, 321, 367.
—— —— of Assynt, 168, 172, 174, 175.
—— —— in Brackanord, 177, 253.
—— —— of Coul, 186, 193.
—— —— of Dachmaluak, 328.
—— —— of Gairloch, 171, 172, 174, 175, 180, 299.
—— —— in Knockbaxter, 201, 202.
—— —— of Scatwell, 168, 172, 174, 175, 177, 198, 201, 233.
—— Margaret, 26, 27.
—— Murdoch, xv, 137 and n, 138, 141, 152, 160, 162, 163, 166-187, 191, 217,
218, 232, 234, 237 and n, 239, 248, 250 *passim*, 286, 290-292, 309, 326, 336, 338, 345.
MacKenzie, Murdoch, of Achiltie, 224.
—— —— in Knockbaxter, 287.
—— —— of Little Findon, 143.
—— —— bishop of Moray, 3, 7, 17, 34, 37, 38, 70, 71, 81, 89, 90.
—— Roderick, xix, xxxiii, 2, 11, 47, 48, 49, 51, 57, 58, 64, 201, 228, 242, 245, *passim*.
—— —— student of theology, 201, 328.
—— —— of Corie, 204-210.
—— —— of Davachmoluagg, 159, 165, 172, 174, 176, 177, 190, 192, 246, 263, 265, 295, 314, 367.
—— —— of Farburne, 159, 165, 172-175, 177, 190, 193, 368.
—— —— of Findon, xxx, 357.
—— —— at Gairloch, 147, 171, 181, 191, 203, 303, 326, 336.
—— —— of Knockbaxter, 254.
—— —— at Moy, 26, 33, 36, 62, 65-67, 73, 82, 84, 88.
—— —— of Redcastle, 186.
—— —— of Tollie, 168, 255, 298.
—— Simon, of Lochslinn, xi, xii, 220 and n, 230 and n, 231, 232, 246, 255.
—— Thomas, of Inverlaoll, 233.
—— —— of Pluscarden, viii, 139 n, 140 n, 154 n, 184.
—— William, 265, 312, 355.
M'Killimichell, Finlay, 106.
—— John, 106.
Mackillican, John, xii-xiv, xx, 269, 271, 273, 274-276, 288, 289, 293-302, 313, 314, 320-322, 336 and n, 337, 345, 362.
Mackintosh, in Conadge, 109.
—— Alex., 49.
—— —— of Farr, xxv, 33, 34, 106.
—— —— of Ochtr. Urchall, 19.
—— Angus, of Daviot, 19, 62, 63.
—— —— in Drummond, 55.
—— —— in Moy, 18.
—— —— M'Allan, 96.
—— Donald, 104.
—— Hector, in Craggie, 19.
—— —— in Breachly, 109.
—— James, 106.
—— Janet, in Moy, 97.
—— John, xvii, 14-17, 31, 33, 34.
—— —— in Dallichield, 109.
—— —— in Elrig, 106.
—— Kenneth, 104.
—— Lachlan, 2, 38.
—— —— of Aberarder, 19, 62, 72, 106.
—— —— in Drumbog, 19.
—— Malcome, in Dores, 55.

Mackintosh, Martin, in Fleemintoun, 109.
—— William, of Borlome, 8, 55.
—— —— of Corribroch, 17.
M'Kivirrich, Lachlan, 106.
M'Krishe, Rorie, 264.
M'Kvarran, James, in Drumcharduy, 108.
M'Lauchlan, Alex., 178, 179, 181, 183, 185-187.
M'Lean, Alex., 104, 340, 341.
—— Charles, 294.
—— Donald, in Balnichrie, 109.
—— Hector, 91, 357.
M'Leich, Donald don, 310.
M'Lennan, Alex., 194.
—— Allan, 246-249.
—— Donald, 149, 191, 247, 365.
—— Ferq^r., moderator of Dingwall presbytery, xxvi, 136-149, 185, 187, passim.
—— James, 327.
—— Murdo, 194.
M'Leod, Neil, schoolmaster at Tarbat, 167.
—— Rorie, 147, 152, 217, 218, 231-233.
—— William, xxxii, 309.
M'Ley, Anne, convicted of using charms, 333.
—— Donald, 334, 335, 364.
Macmiller, William, xlii, 341.
M'nakaird, Finlay, 368.
M'Naoise, Thomas, xviii, 176, 180.
M'Neil, Donald, 206.
M'nicoll, Donald, 367.
M'phail, Angus, in Inverarny, 106.
—— D., 38.
—— Donald, in Home, 79, 108.
—— —— in Meikle Garth, 54.
—— Duncan, 106, 312.
—— —— of Invernie, 19, 62.
—— John, 354.
M'Phatricke, John, 331.
M'Pherson, Andrew, notary public, 46.
—— Donald, 35, 104.
—— Even, of Fleichitie, 19, 106.
—— John, 48-50, 104.
—— Lachlin, in Easter Urchol, 106.
—— William, xxxiii, 60, 84.
M'Phoid, Duncan, 367.
Macqueen, Archibald, at Snizort, 150 and n.
—— Donald, 324.
—— —— of Corribroch, 109.
—— Duncan, Raigmore, 109.
—— Isobell, 99, 100.
—— John, 18.
—— Lachlan, 18.

Macrae, Donald, ix, xi, xv, xxvi, 136-149, 199-210 passim.
—— Farquhar, 147, 149, 155, 171, 191, 193, 220, 231, 246, 283 n-285, 296.
—— John xii, xiii, xviii, xxvi, 136, 138, 152, 154, 156, 161, 162, 173, 178-180, 194, 199, 202, 203, 205, 207, 209, 210 passim.
—— —— schoolmaster at Dingwall, xlviii, 306-308, 318, 319, 321, 324.
M'Ridler, John, 368, 369.
M'Ritchie, Alex., 368.
—— Donald, 368, 369.
—— John Bayne, 368.
—— Murdo, in Ardnacraick, 368.
—— William, 368.
M'Ronald, Alex., 252.
—— Allan, of Teachknock, 141.
—— James, in Knockie, 54.
—— John, 160.
—— Ronald, 136, 141, 204-216.
—— —— in Teachuick, 240.
M'Rorie, Donald, in Kinkel, 143.
—— Gillipadrick, 280.
—— John, in Glencannich, 281.
—— Lachlin, in Altirly, 109.
M'Shoirle, Donald, 28.
—— —— in Bellvraid, 368.
—— —— in Lemnech, 79, 108.
—— John, 79, 107.
M'thomas, Donald, in Donaldstoun, 108.
M'Tormoid, Donald, 368.
—— John, 368.
M'Warron, Thomas, 28.
M'William, Donald, 18, 82.
—— Hutcheon, 142.
—— John, 92, 144.
M'wyre, William, 82.
M'Zlassich, John, 247.
M'Zowne, Donald, in Auchnafoile, 260, 261.
Main, in Strathconan, 328.
Malcome, John, 249.
Malignants, viii, 139 and n, 140, 153, 159, 162, 163, 168-177, 182,185, 187-189, 191, 197, 369, 370.
Man, Alex., student, 116.
Maolrubha, St., xxxvii, xxxviii, 279 and n, 280 and n, 282.
Margret nin Thomas, 364.
Marion nin Archie, 357.
Marjorie nin William, 339.
Marriage, breach of promise of, xlii, 303, 305, 313; marriages by priests, 92, 94, 99, 112; regulation concerning marriage of a widow, 102; irregular marriages, xxxiv, 2, 133, 134, 138.

INDEX 381

Marshall, Gilbert, minister at Inverness, 45, 46, 48, 49, 51, 57-63, 68, 73, 74, 82, 89, 91, 107, 112, 114, 115, 117, 122, 125, 133-135.
—— Johne, minister of Dundurcos, 121 *n.*
Marie neine Donill Roy, 196.
—— Donald vic Wurchie, 230, 231.
—— nien Dul vic ean vore, 348.
—— nien Dhonchie roy, 364.
—— nin doil uyre, 359.
—— neine Ferq^r., 196.
—— nien Khenich ghlaise, 303, 305.
—— neine vic neill, 196.
Massie, Andrew, 47.
Mathesone, Donald, 312.
—— Murdo, 191.
Maxwell, John, bishop of Ross, vii.
Meldrum, George, 69.
Mersall, John, 369.
—— —— M'William, 368.
Midsummer fire superstition, xl, 268, 323.
Miller, Donald, xxxi, 71, 72.
—— Hutcheon M'Ean, 92.
—— John, 82, 160.
—— William, 301.
Moir, William, 25, 368, 369.
Monmouth's rebellion, xix, xxiii, 357 *n.*
Monro. *See* Munro.
Montrose, assistance for merchants of, 101.
—— marquis of, rebellion of, vi, viii, 157, 158, 160, 162, 165, 168, 170, 172, 177, 180, 191, 201, 209, 369; lands in Caithness, 182; defeated at Carbisdale, 184.
Moray, earl of, xxxv, 17, 49, 51, 57, 68, 70.
More, Mary, 92.
—— Thomas, 92.
Morrich, Andrew, 327.
Moy, vi, xvi, 18, 95-97, 103.
Muckovie, 30.
Mulroy, xix.
Munro, Agnes, 91.
—— Alex., 208.
—— —— in Foulis, 339.
—— —— principal of Edinburgh university, 131.
—— Andrew, 172, 174, 231, 234, 236, 242, 244, 254, 263.
—— —— in Culcairnie, 114, 138, 156, 160, 259.
—— —— in Milchaith, 143.
—— —— in Teanuar, 156 and *n*, 160.
—— —— in Thurso, 314.
—— captain Andrew, 159.
—— Christiane, 289.

Munro, David, 140, 186, 187, 208, 287, 312, 321, 367.
—— —— of Killichoan, 347, 353.
—— Donald, xlvii, 157, 192, 325, 329, 347, 367, 369.
—— Ferqhair, of Teahnaird, 139, 156, 160, 183, 259.
—— Florence, 165.
—— George, 136, 145-147, 163, 193, 194, 198, 207, 208, 210 *passim.*
—— —— in Alness, 294.
—— —— in Rosemarkie, 168, 292.
—— —— of Teanowar, 256 and *n.*
—— —— at Urquhart, 136, 138-143, 185, 186.
—— —— in Commer, a papist, 91.
—— —— M'conill, 368.
—— Hector, 168, 369.
—— —— of Coul, 210.
—— —— of Drummond, 339, 353.
—— —— of Eddertayne, 270.
—— —— in Kiltearn, 193, 353, 368.
—— —— in Kincardine, 164, 233 and *n*, 235, 250, 251.
—— Hew, 258.
—— —— of Foiris, 156, 160.
—— —— in Foulis, 139.
—— —— in Katuell, 139, 156, 160.
—— —— of Swardale, 353.
—— —— of Teamerchies, 139.
—— —— of Teannich, 156, 157, 160.
—— —— of Tearibban, 353.
—— Hutcheon, 367.
—— Janet, 347, 348.
—— John, 164, 288.
—— —— in Alnes, 164, 178, 180, 186, 192, 199, 292, 302 *n*, 313.
—— —— in Ardully, 157.
—— —— in Culnaskeah, 157.
—— —— in Dingwall, xxvi, 141, 143, 145-149, *passim.*
—— —— in Kinkel, 143, 156, 160.
—— —— schoolmaster at Kiltarlity, 1, 77, 93, 95.
—— —— of Lemlair, 158, 174, 193, 251, 256, 289.
—— —— in Newtoune, 156, 160.
—— —— of Sordell, 139, 141, 156, 160, 183.
—— —— sir John, of Foulis, vii, 353.
—— Katharin, 325, 349-352.
—— Margaret, in Culcraiggie, delated for charming, 156.
—— —— papist, 91.
—— Neill, of Findon, 158, 287, 295.
—— Robert, 99, 123, 133, 134, 155, 157, 163, 174, 256, 262, 278, 288.
—— —— a Roman catholic priest, xxxv, 45, 46, 48-50, 68, 69, 100, 332.

Munro, Robert, of Abertarff, and Glenmoriston, iii, xvi, 65-68, 70, 80, 82, 91, *passim*.
—— —— of Baillchladdich, 183.
—— —— of Clyne, 353.
—— —— of Kiltearn, xxi, 136, 137, 139, 160, 168, 234-238, 242, 244.
—— —— of Lemlair, 160, 353, 367.
—— —— of Obstill, 156, 161, 163, 183, 186.
—— —— of Roskeen, 267, 270.
—— —— at Urquhart, 249.
—— William, of Keatwall, 353.
—— —— of Teanaird, 353.
Murders, xxx, 92, 97, 254, 255.
Murdo M'Conill oir, 367.
—— M'Conill v^c Wurchie v^c Conill v^c Allister, 281.
—— M'eane Woire v^c eane Zlaiss, 280.
—— M'eane roy, 280.
—— M'ferq^{re} v^c conill oire, 280.
Murray, earl of. *See* Moray.
—— James, 154, 186.
—— captain William, xlv, 320.

NEILSON, JOHN, 50.
Nickphaill, Elspit, xliii, 6, 8.
Nigg, 361.
Noble, Alex., 63.

OBSTINATE DELINQUENTS, 3, 6, 10.
Ochtera, 91.
Ogilvy, Alex., 319.
O'Neil, a Roman catholic priest, xxxv, 100.
O'Rien, father Hugh, xxxv, 100.

PAPE, CHARLES, at Cullicudden, 270.
—— Thomas, at Cullicudden, 249.
Papists, xiv, xxxiv, 23, 43-48, 57, 60, 61, 68, 69; lists of, to be prepared, 2, 3, 103; convention of, in Inverness castle, 43, 44; proclamation on, 90; papists in Abertarff, Glenmoriston, and Kiltarlity, 91, 103; in Glengarry, 127; in Kilmorack, 330, 331, 333; in Strathglass, 345.
Parish registers of Daviot and Wardlaw, 107 and *n*.
Paterson, John, bishop of Galloway, 339, 340.
Peiric, Andrew, in Bunchrue, 79.
—— —— in Rindony, 108.
Penalties, uniformity of, 144.
Penny weddings, xxiv, 120 and *n*.
Perjury, 198.
Peterhead bulwarks, 340.
Petrie, Wm., 193.

Petty, xxii, l, 109, 114, *passim*.
Pitglassie, 180.
Plague in England, xxiii.
Polson, Robert, of Clyne, 353.
Popery, xxxvi, 51, 77, 82, 84, 87, 88, 103; the popish plot, xxiii.
Portpatrick, 308.
Portsoy harbour, 99, 102.
Presbytery meetings, difficulties connected with, xxvi-xxviii.
Proclamation concerning papists, 90; against leasing-makers, 124, 128, 130, 135; on seditious books and libels, 135; for a fast, 310 and *n*; on the defeat of the Dutch navy, 311 and *n*; for victory at Sedgemoor, 357 and *n*.
Prot, Jane, in Petty, 113.
Psalms, metrical version of, 184 and *n*, 185.
Punishments of evildoers, xxxiii.
Pyper, Angus, kirk officer, 141.

RAFART, 63.
Ranald M'conchie vic Ranald, 369.
Ranaldson, Alex. Bayne, 171, 369.
Rasay, 276.
Reay, lord, viii, 139 *n*, 140 *n*, 154, 229.
Reid, William, xlvii, 164, 231, 248.
Reidcastle, 203.
Reildach, Muirach, 354.
Remonstrance against Charles II., 204 and *n*.
Restoration of Charles II., thanksgiving for, 321.
Reuch, Margaret, 92.
Ritchie, Charles, student in divinity, 65, 71, 72.
—— —— schoolmaster at Wardlaw, 29.
—— Margaret, 45.
Robertson, Gilbert, 359, 360.
—— Isobell, 47, 57-59, 69, 70, 92.
—— James, of Cults, 69.
—— Katrin, 334.
—— Mathew, of Dochcarty, 314, 328.
—— Wm., 22, 38.
Robinson, Dr. John, 131.
Rorie, Tho., 280.
—— M'Alister v^c Rorie, 92.
—— begg M'eachin, 368.
—— M'Jock, 368.
Rosemarkie, 175.
Ross, kirks of, 162, 163, 165, 166.
—— Alexander, l, 22, 23, 28, 29, 31, 33, 34, 42, 62, 87, 97, 132, 265.
—— —— of Clava, 104.
—— —— in Culechuinacke, 19.
—— —— of Holme-Rose, 104.

INDEX

Ross, Andrew, 114, 267, 270, 352, 353.
—— Arthur, archbishop of St. Andrews, 130, 131.
—— David, 267, 269, 270, 286.
—— —— of Earlesmill, 42.
—— Donald, xviii, xx, xxiv, xxviii, 137, 141, 143, 147, 185, 187-189, 191, 193, 194, 197-201, 203-210, 214, 216-218, 220-221, 223-230, 274, 276, 279, 286, 289 *passim*.
—— Hugh, 41, 93, 109, 176.
—— John, 191, 199, 316.
—— —— Dow, 104.
—— Katherine, 315-317, 560, 561.
—— Robert, 22, 249, 295, 296, 301-303, 305.
—— Thomas, 137, 153-155, 161, 162, 192, 233 *n*, 264, 270, 367.
—— Walter, 308, 309, 313, 317, 322, 326, 336, 337, 345, 355, 358.
—— William, 19, 104, 168, 270.
Rosskeen, 236, 269, 278.
Rous, Francis, 184 *n*.
Roy, Donald, 343.
—— —— a sheriff officer, xxxii, 78.
—— Even, 18.
—— Finlay, trumpeter, 238, 239, 240, 241.
—— John, in Teanaird, 139, 183.
—— William, 369.
Rye-house plot, xxiii, 115.

SABBATH-BREAKING, xxiv, xxv, 41, 54, 99, 102, 137, 143, 144, 148, 190 and *n*, 196, 327, 331, 332, 343, 344.
Sackcloth to be provided for delinquents, 19, 20.
Sacrament of the Lord's supper, xxi.
St. Ruffus island, 338.
Schevies, Thomas, of Moortowne, 22.
Schisome. *See* Chisholm.
Schools and schoolmasters, xlvi-lii, 18, 20, 23, 28, 93, 94, 99, 105, 107, 108, 110, 156, 161, 162, 164, 167, 172, 174, 175, 257-259.
Seaforth, earl of, 133, 157 *n*, 159, 173, 175, 179, 237 *n*, 241, 254, 255, 268, 269, 273-275, 277, 293, 297, 308-340.
—— lady, xxx, 321.
Seaforth's Remonstrance, viii, 157 and *n*, 168, 172.
Seminary priests, xxxv, 84, 87, 103, 112.
Shaw, Duncan, in Knocknikeall, 97.
—— Robert, 38.
—— —— of Tordarroch, 19, 106.
—— —— of Wester Leyes, 104.

Shiack nein Do^d, in Tarvie, charmer, 181, 182.
—— nein finlay vic George, 181.
Skinner, Patrick, 368, 369.
Slander, cases of, xlii, 84-87, 321, 325, 341, 349, 350.
Smith, Alex., in Donaldstoun, 108.
—— in Home, 79.
—— Donald, in Applecross, 282.
—— James, minister at Dores, 3-6, 8, 9, 11, 21, 22, 24, 26, 27, 30, 31, 34, 48, 49, 51, 62, 73, 74, 88, 90, 96, 110 and *n*, 112, 113, 116.
—— John, 142.
—— William, 160.
—— —— minister at Duthell, xxiv, 49, 50.
Snizort, 274-276.
Solemn League and Covenant, viii.
Spense, James, in Achnigarn, 108.
Ssoiles, Arthur, in Obstell, 349.
Stewart, Anna, excommunicated, 45.
—— James, chancellor of Moray, 65, 70, 71.
—— —— minister of Inveravon, 30, 32.
Stonehaven bulwarks, contribution for, 340.
Strachan, James, of Thorntowne, 44.
—— John, prof. of divinity at Edinburgh, 131.
Stragairve, 220.
Strathconan, xii, 146, 166, 181, 220, 294, 307, 315, 328, 329.
Stratherrick, v, 30.
Strathglass, vii, xxxiii, xxxiv, xxxvi, 64, 77, 88, 100.
Strathnaver, 169, 206, 229.
Stricken, laird of, 116, 117.
Struy. *See* Fraser, Hugh.
Stuart. *See* Stewart.
Suddie, 237, 247, 286.
Superstitious customs, xxxvi-xli, 88 and *n*, 156, 196, 268, 279-282, 287, 338, 344.
Sutherland, 259, 261, 262.
—— earl of, 261, 262.
—— Alexander, 41.
—— Arthur, 358.
—— Hector, in Catwell, 339.
—— James, minister in Inverness, 2-4, 15-17, 26-29, 36, 39, 40, 46, 69.
Sympson, Alex., 92.

TARBAT, 175.
—— *See* M'Kenzie, sir John.
Taylor, David, 142.
—— Donald, 312.
—— Hector, 370.

Taylor, John M'in, 6.
Test, the, letter on, from the bishop of Ross, 346.
Thomas M'Kean vickonil in Craggag, 108.
—— Mac ean vic Gillereach, 347.
—— M'Kean vore, in Grome, 108.
—— M'farq^r. vane in Ardochie, 82.
—— M'hutcheon moir, 329, 331.
—— roy M'conill vaine, 159, 368.
Thomson, Alexander, 1, 25.
Tod, Alexander, 62, 104.
Tollie, 228, 329.
Troupe, William, 2.
Tulloch. *See* Bain, John.
—— tutor of, 360.
—— Lewis, in Cantra, 104.
—— Samuel, 132.

UNITED PROVINCES, war with the, 310 and *n*, 311 and *n*.
Urquhart, vi, li, 12, 15, 21, 30, 32, 36, 123, 234, 277, 280, 287, 295, 296, 299, 307, 309, 340; list of 'engagers' in, 158, 160, 368.
—— of Ferintosh, xxv, xxx, xlvii.
—— Donald, 197.
—— James, 338 and *n*, 339.
—— Janet, xliii, 317.
—— John, 368, 369.
—— Murdo, 367.
—— Shihag, in Delines, accused of charming, 156.
—— Thomas, 336, 337.
—— William, 353, 368.
Urray, vi, viii, ix, 145, 170, 171, 233, 234, 254, 269, 271-274, 283, 289, 295, 304, 305, 311; list of 'engagers' in, 158, 159, 367, 369.
Usie, 252, 254, 255.

WALLACE, DAVID, 238-240.
—— Francis, 92.
—— James, minister of Orkney, 87.
Wardlaw. *See* Kirkhill.
Water of Ness, 63, 64.
—— of Oviach (Oich), 83 and *n*.
Watson, Thomas, 48-50, 349, 350.
Wause, James, 25, 26.
Wells, pilgrimages to, xxxviii-xxxix, 88 *n*, 136, 144, 280.
Whyte, Donald, 351, 352.
William M'alister vic William vic Finlay, 367.
—— M'conill oire, 280.
—— M'connill vaine, 369.
—— M'conill vayne vic ean Vreick, 159, 367.
—— M'Do^d vic rorie, 370.
—— M'ean vic Gillimichaell, 368.
—— M'ean vic William, 191.
—— M'Hucheon v^c William roy, 92.
—— M'jock, 368.
—— more M'ean v^c William, 92.
—— roy M'George, 368.
—— M'thomas, in Urquhart, 368.
—— M'Wm. vic cay, 368.
Williamsoune, Robert, 270.
Witchcraft, xxii, xl-xlii, 153, 156, 167, 181, 196, 326.
Worcester, battle of, viii, xii, 188.
Wright, Alex., 28, 79.
—— John, 107.

YOUNG, J., 168.

Scottish History Society.

THE EXECUTIVE.

President.
THE EARL OF ROSEBERY, K.G., K.T., LL.D.

Chairman of Council.
DAVID MASSON, LL.D., Historiographer Royal for Scotland.

Council.
G. W. PROTHERO, Professor of History in the University of Edinburgh.
J. R. FINDLAY.
P. HUME BROWN, M.A.
J. FERGUSON, Advocate.
Right Rev. JOHN DOWDEN, D.D., Bishop of Edinburgh.
Professor Sir THOMAS GRAINGER STEWART, M.D.
J. N. MACPHAIL, Advocate.
Rev. A. W. CORNELIUS HALLEN.
Sir ARTHUR MITCHELL, K.C.B., M.D., LL.D.
Rev. GEO. W. SPROTT, D.D.
J. BALFOUR PAUL, Lyon King of Arms.
A. H. MILLAR.

Corresponding Members of the Council.
C. H. FIRTH, Oxford; SAMUEL RAWSON GARDINER, LL.D.; Rev. W. D. MACRAY, Oxford; Rev. Professor A. F. MITCHELL, D.D., St. Andrews.

Hon. Treasurer.
J. T. CLARK, Keeper of the Advocates' Library.

Hon. Secretary.
T. G. LAW, Librarian, Signet Library.

RULES

1. The object of the Society is the discovery and printing, under selected editorship, of unpublished documents illustrative of the civil, religious, and social history of Scotland. The Society will also undertake, in exceptional cases, to issue translations of printed works of a similar nature, which have not hitherto been accessible in English.

2. The number of Members of the Society shall be limited to 400.

3. The affairs of the Society shall be managed by a Council, consisting of a Chairman, Treasurer, Secretary, and twelve elected Members, five to make a quorum. Three of the twelve elected Members shall retire annually by ballot, but they shall be eligible for re-election.

4. The Annual Subscription to the Society shall be One Guinea. The publications of the Society shall not be delivered to any Member whose Subscription is in arrear, and no Member shall be permitted to receive more than one copy of the Society's publications.

5. The Society will undertake the issue of its own publications, *i.e.* without the intervention of a publisher or any other paid agent.

6. The Society will issue yearly two octavo volumes of about 320 pages each.

7. An Annual General Meeting of the Society shall be held on the last Tuesday in October.

8. Two stated Meetings of the Council shall be held each year, one on the last Tuesday of May, the other on the Tuesday preceding the day upon which the Annual General Meeting shall be held. The Secretary, on the request of three Members of the Council, shall call a special meeting of the Council.

9. Editors shall receive 20 copies of each volume they edit for the Society.

10. The owners of Manuscripts published by the Society will also be presented with a certain number of copies.

11. The Annual Balance-Sheet, Rules, and List of Members shall be printed.

12. No alteration shall be made in these Rules except at a General Meeting of the Society. A fortnight's notice of any alteration to be proposed shall be given to the Members of the Council.

PUBLICATIONS

OF THE

SCOTTISH HISTORY SOCIETY

For the year 1886-1887.

1. BISHOP POCOCKE'S TOURS IN SCOTLAND, 1747-1760. Edited by D. W. KEMP. (Oct. 1887.)

2. DIARY OF AND GENERAL EXPENDITURE BOOK OF WILLIAM CUNNINGHAM OF CRAIGENDS, 1673-1680. Edited by the Rev. JAMES DODDS, D.D. (Oct. 1887.)

For the year 1887-1888.

3. PANURGI PHILO-CABALLI SCOTI GRAMEIDOS LIBRI SEX. — THE GRAMEID : an heroic poem descriptive of the Campaign of Viscount Dundee in 1689, by JAMES PHILIP of Almerieclose. Translated and Edited by the Rev. A. D. MURDOCH. (Oct. 1888.)

4. THE REGISTER OF THE KIRK-SESSION OF ST. ANDREWS. Part I. 1559-1582. Edited by D. HAY FLEMING. (Feb. 1889.)

For the year 1888-1889.

5. DIARY OF THE REV. JOHN MILL, Minister of Dunrossness, Sandwick, and Cunningsburgh, in Shetland, 1740-1803. Edited by GILBERT GOUDIE, F.S.A. Scot. (June 1889.)

6. NARRATIVE OF MR. JAMES NIMMO, A COVENANTER, 1654-1709. Edited by W. G. SCOTT-MONCRIEFF, Advocate. (June 1889.)

7. THE REGISTER OF THE KIRK-SESSION OF ST. ANDREWS. Part II. 1583-1600. Edited by D. HAY FLEMING. (Aug. 1890.)

For the year 1889-1890.

8. A List of Persons concerned in the Rebellion (1745). With a Preface by the Earl of Rosebery and Annotations by the Rev. Walter Macleod. (Sept. 1890.)
   Presented to the Society by the Earl of Rosebery.

9. Glamis Papers: The 'Book of Record,' a Diary written by Patrick, first Earl of Strathmore, and other documents relating to Glamis Castle (1684-89). Edited by A. H. Millar, F.S.A. Scot. (Sept. 1890.)

10. John Major's History of Greater Britain (1521). Translated and Edited by Archibald Constable, with a Life of the author by Æneas J. G. Mackay, Advocate. (Feb. 1892.)

For the year 1890-1891.

11. The Records of the Commissions of the General Assemblies, 1646-47. Edited by the Rev. Professor Mitchell, D.D., and the Rev. James Christie, D.D., with an Introduction by the former. (May 1892.)

12. Court-Book of the Barony of Urie, 1604-1747. Edited by the Rev. D. G. Barron, from a ms. in possession of Mr. R. Barclay of Dorking. (Oct. 1892.)

For the year 1891-1892.

13. Memoirs of the Life of Sir John Clerk of Penicuik, Baronet, Baron of the Exchequer, Commissioner of the Union, etc. Extracted by himself from his own Journals, 1676-1755. Edited from the original ms. in Penicuik House by John M. Gray, F.S.A. Scot. (Dec. 1892.)

14. Diary of Col. the Hon. John Erskine of Carnock, 1683-1687. From a ms. in possession of Henry David Erskine, Esq., of Cardross. Edited by the Rev. Walter Macleod. (Dec. 1893.)

PUBLICATIONS 5

For the year 1892-1893.

15. MISCELLANY OF THE SCOTTISH HISTORY SOCIETY, First Volume—
    THE LIBRARY OF JAMES VI., 1573-83.
    DOCUMENTS ILLUSTRATING CATHOLIC POLICY, 1596-98.
    LETTERS OF SIR THOMAS HOPE, 1627-46.
    CIVIL WAR PAPERS, 1645-50.
    LAUDERDALE CORRESPONDENCE, 1660-77.
    TURNBULL'S DIARY, 1657-1704.
    MASTERTON PAPERS, 1660-1719.
    ACCOMPT OF EXPENSES IN EDINBURGH, 1715.
    REBELLION PAPERS, 1715 and 1745.   (Dec. 1893.)

16. ACCOUNT BOOK OF SIR JOHN FOULIS OF RAVELSTON (1671-1707).
    Edited by the Rev. A. W. CORNELIUS HALLEN.
                                                (June 1894.)

For the year 1893-1894.

17. LETTERS AND PAPERS ILLUSTRATING THE RELATIONS BETWEEN CHARLES II. AND SCOTLAND IN 1650. Edited, with Notes and Introduction, by SAMUEL RAWSON GARDINER, LL.D., etc.
                                                (July 1894.)

18. SCOTLAND AND THE COMMONWEALTH. LETTERS AND PAPERS RELATING TO THE MILITARY GOVERNMENT OF SCOTLAND, Aug. 1651—Dec. 1653. Edited, with Introduction and Notes, by C. H. FIRTH, M.A.   (Oct. 1895.)

For the year 1894-1895.

19. THE JACOBITE ATTEMPT OF 1719. LETTERS OF JAMES, SECOND DUKE OF ORMONDE, RELATING TO CARDINAL ALBERONI'S PROJECT FOR THE INVASION OF GREAT BRITAIN ON BEHALF OF THE STUARTS, AND TO THE LANDING OF THE EARL MARISCHAL IN SCOTLAND. Edited by W. K. DICKSON, Advocate.

20, 21. THE LYON IN MOURNING, OR A COLLECTION OF SPEECHES, LETTERS, JOURNALS, ETC., RELATIVE TO THE AFFAIRS OF PRINCE CHARLES EDWARD STUART, by the Rev. ROBERT FORBES, A.M., Bishop of Ross and Caithness. 1746-1775. Edited from his Manuscript by HENRY PATON, M.A. Vols. I. and II.
                                                (Oct. 1895.)

PUBLICATIONS

For the year 1895-1896.

22. THE LYON IN MOURNING. Vol. III.

23. SUPPLEMENT TO LYON IN MOURNING—ITINERARY AND MAP. Edited by W. B. BLAIKIE.

24. EXTRACTS FROM THE PRESBYTERY RECORDS OF INVERNESS AND DINGWALL FROM 1638 TO 1688. Edited by WILLIAM MACKAY.

25. RECORDS OF THE COMMISSIONS OF THE GENERAL ASSEMBLIES (*continued*) for the years 1648 and 1649. Edited by the Rev. Professor MITCHELL, D.D., and Rev. JAMES CHRISTIE, D.D.

In preparation.

JOURNAL OF A FOREIGN TOUR IN 1665 AND 1666 BY JOHN LAUDER, LORD FOUNTAINHALL. Edited by DONALD CRAWFORD, Sheriff of Aberdeenshire.

JOURNALS AND PAPERS OF JOHN MURRAY OF BROUGHTON, PRINCE CHARLES' SECRETARY. Edited by R. FITZROY BELL, Advocate.

NOTE-BOOK OR DIARY OF BAILIE DAVID WEDDERBURNE, MERCHANT OF DUNDEE, 1587-1630. Edited by A. H. MILLAR.

SIR THOMAS CRAIG'S DE UNIONE REGNORUM BRITANNIÆ. Edited, with an English Translation, from the unpublished MS. in the Advocates' Library, by DAVID MASSON, Historiographer Royal.

A TRANSLATION OF THE STATUTA ECCLESIÆ SCOTICANÆ, 1225-1556, by DAVID PATRICK, LL.D.

DOCUMENTS IN THE ARCHIVES OF THE HAGUE AND ROTTERDAM CONCERNING THE SCOTS BRIGADE IN HOLLAND. Edited by J. FERGUSON, Advocate.

THE POLITICAL CORRESPONDENCE OF JEAN DE MONTREUIL WITH CARDINAL MAZARIN AND OTHERS CONCERNING SCOTTISH AFFAIRS, 1645-1648. Edited from the originals in the French Foreign Office, with Translation and Notes by J. G. FOTHERINGHAM.

SCOTLAND DURING THE PROTECTORATE, 1653-1659; in continuation of SCOTLAND AND THE COMMONWEALTH. Edited by C. H. FIRTH.

RECORDS OF THE COMMISSIONS OF THE GENERAL ASSEMBLIES (*continued*), for the years 1650-53.

REGISTER OF THE CONSULTATIONS OF THE MINISTERS OF EDINBURGH, AND SOME OTHER BRETHREN OF THE MINISTRY FROM DIVERS PARTS OF THE LAND, MEETING FROM TIME TO TIME, SINCE THE INTERRUPTION OF THE ASSEMBLY 1653, ON THE PUBLIC AFFAIRS OF THIS DISTRESSED AND DISTRACTED KIRK, WITH OTHER PAPERS OF PUBLIC CONCERNMENT, 1653-1660.

PAPERS RELATING TO THE REBELLIONS OF 1715 AND 1745, with other documents from the Municipal Archives of the City of Perth.

THE DIARY OF ANDREW HAY OF STONE, NEAR BIGGAR, AFTERWARDS OF CRAIGNETHAN CASTLE, 1659-60. Edited by A. G. REID from a manuscript in his possession.

A SELECTION OF THE FORFEITED ESTATES PAPERS PRESERVED IN H.M. GENERAL REGISTER HOUSE AND ELSEWHERE. Edited by A. H. MILLAR.

A TRANSLATION OF THE HISTORIA ABBATUM DE KYNLOS OF FERRERIUS. By ARCHIBALD CONSTABLE.

DOCUMENTS RELATING TO THE AFFAIRS OF THE ROMAN CATHOLIC PARTY IN SCOTLAND, from the year of the Armada to the Union of the Crowns. Edited by THOMAS GRAVES LAW.

www.ingramcontent.com/pod-product-compliance
Lightning Source LLC
Chambersburg PA
CBHW020525300426
44111CB00008B/553